A HISTOR...
ISRAEL

By W. O. E. OESTERLEY

and THEODORE H. ROBINSON

D1485792

VOL. II

From the FALL OF JERUSALEM, 586 B.C. to the BAR-KOKHBA REVOLT, A.D. 135

By W. O. E. OESTERLEY

Pp. 516, with 11 maps

FIRST EDITION 1932
REPRINTED 1934, 1938, 1945, 1948, 1951, 1955, 1957

A HISTORY OF
I S R A E L

VOL. I

From the Exodus to the Fall of
Jerusalem, 586 B. C.

BY

THEODORE H. ROBINSON

Litt.D. (*Cantab.*), D.D. (*Lond.*), Hon. D.D. (*Aberdeen*)
Hon. D.Th. (*Halle*)

*Professor of Semitic Languages, University
College, Cardiff*

OXFORD
AT THE CLARENDON PRESS

Oxford University Press, Amen House, London E.C.4

GLASGOW NEW YORK TORONTO MELBOURNE WELLINGTON

BOMBAY CALCUTTA MADRAS KARACHI

CAPE TOWN IBADAN NAIROBI ACCRA SINGAPORE

PRINTED IN GREAT BRITAIN

To

THE SOCIETY FOR
OLD TESTAMENT STUDY

this work is
gratefully dedicated

GENERAL PREFACE

AT its winter meeting in December 1928 the Society for Old Testament Study discussed, among other matters, the supply of works on the History of Israel. It was felt that there was need of a substantial book on the subject in English. During the discussion Dr. Robinson stated that he had been planning such a book and collecting material for many years, but had been deterred from completing the work mainly by two facts. One was his inability to secure an adequate period of continuous leisure, since such a work required practically uninterrupted attention during the actual writing; the other was that his special studies had been limited to the pre-exilic period. It transpired almost at once that Dr. Oesterley had been working for many years on similar lines, dealing with the history of Israel after the Exile. The two were encouraged by the Society to proceed in co-operation, and to produce the whole as soon as was reasonably possible.

We have divided the period covered into two distinct parts, and each of us is solely responsible for the volume which bears his name. At the same time we have worked with a single purpose, in close co-operation, consulting and criticizing one another, and we hope that, in spite of the divided authorship, we have succeeded in producing a single work which shall meet one of the present chief needs of Old Testament studies in the English-speaking world.

W. O. E. O.

March 1932.   T. H. R.

NOTE

THE printing of this book was already well advanced when the results of Professor Garstang's work at Jericho were made available for the general public. Had they appeared earlier, much of what has been said below on the fall of Jericho would have been re-written, but in the circumstances it has been possible only to refer to the work in a few footnotes. Two remarks, however, may be made. In the first place, Professor Garstang's opinion as to the date of the destruction of the city is much more in harmony with the period to which the other indications seem to point, i.e. to the first half of the fourteenth century. In the second place, his judgement, as reported in the *Daily Telegraph* for April 4, that the walls were destroyed by an earthquake, tends to confirm the conjecture mentioned on p. 123.

T. H. R.

NOTE TO SECOND IMPRESSION

I AM indebted to many friends, reviewers, and others, for suggestions and corrections. Archaeology, it may be remarked, has made such strides, even since this book left my hands, that much of what is said in the introductory section must be regarded as being out of date. So rapidly, however, is progress being made, that a complete revision, though desirable, would be practically useless until the results of recent and current excavation can be more exactly determined than is possible just yet. The text has been allowed to stand, therefore, substantially as originally printed, while the reader may be referred for more accurate information to such works as Olmstead's *History of Palestine and Syria* and Albright's *Archaeology of Palestine and the Bible*.

NOTE TO THIRD IMPRESSION

I HAVE taken the opportunity, kindly afforded by the Clarendon Press, of adding a few more notes and making one or two necessary corrections.

PREFACE

Few more difficult tasks can be presented to a student than the writing of a history. Two objects, apparently so different as to be almost opposed to one another, have to be kept in view. The facts must be correctly stated, and every detail must be duly checked that the highest degree of accuracy may be attained. At the same time these must not be allowed to obscure the broader outlook, and the period must be visualized as a single whole, into which the details must fit as necessary component parts. The historian's vision must be at one and the same time microscopic and telescopic; failure in the one respect means unsound conclusions, and failure in the other reduces the work to a Chronicle or a set of Annals. The laws which govern the evolution and progress of human society are as rigid as those which obtain in the physical world, though they are far more complex and elusive than the principles of material Nature. It is the duty of the historian to discover, propound, and illustrate those laws, in so far as they affect the people and the age which he has under review.

The supreme contribution of Israel to human thought lies in the sphere of religion. It is her faith which has made her unique, and has given her the place she deservedly holds in the story of mankind. But Dr. Oesterley and I have already given (albeit in summary form) our estimate of Hebrew Religion, and we have therefore felt it advisable to exclude that side of the subject as far as possible, for to have given it due place and proportion would have meant the expansion of the book to inordinate size. It is, however, impossible to leave the religious aspect out of the history of Israel, just as the story of Europe in the sixteenth and seventeenth centuries cannot be considered apart from the Reformation. I have, nevertheless, reduced my discussion of this matter to a minimum, in the hope that the reader will regard what I have written as a background for the more important study.

There still remain other aspects of the subject. The Old Testament, especially in those portions which deal with pre-exilic days, presents us with a situation which is almost unparalleled in the ancient world. We have a people passing from the simple nomad plane to a more complex agricultural and commercial order, and still maintaining certain contacts with their older life. The key to the history of pre-exilic Israel, both in religion and in secular affairs, is to be found in the reaction of these two points of view upon one another. There were elements in her pastoral life, commonly absent from the settled communities of the ancient world, which man dare not suffer to perish, and though Israel failed in her effort to apply them wholly to the new order, she did at least point the way to prosperity and to stability in Church and State.

In the attempt to develop this thought I have touched but lightly on many subjects of interest. Archaeology, philology, geography, textual and higher criticism, and other subjects have been mentioned only so far as they seemed to me to bear directly on what I conceive to be the central principle in the history of Israel, and in dealing with many points (e.g. such matters as the location of Sinai) I have deliberately avoided elaborate discussion. Where I have felt that extended treatment is necessary for the justification or explanation of my point of view, I have normally relegated to a footnote, or to an 'Additional Note', my contribution to the debate.

It may seem to some readers that in the earlier part of the book I have given too much weight to the Biblical narratives. It may be true that these narratives in their present form do not go further back than the period of the Monarchy, but they are certainly based on traditions which are much older. The traditions themselves are facts. To the scientific mind every fact requires an explanation, and the simplest and most obvious explanation of a tradition is an event. The event may have been very different from that which is actually described for us; in these long race-memories there may be comparatively few details which we can trust. Yet it behoves us, taking into account all the evidence and the various tendencies which have been at work upon the story, to make the best guess we can at what the event actually was. Where, then, there has seemed to be no valid ground for rejecting any element in the ancient narratives, I have assumed that the balance of probability lies on the side of its acceptance. For example, I have not the slightest doubt that among those who in the remote past contributed to the future Israel, there were men named Abraham, Isaac, and Jacob, though I am equally convinced that some of the stories which have gathered about them are not historical in every detail. No one is more keenly alive than I either to the element of subjectivity in the process of conjecturing the actual events, or to the fallibility of my own judgement, yet I have felt it incumbent upon me to do the best I can with the material at my disposal.

The following pages are the result of study and reflection extending over a period of rather more than a quarter of a century. But the drafting, if not the actual writing, of an historical work demands a continuous period which is practically free from all distractions; otherwise the perspective may be lost. The kind invitation of the University of Chicago to a Visiting Professorship in the summer of 1929 gave me an opportunity of preparing a rough draft of a book. I have to acknowledge with sincere gratitude not only the magnificent equipment of the Oriental Institute of the University of Chicago, but also the kindness and helpfulness of a body of experts both in the Old Testament and in other fields, particularly in Egyptology and Assyriology. I must mention in particular Professors J. M. P. Smith, Chiera, and Poebel, and Mr. Jacobsen. Needless to say, while the main outline of the book has remained unchanged, it now has a very different form from that which it presented when I returned to Europe. I have to offer the warmest thanks (in which every reader has abundant cause to share) to a number of friends who have offered valuable and helpful criticism, suggestion, and advice.

I would name especially Mr. G. R. Driver (especially on matters where a knowledge of Assyriology is essential), my colleague Mr. H. Bruce, Professor of History in Cardiff, Professor H. J. Fleure of Manchester, whose encyclopaedic knowledge of geography and anthropology has been placed freely at my service (there are, indeed, paragraphs in Chapters II and III to which Professor Fleure's name might justly have been appended. The critical reader may like to exercise his ingenuity in identifying them!), the Rev. Principal W. L. Wardle of Manchester, and the Rev. Principal H. Wheeler Robinson of Oxford.

I should add that, for the map of the Assyrian Provinces on p. 381, I am indebted to the kindness of Professor Forrer, who generously placed at my disposal a series of his maps in MS.

The whole has undergone a revision of very great value through the generosity of the University of Halle, where I lectured as a Visiting Professor on the subject of this book during the Summer Semester of the year 1931. This gave

me the opportunity of testing my work, not only through
the exercise of trying to put my ideas into a foreign language,
but through the extraordinary kindness of Professor Eissfeldt.
He gave me freely of his time, busy as he was, and we met
nearly every day. While his primary object in these conversa-
tions was to ensure as far as possible that my lectures should
be offered to the students in intelligible German, they had the
additional advantage that practically every point was talked
over between us, and, though he must be acquitted of complicity in my opinions, there is no part of the work which does
not owe him much. I may add that I was privileged also to
discuss isolated points with Professors Gunkel, Hans Schmidt,
Hempel, Galling, Alt, and Puukko.

I must also gratefully acknowledge my indebtedness to those
who have been good enough to lend me their assistance in the
arduous task of proof-reading. I should mention first my wife,
who has read every word with me more than once, and checked
all the Biblical references. Dr. Oesterley and the Rev. H. H.
Rowley have also read the proofs with great care, and all three
have made valuable corrections and suggestions. Finally, the
readers of the Clarendon Press have shown that combination
of technical skill and expert knowledge which I have long ago
learnt to expect from them, and I owe not a little to their
criticisms.

Even so, there is a great gulf between the book I have written
and the book I should like to have written. Nevertheless, in
the consciousness that no amount of revision or of modification
would render it a work that would satisfy its author, I send it
out, hoping that it may play its part in the interpretation of
that people whose full meaning became manifest only in the
Incarnation.

T. H. R.

CARDIFF,
March 1932.

CONTENTS

BOOK IV. THE ISRAELITE MONARCHIES: THEIR DECLINE AND FALL

LIST OF MAPS

ABBREVIATIONS

ABAT   Gressmann, *Altorientalische Bilder zum Alten Testament.*

AHNE   Hall, *Ancient History of the Nearer East.*

AHT   Hommel, *Ancient Hebrew Tradition.*

AJSL   *American Journal of Semitic Languages.*

ARA   Luckenbill, *Ancient Records of Assyria and Babylonia.*

ARE   Breasted, *Ancient Records of Egypt.*

ATAT   Gressmann, *Altorientalische Texte zum Alten Testament.*

A.V.   Authorised Version.

BA   *Beiträge zur Assyriologie.*

CAH   *Cambridge Ancient History.*

Cent. Bib.   *Century Bible.*

DB   *Hastings' Dictionary of the Bible.*

EB   *Encyclopaedia Biblica.*

ERE   Hastings' *Encyclopaedia of Religion and Ethics.*

E.T.   English Translation.

E.V.   English Versions.

GA   E. Meyer, *Geschichte des Altertums.*

GVI   *Geschichte des Volkes Israel.* (Stade, Kittel and Jirku wrote under the same title, but wherever one is quoted, the author's name will be attached.)

HE   Breasted, *A History of the Ancient Egyptians.*

HGHL   G. A. Smith, *Historical Geography of the Holy Land.*

HI   Wellhausen, *History of Israel.*

HK   *Göttinger Handkommentar zum Alten Testament.*

HPH   Desnoyers, *Histoire du Peuple Hébreu.*

ICC   *International Critical Commentary.*

IN   E. Meyer, *Die Israeliten u. ihre Nachbarstämme.*

JAOS   *Journal of the American Oriental Society.*

JEA   *Journal of Egyptian Archaeology.*

JRAS   *Journal of the Royal Asiatic Society.*

KAT   Schrader, *Keilinschriften u. d. Alte Testament* (3rd ed. by Winckler and Zimmern, 1903).

KHC   *Kurzer Hand-Commentar.*

LXX   Septuagint.

MI   Inscription of Mesha.

MT   Massoretic Text.

NSI   G. A. Cooke, *North Semitic Inscriptions.*

O. and R.   Oesterley and Robinson, *Hebrew Religion.*

RB   *Revue Biblique.*

SA   King, *A History of Sumer and Akkad.*

ZAW   *Zeitschrift für die Alttestamentliche Wissenschaft.*

ZDMG   *Zeitschrift der Deutschen Morgenländischen Gesellschaft.*

BOOK I

ISRAEL'S HERITAGE

Chapter I

INTRODUCTORY

SUMMARY

[The aim of this chapter is to obtain such a conspectus of history that we can place our subject rightly in its course. We distinguish three main periods: (*a*) that in which the centre of interest lay between Mesopotamia and Egypt, i.e. in Palestine, (*b*) that in which the centre is the Mediterranean, (*c*) that in which it is transferred to the Atlantic. Our subject falls within the first of these, at which we glance in a little more detail.

After the expulsion of the Hyksos from Egypt, about 1600 B.C., the Egyptian kings, especially Tutmose III, tried to establish their authority over Palestine and north-eastern Syria as far as the Euphrates. The weakness of the later kings of this dynasty (XVIII) permitted the country to be overrun by nomad tribes from the eastern wilderness and to fall under the dominion of the Hittites, whose power was at length checked by Ramses II (*c.* 1250 B.C.), and finally broken by the Philistines (*c.* 1200 B.C.). Palestine remained nominally under the suzerainty of Egypt, though the authority of the Pharaohs was seldom recognized or enforced. For three centuries (1150–850 B.C.) Palestine was largely free from external control.

It was this period which witnessed the rise of the kingdoms of Edom, Moab, Ammon, Damascus, and the Philistine cities. In the ninth century the Assyrian power began to make itself felt effectively on the Mediterranean coast-lands, and its first great movement westwards culminated in the defeat and submission of Damascus in 841 B.C. For a century internal weakness prevented the extension of Assyrian power, but with the accession of Tiglath-pileser III in 745 B.C. the advance was renewed. This king subdued Damascus and reduced Israel to very narrow limits in 732 B.C., while Sargon captured Samaria in 721 B.C. and Ashdod in 711 B.C.; forty years later Esarhaddon successfully invaded the Egyptian Delta.

From this point the power of Assyria began to decline, and in 612 B.C. Nineveh fell before a coalition of Medes and Babylonians, the latter under the Chaldean prince, Nabopolassar, father of Nebuchadrezzar. Necho, king of Egypt, tried to save the falling power of Egypt, but failed, and his defeat at Carchemish in 605 B.C. marks the end of the age during which Egypt could be accounted a first-class power. The subjugation of Palestine soon followed, and the fall of Jerusalem in 586 B.C. left the Babylonians on the threshold of Egypt itself, though the conquest of that country was carried out only by the Persians.]

MODERN history properly begins with the year 1479 B.C., and treats of that epoch in the story of our race which we may call the era of territorial imperialism. For thirty-four centuries, all political ambition, whether of the individual or of the race, has aimed at geographical extension, and at the subjugation of neighbouring tribes and peoples. There have been other theories in men's minds, dim adumbrations of new conceptions of human society, ideas of nationalism and of republicanism, doctrines of liberty and of self-determination, but all have had as their basis the occupation of land, and the different social organisms have been separated one from another by more or less clearly marked geographical frontiers. To-day, it seems, we stand on the verge of a wholly new order, in which the division of mankind is to be neither geographical nor racial, but industrial. And it may well be that the historians of our age, writing in millennia still far distant, will look back on the year 1918 as the landmark which parts the old world from the new, and will assign to the audacious swoop of Allenby's cavalry through the gorge above Megiddo an importance equal to that of Tutmose III's bold passage of the same ravine. The latter was the movement leading to the victory which inaugurated the age; the former was the turning-point in the military action of a war which may well prove to be its close.[1]

The history of this age falls into three well-marked periods. During the first, which lasted roughly down to the end of the third century B.C.—though it is difficult to define a limit with any accuracy—the scene of the drama lay to the east and south of the Mediterranean. For centuries the rivalry between the African power of Egypt and one or other of the great Asiatic empires remained undecided, though the latter gradually increased in strength, until the question was finally settled at the battle of Carchemish in 605 B.C.,[2] when Nebuchadrezzar inflicted a crushing defeat on Pharaoh Necho, the last Egyptian prince to make any serious bid for the hegemony of civilization. The new Babylonian empire, which had succeeded that of Assyria, gave way in turn to Persia. Though Cyrus was the great conqueror, the importance of Persia for the history of the

---

[1] It is a curious coincidence, as Professor H. J. Fleure has pointed out, that this is also the age in which the horse plays a prominent part, both in civil life and in war. Earlier ages moved on foot; later generations, it seems, will rely on machinery for locomotion.　　　　　　　　　　　　　　　　　　　　　　[2] Cp. Jer. xlvi. 2.

whole imperial age centres round Darius I. Egypt, Assyria, and Babylon had maintained their authority mainly by a series of plundering raids, though there was some attempt at organization by Tiglath-pileser III and his successor. In a few cities garrisons were established, and during the last century of the Assyrian empire provinces were formed and governors appointed, but often the subject dominions were left in the hands of vassal sovereigns, usually natives of the countries they ruled. The sign of their fealty was the payment of tribute, and when this was withheld, the suzerain had no course open to him except to lead an army into the rebellious land, punish the ruler, and take his tribute by force. It is noticeable that nearly every great Assyrian king found himself faced with a general revolt on his accession, and had to devote the first few years of his reign to a fresh subjugation of the tribes and kingdoms whose allegiance he claimed. With Darius, however, we have an organization duly systematized and centralized.[1] The whole empire now consisted of great provinces, administered by officials directly appointed from Susa, and always immediately responsible to the court. The relation between the ruler and the subject was no longer merely financial; it included all branches of government, and, while subordinate posts might be held by natives, the higher officials were always the direct servants of the dominant power. Darius succeeded thus in welding his heterogeneous realms into a single whole, and his organization proved to be the model for all later empires. In its main outlines, its constitution was not very different from that of the Roman government in the Mediterranean world, or the organization of British India to-day.

Persia was followed by Greece—still, in the main, an Asiatic power—though there was no longer the same unity in the world after the death of Alexander. The age of the Diadochi was an interval during which several more or less evenly balanced powers rivalled one another, none attaining to supremacy until the rise of Rome once more established a single political authority in the world. At once the centre of interest began to move westwards, and, instead of being located in the eastern Mediterranean and in south-western Asia, it was to be found in the Mediterranean as a whole. In spite of the violent dislocation produced by the rise of Islam, the situation remained

[1] Cp. vol. ii, p. 63.

substantially unchanged until the discovery of America gave
a new importance to the maritime countries of western Europe,
and transferred the arena of conflict to the Atlantic. And, were
it not that the whole age is fast merging into an utterly new one,
that of the industrial order, there can be no doubt that the world
would have seen a struggle of some centuries' duration whose
centre would have been the Pacific.

It is but recently that we have been able to appreciate the
importance, almost, indeed, to recognize the existence, of the
first of these three periods in the history of the epoch. The
discovery of the forgotten cities of Mesopotamia, and the reading
of the hieroglyphic and cuneiform systems of writing, are very
modern achievements, and it is these newly available sources of
information which have made it possible for us to reconstruct
the history of the age. Of much we were dimly conscious, even
on the basis of such records as those of Herodotus and of our
Bible, but now, with some notable gaps, the whole lies before
us, and a large part of the period is better documented than is
much of the history of medieval Europe. Since it is wholly
within this era that the history of Israel as an independent nation
falls, we shall do well to glance at its main outlines.

We may start from the expulsion of the Semitic kings of Egypt
at the beginning of the sixteenth century B.C.[1] For a hundred
years the kings of the eighteenth dynasty[2] were content to hold
the Asiatics at bay, with occasional raids northwards into
Palestine, but with Tutmose III begins a real era of conquest.
His expeditions were directed against a Semitic kingdom which
had its centre at Kadesh on the Orontes, but held the country as

---

[1] I am indebted to Professor H. J. Fleure for the following note: 'C. 1800–1600
was a time of great unrest on the Egyptian border. The Mitannic power was growing near the upper Euphrates (a better watered region), the European steppe was
apparently emptying or empty. Probably soon after this the Aryan steppe people
reached India. It was probably a period of dry seasons. Legendary history suggests
a steppe-landers' invasion of China c. 1750 B.C. I think dry conditions continued
to about 1250 or so, and am interested in the relation of the Hittite power in the
Taurus region to this. I think that later on, about 1000–850 B.C. was a cooler,
rainier period. It was a time of organization (Chow) in China, of the disappearance
of Swiss lake dwellings because of the rise in the lake levels, of the decline of the
brilliant bronze-age culture of Denmark and of a marked rise in importance of the
English Channel region, of the streaming of peoples down from the mountains in
south-east Europe, of prosperity in Palestine. I fancy it was a time when the latitudinal belts of climate stretched a little further south than now, and conditions
such as obtained in early A.D. 1929 reigned around the Mediterranean. A spread-
ing of Hittites to Palestine (see pp. 41 ff.) fits in with this.'   [2] c. 1600–1350 B.C.

far south as Palestine. In his first campaign the Egyptian king broke the power of the Syrian armies and won Palestine at the battle of Megiddo, 14 May 1479 B.C. In a series of annual campaigns, some of which were no more than military demonstrations and involved no fighting, Tutmose completely established the Egyptian power in Palestine and Syria, and for more than a century its authority was fully accepted. But changes gradually took place. The Syrian power at Kadesh had been broken, but a new rival arose to the north as the Hittite kingdom of Asia Minor grew to imperial stature. On the upper waters of the Euphrates the Mitanni, an Indo-European people, formed a strong kingdom, and the wandering tribes of the half-desert on the inner edge of the Fertile Crescent[1] began to exhibit that restlessness which comes over them from time to time. When, in the middle of the fourteenth century, the curtain is lifted for us by the Tell-el-Amarna letters, it is clear that, while Egypt was still nominally the greatest of the world powers, her position was by no means unchallenged or secure. The vigour had died out of the eighteenth dynasty, and while Amen-hotep III was still able to correspond with the kings of Babylon (now held by the Kassite dynasty) and of the north on equal terms, his son, the famous Ikhnaton, was more interested in theology than in the practical government of his dominions. The result was inevitably the loss of a large part of the Asiatic territory which had accepted the lordship of Egypt, and the diminution of prestige among the great powers.

The decisive factors in the situation were two: the personality of the Hittite king, Shubiluliuma, and the irruptions of the nomad tribes from the edge of the Fertile Crescent. Shubiluliuma was a clever politician and a wise statesman. He made little attempt to secure his aims by methods of direct conquest, but contrived by intrigue to weaken his enemies till they were unable to resist him, or fell of their own accord. The two powers which seemed to bar his way to general supremacy were Egypt and Mitanni. Shubiluliuma took advantage of the death of the Mitannian king, Tushratta, to foment civil war in the country, and, by marrying his daughter to the leader of the more powerful

[1] A term first used (it seems) by Breasted to describe the great horse-shoe of arable land which includes the Mesopotamian river valleys, the country immediately south of the mountains of Asia Minor, Syria (including Palestine), and Lower Egypt (cp. pp. 21 ff.).

faction, succeeded in obtaining practical control over the policy of the country, which had hitherto been friendly to Egypt.

Shubiluliuma was now master of Asia Minor and of the north-western portion of the Fertile Crescent. Farther to the south-east his progress was barred by Assyria, still a small state, though not lacking in vigour. To the south lay Palestine, nominally an Egyptian possession, which seemed to offer better opportunities. Here again direct assault was unnecessary, for the country was already being invaded by enemies from outside. These were a people described sometimes by the ideographic term SA-GAZ, and (in correspondence emanating from Jerusalem) by the phonetic name Ḫabiru.[1] The latter word appears in much more ancient Mesopotamian documents with reference to a tribe or group of tribes belonging to the half-desert. Philologically there seems to be no doubt that it is equivalent to the word Hebrew, and the possible connexion with Israel is a point that must be mentioned in discussing the history of that people. For the present it is enough to note that their repeated attacks were causing the gravest danger to the Egyptian interests in Syria and Palestine. The country was none too secure, for the Egyptian government left the local dynasts a large measure of freedom. It is difficult to disentangle the complicated web of intrigue, but it seems quite clear that many, if not most, of the native rulers were false to their suzerain, and, with that short-sighted policy which so often characterizes little men with great ambitions, each was thinking only of his own power, and trying to establish himself in a strong position at the expense of his neighbours. Perhaps the only man whose loyalty to Egypt remained unshaken was Rib-addi of Byblos. His letters form a series of appeals for help from Ikhnaton, each more urgent and despairing than the last. The series ends suddenly, and, though we have only a small part of the original correspondence, there can be little doubt that Rib-addi paid for his loyalty with his life. The Egyptian king seems occasionally to have sent commissioners to examine the actual state of affairs, but was either too busy to lead an army into Palestine or too uncertain of his position in his own land. He had set himself to break the power of the priesthood of Amon at Thebes, and was fighting a losing battle, whether he knew it or not.

---

[1] For divergent views as to the etymology of this name cp. Burney, *Judges*, pp. lxxiv f. (n.), and Dhorme, *RB.*, 1924, pp. 14 ff.

The result of Ikhnaton's inaction was easy to foresee. Egyptian garrisons continued to hold a few important strongholds, but the country as a whole was practically lost. The invaders from the east made good their footing, but do not seem to have established any strong political power. The people who reaped the fruits of their success were the Hittites, and it is to the century which followed the time of the Tell-el-Amarna letters that we must ascribe the extension of Hittite influence over Palestine. We have, as yet, no records of a Hittite conquest, but the fact is indisputable, for with the rise of the nineteenth dynasty we find that Hittite influence is predominant, and it is perfectly clear that there was at some time an Anatolian occupation of Palestine which left an indelible mark on the inhabitants of the land. We know of no period in the history of the country which leaves room for such events, except that which includes the end of the eighteenth Egyptian dynasty and the beginning of the nineteenth.[1]

The line of Tutmose III came to an end before 1350 B.C., and for a generation no serious attempt was made to recover the lost territories; there was too much to be done in restoring order and prosperity in Egypt itself. But the military expeditions of Seti I and Ramses II succeeded in subduing Palestine as far north as the Lebanon, though they failed to shake the great Hittite power at its centre. Till the end of the thirteenth century B.C. the frontier between the two powers remained unchanged, and Ramses was the last king of the age who attempted any serious conquest north of the Lebanon.

Meanwhile great events were taking place in the world of the eastern Mediterranean. That old Aegean civilization which has been but recently laid bare before us had reached and passed its zenith, and was falling into decay.[2] Stronger but ruder tribes from the north were making their way into Greece and the coasts of Asia Minor, and there was a general movement of the peoples. Already in the fourteenth century there had been vast combined attacks on Egypt by sea, made apparently by tribes whose occupation of their own lands was threatened by

[1] *c.* 1350–1200 B.C. J. L. Myres, however (cp. *Who were the Greeks?*, pp. 62 ff.), calls attention to the fact that the 'Armenoid' type existed in Palestine from neolithic times, and that the repeated Semitic invasions failed materially to modify it.

[2] The Cretan civilization fell before the attacks of its children, who became the Mycenaean princes. See Nilsson, *The Minoan-Mycenean Religion.* Cp. also, for the whole period, J. L. Myres, *Who were the Greeks?*

invaders from the north, and with the period which saw the fall
of Troy these assaults were renewed. But this time the invaders
came not only by sea but also by land, and they moved less as
an army than as a migrating people. Their fleet sailed down the
coast towards Egypt, and was accompanied by a great host
marching down the maritime plain. They were met and
repulsed by Ramses III, at a point which has not been identified,
but was probably not far from the frontier of Egypt itself
(*c.* 1190 B.C.). They were kept out of the Nile valley, and the
first advance seems to have been driven far back, but if so they
returned to southern Palestine, and made good their footing at
many places on the Palestinian seaboard, especially towards the
south. Here they settled in the cities they captured or built, and
formed the people known to history as the Philistines. They had
swept the Hittite empire completely away, and, from the five
chief cities they made their own, they gradually spread inland,
subduing the country and taking possession of the strong points.
They even made their way right across the land and captured
Beth-shean, thus securing the most important passage of the
Jordan, and bringing to an end the effective Egyptian occupation of Palestine. The south of Palestine remained nominally
dependent, and one of the last kings of the twenty-first
dynasty took and destroyed Gezer, on the pretext that it had
'revolted' against him.[1] But, though they never succeeded in
forming a new world empire for themselves, the Philistines did,
for practical purposes, shake beyond recovery two of the old
claims for supremacy, that of the Hittites and that of Egypt.

For the next three hundred years there is no great power
which can even claim a dominant position. Egypt has as much
as she can do to protect her own frontiers, north, south, and
west. There is no great state in Asia Minor; the Greek cities,
while evolving a culture and a polity of profound importance to
the human race, yet lacked the power of cohesion which could
weld them into an imperial nation. Assyria, having conquered
Babylon, herself fell into a period of comparative decay, from
which she did not recover till the end of the tenth century. It
was an age of small peoples, each striving to maintain its independence and to imitate the great empires by conquering its
immediate neighbours. In the absence of any world power to
hold them in check, the nomad tribes of the inner edge of the

[1] Cp. 1 Kgs. ix. 16.

Fertile Crescent again broke into activity, and their repeated movements and inroads were a constant source of anxiety to the more highly cultured communities of the settled lands. Syria was broken up into small princedoms and city states, and the hopeless weakness of Egypt is nowhere better shown than in the pathetic record of the voyage undertaken for commercial purposes by the Egyptian prince Wen-amon, especially in the story of his visit to Byblos. Western Asia lay ready as an easy prey to any power strong enough to grasp the authority which had fallen from the nerveless hand of the kingdom on the Nile.

The failure of Egypt and the Greek instinct for the city-state meant that Mesopotamia was the only quarter in which the new empire could arise. This may be said to begin with the accession of Adad-nirari II (911–889 B.C.). Assyria had been reduced to very narrow limits, and the efforts of this king and of his successor, Tukulti-ninurta II (889–884 B.C.), were devoted to re-establishing the old extent of the kingdom and strengthening the immediate frontiers. With Ashur-naṣir-pal II (884–859 B.C.) the work of conquest began. In a series of campaigns the boundaries of Assyria were gradually extended, the new states produced by the settlement of Aramaeans from the half-desert were conquered, and one expedition even reached the shores of the Mediterranean, where Tyre and Sidon paid tribute and a memorial-stone was set up on Mount Amanus. The work was carried still further by Shalmaneser III (859–824 B.C.), who attempted the serious conquest of Syria and Palestine. Checked by a combination of states under the leadership of Damascus at Ḳarḳar in 853 B.C., he made repeated attempts to overcome the opposition, and succeeded only in 841 B.C., when the breaking-up of the old coalition left Damascus to stand alone against him. The rest of Palestine acknowledged his authority, and his monuments include the earliest external mention of an Israelite king, for they not only name Omri and Ahab, but also depict the payment of tribute by Jehu.

The immediate successors of Shalmaneser III were strong men, but after Adad-nirari III (811–782 B.C.), who struck Damascus down in 805 B.C., the throne was occupied by a series of less vigorous monarchs. At the same time there was a recrudescence of power in Urartu,[1] the mountain-land which lay on the northern

---

[1] The Biblical Ararat, cp. Gen. viii. 4.

Assyrian frontier. Babylon, always the most restless of the subjects of Assyria, also gave trouble, and by 750 B.C. it seemed almost as if the rule of Assyria might definitely be broken. From this fate she was saved by the appearance of a king of a new line, Tiglath-pileser III (745–727 B.C.), one of the greatest monarchs who ever wore the Assyrian crown. Within seven years he had restored the old boundaries of the empire, and by 732 B.C. he had brought to an end the native government of much of Palestine, and organized a series of Assyrian provinces which included not only the old territory of Damascus but also Syria as far south as the plain of Esdraelon, while the rest of the country acknowledged his suzerainty. His successors, Shalmaneser V (727–722 B.C.) and Sargon II (722–705 B.C.), carried the Assyrian arms to the very borders of Egypt, though they still left a few tributary princes in the far south of Palestine. In spite of a widespread revolt at the beginning of his reign, Sennacherib (705–681 B.C.) maintained the empire with increased strength, and in 671 B.C. Esarhaddon (681–669 B.C.) actually subdued the Egyptian Delta.

But this last conquest proved the undoing of Assyria. Her empire had become too large and unwieldy to be maintained on the narrow basis of her own land and population. The new territory was difficult to hold, and Esarhaddon himself died in the course of an expedition undertaken to quell a revolt in Egypt. His successor, Ashur-bani-pal (669–626 B.C.), gave up the attempt to hold Egypt before 650 B.C., and it is clear that by the time he died (626 B.C.) the days of imperial Assyria were numbered. Hordes of wild barbarians from the north broke into the Fertile Crescent, and though they failed to occupy the land permanently, the effect of their inroads was to deal a fatal blow at the old empire. Babylon, under Nabopolassar, the first king of the new Chaldean dynasty, recovered her independence on the death of Ashur-bani-pal (626 B.C.), and, in alliance with the Medes, attacked the heart of the Assyrian power. The city of Ashur fell to the Medes in 614 B.C., and in 612 B.C. a joint effort brought about the final ruin of Nineveh. An attempt was made, with the help of the Egyptian king Necho, to maintain the struggle from Harran, but this too was captured in 610 B.C., and Necho's aspirations were utterly shattered by Nebuchadrezzar at the battle of Carchemish in 605 B.C. Never again did Egypt take front rank among the nations, and

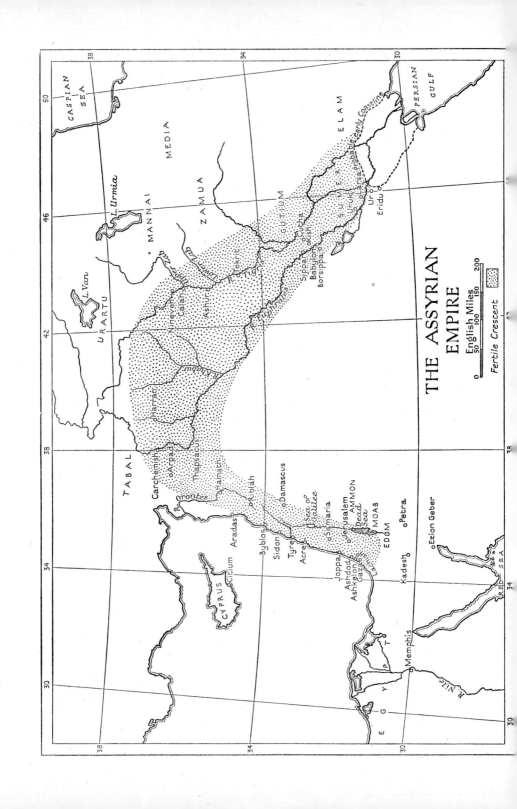

THE ASSYRIAN
EMPIRE

English Miles
0   50 100 150 200

Fertile Crescent

for two generations Babylon remained supreme without a rival.[1]

It is, then, against a background of great events and creative movements, to some of which we shall have to refer repeatedly, that we must view the history of the little people of Israel. It is well that we should see them, as far as we may, through the eyes of their contemporaries. They formed one of a group of western states, lying on the road between Mesopotamia and Egypt, a group which included also Damascus, Phoenicia, the Philistine cities, Moab, Ammon, and Edom. While the Israelites, at the height of their power, proved stronger than any of their neighbours, except possibly Damascus, the difference was never so great as to give them an unchallenged supremacy. The Phoenician cities, indeed, always maintained their independence, but their outlook was westwards, and, provided that they were not actively molested from the east, they took little trouble to interfere in international politics. They were at two periods definitely allied with Israel, but we hear nothing of Phoenician armies in the whole course of Israelite history. Among the rest, Moab, lying to the east of the Dead Sea, and more truly pastoral than Israel, was sometimes subordinate, but normally independent. Edom seems to have been nominally subject to Judah throughout a large part of the monarchic period, but the wealthy Philistine cities (except possibly Gath) never formed a part of the Hebrew kingdoms, and the

[1] It is to the former half of the first millennium B.C. that we must look for the formulation and crystallization of many of those tendencies which did so much to make the age of territorial imperialism what it was. Not in western Asia nor in the eastern Mediterranean alone, but wherever the human race attained to a high level of civilization and culture, there was a movement in the heart of the peoples, a stirring of the spirit of the race. As we have seen, it was under men like Darius that a definite imperial organization was fully developed, and Darius does not stand alone. The Chow period in China is one of social and national organization, and the impulses to which this age gave birth manifest themselves unmistakably in the next few centuries from the Atlantic to the Pacific. Still more striking is the leap made by human thought, its incipient efforts towards a harmonious explanation of the universe, and its development of the abstract from the concrete. It can hardly be an accident that we must place within these few centuries such men as Confucius, Lao Tze, Sankara, Siddharta, Zoroaster, the early Ionian philosophers, and, we must add, the great prophets of Israel. More than any others, save only the Founder of Christianity, these are men whose thought has dominated the world, and moulded the philosophy and the religion of humanity. Even Plato owed much, possibly more than he himself knew, to his predecessors in other lands, and it may well be maintained that no other single mind has ever exercised so vast an influence over later thinking.

Ammonites were too far out towards the desert to be an easy prey to any settled state.

Yet, small and insignificant among the nations of the world as Israel was, without political influence or extended power, it may safely be said that no other people of antiquity holds a place of such profound importance in the history of human thought. It was Israel who gave to the world a religion which has directed the spiritual life of nearly half mankind, and, not only among the Jews themselves, but in the two daughter faiths of Christianity and Islam, has moulded the beliefs of men in every continent save central and eastern Asia. Of Israel's creed it is no part of our task to speak in detail, though the history of Israel can no more be told without reference to religion than can that of Europe in the sixteenth and seventeenth centuries. But every side of the life of this people must be of interest to us, and we need to trace the development of the nation, as a nation, if we would win an adequate background for the record of her spiritual life. We must consider those elements which went to make her what she was, her geographical and racial inheritance, the culture which she adopted, and the traditions which inspired her. We must trace from the earliest point at which it is discernible the story of her organized national life. We must see how the prospect of political influence in the ancient world opened before her, and how she failed to make good her early promise. We must watch her as she struggled, no longer for supremacy, but for bare independent existence, until her internal weakness and the external pressure both became too great, and she fell, never to rise again as a political force in the world. Yet, even as we reach the end of the story of the Israelite monarchies, we must remember that in a very real sense the apparent ruin is but the beginning of her life, and that in the ages which followed the extinction of her political power she was the better able to give herself to the cultivation of those spiritual elements which made her in the long run the most influential nation of the ancient world.

Chapter II
THE LAND OF PALESTINE

SUMMARY

[As far as we can tell, it was in the great river valleys of Egypt and Mesopotamia that man first passed from the stage of the pastoral nomad to that of the farmer. These two early centres of culture were separated from one another by a wide desert stretch, broken only by the comparatively fertile strip of land between the Jordan and the Mediterranean. Hence, while there were caravan routes across northern Arabia, the real land bridge between Asia and Africa was always Palestine, used alike by the merchant, the soldier, and the politician.

South from Anatolia and the Taurus mountains runs a crack in the surface of the earth, known as the Great Rift. The mountains forming its western wall serve to catch rain, and the whole is therefore sufficiently fertile to support human communities, at least on the pastoral scale. Palestine proper, whose backbone is this ridge, thus forms a part of what is called the *Fertile Crescent*, whose southern horns are the valleys of the Euphrates and the Nile.

On the level of the southern end of the Sea of Galilee the main ridge is broken by a stretch of comparatively level country, down which the great trade route passes. South of this are the highlands of Ephraim and Judah, whose western side slopes down through the Shephelah, or foot-hills, to the coastal plain. A number of valleys lead up into the hills through the Shephelah. To the north of Esdraelon the country is more broken, with a few outstanding peaks.

The country to the east of Jordan rises very steeply from the river-level, but the wall is broken by three main valleys, those of the Arnon, the Jabbok, and the Yarmuk. Except in these depressions and a few other spots the land is unsuited to agriculture, though it affords a fair livelihood to nomads.

The most prominent feature of the climate is the rainfall, which is comparatively gentle in autumn and spring, but very heavy in winter. Life in Palestine is almost entirely dependent on these rains, and the agriculturist is thus presented with problems to which Egypt and Mesopotamia are strangers. The centres of importance, agricultural, commercial, and political, are necessarily to be found in the better watered spots, such as the plain of Esdraelon and the hills immediately to the south of it.

It is to its position that the country owes its importance in world history, for its possession is vital to the success of any conqueror who wishes to pass either from Europe or Asia into northern Africa or vice versa.]

FOR some ten or twelve degrees north of the Tropic of Cancer there stretches from the Atlantic to the central Asiatic mountain-massif a strip of territory which is fairly uniform in its external features. In modern times it is mostly dry, and can support little vegetation, except a scanty grass which is nurtured by the sparse rainfall; but in earlier ages it seems clear that it was well within the area reached by moisture-bearing winds, and was far richer in varied forms of life than it is to-day. It must have been at one time a great prairie, broken by ranges of mountains and by two great river valleys, in addition to many smaller streams, and even to-day there are left many relics of the older, richer type of land.[1] Along the north coast of Africa we meet from time to time with fertile spots, clearly more numerous and better watered in classical times than they are now. In earlier ages the mountain ranges seem to have been thickly wooded, while throughout the modern period they exhibit little more than bare heights where the grass will grow after rain, though at other seasons there is little vegetation. No doubt there are portions of the land in which the present appearance has been largely due to human action, for it is a well-established fact that the deforestation of a country often means a decrease in its fertility, possibly owing to a lower rainfall, and certainly to the ease and rapidity with which the rocky hills are denuded of fruitful soil. Some, at least, of the mountain ranges of this area were sources for the supply of timber, which had often to be carried many hundred miles before reaching the spot at which it was to be employed. So freely have these supplies been used that they have been exhausted, and it is often doubtful whether re-afforestation is at all possible. But in the main this great stretch of territory must have presented for many ages the same general appearance—grass-lands of varying richness, suitable primarily for the life of the hunter and of the shepherd.

In two districts we find country of a different type. These are the two great fertile river valleys to which allusion has been made, that of the Nile in Africa and that of the Tigris and Euphrates in Asia. Here the soil is regularly irrigated by the rivers, and, being independent of the local rainfall, it is suitable

[1] The evidence, especially that collected by Miss Caton-Thompson, goes to show that parts of the Sahara were grass-land in palaeolithic times, and became desertic when the latitudinal belts of climate moved northwards as the level of the land sank in north-west Europe and the Gulf Stream was able to influence Europe more closely. (Note for which the writer is indebted to Professor H. J. Fleure.)

for the production of crops. Archaeologists do not seem able to agree whether it was in Egypt or in Mesopotamia that man first took to the operations of agriculture, but it seems to be clear that systematic tillage began in one or the other, perhaps in both independently. Judging from the remains which have survived, the earliest grain to be thus grown was barley, and at a later stage wheat followed. Wild forms of both plants are still found in the Lebanon and neighbouring lands, while the evidence seems to show that the actual cultivation of corn was first practised in the district of Susa. Here the spade of the excavator has disinterred traces of what is claimed to be the earliest site of a settled human community. The locality is towards the eastern edge of the area we are considering, and lies among the hills that lead up to the central Asiatic massif.

It was, then, in this stretch of country that, so far as we know, man made one of his great experiments in the social order. His earliest means of securing a livelihood was necessarily the collection of food, in which he stood on the same level as the animals. He was at this grade essentially a food-gatherer, hunting the beasts he sought for food, and plucking what fruits or leaves he found to his hand. Eventually he began to take measures for the care and protection of the things he needed, following the companies into which edible animals naturally group themselves, and gradually taming them to his needs, tending them when opportunity offered and reducing them to subjection. In some instances he seems almost to have been a parasite on the animal,[1] spending much of his time on its back, if it were large enough, and deriving his sustenance from the supply Nature had provided for its offspring. The camel, the horse, the goat, the sheep, and the ox he thus made members of his own community, and his organized life centred round his droves of cattle. The dog was an inheritance from the purely hunting stage, and was seldom an article of diet, but the rest were possessions which changed the whole character of his existence. And so, with the development of the art of food-producing, life became more stable and assumed new shapes.

The passage from the life of the food-gatherer to that of the pastoral nomad made comparatively little difference to the actual social order. Both necessarily involve constant movement, and demand wide areas over which the community may range.

[1] Cp. Myres, *CAH*. i. 22.

For though pastoral man has provided the means of his own sustenance in his cattle (living mainly on their milk), they in turn are food-gatherers, and may have to wander far in order to satisfy their needs. With them, naturally, go their attendants —alike their masters and their dependants—and, as the generations pass, men become almost as wise as the beasts and as skilful in the quest of grass and water, leading and not following their flocks.

The greater change in human life took place when man embarked on the provision of vegetable food. The transition, no doubt, was slow. He must have marked those species of plant which gave him fruit of one kind or another. He next recognized them in seasons of the year when no fruit was available, and eventually in their earlier growth. Where a specimen or a group of specimens was found, he would begin to care for it, removing the useless vegetation about it and doing his best to protect it till it was full grown. Finally, he would note that plants grow from seed, and would assist nature by sowing and caring for the fruit of his cereals, and, gradually eliminating other growths, would bring to full fruition that which he required for himself.[1]

All this, however, demands a more or less continuous residence in or about the same spot. The length of time needed and the extent of ground covered will vary with different crops. There are places where corn may be sown and reaped within a few months, but for those months it is necessary for the group to suspend its migrations and stay in the same neighbourhood. Both the cereal crop itself and the fodder for the animals demand special conditions, including fertile soil and an adequate water supply. These things are not found everywhere in the great steppe country, though the water supply can often be secured artificially by digging wells, and by constructing reservoirs for rain-water. Such devices are obviously comparatively late developments, and the earliest agriculture must have depended on rain or on the presence of rivers and natural fountains.

Cereals thus require an extended habitation in the same spot, though until man learns to cultivate the soil and renew its productivity by artificial means, it frequently becomes exhausted in a comparatively short time, and the cultivators must move

---

[1] Peake and Fleure (cp. *Corridors of Time*, vol. iii) doubt whether this sequence of stages is invariable. But it certainly seems to be true of the Aramaean element in Israel, whom all tradition regarded as nomads, later settling down to agriculture.

elsewhere. But fruit-trees, including especially the date, the vine, and the olive, demand a permanent home, and with the culture of these plants man passes definitely out of the nomad stage. Date-culture is characteristic especially of early Meso-potamia, and there is a school which holds that all early Sumer-ian and Babylonian thought was dominated by it.[1] Whether this theory be finally sound or not, there can be no doubt of the primary importance of this fruit in the southern parts of the nearer east. The vine and the olive seem to have come from the north, and to have had their earlier home in the mountains of Anatolia and Armenia. In the fully developed civilization of the Nearer East these two products play a part whose impor-tance is second only to that of the cereals.

So in Mesopotamia man passed from the nomad to the agri-cultural order. Roughly at the same period a like change took place in the other great river valley, that of the Nile. Here the process seems to have been not unlike that which led to the Mesopotamian developments, but arboriculture is far less prominent.[2] Egypt was famous for its vegetables[3] and for its cereals, but tree-borne fruit, though always present, does not play so large a part in the life of Egypt as in that of western Asia.[4] It is worth observing that, while in later days communi-cation between Egypt and Mesopotamia was frequent, the two cultures seem to have arisen independently of one another.

This conclusion is supported by the fact that between the two great civilizations there lies a stretch of territory which is (and, apparently, always has been) practically desert. Rain falls so rarely as to give no opportunity even for the scanty growth which suffices the goat for a living, and the absence of any kind of regular water-supply makes the passage of the country almost impossible except to carefully organized caravans. During the Great War, the Allied attack on the Turkish empire was directed along two lines, from Egypt and from the Persian Gulf. But there was, and could be, no direct communication

---

[1] Cp. especially Barton, *A Study of Semitic Origins* (1902).

[2] The artistic remains which survive from the time of the Old Kingdom seem to suggest that fruit of various kinds was a luxury rather than a necessity.

[3] Cp. Num. xi. 5.

[4] Even as late as the fifth century B.C. the accounts and indents in the Elephan-tine papyri show that the staple was barley, and that dates occupied a very subordi-nate position, though there is frequent mention of wine and other beverages which may have been tree products.

between the two bodies, save possibly by air. The desert is a more effective barrier than the ocean.[1]

In one place only is this stretch of desert broken. The borders of Asia and Africa are scarred by one of the most impressive features of the earth's surface, known to specialists as the Great Rift. Parallel fractures, a varying number of miles apart, have been accompanied by the sinking of the narrow belt between them, leaving great walls of rock on either side. The Rift stretches from Syria through El Ghor (the Jordan valley) and the Dead Sea to the Gulf of Akaba. The Red Sea continues the same feature on a larger scale, and it goes on into east central Africa, with the great lakes Rudolf, Tanganyika, and Nyasa in its branches. Just as the Judaean, standing on the Mount of Olives, may look across the depth of El Ghor to the heights of Pisgah in the land of Moab, so, west of Nairobi in Kenya, we come suddenly upon a sharp edge with a clear view of the great peaks of Longonot and Eburru on the other side of a long ribbon of lower scrubland. To the north the Rift is continued between Hermon and Anti-Lebanon on the one hand and Lebanon on the other, till it fades away as we approach the Taurus mountains and the highlands of Anatolia.

On the eastern side of the Rift the high tableland of Arabia with its wastes of sand dominates the scene. Near the edge are outpourings of lava that give wild rocky areas, such as the Harras (near Mecca), and El Leja (Trachonitis) in what was once Bashan, east of the Sea of Galilee. The sunken zone lies deepest in the Dead Sea, a pit whose surface is 1,292 feet below the level of the Mediterranean. The lands to the east are favoured with rain on the high edges, and the waters of Abana and Pharpar[2] are as famous in history as the dews of Hermon,[3] the balm of the forests of Gilead,[4] and the pools of Heshbon.[5] Had we the traditions of Moab and Ammon along with those of Israel, no doubt there would be other names to be added here. Most of the watercourses, however, on both sides of the Rift, are seasonal *wadis*, valleys down whose limestone beds great torrents of water pour in the rainy season, while for many months they remain lines of dry boulders. Even of the perennial

---

[1] It should be noted, however, that from very early times there were caravan routes across northern Arabia, though no permanently settled communities could be formed in this region.　　　　　[2] Cp. 2 Kgs. v. 12.
[3] Cp. Ps. cxxxiii. 3.　　　　[4] Cp. Jer. viii. 22, xlvi. 11.　　　　[5] Ct. vii. 4.

streams not all are serviceable; the Jordan, in particular, flows for the greater part of its course at the bottom of a deep gorge, with a very swift current, there are comparatively few places where it can even be crossed, and it is quite useless for any kind of transport. But there are others, especially the Litany (though this lies too far north to exercise any influence on the history of Israel) and the Kishon, which contain some water all the year round, and the land is fairly well supplied with fountains. The hills are (or rather were) well wooded, and normally rain is regular, falling at two seasons.[1] In the autumn there is a very heavy downfall, which serves to start the growth of the corn in arable lands, and in February a series of gentler showers which help to swell the grain before the heat of the early summer ripens it. A people of energy and ingenuity can store enough for their needs; Jerusalem has but one small spring in its immediate neighbourhood and has been for many centuries mainly dependent on supplies of rain-water preserved in large tanks or reservoirs. Though inferior to Mesopotamia and Egypt, Palestine yet affords, at least in some districts, the means of livelihood to a settled agricultural community.

The geography of the Nearer East thus presents us with what Professor Breasted has so happily called a Fertile Crescent. Starting in the south-east at the extremity of the Persian Gulf, it follows the great rivers, broadening as they diverge, with its western limit bending still further as it approaches the mountains of Asia Minor. With an exceptionally luxurious patch in the Damascus district, watered by the Abana and the Pharpar, it turns southwards in a somewhat broken line, until it reaches Egypt, where its course is continued up the Nile into the heart of Africa. It is, curiously enough, practically conterminous with the Babylonian empire at its greatest extent.[2]

As we have seen, this Fertile Crescent has two main centres, alike of population and of culture, one Asiatic, the other African. And there is, as it were, only a single land-bridge between them, that formed by Palestine. A glance at the trade routes of the ancient East will show the primary significance of this land for commerce. The main road between Mesopotamia and Egypt ran westward through Damascus, crossed the Jordan just below

---

[1] Rain in the wheat harvest (April to May) is counted a miracle; cp. 1 Sam. xii. 17.

[2] i.e. at the time when the influence of moister conditions had accumulated.

the Sea of Galilee, passed across central Palestine, and followed the coast through the Philistine cities of Ashdod and Gaza. There is to-day another route passing to the east of Jordan from Damascus, but this is mainly a pilgrim route to Mecca (though it is now followed by a railway) and can never have been as well frequented as the western road.[1] There is again a line of traffic which enters from the north, and passes through Phoenicia to meet the first great route near Megiddo. Another route through Dedanite country ran east and west across the northern end of the Arabian Peninsula. Palestine is, as it were, a ganglion of commercial routes, and as long as there has been any communication between Asia and Africa, the country has formed one of its main channels.

It follows that the land has had a similar importance—even a greater importance—for the soldier and for the politician. As we have already seen, the battle which opened the era of territorial imperialism was fought on its soil. So also was the engagement which, thirty-four centuries later, proved to be the decisive military action of the greatest war the world has ever seen. Through the ages armies have passed over its roads, and every imperial nation has tried to make good its footing there. Great conquerors—Alexander, Pompey, Caesar, Napoleon—have sought to make the land their own, for all have realized that in a very vital sense it is the key to the East. The politicians of the ancient world found it always the buffer-state between any great Asiatic empire and Egypt. Whenever there has been a strong power on either side, the land has been an object of contention between them, and its possession has been a symbol of supremacy. Seldom has an independent state been possible there, for the condition precedent has always been national and military weakness on the south, north, and east. While the medieval cartographer was, no doubt, led by theological motives to make Jerusalem the centre of the human universe, his view has been confirmed by the secular judgement of the historian. Palestine was the commercial, military, and political centre of the ancient world, and on it focused all the greatest movements of the peoples.

West of the Rift and north of the Red Sea, a belt of highland remains upstanding between El Ghor and the Mediterranean. The southern portion is the wilderness of Arabia Petraea,

---

[1] Cp. Burkitt, *Palestine in General History*, pp. 90 ff. (1929).

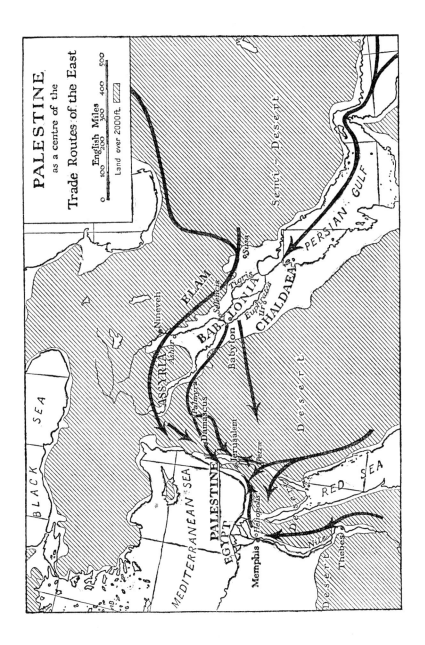

PALESTINE
as a centre of the
Trade Routes of the East

English Miles
0   100   200   300   400   500

Land over 2000 ft.

BLACK SEA

MEDITERRANEAN SEA

PALESTINE

EGYPT

Memphis
Heliopolis
Thebes

Desert

Desert

RED SEA

NILE

Jerusalem
Pelusium

Damascus
Palmyra

ASSYRIA
Nineveh
Asshur

ELAM
Susa

Seleucia
Tigris
Babylon
Euphrates
Ur
BABYLONIA
CHALDAEA

PERSIAN GULF

Semi-Desert

Desert

declining from its majestic southern heights of Sinai (over 8,000 feet) northwards through Edom or Seir to the narrow belt between the Philistine and Phoenician coasts on the west and the Jordan valley on the east. This is Palestine, upstanding between two sunken zones, and remarkably dissected. It is cut into two main portions by a belt of lower land, forming the valley of the Kishon, and known as the plain of Esdraelon or of Megiddo. This affords a lowland route south-east from the Mediterranean near Haifa to the Jordan valley near the southern end of the Sea of Galilee, where stands the ancient fortress of Beth-shean (modern Beisan), 322 feet below sea-level. The south edge of the plain is marked by the Carmel range and Mount Gilboa; between these two lies the so-called plain of Dothan, which thus connects Esdraelon with the coastal lowlands.

South of Esdraelon we shall best understand the configuration of the land if we realize that it consists of a series of more or less parallel belts, all running roughly north and south. To the west we have the strip along the coast, which, in not a few places in the south, has its shore belt encumbered with sand, but elsewhere offers rich soil to the cultivator. Above this rise the lower hills with comparatively gentle slopes, known as the Shephelah, while yet higher (up to 3,000 feet) stand the mountains of Ephraim and Judah, a mass of limestone rocks, often presenting a sharp edge to the west. To the east there is a sudden drop into the Jordan valley, whose wall is seldom broken on this side. No river worthy of the name runs into the Jordan from the west. There are paths and roads leading up into the hills from several points, notably from Jericho and from Engedi, though the latter stands on the shore of the Dead Sea and not in the Jordan valley proper. The Wadi Farah affords access into the hills of Samaria from Adam, but is of no great significance inasmuch as no main trade route runs that way. But the fords below the Sea of Galilee are supremely important, since they offer the easiest way of crossing the Rift, and so form a vital point on one of the world's great highways.

The slope that leads down to the sea on the western side is comparatively gentle. Jerusalem stands some 2,000 feet above the level of the Mediterranean, and therefore more than 3,000 above the point at which the Jordan enters the Dead Sea. Yet the city is less than twenty miles in a straight line from Jericho, while it is between thirty-five and forty from the coast. Through the Shephelah a number of valleys lead up into the heart of the hills of Ephraim and Judah. The most northerly is the Wadi es-Sha'ir, opening into the Samaria district. South of this we have the Wadi Ishar, which forms one of the natural frontiers between Judah and Samaria. Next comes the valley in which the Beth-horons stand—a notable road for invading armies—which itself may be approached from several directions. Only a few miles farther south we have the Wadi Ali, one of the historic gates of the Jerusalem country. The easiest route is that followed by the modern railway, past Beth-shemesh and Kirjath-jearim. Southern Judah may be reached through the Wadi es-Safieh, or, more naturally, by the road that leads north from Beersheba, but the southern approaches are generally well protected by the desert land lying between Palestine on the one hand and the Sinai peninsula on the other.

Even south of the plain of Esdraelon, a few miles north of Bethel (2,890 feet), the stream valleys giving on the Jordan and the Mediterranean almost intersect, so that, in place of a continuous highland, there are more isolated hills, such as Ebal (3,077 feet) and Gerizim (2,849 feet), and the area of fertile land is larger and better. To the north of the plain, between Galilee and the Mediterranean, there is space but for a fragmented highland, with one height at Tabor and another behind the ledge whence Nazareth looks southwards over the lowlands.

The land east of Jordan consists chiefly of the sharp slopes down to El Ghor. The hills on this side rise even more steeply than those on the west, and attain a greater height, at isolated points being above 3,000 feet. The wall facing El Ghor is broken by several river valleys, of which three are more important than the rest. The first of these (from the south) is the Arnon (modern Wadi Mojib), which flows into the Dead Sea about half-way down its length, the second is the Jabbok, now known as the Wadi Zerka, and the third, flowing into the Jordan just below the Sea of Galilee, is the modern Yarmuk. This last does not seem to be mentioned in the Old Testament, but was known in Greek times as the Hieromax. The other tributary streams are mere *wadis*, and have no significance for history.

North of the Yarmuk lies the rich cornland of Bashan, half Syria, yet not quite Syria, probably in part because of the volcanic wilds of El Leja, set in its midst. The district was famous in ancient times, not only for its crops but also for its large cattle;[1] the ox in western Asia belongs to the agriculturist rather than to the nomad. South of the Yarmuk there are a few fertile spots, especially in the river valleys, while Heshbon was famous for its luxuriance. But apart from these isolated patches of arable land, the country is mostly dry and the vegetation scanty, seldom affording sustenance to any communities other than the shepherd tribes of the wilderness. Throughout its history, the land of Moab was essentially a pasture country.

The art of cultivation, and with it the settled life, first arose, as we have seen,[2] in the riverine lands of Mesopotamia and the Nile, with their regular annual fertilizing floods which simplified the problem of irrigation. The highland steppes of Arabia, on the other hand, became the home of pastoral nomads. Palestine presented special opportunities and special problems for both types of life. If he could fight his way in, the nomad could wander in a limited space. To the south, on the hills of Judah, the harshness of the winter and the bareness of the surface made shelter important, and the cultivation of any small fertile tracts a valuable supplement. It was therefore often found convenient to live in small cities near patches of cultivable land, without entire abandonment of the semi-nomad herding life. Farther north there was less extreme climate and more pasture, but the pastures were intermingled with larger stretches of arable soil.

The cultivator of Palestine had problems very different from those of Egypt or of Mesopotamia. The writer of Deut. xi. 10–12 points out that, unlike Egypt, the country depends directly upon God for its water: 'it drinketh water of the rain of heaven'. It seems that the Israelites made their entry into the land during a 'pluvial' period,[3] when the annual rainfall was at a maximum, and Palestine is probably somewhat drier to-day than it was during the early Israelite occupation. But the order of the seasons remains unchanged, and there were, as now, two rainy periods in the year. The violent rains of mid-winter are often more destructive than helpful, washing soil down the slopes, and even breaking down buildings on rocky ledges, unless the builder has taken care to remove the sand and loose stones from his site.[4] Fortunately, in a good year they are

---

[1] Cp. Am. iv. 1; Ps. xxii. 12 (Heb. 13).   [2] Above, pp. 16 ff.
[3] Cp. Myres, *Who were the Greeks?*, esp. p. 503.   [4] Cp. Matt. vii. 24–7.

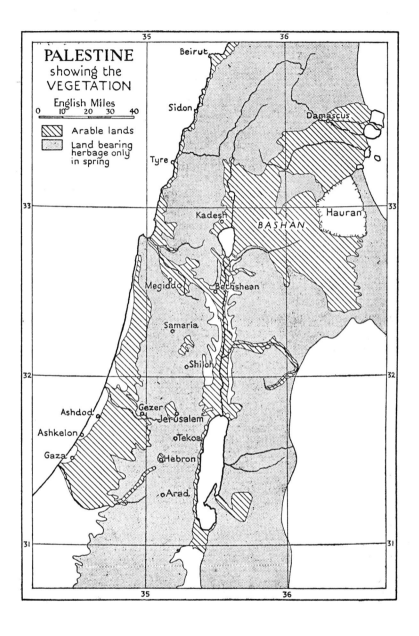

PALESTINE
showing the
VEGETATION

English Miles
0 10 20 30 40

Arable lands

Land bearing
herbage only
in spring

Beirut

Sidon

Damascus

Tyre

Kadesh

BASHAN

Hauran

Megiddo

Bethshean

Samaria

Shiloh

Ashdod

Gezer

Jerusalem

Ashkelon

Tekoa

Gaza

Hebron

Arad

preceded and followed by more moderate rains, during which milder temperature conditions rule. These are the former and the latter rains; the first soften the earth for ploughing, the second help the growth of crops in the spring. A short season of joy and beauty is then followed by a summer that becomes drab and weary ere it closes. It thus comes about that Palestine is, to a special degree, dependent on 'marginal' rainfall, rather, perhaps, than on the main rainfall, and so it is a land peculiarly liable to react to fluctuations of the seasons. Here the nomad and the settled were face to face in olden times, now with a slight advantage on the one side and now on the other. It was probably the nomad, however, who appreciated the country most. Israelite writers loved to speak of their home as a 'land flowing with milk and honey',[1] and therefore ideal from the pastoral point of view.

A glance at a vegetation map of modern Palestine (and, in spite of a slight shrinkage in rainfall, it is not likely that there has been much change in the distribution of pasture and arable land) shows that the greater part of the country consists of limestone hills, covered after the rains with grasses and other low plants on which cattle can feed. Here and there lie more fertile areas. The largest of these is to the north-east, where the soil of Bashan yields rich harvests. Next in importance is the maritime plain, especially south of Carmel. Historically neither of these was a permanent possession of Israel, for dominion over the one was claimed by the Syrians, while the other was in the hands of the Philistines and the Zakkara. But truly Israelite agricultural land was to be found in the plain of Esdraelon, and in patches, decreasing in size and fertility towards the south, in the central range from Samaria to Hebron, and even beyond that city. It is here that we must look for the chief centres of population, for cities can exist only in such districts or on the great trade routes. The economic heart of Palestine was thus the plain of Esdraelon and the hills of Samaria. Here was a land of 'great and goodly cities . . ., of houses full of all good things . . ., of cisterns hewn out . . ., of vineyards and of oliveyards'.[2]

We have thus a general picture of the land which Israel has regarded as her own for thirty centuries. It was a country of mountains and of dashing torrents, of woods and of open spaces,

---

[1] The phrase occurs some twenty times in the O.T., e.g. Ex. iii. 8 (J), Num. xiii. 27 (JE), Lev. xx. 24 (H), Deut. vi. 3, Jer. xi. 5, Ez. xx. 6, 15.   [2] Deut. vi. 10–11.

of scanty pasture lands and of rich cornfields. It was difficult of access for the most part, and easily defensible; when reached, it had little in itself to attract the civilized invader, though it offered a combination, almost unique in the ancient East, of a land suited to the needs of the hunter, the shepherd, the farmer, and the trader. It was, however, of profound importance in the earlier part of the great age of territorial imperialism, an importance which it owed to its position. If ever one of the great world powers in the first period of that age sought to reach the other in peace or war, its easiest route lay through the plain of Esdraelon and past the Judaean hills. The possession of the former was indispensable, the control of the latter desirable, to any who sought world empire, and the whole history of the land, from the fifteenth century b.c. to our own day, has been conditioned by its geographical position.

The cities of the world's wastes are of special interest in matters of religion, and no doubt owe much to the special energy of the religious motive, potent at all times in overcoming obstacles. Mecca, Lhasa, Samarqand, Ghardai'a, spring to the mind at once, and Jerusalem is of the company. Indeed, in view of its sanctity to Judaism, Islam, and Christianity, it may be said to be the greatest of them all. Its position on the northern front of the highland of Judah, above the long way down to the ford of Jordan at Jericho, gave it a special importance among the fortresses of Judah; and when, in Abrahamic times, nomad shepherd traders moved along the highland belt from Shechem to Hebron and Beersheba, it no doubt shared with Bethel a considerable importance as a station and religious centre. The development of trade in horses and chariots under Solomon increased the importance of the coastal plain. Thence the trade route went through Jezreel towards Damascus, so that Jerusalem came to be a lonely fortress living on its memories of the past, and the northern kingdom broke away from its poor and rather backward relation in the south. But this turn of the wheel of fate helped not a little to make Jerusalem treasure its heritage of ritual and law, with the most impressive consequences for the religion of mankind.

Chapter III
THE RACES OF PALESTINE

SUMMARY

[While both Egypt and Mesopotamia knew Palestine and used the country as a means of communication, neither tried to conquer it before the fifteenth century B.C. The land was not, however, un-inhabited. The earliest occupants seem to have been cave-dwellers of large stature whose culture was probably neolithic, but their remains have hardly been identified. The next settlers were Semites, who seem to have migrated from Arabia in three successive waves. The first settled in Mesopotamia, and, mingling with earlier in-habitants, formed the Babylonian and Assyrian peoples. The second, whom we may call Amorites, lived long as nomads wandering round the inner, or desert, edge of the Fertile Crescent, but many of them actually settled in Palestine, where they developed an agricultural and commercial civilization, tilling the land and building strong cities whose remains are now being excavated. The third, or Ara-maean wave, followed the same course, but settled less. The only district in which they were the dominant element was the north of the Fertile Crescent, from the Anti-Lebanon mountain range to the Euphrates, though Aramaean invaders and settlers exercised a profound influence on Palestine itself.

Though the Egyptians conquered Palestine, they do not seem to have made a permanent home there, but held the country by means of fortified posts and garrisoned cities. We have little or no record of the next invaders, the Hittites, though they must have settled in numbers, since they have left their mark on the physical build of the Palestinian peoples. It was only during or after this Hittite period that the Aramaeans entered the country.

Finally, early in the twelfth century, the Philistines came into the land. The popular application of the word 'Philistine' to uncultured and inartistic people is as unjust to the facts as the application of the word 'Jeremiad' to a complaint or a pessimistic outlook. They were the survivors of the Aegean civilization, who, driven from their old homes on the shores of the Aegean Sea and the 'Greek' islands, sought new lands to the south. They were beaten back from Egypt by the early kings of the twentieth dynasty—especially Ramses III—but eventually made good their footing on the maritime plain to the south of Carmel. Like their predecessors, they contributed in some measure to the blood of the Israelite people.]

ONE result of the peculiar position of Palestine in the ancient world was that it witnessed the ebb and flow of many national and racial movements. Those who entered the land were not all representatives of the great empires, seeking to extend their conquests, for many of them were of less notable tribes who desired to make their home in a land better at least than that to which they had been accustomed. They came from every part of the Nearer East, and, even though a particular people may have been rolled back from the territory it once occupied, it not infrequently left its mark behind it, either on the physical aspect or on the culture of the people.

Prior to the opening of the fifteenth century B.C. there was comparatively little contact between Egypt and Mesopotamia. The people of both countries knew and entered Syria, and especially drew supplies of timber from Lebanon. The centre of trade at this epoch seems to have been Byblos, and many of the objects recently discovered there show signs of both Egyptian and Mesopotamian influence. In Egypt itself traces of contact with Mesopotamia have been observed in the famous ivory knife-handle discovered at Gebel Arak, dating from the Old Kingdom of Egypt, and in the palette of Narmer, the founder of the first dynasty. The figures engraved on these objects, though undoubtedly of Egyptian workmanship, suggest designs common in the Sumerian world, and seem to indicate some kind of cultural communication between the two river valleys. This probably passed through Palestine, though it may have been brought by sea from Byblos.[1]

Yet the two peoples remained apparently unconscious one of another, and apart from a doubtful reference which has been held in some quarters (though on grounds hardly adequate) to imply the conquest of Narmer by a Babylonian king, no mention is made of either in the other's records. In fact Palestine, unproductive and mountainous, was a no-man's-land, and came into political prominence only when a strong power first established itself behind the Hyksos kings of Egypt. This does not mean that the country was uninhabited. As far back as the fifth dynasty we have a Syrian village depicted in a painting on the tomb of Inti,[2] and from the twelfth dynasty (roughly about 2000 B.C.) we have the old story of Sinuhe,[3] an Egyptian noble

---

[1] Cp. Frankfort, 'Egypt and Sinai in the First Intermediate Period', *JEA.* xii. 80 ff. [2] Cp. Petrie, *Deshâsheh*, pl. iv.
[3] Cp. Gressmann, *ATAT.*, pp. 55 ff., Erman, *Literature of Ancient Egypt*, E.T. (1927), pp. 14 ff.

who was compelled to flee from home and take refuge in
Palestine. Here he wandered from one tribe to another, always
well received and kindly treated, till he made his home with a
clan domiciled somewhere in the country, apparently about
the Esdraelon district. We get exactly the same impression
that we should receive from the story of an eighteenth-century
American who, for one reason or another, had fled for refuge
to the wigwams of some Indian tribe. The natives are felt to
be kindly savages, who appreciate the honour done them by the
presence of the distinguished Egyptian, and are most grateful
for the help he can give them in overcoming their enemies.
Further evidence to the same general effect is supplied by the
early pottery, which seems to be indigenous, showing little or
no trace of Egyptian influence.[1]

We need not consider the palaeolithic peoples of whom
remains have been found in Galilee and on the slopes of Mount
Carmel, since there seems to have been no connexion between
them and their ultimate successors. The earliest stratum of
population which formed a serious element in the blood of the
later inhabitants of Palestine appears to have consisted of a
neolithic people of large stature but of low culture.[2] The
Hebrew archaeologist applied to them the general term
'Rephaim' ('ghosts') but recognized that they had local names.
Thus we hear of the 'Emim' ('the horrors') as the predecessors
of the Moabites,[3] the 'Horim' ('Troglodytes') in the country of
Edom,[4] and the 'Zamzummim' ('Howlers') in the territories of
the Ammonites.[5] To those living in southern Palestine Israel
gave the name 'Anakim' ('the long-necked'?), but recognized
that they belonged to the same general group as the rest.[6] Of
these aborigines we know very little, beyond the fact that they
seemed abnormally tall to the Israelites, and the probability
that many of them were cave-dwellers. Archaeology does not
seem as yet to have identified any of their remains with certainty.[7]

---

[1] Cp. Bliss and Macalister, *Excavations in Palestine*, pp. 77 ff. (1902), and the
wealth of early remains recently excavated at Beth Pelet by Sir Flinders Petrie.

[2] To judge from the Cro-Magnon and other remains there were folk of large
stature in palaeolithic times, and some of these may have survived in Palestine.
Cp. British legends of giants in Cornwall, and see Peake and Fleure, *Corridors of
Time*, vol. ii (Hunters and Artists).   [3] Gen. xiv. 5, Deut. ii. 10 f.

[4] e.g. Deut. ii. 12.

[5] Deut. ii. 20; the Zuzim of Gen. xiv. 5 may be the same people.

[6] Cp. e.g. Deut. ii. 11. Possibly a false interpretation of בני ענק. See p. 44.

[7] Cp. Macalister, *A Century of Excavation in Palestine* (1925), pp. 148 f., 224 ff.

The next group that we have to consider were the Semites. Briefly to rehearse what is so familiar, we note that the Semitic peoples spread from a common centre, probably Arabia, in several waves.[1] The first, proceeding north-eastwards, settled in the lower Mesopotamian valley, and gradually spread northwards, subduing their predecessors, the Sumerians and others. The second wave of immigrants took a more westerly route, as it seems, and made their homes in Palestine and Syria though some of them seem to have wandered round the Fertile Crescent from the east. They were followed by a group who maintained the nomad habits of their Bedawin ancestors, and remained on the inner edge of the Fertile Crescent. All of these, in one way or another, had their influence on Palestine.

Egypt was near to Palestine and Mesopotamia far away. Yet while the cultural influence of the great African state on the pre-Israelite inhabitants was negligible, that of the first wave of Semitic migration was of the greatest importance, and shows that there was free intercourse between the west and the east of the Fertile Crescent before the end of the third millennium B.C. Whether the movement of the Amorites, the next group of Semites to leave their ancient home, was from west to east or vice versa, they may be regarded as the great carriers of civilization for this early period.[2] At the same time it is clear that the greater Mesopotamian kings must have exercised some kind of authority over Palestine, though even in the case of Ḥammurabi we find it difficult to define that authority with exactness. It does not seem that there was any formal occupation of the land, or that the Mesopotamian kings deliberately made settlements there, but the influence is so well marked as to prove fairly close contact, or at least the regular transmission of ideas. It is true that this influence did not extend to material affairs. The building arts of Palestine remained in a comparatively primitive condition till a far later age, and, although the country is richly endowed with stone, its people continued to use sun-dried brick for centuries. The pottery appears to be *sui generis*, until it begins to be affected by the art of the Aegeans, probably entering through Phoenicia.[3] Metalwork was rare, and, we may guess, costly; flint implements continued to be

---

[1] Cp. Winckler, *Die Keilinschriften und das Alte Testament*[3], pp. 11 ff.
[2] See below, pp. 36 ff.
[3] Cp. Bliss and Macalister, *Excavations in Palestine*, pp. 72, 84 ff.

used till a point late in the history of the Israelite monarchy, though both bronze and iron were well known.

In other ways, however, the effect of contact with Mesopotamian culture is undeniable. We may note first that the traditions of the Creation and of the early experiences of the human race, as preserved in Genesis and reflected elsewhere, show resemblances to the Sumerian stories which we know best through Babylonia. It is true that they have acquired unique features, and when we compare the Biblical narratives with those of the East, we are struck by the differences as much as by the resemblances. This goes to prove that while a common origin is certain, there must have been a very long period during which the two types of tradition remained unaffected by one another. In other words, the form in which these stories appear in Hebrew literature must have had a long history in Palestine after being brought thither from Mesopotamia, and we must throw their importation well back into the pre-Israelite age.

The second sphere of influence is that of Law. Throughout the whole of western Asia in historic times we have a general standard of civil and criminal law. It varies in details, and comes to us in several different forms. We have codes, whole or fragmentary, from the Sumerians, the Babylonians (the famous 'Code of Ḥammurabi'), the Hittites, the Assyrians, and the Israelites. While, as in the case of primitive traditions, the resemblances are so great as to make a theory of independent origin practically impossible, the differences equally preclude the hypothesis of direct borrowing. Each has developed by itself from a primitive and common body of legal principles which may have been expressed in an early code. It should be observed that in all forms of the laws, the state and order of society presupposed is that of the agricultural and civic life, and hence we are again led to the conclusion that the Old Testament form of law is, like its primitive tradition, derived from the common source through the medium of the pre-Israelite inhabitants of Palestine. There are grounds for believing[1] that the Old Testament presents us with this original *corpus* of law in an earlier form than any other of our sources. Now the Code of Ḥammurabi dates from the end of the third millennium B.C.

[1] See especially Anton Jirku, *Das weltliche Recht im Alten Testament* (1927). Without committing ourselves to an acceptance of the whole of Jirku's theory, we may remark that here he seems to be on sure ground.

or the beginning of the second, and we are thus forced to the conclusion that the most important era of Mesopotamian influence was at least some centuries earlier than this date, i.e. it can hardly have been later than the middle of the third millennium B.C.

We are next led to ask how this influence was exercised or transmitted. Three possible answers to this question present themselves: (a) the activities of travellers, (b) direct migration by the population of one district to the other, (c) conquest, and dominion held long enough to have affected the life of the subject people. Of the three, the first might account for the presence in the west of Mesopotamian traditions regarding the Creation and similar subjects. But the traveller is not likely to have imposed a *corpus* of law on the countries he visited. Further, the great trading movements of the ancient world seem to have lain very largely in the hands of the nomad or semi-nomad elements in the population, and the type of law for whose spread we have to account is that of the settled community, not that of the wanderer.

Direct migration would account for the presence, both of ancient legends and of ancient law in the newer country. But in such a case the immigrants usually bring with them also a large amount of their material culture. In this respect, as we have seen, Palestine owed little or nothing to Mesopotamia. Neither its architecture nor its pottery shows obvious signs of influence from the East, and the absence of this connexion makes a theory of direct migration practically untenable.

We are thus left with the third possibility, that of an externally imposed dominion, whose influence was perhaps reinforced by other means of communication. Our data from Mesopotamia itself are scanty, but they do, nevertheless, offer evidence which helps us to a conclusion. We hear of an expedition by Lugal-zaggisi[1] of Umma, who claimed to rule from the Persian Gulf to the Mediterranean. His 'conquest' may have been little more than a raid, but it seems clear that the dynasty of Akkad, founded by Sargon I, did exercise effective sovereignty over Syria and Palestine.[2] Dates are disputed, but Sargon and his

[1] Cp. King, *SA.*, pp. 197 f., *CAH.* i. 226 (S. A. Cook), 402, 404 (Langdon).

[2] Cp. King, *SA.*, pp. 233 f., 335, *CAH.*, p. 404, &c. Further evidence may be derived from a seal-cylinder, found at Taanach, attributed to the end of the third millennium B.C., bearing the inscription 'Atanahili, son of Habsi, servant of Nergal'. See Sellin, *Tell Ta'annek*, i. 27 f. (1904).

immediate successors cannot be placed later than the middle of the third millennium B.C., and it is to this period that we can best ascribe the introduction of Mesopotamian tradition and law into the Mediterranean coastlands, for it is not until the latter part of the Hebrew monarchical period that the political dominance of the East again appears.

When we turn to those racial factors which actually contributed to the blood of later Israel, we find first groups of early inhabitants in Palestine to whom the Hebrews gave several different names. Tradition, which we may trace back at least to the latter half of the seventh century, had a list of seven peoples expelled or destroyed by invading Israel, though it is rarely that we meet with the whole number.[1] The names are: Hittites, Girgashites, Amorites, Canaanites, Perizzites, Hivites, and Jebusites. Some of these seem to be merely local tribes, e.g. the Girgashites, Hivites, and Jebusites. Perizzite may be a general term for countryfolk living in unwalled villages.[2] Canaanite, Amorite, and Hittite, however, have a wider designation.

The first of these three, Canaanite, is sometimes used as general name for the pre-Israelite inhabitants of Palestine, but in this sense it is practically confined to that element in the Hexateuch which we call J. It seems to include—indeed to be especially applicable to—the Phoenicians, and it is possible that the word means 'traders'. This would be particularly suitable to the Phoenicians, though it would not describe so well the other inhabitants of the country.[3]

It is the term Amorite which has given ground for most extensive discussion, since it is used from early times, not only by Hebrew writers, but also in Mesopotamian documents. In the middle of the third millenium B.C. the name is applied to a group of Bedawin on the borders of Mesopotamia.[4] Sargon of Agade alludes to them in terms which imply that they are a people of Syria.[5]

In the time of Gudea they are domiciled in the far west[6] and

---

[1] The list certainly occurs in passages attributed to JE, but appears to be sometimes, if not always, a later insertion. The only passages in which all the names stand are Deut. vii. 1, Josh. iii. 10, xxiv. 11. For a discussion see Driver, *Deuteronomy* (*ICC.*), (1902), pp. 97 f. [2] See p. 44.

[3] Cp. Driver, *op. cit.*, pp. 11, 13 f., and especially Budde, *Die biblische Urgeschichte* (1883), pp. 344–8.

[4] E. Meyer, *GA.* ii¹ (1921), § 396.

[5] Meyer, *op. cit.*, ii¹, § 398; L. W. King, *SA.*, pp. 225, 233; *Chronicles*, ii. 27 ff.

[6] Meyer, *op. cit.*, ii¹, § 410; L. W. King, *op. cit.*, p. 261; *CAH.* i. 428, Langdon.

'Amorite Walls are built by Gimil-sin.[1] About 2225 B.C. an Amorite dynasty was established in Babylon, to which Ḥammurabi himself belonged,[2] and it is commonly held among Assyriologists that their names show them to have belonged to a stock better represented among the western Semites than among the earlier inhabitants of Mesopotamia.[3] In the twelfth century the mention of these people by Tiglath-pileser I suggests that they are to be found at intervals, if not continuously, from the Euphrates to the Phoenician coast.[4] At the end of the eighth century the term occurs with a limited application in the famous description of Sennacherib's great campaign in Palestine,[5] and we may take it for granted that his language represents the geography and the ethnology of the age in which he lived. Here the word is applied mainly to Palestine south of the plain of Esdraelon, the country north of this being summed up in the other name, Hittite. We think inevitably of Ezekiel's fierce sneer against later Israel, 'The Amorite was thy father and the Hittite thy mother'.[6] Sennacherib includes Jerusalem and some (though not all) of the Philistine cities in 'the land of the Amurru'.

[1] Meyer, *op. cit.*, § 415; L. W. King, *op. cit.*, p. 300.

[2] Meyer, *op. cit.*, ii². 1, pp. 18 ff.

[3] This view is challenged by Th. Bauer in *Die Ostkanaanäer*, a searching study of the linguistic evidence available. He reaches certain definite conclusions: (*a*) that there was no western kingdom of Amurru in the third millennium B.C.; (*b*) that the term (*Kur*) *Mar-tu* (*ki*), which may best be rendered 'Mountain of the Amurru', refers to the hill country, or to a district in the hill country, to the north-east of Babylon; (*c*) that the people known as the *Mar-tu*, or Amorites, came originally from this district, not forming a separate race, but being a branch of the Akkadians; (*d*) that the west-Semitic names in the age of Ḥammurabi do not belong to the older Amurru, but to a separate folk altogether (the 'Amorite' dynasty Bauer believes to have come from Larsa, p. 86); (*e*) that the well-known later kingdom of the Amurru, which is certainly to be located in the Lebanon, has nothing whatever to do with these earlier peoples. While some of Bauer's arguments (e.g. the distance from which Gudea is said to have brought stone for his buildings) appear to have some cogency, we must wait for fuller discussion by the Assyriologists before accepting his conclusions as final. If he is right, then the Amorites may have been an early Nordic people, and in this connexion it is worth recalling the blue-eyed, brown-haired peoples depicted on some Egyptian monuments of the eighteenth dynasty. Myres and Salaman appear to agree, but, nevertheless, such evidence as can be gained from philology (though this is seldom reliable) is on the other side. The presence of west-Semitic names in Mesopotamia in the second millennium is surely important, as these would hardly have been borne by a non-Semitic folk from the north-east. Such immigrants would use either their own earlier names or those which they adopted from the country in which they settled.

[4] Cp. Luckenbill, *ARA*. i. 92, 94, 99, 103, §§ 263, 287, 308, 328.

[5] Luckenbill, *op. cit.*, ii. 19, § 239.   [6] Ez. xvi. 3.

Within Israel we have the term applied to the pre-Israelite inhabitants of Palestine in the E sections of the Hexateuch (J uses 'Canaanite'). But, further, it is employed in a specialized and limited sense in the Pentateuch[1] of the kingdom of Sihon to the east of Jordan and to the north of Moab. The limitation is the more important inasmuch as it is frequently paralleled by reference to Og, king of Bashan, who first appears in *Deuteronomy*. If Bashan was recognized as a limited territory, as it undoubtedly was, should not the same restriction be assumed in the case of 'Amorite' at the end of the seventh century in Israel? The former is the name of a locality and the latter that of a people, but we are left with the possibility that in certain circles the word was confined to inhabitants of the district round Heshbon.

These considerations lead us to suppose that the name Amorite was generally applied to a large group of Semites, those, in fact, who formed the second great wave of migration from the Arabian peninsula, whence they emerged not later than the beginning of the third millennium B.C. Like their successors the Aramaeans, they lived at first the life of the Bedawin and of the shepherds, but gradually settled down in various parts of the Fertile Crescent, establishing their homes at many points in its circuit. As time passed they mingled so completely with their predecessors in most districts that their identity was lost, but it remained in certain parts, and the application of the term was gradually limited until it was confined to a small territory to the east of Jordan.[2]

These Amorite races belong physically to that type which we recognize as Semitic. To-day we find the pure stock only in Arabia, and, occasionally, in other lands occupied by Moslem invaders, e.g. in India. The frame is small-boned, slender, with delicately formed limbs and features, thin lips and straight nose, the whole giving an impression of a clear-cut face. Semites are clearly represented in the mural paintings characteristic of Egyptian art down to the end of the eighteenth dynasty, and we can identify the type, as has just been remarked, with that of the modern Arab.

We may gain some clue to their distribution, or at least to

---

[1] In Num. xxi. 25 it is possible that the term Amorite is used by J in this limited sense, but see E. Meyer in *ZAW.* for 1881, while Wellhausen, *Composition of the Hexateuch*, p. 110, ascribes the word to redaction.

[2] On the whole subject cp. also Böhl, *Kanaanäer und Hebräer*, especially pp. 31–63; Jirku, *GVI.*, pp. 40–2, especially footnote on p. 41.

their colonization of the west, from their language. This is by no means always a safe guide, for we not infrequently find an immigrant people adopting the speech of its predecessors. Thus, if we are right in ascribing the Mesopotamian Amurru and the Palestinian Amorite to the same stock, we shall have to admit that the former adopted the language of their predecessors. For one of the certain conclusions of Semitic philology is that the Mesopotamian group diverged from the main type at a stage when the accidence was still in process of development from being agglutinative to becoming fully inflected. But we have in and about Palestine a group of tongues which clearly belong to a common stock. These include Phoenician, Hebrew, and Moabite. The first is known to us through a large number of inscriptions, the last through a single one, the famous Moabite stone, or inscription of Mesha, discovered at Diban by M. Clermont-Ganneau. Hebrew is known to us through Israelite literature, but there is reason to suspect that it was not originally spoken by Israel—at least not before the conquest of Palestine. Certainly, as the evidence of the Tell-el-Amarna tablets shows,[1] it was the language of the pre-Israelite inhabitants of Palestine, and here again we are probably right in supposing that the invaders adopted the speech of their predecessors. We have no direct evidence as to the language of other peoples and tribes settled in this region, for no Edomite or Ammonite inscriptions have yet come to light, and only a word or two of Philistine has come down to us.[2] It is quite possible that these invaders also adopted the language which they found in the land before them, retaining one or two technical terms for which no equivalents were available.

Of the culture of the Amorites abundant evidence has come to light in recent years.[3] The breaking up of the Turkish empire

[1] The language of most of these is Akkadian, but the Palestinian scribes occasionally added to an unfamiliar word its equivalent in their own vernacular. These are the so-called 'Canaanite glosses', and they are clearly Hebrew, though perhaps they represent a somewhat earlier stage than the language of the Old Testament.

[2] Perhaps the only word we can with any certainty regard as Philistine is the word for 'prince' or 'king'—*seren*, which some would identify with the word τύραννος, surviving in Greek, though, apparently, of non-Hellenic origin. See also p. 44.

[3] It is, of course, impossible here to enter into any detailed account of the material culture of Palestine before the entry of Israel. The reader is referred to the standard works on Palestinian archaeology, e.g. Bliss and Macalister, *Excavations in Palestine*; Thomsen, *Kompendium der palästinischen Altertumskunde*; Benzinger, *Hebräische Archäologie*; Volz, *Die biblischen Altertümer*; Père Vincent, *Canaan*; the *Quarterly Statements of the Palestine Exploration Society*; the *Annual of the American Schools of Oriental Research*;

has given new opportunity and stimulus to archaeological research, and while a number of the sites excavated are primarily
Israelite, e.g. Samaria and Megiddo, there are others, such as
Jericho, Jerusalem, Beth-pelet, and Gezer, which belong to the
earlier people. The remains show them to have been a race
capable of a fairly high degree of culture; in particular they were
experts in building. The city walls of Jerusalem and of Jericho
were of considerable thickness, and those of Jerusalem very
lofty. The method of construction shows that the builders were
masons of no mean order, and the stone was often carefully
dressed. Cities were small, and within them the houses were
closely packed, leaving very narrow streets and passages.
Houses were built either of stone or of burnt brick in their lower
courses, while the upper parts (as was almost universal in the
ancient world) were composed of sun-dried mud. This, in the
course of ages, has sunk with the weather, with the result that
most of the cities are nothing more than mounds of earth concealing the more solid foundations. The objects of art, whether
of pottery or of metal, are nearly always local copies of forms
current elsewhere,[1] occasionally varied by much more delicate
and artistic imported objects. Neither at this or at any subsequent period did the inhabitants of Palestine show signs either
of artistic originality or of artistic appreciation.

As we have already seen, the first people to secure external
dominion in Palestine were the Egyptians, and it is interesting
to see how small was the permanent effect produced by their
presence. The Egyptian element in the later life of Israel was
comparatively slight, in spite of the close connexion between the
two countries in history and in commerce. And in these earlier
times the interest of Egypt was confined to exacting tribute.
In a few cities garrisons were placed, especially in Beth-shean,
and substantial evidence of Egyptian occupation has come to
light. But the Egyptians did not mingle with the people, and
even where they were established, the two cultures lay side by
side, producing no mixed forms. The Egyptian occupation
persisted till long after the Israelite conquest, and it is possible

and the detailed accounts of separate excavations, such as Petrie, *Tell-el-Ḥesy* (1891);
Bliss, *A Mound of Many Cities* (deals with the same site as the last) (1898); Macalister,
Excavations at Gezer; Sellin, *Tell Ta'annek* (1904–5) and *Jericho* (1913); and others too
numerous to mention. It is curious that a large proportion of the sites hitherto excavated are as important for their pre-Israelite material as for that which dates from
the Israelite occupation.   [1] This is especially true of the 'later pre-Israelite' period.

that 'Sisera' is a corruption of some Egyptian name, but, taking the whole of the country, we may safely say that the contribution of Egypt was negligible. Strange as it may seem, the civilization of Palestine, in spite of the conquests of the eighteenth and nineteenth dynasties, remained emphatically of the Mesopotamian, not of the Egyptian type.[1]

When we know more of the Hittites, we may have fuller details as to their hold on Palestine. It is, however, clear that they came not merely as conquerors but also as colonists, and that many of them made their home in the land. The stories of Abraham located a Hittite population in southern Palestine,[2] and at the end of the thirteenth century the dominant power in the land was that of the Hittite kingdom of Kadesh on the Orontes.

The most striking and obvious effect of this Hittite occupation is to be seen in the Jewish physiognomy. The broad, rather short, full-fleshed figure, and the heavy face with the large hooked nose, have practically nothing in common with the true Semitic type as we know it from the Arab and from the earlier Amorite. On the other hand, they are practically identical with the forms found on Anatolian monuments, and with representations of the ancient Hittites as we find them elsewhere. We may have no details as to the Hittite invasion, but it has left its stamp so clearly impressed on the faces of the people that we hardly need further evidence of its historicity.[3] Further, we find Hittites in Palestine throughout the history of Israel, and we must regard these as pools left by the retreating tide after the victories of Ramses II. The interval between

---

[1] It may be remarked that in Israelite, especially later Israelite, times, there seems to have been a good deal of interchange of thought between Egypt and Palestine, and perhaps even literary connexions.

[2] The passage in which the mention of the Hittites occurs is Gen. xxiii, where Abraham buys the cave of Macpelah from Ephron the Hittite. In its present form the narrative belongs to P, but may embody a very ancient tradition which has not survived in sections taken from other sources.

[3] An alternative suggestion as to the origin of the 'Hittite' element in Biblical Palestine has been made by Hempel, who thinks (cp. *Die Althebräische Literatur*, p. 8) that it was due to the presence of a Mitannian admixture in the nomad invaders among whom the later Israel is to be classed. The balance of evidence would seem, however, to be in favour of the view taken in the text, since the anthropological features of the case point to Anatolian rather than to Mitannian origin. Myres believes that this type of countenance may have been an inheritance from neolithic times. Against this view is the fact that the Palestinians figured in Egyptian monuments down to the eighteenth dynasty clearly belong to a pure Semitic stock.

Ikhnaton and Ramses II seems to be the only point at which this influx of Anatolian settlers can have taken place, and it is worth remembering that, even when her hold was weakest, Egypt still claimed the land, and actually maintained garrisons in one or two fortresses.

Two other racial elements are worthy of special mention. The first is that supplied by the more or less constant inflow of population from the wandering tribes on the inner edge of the Fertile Crescent. In the second millennium B.C. these belonged to that third wave of Semitic migration from Arabia to which the name *Aramaean* is commonly given. Except in one or two districts in the north (Damascus is the best known), they remained for the most part Bedawin, or pastoral nomads. Their continuous movement made them, apparently, in later times the great carriers and caravan leaders of the ancient East, and their tongue, or some of its dialects, became the language of diplomacy and of international commerce, superseding the Akkadian which had served this purpose at least as late as the fourteenth century B.C. Whilst the Aramaeans included the ancestors of Israel proper, we may be sure that other tribes also were concerned. For this influx was not confined to a single period, but, on a small scale, was continuous. There were times when the weakness of the defenders made access to the cultivated lands particularly easy, as in the days of Ikhnaton and the Israelite 'Judges', but all through its history Palestine has been exposed to inroads from the east, and from time to time the invaders have not been content merely to acquire booty, but have settled down in the land. The Aramaeans were a fairly pure Semitic type, and their language seems to have been a development from the main stock later than Hebrew. They maintained for the most part their hunting or pastoral habits, and for centuries small groups of them continued to find homes in the barer parts of the land.

The last group of settlers are those who, curiously enough, gave their name to the whole country—the Philistines.[1] It is only within comparatively recent years that we have been able to identify them, and to assign to them their true place in history. The researches of the last generation have revealed to us a whole civilization, with centres in Crete, Asia Minor, and the Greek mainland, which had been almost entirely lost to

[1] The name Palestine was first used by the Greeks.

sight. It was known to us only conjecturally through the Homeric poems, till excavations in the Troad, in Crete, and in the Peloponnese, brought it to light. The name Aegean is commonly used to cover the whole, though its parts seem to have been fairly distinct. It began to break down under the pressure of wilder tribes from the north, and from the thirteenth century onwards its survivors made constant attempts to secure homes to the south. Ramses III (early twelfth century) repelled a great assault made by land and sea, or they would have made good their footing in the delta of the Nile.[1] But though they were prevented from entering Egypt, and for a time beaten back, it is clear that they returned and, moving along the coast roads, settled between the Carmel range and the Egyptian frontier. Immediately south of Carmel the new-comers belonged to a people known as the Zakkara; farther south the Philistines established themselves particularly at five centres, Gath, Ekron, Ashkelon, Ashdod, and Gaza.[2]

Their appearance is familiar to us from the battle scenes of Egypt, and they are characterized by a feathered head-dress which reminds us somewhat of the crested helmet which we associate with the Greeks of the heroic age. Their entry into Palestine was a migration rather than an invasion, for they came with great wheeled vehicles, in which they transported their wives and their movable property.[3] Their pottery identifies them as belonging to the latest Aegean age, and we can hardly doubt that in these Philistines we have all that really survived of one of the greatest civilizations of the ancient world. They spread over the whole land, and might have established a new empire but for the rise of Israel. The five cities formed a confederacy which had, apparently, no real organic unity, though its members used to take counsel and act together in any matter which seemed to affect their common interests, while retaining complete autonomy when they so desired. While the Philistines were never formally members of the Israelite state, there can be little doubt that they contributed something to the blood of the later people. The stories of Samson illustrate at least the possibility of intermarriage, and it seems

[1] Cp. the name *Purusati* among the enemies defeated by Ramses III, *Papyrus Harris*, pl. 76, 17; Breasted, *ARE.* iv, § 403.

[2] Myres, *Who were the Greeks ?*, pp. 130 f., calls attention to the fact that early Philistine pottery shows very clearly the influence of the Minoan pottery of Cyprus.

[3] Cp. illustrations on pp. 112–15 of E. Meyer, *GA.*, from Medinet Habu.

that David had Philistine connexions of some kind, though possibly not of actual blood. Certainly he relied on Philistine help; the royal bodyguard which he established was largely drawn from that source, and in his greatest difficulties he retained the loyal service and affection of Philistine friends.

There were other and later immigrants, especially those who were settled in Galilee and Samaria after the fall of the northern kingdom. But there was a decided effort made in post-exilic times to exclude them from the official Jewish community. We cannot suppose that these efforts were wholly successful, and in considering the ancestry of the more modern Jew, we must allow for the possibility of this element. Yet for the purpose of our present study, the story of Israel down to the end of the monarchic period, these factors are negligible. Without them the admixture of races was sufficiently complex, and it may be doubted whether any people composed of such diverse elements has ever played so important a part upon the stage of history.

ADDITIONAL NOTES

Page 32, note 6. *Add*: These popular etymologies are hardly reliable; the Horites, for example, may be connected with the Hurrians of the north.

Page 36, note 2. *Pirizzi* occurs as the name of a messenger sent by Tushratta of Mitanni to Amenhotep IV. Cf. Knudtzon, 27, 89, 93, 100; 28, 12; 29, 91, and Dhorme: *L'Évolution religieuse d'Israël*, pp. 119 f.

Page 39, note 2. *Add*: Possibly also פִּילֶגֶשׁ, 'a secondary wife'.

Chapter IV

TRADITIONS OF ISRAEL'S ANCESTRY

SUMMARY

[Though the racial ancestry of Israel was so mixed, most of her early traditions belong to one group—the Aramaeans. Abraham, Isaac, Jacob, and the twelve patriarchs, may be regarded for the most part as historical personages, though the stories told of them (except Abraham) may often be interpreted as tribal rather than individual history.

Traditions carry back the Aramaean ancestry of Israel to the district of Ur in southern Mesopotamia. Thence they moved, perhaps about 2350 B.C., northwards to Harran, and a group of them continued their wanderings round the Fertile Crescent as far as Egypt. Many places in Palestine had traditions of the presence of Abraham and Jacob; Isaac was known chiefly in the far south, near Beer-sheba.

The stories of Jacob and his sons, especially, seem to reflect tribal interrelationships. These seem to indicate a sense of common blood among them all, though they fall into groups within which the alliance is closer. One group seems to have consisted traditionally of Reuben, Simeon, Levi, Judah, together with Zebulun and Naphtali, Gad, and Asher being attached as subordinate tribes. The other group contained Joseph (later Ephraim and Manasseh) and Benjamin, to whom were appended Issachar and Dan. To some extent this theory is borne out by history, since Simeon and Levi disappeared very early as tribes, and Reuben vanished before the establishment of the monarchy. The two leading elements are those of Joseph and Judah, though the latter may have been originally a Canaanite people, imported into the community of Israel at a comparatively late date, and reaching eminence only in the time of David.

Some of the tribes—belonging to the Joseph group—settled on the borders of Egypt, probably during the Hyksos age. After the rise of the eighteenth dynasty (1600 B.C. onwards) they were much exposed to Egyptian violence, and many of them were forced into slavery. At the same time they retained their sense of kinship with the rest, and even with other tribes still farther from the frontiers of Egypt and nearer to Palestine itself.]

Sources. For this subject we are practically confined to the book of *Genesis*. Here we have, as is generally agreed, narratives emanating from at least three distinct sources, (*a*) traditions preserved and collected in southern Israel ('J'), (*b*) similar traditions originating in northern Israel ('E'), and others which have reached their present form through priestly redaction, though it is not disputed that the

material which they embody—or at least a part of it—may be far
more ancient than the actual compilation in which they have been
preserved. It is also possible that we have some genuine historical
tradition lying behind Genesis xiv, a chapter containing two narratives which cannot be assigned to any of the other recognized groups.
If this is so, we have in one of them our only direct contact with any
historical figures known to us from outside Israel, for the kings
against whom Abraham is represented as fighting bear names
familiar to us in Babylonia at the beginning of the second millennium
B.C. At the same time it must be observed that their identification
raises difficulties, since the kings whose names most resemble Chedorlaomer (this name has not been discovered, though it is a natural and
suitable Elamite formation), Amraphel, Arioch, and Tidal, were not
contemporary with one another. There does, however, remain the
possibility that ancient tradition placed Abraham, perhaps rightly,
in the age of Ḥammurabi. Apart from this we have no external
evidence available for the time of the patriarchs.

OUR sketch of the physical ancestry of Israel has helped us to
see that it contained an extraordinary mixture of blood.
Aboriginal—of Armenoid or other race—Semite (Amorite and
Aramaean), Hittite and Philistine all contributed their quota.
The historic language of the people was a dialect of the western
Semitic or Amorite. The physiognomy characteristic of the
Jew is either primitive Armenoid or, more probably, Hittite—
perhaps both. The culture of Palestine in the historic period
owed much in tradition and in law to a Mesopotamian, and
ultimately to a Sumerian source. The name by which the land
is commonly known is derived from one of the Aegean peoples
who were among the last to colonize the country.

Neither common blood, common culture, common language,
nor common political organization can, separately or together,
make a nation. It is true that for four or five centuries Israel
was organized into one, or rather two, states, but this was the
effect, not the cause, of the sentiment of nationality. There is
a subtle factor in the consciousness of every people, which,
though it may escape definition and defy analysis, is yet most
real, and, indeed, determines the essence of what we call a
sense of nationality. As the most recent anthropological research[1] has shown, the Greeks had an ancestry almost as complicated as that of Israel, spoke widely different dialects, and
clung passionately to the autonomy of the city state. Yet from

[1] Cp. especially Myres, *Who were the Greeks?*

the time when the history of Greece proper begins we can see that, behind all these separate, warring little communities, with their mutual jealousies and rivalries, there lay a sense of oneness as against the rest of the world. There was a Pan-hellenic feeling which found its clearest expression in the Persian wars, but was never wholly lost. Much as the individual Greek city might dislike its neighbours, it still recognized the distinc-tion between Greek and barbarian, and no difference of dialect, habit, or polity, ever obscured the sense of the fundamental unity of the Greek nation. It was tradition more than anything else which made the Greeks a self-contained people, and though the oldest (and, in some ways, the most powerful) elements in that tradition belonged rather to their predecessors than to the Greeks proper, they served to create and to maintain Greece as a spiritual entity.

So it was with Israel. The controlling factor in her recogni-tion of herself as a nation was that supplied by Aramaean blood and, still more, by Aramaean tradition. As far as physical ancestry was concerned, that element seems to have been com-paratively slight. The invaders from the 'wilderness' can hardly have been very numerous, and, after their first inroads, their 'conquest' was achieved rather by the assimilation of the earlier population than by military triumphs. Their victory was not won by force, it was the imposition of a national sentiment on an alien people. It was their ideas, not their armies, that secured their ultimate supremacy over their predecessors, and made them the power they became. We need not dwell here on the details; it will be necessary for us to discuss those at a later stage. But, at the outset, it is of the highest importance that we should recognize the main fact.

When the pious Israelite of later days brought to the common sanctuary his offering of thanksgiving for the mercies vouchsafed to him during the year, he began his recital of the benefits he had received with the words 'A lost Aramaean was my father',[1] and the phrase is all the more striking inasmuch as the gifts for which he expressed his gratitude were those especially sought by the agriculturist, not by the shepherd or the hunter. It was his corn, his wine, and his oil, the produce of

[1] Deut. xxvi. 5. The passage in its present form dates from the seventh century B.C., but, in view of the persistence of Israelite tradition, we may suspect that the formula itself was much older.

the ground on which he had settled, that he attributed to the beneficence of his God. It is the conjunction and the combination of these two interests and points of view which form the key to the whole history of Israel, which made her unique among the nations of the ancient world, and rendered possible the message she had to give mankind in economics, in politics, and, above all, in religion.

The Aramaean was essentially a wandering shepherd. He may have reached a plane somewhat higher than that of the pure Bedawin, and there is a tendency to-day to see in him a representative of the type known as the 'half-nomad'. But, even while we recognize that he was not simply the wild inhabitant of the wilderness,[1] we must remember that his life and outlook did not differ very greatly from those of the Bedawin, and that he was more closely allied to them in general thought than to the settled farmer. As he entered Palestine, he brought with him much of his traditional attitude towards personal relationships, whether these concerned man or God. He retained in an almost unique degree the social theory and the religious outlook of the nomad age, and, as he absorbed the agricultural and civic peoples who were in the land before him, he introduced and insisted upon his philosophy of life. It is true that such language as we use would have been unintelligible to him, for his modes of thought were very different from ours. He acted without conscious premeditation, but this very lack of deliberate purpose serves only to indicate more clearly the overwhelming force of the spiritual power within him. The new principles which he brought into the life of the country were not expressly set forth or elevated into constitutional law; they were the inevitable outcome of instincts developed by generations of nomad life, and woven into the very fabric of his being.

Now it is true that, in all probability, other elements in the population of Palestine had at one time or another passed from the life of the nomad to that of the agriculturist. It is hardly possible to doubt that the Amorite stratum, for instance, had in the distant past made the same changes in its life as did the Hebrew. But there was one outstanding difference, and it is to

---

[1] It may be worth while remarking that the 'wilderness' of the Old Testament is not absolutely barren, waterless desert, but land which, though not suited for cereals and other crops, yet afforded the scanty herbage on which the small cattle of the nomad could subsist.

this that we may attribute the uniqueness of the history of Israel. When the Aramaean nomad settled in western Palestine, he left not a few of his brethren behind. The circumstances of the conquest were such as to bring only a portion of the Israelite confederacy into the richer corn-lands, and it was many generations before the whole came under a single sway. At the same time an appreciable and influential section of the people remained on the pastoral plane, especially in the east and south. The shepherd of Gilead or of the Negeb, the farmer of Esdraelon, and the merchant of Shechem or of Samaria, all recognized themselves and one another as true Israelites, and felt themselves bound together into a single nation as against the rest of the world.

By far the most powerful factor in maintaining this unity of the agricultural and the pastoral Israel was their common acceptance of Yahweh as their national God. We find, even in western Palestine, from the early days of the Aramaean settlements down to and beyond the end of the monarchical period devotees of Yahweh who insisted on a whole-hearted devotion to Him, and gave themselves to the maintenance of the old traditions. In the earliest literary form in which we can trace them, our stories of the patriarchs—the Aramaean ancestors of Israel—come from the time of the monarchy. Yet, with one consent, they present the life of the 'wandering Aramaean' as the ideal, and the tent-dwelling shepherd as the model Israelite. We may justly suspect that one or two of them originated in agricultural Palestine before the Conquest, and that these had, in the first instance, no reference to pastoral Israel,[1] but the significant fact is that they have been so modified as to bear a superficial appearance of dealing with that plane, and have been woven by the compilers into the general fabric of the patriarchal age.

The history of Israel, then, is the record of the interaction of these two orders of society, or rather of the spiritual principles which they embodied. In many ways the contrast between the two amounts to conflict. Nomad conceptions of sexual morality, of the position of property, of the rights of personality, of the

---

[1] The Creation, Eden, and Flood stories are hardly 'national'. The traditions of the origins of the tribe of Judah, preserved in Gen. xxxviii, seem to be drawn from a non-Aramaean source, and to belong to the earlier Canaanite stratum of the population. It is possible that the account of the sack of Shechem in Gen. xxxiv, and a number of the notices which account for the more famous sanctuaries in Israel have a similar provenance. For an alternative explanation see p. 60, n. 2.

substantial equality of all members of the community, were diametrically opposed to the theory and practice of the more highly organized agricultural and monarchic states of the ancient world. We shall find, even in western Palestine, factors which tended to preserve the traditions of the wilderness, but at times their influence weakened, and they themselves fell captive, as it were, to the life of the world about them. But within Israel, though outside the agricultural community, there still remained those who stood for the old ideals, and when the lowering moral and spiritual influences of the new life seemed most to threaten the principles which the nation claimed as its own, there came from the half-desert an Elijah or an Amos to reiterate the old demands of Yahweh.

Israel thus entered on a great experiment, the passage from a simple order of society to one far more complicated and difficult. Others had passed through the same transition, but her effort was peculiar, inasmuch as it involved an attempt, perhaps half-unconscious but very real, on the part of a section of her people to apply to the new life principles in religion and in social ethics which had proved successful in the old. The experiment ended in apparent failure, and the fall of the Hebrew monarchy in 586 B.C. marked the extinction of any political hopes the prophetic party may have cherished. But the spirit and the ideals survived, and, in a sense, it was only when Israel had ceased to be a nation to the outward eye that she began her great task in the world. For six centuries longer she remained a subject-people in her national home, developing and enlarging her religious conceptions. But the conditions of her life and the complex tradition which she inherited precluded a general transmission of her message to the outside world. In a certain sense the breaking loose of the Christian Church from the Jewish community was the liberation of the ideals which counted for most in Judaism itself. Then, and only then, were these essential principles in religion and ethics made available for the great mass of humanity. While the modern exponent of Christian theology is justified in refusing to see the whole of the Gospel in the book of *Genesis*, he must admit that the Hebrew presentation of the patriarchal age contains at least the seed from which the great tree ultimately sprang.

It is a task of peculiar difficulty to determine the actual value of these traditions for history. Whilst it seems that in each of the main sources of the Hexateuch the different elements were so arranged as to produce a continuous narrative, we need to remember that this represents the opinion of a comparatively late age—probably the former half of the monarchical period. The Hexateuch documents are eloquent testimony to the skill with which writers of that period constructed their stories, giving them the impress of an almost unbroken record of events, and fitting into place the various tales which they collected. They have, indeed, succeeded in offering their readers something like written lives (on a small scale) of Abraham, Jacob, and Joseph. But when we examine our documents rather more closely, it becomes evident that this appearance of straightforward biography may be at times misleading. The elements which are woven into the narrative seem to have been drawn from a variety of sources and cannot all be interpreted in the same way.

Broadly speaking, we may say that the narratives fall into two classes. Some of them were from the first what they are still, stories about individual men and women. Others seem to be memories of tribal history, thinly veiled under the cloak of personal experiences. Most of the former class seem to have been told in the first instance with some special purpose, often supplying the explanation of some natural fact or traditional custom. Thus we may assume that the narrative which describes the destruction of the cities of the plain, with its appended note concerning Lot's wife, was an attempt to account for the desolate country to the south-east of the Dead Sea, based, perhaps, on dim memories of some tremendous natural convulsion. With this men connected a story explaining the existence of some upright block of stone in which a fanciful eye might detect a resemblance to a human figure. The Penuel narrative in Gen. xxxii. 24–32 gives a reason for a curious food-*tabu*—later Israel avoided eating a particular part of the thigh, because it corresponded in the animal to that which was touched by the river-spirit in his struggle with Jacob. We may suppose that such stories of the conflict between men and the countless spirits of nature were common, and one of them has been used for this particular purpose. A number of the statements and narratives in Genesis are clearly the ἱεροὶ λόγοι of different sanctuaries, told by the attendant priests to the faithful in order to explain how it was that the presence of a *numen* had originally been identified. Thus a divine revelation given to Abraham was held responsible for the sanctuaries at Shechem,[1] Bethel,[2] Mamre,[3] Beer-sheba,[4] and perhaps Moriah.[5] The best known of all these stories is, of course, the narrative of Jacob at Bethel, and it is noticeable that it was current both in the north and in the south, though the two forms differed slightly from one another. But in considering these we have always to be alive to one possibility. It is beyond doubt that some of the Israelite sanctuaries had previously been centres of Canaanite worship, and the stories in themselves may thus be more ancient than the Israelite form of them. They may have contained other names, changed to those of the patriarchs after the supremacy of Israel had been well established in the land.[6] This certainly seems to be true of Shechem, and also of Jerusalem, if we are to place Moriah on the later Temple hill—a very doubtful identification. In no case can we feel confident that we have here a reliable tradition regarding the movements and actions of the patriarchs themselves.

It may also be observed that the names of some of the patriarchs—though not of all—appear outside Israel as those of gods. The place-names Jacob-el and Joseph-el mentioned in an inscription of Tutmose III indicate that there were deities bearing two of these names.[7] Gad is a well-known Mesopotamian god, and was worshipped even on Mount Hermon.[8] Asher is quite possibly a variant pronunciation of the divine name Ashur, and a god Laban is known from Cappadocia.[9] We have, however, no patriarchal story which at all resembles a myth, and, on the

---

[1] Gen. xii. 6; see Driver, *Book of Genesis*, p. 146 [12th ed., 1926].

[2] This apparently is the original intention of the notice in Gen. xii. 8, but since the sanctuary was also attributed to Jacob, about whom a longer story was current, the locality of Abraham's altar had to be shifted slightly eastwards.

[3] Gen. xiii. 18, and perhaps also ch. xviii.   [4] Gen. xxi. 25–33.

[5] Gen. xxii. The site intended seems to be very uncertain. For a discussion of the point see Skinner, *Genesis* (*ICC.*), pp. 328 f., and Gunkel, *Genesis* (*HK.*), pp. 240 f.

[6] It is a curious fact that unless we count Gen. xlix. 10, which does not suggest a theophany, even if the text be correct, the patriarchal narratives have no mention of Shiloh, the one great Israelite sanctuary of which we can say with certainty that it had no Canaanite predecessor.

[7] Cp. below, pp. 90 ff.   [8] Cp. also Isa. lxv. 11.

[9] I am indebted to Mr. G. R. Driver for the following note: '*Laban* occurs as a divine name as a component element in the "Cappadocian" (*c.* 2000–2500 B.C.) proper name *Gimil-Laban* = "mercy of Laban" like *Gimil-Ištar*, *Gimil-Ašur*, *Gimil-Dagan*, and so on (Stephens, *Personal Names of Cappadocia*, 66), where ŠU is the ideogram for *Gimillum*. It was foreshadowed from a glossary in Winckler-Zimmern, *KAT.*³ 363.' In the absence of other conjectures we may guess that Laban was a form of the Moon-god (לבנה).

whole, the best explanation of the facts may be that they represent a stage in Hebrew religion when the objects of worship were the eponymous ancestors of the tribes which bore these names.

It will also be necessary to allow for the possibility that some of the stories were originally pure inventions—to put the matter plainly, short novels. It is, perhaps, only in the narratives which describe the fortunes of Joseph that we are tempted to such an explanation of the facts, but here we certainly have familiar tales from Egypt which present parallels to some, at least, of the events recorded in the life of this patriarch. The best known is the tale of the Two Brothers,[1] where we have a story not unlike that of Joseph and Potiphar's wife.

It will be obvious that narratives which originate as we may guess these to have done will have comparatively little value for the historian. There is, however, the second class, from which we may expect to be able to extract a residuum of historical fact, though even here we may feel that our conjectures are dubious. There are passages in which it seems that the names indicate, not so much individuals as personified tribes. This habit of speaking of a tribe by the name of its eponymous ancestor is common among Semitic peoples, and we have one very obvious and familiar illustration in the use of the name Israel, not for the individual elsewhere designated Jacob, but for the nation which claimed descent from him. While, then, we should probably fall into serious error if we denied the historicity of the patriarchs themselves, we must always allow for the possibility that the narratives concerning them are really traditional accounts of the relations of the tribes to one another and to other peoples. Thus we shall not be far wrong if we interpret the covenant between Jacob and Laban[2] as an early treaty between Israelites and Syrians, delimiting the border to the north of Gilead. Similarly the treacherous assault on Shechem[3] is far more likely to have been the work of the combined tribes of Simeon and Levi than an act perpetrated by two individuals. And we should, perhaps, see in some of the patriarchal marriages and genealogies an ancient account of the combinations and relations of various tribes.[4] It may be that this principle can be pressed

---

[1] Cp. *Select Papyri from the British Museum*, pt. ii; Gressmann, *ATAT.*, pp. 69 ff.

[2] Gen. xxxi. 44–54.   [3] Gen. xxxiv.

[4] This may be illustrated particularly by the marriages of Isaac (Gen. xxiv) and Jacob (Gen. xxix. 15 ff., cp. also xxviii. 1 ff. (P)), which, perhaps, reflect the nomad tendency to endogamy.

too far, but it is certainly a factor for which we must allow in attempting to recover the meaning of Israel's traditions concerning her ancestors.

There is, however, no suggestion that the first of the patriarchs, Abraham, ever represents a tribe, or, indeed, any other than himself—an individual person. He and the others are always depicted as leaders of shepherd clans; their wealth consists in flocks of sheep and goats. In Gen. xxvi. 12 Isaac is said to have sown corn profitably, but this need be no more than the occasional agriculture of the semi-nomad, temporarily settled in an arable district, and nowhere is there a hint that either he, his father, or his son, were anything but wanderers. The word in Deut. xxvi. 5, rendered in the A.V. 'ready to perish' and above translated 'lost',[1] is one which might be used of a sheep or goat which had strayed from its fellows and was homeless. It is admirably suited to the nomad who had no permanent home, but moved from place to place as occasion and the supply of water and food should determine.

We may take it for granted that the wandering Aramaean, though compelled to move over a fairly wide area, often had some civic centre. Especially in districts which lay about a large town or city, he would assume a definite relation, commercial and political, with its people, and would probably be compelled to acknowledge its ruler as in some sense his own overlord. The nomad lived within reach of the city, and his safety and well-being were thus bound up with its prosperity, and for him to pass beyond the radius of the city's influence was to journey into a strange land.

The Hebrew tradition connects Abraham[2] and his tribe with Ur, a city in the south of Mesopotamia, and at one time not far from the edge of the Persian Gulf. Later Israelites spoke of Abraham as having been called out of Ur of the Chaldees, but that is not the only form of the tradition. The earliest narra-

---

[1] Heb. אֹבֵד.

[2] It is a little curious that, outside the Hexateuch, we have no mention of Abraham in any passage which we can safely assign to the pre-exilic period. Nevertheless we cannot hold, with Wellhausen, that Abraham is a later importation into the tradition, for the earliest strata in the Hexateuch contain stories of which he is the hero, and Wellhausen would agree that these are older than any prophetic writings. We must assume the omission of his name elsewhere to be accidental. Isaac, Jacob, and Joseph are names found as early as Amos (cp. Am. vii. 16, vi. 8, vi. 6, &c., while Hosea uses 'Ephraim' as parallel, if not as equivalent, to 'Israel', e.g. Hos. v. 3, &c.).

tive[1] has no mention of the place from which Abram was called, emphasizing only the fact that he had to leave his family and his kindred. The narrative of P, on the other hand, distinctly states that it was Terah, the father of Abram who led the migration from Ur, and that he settled with his clan at Harran, in the north of the Fertile Crescent.[2] This may be an ancient tradition, omitted by the compiler from the section he took from J, because it occurred also in his other document. Be that as it may, two facts seem to emerge, one that the tradition carried the family back to Ur, and the other that it was Abraham who headed the latter part of the migration, and ultimately reached the borders of Palestine.

We have no information as to the reasons why the tribe migrated from Ur in the first instance; the further movement from Harran, on the other hand, is ascribed directly to a divine command. But we know from Mesopotamian sources that towards the end of the second millennium great changes were taking place in Chaldaea. The old order, in which the Sumerian cities, Ur, Isin, Lagash, had taken the lead, was definitely passing away. Somewhere about the year 2350 B.C. Ur was overthrown by an Elamite invasion, and though it was not finally destroyed, its political importance came to an end. We may conjecture that the same invasion threatened the wandering tribes whose centre was Ur, and that they felt it advisable to seek new pasture in less troubled lands.[3]

The statement in Gen. xi. 32 that Terah, the leader of the first migration, died in Harran, evidently implies an extended residence in that district, in the view of the priestly writer. In all forms of the tradition Abraham is represented as leading the next great movement, in company with Lot, the ancestor of the kindred tribes of Moab and Ammon. Nahor, from whom the Syrians of the Damascus district are to spring, remains behind, though the narratives assume that there was a later migration westward by these people also.

The story of Abraham in Canaan is clearly produced by a compilation of narratives derived from various local traditions. There were, as we have already seen, sanctuaries in the land which claimed him as their founder, and it was assumed that he made a regular progress through the country, making a stay at

---

[1] Gen. xi. 28–30, xii. 1–3. Note that in these passages the form *Abram* is used. Cp. also the Shishak stele; Breasted, *HE.*, p. 363.
[2] Gen. xi. 31.   [3] Cp. L. W. King, *SA.*, p. 304 [1923].

each of these in turn. Palestine at this time, i.e. probably at the end of the third or the beginning of the second millennium, seems to have developed that civic life which is so prominent a feature in the correspondence of seven centuries later, though we may conjecture that the cities were fewer and the population more sparse than in the Tell-el-Amarna period. At the same time there is no impossibility in the suggestion that a pastoral tribe should find sustenance and be able to move with some freedom, since large tracts of country were suited only to the shepherd.[1] We have thus a station beside the Oracle Terebinth near Shechem,[2] another twenty miles farther south, between Bethel and Ai,[3] and there is a third by the terebinth of Mamre near Hebron.[4]

In Gen. xiv. we have a passage which is unique in the patriarchal narratives. It contains two stories, one of which brings Abraham into conflict with a coalition of Mesopotamian kings, while the other tells of his visit to 'Salem', i.e. probably Jerusalem,[5] and of his relations with Melchizedek, king of that city. The latter of the two is inserted in the middle of the former, and, though they may originally have been independent, they were intended by the actual writer to form a continuous narrative. Critically, the chapter cannot be assigned to any of the other recognized sources, and it has certain marks of lateness. But this does not prevent us from supposing that it contains a very early tradition, though what we know at present of Mesopotamia at the end of the third millennium B.C. suggests that there has been a good deal of confusion. The names of the four kings are generally interpreted as follows. Chedorlaomer is a Hebraised form of the Elamite Kudur-Lagamar, though no reference to an actual king of this name has yet been discovered. Amraphel may be Ḥammurabi, Arioch closely resembles Eri-aku, the Sumerian form of the name of Arad-Sin, a king of Larsa who lived not long before Ḥammurabi, while Tidal is probably the same word as Tudḥula, though no king of this name is yet

---

[1] Palestine in the early patriarchal period is sometimes described as a well-populated country. For this we have little evidence, since our earliest full details come from the fourteenth century, and even then there is opportunity for the wilderness peoples to enter the land and make their home in it. The Sinuḥe story suggests a much wilder country, and a lower level of culture. Cp. Stade, *GVI.*, p. 139 [1886].

[2] Gen. xii. 6.   [3] Gen. xii. 8.   [4] Gen. xiii. 18, xviii. 1.

[5] Cp. Driver, *Book of Genesis*, p. 164 (12th ed., 1926); Skinner, *Genesis (ICC.,* 1910), p. 268.

known.[1] A western expedition by a Mesopotamian coalition which included Hammurabi is by no means impossible, though we have no evidence of an attack on south-eastern Palestine from Babylonian sources of this period. But we do know enough to make it clear that in details the narrative is untrustworthy.[2] Further, the picture of Abraham as a bold and successful warrior is not quite consistent with the usual presentation of the patriarchs as peaceful shepherds.[3] We can say only that the narrative may have a substratum of historic fact, though it is no longer possible to recover the actual events in detail. More interesting still is the tradition which carries Abraham down to Egypt,[4] and thus begins the long association of Israel with that country. One form of his story also locates him at Gerar,[5] and the foundation of Beer-sheba is ascribed to him.[6] It is possible, though by no means certain, that the story of Gen. xxii. is intended to bring Abraham into connexion with Jerusalem.[7] Generally speaking, however, it is Hebron with which he is most closely associated.

Isaac, on the other hand, has little said of him, and most of what is said is more or less a repetition of stories which have already appeared in the life of Abraham. All, however, centre round Beer-sheba and Gerar.[8] Here we have the same attempt to deceive Abimelech (the king of Gerar has the same name in both narratives)[9] and the same strife over the wells which have already been described of his father, though in different terms. We may, in fact, say that there is one item only in the life of Isaac proper which shows independence of the Abraham narratives, and that is the mention of his having some success in agriculture, Gen. xxvi. 12.

The story of his marriage,[10] however, is significant, though, as

---

[1] Böhl (ZAW. 42 (1924), pp. 148 ff. suggests Tud'alia, a Hittite king of the seventeenth century B.C.

[2] The question has been studied by all recent commentators on Genesis, the fullest and most elaborate discussion being that of Skinner, *Genesis* (ICC.), pp. 255–76, esp. 278 ff.

[3] Of course, shepherd peoples are not necessarily peaceful. But Israelite tradition did normally represent its ancestors as being unwarlike, cp. the contrast between Jacob and Esau in Gen. xxxiii.

[4] Gen. xii. 10 ff.   [5] Gen. xxi.   [6] Gen. xxi. 22–33.

[7] For a discussion of the various theories as to the location of the 'land of Moriah', see Skinner, *Genesis*, pp. 328 f. [1912].   [8] Gen. xxvi. 6.

[9] For the relation between the three stories in which a patriarch lies about his wife to ensure his safety, cp. Wellhausen, *HI.* (E.T.), p. 320 n.; Skinner, *Genesis*, pp. 364 f.; Procksch, *Die Genesis*, pp. 94, 150, 297 [1913]; Gunkel, *Genesis*, pp. 225 f. [1910]; Eissfeldt, *Hexateuch Synopse*, pp. 9 ff., 89 [1922].   [10] Gen. xxiv.

it now appears, it is rather included in the life of Abraham. We may have in it a reflection of a later feeling against the pre-Israelite inhabitants of Palestine, or, more probably, we have a genuine tradition, cast in the form of a personal narrative, of a fresh racial movement. Abraham will not allow his son to marry any of their neighbours,[1] and insists on his taking a wife from among his own kindred. Accordingly Rebecca is brought from 'Aram Naharaim'. This is apparently on the upper waters of the Euphrates, and the 'city of Nahor', which is unnamed in the narrative, is probably intended to be Harran.[2] Does not this point to a fresh migration from the locality at which the clan had divided, a smaller group following in the footsteps of the company led by Abraham, and uniting with the larger in the south of Palestine?

In the narratives of the children of Isaac it seems to be clear that the tribal *motif* has become much stronger, and, though the stories have grown to be extraordinarily vivid pictures of individual nomad life, the events which they describe are rather to be interpreted for the most part as affecting whole clans and not merely isolated persons. Thus, at the outset we have the contrast between Jacob and Esau.[3] The one is a 'civilized' man, living in a tent, which is the proper dwelling for the good nomad, the other is a 'wild man', a hunter, with not even the tent for a home. Esau does not understand the cookery of the higher levels: a dish of lentils is to him simply 'that red stuff'. The contrast is between the two cultural orders, that of the food-gatherer and that of the food-producer. The narratives of the sale of the birthright (Gen. xxv. 29–34) and the stolen blessing (Gen. xxvii.)[4] are intended to describe the gradual growth of

---

[1] Professor H. J. Fleure suggests that the story of Isaac and Rebecca is evidence 'of the endogamous tendencies which are fairly widespread among nomads and pastoralists generally'.

[2] The name Naharaim is clearly identical with the Egyptian Naharin—Nahrima in the Tell-el-Amarna tablets—and is to be located, not in Mesopotamia proper, but on the Euphrates itself. Cp. Ed. Meyer's identification, *GA.* i. 2², §§ 334, 463, and Skinner's additional note in *Genesis*, p. 342. For the identification with Harran cp. Gen. xxvii. 43, xxviii. 10, xxix. 4. Skinner's suggestion that עִיר נָחוֹר 'is probably an Elohistic variant to '*Aram Naharaim*, in which case a much less distant locality may be referred to' is beside the point, since, wherever the city is, it must be that which Israelite tradition regarded as the proper home of the Aramaean group from which Abraham himself had sprung.

[3] Cp. esp. Gen. xxv. 27.

[4] This latter was evidently a favourite theme with Israelite story-tellers; it appears in both the ancient traditions, J and E, with slight variations.

Israel as compared with Edom. The latter was the older as an organized and settled state,[1] but was subdued by David, and from his time onwards, down to the fall of Jerusalem in 586 B.C., was always liable to hold a subordinate position. Israel was thus the younger and the stronger of the two peoples.

We are probably justified in assuming that a similar interpretation is to be placed on the story of Jacob's domestic life. We need not question the historicity of Jacob himself. The twelve (thirteen?) patriarchs are more doubtful; some may have been gods, some totem animals, some human ancestors, but it may be doubted whether any of the latter were actually Jacob's sons. It would seem that the later Israel was formed by the federation of several groups of clans. There is a suggestion of a primitive totemism in the names of the two chief 'mothers', for Leah seems to mean a 'wild cow', while Rachel certainly signifies 'ewe'. In that case the names of the sons will be those of the subordinate clans united under the same totem, while the sons of the slaves, Bilhah and Zilpah, will represent tribes which occupied a lower standing in the eyes of their fellow-Israelites.[2] It is, of course, clear that this interpretation is by no means dependent on the totemistic view, and that it is equally valid (or invalid) whatever be the original motive for the giving of the names. We may go further, and say that the order in which the children are born indicates the ancient view of the way in which the individual groups came gradually into existence.

From this fluid tradition we may, then, venture to crystallize out a residuum, if not of actual history, at least of the view of history commonly held in the Israel of the eleventh century.

---

[1] Cp. Gen. xxxvi. 31, and the tradition which made Israel ask for a passage through the settled Edomite territory, Num. xx. 14–21, xxi. 4, Deut. ii. 2–8.

[2] The totemistic view is championed by Robertson Smith, *Kinship and Marriage in Early Arabia*, pp. 218 ff. [1903], *Journal of Philology*, ix. 80, 96, who adds the name of Reuben as that of a hybrid between wolf and hyena; Stade, *GVI*. i. 152, 408. Nöldeke, *ZDMG*. xl. 165 ff., while not denying the possibility of totemism, doubts whether it is to be found here, and the view is contested by Haupt, *Nachrichten der kön. Gesell. zu Göttingen*, 1883, pp. 100 ff., and by Ed. Meyer, *IN.*, pp. 308 ff. Meyer believes that these animal-names were given in ancient Israel either in mockery or as titles of honour to individuals, which were then handed on to their descendants, the original purpose of the names being forgotten, and he quotes parallels from Arabia. It may also be suggested that animal names were sometimes given in order to deceive the demons who watch over the birth of a child with hostile intent. This is certainly the explanation of some of the contemptuous names ('Three-cowry', &c.) found in modern India. See further G. B. Gray, *Hebrew Proper Names*, pp. 101 ff., 253 ff. (1896).

The future Israel consists of four groups of clans, recognizing a common blood among themselves, but still standing apart one from another. Six of the names are attached to one group and two to another, while to each of the two more important there is attached a smaller and more insignificant pair of associated clans. The first group is that which bound itself together, though very loosely, under the name of Leah. It included originally only four of the independent tribes, Reuben, Simeon, Levi, and Judah,[1] but at a later period two more were added, Zebulun and Naphtali, and, finally, it absorbed the subordinate tribes of Gad and Asher. At the outset Reuben is the most prominent, but a too hasty grasp at the privileges of supreme power led to its decadence, and, ultimately, to its disappearance. The next two are characterized by extreme and brutal cruelty, illustrated in history by the sack of Shechem.[2] They too vanish, and the headship of the group is left with Judah. The affiliations of the other four are obviously much later, and may equally well be fictitious. In the Rachel group the headship from the first is with Joseph, which later divides into two,[3] Ephraim and Manasseh, but eventually the tribe of Benjamin attains to a position of authority, though it is not permanently a leader in Israel.

This reconstruction is, in the main, borne out by what we know of the history of the tribes from references outside the Pentateuch. Reuben is last mentioned in the Song of Deborah, and, though its original territory is placed between Gad and Moab, yet in the ninth century[4] there is no interval between Gad and Moab; the very name of Reuben has disappeared. The original tribe of Levi vanished at a very early date, though the name was preserved in that of the professional priests, who developed into a hereditary ecclesiastical body and ultimately ranked

[1] As we shall have occasion to observe later (cp. pp. 134 f., 169 f.), this can hardly be the earliest form of the national tradition, since we are led to suspect that there was a time when the name 'Judah' did not apply to any section of the stock recognized as Aramaean, but rather to one element in the peoples who were found in Canaan by these nomad invaders. Possibly 'Judah' is the latest insertion of all into the list.

[2] Cp. Gen. xlix. 5-7. Perhaps the attack on Shechem described in Gen. xxxiv is a piece of later history thrown back into the patriarchal age, and modified like the other primitive histories. For a full discussion see Skinner, *Genesis*, pp. 421 f.

[3] This is a reversal of the process observable elsewhere, but it seems to be the actual fact. In Gen. xlix. the tribe of Joseph is one, while in the somewhat later Blessing of Moses, Deut. xxxiii, though there is much similarity between the two passages, the two names Ephraim and Manasseh appear in the last line—possibly as an afterthought or an appendix.   [4] Inscription of Mesha.

as a tribe, perhaps through its similarity to one of the Semitic words for 'priest'.[1] Of the tribe of Simeon we hear for the last time in Judges i. 3, where it combines with Judah in an invasion of southern Palestine.[2] Clearly the attempt failed, and Simeon was destroyed or dispersed. Judah, if we may judge from Gen. xxxviii, was settled in Palestine long before the main conquest of the land, and may have been originally Canaanite rather than Aramaean in blood. For this or for some other reason, it stood apart from the more northerly tribes, and took no leading position till the time of David,[3] when it became the dominant element in all Israel.

In the early days the most influential group was certainly that of Joseph. To it Joshua belonged, and it must have taken the lead in the conquest of central Palestine, while the first attempts at the establishment of a monarchy are to be seen in Gideon and Abimelech who belong to that group. Its claim to permanent headship is illustrated by its quarrel with Jephthah,[4] which led to a disaster that may have reduced the tribe temporarily to the second rank. Benjamin comes into prominence only with Saul, and during his reign holds the premier position, though it fails to maintain its power. We thus conclude that the patriarchal narratives reached their final form not earlier than the eleventh century, and, possibly, as late as the tenth, when, in the early monarchy, the tribes had fallen into their respective positions.

Such a reconstruction is admittedly conjectural,[5] and can claim no more than probability. As we have had occasion to remark, there are points which remain unexplained, and uncertainties which, as far as we can tell, may never be dissipated. But the basis on which it rests, the conception that many of the narratives are to be interpreted as tribal tradition rather than as personal biography, is a plausible hypothesis, and fits in with

[1] The Minaean *lawiya*. For a full discussion cp. Gray, *Sacrifice in the Old Testament*, pp. 242 ff. (1925).

[2] This tradition is somewhat difficult to reconcile with the view that Simeon and Levi were central Palestinian tribes which perished as a result of their aggressions in the Shechem district. Clearly we have two entirely independent lines, and the fact that they diverge so far tends to show how early was the disappearance of Simeon and how uncertain was its fate. 2 Chron. xv. 9 and xxxiv. 6 imply a tradition of Simeon in central Palestine. See also p. 119 f.

[3] The early heroes of the south are not strictly Judahites at all, but Kenites, Kenizzites, Calebites, or perhaps even Jerachmeelites. See below, esp. pp. 120, 134 f., 169 f. Cf. also 1 Chron. ii. 18 ff., 42 ff. and iv. 13, where Caleb and Kenaz seem to be artificially imported into the genealogy.   [4] Jud. xii. 1–6.

[5] See Skinner, *Genesis*, pp. 440 ff.

what we know of the east from other sources.¹   There are, of
course, narratives, especially among those dealing with Jacob,
which must be regarded as purely personal.   Such are the
theophany at Bethel, which was undoubtedly one of the ἱεροὶ
λόγοι of the shrine located there, a story told by the official
resident priesthood.

One fact emerges with unmistakable clearness. Like Abraham
(Isaac is more stationary) Jacob is a wanderer. There is a war-
like element in the clans grouped about him, but as a rule they
avoid conflict, and are only too thankful when they can persuade
their enemies to be merciful, as Esau was,² or can conclude a
peaceful treaty with them, as Jacob did with Laban.³   The
ancestors of nomad Israel are essentially shepherds, wanderers
who find themselves now on one side, now on the other, of the
river Jordan. Their range is from near the plain of Esdraelon in
the north-west and the borders of Syrian territory in the north-
east, down to the edge of the country included in the Egyptian
kingdom.   From time to time they cross the Egyptian border,
and they are always in some degree familiar with the land.
When the final migration comes, and they definitely settle
within the dominions of the Pharaoh, it is with no strange place
or people that they take refuge.

The patriarchal age closes with the descent into Egypt. The
familiar Biblical narrative tells how⁴ Joseph was either sold by
his brethren to Ishmaelites (J) or abandoned by the other sons
of Jacob and rescued by Midianites (E), both traditions describing how he was taken down into Egypt, and, from being
a slave, attained to a high position in the royal court. Driven
by famine, his brethren went down to Egypt, were recognized,
and ultimately they and their father followed the younger son
into prosperity, being accorded wide grazing lands on the north-
east frontier of the country.

The *motif* of the story is familiar, but hitherto no confirmation
of its details has been found among the Egyptian records,
though an interesting parallel may be seen in the Egyptian
story of the Two Brothers, and possibly elsewhere. There is,
however, no reason to suspect the substantial historicity of the
narrative. It would be unusual, but by no means impossible,

---

¹ For an extended presentation of the general position cp. Steuernagel, *Die
Einwanderung der israelitischen Stämme in Kanaan* (1901).
² Gen. xxxiii. 1–16.   ³ Gen. xxxi. 44–54.   ⁴ Gen. xxxvii.

for an individual to rise from a lowly position, and the process would, no doubt, be facilitated if the new-comer were an Aramaean, and the time were that of the Hyksos dominion in Egypt.[1] As a matter of fact, on every ground this seems the best, if not the only period, to which we can assign the entry of the ancestors of Israel into Egypt, for the hostility to the Asiatics roused by the Hyksos dominion was so great that it is almost inconceivable that any king of the eighteenth dynasty should have welcomed a Semitic tribe for any reason whatever, though they might well impress them as slaves.

It is clear that the ancestors of Israel—or some of them—settled in the pasture-lands to the east of the Delta, the country which we know as Goshen.[2] It is possible that in the Joseph-story we have a tradition of a double migration, the tribe of Joseph leading the way, and being followed by others. It has been held that it was this tribe alone that was involved in the Egyptian period. In particular it seems probable to some scholars that the story of Judah and Tamar in Gen. xxxviii implies that this tribe, and therefore possibly all the Leah tribes, were never in Egypt at all, but remained permanently in Canaan.[3] On the other hand, there can be little doubt that the story of the Exodus contemplated a union of the escaping Israelites with kindred tribes. We shall, on the whole, be on safer ground if we accept without qualification the tradition that at least the Rachel tribes migrated to Goshen, and leave open the possibility that others of their kinsmen came with them. The motive assigned, i.e. famine, is a very natural reason, and we have in Egyptian records the account of permission given by an official of Merneptah II to certain Edomites to enter the borders of Egypt in order that they might find sustenance for their cattle.[4]

The story of the fortunes of Israel in Egypt is too well known to need elaboration. 'There arose a new king over Egypt who knew not Joseph'[5]—a vague phrase, for the Israelite narrator

---

[1] It is interesting to observe that one of the Hyksos kings bore the name Jacob-her or Jacob-el.

[2] Gen. xlvi. 28, xlvii. 4, 6, 27. Goshen has been identified with the district round the Wadi Tumilat from early times, though more recently this has been disputed. Cp. Peet, *Egypt and the Old Testament*, pp. 78 ff.

[3] Cp. E. Meyer, *IN.*, pp. 104, 204 f., 433; H. Guthe in *EB.*, article 'Israel', vol. ii, col. 2219; Procksch, *Genesis*, p. 205 [1913]. See also below, pp. 75 ff.

[4] *Pap. Anast.*, vi. 4, 14.   [5] Exod. i. 8.

could not be expected to be familiar with the details of Egyptian history. But we may be fairly certain that the words cover the great change in Egyptian politics which took place with the expulsion of the Hyksos and the establishment of the eighteenth dynasty by Ahmose. The impression made by the Asiatic rulers on their subjects was so terrible that the very name of Asiatic became abhorrent, and, though the phrase is an anachronism in Gen. xlvi. 34, it became true that 'every shepherd was an abomination unto the Egyptians'. These nomads, then, who (unless we are to identify the expulsion of the Hyksos with the Exodus[1]) remained on the borders of Egypt, were looked upon as natural enemies and almost savages.

There is no reason to suppose that the bondage of Israel in Egypt involved the whole people, or even a large proportion of those whose pasture-lands were in the border-country. We know that from very early times slave-labour was recruited by raids into Semitic territory, and we must suppose that the kings of the eighteenth dynasty continued the policy.[2] Our acceptance of the tradition preserved in Exod. i. 11, which states that the Israelites were employed in the construction of the treasure cities of Ramses and Pithom, must depend on the date we assign to the Exodus, and will be discussed later. It is enough to remark here that there is archaeological evidence for the view that Asiatics, and indeed Semites, were employed on the buildings at Pithom and Ramses, but it does not necessarily follow that these were Israelites, and, as a matter of fact, opinion is steadily tending in the direction of a belief that the Exodus took place long before the accession of Ramses II, the founder of these cities. The absence of any exact definition of the Egyptian kings in the narratives of the Pentateuch makes it impossible to date events with any certainty, but, when all the facts are taken into account, it seems probable that the mention of these places is due to a comparatively late scribe or author, who knew something of Egyptian conditions, but not enough to make him accurate in his historical references.

[1] See below, pp. 71 ff.
[2] For an early raid on a Semitic village cp. the mural decoration in the Tomb of Inti (fifth dynasty, c. 3600), Flinders Petrie, *Deshâsheh*, pl. iv.

BOOK II

THE BIRTH AND GROWTH OF THE NATION

INTRODUCTORY REMARKS

ISRAEL came into existence with Moses, but she was far from reaching her full stature when she entered Canaan. It is with the exodus that her history begins, but we can regard this only as the commencement of a process which was not complete until the establishment of the monarchy. We must therefore trace, not merely the passage from Egypt to Palestine, but also the conquest and the gradual process by which the Israelite tribes settled down and found their final position in the land. This was necessarily a work of centuries, and was probably in most of its stages accomplished but slowly.

Our main source continues to be the narrative of the Hexateuch, to which the book of *Judges* and the first few chapters of *1 Samuel* must now be added. In the main these present us with the same features that the critic observes in *Genesis*. Leaving aside the vexed question as to whether J and E are continued into *Judges* and *Samuel*, we find that the more important events (at least down to the conquest) have the double attestation of both the older sources, though with occasional variation in details. In the book of *Judges* it sometimes appears that a narrative is composite,[1] though we suspect in some instances that two accounts originally referring to different events have been interwoven to form a single narrative. An obvious illustration occurs in the story of Gideon. Similarly in the narratives of 1 Sam. i–vii we are clearly following several lines of tradition, originally independent, which leave us in some doubt as to the original Hebrew view of the details. But, generally speaking, as we pass down the stream of tradition, its course becomes clearer, and we feel more confidence in relying on details.

In this period we are able to add one authority from outside Israel which is of the first importance. This is the correspondence of the court of Amenhotep III and Ikhnaton, which we commonly call the Tell-el-Amarna tablets. The extent to which we regard these as direct evidence for the history of the Israelite conquest necessarily depends on the date to which we assign the entry into Canaan, but even if the evidence be not direct, it throws invaluable light alike on the conditions of the period in general and on the way in which the wilderness tribes constantly pressed into the land.

[1] For the most recent and thorough analysis see Eissfeldt, *Die Quellen des Richterbuches* [1925].

Chapter V

THE EXODUS

SUMMARY

[The national life of Israel begins with the Exodus, and, after a short summary of the Biblical narrative of Israel's escape from Egypt, the date of the event is discussed. Various theories are propounded, and the available evidence reviewed, the general conclusion reached being that, though there can be no certainty on the point, the main exodus of Israel from Egypt is to be placed comparatively early in the eighteenth dynasty (*c.* 1600–1350 B.C.).

The personality of Moses is then discussed. He was clearly an Israelite with some Egyptian affiliations, and, while the story of his early days has parallels in the folk-lore of many nations, there is no reason to doubt his historicity. He was also, during a period of exile from Egypt, brought into contact with a Deity named Yahweh, whose home lay in the wilderness to the south of Palestine, from whom he received a commission to deliver Israel—or such Israelites as were in slavery. The plagues which preceded the escape are practically all natural events; the miraculous element in the story is due to their coincidence at a point so critical for the Israelites. An analysis of the text shows that the earliest form of the narrative gives a simple and consistent account of the crossing of the Red Sea, which was facilitated by exceptionally high winds. To the fact that the Mediterranean, the sea with which the Israelites were most familiar, was practically tideless, we owe the impression of miracle which these events produced on later generations.]

ISRAELITE tradition universally connected the Exodus with the work of Moses. It told of the oppression of the Pharaoh (whose name is not given, though he clearly belonged to another dynasty than that which welcomed the Hebrew immigrants), and of the attempt to exterminate Israel by the slaughter of all the male children. The two policies seem to be hardly consistent,[1] for no king would wish to extinguish his supply of forced labour, and we may suppose that the destruction of the children is a misinterpretation of a custom by which human sacrifices were offered to the river god or to the crocodile god. In any case, through the care of his mother, Moses escaped this fate, and was fortunate enough to be adopted by a daughter of Pharaoh—again unnamed. He was brought up in the royal

---

[1] Probably two narratives are interwoven in Exod. i, see E. Meyer, *IN.*, pp. 41 ff. (1906).

court, but did not forget his ancestry, and, at the age of forty, rescued one of the Hebrews who was being ill-treated by an Egyptian. Like Sinuhe, centuries earlier, he was forced to flee, and took refuge with a Midianite priest whose name is variously given as Jethro, Reuel, and, possibly, Hobab. The story of his introduction to his new protector strongly recalls that of the meeting between Rachel and Jacob, and the two may have been accommodated one to another. Moses marries Zipporah, one of the priest's daughters, and for another forty years lives the life of a shepherd. At length, as he leads his sheep 'to the back of the mountain', he receives a divine revelation in a bush that burns with fire, but is not consumed.

There is possibly some variation in the details of the traditions which we have traced up to this point, but the main outline is clear; the different stories are supplementary rather than contradictory. They continue to tell us that in the name of the God who thus speaks to him (in two forms of the tradition that name is as yet unknown to any Hebrew), Moses is bidden to return to Egypt and demand the release of the Israelites now held in serfdom. He is given power to work miracles which shall convince the king of the authority that lies behind him. The pretext named is that Israel must go three days' journey into the wilderness,[1] i.e. presumably to the site of the theophany, and there sacrifice to the God whose name is now revealed as Yahweh. Moses carries out his instructions, Pharaoh refuses to let Israel go, and he and his people suffer from a series of divinely sent plagues. These in themselves (except, possibly, the last) are natural events, but their violence and coincidence show them to have been the work of Yahweh. Finally, since the appointed time has arrived, and the people have not been suffered to visit the home of Yahweh in the wilderness, they make such preparation as they can in Egypt, and Yahweh comes to them, destroying the firstborn in every house which has not protected itself by the due ritual of the festal sacrifice.

In these circumstances the Israelites make good their escape. But they are followed by an Egyptian army, and when their course has led them to the Red Sea they are helpless. But a strong wind dries a path for them and they cross in safety. The Egyptians attempt to follow, but the wind changes, and the water comes in under the sand and makes it a quicksand which clogs

[1] Exod. viii. 27.

the wheels of the chariots, the pursuers attempt to escape, but
they are caught and drowned by the returning waves. A song
of triumph is sung by Israel over the bodies washed up on the
shore.[1]

It is quite impossible to deny either the fact of the Exodus or
the historicity of Moses. An event which stamped itself so
deeply on the consciousness of the people as to control all its
later thinking, to ratify its religion, and to dictate its theory of
history, can by no possibility have been a mere invention. It
is quite true that, in all probability, we have no reference to
this occurrence in Egyptian records, but it is easy to understand
why it should have been overlooked. It was to Egypt a trifling
affair, and the ancient world, like the modern, preferred to
dwell on big things. Moreover, it was not a great success for
the Egyptian power, and the historians of that country seldom
recorded facts on their monuments unless they could be turned
to the honour of the king and of the people. And even so, our
knowledge of Egyptian history is not so complete that we can
venture to state dogmatically that an incident was never recorded simply because we have not discovered the narrative. It
is not too much to say that without this deliverance, apparently
so miraculous, there never would have been an Israel at all.[2]
A like remark may be made of the personality of Moses. The
work which he accomplished in the formation of Israel as a
people was such as to demand the power of a single genius, not

[1] The account here followed is that of E. P's narrative, interwoven with it,
speaks of walls of water standing up on either side, a presentation which is quite
inconsistent with that of the earlier tradition. Gressmann (*Mose*, pp. 108 ff.) supposes that the escape of the Israelites was facilitated by volcanic action. Placing
the scene of the crossing near the head of the Gulf of Akaba, he suggests that a
mountain in eruption was visible from the far side, i.e. from the western shore. As
so often happens in severe earthquakes on a coast, the sea first receded from its
normal bed and then returned with extraordinary violence. The Israelites thus
connected this phenomenon with the God who dwelt in the volcano, and recognized that it was He who had brought them safely out of their difficulties. This is a
brilliant and not impossible explanation. But Gressmann's view is not decisive
in other respects. To associate the earthquake with the eruption requires some
degree of scientific knowledge, and ascribes to primitive Israel a rather high
standard of intellectual attainment. The narrative (at least in the earlier tradition)
is quite simple and straightforward. It is possible that the tide which, though not
high at Suez, still appears, played its part with the wind.

[2] For a fresh discussion of this tradition and its place in the thought of Israel see
Kurt Galling, *Die Erwählungstraditionen Israels* (1928). Galling contends that it was
in northern Israel in particular that this tradition was most strongly maintained,
thereby lending strength to the theory that the Exodus concerned primarily the
Joseph tribes.

merely brilliant in conception, but also endowed with a compelling personality. Once only in later history has an achievement of similar magnitude been accomplished in the Semitic world, and that was the union and organization of the Arab tribes by Mohammed. If we had no account of Moses at all, it would have been necessary to assume the existence of a person such as he is said to have been.

This assurance, however, still leaves us with a number of problems which ask for some attempt at solution. What was the date of the Exodus? How far can we accept the details as they have been handed down to us in the Old Testament? These details concern both the life of Moses and the record of the events, and we shall need to examine with some care the statements regarding the incidents of the Israelite escape and the Egyptian disaster.

The actual date of the Exodus, and even the identification of an approximate period, may never be certainly attained.[1] Direct evidence is almost entirely lacking, whether from Egypt or from Israel, and we shall have to be satisfied with conjecture based on other data. Such a conjecture was made in ancient times by Josephus, who identified the escape of the Hebrews with the expulsion of the Hyksos. He quotes verbatim from the account given by the Egyptian historian Manetho, who was naturally hostile to the Asiatics, and would therefore give a very different colour to the story from that which we find in the Old Testament.[2] The theory has found some support in our own day,[3] but it cannot be accepted without discarding the whole tenor and purport of the Biblical narrative. The essence of the Hebrew tradition lies in the reluctance of the Egyptian king to let his slaves go free. The oppression is a feature of the story which is fundamental to the meaning of the whole. Apart from it the deliverance could never have made upon later Israel the impression which it actually did make, and we can hardly imagine a people inventing a narrative which traced its own origin back to a period of slavery. It is inconceivable

[1] The best modern discussion of the subject is to be found in J. W. Jack, *The Date of the Exodus* [1925]. For a shorter, but yet both acute and cautious statement of the problems involved, cp. Peet, *Egypt and the Old Testament*, ch. v, pp. 105–45 [1922].

[2] *Contra Apionem*, i. 26 ff. Manetho seems to have blundered sometimes, e.g. in making the king who expelled the Hyksos Amenhotep, the father of Ramses.

[3] Cp. Hall, *AHNE.*, pp. 213, 408 n. 'Montet's vindication of the old equation Avaris = Zoan = Ramesses goes far to corroborate this view.' (A. H. Gardiner, privately communicated.)

that an event which played so large a part in forming the
national consciousness should have been so twisted by tradition
as to present an appearance almost exactly the opposite of the real
facts. As we have seen, the Hyksos age is the most probable for
the residence in Egypt, and the oppression is almost unintelligible unless it followed the expulsion of these Semitic rulers.
Yahweh brought Israel out of Egypt, out of slavery, against the
will of the Egyptian government of the time—'with a high hand'
—and it was this event which at once proved His power and
impelled Israel to adopt Him as the national God.

We must, then, regard the expulsion of the Hyksos (roughly
c. 1600 B.C.) as the earliest date for the oppression, and our
terminus a quo for the Exodus will be at least a generation later.
That is to say, the first date we can consider will lie somewhere
about the middle of the sixteenth century B.C. For a *terminus ad
quem*, we must rely on such data as are available for the conquest
of Palestine, again remembering that we shall have to allow a
space of at least a generation for the nomad period of Israel's
life. Indeed, the high place given in Israelite theory to the
pastoral life[1] suggests that the nation, or what was the ideal
nucleus of the nation, spent a longer rather than a shorter time
in the wilderness. It is clear that in order to discuss the Exodus
at all, we must anticipate so far as to look also at the possible
dates for the conquest of Palestine.

As we have already seen, direct evidence of the Exodus from
the Egyptian side is, up to the present, entirely lacking.[2] There
are, however, one or two references in the Old Testament itself
which, taken together with certain Egyptian data, may bear on
the question. We have in Exod xii. 40 the statement that the
residence in Egypt lasted for 430 years.[3] If the descent into
Egypt is rightly placed in the Hyksos age, i.e. between 1800 and
1600 B.C., this gives us roughly a time between the middle of the
fourteenth century and the middle of the twelfth, while the
acceptance of the LXX figure would throw the date back by
a couple of centuries. Further, in 1 Kgs. vi. 1 it is said that the

[1] Cp. pp. 47 ff.
[2] We can hardly take seriously the suggestion that a name MNŠH found in
inscriptions on Mount Sinai, dating from the reign of Queen Hatshepsut (*c.* 1500-
1480 B.C.), really refers to Moses. Cp. Grimme, *Althebräische Inschriften vom Sinai*
(1923), &c., and, for the opposite view, Gardiner (*JEA*. iii. 1-16).
[3] So the MT.; the LXX includes in this period also the time spent by the patriarchs in Canaan before the descent into Egypt, and gives 215 years to each part.

building of the Temple was begun 480 years after the Exodus. This would yield a date about the middle of the fifteenth century. Unfortunately figures of this kind in ancient traditions are seldom reliable, and are very easily affected by textual corruption. The second of the two mentioned looks artificial, since it appears to represent a space of twelve generations, and may well have formed part of an ideal scheme of Israelite chronology.

More significant is the statement in Exod. i. 11 that the Hebrew captives built for Pharaoh store-cities whose names were Pithom and Ramses. The latter name strongly suggests a king of the nineteenth or twentieth dynasty, and it has generally been assumed that Ramses II is intended. This view has been confirmed by the discovery at Beth-shean of a stele of Ramses II, which mentions the building of a city bearing the king's name, and suggests that Semitic labourers were employed in the work.[1] When Naville identified the site of Pithom as a city in the Wadi Tumilat, built by Ramses II[2] with the use of Semitic labourers, the question seemed settled, and many, if not most, modern writers on the history of Israel have accepted without further discussion Ramses II as the Pharaoh of the oppression and his son Merneptah as the Pharaoh of the Exodus. Further investigation, however, has tended to shake our belief in the accuracy of this view. The identification of the city in question has not passed unchallenged,[3] and it has been pointed out that Semitic labourers, even though they are described by a name philologically equivalent to 'Hebrew', were not necessarily the ancestors of Israel. We must also beware of laying too much stress on our present text of Exod. i. 11. The names of the two cities are not necessary to the sense of the verse, and they may quite well have been inserted by an editor or copyist. It is clear that we owe a good many details in the life of Joseph and in the first chapters of Exodus to Israelite scholars who lived in the period of the Monarchy, and we can without serious risk of error attribute the mention of Pithom and Ramses here to such a student of Egyptian affairs. While, in the absence of all other evidence, the data furnished by a comparison of this verse with known Egyptian

[1] Cp. *The Museum Journal*, Philadelphia, 1913, p. 245; Gardiner, *JEA.* x (1924), p. 93; Gressmann, *ATAT.*, p. 96, fig. 98, pl. xlii.
[2] *The Store City of Pithom and the Route of the Exodus* (1883).
[3] Cp. especially Peet, *Egypt and the Old Testament*, pp. 83–91.

records might be allowed to form the basis for a conjecture, they cannot be permitted to bear the whole weight of a theory if there are serious considerations which point in other directions.

We turn, then, to our *terminus ad quem*, the entry of Israel into Palestine. Here we have a number of data which may indirectly throw light on the problem. And we shall do well to consider first the periods which our knowledge of Egyptian history in general allows us to regard as possible. The history of Egypt, at least from the expulsion of the Hyksos onwards, presents us with a series of waves of prosperity, brilliant success alternating with times of deep depression. Each new dynasty, as it came to the throne, had first to establish its own power, and was only then in a position to embark on a career of foreign conquest. Thus Tutmose III was the first to undertake a serious campaign in Palestine, with a view of adding the country to his dominions, and we have seen the importance of his work for an understanding of general history. But his successors could not permanently keep Palestine in full subjection, and after the death of Amenhotep III the Egyptian power was so weak that in the end only a few fortresses remained in the Pharaoh's hands. The country was overrun by invaders from the east, and there seems to have been a real Hittite occupation, though the northern kingdom may not have claimed the country formally as its own. With the accession of the nineteenth dynasty we have a recovery, and Seti I, and still more Ramses II, reasserted the old dominion. But after the death of Merneptah, son of Ramses II, we find another period of weakness, due largely to the Philistine immigrations. Though beaten back from the borders of Egypt by Ramses III, they made good their footing in the coastal plain, and the Zakkara (apparently an 'Aegean' people) south of Mount Carmel, and the Philistines proper still farther south, became the possessors of the maritime plain.

Now it is obvious that the Israelite settlements could not have been made during the times of greatest Egyptian activity. It was only when their forces were withdrawn, and the government was too deeply concerned with domestic matters, or too seriously involved in other struggles to pay due attention to Palestine, that an immigration from the wilderness was practically possible. We are thus reduced to three periods, (*a*) from the expulsion of the Hyksos to the conquests of Tutmose III, roughly 1600 to

1480 B.C., (*b*) from the decline of the eighteenth dynasty to the time of Seti I and Ramses II, about 1380 to 1300 B.C., (*c*) the end of the nineteenth dynasty onwards, i.e. after *c*. 1200 B.C. We have a certain amount of evidence which may be derived from Egyptian inscriptions, referring either expressly by name to Israel or to movements which may be connected with their immigration into western Palestine. We may glance first at a stele of victory set up by Merneptah (*c*. 1200 B.C.). Here we have a poem in which the king speaks of his defeats of the Libyans who had attacked Egypt from the east, and goes on to describe the conquest of certain peoples in Palestine:

> The kings are overthrown, saying 'Salâm!'
> Not one holds up his head among the nine nations of the bow,
> Wasted is Tehenu,
> The Hittite land is pacified,
> Plundered is Canaan, with every evil,
> Carried off is Askalon,
> Seized upon is Gezer,
> Yenoam is made as a thing not existing.
> Israel is desolated, her seed is not,
> Palestine has become a (defenceless) widow for Egypt.
> All lands are united, they are pacified;
> Every one that is turbulent is bound by king Merneptah.[1]

The sites of Askalon and Gezer are familiar to us; Yenoam seems to have been not far from Damascus. The conclusion is irresistible that Israel too is to be regarded as a people already settled in the country, and, apparently, confined to a somewhat circumscribed district, probably in the centre of the land. It is, of course, open to us to believe that a people called Israel had long been settled in Palestine, and that the fugitive Hebrews on their arrival coalesced with them, adopting their name and identifying their eponymous ancestor with Jacob, but this appears to be an hypothesis rather too remote for ready acceptance unless other indications point unmistakably in the same direction.

With this mention of Israel we must class also the appearance of the name Asher on inscriptions of Seti I and Ramses II.[2]

---

[1] Breasted, *ARE*. iii. 603 ff., 616–17.

[2] Cp. W. M. Müller, *Asien und Europa*, pp. 236 ff. Among the relevant monuments is a temple at Abydos, consecrated by Ramses (or some predecessor?) to Osiris. On the base of one of the pylons is a line of captives, with ropes about their necks, apparently being led before the king. Each figure represents a conquered

Here, too, it is possible to assume that the tribe was no part of the original Israel, but was adopted after the conquest of Palestine. Again, it may be remarked that while this explanation will have to be adopted if it can be held proved that Israel did not leave Egypt before the reign of Merneptah, it more naturally affords evidence of an earlier date for the Exodus and for the conquest of Palestine by the Hebrews.

Next, we should note the mention of the Ḥabiru as invaders of Palestine in the communications of Abdikhiba of Jerusalem preserved in the Tell-el-Amarna tablets.[1] Throughout the reign of Ikhnaton Palestine was subject to raids from dwellers in the wilderness, and faithful subjects of the Egyptian king made

tribe, whose name is inscribed on it. The eighth is called 'srw, almost certainly to be vocalized Asher (the w is the sign of the plural). See Marriette, Abydos, ii, pl. 2a. There is also a reference in Papyrus Anastasi, i. 23. 8, where the name 'srw is used as a term of contempt. This apparently dates also from the reign of Ramses II. There is, further, an inscription in the first chamber of a temple built by Ramses' father, Seti I, at Redesieh in the desert (Lepsius, Denkmäler, Bd. VI, pl. 140a), showing the king holding a group of captives by the hair and threatening them with a club or some similar weapon. Opposite him stands a figure of Horus brandishing a scimitar and leading eight captives bound by cords. Evidently we have here a representation of one of those sacrifices of captives which were practised by the Egyptian kings of the Empire. The captives are called 'srw, and though the spelling of the names in the three places varies there can be no doubt as to their identity, and it is clear that they came from northern Palestine, much the same district as that in which the tribe of Asher was located during the Israelite period. Five names inscribed on the 'labels' of Horus' captives are certain, Shinar (the Hermon district? Cp. Deut. iii. 10, &c.), Kadesh (probably Kadesh Naphtali), Shasu (a general term for the shepherd peoples of Palestine), Megiddo, and Asher. Breasted (ARE., § 165, n.), curiously enough, vocalizes this last name as Ashur.

[1] It is curious that it is only in the letters of Abdikhiba that the name Ḥabiru is used. Other correspondents speak of the Gaz or Sa Gaz; see Knudtzon, Tell-el-Amarna Tafeln, 286, 19, 56; 287, 31; 288, 38, 44; 289, 34; 290, 13, 24. These seem to be the only passages in the surviving tablets where the name Ḥabiru is used. It occurs, however, in Mesopotamian documents from comparatively early times. Ḥabiru are mentioned, apparently as mercenaries, in a document dating from the reign of Rim-Sin (cp. Scheil, Revue d'Assyriologie, xii. 114), and the contract tablets (of the fifteenth century?) discovered on the site of the ancient Nuzi, near the modern Kirkuk, include references to Ḥabiru slaves torn from their homes by Assyrians (cp. Chiera and Speiser, JAOS. xlvii. 44, nos. 7, 8). This last reference makes it impossible to identify the Ḥabiru absolutely with the Israelites, for the ancestors of Israel must have been in the west before the time of these records. We should also, perhaps, identify with the Ḥabiru the Aperiu who appear on inscriptions of Ramses III (cp. CAH. ii. 328, 357), where they are imported labourers. We might also mention the theory of Landsberger (cp. Hempel, Die althebräische Literatur (1930), p. 9) that the term Ḥabiru does not imply a tribe or a group of confederates, but refers to a social and economic grade. Against this we have the mention of 'gods of the Ḥabiru' (first noted by Winckler) in Hittite documents and elsewhere, cp. CAH. ii. 311; Gustav, Was heisst ilâni Ḥabiri?; ZAW. xliv (1926), pp. 25 ff.

constant complaints of the danger which threatened the empire. There is no doubt that, philologically speaking, the word *Ḥabiru* may be identified with *Hebrew*, but it does not follow that the enemies of Abdikhiba were the tribes of Israel. It will be remembered that in Gen. xiv. 13 Abraham is already described as 'the Hebrew', and there is a growing feeling that, while this passage may not be historical in all its details, it has behind it an ancient tradition. Other references make it clear that we have to regard the Ḥabiru as belonging to the wandering tribes of the inner edge of the Fertile Crescent, and we need not doubt that their attempts to enter the cultivated lands were constant, being repeated over many generations. At the same time, there is, as far as we know, no serious obstacle to our acceptance of the identification of some portions of Israel with some—or indeed all—of the Ḥabiru of the Tell-el-Amarna age. Probably the safest solution of the problem is that suggested by Dr. Wardle,[1] namely that the two terms, Ḥabiru and Israel,[2] overlap, each including a part of the other. But while this view would be very strongly in favour of an early, or comparatively early, date for the Conquest, it would probably not be decisive if it stood alone.

These data all point to a period earlier than the nineteenth dynasty, and if the attacks from the desert alluded to in the Tell-el-Amarna letters are held to include some or most of the events recorded in the book of *Joshua* and Judges i, then they indicate a date somewhere in the middle of the fourteenth century. A yet older invasion, however, is suggested by the excavations at Jericho. The masonry, pottery, and other objects discovered there show, in the opinion of some of our best archaeologists, that the last pre-Israelite city was overthrown about the beginning of the fifteenth century, and that the site was not re-occupied, at least as a fortified city, until the ninth century. This last date goes to confirm the statement of 1 Kgs.

---

[1] *Israel and Babylon*, ch. iii.

[2] We may notice here a theory held by Jirku (cp. *GVI.*, pp. 51 ff.) that the Aramaeans and Hebrews are to be distinguished from one another. He admits that Israelites and Hebrews are often identified, but calls attention to one or two passages where they seem to be contrasted, especially 1 Sam. xiii. 7, xiv. 21, Num. xxiv. 24. In the first passage the accuracy of the text is disputed, and in the last the term עברי is placed in the mouth of a non-Israelite. In any case, it is surely more probable that the 'Israelites' were a *branch* of the Hebrews? The fact that both Gittites and Philistines are mentioned in the O.T. certainly does not imply that they are contrasted with, or differentiated from, one another.

xvi. 34 that Jericho was restored in the reign of Ahab,[1] and if the former be established the fall of this city must be thrown back to a time a century and a half before the Tell-el-Amarna age. Three possibilities are open to us. We may dissociate the fall of Jericho from the Israelite invasions altogether, and assume that the Hebrews adopted a tradition from some of their predecessors. We may assume (and, in effect, this view will have the same general result as the last) that the Israelite conquests extended over a long period. Or we may deny any connexion between Israel and the Ḥabiru of Abdikhiba's letters, and suppose that, while the eastern invasions of this period illustrate the same process as that which brought Israel into western Palestine, they have nothing to do with that group whose tribal and national inspiration was the memory of an escape from Egyptian bondage and a covenant with the God who had delivered them.

Lastly, we may consider such data as may be derived from the Old Testament itself. For this purpose the narratives of the book of *Joshua* and of Judges i are clearly useless, since they offer us no contacts with peoples in whose history we can date events. They are serviceable only in general, and even so are valueless for chronology unless we can link Israel with the invaders of the Tell-el-Amarna letters. But we have one or two ancient songs which come to us from very early periods. Of these we may mention two, the song of Deborah[2] and the so-called Blessing of Jacob.[3] The former is admitted on all hands to be the work of a poet who actually witnessed the defeat of Sisera, and though the text has suffered in course of transmission, it remains a document of the highest importance. The latter is a collection of tribal songs and sayings, of which different parts demonstrably belong to different periods, some being much older than others.

Now in Judges v we have references to several of the tribes, and verse 17 refers to Dan and Asher. Both are situated on the coast, and the language used implies that they are in undisturbed possession of their lands. There is no reason why they should not have come to the help of Israel in the struggle against Sisera. Such a situation is inconceivable after the advent of the Philistines and kindred peoples, nor could the two invasions have been simultaneous. It is true that the Danites and the

---

[1] For the general results of the excavations at Jericho cp. W. F. Albright, *Annual of the American Schools of Archaeology*, vi (1924–5), p. 49.   [2] Judges v.   [3] Gen. xlix.

Asherites may not have been completely dispossessed by the first migrations of the Philistines, and that they were only gradually thrust inland. But they could not possibly have retained the reputation of being primarily a maritime people after 1192 B.C. In Gen. xlix. 17 Dan is mentioned, no longer as a seafaring people, but as a tribe which is in a position to raid passing caravans. This must, it is true, be earlier than their migration northwards, but, like the Samson stories, it illustrates the position into which the clan was forced by the new invaders. Throughout the whole of Judges v there is no suggestion whatever, direct or indirect, of the presence of Philistines in the land, and we are compelled to date the poem before their appearance. As against the doubtful evidence of Exod. i. 11 this must be held to be decisive. The whole theory of a nineteenth dynasty date for the Exodus rests, as we have seen, on two names in that verse, and we have already noted the weakness of its foundation.

As between the other two possible periods, 1600–1480 B.C., and 1380–1300 B.C., it is much less easy to decide. The date given by the archaeologists to the fall of Jericho [1] is in favour of the former, the possible identification of Israel with a portion of the Ḥabiru supports the latter. If it be necessary to make up our minds we must depend on general considerations. In the first place, we may note that the conquests of Tutmose III have left no mark whatever on Hebrew tradition. The same remark may be made of the movements of Ramses II, but the conditions were different. Some of the greatest battles of the earlier king were fought on Palestinian soil, while the latter simply marched through the country to an objective much farther north, in the Orontes valley. No doubt he received the submission of cities and tribes which had not recognized the authority of Egypt for some time, but he engaged in no great conflict in the land itself. It is true that the Israelite settlements may have been first made before 1479 B.C., and that they had not progressed far enough to come within the conqueror's range, but the balance of probability here lies on the side of the later rather than on that of the earlier date.

[1] The publication of Garstang's valuable and stimulating *Joshua and Judges* [1931] has greatly simplified this question. He dates the fall of Jericho in 1407 B.C., which brings it within the same general period as the date suggested in the text above as the least improbable for the invasion of Palestine by Israel.

Another consideration points in the same direction. The earlier date hardly gives us enough time between the expulsion of the Hyksos and the fall of Jericho. We have to allow for the oppression, for the Exodus, for the period of the wanderings, for the conquest of Transjordania, and for a residence of some length in the newly-won territory. While no reliance can be placed on the traditional length of the life of Moses, the familiar figure of 120 years is not too long for these events, and while they may have been compressed within a century, the probability lies on the other side. We may, perhaps, escape from our difficulties and still ascribe the destruction of Jericho to Israelite forces, by supposing that the fall of the city was the result of a raid across the Jordan, undertaken at the same time as the conquest of the eastern territory. But we must admit that we are in no position to dogmatize on this point, and that, while the general tendency of the data at our disposal is in favour of a fourteenth-century date for the Conquest, the margin of probability is very small. But in any case the date of the Exodus can hardly have been later than the early part of the fifteenth century.[1]

Moses[2] claims our attention, as one of the most remarkable figures that have ever passed across the stage of history. Hebrew tradition assigns him to the tribe of Levi, but this may have been an accommodation to a later theory of the priesthood, and it has been suggested that he was really connected with Ephraim. The *descendants* of Moses were Levites (cp. Judges xviii. 30),[3] but the term may have an official and not originally a tribal application. It is noticeable that his attendant, Joshua, is always represented as an Ephraimite, and E. Meyer[4] advances

---

[1] See p. 87.　　　　　　[2] For an acute and detailed study of the subject cp. Gressmann, *Mose und seine Zeit* [1913].

[3] In Judges xvii. 7 the MT. makes this young man a Judahite, but the Vatican MS. of the LXX and the Peshitta omit the term, possibly because of the difficulty of reconciling the statement with the theory that Moses was a Levite. As a matter of fact we may doubt whether the term Levi in reference to Moses and his descendants originally implied the tribe. There was, no doubt, a tribe of Levi, but it seems to have disappeared at an early date, if we may trust Gen. xlix. 5–7, along with the tribe of Simeon. The word, *lawiya*, however, is found in Minaean inscriptions in the sense of 'priest', and it may be that the similarity of the two led to confusion, the later office being supposed to imply the tribe. This would not be difficult after the office had become (as it certainly did) hereditary. For a discussion of the two terms see Gray, *Sacrifice in the Old Testament*, pp. 242 ff.; E. Meyer, *IN.*, pp. 51–3; and on the general subject, Wellhausen, *Prolegomena to the History of Israel*, E.T., pp. 141–3.　　　　　　[4] *IN.*, pp. 118–20.

reasons, not wholly conclusive, for the assignment of Moses to that clan. But, whatever the precise tribe be, it is clear that Moses was an Israelite. It is also clear that he had Egyptian affinities. The derivation of his name in Exod. ii. 10 is hardly meant to be taken seriously; it is surely an obvious Egyptian name, possibly a shortened form of a name like several of the royal names of the eighteenth dynasty[1]—Ahmose, Tutmose— while in the nineteenth and several subsequent dynasties we have the common name Ramses, containing the same element. Its prevalence in names of the eighteenth dynasty may possibly be a further hint at Moses' date. The word in itself means 'son', and is not likely to have been used alone, while, if the first element were the name of an Egyptian god, we can understand why it should have been dropped.[2]

The story of Moses' birth and preservation[3] has parallels in the folk-lore of many nations, eastern and western. One of the closest is to be found in Sargon's account of his own early days, but many others are known, and the *motif* extends even to early Celtic literature.[4] In the case of Moses it is peculiarly appropriate, for the two elements, Hebrew and Egyptian, are clearly combined in him. A period of separation from Egyptian court surroundings was indispensable if he was to win a right perspective, and to do his work as a deliverer of his own oppressed people. Stories taken from general folk-lore tend to attach themselves to every great historical character in early

[1] Roughly 1600–1350 B.C.

[2] For an abbreviation made in Israelite tradition on theological grounds, cp. Ahaz. His name, as shown by Assyrian documents, was Jehoahaz, but the first element has been eliminated in our Biblical records, presumably because he had so bad a reputation. See below, p. 375.   [3] Exod. ii. 1–10.

[4] For the whole story cp. W. J. Gruffydd, 'Moses in the Light of Comparative Folk-lore', *ZAW.* xlvi (1928), pp. 260 ff. Professor Gruffydd starts his research with the old Welsh Mabinogi of Math, and his thesis is that the original form of the story always involved the presence of a foreign and oppressive king. A child is born of mixed parentage, his mother (or his father) being a child of the king, and the other parent one of the oppressed race. It is foretold that this child will one day destroy his grandfather and deliver the oppressed nation, and in one way or another the prophecy is fulfilled. Professor Gruffydd conjectures that some such story may have been current in Egypt, and have been adopted by Israel for its own national hero. If he is right, we may add the further guess that the Egyptian child of fate was originally Ahmose, and that the oppressor was a late Hyksos king. See further W. J. Gruffydd, *Math fab Mathonwy.* Even if the suggestion is correct, the historicity of Moses is not thereby invalidated, nor does it necessarily follow that the events of his birth and upbringing are not as described in the Biblical narrative. All that can justly be contended is that the story of his life may have been modified by contact with a tale which has not survived in Egyptian literature.

days, and there is hardly a detail in the life of Moses for which a parallel cannot be found elsewhere. His flight from Egypt and his protection by the chief of a wilderness tribe[1] may be compared with the story of Sinuhe,[2] the actual scene which introduces him to the family of his protector with the narrative of Jacob's meeting with Rachel.[3] Of course, each story has its own peculiar features, but the general outline is the same. It is quite possible that the narrative in Exod. ii. 1–10 conceals an early belief that Moses was of Egyptian as well as of Israelite descent, and certainly all later tradition, following the suggestion of the narrative, made him an expert in those arts which were held to be characteristic of Egypt.

To these two factors in the personality of Moses we must add a third, that which he acquired after his flight from Egypt. In a certain sense this is the most important of all, for it was in this period that he came into contact with that religion which inspired him and enabled him to do his work. In the land of Midian he enters the family of a priest—*the* priest in Exod. ii. 16 —who is called Reuel, marries his daughter, Zipporah, and settles down as a herdsman of his father-in-law's flock. Here is vouchsafed to him a revelation in the thornbush,[4] and we can hardly doubt that, to be intelligible, the God who appeared to Moses there must have been in some way familiar to him.

The site of the 'Mount of God' is by no means certain. The earlier sources of the Pentateuch use different names, J speaking of Sinai and E of Horeb. D follows E, and P follows J. Both names are found outside the Pentateuch; in the Song of Deborah we have Sinai,[5] and Elijah flees to 'Horeb, the mount of God'.[6] These references clearly imply that it lay to the south of Palestine. The traditional site is the Jebel Musa, in the southern portion of the Sinai peninsula, but this identification cannot be traced farther back than the third century A.D. Josephus speaks of the Midianites as living to the east of the Gulf of Akaba, and some would place Horeb in that locality. But the Midianites may well have changed their ground more than once, as the nomad Israelites are said to have done, and we

---

[1] Exod. ii. 11–22.   [2] Cp. Gressmann, *ATAT.*, pp. 55 ff.
[3] Gen. xxix. 1–14.
[4] The Hebrew word סנה is used only here and in Deut. xxxiii. 16, where Yahweh is mentioned indirectly as the 'dweller in the thornbush'. The fact that this phrase occurs in the Blessing of Joseph may lend a certain colour to the theory that Moses himself was an Ephraimite.   [5] Judges v. 4.   [6] 1 Kgs. xix. 8.

cannot be sure that they were to be found there in Moses' day. At the same time, the mention of Horeb as being eleven days' journey from Mount Seir in Deut. i. 2 suggests a site in the far south. But the incidents of Exod. xvii and xviii, in so far as they are drawn from E—the smiting of the rock, the battle with Amalek and the visit of Jethro—seem to be placed in the same district as the sacred mountain, and the names mentioned, Massah, Meribah, and Rephidim, appear to indicate places in the same general locality. To judge from Num. xx. 1–14 these places lay near Kadesh. A similar view emerges from the references in P, which connect the wilderness of Sin and Paran with Kadesh, as well as Meribah.[1] To these references we may add Judges v. 4 and Deut. xxxiii. 2, which seem to place Sinai in the Edom territory. It is possible that variant traditions were current at different periods in the history of Israel or perhaps in different parts of the country. But for us the important question is, not Where was Sinai? but What happened at Sinai? The exact site is quite unimportant, while the events which took place at the sacred mountain were of profound significance for the later history of Israel.[2]

The three main authorities in our present text differ as to the amount of knowledge that Moses had of Yahweh before the theophany. J (e.g. Exod. iv. 1) assumes that Israel is already familiar with the divine name Yahweh; E suggests that it was unknown, and that it was revealed only now, though Yahweh had, as a matter of fact, been the God of the patriarchs (Exod. iii. 6, 15); the theory of P is that though Yahweh was the God of the patriarchs, He had never allowed them to know His real name, permitting Himself to be worshipped under the title El Shaddai (Exod. vi. 2, 3), a modification of the view expressed in E.

All are agreed, however, that Moses was commissioned in the name of Yahweh to deliver Israel from the Egyptian servitude, and to bring the people to the sacred mountain. All send Moses back to Egypt to accomplish his mission. J, however, introduces a very ancient and primitive story, according to which Yahweh met Moses when he and his family encamped for the night and

---

[1] Cp. Num. x. 12, xxvii. 14, xxxiii. 36, &c.

[2] Discussions of the location of the 'Mount of God' are to be found in most histories of Israel and commentaries on the book of *Exodus*. We may select as among the most useful those of McNeile, *The Book of Exodus* (Westminster Commentaries), pp. ci–cvi (1908), and A. Lods, *Israël*, pp. 199–205 (1930).

tried to kill him because he was still uncircumcised,[1] and attributes his safety to the ready wit and prompt action of his wife.

From this point the story proceeds with a series of events which are in themselves perfectly probable and, indeed, natural, due allowance being made for the normal colouring which an ancient author's mind inevitably gives to facts. Moses demands in the name of Yahweh that the Israelites shall be released, and the first effect is to irritate the authorities. He then begins to threaten Egypt with the plagues which follow on the repeated refusals of Pharaoh to accede to the demand of Yahweh that Israel shall go three days' journey into the desert in order to observe a festival,[2] presumably at the mountain where Moses received his theophany. This is an element which must belong to the very earliest form of the story, since on it turns the later development. As the list now stands, ten plagues are named.[3] No one of the three sources contains all ten, and the number seems to be fortuitous. The distribution is as follows, several being drawn from more than one source:

J	E	P
1. Water turned to blood.	As in J.	As in J.
2. Frogs.		As in J.
3.		'Lice.'
4. Flies.		
5. Murrain.		
6.		Boils and blains.
7. Storm.	As in J.	
8. Locusts.	As in J.	
9.	Darkness.	
10. Death of Firstborn.	As in J.	As in J.

From this list it will be seen that E has one plague only which is not in J, while J has three which are not in E. It may be that the accounts of these four were so similar that the compiler drew on one only of his sources. Of the four which are found

---

[1] Exod. iv. 24b-6. As the story stands Zipporah circumcised her son in lieu of her husband, but we may suspect that in its earliest form she circumcised Moses. Probably we have here an ancient explanation of the origin of circumcision in Israel; it was a rite that must be performed before marriage, or the bridegroom would risk the anger of one of the spirits that watch the bridal chamber. We may remark also that the story possibly indicates the change which took place when circumcision was performed in infancy instead of during adolescence.

[2] Exod. v. 3.

[3] Exod. vii. 14—xii. 30.

in P, two appear also in J, while the other two are variants of J plagues. The 'lice' are simply flies, under another name, and the 'boils and blains' are clearly another version of the 'murrain' of J.

None of these plagues, except the last, contains anything strange or abnormal; all are events which may naturally take place at the end of the inundation of the Nile. The stagnant water left as the river goes down often reddens with infusoria, and becomes undrinkable, while fish that have been caught in the pools will, of course, die as the ground dries. Frogs naturally find their way from the water on to dry land, and may easily be so numerous as to be a nuisance. The pools breed quantities of mosquitoes, and these, in turn, produce distressing forms of skin disease. Thunderstorms, accompanied by heavy hail, are rare in Egypt, but they do occur,[1] and are naturally alarming. Sand and dust storms which produce deep gloom may quite well take place to the east of the Delta, while locusts are only too frequent a scourge. In all this there is nothing to awaken incredulity; the 'miracle' will consist in nothing more than the coincidence of all these events, and their exceptional severity.

At the same time it is hardly possible to accept in detail the narrative as it stands. The district in which Israel is represented as living, even if it be as far west as Pithom, is still a long way from the Nile, and the picture of the court of Pharaoh being always ready and at hand for the convenience of Moses gives an impression of improbability which it is hard to shake off. Nor can we easily interpret the last calamity of all, though we may conjecture that originally it was the first-born of Pharaoh alone who perished. No doubt, tradition told of some disaster which fell upon Egypt at a critical moment, thus facilitating the escape of the fugitives, and the imagination and knowledge of Egypt possessed by later generations readily filled in the details. The impression, however, made on the mind of Israel is unmistakable. They were the people of Yahweh, chosen and protected by Him. He had summoned them formally to enter into relations with Him at His home in the sacred mountain, and it was their earnest desire to obey the call. But they were prevented by

[1] The present writer, while passing through the Suez Canal, from which the ancient Pithom is but a few miles distant, witnessed a severe thunderstorm in May 1914, and persons acquainted with the country commented on the rarity of the phenomenon.

no fault of their own, and since they could not go to Yahweh, Yahweh came to them. He is presented at once as a mighty, terrible and capricious deity; there is something of the demon[1] in Him, and the perils of His proximity can be avoided only by the prophylactic sacrificial blood upon the doors.[2] Where this blood was wanting the Destroyer entered, and while the Israelites celebrated, as best they could in a profane land, that Passover which should have been observed at a Yahweh sanctuary or on Yahweh's soil, the God Himself swept through the land, bringing death into every unprotected home. We may not feel justified in trying to reconstruct the whole picture in detail, but we may be sure that something happened, something which made the most profound impression on the national consciousness of Israel.

The Passover night was one of the two great events of the Exodus; the other was the crossing of the Red Sea. Once more we may say that it is impossible to be sure that the details handed down to us are historically accurate, and once more we should have no doubt as to the essential fact. And again, we may say, there is nothing in E's story of the crossing to rouse suspicion,[3] for the only 'supernatural' feature of the story is to be found in the pillar of fire and cloud, and even this may be based on a phenomenon which has been observed in modern times. When it is remembered that Yahweh was always (among other attributes) a fire God, it will be seen that tradition had no

---

[1] Cp. Volz, *Das Dämonische in Jahve* (1924).

[2] Beliefs of this kind are widely spread in the east, cp. Gray, *Sacrifice in the Old Testament*, pp. 361 ff.

[3] It may be as well here to reproduce the whole of the JE portions of Exod. xiv. 15–30, in so far as they can be disentangled from the interwoven account of P: 'And Yahweh said unto Moses, Wherefore criest thou unto me? Lift up thy rod. And the angel of God which went before the camp moved and went behind them, and the pillar of cloud removed from before them and came behind them, and came between the camp of the Egyptians and the camp of Israel, and there was cloud and darkness and it lit up the night, and they could not approach one another all the night. And Yahweh drove the sea back with a strong east wind all the night, and made the sea into dry land. And in the morning watch Yahweh looked out on the camp of the Egyptians through the pillar of fire and smoke, and threw the Egyptian camp into a panic. And he bound' (reading, with the Samaritan text and the chief ancient versions, ויאסר for ויסר) 'their chariot wheels and made them drive heavily, and the Egyptians said, Let us flee from the face of Israel, for Yahweh is fighting for them against Egypt. And as the day broke the sea returned to its bed, while the Egyptians fled towards it. And Yahweh overthrew the Egyptians in the midst of the sea, not one of them survived. And on that day Yahweh saved Israel from the power of Egypt, and Israel saw the Egyptians dead on the sea-shore.'

better way of expressing its conviction that He was present and at work, especially in producing panic in the Egyptian force, than to speak of this pillar.

We have no means of knowing for certain where the crossing took place. Those who would locate Sinai to the east of the Gulf of Akaba will naturally find the spot at the northern end of that gulf. On other grounds, the more natural place will be north of the modern Suez. The sandy stretch between Suez and the southern end of the Bitter Lakes is raised only a few feet above sea-level, and was probably wholly or partially covered with water in ancient times. Shallow water of this kind may easily be driven back by a strong wind, leaving the sand bare.[1] With the dropping of the wind the water returns, coming, probably, under the sand first, as it does in so many such places with the tide, and forming a quicksand in which the wheels of the chariots would first sink. Finally, as the dried space filled with water, the infantry and others would be caught and drowned. We must remember that, for the most part, Israel was unfamiliar with the sea, and movements of this kind would almost inevitably appear miraculous. There can be little doubt that some unusual coincidence facilitated the escape of at least a portion of the tribes, and that this was ever afterwards remembered as the first great interference of Yahweh on behalf of His people.

[1] Cp. C. S. Jarvis, in *Blackwood's Magazine*, Feb. 1931, who has observed phenomena in the district which would account completely for the drying of the sea and the pillar of cloud, &c.; also the same author's *Yesterday and To-day in Sinai* (1931), pp. 158 ff. Major Jarvis places the scene of the crossing at the modern Bardawil Lake, which is separated from the Mediterranean only by a narrow strip of sand. For the tides in the Gulf of Suez, and the variations of sea-level, cp. the *Red Sea and Gulf of Aden Pilot*[5] (1900), pp. 17, 18, 85 (for the Gulf of Akaba, p. 244). Eissfeldt (cp. *Baal Zaphon*, 1932) adopts a similar view, believing that the true site is on the Serbonian marsh.

ADDITIONAL NOTE

Page 80, note 1. But cf. for a recent defence of the later date, H. H. Rowley, *Israel's Sojourn in Egypt*, Bulletin of the John Rylands Library, vol. 22, No. 1, April 1938.

Chapter VI

THE COVENANT

SUMMARY

[The escape from Egypt is but the preliminary to the Covenant at
the sacred mountain, which forms the real beginning of the Israelite
nation. Probably the number of fugitives, and even of the tribes
represented among them, was a good deal smaller than later Israel
supposed, and they may have united with other nomads before
reaching Sinai or Horeb. But, when they did arrive at the sacred
mountain, Moses bound them into a single whole by means of a new
religion.

Before the time of Moses we have little indication of the objects of
tribal worship, but there is ground for the suggestion that some of
the clans recognized their own eponymous ancestors as their proper
gods. Yahweh, on the other hand, was probably a Midianite or
Kenite deity. The Covenant consisted in the mutual adoption of
God and people; Yahweh *became* the God of Israel; Israel *became*
the people of Yahweh—on certain conditions. The divine promises
are not explicitly stated; of the human undertakings we have two
accounts, one in Exod. xx–xxiii, the other in Exod. xxxiv. Probably
both, in their present form, are later interpretations of the original
terms, since they presuppose a settled agricultural community rather
than a nomad people. We may say, however, that in all probability
the familiar Decalogue does represent the moral standard required
by Yahweh of His new people.]

THE Exodus was but the preliminary act in the work of Moses.
There still remained his great achievement, the formation of
the people of Israel. His task was to take a number of more or
less isolated tribes, and to weld them together into a single
whole, giving them an organic unity which should prove to be
stronger than the claims of the old tribal patriotism. The
difficulties in the way of such an achievement would seem at
first sight to be insurmountable, for, in all probability, the
independence of the tribes was not merely political but also
religious, and the combination of the two, while not precluding
friendly relations and some degree of co-operation, could not
but prove a most serious obstacle to a more intimate union. As
a matter of fact the tribal sense long remained, and it was only
some centuries after the settlement, with the rise of the monarchy,
that the unification approached completeness. But had it not
been for the work accomplished by Moses, the task even then

would have been impossible, as the whole earlier history of Palestine shows. At no date prior to the Israelite settlement, does there seem to have been the slightest evidence for a real unification of Palestine; each town and princedom stood by itself against its neighbours.

We have no means of knowing the number or the tribal identity of the fugitives delivered by Moses. In Num. i. 20–47 we read of 603,550 fighting men of twenty years old and upwards, which would mean a total of certainly not less than 2,000,000. This figure is due to P and is clearly unhistorical. Apart from the problem of sustenance in the wilderness through which Israel had to pass in order to reach the sacred mountain, the arranging and moving of such a host from Egypt would have been impossible. So far from accepting this figure, which is based on the assumption that all the tribes moved together[1] from Egypt, we may be fairly certain that it was only a limited number of them that were represented among the captive labourers who escaped under Moses, and even so we may suspect that the fugitives included only a small portion of the tribes to which they belonged. The deliverance of even a small force would have all the effect that is ascribed to the Exodus, for it would illustrate to all the power of the God under whose aegis it had been carried out.

We may suppose, from indications afforded by the narrative, e.g. in the account of the visit of Jethro,[2] that on their departure from Egypt the tribes met with others whose kinship they recognized, perhaps already near the sacred mountain. Probably the wanderers gathered strength as they went, and they may have continued to absorb fresh elements till after the settlement in Palestine. As we have seen, it is not impossible that the nucleus was formed by Joseph tribes and those most closely related to them. It is clear that there must have been some

---

[1] The actual figures given by P (Num. i. 20–47) are: Reuben 46,500, Simeon 59,300, Gad 45,650, Judah 74,600, Issachar 54,400, Zebulun 57,400, Ephraim 40,500, Manasseh 32,200, Benjamin 35,400, Dan 62,700, Asher 41,500, Naphtali 53,400. The tribe of Levi is expressly excluded, presumably because on the theory of P they were not regarded as combatant units, and the enumeration is that of the military force of Israel. The order is peculiar, and there seems to be no particular reason for the displacement of certain of the tribes from their natural positions. The suggestion that the word אֶלֶף means not 'thousand', but family, will not apply here since it does not account for the odd hundreds and even an odd fifty in the tribe of Gad. It must be admitted that the list has no historical value.

[2] Exod. xviii. 1–12.

amalgamation of tribes, and we must allow for the possibility
that later assimilations of the same kind were thrown back by
tradition to this point.

The instrument used by Moses was religion, in fact the only
means by which he could have accomplished his purpose. It
was in association with a new God, and in nothing else, that
these tribes could find their unity, for the basic principle, one
people, one God, seems still to have governed the polity of the
tribes. Religion entered so largely into the life of the ancient
peoples that no valid transaction of any size was possible
without it, and almost every type of action had its special
relation to the object of tribal worship.

The Biblical record tells us practically nothing of the deities
worshipped by the tribes before the time of Moses. In Gen.
xxxv. 2 Jacob exhorts his clansmen to put away the strange
gods who were among them, as they were about to approach
the sacred spot of Bethel. It may be that we have here, reflected
back into the patriarchal age, a transaction which properly
belongs to the period of the Exodus, and the impression
is heightened by a repetition of the same words at the same
place by Joshua.[1] But who were these strange gods? There
seems to have been an early connexion between the Aramaean
nomads from whom Israel's ancestry is traced and the worship
of the Moon-god. Ur was the most important centre of the
cult of Sin in early Mesopotamia, Harran was another city
devoted to the same deity, while the relation between Sin and
Sinai seems obvious.[2] But even if the Moon-god be admitted as
one of the objects of worship, he is only one, and a number is
implied. Perhaps the most plausible conjecture is that some
of the tribes, possibly all, worshipped their own eponymous
ancestors. There are several indications which seem to point
in that direction. The ordinary Hebrew word for God is a
plural form, *'Elohim*, and though this may be a 'plural of
majesty', it is at least possible that it points back to a poly-
theistic or rather a polydaemonistic age. The original meaning
of the term is not certain; perhaps the only clear light is thrown
by 1 Sam. xxviii. 13, where the witch consulted by Saul tells
the king that she sees *'Elohim*, i.e. a ghost. This suggests that
originally the term was one of those animistic plurals for the
dead, regarded as objects of worship, such as we find in other

[1] Josh. xxiv. 23.   [2] It is, however, disputed.

forms of primitive religion, cp. the Roman *Manes* and *Larvae*. The early Semite had many objects of worship, and his religion was on a stage in which an animism was passing into a polytheism, with certain deities to some extent individualized but not fully isolated. Some form of cult of the dead seems to be found in every known type of animism, and we find Israel constantly falling into spiritualism (necromancy). It is true that the term *'Elohim* is never used elsewhere in this connexion, but it is easily to be understood that, after it had been applied to the single deity Yahweh, men would avoid applying it to the spirits of the departed. It is to be regarded as an accident that it has survived in the one passage cited.[1]

We may, perhaps, find some further evidence in the fact that several of the tribes bear names known elsewhere to be divine. The lists of 'Retenu', Palestinian tribes, subject to Tutmose III, include two sites named respectively Joseph-el and Jacob-el,[2] which are best interpreted as the homes of tribes bearing the ancestral names 'Jacob is El' and 'Joseph is El'.[3] Divine names which take the form of verbal imperfects are by no means uncommon in Semitic speech, and a familiar example is found in the name of Yahweh Himself. It would seem, then, that there were two gods, albeit obscure, known as Jacob and Joseph. Asher may quite well be a modification of the name of the great Assyrian eponymous deity Ashur, while Gad is a familiar Semitic divinity, best known as the god of good luck,[4] with a place in the Hermon district especially consecrated to him—Baal-Gad. Laban, if not actually one of the ancestors of Israel, is yet closely akin to Jacob, and represents the Aramaean affiliations. He also bears a theophorous name, known to us from Cappadocian tablets belonging to the latter half of the third millennium B.C.[5] We have, it is true, no evidence at present in respect of the other names (though it has been suspected, on quite inadequate

---

[1] But cp. also Isa. ix. 19.

[2] See for Jacob-el, Mariette, *Les Listes Geographiques des Pylônes de Karnak*, p. 40 (No. 102). The transliteration of the former is disputed, it being contended that the Egyptian sibilant represents the Hebrew שׁ, not ס. The actual forms are, of course, written without vowels, and are *Y-sh-p-ʾ-r* and *Y-ʿ-ḳ-b-ʾ-r*, the Egyptian *r* corresponding to the Semitic *l*. The name *Yakub-ilu* is said to occur in Babylonian texts of the age of Ḥammurabi, cp. *E.B.*, art. 'Jacob', col. 2,306; Hommel, *A.H.T.*, p. 96, and Burney, *Judges*, pp. lxvi, lxviii, ciii, civ, cxi, cxv.

[3] For a discussion of these names cp. E. Meyer, *IN.*, pp. 249 ff., 292.

[4] Cp. Isa. lxv. 11 and Mordtmann in *ZDMG.* xxxi. 99–101; Nöldeke, *ZDMG.* lii. 474, 478 ff.   [5] See above, note on p. 52.

grounds, that Dan is a divine name), but what is certainly true of these five is not impossible of the rest.

Whether the suggestion contained in the last two paragraphs be correct or not, it may be taken for granted that the tribes— or such of them as Moses had collected—worshipped different gods, and his task was to introduce them to the cult of a new deity, who should combine them into a single whole from the religious, and so from every other point of view. It was inevitable that the God chosen for the purpose should be He whom Moses had learnt to know during his exile, He who had given Moses his commission, He whose power had rescued 'Israel' from Egypt and taken vengeance on their pursuers.

This was Yahweh. His name and original worshippers have been the subject of much discussion.[1] He seems to have been the local El of the sacred mountain and of its neighbourhood, especially of the tribe of Midian or, perhaps, of the Kenites. The latter suggestion rests on several important facts. The Kenites were the smiths of the ancient nomad tribes of the east. That is to say, they probably resembled the wandering smith clans whom Doughty found in Arabia,[2] a people who moved from one tribe to another as their services were required. More than any others of that age and district they were in the habit of using fire, and undoubtedly Yahweh is a fire-God, though He has other attributes as well.[3] In Judges iv. 11 the father-in-law of Moses is called Hobab the Kenite, and in Judges i. 16 he is an unnamed Kenite, though the Alexandrian MS. of the LXX and some others prefix the name Hobab. These facts make it clear that in one form of the ancient tradition it was among Kenites that Moses learned to know Yahweh, and this tradition may be the earliest. Certainly Israel always had Kenite allies and friends, and a common religion would serve as the strongest bond of union between the two peoples.

---

[1] For various theories and the evidence adduced in their support see E. Kautzsch in *EB.*, art. 'Names', §§ 108 ff., esp. n. 3, col. 3,322, and, for more recent discussion, with special reference to the Mesopotamian evidence, G. R. Driver in *Old Testament Essays* (pub. Griffin), pp. 18–24. See also König, *Geschichte der A.T. Religion*, pp. 160–9 (1912).   [2] Cp. *Travels in Arabia Deserta*, i. 281 ff.

[3] Budde has advanced reasons for believing that the Sabbath, with its special *tabu* on fire, was a specifically Kenite institution, and contends that only so can its presence in Israel be satisfactorily explained. Cp. 'Sabbat und Woche' in *Die Christliche Welt*, Nr. 5, 6, 1929. For other views see Hommel, *Die altorientalische Denkmäler und das alte Testament*, pp. 18, 19; Nielsen, *Die altarabische Mondreligion*, pp. 87 ff., 251 ff.

We may remind ourselves also that the Kenites played an important, if obscure part in the tribal constitution of the later Israel. As we shall have occasion to observe, they were in some way linked with the tribe of Judah, and may have formed an element in the original nucleus out of which that clan grew. If that be so, then it is at least possible that others of the Leah tribes were at one stage in the history connected also with the Kenites; in other words, Yahweh was originally a deity who was worshipped among the Leah tribes. Every attempt to solve the question which we have immediately before us must rest on conjecture, but that which gives us the most complete explanation is the supposition that Moses, by birth a member of a Rachel tribe, by training an Egyptian, and by force of circumstances an adherent of a Leah cult, led his own clansmen out of Egypt, and united them to a group which claimed a common, though more remote, kinship with them.

The name Yahweh, too, has been a matter of dispute. In various forms the element YHW is said to be found in Mesopotamian documents dating from comparatively early times. It is clearly a verbal form, but there are parallels elsewhere in the ancient Semitic world. The root from which it comes is quite uncertain; the paranomasia of Exod. iii. 14[1] was hardly intended to be etymology, and the word has been variously identified as one meaning 'to be', 'to blow', 'to fall'. But whatever its exact origin may be, the characteristics of Yahweh Himself are clear: He is a storm-god, a mountain-god, a fire-god, and a warrior-god. As a denizen of the wilderness He might be expected to know its paths and to be an efficient guide to water and to pasture. He was, in a word, just the deity to meet Israel's needs during the nomad period of her history.

The actual ceremony by which the union of Israel and Yahweh was accomplished is described in Exod. xxiv. 3-8.[2] It consisted in a form of covenant ritual, embodying a symbolism such as is not infrequent among Semitic and other peoples. Allowing for certain details which must be ascribed to a later time, it was much as follows: An altar was erected, representing the deity, and over against it stood the people. Victims were slain and their blood was drained off into bowls. Part of this

---

[1] 'I am that I am'—אהיה אשר אהיה.

[2] A simpler ceremony, consisting of a sacred meal, is probably indicated in Exod. xxiv. 9-11.

blood was then dashed against the altar, and the rest flung over the heads of the people. The ritual may have included other sacrificial features, but its essence lies here. The symbolism is obvious. The life of the victim has been used to cover and include both the contracting parties. Each, passing beneath its blood, has become essentially identified with it, and since both are thus one with a third party, they are one with each other. Before the ceremony they were to be regarded as separate entities; they are so no longer, for they are one. A single essence runs through them both, and they are no longer merely contiguous, but vitally continuous. Henceforth Yahweh is a blood-member of the tribe gathered at His seat.

The conception of the god as member of his tribe seems to have been common to many, if not to all, the Semitic peoples. But in other cases the connexion is natural, for the human members of the tribe are regarded as being literally the physical descendants of the deity. That is not so with Israel; the bond is not natural but artificial. There had been a time when Israel had not been the people of Yahweh, and Yahweh not the God of Israel. Their connexion was based on a deliberate act of choice by the God and a voluntary acceptance by the people. It was a partnership into which both parties had willingly entered, based upon conditions offered on the divine side, which had been freely accepted on the human. In its simplest form the Covenant is expressed in a phrase which does not actually meet us in the extant literature until the seventh century B.C., but which sums up the whole history of the religious life of Israel, 'I will become their God, and they shall become my people.'[1] Since the association was voluntary, based on the performance of certain duties, each to each, it followed that any breach of the conditions would automatically terminate the connexion, unless the injured party chose to renew it. And while, through her history, Israel ever found in Yahweh a God who 'observed covenant and love',[2] its terms were violated again and again on the human side, and it was shown that man could not be brought to maintain a standard which was merely written on some outward substance. Thus the climax of Israel's spiritual history is reached when Jeremiah lays down

[1] Cp. e.g. Jer. xxxi. 33.
[2] Deut. vii. 9, 12, 1 Kgs. viii. 23, Dan. ix. 4, Neh. i. 5, ix. 32, 2 Chron. vi. 14.

the principle that a truly valid covenant must be put in men's inward parts and written on their heart.[1]

What, then, were the terms of the Covenant? On the divine side they are never stated, but it may be assumed that they are summed up in the duties and responsibilities which naturally and inevitably fell to a god among his people. Nor is it clear what human obligations were involved in Moses' day. Later tradition spoke of the 'tables of the Covenant',[2] assuming that the two tables of stone contained the conditions on which Israel had been accepted. Even Exod. xxiv. 7 spoke of the 'Book of the Covenant', and it is possible that the reference is to the short code contained in Exod. xx–xxiii, which the writer may have referred to Moses' day. But a cursory examination makes it most improbable that this was imposed on Israel in the nomad period. Not only are many of the laws designed for an agricultural and commercial community, and none of them confined to a nomad tribe, but they closely resemble that type of code which we know to have been generally current in western Asia.[3] Four forms are known—a fragmentary Sumerian code, that of Ḥammurabi, proper to Babylonia, an Assyrian code, and a Hittite code. Of the four, that of Ḥammurabi is much the oldest in the form in which we have it, and there can be little doubt that, in the main, Exod. xxi–xxiii (Exod. xx consists of the 'Ten Commandments', together with a few simple regulations for the cultus) represents the law as current in Palestine before the advent of Israel, adopted, along with other elements of Canaanite culture, by the invaders.[4]

Two still shorter summaries of law are found in *Exodus*, the one being the familiar Decalogue, the other a list of regulations to which, apparently, the name 'ten words' was originally intended to apply. The former appears in two slightly differing forms—both of them probably expanded in one or two items— in Exod. xx. 3–17 and in Deut. v. 7–21. These latter are stated to have been written on the two tables, and it is clearly the view of the Deuteronomist that they are the articles of the covenant. E, on the other hand, suggests that it is the whole of Exod. xx–xxiii which formed the basis of the agreement. The other

---

[1] Jer. xxxi. 31–4. [2] Deut. ix. 9, 11, 15. [3] See also pp. 34 f., 326 ff.
[4] The investigations of Jirku (cp. *Das weltliche Recht im Alten Testament* [1927] have shown, however, that the *sources* of Israelite law go back to a much more primitive stage than that represented in the Code of Ḥammurabi.

'code' is to be found embedded in Exod. xxxiv. 10–26. It has clearly been considerably expanded from the original form (J), and the writer regards it as the basis of the covenant, while in verse 28 the term 'ten words' (E.V. 'Ten commandments') is applied to it.

The outstanding difference between these two is that the commands of Exod. xxxiv are all cultic, while those of Exod. xx are mainly ethical, ritual appearing in only two of them. Further, the ritual of Exod. xxxiv is essentially that of an agricultural people, laying, as it does, great stress on the observance of the three chief agricultural festivals and the duty of every good Israelite to present himself at the sanctuary on the occasion of each. This, then, like Exod. xxi-xxiii, we must assign to the period of the settlement in Palestine. But the moral code in Exod. xx is timeless, and its provisions are valid for any condition of organized human society. There is, then, nothing in the code itself to prevent its having been promulgated by Moses, especially if the first few commandments are reduced to a simpler form. The explanation and reason given for the Sabbath, in particular, are almost certainly due to later redaction, as the variant in *Deuteronomy* shows. There is a tendency among modern critics, then, to ascribe the Decalogue of Exod. xx to Moses himself, and to assume that this was the basis on which the Covenant was established.[1] Of this theory it can only be said that it seems to be capable neither of proof nor of disproof, and even some of those who find it impossible definitely to ascribe the written document to Moses would agree that at least it represents the general moral standard set before Israel during their nomad period.

---

[1] Volz (cp. *Mose*, p. 70 [1907]) apparently regards the whole of Exod. xx-xxiii as Mosaic; and Sellin alludes sympathetically to the view that Moses is the author of the Decalogue, though he does not definitely commit himself (*Introduction to the Old Testament*, E.T., pp. 40 ff. [1923]). The Mosaic authorship of the Exod. xx Decalogue (in a simple form) is accepted also by Gressmann (*Mose*, pp. 475 ff.) and Kittel (*GVI.* i.³ 581 ff., 651 ff.). So also Jirku (cp. *Das weltliche Recht im Alten Testament*, pp. 150 ff.; in *GVI.* 81 ff. [1931]; he accepts those laws in Exod. xx-xxiii which bear the 'If-formula' as forming the original Mosaic Book of the Covenant).

Chapter VII

NOMAD ISRAEL

SUMMARY

[We know very little about the actual life of Israel during the wilderness period. Most of the stories we have seem to be thrown back into this time from a later age, and we must rely largely on what are clearly survivals in the later life of Israel, and on the analogy of similar peoples whom we can study to-day. We do not even know the tribal composition of the people; our earliest records omit some of the familiar names, especially that of Judah, and include others— e.g. Kenites, Kenizzites, and even Amalekites—who are not reckoned later as independent tribes. In these early times the nation seems to have been in a fluid state, and the familiar constitution may not have emerged till long after the first invasions of Palestine.

In such a community as that of nomad Israel, judicial functions are exercised by the religious authorities. Property is nearly all tribal rather than personal, and there are recognized clan leaders or Sheikhs. These features are common to many nomad tribes, but the religion of Israel presented unique features.

In later times there were three objects which were worshipped as representing Yahweh, the Bull, the Snake, and the Ark, a box containing a stone—or two stones. For each it was claimed that it went back to nomad days, possibly to Moses himself, and, of the three, it is most probably the Ark whose claim is best justified. It was kept in a special tent and had special attendants, the priests. Through it Yahweh was the supreme court of appeal in judicial matters, the guide through the wilderness, and the leader in war. He was also the guardian of the moral standard which, as is usual among peoples on this level of civilization, was rather higher than that commonly found in agricultural and civic communities. While we should not detract from the merit of this superiority, we must recognize that it was in part due to the fact that the life of the pastoral nomad is very much simpler, and is exposed to much fewer complications and temptations than that of the farmer or of the merchant.]

IT was with the work of Moses at the sacred mountain that Israel as a nation came into being. Of that we may be certain, for the events of those days stamped themselves deeply on the national consciousness. Ever afterwards men continued to look back on the deliverance from Egypt as the first great manifestation of the power of the national God, and to regard the covenant as the constituent act on which the whole of the later history was based. Till the ninth century, and possibly later, there were sections, at least, in Israel which thought of Yahweh as dwelling in the far south, as passing through the territory of Edom when He came to the help of His people, and as being most readily and certainly consulted by His chosen prophet in the 'Mount of God'.[1]

But of the history of Israel during the period that we commonly call the 'Wanderings' we know practically nothing, and are forced to fall back on conjecture and analogy for our reconstruction. All we can say is that the traditional period of forty years—one generation—must be regarded as a minimum, and, while it may have been more, it can hardly have been less. From one point of view these years have left little mark on Israel's traditions, beyond the story of the spies and of an abortive attempt to enter Palestine from the south.[2] There are incidents ascribed to the age which belong to the domestic history of Israel, but most of these, if not all, are evidently stories intended to explain some feature in the life and organization of the later Israel. Under this head we may include such incidents as the rebellion of Korah, Dathan, and Abiram.[3] Here two narratives have been interwoven. One deals with Korah alone, and comes from priestly sources. Its purpose is to illustrate and to explain the unique ecclesiastical position held by the family of Aaron. The fortunes of Dathan and Abiram belong to that type of tradition which is a form of early tribal history. The rebels are Reubenites, and we cannot help connecting the story with the references in Gen. xxxv. 22 and xlix. 3. It seems that the national memory of Israel recorded a time when the leadership was in the hands of this tribe, but that its arrogance made it insecure and brought about its fall. This tradition must have been handed down from the pastoral age, for Reuben was never an agricultural tribe. Its power had already weakened when reliable history begins, and before the middle of the ninth century it had disappeared.

We may accept as historical the tradition which makes Kadesh the 'home' of Israel during this period, or the greater part of it. This does not mean that the tribes abandoned their wandering habits and took to a settled life in the oasis. We must assume that they made Kadesh the centre round which

---

[1] Cp. e.g. Judges v. 4, 1 Kgs. xix. 8.   [2] Num. xiii, xiv.
[3] Num. xvi. 1–35.

they spent their time, moving from place to place within a comparatively small radius, as opportunities for fodder and water presented themselves. As we have seen,[1] there are reasons for conjecturing that the sacred mountain lay in this neighbourhood, and for a time they would wish to be within reach of it. Moreover, with the supplies available at Kadesh during the drier parts of the year, there would be little attraction for the tribes to migrate to other spots. It may be that an increase in their numbers or a succession of dry seasons at length compelled them to look elsewhere for a better home.

As we have remarked, we do not know how long the Kadesh period lasted. It was one of those times of silent assimilation and consolidation which are necessary before a new idea can effectively influence history. An immediate conquest of Palestine might have proved fatal, for the formal combination of the tribes and the adoption of a new deity were still too fresh to have made a permanent impression on the national consciousness. Cities might have been stormed and territories conquered, but the later history of Israel shows how great were the risks run even after a generation or more of further wilderness life. After the conquests it was only the repeated assaults of enemies within and without which threw the tribes back on their common inheritance of blood, religion, and tradition, and welded them into a single whole. There was always a disintegrating force at work, manifesting itself after the death of Solomon in the division of the kingdom, and culminating in the bitter hostility of the Jew and the Samaritan. Only a firm conviction and a strongly rooted tradition could have sufficed to give Israel even that measure of unity in politics and religion which she actually achieved. The enthusiasm engendered by the circumstances of the Exodus and by the great covenant might have carried the nation safely into the promised land, but there the centrifugal tendencies which were always so marked a feature of Palestinian life would have prevailed, and there would have been but one more element added to the mixed blood of a number of isolated and mutually jealous little communities, standing apart from one another both in religion and in political organization. Hostile aggression, particularly that of the Philistines, would have dissolved instead of strengthening the ideal unity of the people, and in the end the Aramaean wave

[1] Cp. above, pp. 82 f.

of immigration would have contributed no more to Palestine
and to the world than did its Amorite predecessor.

As we look over the narratives which deal with the early days
of the settlement in Palestine, we meet occasionally with references which may throw light on the constitution of Israel in the
wilderness. We note, for instance, in Judges v that there
are significant omissions. Of the four senior Leah tribes,
Reuben alone is mentioned. Our evidence suggests that
Simeon and Levi disappeared at an earlier period, but the
absence of Judah is not to be explained in this way, and we can
only suppose that it was not yet fully recognized as an Israelite
tribe. Further, the tribal song of Judah in Gen. xlix describes it,
not merely as a powerful warrior people, but as a grower of the
vine[1]—the only mention of viticulture in the book except in the
story of Noah.[2] This, even more than the growth of corn,
signifies a long settlement in the land, and confirms our impression that Judah formed no part of the community in the
wilderness. It may be that the 'junior' Leah tribes and the
'subordinate' tribes of both groups entered the general body
later than the rest, but their connexion with the others goes
back to the nomad stage. The prominent part played by
Zebulun, Issachar, and Naphtali in the defeat of Sisera, and the
close traditional connexion between Dan and Naphtali, on the
one hand, and Gad and Asher on the other,[3] seem to preclude
the idea that any of them was originally of Palestinian origin.
All must have been traditionally members of the Aramaean
pastoral group which we call Israel.

On the other hand, there are suggestions of tribes which were
never reckoned as fully Israelite, but yet seem in a sense to be
included. Thus, if we may trust the MT. of Judges v. 14, there
is some kinship between Ephraim and Amalek. In Num. xxiv.
20, a kind of appendix to the panegyrics he utters over Israel,
Balaam pronounces a blessing on Amalek. In Judges xii. 15
a 'mountain of the Amalekite' is placed in 'mount Ephraim'. It
is true that from the days when Israel first left Egypt the

---

[1] Gen. xlix. 11 f.   [2] Gen. ix. 20.

[3] This tradition of full brotherhood is particularly important. Throughout the
period of the settlement these two tribes were widely separated from one another,
and Gad always remained on the pastoral plane. The tradition of the relation-
ship, then, cannot be explained, as might that of Dan and Naphtali, on the
ground of proximity in Palestine, but must go back to the period before the
conquest.

Amalekites are represented as permanent enemies,[1] but it is possible that we have two conflicting lines of tradition, of which that hostile to Amalek ultimately prevailed. The position of the Kenites is less equivocal. As we have seen, there are grounds for suspecting that the family into which Moses married was Kenite—one form of the tradition certainly took this view —and there is yet further evidence. Balaam pronounces a blessing on the Kenites in Num. xxiv. 21 f.; Kenites are said to have united with Judah in the conquest, and, as a matter of fact, Caleb and Othniel, the early heroes of the south, are Kenizzites,[2] not strictly Judahites, and it is not impossible that this is another form of the same name. A Kenite woman slays Sisera, though the prose version of the story is careful to explain how she came to be so far away from the usual haunts of her clan;[3] and when Saul sets out to exterminate the Amalekites, he warns the Kenites who are with them to make their escape before the assault is delivered.[4] Finally, when David wishes to make Achish believe that he has committed unpardonable offences against his own people of Judah, he tells him that it is against the Kenites, among others, that his raids have been directed.[5] The same passage mentions also the Jerachmeelites, an obscure tribe of whom we hear only in this verse, in 1 Chron. ii. 9, 25, 26, 27, and in 1 Sam. xxx. 29, where they are mentioned among the clans benefited by David's generosity.[6]

We have thus certain elements in the population which seem to be on the border line, partly included in Israel and partly excluded. Their presence in the Biblical narrative serves to illustrate the fluidity of Israel in the thought of earlier days. It seems that it was only gradually that the traditions crystallized into the form in which we now have them, and that they underwent considerable modification in the course of centuries, particularly during the monarchy. It is comparatively late in the history of the people that the familiar organization is fully developed, and it may be that it was only after the nation had

---

[1] Cp. the story of the battle of Rephidim in Exod. xvii. 8–16, the repeated wars against the Amalekites, concluding with David's vengeance for the sack of Ziklag, 1 Sam. xxx, and the Deuteronomic injunctions to destroy Amalek, Deut. xxv. 17, 19.

[2] Cp. Num. xxxii. 12, Josh. xiv. 6, xv. 17, Judges i. 13, &c.

[3] Jud. iv. 11. But cp. Garstang, *Joshua and Judges*, p. 301 (1931).

[4] 1 Sam. xv. 6.   [5] 1 Sam. xxvii. 10; cf. also 2 Chron. ii. 55.

[6] No reliance is to be placed on that theory of Israel's history, so keenly advocated by Cheyne, which gives a leading part to Jerachmeel. But possibly Samuel's ancestor, Jeroham (1 Sam. i. 1) was originally Jerachmeel (cp. LXX).

lost its independence, and some of the tribes had disappeared for ever, that the ideal Israel assumed the form we know so well.

When we turn to the life and political arrangements of the period, we are compelled to rely on two sources of information, neither of them directly taken from the time in question. One is to be found in the relics of tradition which we may glean from later writings, and the other is the general condition of existing tribes on the same level of civilization. Fortunately the two agree fairly closely, and we are enabled to reconstruct a picture of Israel which, though conjectural, can yet claim a measure of probability.

Such organization as there is has the family or the clan as its basis.[1] It always assumes a common blood and a common descent. It often happens that strangers and foreigners are introduced into the community, but this is done through a ceremonial which implies an artificial application of the essential principles, a fictitious blood-relationship. The head of each family has certain rights and privileges, but these extend officially only to his own immediate descendants, and do not allow him any formal control over other members of the group. The heads of the families tend to form an inner council of the tribe, the 'Elders', but there is no formal limitation or right assigned to them, and any opinion, if valid in itself, is given due weight, no matter the quarter from which it proceeds.

The meetings of such a council are usually quite informal. Members gather in a semi-social way in the tent of one or another, and in general conversation topics of interest to the whole group are discussed. While the views of the older and more experienced naturally receive most consideration on any matter of practical policy, there is no formal vote, still less an autocratic decision given by the chief of the clan, a strong contrast to the situation represented, for example, in the Homeric poems. Action is taken on the general opinion, and each person present has an equal right to contribute to the formation of that opinion. There are, among the modern Bedawin, families which claim a kind of social superiority, as belonging to 'sheikhly' groups,[2] but 'the dignity of a Sheikh in free Arabia

---

[1] Only a brief outline is attempted in the following pages. For an admirable account of the probable constitution of nomad Israel see A. Lods, *Israël* (1930) pp. 216–40.

[2] Cp. e.g. Doughty, *Travels in Arabia Deserta*, i. 251, &c.

is commonly more than his authority'.[1] It goes without saying that there is a nominal head to the group, a Sheikh who acts as leader, but he can seldom claim any power except over his own children, and on the larger questions, such as peace, war, and migration, his word prevails only in so far as it commends itself to the great mass of his fellow-tribesmen.

Military organization seems hardly to exist. Every man is naturally a soldier, and will go out to fight when the tribe is at war. Probably the members of each family tend to stand side by side in actual battle, and there is inevitably a leader. But his position depends on personal qualities, not on his age or descent; and the tactical and strategic methods employed are normally very simple. It is only with the greatest reluctance that the tribesmen submit to any kind of discipline, and then only from a sense of personal loyalty to their leader. A chief is followed because he is worth following in himself, not because of the rank which he holds.

Disputes between members of the clan are commonly settled in much the same way as other matters affecting the general welfare. It seems, however, that even in nomad days Israel had begun to develop something like a judicial system. The appointment of Judges is carried back to Moses in tradition,[2] and is placed even before the great assembly and covenant at the sacred mountain. The responsibility for dealing with differences between individuals would naturally fall upon the senior members of each family, and here we may find the germ of a much larger and more complicated organization. Tradition also assigns to Moses the position of a supreme court of appeal. Here he exercises one of the regular functions of the priesthood.[3] In the last resort one of the essential duties of the tribal God was judicial. Cases which could not be decided otherwise were brought to Him, and He would make His will known on each. His method was usually through the application of the sacred lot, or some other means which was clearly beyond human control.

Private property in such a community hardly exists. A man may claim as his own personal possessions such articles as clothes, weapons, cooking utensils, and, perhaps, a tent, though this is more likely to be owned by the whole family. The wealth of the community consists primarily in its animals, and these

[1] Op. cit., ii. 662.   [2] Exod. xviii. 25-7, Deut. i. 9-18.
[3] Cp. Exod. xviii. 13-16.

cannot be claimed by any individual; they belong to the group as a whole. There is certainly no private ownership of land, and the very idea is foreign to the nomad. The flocks, usually of camels, sheep, and goats (the last is the commonest), have to find pasture where they can, and it is inconceivable that any individual should have the right to forbid the cattle of other members of his clan to graze where they can find fodder. Wells, in particular, belong to the whole group, and are jealously guarded on their behalf. They are, naturally, a frequent ground of dispute as between different tribes, and men may often have to fight for their possession,[1] but within the group no member can claim rights of priority.

The note contained in Gen. xxvi. 12, which states that Isaac sowed corn and reaped in the same year a hundredfold, may be held to suggest that the tradition described early Israel, even in the wilderness, as half-nomads rather than as a shepherd-tribe pure and simple. A group which has control of an oasis may raise a few occasional crops, even though its main dependence is on its flocks. Date-palms are almost certainly grown, and, in ancient times, probably no other fruit. Barley may be sown and reaped within a few months, and it is possible to cultivate some vegetables. All these together form a welcome change to a diet which consists mainly of milk in various forms, liquid and solid, with occasional game and the very rare (probably only annual) meal of the flesh of the domestic animals taken under sacrificial conditions.

The clothing of the nomad may include the skins of his animals or of the wild creatures whom he hunts for food, but is more usually a cloth woven of wool or of hair. The tents in which he lives are generally of this latter material, and the tents of the Bedawin are characteristically black, since this is the commonest colour of the goat. Linen may be obtained by trade with agricultural lands if there are any near enough to the centre of the tribe's range. Apart from spinning and weaving, the chief arts are those of the potter and of the smith. The latter is the more highly specialized, and belongs properly to a wandering tribe which carries its craft with it. In general, we may say that the life of the nomad and of the semi-nomad is simple, and its political organization elementary. There is thus comparatively little room for the complications which beset a more

---

[1] Cp. e.g. Gen. xxvi. 15–22.

advanced order of society, and free play is given for individual responsibility and enterprise.

It is on this last point that we need to lay the greatest stress in our study of Israel and of her history. Her ideal ancestors belonged to an order of society in which the value of persons far outweighed that of things. There was a passion for freedom, a love of independence, an impatience of external control, which distinguished the shepherd races from those of the more settled lands. Authority might in certain circumstances be exercised, and by certain persons, but it was always strictly limited, and, except within the actual family, none had rights over the person of another free member of the tribe. The conception of a governing class was foreign to their thinking, and an autocratic power was repulsive to their instincts. To one another the members of the tribe were brethren, and while they might accept the command of one of their number for special occasions, such as war, the restraints of authority were unnatural to them. Slavery was common, but it may be taken for granted that the slave was a foreigner, or of foreign descent, being often the son of a captive woman taken in war. But this fact does not affect the essential attitude of the old Semitic nomad. The Greek ideal was the autonomy of the city-state; that of the Aramaean nomad was personal and individual liberty, and he could not bear the curtailment of his independence by any other member of his clan. This feeling, wherever it has appeared, has undoubtedly brought grave dangers with it, and has often proved a drawback to the development of the people. It has prevented them from forming anything like a strong centralized state, and has helped to keep them organized into very small and rather unruly communities. But there is in it an element without which no society can be really stable, a respect for personality as such, and an insistence on the rights of the individual, which must be cultivated if the community is to retain its real strength. The ancient Semitic nomad would not have understood the term *democracy*, but he had deeply planted within him an unconscious theory of life which corresponded to the attitude which that word indicates in common speech. That which the free Athenian citizen of the fifth century B.C. boasted as his highest achievement was taken for granted by the ideal ancestors of Israel. It will be necessary to bear this fact in mind as we follow the course of Israelite history, for the presence of this feeling—

it was hardly an idea, and developed no vocabulary—was of profound importance both to the actual life of the nation and to the message which the Hebrew had ultimately to give to the world.

It is obvious that in so simple a social constitution as that of the wandering shepherd, or Bedawin, life is free from a vast number of difficulties which beset man in the more complicated agricultural and industrial orders. He has not yet entered a field of which every yard is set with pitfall or with trap, and a social ethic can hardly be said to have begun. Morality deals mainly with matters which affect the tribe as a whole. The questions of primary importance are those which concern the actual life of the community, those which bear on its man-power or the purity of its blood, in other words those which deal with sex-relations and with murder. In the former of these two classes the pastoral tribes as a rule seem to have a comparatively high standard, normally above that observed among agricultural peoples.[1] Life is more severe, with less of ease and luxury, and the constant unending struggle for existence, lacking even the seasons of comparative plenty which enable the farmer to relax his efforts for a short time, tends to weaken the force of natural passion, while the absence of alcohol[2] from the normal life of the nomad contributes to his powers of self-control. The community may be polygamous or even polyandrous (though it may be doubted whether polyandry was ever found among the Semites), but its sex behaviour is regulated by strict rules, and the rules are observed. One of the darkest features of the agricultural life of the ancient world is to be found in the low sexual standard set by its religion, and nearly everywhere in the ancient east we find the cult of fertility deities, involving sacramental fornication. Such a practice is not merely foreign, but utterly abhorrent, to the mind of the nomad, and through all her history there was an element in Israel which revolted against the ritual in vogue at the great sanctuaries of the agricultural world.

The demand for the maintenance of the man-power of the tribe is closely connected with animistic or even pre-animistic

[1] It is said, for instance, by persons familiar with Africa, that the Masai, who are nomads, have a higher standard of sexual morality than the agricultural tribes of central Africa.

[2] This is not invariable; cp. the intoxicating spirit made by the Mongols from mare's milk.

ideas about blood. As one of the 'givers of life' blood has a mysterious essence and power, almost amounting to a personality. We hear the blood 'crying from the ground', and unsatisfied until it is avenged. The rule that nothing can atone for the blood that has been shed except the blood of the slayer is primitive, and it is only later that the possibility of any commutation enters men's minds. But as the theory weakens, the importance of maintaining the life of the tribe grows, and it is clearly impossible to allow its men to be killed with impunity. Long after the cry of the blood has lost its power, men continue to demand reparation, partly as a deterrent and partly as compensation. It is not always the life of the slayer; a sum of money may be laid upon him as a fine,[1] and it is noticeable that at this stage it is the dead man's relatives who decide whether it shall be accepted. It is they who have suffered, no longer the dead, and it is they who must be satisfied.

Our interpretation of the political and social condition of Israel in the nomad period necessarily depends largely on analogies drawn from the modern Bedawin. But there is one outstanding difference between the ancient and the modern nomad, probably applying to all such peoples in the ancient world, and certainly to Israel. That difference lies in the part played by religion. There are, it is true, numerous rites and ceremonies to be observed by the modern Bedawin, many of them relics of pre-Moslem days, and there are numerous shrines consisting of the tombs of saints, at which prayer is especially meritorious. But the ancient nomad went much further. While he recognized that his deity had a special home, and could be most safely approached in a particular spot, he seems always in a sense to have carried his god with him. There was a sacred emblem, some article which, though it might not in itself be an object of worship, yet served as an outward symbol of the presence of the god, and could be treated as though it were the god. There can be no doubt that Israel believed that they carried Yahweh with them, though this did not prevent them from feeling that it was at the sacred mountain that they could come most surely into touch with Him. In Exod. xxxii. 12–16 we have Moses pleading for some assurance of the presence of Yahweh with him and his people in their wanderings through

---

[1] Cp. the Anglo-Saxon 'Wergild' and similar payments among other early Germanic peoples.

the wilderness. Moses asks for the 'presence' (literally, 'the face'), and this is promised to him.[1] In Exod. xxiii. 20 ff. the 'angel' of Yahweh is promised as a guide. But neither of these can be regarded as being actually an emblem or symbol of Yahweh, still less Yahweh Himself. All we know of the primitive mind leads us to seek for some material object which could be carried about with Israel through their wanderings, performing the normal functions of the tribal god and receiving divine honours.

In later Israel, three such objects claimed to date from the period of Moses. These are the Bull, the Snake, and the Ark. The first was revered at a number of sanctuaries, the second at Jerusalem (and possibly elsewhere), and the third also had its home during the monarchical period in the Judahite capital. It was the last which finally made good its claim as against the others, and it is interesting to note how the old traditions respecting the other two were preserved, though almost certainly in a form adapted to the triumph of the Ark.

In Exod. xxxii we have the tragic story of the people who had been led from Egypt to find a new god, losing their leader without having discovered their deity. They resort to another method, and Aaron makes a golden 'calf'. Discovery and terrible punishment follow when Moses actually returns. Now we may with reason suspect that some such story was told at Bethel, and possibly at other Bull-sanctuaries, to explain why Yahweh was worshipped under the form of an ox. But there would have been striking differences. The making of the image would not have been an act of apostasy, but a legitimate method of worship, and the story itself still contains evidence of the theory underlying the action. Aaron is represented as saying in his defence that 'there came out this calf' (Exod. xxxii. 24), suggesting that he had poured the molten metal into water and been guided by the form it assumed on its sudden cooling, in the belief that the new God Yahweh would thus reveal the shape under which He would be adored. But we may further suspect that in the original story, as told at the Bull sanctuaries, it was not Aaron (who in tradition is always elsewhere an ecclesiastical figure rather than a real man) but Moses himself

---

[1] For a new theory, interestingly propounded, of the 'presence' see Morgenstern, *The Oldest Document of the Hexateuch*, pp. 8–12, 44–7, where the 'Panim' of Yahweh is held to be a technical term for the Kenite priesthood.

who performed this operation. Certainly there was in the mind of Israel, prior to the latter part of the eighth century, no thought of possible impropriety in the cult of Yahweh as a Bull-god. Even in the form in which the tradition has been handed down to us, the original snake[1] is the work of Moses. But in the story of Num. xxi. 4-9 the bronze serpent is constructed in order to save the people from the effects of snake-bite—a piece of 'medicine' which is redolent of sympathetic magic. Yet the actual worship of the snake had a strong hold on Judah, as we see from 2 Kgs. xviii. 4, where Hezekiah breaks it in pieces,[2] and we are probably justified in assuming that popular tradition told of its establishment by Moses as an object of worship.

We are thus left with the Ark. Now the Ark was simply a box, and it may be taken for granted that its sanctity was not independent, but was derived from that which was carried in it.[3] Tradition stated that it contained two stones, and the orthodox form of the story held that they were the stones on which the terms of the Covenant were inscribed. An older belief, however, was that the Ark contained the very presence and person of Yahweh Himself. Thus when the Ark moved out to battle, the formula recited over it was '*Arise, O Yahweh, and let thy enemies be scattered, and let them that hate thee flee before thee*', the corresponding formula when it returned from battle being '*Return, O Yahweh, to the myriads of the families of Israel*'.[4] When the sons of Eli take the Ark into battle, the Philistines recognize that the God of Israel has come into the camp.[5] Though they capture the God of Israel, He is not defeated, and exhibits His authority on the Philistine god Dagon, forcing him to do homage. Most instructive of all is the story of the return of the Ark from Philistine territory.[6] It is placed on a cart, two cows are harnessed to it, and their calves shut up behind them. In spite of the mother passion which would naturally impel them to rush at once to their calves, they move away, no man laying a hand

[1] Serpent-worship is very widely spread. There was, for instance, a serpent goddess worshipped in Crete. Cp. *CAH*. Plates, vol. i, pp. 116-19. Jerusalem seems to have had Philistine affinities before the time of David, and the Bronze Snake may have had ultimately a Cretan ancestry.

[2] It is worth observing that the attendants of Yahweh in Isa. vi are beings which apparently belong to the same species as the snake of worship—the 'seraph'.

[3] The tendency to regard the Ark as empty, and to hold that no material object was used to represent Yahweh, seems to ascribe far too lofty a conception to a primitive people.   [4] Num. x. 35, 36.   [5] 1 Sam. iv. 7 ff.   [6] 1 Sam. vi. 10-14.

on them, down the middle of the road, without swerving to right or left, towards Beth-shemesh. They are quite helpless and can indicate their misery and express their instincts only by continuous lowing. Clearly they are being driven, and by a power greater than any human force, for no man could so control cows robbed of their calves. No mere stones, however sacred be the inscription they bear, are thus driving the animals; it is an intensely powerful personality.

At a later day, then, the stones were held to embody the very presence of Yahweh, and it is they rather than the Ark itself which are the real objects of worship. Now the bull and the snake, in one form or another, are familiar in the nature-worship of the agricultural Canaanites before the advent of Israel,[1] and we are justified in concluding that they were adopted by the immigrants from their predecessors, along with much else in the spheres of social and religious life. Of the three claimants for originality, it is almost certainly the stones which have the best title to being called Mosaic, and we may regard it as highly probable that Israel carried the box which contained them throughout their nomad period, from the days of the Covenant till it found its final resting-place in Solomon's temple.[2]

It goes without saying that Yahweh must have had His own tent and establishment. Hence the tradition of the Tabernacle. We need not assume the historicity of the details given in Exodus and Numbers, for these come from a later time (P), and obviously reflect the temple of Solomon. But we may be sure that there was a sacred tent, and that the God who dwelt in it had His own attendants. Concerning them we have two traditions, the one stating that it was Joshua who made his home in the tent,[3] while the dominant theory was that the responsibility devolved on the family of Moses. The introduction of Aaron may be due to a tradition which developed at a later period, but, in any case, the connexion with Moses remained. He was the first priest, and even Aaron derived his sanctity from him.[4]

---

[1] Numinous stones, too, are common enough in pre-Israelite Palestine, though they seem to be sacred objects rather than actual deities, especially in the form of Masseboth. But stones are more likely to have been carried by nomads.

[2] We have no reason to suppose that the earliest traditions stated that the Law or any part of it was inscribed on the stones. This theory seems to be the attempt of a later age to avoid the impression of 'idolatry' which would be involved in ascribing to Yahweh any material form.

[3] Exod. xxxiii. 11.

[4] Cp. G. B. Gray, *Sacrifice in the Old Testament* (1925), pp. 194–210.

The functions of the Ark in the Israelite community may be briefly sketched. In domestic matters it was the supreme authority, and so became inevitably the chief judicial tribunal. A case at law might be terminated by an oath taken in the presence of Yahweh; perjury was so terrible as to be unthinkable —or if the decision turned on an obscure point of law rather than on a point of fact, the sacred lot would be called into action, and this, being controlled by no human power, would be held to indicate the will of Yahweh. No treaty could be made without His consent.[1] War was necessarily a sacrament, and could be undertaken only under Yahweh's auspices. At critical times He himself might take part in a battle and turn the tide in favour of His own tribe. In early warfare it seems that the two sides would face one another, and the battle would begin with a charge made by one of the two or by both simultaneously. But before actual contact took place one or the other often lost heart and turned in flight.[2] Hebrew had a regular technical term for this battle panic, which, like all other inexplicable psychological states, was attributed directly to divine activity.[3] Thus leading His troops, Yahweh performed one of the primary duties of ancient oriental royalty, and here as in all else, the Israelite constitution was an absolute monarchy, with Yahweh as the King.

[1] Cp. Josh. ix. 14, where Israel is trapped into the Gibeonite treaty through failure to consult Yahweh, though no further penalty is imposed on the people.

[2] Cp. e.g. Josh. vii. 4, 1 Sam. iv. 2, 10, &c.

[3] Cp. T. H. Robinson, 'Note on the use of the Hebrew root NGP.', *AJSL*. xlvi. (1929–30), pp. 198 ff.

Chapter VIII

THE CONQUEST OF PALESTINE

SUMMARY

[Our records tell us of an abortive attempt to conquer Palestine from the south, and we have no reason to question their historicity on this point. But the main assault was delivered from the east, and falls into three periods, (*a*) the conquest of Transjordania, (*b*) the establishment of the tribes in western Palestine, (*c*) the rise of Israel to dominance.

(*a*) Several semi-nomad peoples, especially Edom, Moab, and Ammon, seem to have settled in the neighbourhood of Palestine before the advent of Israel. The latter made no attempt to occupy their territory, but, moving northward to the east of Jordan, defeated an Amorite king named Sihon and took possession of his land. The boundary between eastern Israel and Moab was always in dispute, however, and fluctuated from the Arnon nearly as far as the Jabbok.

(*b*) There seem to have been three distinct waves of invasion. The first probably came from the south, and was made by tribes such as Kenites and Kenizzites who were later absorbed in the general term Judah, though the original Judah seems to have been a settled Canaanite people rather than a clan of nomad Aramaeans. This advance secured the country to the south of Hebron.

The second and most important of the three was the invasion of the Joseph tribes under Joshua. Crossing the Jordan at a time when the river was dammed by a landslide near the mouth of the Jabbok, Joshua made himself master of Jericho and the plain about it, and then moved up into the central range. Here he captured Ai, and secured an alliance with Gibeon, which gave him command of the middle of the mountainous district. A coalition of the kings of the district was defeated at Beth-horon, and Israelites were now masters of the hills in the centre of Palestine, whence they spread northwards, though their progress was checked by the line of fortresses covering the plain of Esdraelon.

The third wave occupied the extreme north. The conquest, though ascribed to Joshua, was probably the work of a later generation, since there appears to be a reference to it in Judges iv. We have thus three centres of Aramaean settlement, the north being cut off from the centre by the fortresses which stretched from Beth-shean to Megiddo, and the centre from the south, probably by Judah, which remained Canaanite till nearer the time of David. This latter division persisted, with more or less prominence, throughout the whole history of Israel.

(*c*) The dominance of the Aramaean invaders over their predecessors was secured during what we call the period of the Judges. These were inspired military heroes who rose from time to time to deliver Israel from foreign oppressors. Seldom was the enemy a Canaanite, most were invaders from across the Jordan, seeking to do what Israel had already done. In these cases Israel was fighting the battle of the Canaanites as well as her own, and the repeated struggles went far to weld the whole population into a unity.

The climax was reached with the coming of the Philistines. For the moment there was no external power which was strong enough to make good a claim to Palestine, and, but for the resistance made by Israel, the Philistines might have established a new empire there. It was after the repulse successively of Moab, and of various nomad tribes, that the serious struggle against the Philistines began, but in these earlier conflicts we have already the first tentative efforts towards a monarchy which should unite all races and all parts of the country. This tendency is especially manifest in the stories of Gideon and of Abimelech.

In the stories of Samson we find ourselves at a point where the Philistines were pressing Israel hard, and the tribe nearest to them, that of Dan, was reduced to very small limits. Not long afterwards they were compelled to migrate and to find a new home in the far north. The Philistines continued their advance, and finally completed their conquest of the country by their victory at Ebenezer and the destruction of Shiloh. Archaeological evidence shows that they went still further, and, since they certainly took Beth-shean from the Egyptian garrison, they probably made themselves masters of the whole country.

As compared with her predecessors, Israel had now made good her position as that of a military aristocracy. Her lack of co-ordination had led to her failure against the Philistines, but there were signs that a real unity would be achieved. She had brought into Palestine something of the vigour and *élan* of the nomad, a sense of a common blood, and, most of all, a unifying force in her recognition of Yahweh as her national God. It is true that in His worship she had largely adopted Canaanite ritual and theory, but the unity was there in embryo, and there was the possibility that in due time it would produce its effect.]

W E cannot be sure how long the purely nomad period of Israel's history lasted. Biblical tradition puts it down at forty years, i.e. to a whole generation; the period may have been longer, it cannot have been shorter.[1] The Old Testament narrative states that after the ratification of the Covenant, the

---

[1] Num. xiv. 32, 33, &c.

people remained for some time in the neighbourhood of the sacred mountain, and then sent out spies to examine the land.[1] The report that came back was so discouraging that they refused to make an attempt on the country, in spite of the advice given by one of the spies, Caleb,[2] and the direct command of Yahweh.[3] Yahweh's anger was manifested, and they were condemned to wander in the desert till all the adult members of the community had passed away. Hearing this sentence they changed their minds, and determined to make the attempt. But it was too late; Yahweh refused to go with them, and they were defeated with slaughter. There followed a period of thirty-eight years[4] wandering in the wilderness, at the end of which Caleb and Joshua were the only survivors of the generation with which the Covenant had originally been made.[5] They found themselves once more in the neighbourhood of the sacred mountain,[6] and then turned eastwards, circling round the south of Edom[7] and the east of Moab,[8] in order to avoid conflict with kindred tribes. In Gilead, however, they met with Sihon,[9] king of the Amorites, and to the north with Og, the gigantic king of Bashan.[10] Both of these they conquered and took their territory. They then prepared to cross the Jordan, but two tribes, which preferred to retain their pastoral life, Reuben and Gad,[11] received permission to make their permanent home to the east of Jordan, on condition that their fighting forces should unite with the rest in the conquest of the land.

At this point Moses died,[12] and his place was taken by Joshua, who led the people across the Jordan and proceeded to conquer the land. For the story of the actual conquest we have two different presentations. According to the one, which is confined

---

[1] Num. xiii, xiv.

[2] So the older narrative (JE; e.g. Num. xiii. 30); the later (P; e.g. Num. xiv. 6) adds Joshua.

[3] The account in Num. xiii is composite, one element being P, the other a combined JE in which the two original sources are no longer distinguishable. According to P the spies reported that the land was not worth occupying, 'it is a land that eateth up the inhabitants thereof' (v. 32); according to the older sources, they stated that it was a good and luxuriant country, but that the inhabitants were too powerful to be successfully attacked (v. 31).

[4] Deut. ii. 14.   [5] Cp. Num. xiv. 30, 38, xxxii. 12.   [6] Num. xx. 1.

[7] Num. xx. 14–21, Deut. ii. 4–6.   [8] Deut. ii. 9.

[9] Num. xxi. 21–6, Deut. ii. 26–36.   [10] Num. xxi. 33–5, Deut. iii. 1 ff.

[11] Num. xxxii. The 'half tribe of Manasseh' (Machir) seems to be a later addition, and may have re-crossed the Jordan from the west.   [12] Deut. xxxiv.

to the book of *Joshua*, the Israelites conquered all the land in a few short campaigns, exterminated their predecessors, and proceeded to divide up the whole country between the tribes. According to the other, which is represented in certain passages in the book of *Joshua* and in the book of *Judges*, the conquest was partial, incomplete, and slow, extending over many generations, and resulting as much in the fusion of the old inhabitants with the new as in the supersession of the one by the other. It is generally recognized that the former of the two is late and highly idealized, while the second (almost certainly the earlier in date) not unfairly represents the actual course of the events.

The whole period clearly falls into three divisions, (*a*) the conquest of Transjordania, (*b*) the establishment of Israelite tribes in western Palestine, (*c*) the rise of Israel to predominance in Palestine. The first of these is covered by the last seventeen chapters of the book of *Numbers* (except the ritual sections which belong clearly to P), the second roughly by the book of *Joshua*, and the third by the book of *Judges* and the first few chapters of *I Samuel*.

(*a*) THE CONQUEST OF TRANSJORDANIA

Israel was not the first Aramaean group to seek and to find a settled home in the west. They were preceded by three peoples whom they recognized as akin to them, though two, Moab and Ammon, were but distantly related to Israel in tradition, being descended from Lot, the nephew of Abraham. Edom, on the other hand, was held to be a very near relative, as its ancestry was ascribed to Esau, the brother of Jacob. Of the three, Moab seems to have been much the most advanced, for while the greater part of the country the tribe occupied was fit only for pasture,[1] there are fertile spots where the soil can be and is regularly cultivated. The land of Edom, except about Petra,[2] is rocky and wild, and the people can never have advanced far beyond the nomad stage. Ammon, while it had a city, Rabbah, hardly rose above the level of the modern Bedawin, and ranged over a country whose frontiers are very difficult to define. They had, nevertheless, to be taken into account by the advancing

---

[1] Cp. 2 Kgs. iii. 4.
[2] For the most recent account of Petra see Burkitt, *Palestine in General History*, pp. 87–98.

Israelites. Both Moab and Edom[1] seem to have developed into organized states, with an established monarchy, before the appearance of Israel.

In the circumstances it is not surprising that the narrative speaks of Israel as making a circuit about the lands of these two peoples. The frontier of Moab, however, was always uncertain, since there was a large district claimed by both Israel and Moab. The former insisted that their territory east of Jordan extended as far south as the Arnon, i.e. half-way down the eastern side of the Dead Sea. This claim was made throughout Hebrew history,[2] but it can seldom have been enforced. Even in the ninth century, Mesha[3] speaks of certain cities well to the north of the Arnon as having been wrongfully seized by Israel and recovered by him, and his native city of Dibon itself lies to the north of the main stream. It may be doubted whether this place was ever in Israelite hands. In Num. xxi the claim is based on the fact of a double conquest. There is no doubt of the defeat of Sihon, king of Heshbon, by Israel, and the account of this is immediately followed by an ancient song, taken apparently from the folk-lore of the district, which commemorates a victory of Sihon over Moab.[4] The argument is that since this land had been given to Sihon, it must belong to his conquerors, i.e. to Israel—reasoning which may have had a certain logical validity, but lacked the strength afforded by actual possession of the object in dispute. The site assigned to the battle in which Israel defeated Sihon is Jahaz, which appears to have been in or near one of the upper valleys leading down into the Arnon.[5] Heshbon, indicated as Sihon's capital, is almost on a level with the northern end of the Dead Sea, and there seems no doubt that Moab's territory seldom if ever stretched north of that

---

[1] Cp. the Israelite tradition of Edomite kings, preserved in Gen. xxxvi. 31–9, and the evidence in Judges iii. 12 ff. for a Moabite monarchy in the period of the Judges.

[2] Cp. e.g. Num. xxi. 24, Josh. xii. 1, Judges xi. 22, 2 Kgs. x. 33.

[3] Cp. MI., l. 8 (Ba'al-Me'on), l. 11 ('Aṭaroth), l. 14 (Nebo).

[4] There is in some quarters a tendency to interpret this as evidence that Sihon was really king of Moab, and that the conquest of this district did not actually take place till the accession of the dynasty of Omri. Cp. E. Meyer, *IN*., p. 530 f. But this is to misunderstand the song in Num. xxi. 27–30, and we may suspect that Meyer's date (ninth century) is much too late. It is possible that the first clause, in v. 27*b*, is no part of the original song, but was prefixed by the Israelite editor. The rest clearly indicates that Moab had suffered from the invasion of Sihon, who had seized not only Medeba, but even Dibon and the whole territory down to the Arnon.

[5] Cp. G. A. Smith, *HGHL*., p. 559, n. 8.

point, though it must at one time have extended far enough to enable Moab to hold the fords of Jordan near Jericho.[1] In after days the whole of this country was occupied by Damascus,[2] but that does not invalidate the claim of Israel, since this is recognized on all hands as being a late conquest. But with respect to the country above the eastern coast of the Dead Sea, the utmost that can be admitted is that it may for a time have been in the hands of Israel in the days of the early conquest.

It was in connexion with this first of Israelite conquests that the Hebrew tradition introduced the familiar incident of Balaam. The story needs no repetition; suffice it to say that the prophecies of Balaam are brought into the narrative at this point probably in order to emphasize the authority which Israel claimed over Moab in the ninth century and, perhaps, earlier.

Deuteronomic tradition[3] recorded a conquest still farther to the north, the kingdom of Og in Bashan being occupied by Israel after that of Sihon. The decisive battle is said to have taken place at Edrei, which lies east of the source of the Yarmuk.[4] There is no early record of the occupation of the country lying between the Jabbok and the Yarmuk, still less of the seizure of Bashan, yet in later times both were claimed for Israel. It is sometimes supposed that these districts were taken by settlers who crossed the Jordan from the west, and that their conquest was read back into the story of Moses by later Hebrew tradition.[5] Certainly, the northern half of Gilead played a very important part in the later history of the monarchy, while the district about the Jabbok was one of the strongholds of the house of Saul. But the territory to the east of Jordan was always a doubtful possession of Israel, for it was threatened from the south by Moab, and from the north by Damascus, while it was exposed to Ammonite raids from the east. At the same time we must recognize the fact that there were clans, mainly of nomads,[6] to the east of Jordan, who claimed kinship with Israel, and regarded themselves as worshippers of Yahweh.[7] This fact had, as we shall see, a profound influence on the later development of Israelite thought.

[1] Cp. Judges iii. 13.
[2] Cp. 2 Kgs. x. 33.
[3] It is now generally held that Num. xxi. 33–5 is taken from Deut. iii. 1–3.
[4] See G. A. Smith, HGHL., p. 576.
[5] For a discussion of this point see G. A. Smith, op. cit., pp. 577 f., n.
[6] Cp. Num. xxxii. 1, Judges v. 16, 17a.   [7] Cp. MI., l. 18.

(b) THE CONQUEST OF WESTERN PALESTINE

Whether we identify the Israelite invaders of Palestine with the Ḥabiru or not, it is clear that their attacks illustrate the Aramaean invasions which resulted in the establishment of Israel to the west of the Jordan. The conquest was a long and slow process, and while we may date its commencement from the first assaults made by the tribes, we cannot hold it to have been complete until after the establishment of the monarchy. Jerusalem was captured only by David, and Gezer did not pass into Israelite hands until Solomon was on the throne. It must be remembered that throughout the whole period Egypt claimed suzerainty over Palestine, and while we have reason to believe that, partly owing to internal weakness, partly to Hittite intrigue, and partly to Philistine invasion, that authority was often no more than nominal, it was liable to be asserted by military force whenever Egypt was strong enough to send an army across the isthmus of Suez. It was such an exhibition of force, probably under one of the last kings of the twenty-first dynasty, which secured Gezer for Solomon, and so provided his dominions with a fortress which could protect him from Philistine attacks.

The grounds for holding that Israel was in Palestine before the time of the nineteenth dynasty have already been discussed.[1] Traditions preserved in Israel and traceable at least as far back as the eighth, or even the ninth, century B.C. suggest that the attack was delivered in successive waves, probably all independent one of another, and, further, that none of them was wholly successful in conquering the land. The invasions of the south, the centre, and the north appear to have had little or nothing in common, though tradition has naturally tended to ascribe them all to the progress of the best known of the heroes of this age, Joshua the son of Nun.

We have in Num. xiv. 39–45 an account of an abortive attack from the south, placed by the writer immediately after the incident of the spies. It is stated here that the Israelites went up into 'the mountain', i.e. the hill country lying between Kadesh and Palestine proper, and that they were repulsed by the united forces of the Amalekites and the Canaanites, being pursued as far as Hormah.[2] Num. xxi. 1–3 describes a raid made on Israel

---

[1] pp. 74 ff.

[2] Site unknown, but cp. Garstang, *Joshua and Judges*, pp. 82, 216 [1931], where the possible location at Kh. Melh is mentioned.

by 'the Canaanite, the king of Arad', who took captive a number of Israelites. Thereupon Israel attacked him in turn, and devoted Hormah to the ban, leaving it utterly desolate. In Judges i. 1–3 we read that Judah was the first to enter the land, in company with Simeon,[1] and in verses 16 f. it is said that, joined by the Kenites (with whom Moses was connected by marriage), they attacked Arad,[2] and then these united tribes proceeded to lay waste the city of Zephath, to which they then gave the name of Hormah.

We have thus three different narratives, each of which gives an account of the name Hormah, and all seem to represent different forms of the tradition. A combination of the first two suggests that Israel took vengeance for a defeat at Hormah, and the third implies that it was not the whole of Israel that was involved in these operations, but merely a group containing Judah, Simeon, and some of the Kenites. This leads us to believe that at one stage in the growth of tradition Judah was held to have made an independent attack on the south and to have sacked Hormah. This form of the story may well have described further conquests in the south by the same group, and have been modified later in the interests of the dominant theory that the whole people moved together under Joshua, and that the only assault was that delivered across the Jordan, through the plain of Jericho. But we have already seen[3] that Judah was held, in some forms of the tradition, to have been resident in the land long before the general immigration, and the narratives taken together may imply an entirely independent invasion of the country, which had nothing to do with Joshua and may have taken place even before the Exodus itself. The expedition was not wholly successful, since Simeon disappears from history after this point. The mention of these tribes may be due to the later theory of the conquest, or it may originate in an earlier belief that the two clans did actually

---

[1] We have, on the other hand, a very ancient tradition to the effect that Simeon and Levi were responsible for the overthrow of Shechem (Gen. xxxiv. 25 f.), and we are probably justified in assuming that this is to be interpreted as the action of tribes rather than that of individuals (see above, pp. 53 ff.). The condemnation of these two tribes in Gen. xlix. 5–7 seems to refer to some such story, and the divergent tradition presents us with a problem for which no easy solution is obvious. This is, however, the less serious in view of the fact that, whenever it was that Simeon entered Palestine, the tribe seems to have disappeared at an early date.

[2] The text of the passage is somewhat uncertain, but this seems to be the general meaning of that used by the LXX. Arad is the modern Tell Arad. [3] p. 61.

conquer the cities of the maritime plain mentioned in Judges
i. 18, retaining them until the arrival of the Philistines, though
it is unlikely that so extensive an occupation really took place.
Verse 19 tells us that the lower land was not taken, because its
inhabitants possessed iron chariots, and we may doubt whether
in the earliest times Judah was held to be a part of Israel at all.
In any case, all the traditions point to an attempt made from
the south, attended by indifferent success, and some forms of
tradition connect this assault with the tribe of Judah.

Some further light may, perhaps, be thrown on this question
by the narrative of Judges i. 11–15, which records the capture
of Kiriath Sepher, or Debir. The site has not been identified
with certainty, though it has been located at the modern ed-
Daheriyah,[1] but clearly it lay to the south of Hebron, and was,
except for springs, a dry district. It was occupied, not by
Judahites proper, but by Caleb and Othniel, who were Kenizzites. In Gen. xv. 19 this tribe is enumerated, along with the
Kenites, as a people resident in Palestine before the advent of
Israel, and the priestly genealogy regarded them as an Edomite
clan.[2] All tradition thus tends to show that they were among
those southern groups which were on the border-line of Israel
and were partially absorbed into Judah, and thus supports the
view that there was an element at least of the later Judah already
in Palestine before the days of the invasion under Joshua. A
tradition preserved in Josh. xv. 13 assigns Hebron also to Caleb.
This, however, is inconsistent with the statement in Josh. x. 3
that the king of Hebron was among the vassals summoned by
the king of Jerusalem to the assault on Gibeon, and we may
suspect that the city was not reckoned Israelite (or should we
rather say Calebite?) until a later day, whether it was taken by
conquest or incorporated through more peaceful means. The
early history of the tribe of Judah is even more obscure than
that of most of the others, and we have to wait till the time of
David before we have unmistakable evidence of its existence
and of its self-consciousness.[3] Once its unity was recognized,
and its supremacy secured through David, the accretion of many
southern traditions would follow inevitably.

[1] Cp. G. A. Smith, *HGHL.*, pp. 279 f., and, for objections to this view, Cheyne
in *EB.*, art. 'Kiriath Sepher', cols. 2,681 f. Albright believes it to have occupied the
site of the modern Tell Beit Mirsim. See *Bulletin of the American Schools of Oriental
Research* No. 15 (Oct. 1924), pp. 4 f., No. 31 (Oct. 1928), pp. 1 ff.; Garstang, *op. cit.*,
pp. 211 ff.   [2] Gen. xxxvi. 11.   [3] See Additional Note A, pp. 169 f.

The second wave of invasion was that in which the Joseph tribes were prominent, under the leadership of Joshua. Tradition is fairly full, and probably reliable in outline, except for the ecclesiastical elements due to the presence of a priestly element in the story as we have it. Possibly, also, in the account of the fall of Jericho we have a tradition which belongs to an earlier age than the rest. It begins with the crossing of the Jordan, and tells[1] how the stream was dammed, and allowed the Israelites to cross over dryshod. As Cheyne has pointed out,[2] there was no need of a miracle to enable Israel to cross the river, for there are at least two fords opposite Jericho, which would have been practicable for the people. Some unusual event, therefore, must be behind the story of the stoppage of Jordan, and that may be found in the mention of Adam opposite Zarethan, sixteen miles above the Jericho fords, at the point where the Jabbok enters the river. Within historical times it has happened that a heavy fall from the hills has thrown a dam right across the river, and checked its current for a time, and we need not doubt that the memory of some such event in the distant past remained in Israel. It is quite possible that one or other of the marauding bands crossed the river bed in such conditions.

The crossing of the river is immediately followed, as the story runs in our Bible, by the circumcision of the whole people. We have here[3] a third account of the origin of the rite. In Exod. iv. 25–6 (J) it is traced back to Moses, while in Gen. xvii. 9–14 its introduction is ascribed to a divine command given to Abraham (P). The present passage must, therefore, be E's account of its institution. The custom is, of course, very widely spread, especially among African peoples, and it is worth observing that only those Semites who were within the reach of Egyptian influence practised it. We do not hear of it in Mesopotamia, and we have no evidence of it from early southern Arabia. On the other hand it was normal in Egypt, and among the Palestinian tribes. Indeed, until the Israelites came into close contact with the Assyrians, the Philistines were the only people familiarly known to them who refrained from it. Josh. v. 9, with its phrase 'the reproach of the Egyptians', may imply that in the writer's view

---

[1] Josh. iii. 16.   [2] EB., art. 'Jericho', cols. 2,399 f.
[3] Josh. v. 2–9. Verses 4–7 are generally regarded as a later insertion, probably due to the compiler of the whole book, designed to explain the apparent discrepancy between the different accounts of the institution of the rite.

the absence of circumcision had been a ground for contempt during the residence in Egypt. But it seems equally possible that the people recognized that they were now entering a country where Egyptian influence was nominally dominant, and that they were glad to avoid the sneer which would have been levelled against them by their enemies. It is in modern times the mark of both Jews and Moslems,[1] and there can be little doubt that elsewhere, as well as among Israelites, it was held to have a religious significance. It certainly implied to the ancient Israelite the removal of a religious impurity,[2] and the insertion of the narrative in Josh. v. may be attributed to the feeling that the holy land must not be profaned by a people ceremonially unclean.

The circumcision of the people is placed at Gilgal, a few miles from Jericho, the most important city in the neighbourhood. Gilgal is a word which probably means a 'stone circle', an ancient religious monument of the type best seen at Stonehenge, but by no means uncommon throughout the world. No such monuments are now found in western Palestine, though the occurrence of the name Gilgal in more than one locality certifies their prevalence in ancient times. They seem to belong either to the late stone age or to the early bronze age, and we may conjecture that the 'Gilgals' of the Old Testament were sacred places which were inherited, along with any rites proper to them, by the Hebrews, and that in later times attempts were made to give an account of them which should be more in keeping with the purer faith of later Israel.[3]

It was inevitable that any invader, attempting to enter Palestine by the fords of the lower Jordan, should first become master of Jericho, for as long as this city was fortified, it commanded the roads up into the country, and we can easily understand why the compiler inserted the tradition at this point. Recent excavations have shown that it was of comparatively small size. The walls, however, were very thick, and it must have been a strong place, especially when its besiegers were a

---

[1] Cp. Doughty's account of a modern Arab circumcision, *Travels in Arabia Deserta*, i. 391 f. The modern Arab, according to Doughty, denies that it has any religious significance, *op. cit.* i. 342. For a general discussion of the whole subject see L. H. Gray, *ERE.*, art. 'Circumcision' (Introductory), vol. iii, pp. 659–70.

[2] For other explanations of its origin, based on comparative folk-lore, see p. 84.

[3] For a further account see R. A. S. Macalister, *ERE.* xi, art. 'Stone Monuments (Rude)', esp. pp. 879–81.

simple nomad people, with little military art and no skill or machinery for siege work. The story of its capture seems to be composite, the two elements being J and E. Exact disentanglement is practically impossible, but Holzinger[1] has suggested plausibly that J 'may have narrated how, in accordance with a military custom found also among the Arabs, Jericho was surrounded in the night or in the early morning, and how an entrance was forced either through some divinely sent panic or a military stratagem, and the inhabitants then exterminated, with the exceptions already provided in ch. ii'. It is easy to see how the successful siege of such a city must have seemed miraculous[2] to later generations (the capture of Ai, for instance, was no miracle, being achieved by drawing the enemy out of the city and entering through the open gates), and we can well understand how the present narrative arose as an attempt to explain the facts. It is beyond dispute that the older Jericho was destroyed by violence, probably at the end of the sixteenth or the beginning of the fifteenth century B.C., but this date raises serious questions. If we are to identify the Israelite assaults with any portion of the Ḥabiru attacks, as seems most probable, then we cannot include the capture of Jericho among their successes, unless the archaeologists find reason to put the date of that event a century later than they do.[3] It is possible that we have in this narrative a memory of some earlier attempt to enter the land, perhaps at the time of the conquest of Gilead, which was really unconnected with the invasion under Joshua. The story differs markedly in quality—even in its earlier elements—from the other narratives of the conquest, and the greater prominence of the miraculous element suggests that it has a longer history. There can be no doubt that memories of earlier raids from the east have found their way into the body of Old Testament tradition, and for the further story of the conquest by Joshua it is Gilgal, not Jericho, which is important. The statement that

[1] *Das Buch Josua*, p. 15 [1901], with reference to Jacob, *Altarabische Parallelen*, p. 14.

[2] Do the narratives point to a primitive tradition of an earthquake? Or, as Garstang (*Joshua and Judges*, pp. 146, 404 [1931]) suggests, to the undermining of the walls?

[3] This has now actually been done by Garstang, who definitely dates the fall of Jericho in 1407 B.C. (*Joshua and Judges*, pp. 61, 146 f., &c.). The paragraph above was already in type when Garstang's *Joshua and Judges* came into the author's hands, and though it was too late to re-write the whole passage, it may be remarked here that the new opinion very greatly simplifies the whole position. There is no longer any difficulty in assigning the conquest of Jericho to Joshua.

the city was put to the ban, and therefore could not be used by the Israelites, may be intended as an explanation of the fact that it was not made their head-quarters for the rest of the invasion.[1]

After recording the violation of the *ḥerem* by Achan, the narrative of the conquest proceeds with the attack on Ai. There are three routes leading up into the centre of Palestine from Jericho.[2] One of these leads southwards towards Bethlehem, the middle one almost due west to Jerusalem, and the third up into the hills of Benjamin. The south country was not Joshua's objective, and the strength of Jerusalem was too great for any attempt to be made upon it, while the road that leads to the city is very difficult and at times dangerous, especially to an invading army, for it affords frequent opportunities for ambush. It is a road on which a traveller may easily 'fall among thieves', and where brigands can lurk a defending force may easily hold its position unless opposed by vastly superior numbers. These Israel did not possess, and naturally took the northern route, leading up moderate slopes through fairly open country on to a table-land. Leaving what was later Saul's country on the left, the road passes through Michmash to Ai, about twelve or thirteen miles as the crow flies from Jericho, though the winding road is somewhat longer.

The story of the capture of Ai is familiar, especially because of the failure of the first assault through the sin of Achan. The city was captured by strategy after the first repulse, and free booty is permitted to Israel. The position was well chosen. It stands near the highest part of the central range, but a few miles from Bethel, and affords a useful base for further operations in the very heart of the land. It is, however, comparatively useless while Bethel remains in the hands of the enemy, just as Bethel cannot stand if her flank be turned at Ai or at Michmash. Curiously enough, the fall of Bethel is not narrated in the book of *Joshua*, but in Judges i. 22–6, where the city is said to have been taken with the help of information given by a prisoner seized as he left the gate. Its capture is attributed to the house of Joseph, and we may fairly ascribe it to the same series of events as that recorded in the book of *Joshua*.[3]

After the fall of Ai, *Joshua* (viii. 30–5) records the building of an altar on Mount Ebal, and the solemn reading of the law, in

---

[1] See p. 122.   [2] Cp. G. A. Smith, *HGHL.*, pp. 264 ff.   [3] The fall of Ai is now (1938) ascribed to a much later period than that of Jericho.

fulfilment of Moses' command as given in Deut. xxvii. But this must be an insertion on the part of a redactor. Much country had to be conquered before Ebal was really in Israelite hands, and the immediate operations tended to run in another direction. Bethel stands practically on the water-shed of the central range, and Joshua's next movements were south and west. At this point the men of Gibeon are introduced, who, by a trick, succeeded in obtaining an alliance with Israel. Gibeon lies to the south-west of Bethel, and the story explains the subservient position of the Gibeonites in the later days of Israel, and accounts for the sanctity whose violation called for vengeance on the family of Saul.[1] For the time being its position enabled the invaders to threaten Jerusalem to the south, while it cut one of the main routes into the hills from the Shephelah, the road leading through the Beth-Horons. The natural result was the formation of a coalition between a number of the chieftains in the more fertile lands of the Shephelah, and of the agricultural district of Hebron. The king of Jerusalem, threatened on the north, its most vulnerable quarter,[2] gathered together the kings of Hebron, Yarmuth, Lachish, and Eglon, to meet and overcome the invaders. Clearly this form of the tradition knows nothing of an earlier capture of Hebron by Judahites (Kenizzites).[3] Yarmuth stands on a spur of the hills, west and slightly south of Jerusalem. Lachish (the modern Tell-el-Ḥesy)[4] and Eglon lie a few miles apart on the Shephelah, almost due west

[1] 2 Sam. xxi. 1-11.
[2] With the account of Adoni-zedek, mentioned in Josh. x. 1, &c., cp. the story of Adoni-bezek, king of Bezek, whose fall is described in Judges i. 4-7. It has been suggested that the two are to be identified, the difference in names being due to textual corruption, cp. Holzinger, *Josua*, p. 38; Moore, *Judges*, pp. 15-17; Budde, *Richter*, pp. 3 f.; Burney, *Judges*, pp. 4 ff., 41 ff. Moore prefers the name Adonizedek, on the ground that in proper names אדני is always followed by a divine name, and a Canaanite god צדק is known from Phoenician sources (cp. Baudissin, *Studien*, i. 15; Baethgen, *Beiträge*, 128; Burney, *op. cit.*, pp. 41 ff. Both, however, find the term only in proper names and (Baud.) in Sanchuniathon's cosmology). The other two are non-committal, although the LXX here reads Adoni-bezek. The story in *Judges* seems to dissociate Adoni-bezek from Jerusalem, and records its capture (a reflection back into the early period of a much later event) after Adoni-bezek has been dealt with. But the word בבזק in Judges i. 5 is textually doubtful, being omitted by some MSS. of the LXX and by the Aethiopic version, while in Judges i. 7 the king is taken to Jerusalem and dies there. The differences are not so great as to prohibit a common origin for the two traditions, though no certainty may be attainable as to the actual form of the king's name.
[3] See above, p. 120.
[4] But cp. Garstang (*op. cit.*, pp. 172 f.), who identifies it with Tell el Duweir.

of Hebron. The coalition thus included the rulers of the district to the south and west of Jerusalem, and they were clearly actuated by a fear that the Israelite movement should spread down into the plains.

The attack was not directed immediately against Israel, which still had its head-quarters at Gilgal—possibly owing to lack of a place where the people could safely move, and possibly in order to secure a line of retreat if the new conquests could not be fully consolidated. The confederate kings, however, had a nearer objective in the city of Gibeon, whose defection had made the Israelite threat really dangerous. Immediately on receiving the news, the Israelite force was set in motion, for not only was the loyalty of Gibeon of vital importance to them, but the terms of their agreement with the people demanded that they should offer their protection. The distance they had to traverse was about twenty-five miles, and they had to reach a height of over three thousand feet above the spot from which they started, so that the journey may have been made in two stages—a view which is not prohibited by Josh. x. 9. In any case Joshua so timed his journey as to arrive before dawn, and at once fell on the allied camp. The sudden onrush of the wild tribes in the dark produced a panic, naturally attributed to divine influence, and the united armies fled. It seems that, after going down the valley of Aijalon, past the two Beth-horons, they divided, some making nearly due west to Makkedah, which lies in the plain just south of Ekron, and others aiming at Asekah, which seems to have been not far from Yarmuth. The latter formed the main body, and their discomfiture was enhanced by a devastating hail-storm which swept on them down the valley. The kings, however, made their way to Makkedah, where they were captured in a cave and killed.[1]

[1] It is in connexion with this battle that Josh. x. 12–14 gives the well-known story of the sun standing still at the bidding of Joshua. It would seem that there are two versions, the older embodied in an ancient snatch of song, verses 12*b*, 13, the other a prose amplification and explanation of the poem. The latter has, apparently, as a matter of fact, misunderstood the former. The poem exhorts the sun and the moon to 'be still', not to 'stand still', and it may originally have been a plea for favourable weather during the long pursuit. The Israelite troops had had a tiring night march, and delivered a sudden assault. In the pursuit they found as they ran down towards the plain that the hot sunshine was exhausting, and their leader asked for shade. The answer came in the form of cloud which developed into a hail-storm. The distance of the pursuit is not so great as to require a particularly long day. From this it is easy to see how the later story of the sun and moon standing still as recorded in the 'Book of Jashar' could have arisen. Dr. H. H.

The text of Josh. x. 28–43 describes the conquest of the whole of the south country, stating that it was subdued from Gibeon and Gaza to Kadesh-barnea and Goshen. A number of places are mentioned, including some of the cities of the five kings. Yarmuth and Jerusalem, however, are not mentioned, and, though the king of Gezer is said to have been killed, it is not stated that his city was captured. Nevertheless, it is hardly possible to regard this as an ancient tradition. A comprehensive occupation would scarcely have been possible with Jerusalem and Gezer unconquered. The passage must be regarded as the work of a later editor, who knew the extent of Israelite territory in after years, and wished to ascribe the victory to Joshua.

We have no reason to doubt the general success of this campaign. The invaders had made good their footing in the centre of the land, and from the heights about Bethel could, when opportunity offered, threaten every part of the country as far north as the plain of Esdraelon. The district which includes Bethel and Gibeon is a nucleus of roads leading north and south, and from that point it was possible to spread out in all directions. The main difficulties which Israel had to face came from within, and were due to the lower level of her general culture as compared with that of her predecessors. She had no political unity nor organized and centralized government; apart from her acceptance of Yahweh as the God of all her groups, there was no force which could keep her together. The same remark might be made, it is true, of the Canaanites, but they had the advantage of a higher order of culture and a more elaborate and scientific equipment for war, to say nothing of the presence of Egyptian garrisons at strategic points. In particular there were two factors which must have tended to impede the further progress of the invaders. The first was the presence of walled cities. The art of siege warfare was not yet; it was invented first by the Assyrians. It was only through some exceptional stratagem, as at Ai, through treachery, as at Bethel, or through negotiation, as at Gibeon, that Israel could hope to take possession of the towns. The second factor was the presence of chariots among the dwellers in the plains. We may assume that these were usually Egyptian, and, indeed, the country had to

Rowley has suggested to me that the original prayer was uttered by Joshua as the Israelites drew near the enemy just before dawn. The sun is asked to cease that the darkness may continue and favour the attack. The answer comes in a thundercloud which has the effect of prolonging the night.

rely on its suzerain for much of its defensive material. Chariotry, of course, was futile among the hills, and hence it was there that Israel won her first victories and established her first posts.

Extensive movements are implied in Judges i. 27–9. What is actually recorded is the partial failure of Manasseh and Ephraim, but the partial failure implies a considerable success. Gezer, on the outer edge of the Shephelah, looking over the maritime plain, did not fall, but the Ephraimites must have taken possession of a fairly wide area for mention to be made of Gezer at all. The same remark applies to the fortresses which Manasseh failed to capture. From the Jordan to the sea there ran a chain of strongholds, mostly in the plain of Esdraelon, which served to guard the great trade routes. In Judges i. 27 a number of these are mentioned: Beth-shean, Taanach, Dor, Jibleam, and Megiddo. There is no regular sequence in the names; they seem to have been put together haphazard, and do not include one or two important places, especially Jokneam, which commands one of the roads across the Carmel range. These cities are named as not being subdued by Manasseh, but they are a long way north of Bethel and its district, and the fact that they could be mentioned at all shows how the Joseph tribes were pressing northwards. It is true that their progress was probably slow, and it must have been spread over several generations. We do not know when Ophrah, the home of Gideon, was taken by Israelites, but it seems certain that Shechem, not many miles away,[1] passed into their hands only in the time of Gideon's son, Abimelech. One other success seems to have been achieved in the early days, though, strangely enough, it finds no mention in any list of conquests. When we hear of the tribe of Dan in the stories of its struggles against the Philistines,[2] it is confined to Zorah and Eshtaol, two small villages on the upper slopes of the Shephelah, almost due west of Jerusalem. But if the reference in Judges v. 17 has any meaning at all, it implies that the Danites were in the days of Deborah a maritime tribe, possibly getting their living, in part, by fishing. This means an extension westwards to the coast, and we may conjecture that Danite settlements were found on the shores of the Mediterranean between

---

[1] The site of Ophrah has not been identified for certain, but it is conjectured that it is represented by the modern Ferata, about six miles south-west of Shechem. The present writer is more inclined to accept Dalman's identification with Wadi Far'ah, north-east of Shechem. Cp. also Garstang, *Joshua and Judges*, p. 319.

[2] Judges xiii–xvi, the Samson stories.

Ashdod and Joppa at an early period.[1] About Mount Carmel it seems also that at one period Zebulun[2] and Asher[3] reached the sea, though their occupation was not permanent, while the coast to the south of Carmel, in the Dor district, was Israelite through the monarchical period.

While, then, we should certainly be in error if we supposed that the whole of central Palestine fell into Israelite hands at a single assault, it is perfectly clear that from the first the expedition under Joshua, in which the Joseph tribes took the lead, seized a strategic position in the heart of the country, and held it against all attacks. The line Jericho—Bethel—Beth-horon, with a southward extension to Gibeon, cuts athwart the central Palestinian range, and, while the country it covers is for the most part not rich or fertile, it is fit for shepherds, and in places gives opportunity to the agriculturist. Moreover, it forms a centre from which advance may be made in many directions, and its possession is, in fact, the key to the whole of the hill country lying to the north of the Jerusalem district. This is the work which, on the basis of all the traditions, we may assign to Joshua as the leader of the second wave of invasion. Its completion may well have been marked by the removal of the centre of Israelite worship from Gilgal to some spot in the hills,[4] implying that, in so far as the tribes had a common centre, it was now in the heart of Palestine.

The third wave of invasion dealt with the country north of the plain of Esdraelon, i.e. with Galilee. Josh. xi ascribes this conquest also to Joshua, and depicts a great gathering of the kings of the north, of Madon, of Shimron, and of Achshaph, under the leadership of Jabin king of Hazor.[5] Except for the last, none of these places is familiar. The first may be a spot some miles

---

[1] In the narrative of Wen-amon, Dor is held by the Thekel, or Zakhara, a people allied to the Philistines. The Israelite (Asherite) conquest, then, may have been earlier than the Philistine invasion, and Dor is certainly included in one of Solomon's administrative districts, cp. 1 Kgs. iv. 11.

[2] Gen. xlix. 13, Deut. xxxiii. 18.

[3] Judges v. 17.

[4] Judges ii. 1. The MT., followed by most versions, has *Bochim*, which some think must have been near Shiloh. On the other hand, the LXX has evidence of another reading *Bethel*, which is adopted by a number of scholars. Cp. Moore, *Judges*, p. 58.

[5] Identified by Garstang with Tell-el-Kedaḥ, a few miles south-west of Lake Huleh. See Albright in *Bulletin of the American Schools of Oriental Research*, No. 29 (Feb. 1928), pp. 3 ff.; Garstang, *Joshua and Judges*, pp. 184 ff., and (for the other cities mentioned), pp. 189 ff.

west of the later Tiberias, or the name may be a textual corruption for Maron or Merom. Shimron may possibly be the modern Semunieh, Greek Simonias, to the west of Nazareth; though this involves a slight change in the spelling, no other suitable site is known. Achshaph is still more uncertain; a location has been suggested in the hills north-west of Lake Huleh, on the edge of the Litany valley, but this does not seem to be a likely spot. As far as we know the invaders never seriously attempted to cross the water-shed between the Jordan and the Litany. Hazor was an important town to the west of Lake Huleh, in the same district as Kadesh Naphtali. Josh. xi. 1–15 records the defeat and slaughter of these kings, and the capture of their cities.

We may, however, venture to doubt the tradition which assigns the conquest of this district to Joshua. The barrier presented by the unreduced fortresses of the plain of Esdraelon would prevent any extensive movement of troops from the centre to the north, and the assault of the invaders must have been delivered from the east of this district, i.e. across the Jordan to the north of the Sea of Galilee. Further, in Judges iv. 2 we find a certain king, Jabin, who reigned in Hazor, and was an enemy to the Israelites. The story as it now stands connects him with Sisera, making the latter, whose home was in the plain of Esdraelon, commander-in-chief of Jabin's army. The inherent improbability of such an arrangement has struck many readers, and it is a significant fact that Jabin plays no part at all in the battle subsequently described, and is not even mentioned in ch. v, a poem which is universally assigned to an eyewitness of Sisera's overthrow. It seems, then, entirely probable that two narratives have been interwoven in the first verses of Judges iv; one described the defeat of Jabin and the conquest of Hazor, the other the destruction of Sisera. If there be any truth in this reconstruction of the text, then we are justified in suspecting that the Jabin of Judges iv. 2 and the Jabin of Josh. xi are one and the same person, and that his defeat really took place only after the death of Joshua, i.e. in the so-called period of the Judges.

We may, then, conjecture that this third wave of invasion entered the land by one of the fords to the north of the Sea of Galilee (to the north of Lake Huleh the ground is normally too marshy for an invading army to use) and struck into the hills. We hear in Judges i. 30 of Zebulun's failure to conquer two

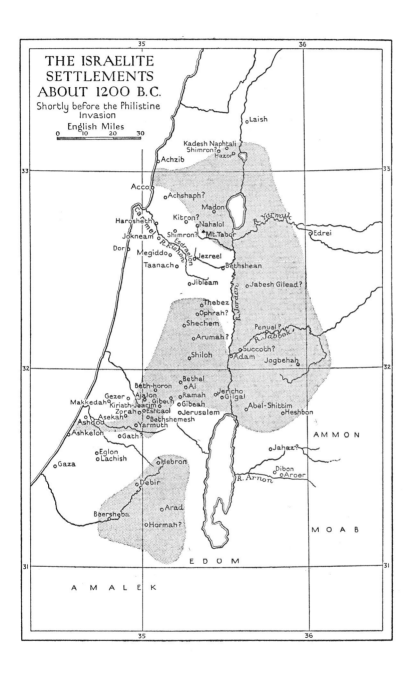

THE ISRAELITE
SETTLEMENTS
ABOUT 1200 B.C.

Shortly before the Philistine
Invasion

English Miles
0   10   20   30

Laish

Kadesh Naphtali
Shimron?
Hazor
Achzib

Acco

Achshaph?

Madon

Kitron?
Harosheth   Nahalol
Jokneam   Shimron? Mt.Tabor   Edrei
Dor   R.Kishon Esdraelon
Megiddo   Jezreel
Taanach   Bethshean

Jibleam   Jabesh Gilead?

Thebez
Ophrah?
Shechem   Penuel?
Arumah?   R.Jabbok

Shiloh   Adam   Succoth?
                    Jogbehah

Bethel
Beth-horon   Ai
Gezer   Ajalon   Ramah   Jericho
Makkedah Kiriath-Jearim Gibeon Gilgal
Zorah Eshtaol Gibeah Abel-Shittim
Asekah Bethshemesh Jerusalem   Heshbon
Ashdod   Yarmuth
Ashkeloh   Gath?   AMMON

Eglon   Jahaz?
Gaza   Lachish
Hebron   Dibon
                   Aroer
Debir   R.Arnon

Arad   M O A B
Beersheba
Hormah?

E D O M

A M A L E K

unidentified places named Kitron and Nahalol,[1] and in the following verse of the inability of Asher to dispossess the inhabitants of some of the coastal cities, especially Tyre and Achzib. Here again we may say that the mention of the failure implies a measure of success, and that these tribes must have made good their footing in the north. And, finally, we have the migration of the remnants of the tribe of Dan, who were compelled by the stress of Philistine pressure to leave their south-western home, and to find a new domicile as far away as possible from their old location, settling at length in the upper valley between the Lebanon and the Antilebanon.

We have thus a point, roughly at the end of the thirteenth century, at which we can speak of Palestine as being occupied, but not yet conquered. There are three main groups of Israelites: a southern, to the south of Hebron; a central, whose chief cities are Bethel and Gibeon, though it extends somewhat farther to the north; and a northern, grouped about the modern Lake Huleh and covering some territory to the west and north. The three sections seem to have been the result of different waves of invasion, and, at first sight, had little to hold them together. But they retained traditions of a common descent, and they had, above all, a common worship. All recognized in Yahweh their own tribal deity, and realized that they must obey Him and respond to His call. Thus the challenge to Israel presented by the oppression of Sisera was answered by tribes of the central hills and by those of the north. Zebulun, Naphtali, and Issachar were joined by the Joseph tribes, while the clans to the east of Jordan and Dan to the south-west were expected to lend their aid. It was in the name of Yahweh that the summons was issued, and it was in Yahweh alone that Israel found their unity. Whatever Moses had done or had not done at Sinai, he had given to all the tribes a common God, valid for themselves and for all who should unite with them in after days, and it was this devotion to a single deity, which, above all else, made Israel a nation.

Politically and geographically, however, there was as yet no unity. We have no suggestion of a common government in these early days, except in much later tradition. 'Every man did that which was right in his own eyes' is the judgement passed by the Hebrew historian on the period.[2] A common centre of worship

---

[1] Cp. Garstang, *op. cit.*, p. 240; Albright, *Cont. Hist. Geog. Pal.*, pp. 26 f. (ap. Garstang, *op. cit.*, p. 397).   [2] Judges xvii. 6, xxi. 25.

may have been supplied by the Ark, the palladium of the Joseph tribes, which had its shrine somewhere in the central range, but, in the nature of the case, this was not always accessible to dwellers in the extreme north and south. Between the Joseph tribes and the settlers in Galilee there lay a chain of Canaanite cities which formed an effective barrier, at least for the time. It stretched across western Palestine over the fertile plain of Esdraelon, from Beth-shean in the east, guarding the main fords over the Jordan, to the slopes of the Carmel range, where Megiddo commands the most important passes in the country, and even to the sea-coast at Dor. These fortresses seem to have been held by Egyptian officers—Beth-shean had an Egyptian garrison till it was captured by the Philistines, and Sisera himself may have been an Egyptian—and so, though they never formed an official kingdom, they may yet have been under the control of a government to some extent centralized. While we cannot suppose that the Egyptian officials were always in harmony one with another, it is clear that the authorities in these posts were able to unite at least in keeping back the hill tribes on either side from the rich agricultural plain, and in preventing them from settling in Esdraelon. Sometimes the guardianship was so close and effective that Israel was denied the use of the main roads altogether, and the tribesmen had to creep by unfrequented by-ways and crooked paths from one place to another[1] if they wished to cross the forbidden land. It is strong testimony to the power of their national and religious sense of unity that, in spite of these obstacles, the two groups, central and northern, never lost the ability to combine with enthusiasm against a common foe.

The separation between the centre and the south, however, had a different cause and proved to be more lasting in its effects. It is true that there were Canaanite cities which remained untaken, particularly Jerusalem and Gezer, while it seems that the acquisition of Hebron itself did not belong to the earliest age of southern immigration. But the geographical conditions in this region are not those of the country farther north. Here we have no break in the line of hills comparable to the plain of Esdraelon, and we cannot speak of a chain of fortresses holding the land. The range is broken somewhat by the valleys that lead from the Shephelah and the maritime plain, but nowhere

[1] Cp. Judges v. 6.

do they present a natural and easily defensible frontier. A glance at the map will show that, even in the early days of the conquests of Joshua, this line—if we can speak of a line at all—was penetrated, for the movement which carried the Ephraimite advance past Gibeon[1] was continued between Jerusalem and Gezer by the Danites. Their last possessions in the southern country were Zorah and Eshtaol, well to the south of the Jerusalem-Gezer line, and if they spread down to the coast (as we believe they did), they must have reached the sea between Ashdod and Joppa. If we may trust our traditions at all, we must assume that, though members of this tribe came into contact with Judah in the Philistine age,[2] their original invasion was connected with the central movement, not with the southern. Even the Philistine occupation of the country, though it seems to have absorbed Jerusalem itself, did not prevent freedom of movement between the centre and the south. Individuals could travel without much fear of molestation, though they preferred Israelite to Canaanite cities,[3] and considerable bodies of troops found it possible to march from north to south in Saul's day.[4]

At the end of the thirteenth century the space between the two occupied areas seems to have extended farther south than Jerusalem. We do not know when the Calebites made Hebron their own, but it was clearly Canaanite in the time of the Ephraimite assaults on Palestine. Even in the early days of the Philistine occupation, we may suspect that there was comparatively little sense of unity as between the south and the centre, though with the gradual spread of the Kenite-Kenizzite influence the Judahite districts were brought into the general body of Yahweh worshippers. At this period there seems to have been practically no connexion between those nomads who entered the country from the south and those who crossed the Jordan under Joshua. As we have seen,[5] there is reason to believe that they were the result of two independent and unconnected movements from the wilderness. In our earliest and most reliable traditions of the conquest the name of Judah is not mentioned; it is Kenizzites and Kenites who are prominent. The evidence of Gen. xxxviii suggests that Judah was resident

---

[1] Desnoyers (*HPH*. ii. 62 ff.) believes that Gibeon remained hostile to Israel, and that it was for this reason that Saul attacked it. But would David have admitted the Gibeonites' claim to blood revenge (2 Sam. xxi. 1–14) if this had been the case?
[2] Judges xv. 9 ff.   [3] Cp. Judges xix, especially verses 11–15.
[4] Cp. 1 Sam. xxiv, xxvi, &c.   [5] Cp. pp. 119 f., and Additional Note A, pp. 169 f.

in Canaan long before the advent of the other tribes, indeed that this clan retained some kind of hold on the country from patriarchal days. The same tradition admits that the tribe which bore this name was at least half Canaanite in origin, for the families which existed in later days all claimed descent from a Canaanite woman.[1] It is not impossible that the story as it stands is a concession to national feeling, and that the original Judah was wholly Canaanite. In the generations which preceded the monarchy, however, the nomad element had made itself felt, and the Kenite, Kenizzite, and, we may add, Jerachmeelite settlers had succeeded in so far modifying the population and its outlook as to bring them all, as far north as the borders of Jerusalemite territory, within the circle of the Yahweh worshippers. It is clear that David, whom we may take as a typical product of the completed process, felt himself to be in a very real sense akin to the Aramaean population farther north, and he was certainly a devoted Yahwist. But, when we consider the ancestry of Judah, as attested by tradition, and the course which the conquest most probably took, the problem is not so much to explain how it was that Judah was separated from the North, as how the two ever became conscious of unity one with another.

As a matter of fact, we may doubt whether that sense of complete oneness was ever attained.[2] As we shall have occasion to observe later, the statesmanship of David devised a course of action which might have welded the two elements into a single whole. Yet even David on two critical occasions seems to have saved his throne by playing off the one against the other, and it is noticeable that when Judah rose against him he received the support of the other tribes and vice versa. It is clear that the ideal unity was far from being achieved in his lifetime, and the policy of Solomon,[3] so far from cementing more firmly the two parties, tended rather to emphasize the distinction between them and to widen the original breach. It is, then, hardly surprising that when the North found the burden of the house of David intolerable, the South should have taken the opposite side and maintained its allegiance to Rehoboam. From that time onwards, though there was a certain sense of unity as against the rest of the world, that feeling never found expression in a single political organization. There were periods in the history of the

---

[1] Cp. Gen. xxxviii.   [2] Cp. vol. ii, ch. xi, esp. pp. 145–151.
[3] See below, pp. 256, 263 ff.

divided kingdom when the two sections worked together in
harmony, though the North seems to have been the dominant
partner, and we may suspect that the co-operation of the South
was not wholly voluntary. But, down to the time when the
kingdom of Israel came to an end, and the Samaritan territory
was incorporated as a province of the Assyrian empire, there
does not seem to have been a single point at which the possibility
of a formal reunion entered men's minds.

It is true that there was a genuine sense of kinship, aided and
supported, no doubt, by the growth and prevalence of the patriarchal traditions as we find them in the ninth and eighth
centuries. A common ancestry was assumed amongst the whole
people, even including Judah, and by the time of the Exile the
ideal nation, especially in prophetic circles, included all Yahweh
worshippers from Dan to Beer-sheba. The fundamental basis
of this sense of oneness lay less in the common descent than in
the common religion. Both sections recognized Yahweh as their
supreme God, and claimed that together they formed His
people. There was free intercourse between the two states, and
it seems as if the frontier between them was often doubtful and
often liable to change. But the policy of Jeroboam in setting up,
or rather in maintaining with royal favour, sanctuaries in the
North, went far to neutralize the cohesive influence of this common worship, and it is not unlikely that there were differences
in the cultus as between North and South which tended to
emphasize rather than to minimize the division.

No event in the course of the monarchic period served to
bridge the gulf between the two kingdoms. Perhaps we do not
realize its breadth and depth until after the fall of the southern
kingdom and the reconstruction of the Jewish people. Historians, Biblical and extra-Biblical, quote different events as
reasons for the later breach, and assign various causes to its
existence. But we may safely say that if there had been at the
outset any realization of the essential unity of the two sections,
none of these would have produced the division as we know it
to have existed in later times. It could be said in the last century
of the existence of a Jerusalem temple that 'the Jews have no
dealings with the Samaritans',[1] and to form a just estimate of the
reasons for this mutual abhorrence we must go back to the very
beginning of Hebrew history. The Judean always had stood

[1] Jn. iv. 9.

apart from the Ephraimite, and, in spite of the power of religion, the two never knew any inclination towards one another. It is true that the facts of the conquest tended to keep them apart, but these would have been quite ineffective if there had been a full sense of brotherhood between the two groups from the first.[1]

(c) THE RISE OF ISRAEL TO DOMINANCE IN PALESTINE

Our study has brought us to the point at which we have, at the end of the thirteenth century, this nomad people, individually strong and vigorous, and united in their sense of a common ancestry and a common faith, yet comparatively low in material culture, and quite unable to meet other inhabitants on equal terms in the plains and more fertile parts of the country. At present they were not fit to occupy the richer lands of Esdraelon and the Shephelah. Generations of the shepherd-life had done little to prepare them for the culture of grain, of the vine and of the olive, and generations must still pass before they would be able to take up to the full the inheritance of the land which, as they believed, Yahweh their God had given them. But there was much land in Palestine which they could occupy and utilize, and there they remained, standing at first aloof from the higher civilization around them, but gradually being drawn into the vortex of Canaanite politics. As a factor in the general military situation they were negligible, for the districts which they held were valueless for the purposes of the great expeditions; and the movements of armies, especially those of Ramses II, left them untouched. Egypt, at the time of her revival, was concerned primarily with an objective farther north than Palestine, and it is only occasionally that we find names suggestive of Israel in

[1] It may be convenient to mention here the theory of Alt (see *Die Staatenbildung der Israeliten in Palästina*, Reformationsprogramm der Universität Leipzig, 1930) that the later monarchy was always composite. From the contrasts drawn between Israel and Judah he believes that there was no organic unity between them, even during the period of the reigns of David and Solomon. On this view the link was simply the personal identity of the king, and the states themselves remained independent of one another. Such 'Dual Monarchies' are found elsewhere in the ancient world, though Alt adduces no exact parallel. The case of Assyria and Babylon is hardly a parallel, for there the king of a conquering people allowed himself to be crowned as monarch over his new subjects in order to conciliate them. We have no suggestion that David conquered northern Israel. The theory is, however, most interesting, and Alt's treatment of it illuminating. If accepted, it would go far to explain the permanent division between the Jew and his kindred farther north. It leaves unexplained, however, the unity between the two peoples of which so many in Israel were always conscious.

the monuments of Ramses II and Merneptah.[1] If we are right
in assigning the first steps of the conquest to the middle of the
fourteenth century, then we shall have to assume that for
another hundred years no serious advance was made.

In the meantime the Hittite power had become dominant in
the land, and had left its stamp upon the people generally.
Egypt had once more recovered her strength under the earlier
kings of the nineteenth dynasty, and had renewed her empire, and
it is not till the beginning of the twelfth century that we can trace
further developments in the internal situation of Palestine.
Even then we shall have to admit that, in the main, progress
was made through a gradual assimilation, not through military
conquest; and the most important element in the task that lies
immediately before us is to trace, as best we may, the change in
the relations between Israel and the Canaanites which in the
end led to the emergence of a genuine Palestinian nation.

The period to which this development must be ascribed is
that which we commonly call the age of the Judges.[2] These men
are the protectors and saviours of their people, and differ

[1] See pp. 75 f.

[2] At the risk of repeating what is very familiar, it may not be out of place to remark that our only evidence for actual events in this period is to be found in the
book of *Judges*, especially chs. ii–xviii, since ch. i is a recapitulation of the story of
the original conquest, and the story of the Benjamite war in chs. xix–xxi, however
interesting as illustrating the condition of Israel during the period, tells us nothing
of the steps whereby they attained to independence and domination. In its present
form the book consists of a number of ancient traditions concerning Israelite chieftains of the period, and of their exploits, particularly in leading the armies of Israel
to victory against oppressive enemies. A 'judge' (שׁפֵט) was practically a local king
for his own lifetime, though he neither inherited his power from his ancestors nor
transmitted it to his descendants. These stories have been woven together by a
compiler who used them to illustrate a theory that Israel constantly sinned in
worshipping the local gods of Palestine—the fertility spirits or Baals so characteristic
of the early Semitic agriculturist—that they were punished for their sin by being
handed over to an oppressor, that they repented and were delivered by a hero, a
'Judge', inspired by Yahweh for the purpose, that they remained faithful to their
spiritual allegiance as long as the Judge lived, and that after his death they relapsed
and the cycle was renewed. While we cannot accept the compiler's view that there
was a succession of Judges in direct line (all seem to have been simply local heroes
with a more or less extensive sphere of activity and influence), and while we
must regard the compiler's system of chronology as being purely artificial,
his point of view does represent a sound philosophy of history. Individually,
Israelites were stronger than Canaanites, but their ignorance of the higher military
arts and their lack of training in them left them an easy prey to others unless they
could present a united front. Their religion was the only unifying force that they
possessed, and when once that was allowed to fall into the background they had
neither the cohesion of the organized nation, nor the wild *élan* of the inspired
warrior, which might make them a match for their enemies.

primarily from kings in that their divine call is personal; they (except Gideon) founded no line, and each received that individual inspiration which made him powerful. They were in no sense constitutional sovereigns, and tradition held that in early days the very idea of constitutional monarchy was abhorrent, for Yahweh alone was the King of Israel.

The age of the Judges is sometimes described as the period in which the conquest was completed. If by this it is implied that it continues the story of the military triumphs of Israel over their predecessors in Palestine, it is hardly correct, for in one instance only is the enemy resident on the soil of Canaan. This one native oppressor is Sisera, and the story of his defeat and death is told us in Judges iv–v.[1] He is the king of Harosheth, a town on the northern slopes of Carmel, to the north-west of Megiddo. Evidently he is the most powerful chieftain in the plain, and it is possible that he was an Egyptian dynast. In the poem of Judges v we have an account composed by an eyewitness of the events, and it is thus one of the most important documents we possess, giving us, as it does, in spite of many obscurities, a striking picture of Israel and her position in these early years. We see first the tyranny of the Canaanites, their policy of disarming Israel, their closing of the lines of communication, so that there should be no collusion between the tribes in the centre and those in the north. We see the position held by the inspired prophetess, and the control she exercised over the man she called to be the leader of Israel's forces. We hear the appeal sent out to gather to the cause of Yahweh, and the judgements pronounced on tribes and districts which fail to respond. We have a picture of the Israelite force, little more than a wild horde, with practically no discipline, its members armed, if at all, with clubs and stones, but terrible in their aspect with their long locks streaming in the wind of their charge. Against them, facing the hills, perhaps at some spot not far from Nazareth, is arrayed the Canaanite army, well trained and equipped, especially strong in chariotry and horses, the arm which the nomad most dreads. But as they thus stand facing one another, the black thundercloud rises over the hills of Ephraim, and the Israelites, already inspired by the call of their prophetess, recognize the coming of Yahweh Himself from His distant home in the south. The storm

[1] Reasons have already been given, p. 130, for supposing that originally Sisera and Jabin had nothing to do with one another.

draws swiftly nearer, till, as it bursts in a fury of light and sound on the Canaanite host, the Israelite army suddenly flings itself upon the line. The horses, panic stricken by the thunder, prance and rear unmanageably; confusion reigns, and each man thinks only of his own safety. Flinging away their weapons, which are picked up and used by the Israelites, they turn south-wards. The Kishon lies before them, and not long before, when they crossed it to meet the enemy, it was parched by the drought, little more than a string of shallow pools. But the storm has made a change here too, and the stream is now a raging torrent. In terror of what lies behind them the fugitives plunge into it, chariots, horses, and men, and are dashed to destruction by the swirling waters. Sisera himself avoids the fate of his army, and seeks safety by another route, only to meet with treachery and death at the hands of a woman.[1]

Such is the story told by the earliest poem of any length that we have from a Hebrew poet. No more vivid picture could have been drawn, and it is not surprising that, out of all the many struggles and conflicts which must have taken place during the early days of the settlement, this alone is familiar to us. Yet the historical value of the event it records is compara-tively slight. It may have opened for a time the roads between the northern settlements and those of the central hills, and its moral effect must have been very great, but we hear of no city captured, no fresh acquisition of territory, no permanent occu-pation of the land held by the defeated Sisera. It was not by force that Israel passed into the fertile plains, but rather by a slow yet steady process of infiltration, of peaceful penetration and of intermarriage. It is true that the military prowess of Israel was a prominent factor in achieving the final result, but the book of *Judges* makes it clear that it was not by defeating the Canaanites, but by defending them, that Israel attained a dominant position in Palestine.

Of the six 'major' Judges of Israel whose exploits are recorded for us, Othniel, it is true, was a conquerer of Canaanites, but he belonged rather to the period of the first invasion and to the first wave of that invasion. We have already glanced at the victory of Deborah and Barak, and the other four are Ehud, Gideon, Jephthah, and Samson, the enemies being Moab, Bedawin

---

[1] For the best modern account of the battle, based on detailed local knowledge, see Garstang, *Joshua and Judges*, pp. 294 ff.

raiders, Ammon (or Moab?), and the Philistines respectively. None of these was a native tribe or race, and in fighting against them the heroes were defending the cause of the Canaanites just as much as that of Israel. In a certain sense all these 'oppressions' (except that of the Philistines) were a continuation of the movement into Palestine which is best represented for us by the immigration of Israel itself. The attacking tribes come from the east, and in the Jephthah story the whole scene is played in Gilead.

We have no indication of the order in which the Judges came, but we may safely assume that the Samson episodes are to be placed fairly late, not more than a generation before the Danite migration. Possibly the Gideon and Abimelech stories are later still, while there is nothing whatever to suggest a date for Ehud and Jephthah. The absence of any mention of Egypt is significant, since it implies that no external authority was being exercised over the country. We know that Egypt was not indifferent to Palestine during this period, as we can see from Merneptah's records,[1] but the Israelite tradition has no allusion to the suzerain, except, possibly, in the case of Sisera. This may partly be explained by the fact that these saviours of Israel (at least, before the coming of the Philistines) looked eastwards, and the Egyptian system of government was such that it was not concerned with matters which did not affect the richer portions of the country. But the later events, and especially those which led up to the establishment of the monarchy, must be dated at a time when there was no external power in a position to claim an effective sovereignty over the whole country. This can have occurred only after the Philistine immigration. It is true that Ramses III repulsed the invaders from the frontiers of Egypt, and that some of the Palestinian fortresses continued to hold out, but the decline had already begun, and the growth of Israelite power received no check from Egypt.

It was, indeed, only in such circumstances as those of the twelfth century B.C. that the rise of an independent and united empire in Palestine was possible. At every other period in her history, from the beginning of the sixteenth century onwards, one or other of the great powers was able to claim, and often to enforce, authority over Palestine. But the general upheaval which ended in the advent of the Philistines wrought such

changes in the ancient east that, for the moment, there was no
people in a position to make an effective bid for world dominion.
Mitanni had long since succumbed to Hittite intrigue, the
Hittite empire itself had been swept away by the migration of
the Aegean peoples from the coast of Asia Minor. Assyria was
still struggling with the mountain tribes on her northern and
eastern borders, and Egypt had much ado to protect her own
nearer frontiers. Time and conditions were ripe for any king or
race of sufficient vigour to establish a principality in Palestine.
It was, perhaps, the only time in the whole long history of the
land that such an opportunity occurred.

To an observer unfamiliar with later history, and contem-
plating only the forces obviously at work in the middle of the
twelfth century, it would have seemed that the way was clearly
open for a new Philistine empire, which might—who knows?—
have spread east and north and even south. The Philistines
themselves were a hardy race of fighting men, well equipped
with the resources of an advanced and ancient civilization.
They were the survivors of heroic wars and of desperate hardships in which the weaker elements must have perished, leaving
only the sturdier and more durable stock. They found themselves in a land which had no organized or settled government,
where, apparently, there could be no concerted effort to oppose
them. To them Palestine must have seemed an easier prey than
was Britain to the Anglo-Saxons after the withdrawal of Roman
forces. A new Troy, a fresh Cnossus—these were well within
the bounds of possibility, and no contemporary of insight and
intelligence would have failed to prophesy the resurrection of
the old Aegean power on the eastern coast-lands of the Mediterranean.

The Philistines very nearly succeeded in forming such an
empire. Our evidence is scanty, mostly indirect, but it is un-
equivocal and decisive. We know that the invaders, in the
generations that immediately followed their first settlements,
spread over the whole country. It was they who brought to an
end the Egyptian dominion in Palestine; the excavations at
Beth-shean [1] show conclusively that a Philistine occupation followed immediately on that of Egypt, and that the latter met
a violent end. An invader from the coast-lands who holds
Beth-shean dominates the rest of central Palestine, and the

---

[1] For a summary of the results cp. Garstang, *Joshua and Judges*, pp. 364 ff.

great fertile plain must have been under their sway. But they also penetrated the hills, for in Saul's day they had a fort at Michmash, on the eastern side of the central watershed, looking down into the Jordan valley. The story of Samson shows us how a tribe (Dan), once, apparently, strong enough to reach the coast itself, was reduced to a couple of villages in the lower Shephelah, and in Judges xvii f. we have the sequel—the tribe is compelled to migrate, and when it does so it contains only six hundred fighting men. Samson had not delivered his people. We have no evidence to show that the Philistines actually captured Jerusalem, but the pottery found on the Ophel of the Jebusite period suggests Philistine connexions, and it may well be that even Jerusalem was included in their sphere of influence.

For the time being the land was theirs. But they could not hold it, and were compelled to yield their place to the growing power of the population whom they found already in possession. The lack of a centralized government may have contributed to their failure, for it would seem that the five divisions, corresponding to the five Philistine cities, acted together comparatively seldom,[1] and though their enemies did not always clearly distinguish between them, yet our references suggest that their conquests were those of the individual city rather than those of the whole nation. The primary cause, however, of the Philistine inability to retain what they had won, must be sought in the rise of Israel. In the long run the Philistines were faced with a power as strong as themselves, if not so highly civilized, and possessing a unity which they always lacked. It is true that in the early days of Israelite occupation the invaders would not have been able to resist Philistine armies, and that the gulf between the Aramaean settlers and their predecessors would have made any united action impossible, but those days were already almost past when the Philistine conquest reached its zenith; and in the end they had to face a united country, whose policy was directed by at least one great statesman, and whose armies were led by at least one military genius.

It was, then, to the repeated attacks of enemies from beyond her borders that Palestine in the end owed her unity. Her population was of blood as mixed as any that history knows,

---

[1] There are reasons for believing, for instance, that in the final struggle which resulted in the supremacy of Israel, David had the support of Gath, partial or complete.

and its varied elements, local and racial, might have stood apart
with no cohesion whatever, had they not been welded into a
single whole by the hammer-strokes of foreign invasion. We
have but few details of the events of the period, and those that
survive must be held to be illustrations of a continuous process,
specimens of a class of events constantly repeated, rather than
an attempt to afford material for the history of the age.

The first attack thus recorded is that of Moab. Just as Israel,
when partially settled in grazing country beyond Jordan, had
sought to find a more permanent home on the west, so Moab
now endeavoured to follow them. Their advance must have
involved the occupation of a large part, if not the whole, of the
territory traditionally assigned to Reuben, and it may have been
at this time that Reuben disappeared. The Moabites spread up
the coast of the Dead Sea, and seized the fords of the Jordan
leading into the plains of Jericho. They penetrated into the
hills, how far we cannot tell, but far enough to make themselves
masters of the land of Benjamin, i.e. probably of Gibeah and
perhaps of Ai, though we may conjecture that they did not take
possession of Bethel. The one place mentioned is 'the city of
palms', often identified with Jericho,[1] but it is unlikely that Eglon,
the Moabite king, was satisfied with the occupation of a ruined
site, and he probably held the western side of the central range
for some distance to the north. This was not his only conquest,
for he was able to summon troops drawn not only from Ammon,
but also from the Bedawin tribes of the wilderness—Amalekites.
His authority was secured by garrisons to the west of Jordan,
and their presence enabled him to exact an annual tribute.

The story of Eglon's assassination by Ehud, told in Judges iii.
15–26, seems to embody a reliable tradition, but unfortunately
we have little evidence as to the situation of the places mentioned. The 'quarries' or 'carved figures' which form a landmark in Ehud's movements, are said to be near Gilgal, and there
need be no uncertainty as to the general locality in which they
lay. Seir, however, is quite unknown; it must have lain to the
north of Ai, since it was within reach of the Ephraimite hills.
But our geographical ignorance is no bar to our acceptance of
the story in its main outlines, and especially we may be sure
that it is accurate when it tells us that the Israelites seized and

[1] Cp. Garstang, op. cit., p. 276, the 'City of Palm Trees . . . would more suitably
describe a new settlement in the cultivable area below the spring towards the east'.

held the fords of the Jordan, and there lay in wait for the fugitive garrisons. It is to be noted that no attempt was made to follow the Moabites across the Jordan, either to carry the war into the enemy's country or to recover lost territory to the east of the river. The Joseph tribes were content with driving Moab out of the land which they themselves occupied.

In Judges xi. 1—xii. 7 we have the story of Jephthah, the hero of the eastern tribes. As it stands it would seem that there have been several narratives compressed into a single story, and that more than one *motif* lies behind them. It is not clear whom Jephthah had to fight, for while the narrative portions of the chapters all speak of Ammon, the argument which is carried on between Jephthah's ambassadors and his adversary in xi. 15–26 seems rather to imply that the enemy was Moab.[1] But we may, perhaps, assume that this whole passage is a later addition to the original story, made by an editor who saw an opportunity of laying down the principles on which the eastern frontiers had been formed.

Jephthah himself is represented as a man of doubtful origin, possibly not wholly of true Israelite, i.e. Aramaean, blood. Expelled from his home by the jealousy of his half-brothers, he took refuge in Tob,[2] where, like David in after days, he lived the life of a chief of banditti. Summoned by his old clan to come to their rescue, he agreed, on condition that he should be accorded some kind of sovereignty in the event of victory. He marched through Manasseh (northern Gilead or Machir?) to Mizpeh in Gilead, and thence launched his attack on Ammon,[3] whom he utterly defeated and drove beyond the recognized borders of Israel.

To this story two other incidents have been attached. The first is the familiar account of the sacrifice of Jephthah's daughter. As it stands it conflicts with what has gone before in giving Jephthah a home in Mizpeh, and it has been suspected, with good reason, that we have here a narrative which was intended

---

[1] For an attempt to explain this discrepancy see Smend, *Beiträge zur Geschichte und Topographie des Ostjordanlandes*, i. *ZAW.* xxii, pp. 129 ff. It is possible that narratives describing two or more different series of events have been combined. Cp. Lods, *Israël*, pp. 403 f.

[2] The site is quite uncertain; for conjectures see *EB.*, cols. 5,108 f.; G. A. Smith, *HGHL.*, p. 587. Most of the sites suggested are to the east of the Jordan, but the interference of the Ephraimites surely implies that it may have lain to the west.

[3] The site of Mizpeh seems to be quite uncertain, cp. G. A. Smith, *op. cit.*, pp. 586 f. The word simply means 'watch-tower', and there may have been innumerable spots to which it was applied.

to account for a custom which was far older than Jephthah, or, indeed, than Israel, i.e. the annual festival of the women's wailing. It would seem that the practice was spread all over western Asia, and belonged to the primitive agricultural ritual of the people. It may be the same custom as that which is known as the wailing for Tammuz, and later Israel would have been glad to get rid of the heathen associations of the rite. If that be so, it must be confessed that to modern minds the new explanation is hardly less objectionable than that which it is supposed to supersede, but it must be remembered that the ancient world, even as its moral sense began to grow, looked on such matters with other eyes than ours. Down to a comparatively late period it would seem that human sacrifice, while rare in Israel, was recognized as legitimate, and it sank into disrepute only under the protests of the great ethical prophets. At the same time we are bound to admit that the evidence does not justify a dogmatic rejection of the historicity of the whole story.

The second incident is that of the interference of Ephraim. A similar story, though with a very different termination, is told of Gideon, and the two may serve to indicate the claim made by Ephraim to supremacy in the days before the monarchy.

As far as our evidence goes, the first serious attempt at the establishment of an Israelite monarchy was made by Gideon, or at least by his son, Abimelech. This clearly does not belong to the early days of the settlement, for the tribe of Manasseh had spread well to the north, and was now not far from Shechem. There had been a good deal of intermarriage between the two races, and Abimelech himself was partly of Canaanite blood While the story of Gideon illustrates the way in which the Israelite warrior took the lead in fighting the battles of the country, the life of his son may perhaps be typical of the interpenetration of the two groups, the old and the new, which ultimately led to the united Israel.

It is clear that there are two narratives about Gideon interwoven one with another. It may even be possible that we have not one but two heroes, Gideon and Jerubbaal, and that the story of Gideon's destruction of the Canaanite shrine has been introduced to explain how the two names came to be applied to the same person.[1] In any case, the narrative gives us valuable

---

[1] For the analysis of the three chapters cp. Moore, *Judges*, pp. 173 ff.; Eissfeldt, *Die Quellen des Richterbuches*, pp. 34 ff. Certain facts are at once obvious. Gideon is

information on the progress that Israel had been making and the position they had attained in the land.

The story—this is probably true of both stories—opens with a statement of the annual invasions of the transjordanic Bedawin at harvest time. They would descend on the land in countless hosts, with camels and other animals, carry off what they could, and destroy what they could not remove. Resistance was certain to be met with violence, and ruthless slaughter without provocation might take place. Then, carrying their booty, they would hurry back across the Jordan to their own wilderness, leaving behind them a grim trail of fire and blood.

It will be observed that such raids as these fell only upon the agricultural community. The Israelites must have taken to the farmer life before they were affected so seriously as to feel that they themselves must take up the defence of the country. Gideon himself was a farmer, and the first scene of the narrative discovers him threshing wheat in a winepress, i.e. in a covered building instead of on an open hill-top, in order to escape the notice of the marauders. Moreover, the whole of the Jerubbaal story implies, not merely the agricultural background, but also a close union between the old and the new elements in the population. The people who resented the insult offered to Baal were not of pure Israelite descent, or, if they were, they had learnt so much from their predecessors as to be indistinguishable from them. The circumstances show that we need not wait for the mention of Gideon's secondary wife in viii. 31[1] to infer that the blood

twice called to the salvation of Israel, once through a theophany given to him as he threshed wheat in a winepress (vi. 11–24), once through a dream which bade him destroy the Canaanite shrine (vi. 25–32). It is this latter which gives him the name Jerubbaal. There are apparently two distinct raids, the first is led by Oreb and Zeeb, and is driven back by Gideon's night stratagem, the second clearly involves (though this part of the story has not survived) an attack on Tabor, in which brothers of Gideon were killed. Here the invading leaders were Zeba and Zalmunnah, and Gideon executed on them the law of blood revenge, after a pursuit which took him far across the Jordan. There is room for the conjecture that the two raids were conducted by different tribes, one by Midianites and the other by Ishmaelites. It may be added that even in the story of the night attack two different accounts seem to be involved, one of which contained the horns and the other the jars and the torches. It is not clear whether some of these differences indicate simply several accounts of the same event, originally independent, or whether they are drawn from separate series of events. It would seem most probable that the two accounts of the night attack really did refer to the same event, but it is equally probable that viii. 4 ff. refer to a different occasion altogether. But no certainty is attainable.

[1] This seems to have been a *mot'a* or *ṣadiqa* marriage, like that which Samson

of the two races was already intermingling. The process of assimilation was now well advanced.

The localities mentioned in the narratives tend to the same conclusion. We do not know where Ophrah[1] was, but it cannot have been at too great a distance from Shechem, though Gideon's marriage with Abimelech's mother may belong to a later period in his life when his authority had extended over a wide area. The actual locality in which the invading army is said to have been destroyed is the valley of Jezreel (vi. 33), which is the lower part of the plain of Esdraelon, leading down to the fords near Beth-shean. Further, in the narrative of viii. 4 ff. Gideon's brothers are killed at Tabor, and there is nothing to suggest that this was not their home. Now Tabor lies to the *north* of Esdraelon, and its connexion with Ophrah implies at least free passage among a friendly folk across the plain. Further, we may ask why the Egyptian garrison at Beth-shean took no part in defending the land. The Philistines had not yet taken possession of this part of the country, and we are compelled to fall back on the belief that the Egyptian forces were too weak to take any decisive action, or, indeed, to do more than protect the town itself.[2] This points to the period of the later Ramasseids, when the feeble Egyptian power in Palestine was on the point of disappearing altogether till revived under the twenty-second dynasty.

We have thus a very different picture from that which is presented to us in the story of Sisera. Egypt has to all intents and purposes vanished, and there is no longer any power in northern Palestine itself which is hostile to Israel. The barrier between Israelite and Canaanite appears to have broken down, or, if it still exists, it has become so slight as to be easily passable, and has no real effect on the relations between the two stocks. The Israelites have taken to agriculture, and are free of the fertile lands, while there are signs that their religion is already entering that syncretistic form which was characteristic of it throughout the early monarchy. It is only in times of special

---

endeavoured to contract (Judges xiv). In this form of marriage the wife remained in her father's home, and was visited by her husband; the children of the marriage belonged to the mother's family, not to the father's. Cp. W. R. Smith, *Kinship and Marriage in Early Arabia*, pp. 83 ff. (1903); S. A. Cook, *CAH*. i. 207 f.

[1] See above, p. 128.

[2] But it will be noticed that in both narratives the invaders flee down the *west* bank of the Jordan, and make no attempt to cross near Beth-shean.

stress that a definite appeal must be made from the local Baal to the great warrior God of Israel, Yahweh. Yet the older inhabitants are comparatively helpless in the face of an invader, and it is only the man with a strong element of Israelite blood in him, still more the man who is subject to the appeal of Yahweh, who dare face the enemy. The two races would appear to have intermingled and become one, except for the fact that the more vigorous Aramaean blood, reinforced by the unity conferred through their common faith in Yahweh, tends to make Israel the natural leader of the people in war. The two racial elements have blended into a new compound, save in so far as Israel remains a military aristocracy in the midst of the composite nation.

The story of Gideon's exploit is very familiar, and is most vividly told, especially where it describes the night attack which threw the hostile camp into a panic and won a great victory without the striking of a blow by the Israelite force. It would seem that the fugitives found it impossible to cross the Jordan near Beth-shean—perhaps the garrison was strong enough to hold the fords, even if it could not prevent the invasion—and fled down the Jordan valley. To cut them off on the flank, Gideon sent messengers to arouse Ephraim, and swarms of fierce warriors descended the slopes to share in the carnage and in the spoil. Among other victims the Ephraimites were fortunate enough to slay the two princes of Midian, Oreb, and Zeeb ('raven' and 'wolf') at spots which ever after bore their names. None of the localities mentioned has been certainly identified, but it is clear that they all lay in the Jordan valley, on the western side. The river seems to be fordable near the mouth of the Jabbok (Wadi Zerka), and the Ephraimites probably came down the Wadi Far'ah, whence a stream, sometimes impassable, flows into the Jordan, and there held the angle formed by the junction of the two, thus preventing access to the Jordan fords. In any case, the defeat was decisive, and survivors of the raiding Bedawin would wait many years before making another venture of the same kind.

Gideon's second exploit was concerned with another raid, and though the first part of the story has not been preserved, yet from what remains in Judges viii. 4 ff. we can trace its course. Here the Bedawin objective is the northern side of the plain of Esdraelon, and during the raid they are unwise enough to kill

Gideon's brothers at Tabor. He follows in pursuit, with three hundred of his clansmen, and crosses the Jordan after them. The route is not clear, for the two places mentioned in the story, Succoth and Penuel, are not identified for certain. The latter clearly lay on the bank of the Jabbok, and the former was probably not far from it. It is significant that though these places lie in Israelite territory, the inhabitants refuse to help Gideon, and scoff at his hopes of overtaking the enemy. But he continues the pursuit southwards, and at Jogbehah, on Ammonite soil, finds them encamped, but so sure are they of their freedom from pursuit that he easily surprises and destroys them. He captures the two 'kings', Zebah and Zalmunna, and returns with them. On the way he punishes Succoth and Penuel, and when he has exhibited his captives to these cities, he puts them to death in accordance with the law of blood revenge.

From the historian's point of view, the significance of Gideon lies chiefly in the fact that he initiated the first tentative movement towards a real Israelite monarchy.[1] It is quite true that he is represented as definitely refusing the title, but the brief account which follows the story of his exploits exhibits him as the typical oriental sultan. He clearly becomes a man of great wealth, and has an extensive harem; no character in the Old Testament is credited with a larger number of children. The language used by Abimelech in Judges ix. 2 is unintelligible unless some kind of sovereignty is ascribed to the house of Jerubbaal, and therefore to Jerubbaal himself. And when Gideon made a metal 'ephod' (whatever an ephod may have been) his action could have only one meaning to his contemporaries. There is no reason to believe that they shared the view of the later writer and regarded this as an act of apostasy, but they must have seen in the inauguration of the new sanctuary a claim for the supremacy of his own home not unlike that involved in the construction of Solomon's temple. Possessing the reality of kingship, Gideon did not need the name.

The truth is, of course, even clearer in the story of Gideon's son, Abimelech.[2] He was of mixed ancestry, and illustrates the

---

[1] It is quite possible that Jephthah's bargain with the elders of Gilead is intended to show that he claimed the powers of a king. But there is no evidence to suggest that he had a successor; tradition expressly denies him a son (Judges xi. 34). And a single personal ruler hardly makes a monarchy, for it does not make a real change in the constitution of the political order.

[2] Judges ix.

general assimilation of the two races one to another. Shechem had been under the authority of his father, and now his half-brothers, seventy in number, had succeeded to the government. Abimelech appealed to Shechem to put him in their place, but he did so, not on the ground that he had Canaanite blood in him, but because his mother belonged to their city.[1] The racial distinction does not appear; it was the local interest on which he relied. We are approaching the stage at which there is no longer any consciousness of diverse ancestry. Men do not ask whether a man is an Israelite or a Canaanite; they ask what is his town.

Abimelech's career opens, in approved oriental fashion, with the removal of possible rivals, in this instance the seventy sons of Gideon—or rather sixty-nine of them, for one, Jotham, makes good his escape. Jotham's fable and prophecy are familiar to every reader, and the event proved that he was right in his estimate of Abimelech, and in the relations which were likely to prevail between the city and its new ruler.

Abimelech was the master of a number of towns, and, unfortunately, we are able to identify the sites of only two, Shechem and Thebez. Besides these there was an open village with a tower in it named Migdal Shechem, which was probably quite near the city, perhaps on the slope of one of the hills above, whence a watch could be kept on the roads. There is also a Beth-millo, which, again, is not far from Shechem, though its actual site is quite uncertain. We may assume that Ophrah recognized his authority, and Abimelech made his head-quarters at Arumah,[2] another site which is still lost to us, though we may, perhaps, conjecture that either this place or Ophrah or both lay between Shechem and Thebez. If we may judge from the instance of Shechem, Abimelech governed through local agents, whom he placed in the towns making them directly responsible to him, and looking to them for information affecting the interests of the overlord. Whether because of this method, or for some other reason, his government became unpopular, and after an interval of three years trouble arose between Abimelech and his subjects.

It seems fairly clear that we have two different accounts of the struggle between Abimelech and the city. Two different

---

[1] For a parallel instance of a man appealing to his mother's kin against his father's family cp. W. Robertson Smith, *Kinship and Marriage in Early Arabia*, p. 86.

[2] Judges ix. 41; so read also in verse 31 for Tormah.

causes for the revolt are given, and two different attacks are
mentioned, the two latter appearing to be mutually exclusive.
The episode of Gaal in ix. 26–41 does not fit in with what
precedes or with what follows. Verse 42 would follow naturally
on verse 25, but the city is not named, and it is just possible that
we have a fragment from the account of Abimelech's reduction
of a totally different place. But this is not at all probable, and
we shall do best to assume that verse 42 is the immediate sequel
of verse 25. In that case the two stories will run much as follows:

(*a*) In verses 22–5, 42–5 the Shechemites show their independence by taking to brigandage. The position of the city on
several important highways made this very easy, but it was a
direct challenge to the authority of Abimelech, who must have
retained the sole right of levying toll on caravans passing through
his district. News was brought to him, and without a single day's
delay he prepared a trap for the Shechemite ambush. Dividing
his forces into three, he placed two companies near the gates of
the city, and set one ready to attack the Shechemite raiders.
When the latter left the city, this party fell upon them and
destroyed them, while the rest fought against the city, and took
it before evening. It was then laid in ruins and left an utter
waste.

(*b*) In verses 26–41 the disaffection is due to a certain immigrant named Gaal, who used his opportunities of sowing distrust
and hostility to Abimelech in private conversation, and then
took advantage of a vintage festival to break into open ex-
pressions of revolt. This was reported to Abimelech by his
governor, Zebul, who urged him to make a night march on the
city and surprise it at dawn. In the morning he succeeded in
lulling the suspicions of Gaal, who saw the army descending
from the heights, and when at last it was impossible to deceive
him any longer, it was too late for him to make any effective
resistance. An attempt was made, but it ended in failure, and
Zebul was able to restore his authority and expel Gaal.

These two narratives are hardly compatible with one another
unless we can assume that a considerable interval of time
elapsed between them. Both, however, serve to illustrate the
friction which attended the government of Abimelech, and
show that his power rested entirely on superior force. Another
narrative tells of the destruction of Migdal Shechem, and yet
another of the attempt to repeat the success at Migdal Thebez,

where, however, Abimelech met his death. It seems that he left no son to succeed him, and the narrative implies the immediate breaking up of any kingdom he may have succeeded in forming. To understand the failure of Abimelech, we need do no more than glance at the outstanding difference between him and the other heroes of the book of *Judges*. The rest were deliverers of their people, saving them from the power of foreign enemies. Such authority as they may have acquired was based, not on their conquest of their neighbours in the land itself, but on the natural respect which their triumphs secured. As long as it was necessary to unite against a common foe, allegiance was freely given, but there was something in the nature of the Palestinian towns and cities, as in those of ancient Greece, which revolted against the idea of control by a single state or individual. The only way in which a complete unity could come about was through foreign pressure by the same enemy extending over many years. The foes hitherto mentioned were but temporary invaders, often only raiders, and the authority of the leader could not long outlast the crisis. Only a generation of struggle could have made Palestine willing to accept a single monarch.

The necessary stimulus was supplied by the Philistines. As we have already seen, these people seem to have been the survivors of a great army of northern invaders who were repulsed from the Egyptian frontier by Ramses III in the eighth year of his reign (1192 B.C.?).[1] It was, no doubt, only after two or three generations that they began to be aggressive and to press seriously inland. The first movements must have been purely local, and aimed at the possession of the coast itself and the lower Shephelah. At this stage the struggle would not assume a national importance, and it was only the tribe in the

[1] In view of the fact that in the eleventh year of his reign Ramses undertook an expedition northwards, and claims to have won back much of the territory possessed by the kings of the eighteenth and nineteenth dynasties, it may be possible that the historic Philistines really planted their colonies in a second wave of invasion, which did not actually attack Egypt. The twentieth dynasty, after Ramses III, was certainly too weak to trouble itself with a foreign people who made no attempt to invade their country. It does not follow that Ramses conquered all the countries claimed for him; the royal scribes probably wished to show that he was no less than the greatest of earlier Pharaohs. It is worth noting that we have no evidence of another expedition, or of any attempt to hold the country, but there must have been some military movement, and the very shortest journey northwards from Palestine would pass through the territory later in possession of the Philistines.

immediate neighbourhood, i.e. Dan, that was conscious of the pressure.

It is in the story of Samson[1] that we first meet with Philistines as serious conquerors of Israel. He himself is a strange figure, with very little resemblance to the other heroes whose exploits form the main theme of the book of *Judges*. He resembles them only in being possessed by a Spirit which seizes him suddenly[2] and drives him to violent action in which he exhibits super-human strength.[3] But his exploits are all strictly personal and individual. He calls none to his aid, raises no army, leads no troops into battle, expels no enemies. All he does is to avenge his own personal wrongs on the Philistines, and though he may be a striking figure in Hebrew folk-lore, he never was in any sense a national leader. Yet the stories which tradition has handed down are of the greatest interest and importance for a reconstruction of Israel's history at this period, inasmuch as they give us a picture of the way in which the Philistine advance was made.

Samson does not appear at the beginning of the Philistine pressure, but shortly before the final expulsion of his tribe. As we have seen, there is reason to believe, from Judges v. 17, that at one time the tribe of Dan had pressed forward to the coast itself. This must have been early in the days of Israelite occupation, and we may suspect that Philistine expansion in the first half of the twelfth century drove the tribe back towards the hills. Even here they could do some damage to passing caravans, and it must have been to this stage in their history that the ancient tribal song preserved in Gen. xlix. 16 f. refers. But in Samson's day they were confined to two small villages, Zorah and Eshtaol, lying on the north side of the Vale of Sorek, and occupying sites which overlook the modern railway from Lydda to Jerusalem. On the hill-side opposite Zorah is Beth-

---

[1] Judges xiii–xvi.

[2] Cp. ‏ותצלח עליו רוח יהוה‎ Judges xiv. 6, 19, xv. 14, contrast xvi. 20.

[3] Samson's name (‏שמשון‎ cp. ‏שמש‎) has suggested to some scholars that we have in him an Israelite form of Sun-myth. For a discussion of the question see Moore, *Judges*, pp. 364 f.; Budde, *Richter*, pp. 109 f. Another line of approach to the problem is indicated by Burney, *Judges*, pp. 391 ff., who sees signs of a connexion between Samson and the Sumerian hero Gilgamesh, especially in the story of the rending of the lion. The utmost that the facts seem to warrant is that possibly some elements of an ancient solar myth attached themselves in the popular mind to an historical character, so Vatke, Budde, Moore, Burney, &c. Cp. also Smythe Palmer, *The Samson Saga* (1913).

shemesh, and the little tribe was at least holding one of the most important gates into the southern hills.

We need not dwell in detail on Samson's exploits; it is enough to glance at the general picture which the stories present. We see first the weak Israelite tribe, still retaining its sanctuary near the ancient rock altar of Zorah. Only a few miles away the inhabitants are reckoned Judahites, for Kiriath Jearim and the rock of Etam are within ten miles of the Danite villages. Every one recognizes the Philistine ascendancy, and it is regarded as a most rash act to provoke them, for they are likely to take swift vengeance for wrong done to them. There is no sign that the Israelites are possessed of any arms; Samson's weapons are those with which nature supplies him, and the situation is not unlike that described in Judges v. 8, and again in 1 Sam. xiii. 19 ff. No resistance against the Philistines is at all possible, if they choose to make a serious expedition into the country. It does not appear, however, that they had adopted any systematic measures for holding the land. Later we hear of garrison posts, and of Philistine governors who occupy them, but at this point the terror of the Philistine name seems to be enough to hold the country.

At the same time there is no bar to communication between Israel and the Philistines. Samson can pass freely to and from the towns and cities, even as far as Gaza. Intermarriage is not prohibited, for Samson's first cycle of exploits[1] is connected with his courtship of a woman of Timnah, four or five miles to the south-west of Zorah. The fact that this is a Philistine town shows how limited was the territory of Dan, and the whole circumstances point to nominally friendly relations between the two races, for Samson chooses Philistine youths as his company for the wedding. The position in general is that the Israelites are dominated but not persecuted, and unless they themselves give offence to the Philistines, they are in no serious danger of attack.

There is no allusion to the political divisions which existed among the Philistines, and they are treated as a single unit. The only one of the 'Five Towns' whose name occurs in the Samson story is Gaza, and Gaza is mentioned as a locality, not as a state; the reference is purely geographical. The 'Five Lords' act together, it is true, but the suggestion is that they

[1] Cp. Judges xiv, xv.

form a supreme Council of State, and compose the Government of a single community. We should probably attribute this vagueness in matters Philistine to the length of time during which the Samson stories remained at the stage of oral tradition, for it is improbable that the five cities ever formed a single closely organized political entity. An official, or semi-official, record might distinguish between the different states included in the confederacy, but to the popular mind of Israel they were simply Philistines, wherever their home might be.

The sequel to the struggle in which Samson played so conspicuous but so futile a part is to be seen in the story of the Danite migration which forms one of the two appendices to the book of *Judges*, chs. xvii. f.[1] Here we have the story of Micah and his sanctuary, attended by a Levite who is none other than the grandson of Moses,[2] and of the theft of both sacred objects and Levite by the Danites. It is clear that the pressure of the Philistines has grown too heavy for the little tribe. The Philistines must have assumed a more aggressive attitude, and have started on the movement which led them ultimately to dominate the whole country. The total population even in Samson's day must have been small, and now there are left only 600 fighting men. A scouting party of five is sent out, and returns with the report that in the far north, in the valleys between the Lebanon and the Antilebanon, there lies a small but rich district about the city of Laish.[3] It is entirely isolated,

---

[1] The dominant theory of the structure of the book of *Judges* is that of Budde, cp. Moore, *Judges*, pp. xxxvi f. This would make the earlier form of the book include the great majority of the stories that we now have, both in the book itself and in the first twelve chapters of *1 Samuel*, though omitting one or two small sections, and without the 'framework' which sets forth the theory of history characteristic of the book as it now stands. The present writer, however, finds it difficult to believe that these two appendices, chs. xvii f. (the Danite migration) and xix–xxi (the Benjamite war), formed a part of the original JE document which Budde and others assume to have underlain the present form. That they come from an early source is not to be doubted, though the second appendix seems to have received later accretions and to be of less value as an historical document than the former. At the same time, both are most valuable to the historian of this period, not only for the actual facts which they record, but still more for the picture they give of conditions in Palestine during this age.

[2] It is perhaps superfluous to remark that the text itself attests the later introduction of the נ into the name of Jonathan's grandfather (or more remote ancestor) in Judges xviii. 30. A later age felt that the sanctuary was illegitimate, and found its traditional connexion with the family of Moses intolerable. This is, of course, the view of the writer's time. In any case the Levite, though he might have been a descendant, could hardly have been a grandson of Moses—the chronology is decisive.   [3] For the location cp. Garstang, *Joshua and Judges*, pp. 245–7 (1931).

having no connexion either with Phoenicia on the west or with Damascus[1] in the east, and can thus easily be overthrown. The whole tribe sets out, taking their women and children with them,[2] and also such cattle as they possess, and on the way, passing near to Micah's home in Mount Ephraim, they are told of the 'house of gods' and of the Levite. They take with them what they want, and when Micah protests he gets nothing but hard words. At length they reach the city of Laish, attack and destroy it, building a new city on its site, to which they give the name of the tribe. They are rough folk, living in a rough age, when 'there was no king in Israel: every man did that which was right in his own eyes'.[3]

This is, no doubt, the story preserved at Dan to explain the origin of the sanctuary, one of the most famous in Israel. It is not connected in any way, as far as we know, with the patriarchal age, as so many of the sacred places of Israel are, and therefore the attribution of the cult to the family of Moses is the more important. There may have been traditions of a Mosaic shrine in Mount Ephraim, and the story explains its disappearance as well as the foundation of the other. There need be no question as to its historicity, at least as far as the migration is concerned. There is indisputable evidence to show that Dan was once located to the south-west of the Joseph tribes, and that later its home was in the far north, and it is clear that it was necessarily the clan most exposed to the early Philistine aggression. The story of Micah may serve as an indication of the fact that the Philistines had not pressed far into the country, for there is no sign of their presence in Mount Ephraim, and the reason why the Danites go to such a distance was not that they found traces of Philistine occupation nearer to their own home, but that they did not discover any other spot which offered such an easy chance of occupation.

So ends the first stage of the Philistine movement. The invaders have not merely made good their footing on the coast, and established themselves in the great cities which are to belong to them for so many centuries; they have begun to extend their authority, and to prove their ability to overcome any single group of their predecessors which may oppose their progress. Judah, i.e. the Shephelah and the lower hills west of Hebron and Bethlehem,

---

[1] In xviii. 7 and 28 read אֲרָם for אָדָם in accordance with what seems to have been the original text of the LXX. [2] xviii. 21. [3] xvii. 6.

recognizes their supremacy, and one fighting tribe has been compelled to give up the struggle and find a new home in the most distant quarter of the land.

The dating of these events must, in the nature of the case, be largely a matter of conjecture. But, as we have seen, no independent empire could possibly have been established in Palestine except at a time of Egyptian weakness. This limits us to the twelfth century B.C. for the beginning of the Philistine movement, and since the foundation of the Hebrew monarchy must be placed not later than the latter half of the eleventh century, the great expansion of Philistine power and the foundation of the short-lived Philistine empire must have taken place before 1050 B.C. We shall not go far wrong if we assign the Danite migration to the third or fourth quarter of the twelfth century. The chronology of the book of *Judges* has been most carefully scrutinized by a number of competent scholars, in the hope of discovering some harmony between it and other known dates and periods. A very adequate discussion is to be found in Moore, *Judges*, pp. xxxviii—xliii. But the only result which seems definitely to emerge from the discussion is that any attempt to make serious use of the figures given in *Judges* is futile.[1] In the nature of the case they have no place in the original folk-tales and traditions on which the compiler has relied for his material, and it seems to the present writer that they are clearly due to the conjectures of a later age, perhaps to the compiler himself. Not only is the transmission of figures in ancient manuscripts notoriously unreliable, but the system of twenties, forties, and eighties which is found in *Judges* has every appearance of being purely artificial. Such dating as we may suggest to ourselves must be based on other grounds, and in the preceding pages an attempt has been made to form an estimate of the probable order of the events described in the book. Further than that, in the absence of information from outside Israel, it seems quite impossible to go.

Our knowledge of the final stage of the Philistine advance is based mainly on the narratives preserved in 1 Sam. i. 1—vii. 1, with some assistance from archaeology. Apart from the Song of Hannah, which, as is generally agreed, is a later insertion in the narrative of ch. ii, there seem to be two main strands from which the text has been compiled. One of these is part of a history of Samuel, and includes chs. i, ii. 11–26, iii. 1—iv. 1a. The second is primarily interested in the fortunes of the Ark, and runs continuously from iv. 1b to vii. 1. Interwoven with the first group there seems to be a series of passages of independent origin, dealing with the corrupt practices

---

[1] Garstang (*op. cit.*), however, accepts the Biblical figures, including those of *Judges*.

of the sons of Eli. It will be noted that we have a direct contradiction between ii. 23–5, where Eli rebukes his sons, and iii. 13, according to which he has not restrained them. This suggests that ii. 22–5 formed no part of the original story of Samuel, but was either a later insertion, coming from an age which failed to realize the heinousness of the offence described in ii. 12–17 (misappropriation of the offerings), and assumed that there must have been a moral offence as well, or else was drawn from an independent source. In the same way it would seem that the rebuke of the unnamed man of God was intended to be a sequel to ii. 12–17, since a ritual sin is indicated in both passages. The two sections, however, do not correspond in style, and whatever be the source of ii. 12–17, it seems likely that ii. 27–36 is later, belonging, perhaps, to the last stage of the composition of the book as a whole. The Samuel story is continued in vii. 2—viii. 22, x. 17–27, xii. In its final form it must be ascribed to a period when the monarchy itself was regarded as an act of apostasy, an attitude which we do not find elsewhere till the time of Hosea. The early stories of Samuel, however, appear to be much older, and we may conjecture that they were adopted by the later writer and incorporated in his work. For full discussions of the question see Smith, *Samuel*, pp. xvi–xxiii; Kennedy, *Samuel (Cent. Bib.)*, pp. 14–19; Budde, *Die Bücher Samuel*, x–xxi (1902); Eissfeldt, *Die Komposition der Samuelisbücher* (1931).

In a certain sense the final act in the drama of Philistine advance centres round Shiloh. In so far as there was any pivotal locality in the Israel of the beginning of the eleventh century, it was there. The Ark had reappeared in history, after not having been mentioned since the days of the first Israelite invasions. Here was a well-built temple, with all the appurtenances and ritual of ancient Semitic shrines, and here men were accustomed to gather from the whole of central Palestine. It was at Shiloh that Samuel, in one of his aspects, the last of the Judges, spent his early years, and so formed a link between the old order and the new. It was, finally, in the tragedy of Shiloh that Israel saw her national ruin for the time, and the fall of the city and its priesthood marked the climax of Philistine power over Israel. There were battles fought later, and, indeed, desperate struggles, but they took the form of revolts against a ruling power; with the fall of Shiloh the Philistines truly became dominant.

It is, perhaps, because Shiloh vanished so completely that we have no surviving early tradition of its foundation.[1] There is,

---

[1] It is interesting to observe that the excavations at Shiloh show no trace of a pre-Israelite sanctuary.

apparently, a reference to Shiloh in Jacob's blessing on Judah, Gen. xlix. 10, but only the most daring would venture to dogmatize on the meaning of this *crux interpretum*. Jer. vii. 12 (cp. xxvi. 6) speaks of its destruction, but not of its foundation. One tradition alone in the whole book of *Judges* is linked with the place, and that is the story of the rape of the women of Shiloh by the Benjamites.[1] In Joshua xviii. 1 the Ark is placed at Shiloh by Joshua, but this is a statement made by P, and though it may be based on older tradition, it is more likely that it offers an explanation of the fact that in later days this was the location of the Ark sanctuary. In Judges ii. 1 we have the statement that the 'angel of Yahweh' went up from Gilgal to 'Bochim',[2] which would imply that this became the chief sanctuary of Israel after the death of Joshua, and that during his lifetime the religious centre had remained in the plain of Jericho.

But if we cannot trace the steps by which the sanctuary reached its fame, we do know that at the beginning of the last stage of Philistine expansion it held an important position. The presence of the Ark alone would be enough to secure a high repute, for while Israel may have had local traditions certifying the validity of other shrines, it is probable that all held the Ark in reverence. The accounts we have of the place also suggest a considerable establishment. There was clearly a well-built temple, perhaps resembling that which has been unearthed at Gezer,[3] though, of course, with its own local and individual peculiarities. It must have included not only the central shrine which was the house of the Ark proper, but also the usual equipment of altars, priestly quarters, place of slaughter and rooms for the worshippers' sacrificial meals. It had a priestly establishment of some size, for not only were Eli and his two sons there to officiate, but they had servants and attendants, probably, in addition to Samuel. While the Shiloh temple may not have been as elaborate as those of later Israel, it was

---

[1] Judges xxi. 16–24. The story is clearly a relic of days when marriage was theoretically marriage by capture. It points to Shiloh as a place of special festival, but the elaborate directions given to those who would find it do not suggest that it was the most famous sanctuary in Israel. The story is either so early that the place was not yet known, or so late that its site was in danger of being forgotten. Though the tradition may be very ancient, yet the form in which it now appears may be comparatively recent, and the second is the more probable of the two alternatives.   [2] See p. 129.   [3] See Macalister, *Excavations at Gezer*.

sufficiently large to prove itself the sanctuary of a people now long settled in the land, who formed the regular agricultural community.[1] The site is usually identified with that of the modern Seilun,[2] which suits admirably the details given in Judges xxi, and it is worth noting that in going to Shiloh from Ramah, which is named as the home of Samuel's parents, it is necessary actually to pass through, or very close to, Bethel. Clearly, the narrative of 1 Sam. i knows nothing of Bethel as a great Yahweh sanctuary, and assumes that worshippers will travel a considerable distance. Elkanah comes up but once a year, and Eli's suspicion that Hannah is drunk suggests that the period was that of the vintage, i.e. of the festival later known as the Feast of Tabernacles. Moreover, he and his family do not start for home on the day of the annual sacrifice, they wait until the following morning before beginning their journey. All these circumstances point to a sanctuary well established and of wide fame, probably the chief shrine for all Yahweh-worshippers in the central hills of Palestine. We receive the impression that this place was the focus for the life of Israel, at least south of the plain of Esdraelon.

The general picture that is presented to us in this narrative is that of a peaceful farmer life. There is a regularity about it which impresses us when we compare and contrast it with the turmoil and turbulence of the days of the Judges. It is possible that the Hebrew historian has done something to idealize the conditions of the age, but the very existence of the Temple as a centre of life in this spot helps to confirm his presentation. We are led to suppose that the Israelite occupation, whether by conquest or by assimilation, is practically complete in the hills of the Joseph tribes, and that when further union takes place it will not be so much between Israelites and Canaanites in the same district, as between the different districts, each of which has by now a mixed but practically unified population.

This quiet agricultural life was destined to suffer a rude

[1] Cp. the offerings mentioned in 1 Sam. i. 24 as presented at Samuel's consecration.

[2] The site was excavated in 1922 and onward by a Danish scholar, Dr. Aage Schmidt. Pottery remains suggest that Israelites were the first to occupy the site, that the main period of their residence came to an end in the eleventh century, and that it ceased altogether about 900 B.C. Cp. Albright in *Bulletin of the American School of Oriental Research*, No. 9, pp. 10 f. (Feb. 1923); Garstang, *Joshua and Judges*, pp. 251, n. 1, 399.

disturbance. The Philistines were now masters of the Shephelah and of the openings of the valleys which led up into the hills. Their power had extended beyond the limits suggested in the Samson story, and it is clear that by this time they held practically all the lower ground towards the sea. The hills were not in themselves essential to their expansion, except in so far as it was necessary for them to secure protection against attacks. Their main objective all along must have been the plain of Esdraelon, with its fertile soil and its great caravan routes. But the Israelite tribes, though probably still far from being politically united, and entirely lacking anything like a centralized government, could yet make difficulties from the hills, and threaten the plains, as the stories of Gideon and Abimelech show. Secure occupation of the country, then, depended on the subjugation of the mountain tribes, and in 1 Sam. iv. 1 we have the first intimation of the Philistine advance.

Two localities are mentioned, Ebenezer, where the Israelite camp lay, and Aphek, the Philistine army head-quarters. These two places cannot have been far apart, but no satisfactory identification has yet been suggested. Aphek in Sharon, on the southern slopes of the Carmel range,[1] and several others among the many places that bore this name, are too far from Shiloh to fit the narrative. The most probable suggestion is that it lay near the present Ain Sinia, a couple of miles to the north-east of Gophna (Ophni). Here one of the branches of the Wadi en-Nimr is crossed by a track leading north from Gophna to Shechem. It is possible that the Israelite force lay across this road in order to prevent further advance northwards. But a path was still open towards Bethel to the south, and it was necessary for Israel not merely to prevent a northward move-ment, but, if possible, to drive the enemy back. The story is vividly told in 1 Sam. iv. The first day's fighting ended in an Israelite panic which came on them as they stood in battle array, and cost them a heavy slaughter. They returned to their camp, which, apparently, was too strong lightly to be attacked, and deliberated on the causes of their defeat. To them it was clear that Yahweh had betrayed them, and it seemed to them that if they brought Him into their midst, then, for His own sake, He would be compelled to fight for them. But

---

[1] Cp. G. A. Smith, *HGHL.*, pp. 350, 400 ff., *EB.*, cols. 192 f., and for a discussion of the whole subject, *HGHL.*, p. 224, n. 2.

they had not allowed for His indignation at the corrupt practices of His priests, Hophni and Phinehas, and when the battle was renewed, not only did He again send panic upon Israel, but even suffered His own Ark to be captured, i.e., to the mind of Israel, He Himself was taken prisoner. Hophni and Phinehas were slain, along with a number of Israelite warriors given as 30,000. The figure was probably very much smaller than this, but it was certainly large enough to prevent any further attempt at defence.

We have no details of the further course of the Philistine invasion. Nor do we need them; the issue is too clear without them. We hear no more of Shiloh, which must have been taken and sacked at this time, its last gift to the world the cry of an unhappy mother who saw in the birth of her child the end of Israel's glory.[1] The defences of the country were cut in two, and an easy road led over a series of open valleys to the north. The whole of the central range must have fallen into Philistine hands, and, as they held also the coast roads, the occupation of the plain of Esdraelon became inevitable. The last vestiges of Egyptian occupation were swept away, and with the capture of Beth-shean the Philistine conquest was complete. There is no evidence that it spread into Galilee, but the western side of the Jordan south of Beth-shean seems to have been completely dominated by the new invaders. A nucleus had been established for a great Philistine empire.

At this point the narrative of *1 Samuel* introduces a deliverance wrought by Samuel.[2] The whole strongly recalls the stories told of the Judges, and is apparently intended to place Samuel as the last of that order, leading up to the establishment of the monarchy. We have the formula which is already familiar to us—the lapse of a period of years, twenty in this instance, the repentance of Israel, and the appearance of the divinely-inspired deliverer. Samuel (of whom we have not heard since the theophany granted to him and the message delivered by him to Eli) summons the people to Mizpah, here, as in Judges xx. 1, regarded as the rallying-point of the whole nation. The site is probably that of the modern Nebi Samwil, about five miles north of Jerusalem. Samuel offers up a yearling lamb as a whole burnt-offering, and receives the answer he requires. Meanwhile a Philistine force is approaching, but the answer of Yahweh is in the form of thunder. The Philistines are thrown into utter panic by the storm, and Israelites, gathering from all parts, pursue

---

[1] 1 Sam. iv. 19–22.   [2] 1 Sam. vii.

them to Beth Car,[1] with the result that the Philistine power is completely crushed and many of the cities on the south-west are recovered
by Israel. Samuel then becomes a judge, and his circuit is organized
to cover Bethel, Gilgal, and Mizpah annually, while his normal home
is Ramah.[2]

It is hardly possible to regard this narrative as being actual history.
All the other evidence points to an unbroken Philistine dominion
from the fall of Shiloh to the rise of Saul, and the statement that the
Philistines 'came no more within the border of Israel: and the hand
of the Lord was against the Philistines all the days of Samuel'[3] is
quite at variance with the conditions reported to us later in the early
days of Saul. We may freely accept the statement of ch. vii. 14b,
that there was peace between Israel and the Amorites, but the story
as a whole must have another origin than fact. It is probably intended to place Samuel on a somewhat higher level than the other
Judges, and liken him rather to Moses. It will be noted that the
victory was won without any human aid; the people do not seem even
to have been armed. Further, it serves as an explanation of the name
Ebenezer, which can hardly be the same place as the scene of Israel's
defeat. In ch. viii, which follows naturally on ch. vii, we have the
view that the monarchy is an act of apostasy, without even the plea
of political and military necessity. What need is there of a king in
Israel, when Yahweh can, through His inspired persons, miracu-
lously defeat any army that may attack them? This also must be
reckoned as a *motif* for the story, which clearly belongs to the later
strata of the book of *Samuel*.

The period ends thus with Israel reduced to the lowest extremity, crushed by the foreign invader, hardly regarded as
free men, forbidden the use of arms, and without a national
sanctuary or any form of centralization. Yet it is worth noting
that certain very marked gains have been secured, and there are
not wanting in Israel signs that there may some day be a revival.
In the first place, there is no longer any hostility between the
older inhabitants and those who claim descent from the
Aramaean invaders. Since the first conquest was made, Israel
has done little fighting, if any, against her immediate neighbours. On the contrary, she has gradually made her way among
them, and has attained a position of something more than
equality with them. She has gained much from others; she has
learnt to till the soil, to sow seed, to reap crops, to prepare food

---

[1] The site intended is quite uncertain, and even the text is doubtful, the ancient
versions offering different readings.
[2] 1 Sam. vii. 15–17.   [3] 1 Sam. vii. 13, 14.

from the grain, to cultivate and use the flax, the vine, and the olive. She is no longer confined to the semi-wilderness, the bare spaces of the east and south and the wooded hills; she has made her way down into the plains, and though her territories have suffered curtailment in the early days of Philistine occupation, she has made good her footing from near Jerusalem to Dan. A few places still hold out against her; particularly Jerusalem, which in Judges xix. 11 f. is still regarded as a hostile city.

If Israel has received something from her predecessors, she in her turn has had gifts to bestow. Among the most valuable has been her military prowess. She has brought from the wilderness a vigour and a battle fury which the centuries of gradual occupation have not yet sufficed to erase. The Canaanites, grown effete and unwarlike by their far longer residence in the land, had grave need of such strength as Israel could afford. Again and again the land has been threatened, and more than threatened, with foreign invasion, and always it has been the Israelite hero, inspired by Israel's warrior-God, who has led the armies to victory and expelled the foreigner. Most of these assaults have come from the east, and have been delivered by peoples on no higher plane than Israel had occupied on her first entry into the land. To her superior morale, Israel has now added superior equipment, learning material lessons from her neighbours, and perhaps some strategy, with the result that the local attacks of the various eastern raiders and oppressors have been easily repulsed by forces which, though drawn from fairly wide districts, not merely from single cities, are still local rather than national. But a new power altogether has appeared, and this cannot be met with the weapons and organization that sufficed to stampede the 'children of the east'. The Philistine invasion is not a local matter, and cannot be handled with local levies, as has been abundantly proved by the failure of the tribe of Dan. If Israel is to be liberated from the Philistines, if the land is to be independent of this foreign control by 'the uncircumcised', then there must be a more complete unity, a oneness of the whole people. A small group may suffice to win a battle; it cannot repel a nation or check the foundation of an empire. Unless and until some steps can be taken towards the unification of the whole land, resistance to the Philistines can never be more than a series of local revolts, which will be put down in every case, possibly rendering less tolerable the lot of the survivors.

Signs, however, are not wanting that the requisite union is at least a possibility. The stories of the Judges show that, in spite of their divisions, the Israelites are capable of more extensive combinations than were their predecessors. The latter had, it is true, formed occasional alliances under the pressure of the early Israelite attacks themselves, but there was nothing in the essential nature of the case which compelled them to harmony in action. It is characteristic of Israel that there is a greater unity among them, a unity which is primarily due to their religion, but which is reinforced by the auxiliary factor of common blood. There is a solidarity in the Israelite tribe, and it can readily be united against a common enemy. Canaanite polity seems to have been organized on a basis of the practically complete isolation of the different towns and villages. While it would certainly be untrue to say that there was now any central authority, there was a sense of oneness which ultimately resulted in a larger political unit. To meet and defeat the Moabites, both Ephraimites and Benjamites combine, and each tribe covers a far wider area than did any one of the old Canaanite cities. It is not the least important of the contributions of Israel that a tribal as well as a local basis now supported the common life, and this is a stage which is well on the way to a complete centralization of the government of the country.

There is one further element in the situation which must not be overlooked. This is the presence of certain of the tribes to the east of Jordan, and their permanent settlement there. Their country was suited primarily to the nomad life; that is the reason given for their choice of it as a home.[1] Reuben, in the Song of Deborah, sits 'among the sheepfolds',[2] and every reference suggests the pastoral rather than the agricultural life. But neither the Jordan valley nor the difference in occupation ever interfered with the sense that they belonged to Israel. They were a part of the nation, and both they and their western kinsmen always remembered the fact. Jephthah takes his place among the heroes of the pre-monarchic age, and Gad and Reuben are expected to share in the perils and the triumphs of the wars of Yahweh. In certain ways, the presence of this transjordanic nomad element was profoundly important to Israel, and some of the most signi-

---

[1] Cp. Num. xxxii. 4.   [2] Judges v. 16.

ficant features of the nation's history are to be explained only by reference to the two Israels, the pastoral and the agricultural. Israelite religion has also undergone a change, and we may assume that, along with the material side of Palestinian civilization, the tribes have taken over also the religious views and practices of their predecessors, practically *en bloc*. It is easy to see that this must have been almost inevitable, as Israel gradually took to the cultivation of the land. A double danger seemed to beset men. The old Baals, the local fertility spirits, losing their accustomed worship, would become hostile, and inflict frightful injuries on those who had neglected them and their just dues. It was such a feeling as this which, centuries later, impelled the colonists of northern Israel to appeal for one who could teach them how the God of the land should be worshipped, for He was sending lions among them.[1] And even if they escaped this danger, there was still the further practical problem presented by the life of the farmer. Yahweh had served them in good stead in earlier years, had brought them safely through the wilderness, had given them victory over their enemies, but men doubted (even as late as Hosea's day[2]) whether he was expert or even competent in the operations of agriculture. This the Baals had been doing for untold generations; it would be safer to continue appealing for their aid, and lending them, through the cultus, the help for which they asked.[3]

In this crude form, the adoption of Canaanite religion soon led to disaster. There were too many Baals, and the wars of Israel required some degree of unity among the people. The Baals were disintegrating forces, and with the lack both of the common loyalty to Yahweh and of the inspiration that He gave men for war, Israel suffered defeat and subjection. The Judges who saved her came in the name of Yahweh and were possessed by the Spirit of Yahweh, and the stern logic of events compelled Israel in the end to a kind of fidelity to her Covenant God.

But the effect was not to revert to the type of religion which had prevailed in the wilderness—at least as far as the agricultural portion of Israel was concerned. Recognizing at length that it was Yahweh who gave her her corn and her wine and her oil, she still saw in Him a God who might demand or even

---

[1] 2 Kgs. xvii. 24 ff. [2] Cp. Hos. ii. 5, 8 [Heb. 7, 10].
[3] Isa. xxviii. 23 ff., and similar passages, attest the ultimate transference of these agricultural functions to Yahweh.

need special treatment in the provision and preparation of these products. To all intents and purposes Yahweh became in Israel's eyes a Baal, differing from His predecessors only in the fact that He was one and they were many. This, of course, meant very marked changes from the ancient cultus of the wilderness. The old rule that no artificial object might be used as a symbol of Yahweh was disregarded or forgotten, and we hear, not only of the 'house of gods'[1] built by Micah for the reception of his molten image and his graven image, but of an 'ephod' made by Gideon himself, of which the historian, writing in the light of a purer faith, says 'it became a snare unto Gideon and unto his house'.[2] At least one solid temple appeared, and it is probable that when the Israelite worshipped at other shrines, he worshipped Yahweh under the name of Baal. A more or less elaborate sacrificial system was adopted. The pre-exilic prophets deny that there was any sacrifice at all enjoined by Yahweh in the wilderness period.[3] Probably the Passover must be excepted, but it must be remembered that till the days of Josiah this was not an offering made at the altar, but a domestic ritual, and it is always the sanctuaries which the prophets contemplate in their denunciations. Sacrifice was now a well-developed institution in Israel. Old rock altars might be used, or new ones might be built, but there was no lack of them, and they were not left always cold. Even human sacrifice was possible, though rare, and resorted to only in case of exceptional peril. Other sacrifices were those of the normal agricultural community, falling into the two main classes of Gift sacrifices and Communion sacrifices. It is worth noting that most of the sacrifices described during this period belong to the latter class. In the early chapters of *I Samuel* we have a very full account of the cultus as it was practised at Shiloh, and it is intimated that this ritual is already ancient and has the authority of long tradition behind it. There was a system of sacred dues, which must be rendered at the sanctuary, and the ordinary offering was an occasion of rejoicing, even of revelry.

With all this the moral standard does not seem to have risen. There is one story of an appalling outrage,[4] and of the vengeance that Israel, as a whole, took upon the perpetrators,

---

[1] Judges xvii. 5.   [2] Judges viii. 27.
[3] For the view that nomad Israel had a somewhat extensive ritual system cp. Lods, *Israël*, pp. 298–356.   [4] Judges xix–xxi.

and on the tribe which defended them. Yet the same story, recording the difficulty created by the extermination of the Benjamite women, finds no horror in the extinction of Jabesh-gilead, and has no condemnation for the rape of the virgins of Shiloh. Samson's amours are frankly mentioned, and there is no reprehension of polygamy such as Gideon's. The laws of blood-revenge and those of sexual morality, as understood in earlier days, are still observed, but Israel has taken no step, as far as we can see, towards the development of new rules for conduct which shall be adapted to the novel life on which she has now entered. The need for such modification, even the possibility of it, does not seem to have occurred to any in Israel until the rise of the great prophets in the eighth and seventh centuries. Till then, Israel maintained her desert standards as far as they were applicable to her new life, and, for the rest, was content to accept those which she found current round about her.

Additional Note A

THE ORIGIN OF THE TRIBE OF JUDAH

THE whole question of the origin of Judah is complicated and obscure. It is beyond all dispute that in the tenth and ninth centuries B.C. Judah ranks fully as one of the tribes; this is clear, not only from the actual records of the fortunes of the kingdom, but also from such passages as Gen. xlix and Deut. xxxiii, where the tribe takes its place among the rest. The beliefs which gave rise to our present narratives have already been discussed (pp. 51 ff.). But such evidence as we can glean from pre-monarchic days suggests that its recognition was comparatively late and that there was a stage of tradition, older than the eleventh century, which knew not Judah. There is no mention of Judah, either for praise or for blame, in Judges v, and we note also the entire absence both of Simeon and of Levi. Reuben is the only one of the four 'major' Leah tribes which is noticed. In Judges i. 1–21 we have an account of the exploits attributed to the tribe in the course of the conquest. Verses 4–7 describe the defeat and humiliation of Adoni-bezek, but this may be regarded as an alternative account of the defeat of Adoni-zedek recorded in Josh. x, with details derived from some other source. Verse 8 speaks of the capture of Jerusalem, and verses 9–10 mention the conquest of Hebron. Verses 11–15 record the capture of Kiriath-sepher, by the family of Caleb. Verse 16 mentions the presence of Kenites; in verse 17 Judah and Simeon together destroy Zephath and call it

Hormah; while in verse 18 they are said to have occupied the whole of the Philistine plain, a statement which is immediately contradicted in the next verse. In verse 20 Hebron is given to Caleb, and verse 21 reverts to Jerusalem, which, it is said, was not captured by Benjamin.

In its present form we cannot trace this tradition back with certainty beyond the seventh century, though it may be somewhat older. Some features of it are certainly comparatively late, e.g. the narrative of verses 8–10. This assumes that the Judahite expedition started with Jerusalem and worked southwards, whereas we know that this city remained untaken till the days of David. We may also doubt the capture of Hebron by the earliest invaders; the original Calebite district is still farther south. We are left with the two sites Hormah and Kiriath-sepher. It is the conquest of the latter of which tradition has preserved most detail, and we may suspect that the introduction of Judah and Simeon into the Hormah story is due to a later theory, dating probably from a time not earlier than that of David.

Our attention is attracted to two other passages in which Judah is mentioned. The first of these is in Gen. xxxviii, where the whole suggestion of the story is that Judah was permanently resident in Palestine, and we are led to suspect that originally the name did not apply to any group of Aramaean invaders, but to a 'Canaanite' clan dwelling in the hills to the south of Jerusalem. In Judges xv. 9 ff. Judahites are introduced into the story of Samson, in a way which suggests that they, like the Danites, are subject to the Philistines.

With these data before us we may, perhaps, venture to attempt some kind of tentative reconstruction of the history of the 'tribe'. It begins with nomad inroads made by the Yahweh-worshipping tribes of the Kenites and Kenizzites—perhaps also Jerachmeelites—in the course of which, after a serious repulse, Hormah is taken and sacked. There follows the capture of Debir or Kiriath-sepher. This brings the nomads into contact with the settled group of Canaanites to whom the name Judah originally belonged, and whose centre is in the Hebron district. This is the situation at the beginning of the twelfth century B.C., but the pressure and domination of the Philistines unites the two groups into a single whole. An old Judahite tradition of the capture of Hebron from its aboriginal inhabitants is transferred to Caleb—now the chief hero of the composite group—the cult of Yahweh is imposed on the whole community, and a number of ancient traditions, the property of Judah, become part of the common stock. We may suppose that this process was, in the main, complete before the end of the twelfth century, though the history of the group still kept it at a distance from the Aramaean settlements north of Jerusalem.

BOOK III

THE ISRAELITE MONARCHY: ITS RISE AND ITS ZENITH

INTRODUCTORY REMARKS

IN the preceding pages we have endeavoured to trace the rise of Israel as a nation. We have seen the Aramaean invaders entering Palestine, partly conquering the country and partly uniting in various ways with their predecessors. We have seen how the distinction between the older and the newer elements in the population gradually broke down under the stress of foreign pressure, and how the superior military qualities of the Israelites enabled them to establish themselves as an aristocracy among their neighbours, so that in time of danger it was naturally they who took the lead. We have observed the elements in Israelite life which made for strength, the tradition of a common ancestry and blood, the worship of a common deity in place of the multifarious Baals of Canaanite times, the wild vigour which they showed in battle, and the extension of the political unit (albeit with the loosest type of organization) to the larger group of the tribe, instead of the city. We have noted the fact that the new-comers were able to impose their own racial and tribal traditions on the mixed race of which they now formed a part, and how they, in return, received from their predecessors much lore in cosmology, a legal code, methods of agriculture, and a religious system. It is noteworthy that they did not adopt the deities they found in the land,[1] but substituted Yahweh at all the sanctuaries of the ancient Baals, probably identifying Him with them.[2] So doing, they made what was, after all, their chief contribution to the life of the people.

[1] This is the impression we receive from the Biblical narrative, but it may be necessary to leave a loop-hole for ourselves. In the Elephantine papyri, which date from the fifth century, we find more than one other deity worshipped alongside of Yahweh. These extra gods (and a goddess) bear Semitic, not Egyptian names, and it may be that they came into Egypt with the Jews who settled on Yeb. If so, it is difficult to avoid the conclusion that they were worshipped in Palestine also, and we must ascribe the absence of their names from the literature to a scrupulous purification by later scribes. It may be remarked that these additional deities include Anath, who was apparently an ancient Syrian war goddess (cp. S. A. Cook, *The Religion of Ancient Palestine in the light of Archaeology*, pp. 104 ff. [1930]). As probable seats of her worship we may mention Anathoth and the Beth-Anath mentioned in Jud. i. 33 as resisting Naphtali (cp. Garstang, *Joshua and Judges*, pp. 243–5). Cp. also vol. ii, pp. 161 ff.

[2] Professor A. C. Welch holds that the Ba'als continued to be worshipped at their old shrines, while the cult of Yahweh was carried on only at a limited number of sanctuaries. Discussion is not possible here; suffice it to say that, while the theory is illuminating and suggestive, the balance of evidence is in favour of the view taken above. See especially *The Code of Deuteronomy* (1924).

We enter now on the period in which this process of unification was carried to the greatest lengths it ever reached in Palestine, when there was not only a common race and a common religion, but a single centralized state. It is true that the unity was retained but for a short time, and that division then appeared; but the political disruption, strangely enough, had comparatively little effect on the national life,[1] and the men of the south continued to take an interest in the north, and to recognize the fundamental unity of the two sections. Amos, the first of the prophets whose work has come down to us in literary form, was a man of the far south, but his message was delivered to the northern kingdom, and as long as Samaria stood, Isaiah had much to say to her and about her. The ideal reconstructions, which later Israel so loved, always included the scattered tribes of the north, even though, as far as our evidence goes, they had long ceased to maintain their independent identity in the midst of the nations among whom they were settled. This sense of the oneness of Israel did not originate with the monarchy, but was enormously strengthened thereby, and without it might not have endured. Later ages looked forward to a reconstitution in which the divinely appointed king should be another David, combining under his rule all of the Israelite name.

The hundred years from 1050 to 950 B.C. presented a unique opportunity for the foundation of a single kingdom and the political unification of the state. The period marks the end of Egyptian domination. The last invasion of Palestine by a Pharaoh (before the rise of Assyria) was, as far as we know, that of Sheshonk in the reign of Rehoboam. A raid had been made on Gezer, in the interests of Solomon, by an earlier king, and these are the only two occasions on which we hear of Egypt taking any part in Palestinian affairs during the first half of the monarchical period. For Egypt had fallen on evil days. The attacks of Libyans and sea-peoples (Philistines and others) in the early days of the twentieth dynasty had been repulsed, but with difficulty, and they exhausted the resources of the country. For the most part her story is little more than a confused record of shadowy kings, of small warring principalities, and of a govern-

---

[1] As distinct from political organization. The relations between Israel and Judah down to the end of the eighth century present a curious mixture of unity and separation. See above, pp. 135 ff., and vol. ii, pp. 145 ff.

ment conducted primarily in the interests of the priests of Amon at Thebes. There were spasmodic revivals, and each dynasty in turn had at its initiation some vigorous action to its credit, but the strongest kings were now foreigners—Lybians or Ethiopians, and their hold on the country was commonly brief. The glory of Egypt had departed, and she was sinking rapidly towards that decay which was to be made manifest to the world once and for all at the fatal battle of Carchemish.[1]

To the east and north the world powers were equally helpless. The general collapse of empires, which accompanied the inroads of the northern peoples and the end of the Aegean age, had swept away the old Hittite empire for ever. Babylon was now subject to Assyria, and Assyria herself was just beginning to rise towards the heights she afterwards held. Ashur-nasir-pal, one of the first of her great emperors, extended his conquests to the Mediterranean, but his armies did not come so far south as Palestine. What Assyria needed was partly a supply of timber, and partly an outlet for her commerce, and she secured the former in the Lebanon and the latter in northern Syria, where she was within easy reach of Cyprus. It was not until the time of Shalmaneser III, in the middle of the ninth century, that any Assyrian king concerned himself with the south-western end of the Fertile Crescent.[2]

The stage was thus clear for the local tribes and races of Palestine to play out their own drama. There would be no interference from the outside, and the future lay with any one element in the population which could create, organize, and hold a centralized government over the land. At the moment the Philistines were supreme, and to all appearance they might remain so, especially in the absence of any external invader of importance. But they could not keep that which they had won. We have not enough detailed knowledge of them to be sure of the causes of their failure—or at least of those features of their character and polity which made for failure. It may have been due to their comparatively small numbers, or there may have been divisions among their own ranks,[3] or again it may be that they made no serious attempt to organize and unify their conquests, but depended, as Egypt and Assyria did after her, on

---

[1] 605 B.C. [2] See above, p. 11.
[3] The five cities were always independent of one another; Gath, in particular, seems to have been at times pro-Israelite. See also pp. 192, 210.

scattered garrisons, supported by occasional demonstrations of military force.

But if we cannot appraise the internal weakness of the Philistine power, we can form a fairly accurate judgement of the forces which confronted and ultimately dispossessed it of the larger part of its territory. It was the native population which rose against the latest immigrants and drove them back to the coast-lands; they were checked by the peoples whom they had defeated in battle, and for a time kept on the level of subjects, almost of slaves. And it cannot be too strongly insisted, or too often repeated, that the element in the native population which gave it strength to accomplish its purpose was that Aramaean blood, tradition, and outlook which Israel had contributed to the common stock. The Hebrews alone brought a sense of unity into the land. They alone had traditions of a common descent. They alone maintained something of that democratic ideal of society which gave to each man a personal dignity and responsibility; they alone provided the strongest of all unifying forces, a common religion.

It falls to us now to attempt to trace what were the steps by which Israel succeeded in establishing a unified state in Palestine, and so created a people who, alone of the ancient nations, have preserved their national identity to this day. We must see how the first revolt against the foreign power was carried at length to a successful issue, in spite of early failure. We must watch the effort put forth, with temporary success, by a man of the highest genius, to unite discordant elements in the people and to overcome the centrifugal tendency which seemed, till his day, to be inherent in the Israelite character. We must try to estimate the greatness of the kingdom thus formed, and see, too, how David's successors, lacking his political wisdom, followed a course which inevitably led to disruption. Yet even so, the task of fusion had been carried through so completely that, in spite of the division of the kingdom, a certain sense of national unity remained, and the two kingdoms, by the middle of the ninth century, reached a height of culture and of power which hardly David had attained.

Our subject, then, naturally falls into two main sections: (a) the establishment of the monarchy, comprising the reigns of Saul, David, and Solomon, (b) the history of the divided kingdom down to the time when the Assyrians stand on the threshold, and are about to enter into the political life of Palestine.

Our sources of information are derived almost entirely from the Biblical records. There is one inscription at Karnak, dating from the reign of Sheshonk, which throws light on the early days of the disruption, and we have the famous inscription of Mesha, king of Moab, from near the end of the period. Other evidence can be derived from archaeology, the discoveries at Megiddo and at Samaria being of primary importance. Our Biblical evidence is contained in the books of *Samuel* and *Kings*, with some doubtful additions from *Chronicles*. But the extent to which this latter compilation can be used as an authority independent of *Samuel* and *Kings* is very uncertain. There may be traditions preserved which have escaped the earlier writers, and their silence must not be held to be, in itself, adequate ground for rejecting any narrative; but the Chronicler's work, as a whole, is to be regarded as an idealized history, written from the point of view held by orthodox Judaism of the fourth century B.C., and additions and discrepancies must be regarded with some suspicion.

In the other books, however, we have material which is often of the highest value. The compilers had at their disposal a number of contemporary records, including the official court documents from the time of David onwards. These seem to have undergone little modification, except that they have been abbreviated—less in the reign of David than elsewhere, with the result that we have a clearer picture of his career than of any of his successors. There are also extracts clearly taken from the archives of the Temple, which are of particular value for one side of the life of Israel, passages from some kind of collection of the lives of the prophets, especially from the lives of Elijah and Elisha, which are profoundly important as giving the point of view, not of the government, but of the common people. Such evidence of popular feeling and conditions is almost without parallel in the ancient world.

A. THE UNITED MONARCHY

Chapter IX

SAUL

SUMMARY

[The yoke of the Philistines does not seem to have been heavy, and though their cattle were to be found in the central range, they governed the country mainly by means of single officers and small garrisons. The element which was most dissatisfied with their rule is to be seen in the ecstatic prophets of Yahweh. To this class belonged Saul, son of Kish. His first exploit was the relief of Jabesh-gilead, besieged by Ammonites. His son Jonathan assassinated a Philistine official, and a strong force was sent into the hills. On the other side, Saul organized an army of some kind, but there seemed little hope of success until Jonathan's exploit at Michmash led to a total defeat of the Philistines and a clearing of the central range. His defeat of the Amalekites further established his power, and in him we have the first real king of Israel.

The Philistines continued, however, their attempts to recover the ground they had lost, and in connexion with one of their efforts David first appeared. But his success, here and later, aroused the jealousy of Saul, and the consequent division in the Israelite ranks ultimately weakened him and his people so much that the Philistines were able to recover their ascendancy. The final battle took place at Mount Gilboa, where Saul and several of his sons perished, and Israel was utterly defeated. Once more the Philistine triumph seemed complete.

Saul's kingdom was not highly organized, though he had something like a standing army, and seems to have exacted tribute from his subjects. But for the real administrative organization, Israel had to wait till the time of David.]

As has already been remarked, the Philistines seem to have employed the imperial methods in use by the Egyptians before them, with this modification, that we find little evidence of their permitting the existence of local kingdoms or principalities.[1] They established garrisons, and appointed (it seems) local commissioners of some kind, but trusted mainly to the disarmament of the population for the security of their power, interfering but little with the ordinary life of the people. They made, as far as we know, little or no attempt to extend their

---

[1] They do seem, however, to have acquiesced in the divided kingdom after the death of Saul.

authority beyond the Jordan, being content to hold western Palestine. As long as he observed the authority of the Philistines, the ordinary Israelite was free to go about his own affairs, to till his own fields, and to manage his local village business. We should never suspect, on reading the records of the early days of Saul, that the country was under a foreign government or, indeed, under any government at all. Yet we know that all the while the Philistine power was in the background, and that its forces could be employed at any time when it seemed necessary to maintain its position, while in some districts Philistines had so far settled as to maintain their own flocks and herds.[1]

The average Israelite might have been content to acquiesce in the conditions prevalent. But there was one element in their national life which would be satisfied with nothing less than complete independence. This was the class of religious enthusiasts known as the *Nebi'im*, or prophets. As far as our evidence takes us, it would seem that this type of enthusiast was not original in Israel, but was characteristic of Canaanite religion before the Hebrews entered the country. Their peculiar feature was an ecstatic condition, in which men lost the normal control of themselves. The attacks might manifest themselves in violent activity, in wild tossing of the limbs, in contortions and strange movements, which tended to become rhythmical, especially when a number were together. In some ways they resembled the 'dancing dervishes' who appeared many centuries afterwards in Islam, though there is no sign of their presence in early Arabia. At a later time these manifestations were to be observed over the whole of the Mediterranean world, but nearly always in the devotees of a few particular deities, Apollo, Dionysus, or the Asiatic Mother goddess. Where they are found in the servants of other gods or goddesses, their presence is generally to be ascribed to syncretism,[2] and this seems to have

---

[1] Cp. 1 Sam. xiv. 32.

[2] Herodotus observed certain Carians in Egypt given to ecstatic behaviour in the worship of Isis, and expressly remarks that this betrays their foreign origin. The best account we have of them comes from Apuleius, where the goddess is again Isis, no doubt assimilated to the Asiatic Mother goddess. The Apollo priestesses at Delphi and Cumae are further instances, and Euripides' presentation of the Bacchants illustrates the phenomenon in the cult of Dionysus. In all cases it can be traced back to Syria or Asia Minor, and the earliest mention we have comes from the report of Wen-Amon in the eleventh century, where it occurs at Byblos. Except in the late story of the seventy elders, we have no reference to the true Nabi' during the nomad period of Israel's history, and it seems clear that the prophetic ecstasy

been true of the Israelite prophets. They were not, however, devotees of Baal, but of Yahweh, and since the ecstatic state was infectious and was enhanced not only by the use of certain drugs and by music, but also by association with others subject to it, they used to go about the country in wild bands, stirring up the people to fidelity to Yahweh, and urging them to action where His name was likely to be brought into disrepute. It seems that their morals were not above reproach, and their social standing was low, but they were respected and listened to, as the mouthpiece of their God. The combination of a high degree of sanctity with a low ethical and social standard is not uncommon in oriental religions, and, little as these men appeal to us to-day, it cannot be denied that in their own age they played a part of primary importance in the development both of the religious and of the political history of Israel. It is to them that we must ascribe one of the strongest impulses to independence in the days of the Philistine occupation.[1]

It was to the class of ecstatic prophets that Saul[2] belonged. We have in 1 Sam. ix f. the story of his being anointed by Samuel, whom he has met more or less by accident in the course of a search for his father's asses.[3] The Seer tells Saul of the high destiny in store for him and indicates several signs by which he may be sure that the prediction will be fulfilled. The last of

was one of the elements of Canaanite religion which Israel adopted after the conquest. For a full discussion cp. T. H. Robinson, 'Baal in Hellas', *Classical Quarterly*, xi (1917), pp. 201 ff.; *Prophecy and the Prophets in Ancient Israel*, ch. 3 (1923), and especially Hölscher, *Die Propheten*, ch. 3 (1914).

[1] It should, perhaps, be remarked that our earliest sources describe Samuel, not as a Nabi', but as a Seer, a class of men possessed of second sight, but not subject to the wilder manifestations of the ecstasy. Indeed, in 1 Sam. ix. 9 (a later gloss) he seems to be clearly, almost sharply, distinguished from the professional prophet.

[2] Lods (*Israël*, p. 411) makes the interesting suggestion that the story of Samuel's childhood really belongs to Saul. This theory, it is true, explains Saul's name, but involves changes in very many details. Cf. also Cheyne in *EB.*, col. 4,303.

[3] We have two accounts of the appointment of Saul, one in 1 Sam. ix. 1—x. 16, the other in 1 Sam. viii, x. 17 ff. The latter is clearly a continuation of that element in chs. i–vii, which makes Samuel the theocratic Judge, and regards the monarchy as an act of apostasy. In the former, Samuel is a seer with a good local reputation, but is not widely known; it appears that Saul has never heard of him before, and his servant has picked up only some local gossip and does not seem to know his name. Samuel, as one of the great figures of early Israel, is presented to us in more than one capacity, as Judge, as Seer, as Priest. On any hypothesis he played an important part in the foundation of the kingdom, but, as far as we can judge, the earliest presentation of him was as Seer, and the other aspects are later interpretations. It was natural that a number of stories should gather round the personality of the real founder of the Israelite monarchy.

these is that, as he nears his home at Gibeah, he will meet a company of prophets coming down from the high place and will be infected with their Spirit. Thereafter he may trust to this Spirit for guidance in action. What Samuel foretold comes to pass, much to the surprise of Saul's kinsmen and fellow-townsmen, and for the rest of his life, for good or evil, he is liable to attacks of the ecstasy.

Saul's first chance came, not from any incident in western Palestine, but from Transjordania.[1] The city of Jabesh-gilead was attacked by Ammonites, and its inhabitants secured permission to try to get help from their brethren across the Jordan; if it did not come within three days, they would submit to a shameful mutilation in token of their submission to Ammon. Messengers were sent through all Israel, and they reached Gibeah[2] and told their story just as Saul came in from ploughing. At once the Spirit 'rushed'[3] upon him, he hewed the oxen in pieces and sent them, like a fiery cross, through all Israel. The rendezvous was at Bezek, on the eastern slope of the central range, whence Jabesh-gilead is almost visible on the opposite hills. By clever strategy Saul utterly defeated the Ammonites, and liberated the imperilled city.

The importance of this victory was very great. It showed Israel that there was a man among them who was capable of taking up the mantle of the old Judges, one inspired of the Spirit, who could fight and win battles for Israel. In future, men would look to Saul as the natural leader of the people, and would recognize in him the divinely-appointed champion of Yahweh and of Israel against their foes. But there was also another

---

[1] Lods (*Israël*, p. 411) finds it difficult to believe that this is Saul's first exploit, and sees reason to doubt many of the details. His chief reason (though not the only one) is that the Philistines would hardly have permitted such an expedition to take place. But, as we have seen, our information does not suggest that their authority was rigorously imposed, until Israel broke definitely into revolt with Jonathan's murder of a Philistine officer. Disarmament probably seemed to be as much as was necessary. To the modern mind the idea of an army without weapons is a contradiction in terms, but more than once the forces of Israel won victories with primitive weapons—stones and clubs. Probably the decisive factor was the rush of a frenzied mob which drove the enemy to flee in panic, and the actual slaughter took place only during the pursuit, when the Israelites would pick up and use any arms the fugitives threw away.

[2] For ancient Gibeah (probably not the same as Geba), as revealed by excavations, see Vincent, 'Fouilles américaines à Tell-el-Foul', in *RB.*, 1923, pp. 426–30; also Desnoyers, *HPH.* ii. 53 ff.

[3] 1 Sam. xi. 6; צָלַח, the technical term for the access of the prophetic Spirit.

aspect of the case. Saul secured the permanent gratitude of the men of Jabesh-gilead, and, indeed, of a large district to the east of Jordan. In after days this was the real stronghold of his house, and in the coming struggle with the Philistines he had secured a base on which he could fall back, outside the territory which they controlled. Once again we note the part played by Israel 'across Jordan', and realize something of the importance of the double settlement. This is the first time that the east has played an important part in the history of the land as a whole, but it will not be the last, and throughout the period now before us we must not lose sight of the fundamental unity of the people, whether to the west or to the east.

Saul's first clash with the Philistines took place at Michmash, and the hero of the story is his son Jonathan. In Saul's own city of Geba or Gibeah there was a Philistine official,[1] who may have had a small bodyguard with him. This man was attacked and killed by Jonathan, and his action lit the train which led to widespread revolt. At once the summons was sent out by Saul, and the men of Israel gathered to him at Gilgal. The spot was probably chosen because it lay near the fords of the Jordan, and offered an easy line of retreat to a country independent of the Philistine power and wholly devoted to Saul. News came quickly to the Philistine authorities,[2] and a force was sent into the mountains.[3] It stationed itself at Michmash, a strong position on the road leading up from the plain of Jericho, which would cut off communication between the Israelite army and the central hills. The immediate result was a panic in the Israelite camp. Many of those who were at Gilgal deserted and crossed the river, for they were unarmed and unused to discipline; the general inhabitants took refuge in caves and dens. Saul, with six hundred men who remained with him, made his way to Geba, two or three miles south of, and above, Michmash. The Philistines were bent on punishment, and sent out three

[1] This seems to be the meaning of the word נציב here (1 Sam. xiii. 3) and in x. 5, cp. H. P. Smith, *Samuel*, pp. 68, 69; Budde, *Samuel*, p. 67, where the suggestion is made that he was the overseer of tribute.

[2] In 1 Sam. xiii. 3 the text is certainly corrupt, though a satisfactory reconstruction is not so obvious. For suggestions cp. Smith and Budde, *ad loc.*

[3] We can hardly suppose that it was exactly that which is described in 1 Sam. xiii. 5, for chariots could not manœuvre in the hills, and, when we next hear of them, the people at Michmash constitute a small garrison, not the large camp of an army. The verse may be a later insertion, and the 'post' at Michmash may have been a part of the regular Philistine establishment.

bands of raiders to ravage the countryside, one to the north, one to the east, and one to the west, leaving only a small garrison at Michmash.

So matters stood for a time, until one day Jonathan was seized with a wild spirit of adventure, and proposed to his squire that they should make some attempt on the Philistine garrison, in the absence of the raiding parties. Between Michmash on the north and Geba on the south stood two pinnacles of rock, and it was not until they had passed these that the two Hebrews became visible to the garrison.[1] The story goes that the audacity of the two men aroused the amusement of the Philistines, and they challenged them to climb the crag to the fort. Accepting this as an omen, Jonathan and his squire scrambled up the cliff, and fell upon the Philistines, Jonathan striking them down as they came within his reach, and his squire behind him despatching the wounded. About twenty were killed in the narrow space, and those who escaped fell into the arms of one of the returning raiding bands and threw them also into a panic.

Geba was too far away for details of the fight to be visible, but the retreating mob caught the eye of the watchman. Saul began to consult the Ephod,[2] but the true state of the case became so clear that he did not carry out his intention, and called all those who were with him to the pursuit. News of what was happening spread quickly, and Israelites began to swarm from all quarters. Some had taken service with the Philistines, and these now turned against their employers. Unarmed as they were, the Israelites came in such numbers as to complete the rout, seizing, perhaps, such weapons as the enemy dropped. Flight and pursuit swept over the hills, past Bethel and past Beth-horon, down the valley of Aijalon, till the survivors of the Philistine host were scattered over the plain.[3]

Two incidents are recorded as connected with this victory. One is the establishment of an altar—a single great stone—by Saul, in order that the people who in their hunger had fallen on the spoil, might duly present the blood to Yahweh. This is important for the history of the cultus, since no objection is taken either to Saul's making the altar or to the people's sacrificing there in the open field.[4] The other

---

[1] Cp. Driver, *Notes on the Hebrew Text of the Books of Samuel*[2] (1913), p. 106 with map opposite.

[2] So, rightly, the text of the LXX in xiv. 18.   [3] 1 Sam. xiv. 4–23.

[4] 1 Sam. xiv. 32–5. The simple rite may be held to represent one of the earliest forms of Semitic sacrifice, viz. the disposal of the blood as a mysterious fluid.

narrative tells us how Jonathan, having unwittingly transgressed the taboo laid on food by Saul, is condemned to death, but is saved by the people. The narrative implies that an animal was offered in his place, and we have an early instance of a surrogate for a human victim.[1]

This victory recovered the hill country for Israel, and restored the people to a sense of independence. It also had the effect of securing the throne to Saul, who henceforward was recognized as the king of Israel. For the time his authority was certainly limited, extending no farther north than the plain of Esdraelon, if so far, and bounded on the south by the Jerusalem district, though the narratives assume that he had free access to the Judahite lands. To the west the Israelites were not yet in possession of the Shephelah, but the territory to the east of Jordan was included in the dominions of Saul. All his life he was engaged in a struggle against the Philistines, with peaceful intervals, but seems to have recovered little further ground except in the Shephelah. The idealized account in 1 Sam. xiv. 47 speaks of conquests of Edom, Moab, and Aramaean kings, but in the absence of any details this statement must be regarded as an anticipation of the achievements of his successors.

We have no reason to doubt Saul's conquest of the Amalekites.[2] He must have had free passage through the hills to the south, for this people belongs properly to the region between Palestine and Egypt. The story is best known for the breach which it produced between Samuel and Saul, a breach which originated as far back as before the battle of Michmash. In failing to slay Agag and destroy the cattle of Amalek on the spot, Saul was guilty of a violation of the taboo, and the result was the loss of his sense of the aid and support of Yahweh. Though in a sense the rupture with Samuel belonged rather to his personal life than to the history of Israel, it had nevertheless a serious effect on the national cause.

From this point onwards, the story of Saul's reign is not to be understood without reference to two personal factors of importance, not wholly disconnected from one another. The first is the gradual change which took place in the man himself. As our narrative stands, this is bound up with his relation to Samuel, who represents the pure, theocratic, aspect of Israelite political theory. From this standpoint, Saul is king, but always subject

---

[1] 1 Sam. xiv. 24–30, 36–45.   [2] 1 Sam. xv.

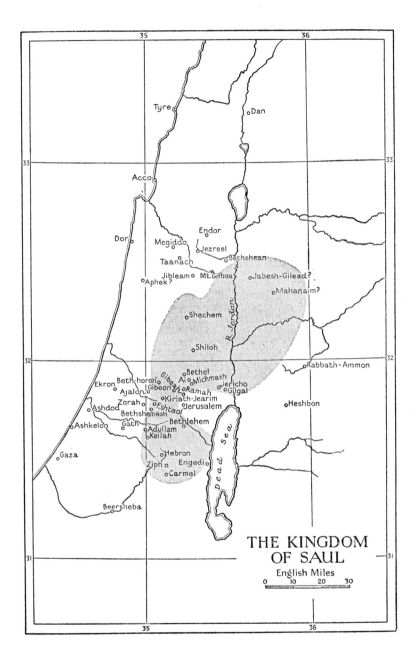

THE KINGDOM
OF SAUL

English Miles

0   10   20   30

to the spiritual power, represented by Samuel, and he must obey and give due honour to the great Seer. The first sign of trouble appears even before the battle of Michmash,[1] when Saul, finding himself in a desperate situation, can wait no longer for Samuel, and insists on offering sacrifice himself. The second and more serious is connected with the Amalekite war. That is undertaken at the behest of Samuel, as the mouthpiece of Yahweh, and Saul's failure to carry out the taboo placed on Amalek leads to a final breach between the two, though Samuel continues to recognize Saul formally as king.

These passages offer an official and theological explanation of a change in Saul which is only too well attested elsewhere. From the first he has been a 'Nabi' ', a person possessed by the Spirit of Yahweh, and liable to sudden attacks of ecstasy. In I Sam. xvi. 14 it is stated that the Spirit of Yahweh has departed from Saul, and an evil Spirit from Yahweh troubles him. This is a later way of saying that the Spirit (for in the early Hebrew belief there is only one Spirit of Yahweh) has ceased to be a help to him, and has become his bane. Saul still 'prophesies',[2] but the prophetic frenzy no longer leads him to feats of valour on behalf of Israel; rather it induces in him conduct which is at best trivial and at worst criminal. Modern psychopathology may well have an explanation for the facts of the ecstasy, and will understand how, when once the primary inspiration is gone from it, the patient may be driven to the opposite extreme. But to the ancient world the explanation must be theological, for all abnormal psychic states were due to the direct action of a

---

[1] The narratives of I Samuel from ch. xi. onwards seem to have been constructed from several different sources, and present a very complicated problem. While in certain respects some agreement between commentators has been reached, that agreement is far from being complete, as may be seen by reference to H. P. Smith, *Samuel (ICC.)*, pp. xxii–xxvi (1899); Budde, *Samuel (KHC.)*, pp. xii–xxi (1897); Nowack, *Die Bücher Samuelis (HK.)* (1902), pp. xiv–xxv, xxx–xxxv); Kennedy, *I and 2 Samuel (Cent. Bib.)*, pp. 13–26, to select four typical modern commentators. Perhaps it should be recognized that, whatever the intermediate stages in the construction of the book, we have behind them all lives of the three main characters, Samuel, Saul, David. These, of course, overlap, and in each mention is made of the subjects of the others—no life of Saul could be written without reference to both Samuel and David. Within each we may find variant traditions, e.g. in the introduction of David to Saul, where there are clearly two narratives, and both belong to a life of David. For the practical purpose of the study of Israel's history, there is little to choose between the stories belonging to a biography of Saul and those which are more concerned with David. The Samuel passages, on the other hand, seem to be written from the standpoint of a religious theory which is probably of later development in Israel than the rest. [2] I Sam. xviii. 10, xix. 24.

superhuman power, and Israel's historians—probably also Saul himself—saw in the change that had taken place in him the evidence of the anger and hostility of Yahweh. The other factor is the appearance and rise of David. There are two accounts,[1] mutually inconsistent, of David's introduction to Saul. Both, however, bring him to the battle of the Vale of Elah and show him as the hero who wins the victory for Israel on that day. One of them connects his coming with Saul's condition, and states that he was brought to the king because of his musical ability. The connexion between music and ecstatic possession is clearly attested elsewhere,[2] and the power that could arouse the spirit could also control and quiet it. Saul is not only refreshed and soothed by David's playing, but is charmed by his personality, and makes him his squire. According to the other account, David is quite unknown to Saul and his officers until he comes with a message from his father to his brothers, hears the challenge of Goliath, and goes out to fight him—apparently without meeting Saul till the Philistine is dead. We have also in ch. xvi. 1–13 an account of the anointing of David, which properly belongs rather to the Samuel group of narratives.

Whichever form of tradition we prefer up to the incident of David's duel with Goliath,[3] after that point the general trend of

---

[1] 1 Sam. xvi. 17–23 and 1 Sam. xvii. 1—xviii. 5, the latter passage including elements which belong to a continuation of the former. The analysis here followed is that of Eissfeldt, cp. *Die Komposition der Samuelisbücher*, pp. 11 ff., 57 (1931).

[2] e.g. 1 Sam. x. 5, 2 Kgs. iii. 15.

[3] In 2 Sam. xxi. 19 we have the record of the slaughter of 'Goliath of Gath, the staff of whose spear was like a weaver's beam', not by David, but by 'Elhanan, the son of Jaare-oregim, the Bethlehemite'. Naturally this has aroused serious doubts in the minds of many commentators. Were there two Goliaths? This is hardly probable. Was it Elhanan (see further, pp. 212, 231) or was it David that slew him? The natural tendency of tradition is to glorify the familiar figure by ascribing all possible feats to him, not to take his actions (unless they are discreditable!) and assign them to a nonentity. The death of Goliath is the only title Elhanan had to fame, and the probability of his having been the original hero is so strong as to amount to practical certainty. Most commentators, therefore, have assumed that the whole story of Goliath has been transferred from Elhanan to David, and then considerably elaborated. It is possible that the process of elaboration has continued beyond the writing of the books of *Samuel* in their original form, for xvii. 12–31, 41, xvii. 55—xviii. 5 are omitted by the LXX, leaving a clearer and more straightforward account. The suggestion is that the LXX represents the earlier form of text, which the Palestinian tradition has expanded (but see Driver, *Notes on the Hebrew Text of the Books of Samuel*, pp. 149–51). The prevailing view is, perhaps, best represented by Stade, *GVI*. i. 227 ff., where other grounds for suspecting the originality of the Goliath-David story are stated. But a solution, ingenious and on

events is clear. David, young as he was, developed into a great warrior, and was given a high position in Saul's army. His wonderful personal charm attracted the whole people, including Saul's own heroic son, Jonathan.[1] At the same time his signal success aroused Saul's jealousy, and he did his best to make away with the younger man, by one means or another. This part of the story is told entirely from the standpoint of David, and it goes on to tell how he was compelled to flee for his life from Saul's court, how he escaped, according to one story,[2] through a trick of his wife's; according to another, through the good offices of Jonathan;[3] how he secured help by a trick from the priests of Nob,[4] thereby bringing down on them the vengeance of Saul;[5] and, finally, how he established himself in the southern 'wilderness' as the leader of a band of brigands.[6] Saul made various attempts to secure and kill him, but David always escaped, and on two occasions[7] (possibly the same event recorded in different sources) exhibited great magnanimity in sparing the life of Saul when the king was in his power. Finally, he took refuge with Achish, king of Gath.[8]

We could wish that we had the story as written from Saul's point of view. If we had, we should probably see the young warrior, receiving every benefit from the king, including the hand of his own daughter, yet seeking to undermine his influence and ultimately to supersede him. It would be clear to us that the distraction in Saul's mind and the division among his people were among the main causes of his fall and final defeat. It may be true that David was not actually among the armies of the Philistines which destroyed Saul, but he had been for some time in the service of the Philistine king, and he was in command

the whole satisfactory, has been proposed by Kennedy (*Samuel*, p. 122), who points out that in 1 Sam. xvii the name of Goliath occurs only in verse 4, and that even there it is parenthetic. He therefore proposes to omit the name, and holds that the giant slain by David was anonymous. Even if it still be held that the story is not historical, Kennedy's solution would get rid of a discrepancy which must surely have been noticed by a compiler, though a copyist might easily overlook it. The same view is held by Desnoyers, cp. *HPH.* ii. 82 n. Further, he suggests that the original text may be represented by LXX[B], according to which David may already have been known to Saul. More probably, however, the narrative in this text has been mutilated in order to remove the obvious discrepancy. For other views, including that which identifies David with Elhanan, cf. S. A. Cook, *CAH.* ii, pp. 393 f.

[1] Cp. e.g. 1 Sam. xviii. 1.
[2] 1 Sam. xix. 11–17.   [3] 1 Sam. xx.   [4] 1 Sam. xxi. 1–9.
[5] 1 Sam. xxii. 6–19.   [6] 1 Sam. xxii. 1–2.   [7] 1 Sam. xxiv, xxvi. 5–25.
[8] 1 Sam. xxi. 10–15, xxvii. 2 ff.—possibly variant traditions of the same event.

of a force which might have turned the day against the enemy. In considering the later life and the death of Saul, we must not lose sight of the fact that the quarrel with David—whatever be its cause, and whoever was to blame—meant disruption and weakness, and contributed in no small degree to the king's downfall.

With these considerations in the backgound, we can return to the story of Saul as it affects more directly the history of the whole people. We hear from time to time of wars against the Philistines, in some of which David plays a leading part.[1] Only two great battles, however, are described; the first is the battle in the Vale of Elah, where the victory was won by David's slaughter of Goliath. The effect of this must have been considerable. The site, near Socoh, is in one of the valleys that lead up into the Judaean hills, where the mountain range is beginning to give way to the Shephelah. It seems that the pursuit carried Israel well down into the plain, and it is clear that, for a time, much of the low-lying country was recovered for Israel. But, though we have no account of actual engagements, the Philistines gradually worked their way back. In particular, it appears that they had never been driven out from the northern territory which they had occupied, and the plain of Esdraelon was in their hands through the whole of Saul's reign. It was, in fact, from that point that the final attack was made. We may suspect that the Philistines used Beth-shean as the base of their operations, and, having failed to penetrate the hills from the west, had decided to try the route directly southwards through the Ephraimite hill country, where the passes are harder to defend and lead to a fairly easy road. There is, in fact, no line which can be safely held against a superior invading force between the plain of Esdraelon and Jerusalem,[2] for the country leads up through a series of small plains separated by low ridges into the tableland of Judah.

The main body of the Philistine army, then, made its way from the coastal plains into the plain of Esdraelon. There are

---

[1] Cp. not only the story of Goliath in 1 Sam. xvii, but also such references as xviii. 27, xix. 8.

[2] Cp. G. A. Smith, *HGHL.*, ch. xii, where the absence of a 'scientific frontier' between Judah and Samaria is clearly brought out. Some of the most successful invaders of Judah (e.g. Sennacherib, cp. p. 396) followed this route, and we need not doubt that it was this which the Philistines sought to use in their reconquest of the country.

three main routes across the Carmel range. That which lies most to the south-east is, strictly speaking, not across the range at all, but through the plain of Dothan which separates Carmel from the central hills. North and west of this is the famous pass to Megiddo, while the third, less easy, is nearer still to the sea, and is guarded at its outlet by Jokneam. While many of the details are obscure, it is hardly likely that the Philistines used the first; it was probably too open to attack from the hills, and the Philistines would wish to concentrate before having to fight a pitched battle. Beth-shean was available as one base of operations, while the main body probably gained access to the plain through Megiddo. It is clear, however, that the great concentration of their troops was in the plain, to the north or north-west of Gilboa.

Our knowledge of the fatal battle in which Saul met his end is derived from I Sam. xxviii–xxxi. Literary criticism of this difficult passage[1] seems to lead us to a reconstruction of the events much as follows. The first great gathering of the Philistines was at Shunem, where the main body, advancing from the south-west, was reinforced by troops from Beth-shean. David, who had followed his immediate overlord, Achish, fell under the suspicion of the other Philistines, and was dismissed, while the main force moved from Shunem to Jezreel. Saul and his men took ground on the lower slopes to the north-west of Gilboa, whence they could watch the larger movements which were made in the plain below them, and cover the road into the hills at any point where the enemy might seek to force an entrance. But Saul, in desperation, made his way to Endor, where he consulted a famous necromancer, who summoned the ghost of Samuel, but all he received was the assurance of his doom. The Philistines made no long delay, but, with archers and chariots, followed the easier slopes up into the hills from Jezreel and the west. They drove back the Israelites, fighting desperately, to the higher ground, where, it seems, the wheeled vehicles were compelled to give up the struggle, and the battle was continued by the archers. First Saul's sons and then the king himself were slain. As to the manner of his death we seem to have two traditions, that given to us in I Sam. xxxi. 4, according to which he committed suicide in despair, and that of 2 Sam. i. 2–10. In the latter passage an Amalekite came to David to tell him that it

---

[1] See Additional Note B, pp. 197 ff.

was he who had killed Saul, at the king's own command. There is no suggestion in the story that the messenger is not speaking the truth, and we have probably an alternative account of the way in which Saul met his end. The day after the battle the Philistines were despoiling the slain, and came across the bodies of Saul and of his sons. The king's head was cut off and sent round the Philistine cities in token of victory. The royal armour was deposited in the temple of Ashtoreth, apparently in Beth-shean, while the headless trunk was hung on the walls of the city. From there it was rescued by the men of Jabesh-gilead, who thus piously requited the service that Saul had rendered to them in his early days.

The Philistine triumph seemed complete. The whole of the Ephraimite hill country lay open to them, and the record states that the cities were abandoned by the Israelites and left to the Philistines.[1] The plain of Esdraelon was theirs, and possibly also the land to the north, though, as we have no mention of Gali-laean tribes or localities (except Shunem), we can only con-jecture that they held this part of the land. Details of this second occupation are lacking; we have no formal mention of Philistine garrisons and officials, but we can hardly suppose it to have been less complete than the first. It is true that the victors appear to have made no attempt to cross the Jordan and subdue Bashan and Gilead. But they now held the whole of the great caravan route through Palestine, and, as it seems, could control the fords of the Jordan. We are not certain whether they occupied the plain of Jericho, and the references to David's early years as king in Hebron suggest that either they were less careful to garrison the country farther south or that they recognized him as a Philistine official. But these were comparatively small points for the time. To all appearance the Israelite attempt at independence had proved a complete failure, and the chains of foreign domination were riveted only the more firmly on the country.

There was thus again presented to the Philistines an oppor-tunity almost unique in the history of Palestine. There was a general stirring of the peoples, and the prize of world dominion lay ready for any power strong enough to seize and hold it. The old empires of Egypt and of the Hittites were no longer serious competitors; the former had been so weakened by the assaults of the Aegean peoples as to be glad to find themselves free from

[1] 1 Sam. xxxi. 7.

foreign invasion, while the movement which brought the Philistines into Palestine had swept the latter power away. Assyria,
though showing signs of vitality, was confined to northern
Mesopotamia, save in so far as she exercised a precarious
authority over Babylonia, and was making strong efforts to
form a durable northern frontier. Nowhere was there a power
of the first rank. Though the territory controlled by the Philistines was comparatively small, its central position should have
made it possible to extend north and south and east. Its people
possessed an advanced and ancient culture,[1] and were skilled
both on land and at sea. They would have needed some
centuries for their development, but, since they held the world's
greatest line of communication, they might have maintained
themselves against attacks from the outside until they had built
up a state internally strong, which, possibly, could have resisted
Assyria at her zenith.

One of the reasons for the ultimate failure of the Philistines may
be found in their own political organization, or lack of organization. The five cities maintained each its own autonomy, and
though they could and did act together in the face of a common
enemy, it seems that there was no complete harmony between
them. It is clear, for instance, that David was a vassal of Gath
rather than of the Philistine power in general, and even to a late
period in his reign he could rely on the fidelity of Gittite troops.
Gath was the smallest of the five towns, and lay nearest to the
central hills, where Israel was strongest in western Palestine, but
its failure to co-operate heartily with the other four must have
meant a serious rift within the Philistine community.

With this lack of a centralized authority we may, perhaps,
connect the Philistine methods of government. Our Biblical
narratives, coming as they do from Israelite sources, make no
clear distinction between the various states. The invaders are
grouped under a single name, and, on the surface, the record
suggests that they governed the country as a single unit.
But we have seen enough to realize that this impression is
unreliable, and that there was no real political unity among
them. They must have, in some way, partitioned the newly-won
land among themselves, and we find no trace of an organized
attempt to hold the country down. We may guess that in each

---

[1] It is a curious irony of fate that the term 'Philistine' should have come to mean
barbaric; in the eleventh century B.C. no race stood higher in culture.

case the dominant city was satisfied with the exaction of tribute in one form or another, and that, in other respects, the Philistines were not greatly concerned with the way in which the country was governed. The conflict between David and Abner implies freedom of movement for Israelite troops, and there seems to have been no interference with David or with Ishbaal until after the death of the latter. Then, it is true, David was recognized as dangerous, but it was too late, and he had already made good his footing, while his military skill enabled him to overthrow enemies who were his equals and, possibly, his superiors in equipment and man-power. The dominion of the Philistines was due, less to organized control, than to a vague and uncertain sense of their superiority, emphasized by a few garrisons and perhaps by sporadic raids. On such a basis no empire could be built up with any real prospect of durability.

The Philistine power was thus in no state to hold its own if faced by a clever and determined enemy. While Israel, divided by faction and seemingly helpless, seemed to have reached the nadir of her national life, there were yet elements within her whose vitality might be, and ultimately was, communicated to the whole body. To the east of Jordan, the family of Saul maintained itself under the nominal kingship of a son of Saul, Ishbaal,[1] but really under the power of Abner, who had escaped the slaughter of Mount Gilboa. Here we have an indication of the importance of that section of Israel which still remained on the semi-nomad plane of the social order. Just as, in the early days of Saul's struggle against the Philistines, the true Israel had found a refuge and a base to the east of the Jordan, so, after Saul had gone, the same districts supplied a home for one of the two factions into which the people were divided. Into the wilderness the Philistines were not prepared to press their conquests, and their failure to do so left a living root of Israelite life.

---

[1] It is generally agreed that this is the original form of the name, cp. 1 Chron. viii. 33, ix. 39. The form which now appears in the text of Samuel is due to the later horror of the name Baal, for which the pious Israelite substituted the word בשׁת—'shame'—even when it occurred in a proper name. It is interesting to observe that Saul and his age felt no objection to the word, and probably regarded it as a synonym for Yahweh. Whatever else Saul may or may not have been, he was a passionate devotee of Yahweh, especially in his younger days. We find also the name Meribaal (1 Chron. ix. 40, the Mephibosheth of 2 Sam. iv. 4, &c.) given to a son of Jonathan, and even David's family included a Baaliada (1 Chron. xiv. 7—Eliada in 2 Sam. v. 16). We cannot accuse David of apostasy!

We have comparatively little evidence of the organization of the kingdom in the days of Saul. In himself he occupies a middle position between the old Judge and the later King. The difference which marked the former off from the latter lay primarily in the fact that his authority was simply personal, and had its origin in a divine call given to him alone. It could not be transmitted to his descendants, and it did not entitle him to any formal or constitutional authority. It was manifested always in the first instance through a deliverance of the oppressed people, and it is best described, to quote an illuminating term used by Alt,[1] as 'charismatic'. The King, on the other hand, was a member of a recognized dynasty, and, even if he did not inherit his power from an ancestor, he expected to hand it on to his successor. His authority was based on popular approval, and in early times it seems to have been attested by the acclamation of the assembled people. Now Saul combined both these characteristics. He had the ecstatic *charisma*, and it was this which gave to him the opportunity of winning his initial victory for Israel at Jabesh-gilead. The steady pressure of the Philistines forced a more enduring régime on the people, and by the time he died, Saul's position had passed from that of the Judge to that of the King.

His power began with a military exploit, and the circumstances of his day made it imperative that he should maintain the character of a warrior. In so far as there was any organized system, it must have been that of an army. Apart from Jonathan we hear of a single military officer, Abner,[2] but he plays only a small part in the story till after the death of Saul. He is mentioned in one form of the story of David and Goliath,[3] as being present at the ceremonial meal which David used to test Saul's feelings to him,[4] and in 1 Sam. xxvi., where he is with Saul at the time when David spares the king's life, merely taking his spear and water-bottle. We suspect that his position is to be ascribed to a comparatively late period in the reign.

Before his death it is clear that Saul had something like a standing army. Its beginnings were very simple; whenever Saul

---

[1] *Die Staatenbildung der Israeliten in Palestina*, p. 9, &c.

[2] The narrative of 1 Sam. xvii. 18, with its mention of a שַׂר אֶלֶף, suggests a real military organization, but the term may be a reflection back from a later time.

[3] 1 Sam. xvii. 55.

[4] 1 Sam. xx. 25, in a passage which is probably later than the main body of the story.

saw a man whom he thought useful, he took him. Even before
the battle of Michmash we hear of a body of three thousand, of
whom one third were under the command of Jonathan.[1] But it
is clear that discipline was not strictly enforced—perhaps could
not be strictly enforced. In the dark days that preceded Jonathan's exploit nearly all Saul's force melted away, and no more
than six hundred still remained with him. The great slaughter
on that day was accomplished by the gathering of indiscriminate
masses from the hills, reinforced by Hebrews in Philistine
service, who reverted to their own people, and the crowd that
pursued the Philistines was in no sense an organized army. But
as time went on it seems that the army developed, and we
certainly get the impression that the force which faced the
Philistines in the Valley of Elah was better equipped and
arranged. Here, it is to be noted, we meet with Abner for the
first time in the story,[2] and the appearance of his name indicates
some degree of organization. But we are struck by the contrast
between the references to Saul's military establishment, and the
accounts we have of David's officers.

We have even less information as to the civil organization of
the kingdom. In the comparatively late account of the establishment of the monarchy[3] mention is made of certain 'sons of
Belial' who brought Saul no tribute, thereby suggesting that
such tribute was recognized as his due. But this may well be a
reflection back into Saul's days of the later practice. On the
other hand, there is a reference in 1 Sam. xxi. 7 to 'servants
of Saul', and especially to Doeg the Edomite, who was the
king's chief herdsman, implying that Saul had extensive
property.

Saul had no palace. Such evidence as we have points to a
continuous residence at his ancestral home at Gibeah, and he
remained a rustic sovereign all his days. There were times when
he needed to meet his officers, and he kept a certain state, with
his councillors—'servants'—about him. But there seems to have
been little formality in his proceedings. He would take his seat
by the 'high place',[4] under a tree, probably a tamarisk, which
was one of the sacred objects of the place, and in this al fresco

---

[1] 1 Sam. xiii. 2.
[2] The mention of Abner in 1 Sam. xiv. 50 f. is a reference to a later stage of
development.
[3] 1 Sam. x. 27.　　[4] Cp. 1 Sam. xxii. 6, reading with LXX בבמה for ברמה.

court would take counsel and give judgement. We hear of sacrificial meals, taken in full assembly on a sacred day, but the analogy of such a passage as 1 Sam. ix. 12 suggests that such meals were taken also at the high place. There is an attractive simplicity about the whole situation in such scenes which reminds us of the pictures of the Homeric kings.

Additional Note B

THE BATTLE OF MT. GILBOA

THERE are two subordinate narratives included in 1 Sam. xxviii-xxxi, the account of Saul's appeal to the witch of Endor (xxviii. 3–25), and that of David's dismissal from the Philistine army and of his vengeance on the Amalekites for the sack of Ziklag (xxix. 2—xxx. 31). Apart from these passages we have the following local references:

xxviii. 1–2 Gathering of the Philistines: place unnamed.

xxviii. 4 The Philistines encamp at Shunem; the Israelites on Gilboa.

xxix. 1 The Philistines are at Aphek; Israel at the Well in Jezreel.

xxix. 11b The Philistines have moved to Jezreel.

xxxi. Saul defeated and slain on Mount Gilboa.

There is a difference of opinion as to whether the narrative forms in the main a continuous whole (e.g. Budde, though with important modifications), or whether it is drawn from different sources. Holders of the latter view (e.g. H. P. Smith, Löhr, Nowack) agree in assigning chs. xxix and xxx to a single source, with modifications in detail. Budde, followed by G. A. Smith (*HGHL.*, pp. 400 ff.), places xxviii. 3–25 between chs. xxx and xxxi. His main reasons are (*a*) that the narrative of xxxi assumes that Saul's consultation of the witch took place on the night before the fatal battle, (*b*) that in xxviii. 4 the Philistines (at Shunem) have advanced some distance beyond the position assigned to them in xxix. 1 (Aphek). Apart from the fact that this is a serious dislocation of the text, which requires very strong grounds for its acceptance, this theory assumes a known site for the Aphek mentioned in xxix. 1. And any theory which involves a single source is open to the objection that the mobilization of the Philistines is mentioned three times, in xxviii. 1, xxviii. 4, and in xxix. 1. This may imply the addition of reinforcements at two of the three places indicated, but the greater probability is that the phrase is used of the gathering of troops at the opening of the campaign. If the narrative is a continuous whole, the only verse where the term is in place is xxviii. 1. Analysis may be difficult, if not impossible, or we may have (especially in xxviii. 4) the accidental insertion of a verse drawn from an account of the battle which has not otherwise survived. But it seems unlikely that these three notices came from the same original narrative. On the other hand, there is no reason to suspect the connexion between xxviii. 2 and xxix. 2, assumed by practically all students of the text, though most make the mistake of prefixing xxviii. 2 to xxix. 1, which, as we have seen, gives an awkward and unusual sense to the term used for mobilization, and Budde's explanation, or rather defence, is hardly justified by the parallels he quotes.

The geographical difficulties are as great as those of criticism. The notice in xxix. 1, which states that the Philistines mobilized at Aphek, while the Israelites encamped at the Well of Jezreel, is confusing. We cannot identify either of the places named. We have already had mention of a battle at Aphek, which seems to have lain at the entrance to one of the valleys leading up from the Shephelah into the Ephraimite hills—certainly far from the scene of Saul's final campaign. There appears to have been a place named Aphek in the plain of Sharon, covering the entries both to Dothan and to the pass of Megiddo, and several commentators (e.g. Budde) assume that this is the place intended. Others (e.g. H. P. Smith, G. A. Smith) find it somewhere in the plain of Esdraelon, in the general locality suggested by the rest of the campaign. The name is a common one, and there is no objection to this assumption. The 'Well which is in Jezreel', however, is another riddle. In xxix. 11 we are told that by the time David and his men left the Philistine army they had already advanced as far as Jezreel, and we are left to conclude that it was from this point that their assault was delivered. The only way in which we can bring Saul and his army into the immediate neighbourhood of Jezreel is to assume that xxix. 1 refers to an earlier stage in the campaign, and that Saul withdrew into the hills when the enemy appeared in force on the plain to the north. If this be the right explanation, then the Aphek of the verse may have lain in the plain of Sharon. But the state of our text forbids us to rely on this as a final explanation of our difficulties, since this verse seems to stand quite apart from the rest of the narrative.

Other views would place the well at some distance from the city of Jezreel, though in the district which bore that name. The Well of Harod and En-gannim have been suggested. The former lies at the entrance to the valley of Jezreel proper, i.e. the *wadi* which leads down from Jezreel to Beth-shean, and is due north of the high ground of Gilboa. It is rather far east for any force wishing to defend the passes into Gilboa, for the easier roads lie to the west, in the direction of En-gannim. The latter spot would be suitable from the strategic point of view, but it lies some distance to the south of Jezreel, and we may doubt whether this name would have been used for it. The name En-gannim does not occur in any document earlier than P, so we cannot assume that it would have been used by the writer of 1 Sam. xxix. 1.

Leaving on one side, then, the question of literary sources in the narrow sense, we have three distinct narratives, which can be treated apart from one another, though a combination of two or more of them may have been employed by the compiler of *1 Samuel*. In the first place, we have the story of the expulsion of David from the Philistine army, xxviii. 1–2, xxix. 2–11*a*, xxx. 1–30. In the second place, we have the account of Saul's visit to the witch of Endor, xxviii. 3, 5–25 ; and in the third place, the narrative of Saul's defeat and death on Mount Gilboa, xxxi. 1–13. As a natural introduction to this last we may take xxviii. 4. xxix. 11*b* may belong to the first narrative, but xxix. 1 seems to come from an entirely independent source. But while we assign these narratives to stories originally independent of one another, there is no need to doubt the substantial historicity of the events recorded in them.

Chapter X

DAVID

SUMMARY

[Later Israel always looked back on David as the ideal Hebrew, and gave him a place in her history second only to that of Moses. His was an intense personality, capable of giving and inspiring deep affection, often showing a high degree of magnanimity to his personal enemies. He was a brave soldier, an able general, and a wise statesman, while all his life he was a passionate enthusiast for Yahweh.

He seems to have been introduced to Saul either as a musician or through his slaughter of a Philistine giant at Elah. His military exploits made him famous, but they aroused the jealousy of Saul, and he was compelled to flee. For some time he lived as captain of an outlaw band, often pursued by Saul, and at length took service with Achish, king of Gath, who assigned to him the city of Ziklag.

After the death of Saul, David became king of Hebron, probably under Gittite protection, while Ishbaal, one of Saul's surviving sons, held court at Mahanaim, to the east of Jordan, and seems also to have exercised some nominal authority over the territory of Benjamin. The main support of his power was Abner, who, however, grew dissatisfied with him, and entered into an intrigue with David, to whom he promised the crown of all Israel. But Abner was assassinated by Joab, and Ishbaal was murdered after a reign of two years, whereupon David became king of all Israel.

The Philistines could not tolerate a united kingdom, and made war on David. After two victories in the Vale of Rephaim, he besieged and took Jerusalem, which he made his capital, installing the Ark in the precincts of his own palace. We have no record of further victories over the Philistines, but it is clear that David conquered the whole country except the maritime plain. He secured his frontiers by subduing Edom, Moab, Ammon and the Aramaean tribes to the north-east, while he entered into alliances with Hamath and Tyre.

His personal life was less happy, especially in his later years. His memory is tarnished by his treatment of Bathsheba and Uriah, while the crime of Amnon led ultimately to the revolt of Absalom. Here he was saved by the loyalty of his own body-guard, and, after the death of Absalom, easily recovered his authority over Israel. Except for the rebellion of Sheba, his throne was not again challenged during his lifetime.

Monarchy in Israel was based on a 'covenant', in which the parties were the people, the king, and Yahweh. The democratic spirit of the old Aramaean tribes was still strong, and the royal prerogative was expressly limited. Within its terms, however, David was able to carry out an effective organization of his army (based on a body-guard of foreign mercenaries), of the civil state, and of the priesthood. Tribal organization disappeared or was submerged, and with David begins the real history of the Hebrew kingdoms.]

WE know more of David than of any other Old Testament character. Later Israel looked back on him as the ideal king, and on his reign as the golden age of the nation's history, at least during its residence in Palestine. It gave to him a respect second only to that accorded to Moses, and even exceeding that which it offered to the memory of Samuel. To many in Israel David was indeed a second Moses; where the one had laid the foundations, making the tribes into a nation, giving them a common religion and laying down for them a law, the other had actually built up the fabric which his great predecessor had planned, had been the true founder of the kingdom, and had carried into effect the whole system, civil and ecclesiastical, which had been foreshadowed at Sinai. And, just as the whole of the legislation and constitution of Israel were carried back to Moses by a later age, so to David was ascribed the foundation of much that can have come into existence only centuries after his time, including, most probably, elements in the national life which did not make their appearance till after the Exile. While the actual erection of the Temple was ascribed to Solomon, his son, the arrangements for it were all held to have been the work of David. He was credited with the organization of the Temple services—to one class in later Israel the most important feature of the national life—and the arrangements for the priestly duties were regarded as his work. Above all, his reputation as a poet, justly high, if we may judge from undisputed poems of his which have come down to us,[1] led men to think of him as the originator of the Temple music, and actually as the author of a large propor-tion of the Psalms used in the cultus. The crowning tribute to him, however, was paid by the dreamers who contemplated the coming of an ideal age in which Yahweh and Yahweh's will should be supreme, when all that was evil should vanish, and men should live a life of perfect happiness and peace. Many of them could find no better expression of their ideal than to say that another David should arise, and that the perfect king who should bring all good to Israel should bear his name and character.

[1] Especially the dirge over Saul and Jonathan in 2 Sam. i. 19–27.

Such is the general picture which has been familiar to many centuries of Jewish and Christian thought. Closer examination of our documents, however, reveals the fact that much of it is the creation of a later age, even of post-exilic Israel, dating from the time when Israel was no longer free and independent and had no king of her own. We may find reason to adopt a very different conception of the man and of his work when we come to study him in more detail, in the light of what we can regard as contemporary evidence. Of this there is no lack, for it is clear that the compilers of the books of *Samuel* had at their disposal a mass of records, official and popular, dating from David's own time, and these afford us ample grounds for forming a judgement as to what he did, and what his deeds were worth to his people. There is, no doubt, much that is left unexplained, and much that arouses question and suspicion in the narratives before us, but a critical study of our texts enables us to reach certain conclusions which we may regard as definite, and to form an adequate estimate of his place in history.[1]

The character of David, as presented in these records, is extraordinarily attractive. No one, least of all the Biblical historians, would deny him faults, and it is quite in harmony with the true Israelite spirit that no attempt is made to conceal or to gloss over even those offences which were condemned by the conscience of his own people and of his own age. He was a singularly vivid personality, in whose veins the red blood ran strongly. The story of lust and treachery told by his adultery with Bathsheba, and his dastardly murder of Uriah, has become one of the classical instances of great sin. We may suspect that in his earlier years he ran the risk of falling into similar pitfalls,

---

[1] It is generally recognized that the bulk of the narratives in *1 and 2 Samuel* which deal with the life of David are to be ascribed to two main sources. These are more easily separable in *2 Samuel* than in *1 Samuel*, for 2 Sam. viii clearly stands at the end of a history and offers a summary of its hero's life. 2 Sam. ix–xx is universally recognized as a continuous and single document, practically contemporary with the life of David. Chs. xxi–xxiv are not homogeneous, and seem to form an appendix drawn from several sources. The analysis of 1 Sam. xiv. ff. is much more complicated, and can be studied in the work of Budde, H. P. Smith, A. R. S. Kennedy, Nowack, Skinner, Eissfeldt, or the relevant articles in the Bible Dictionaries. It is unnecessary to go further here, since for the purpose of reconstructing actual history, both the main sources are most valuable. That represented by 2 Sam. ix–xx is practically contemporary with the life of David, while the other cannot be much later. Where they disagree with one another, it may be necessary to discuss them, but in the main both of these chief sources may be accepted at their face value,

and it is possible that Nabal was saved by his death from suffering a like violence. Here David was condemned by his own conscience, and by the feeling of his people. This in itself is high testimony to the moral standard which the Aramaean tradition had imposed on the true Israel. Nowhere else in the ancient world would a king have felt any compunction at taking the wife of one of his subjects, nor would he have felt it necessary to meet public opinion—even if public opinion had been against him—by getting rid secretly of the injured husband. Still more significant is his own endurance of rebuke at the mouth of a prophet, and his bitter repentance for the wrong he had done. It is noticeable that here, too, David exhibits the attitude dictated by the social and political theory of the semi-nomad. He is only a man, and, unlike other eastern kings, does not regard himself as standing on a plane between the normal human and the divine. He must treat his subjects as free men, in a real sense his equals, and not his slaves, and if he wrongs any among them, he exposes himself to condemnation and even to punishment. The one difference we notice is that, whereas the sin of another might be punished by the king, it is his God who takes vengeance on him. Our narratives, coming as they do from a nearly contemporary source, make it clear that this was the genuine feeling of David himself, not merely a view read back into history by later writers.

His treatment of conquered enemies was sometimes cruel in the extreme, judged by modern standards. We may conjecture that he practically exterminated Amalek, in revenge for the sack of Ziklag; this is the last occasion on which the tribe as a whole is mentioned. On subduing Moab he destroyed two thirds of the men capable of bearing arms. The people of Ammon he reduced to a servitude which must have been hardly less terrible than death to a free nation of the Bedawin type and instincts. We hear of Edom being swept by Joab with fire and sword, and this is a casual reference. But again we must remember to judge David by the standards of his age. His actions in these matters can be more than paralleled by what is told us of other ancient monarchs, and it is significant that they seem to boast of the tortures they have inflicted on people who have resisted them. If David was no better than the men of his time in these matters, he was certainly no worse.

He had that intense temperament which is capable of a great

love and of a great hatred; his emotions were both his inspiration and his temptation. His affections sometimes led him to be weak in action; had he been a less loving father he might have controlled his sons more effectively. Amnon's outrage roused his anger but not his vengeance, and one of the heaviest blows ever struck at him was the death of his rebellious son Absalom. We may well feel that there was a moral weakness here; David was no Brutus, but it is easier to forgive weakness due to affection than strength manifesting itself in cruelty. More than anything else in his story, his friendships impress us. The mutual love of David and Jonathan has become traditional, but David awoke also the enthusiasm of others. Those who gathered about him in the days of his adversity were passionately devoted to him, and would freely risk their lives to gratify his lightest whim. Among the most devoted was that grim and sometimes repulsive fighter, Joab; and the story of the king's humiliation in the days of his flight before Absalom throws into relief the fidelity of many about him. Men of all classes delighted to serve him, and that, as it seems, not merely in the hope of securing the royal favour, but from genuine personal affection. He had a charm which won for him friends outside Israel as well as among his own people, and attracted those whom policy or other motives should have thrown into opposition to him. Saul's own attitude is a curious mixture of love and jealousy, and we note how the former was liable to rise to the surface in David's presence, even when the king was pursuing him to the death. His residence among the Philistines left behind it a heritage of warmly attached adherents, and the narrative shows how completely he won the heart of Achish himself.

The bitterness of David's repentance for the wrong done to Uriah was, in no small measure, due to the fact that he had fallen into a sin which was repulsive to his own nature. His conduct at times showed a magnanimity which was incomprehensible to those about him. Others would have slain Saul, the enemy who hunted him with relentless persistence; Abishai would have taken the life of Shimei, the man who had cursed him, but David was almost incapable of personal vindictiveness. It may be—though we cannot be certain—that he regretted his leniency to Shimei, but not all the harm he had suffered from Saul, not all the persecution to which he had been subjected, ever made him bitter, and his elegy over Saul and Jonathan is the work, not only of a fine poet, but of one who could love greatly and forgive nobly. Treachery of any kind was abhorrent to him—most of all when he committed it himself—and twice at least men who sought to win his favour by acts which brought him advantage felt the weight of his sudden and uncontrollable anger.

David was a man of a high order of intelligence, and, strong as his passions were, they were normally under the control of his will. In personal matters men could appeal to his reason and common sense, and we have no record of any that suffered for speaking truth in his presence. His intellectual powers served him and his people, both in peace and in war. He was a strategist of no mean order, and stands out among the tacticians of the ancient east. Even more striking was his statesmanship. The union of the whole of Israel was a task which no other man of his day could have accomplished, and it was not his fault that the kingdom which he founded did not maintain itself. His dealings with foreign peoples were wise, and, as compared with the standards of his day, not inhuman. Great warrior as he was, he seldom fought if foreign friendship could be secured by peaceful methods. In all probability, it was he who was responsible for the main outlines of the organization of the kingdom, though in its final form it may have owed something to Solomon.

David was an enthusiast for Yahweh, especially for that form of Yahwism which centred round the Ark. It was not without reason that later ages spoke of David as 'a man after Yahweh's own heart'. No doubt his location of the Ark at Jerusalem was a great and successful stroke of policy, but our recognition of this fact must not blind us to the sincerity of the religious motive lying behind his action. The worst thing his enemies ever did to him was to drive him out, 'saying, Go, worship other gods'.[1] We may not be prepared to accept as historical the Chronicler's account of the care he bestowed on the national cultus, but we must admit that he played no small part in the movement which left Yahweh supreme among his people.

Israelite tradition placed the home of David at Bethlehem, and the later genealogists gave him a mixed ancestry which included a Moabite element. He certainly had affinities with

---

[1] 1 Sam. xxvi. 19.

the Philistines, and relied on help secured from them, apart from personal friendships which he formed among them. The tradition which gave him a two years' residence at the court of Gath may imply a close connexion with that city, and certainly his personal body-guard was recruited from people who were strictly from the other side of the Philistine border. Yet, in spite of foreign elements in his ancestry, and foreign affinities which he formed, no man was ever a truer champion of Israel.

His life falls naturally into two parts, the division being at the point where the news of Saul's death was brought to him. Of his early days we have several accounts, all of which are intended to show how he entered into the great life of the nation. The beautiful and familiar story of his anointing[1] belongs rather to the idealized life of Samuel, and conflicts with other presentations. The second narrative brings him into connexion with Saul as a musician, employed in order to assuage the stress of the king's malady.[2] In this he was normally successful, and not only so, but his charm won the king's favour, and he became his personal attendant or squire. In this capacity he slew the Philistine champion in the Vale of Elah. Another story, apparently of later origin, gives quite a different account of the way in which he was introduced to the court.[3] His three elder brothers are serving in the royal army, and he is sent to bring them a message and to carry a present to their officer. He finds the camp in the Vale of Elah, and hears the challenge of the Philistine giant. He is surprised that no one, trusting in Yahweh, accepts the challenge, and goes out by himself, apparently without having met the king.[4] Both these last stories probably recorded his victory, but of the two the former is generally held to be the earlier, and to fit in better with the other incidents of David's life.

The death of the Philistine champion was practically the beginning of David's military life, and he soon showed such ability and achieved such success as to arouse the jealousy and hostility of Saul. Yet he was too popular to be destroyed by direct methods, and the story tells of a number of expedients adopted by Saul for getting rid of him. We need not follow in detail events which are so familiar and so simply and clearly told. At length the hostility of Saul became so great that David felt his life was no longer

[1] 1 Sam. xvi. 1–13.   [2] 1 Sam. xvi. 14–23.   [3] 1 Sam. xvii. 12–31.
[4] For fuller reference to this narrative see above, p. 187.

safe, and, through Jonathan's friendship, he learnt at length that he must flee. He went first to the sanctuary at Nob, where was the Ephod, an instrument of divination, and the most sacred object in Israel after the loss of the Ark. Here he secured food and a sword, by lying to Ahimelech, the chief priest, and continued his journey. At this point the accounts diverge. One (xxi. 10–15) tells us that he went immediately to Achish, king of Gath, and there feigned madness, in fear of the Philistines. This, however, seems to be a variant of an incident which the more continuous history places later in his career, and the original narrative seems to have taken him direct from Nob to Adullam, among the hills that border on the Shephelah, south-west of Bethlehem. Here he was followed by his own family, who had reason to fear the wrath of Saul, and by Abiathar, the sole survivor of the massacre of the priests ordered by Saul when he discovered the help Ahimelech had given David, as well as by numbers of others who had reason to escape from the communities to which they belonged. David thus became the captain of a band of outlaws, and his first experience of government was the control of a company of wild and lawless men. A man who could show himself able to lead such a group had that in him which would make him a successful ruler of far larger bodies. One advantage which accrued to him deserves special mention. When Abiathar escaped he brought with him the Ephod, and its possession gave David not only a means of ascertaining the divine will in a legitimate way, but also a real prestige in the eyes of his fellow-countrymen.

We need not follow in detail the story of David's wanderings. For some years he and his men lived the life of hunted fugitives, and the narrative tells of hairbreadth escapes and of exciting adventures. Sometimes we seem to have duplicates of the same event, as when we hear both in chs. xxiv and xxvi of how David spared Saul's life when he had him in his power. Clearly he was gaining steadily in strength, though never in a position to challenge Saul's position, even had he wished to do so. The story of Nabal[1] shows the influence which he and his men could exert over the pasture lands of the south, and David's marriage with Abigail doubtless brought him some accession of wealth. Scattered all over the south country are places which became memorable as scenes of David's exploits, but he never seems to

[1] 1 Sam. xxv.

have felt safe, and at length took refuge with Achish, king of
Gath, who recognized his value, and assigned to him the city of
Ziklag. The site has not been identified for certain, but it must
have been in the far south, perhaps in the direction of Beer-sheba.[1]
It is possible that this gift is to be regarded as a reward for
services rendered, for David was constantly engaged on raids, and
the way in which the story of 1 Sam. xxvii. 9 ff. is told, suggests
that he and his men returned not to Ziklag but to Gath itself.
David always reported that he had attacked tribes affiliated to
Israel, and it seems more likely that Achish should assign to him
a city of his own only after he had proved at once his fidelity to
his Philistine lord and hostility to his own people. David and
his men did not escape altogether without reprisals, as the
story of the Amalekite raid on Ziklag shows. It was probably
introduced into the narrative in order to explain the origin of
the principle upon which spoil won in war was divided.

As a military officer in the service of Achish, David might
have been expected to take part in the campaign of Mount
Gilboa. That he did not do so is attributed by the Hebrew
historian to the jealousy and fear of the other Philistine princes.
They recognized in David the man who, more than any other,
had successfully fought the battles of Israel against them, and
they believed—perhaps with reason—that he would return to
his old allegiance at some critical point in the battle. Achish did
his best to reassure his colleagues, but to no purpose, and David
was relieved of a difficult situation. It would have been very
hard for him to fight against Saul, whose life he had already
spared, and for whom, in spite of past disagreements, he had a
real affection. Nor can we readily think of him as turning
against a man who had employed him and trusted him for the
last two years.

We may confess that we can hardly escape the feeling that the
story of David's two years' residence under the aegis of a Philistine king implies more than appears on the surface. There can
be little doubt that he succeeded in attracting friends to himself
among the Philistines, especially in Gath, and it may well be
that his influence sufficed to form a party there which was
devoted to him. It is not impossible that the story of his relations
with Achish conceals a division in the ranks of the Philistines

---

[1] Conder's identification of the site with Zuhelike, some miles to the south-east
of Gaza, has not met with general acceptance.

themselves, of which David was skilful enough to take advantage; and this division, if historical, cannot have failed to contribute to the weakening of the Philistine power. Knowing as we do that Gittites, and possibly other Philistines, were numbered among those nearest to David's person in later days,[1] we find it hard to believe that the whole Philistine nation was united against him, when he was struggling to refound the monarchy of a united Israel. Gath, it is true, was one of the less important of the Philistine states, but we may conjecture that throughout his life David could depend on the loyal support of this city, if of no other.

The news of the battle of Gilboa found David at Ziklag, on his return from the punishment of the Amalekite raid. The messenger claimed to have slain Saul with his own hands,[2] but found that he was dealing with a man whose chivalry and reverence for the representative of Yahweh allowed him to see only a sacrilegious murder in the action of his informant. We get the impression that at this time David had not contemplated seizing the vacant throne, and that it was not for some time afterwards that he really aimed at the kingship of Israel. The dirge he pronounced over Saul and Jonathan is one of the loveliest elegies in the world's literature, and its Davidic authorship has never been seriously challenged. It is the outpouring of a poetic soul stricken by the deepest sorrow, and David mourns not only for his loving friend Jonathan, but also for the man who had tried to take his life. This is not the language of one who saw in the death of the king and his sons the removal of an obstacle to the fulfilment of his own ambitions, and additional evidence is supplied by David's message to the men of Jabesh-gilead, complimenting them on their pious action in removing the body of Saul from the wall of Beth-shean.

The political condition of Israel immediately after the death of Saul is far from clear. It is obvious that the Philistines were now masters of the whole land, and, indeed, in 2 Sam. xxiii. 14

---

[1] 2 Sam. xv. 18 ff.

[2] This story is not consistent with the account given in 1 Sam. xxxi. 4, according to which Saul committed suicide. It has been supposed that the messenger was simply lying in the hope of getting a reward from David for good tidings, but most recent opinion tends to regard the two passages as coming from different sources, cp. H. P. Smith, *Samuel*, p. 254. Budde, *Samuel*, pp. 193 f., and Kennedy, *Samuel*, pp. 191 f., are inclined to confine the duplicate narrative to 2 Sam. i. 6–10, and to see in verses 1–5 a natural continuation of the story of 1 Sam. xxxi.

we hear of a Philistine garrison at Bethlehem itself.[1] The Philistine city with which David had the closest affinities was Gath, that one of the five which lay nearest to the borders of Judah, and when David went up to Hebron and assumed a royal state,[2] we are tempted to suspect that officially he was there as a representative of the Philistine, or, more specifically, of the Gittite, government. At the same time, the house of Saul was still represented by Ishbaal, whose head-quarters were to the east of Jordan, and whose forces might be formidable under the veteran soldier Abner. It would seem that to some extent the Philistines were prepared to recognize the authority of Ishbaal also, provided that he, too, held his position as a vassal of one or more of the five towns. It is not impossible that the Philistine leaders deliberately encouraged the two chiefs, in order to prevent the union of all Israel in a single hand. If that were their purpose they should have seen that the two parties were more evenly matched; it was unlikely that a weakling like Ishbaal could long hold his own against a man of David's ability.

It is clear that the house of Saul, though maintaining its position primarily in Transjordania, had access to the west. It is equally clear that the Philistine occupation allowed free passage over the country to the Judahites, and therefore that clashes between the two were almost inevitable. One such is described for us, though it is stated that there was continuous war between the two.[3] Two armed parties, one under Abner, the other under Joab, met by the pool of Gibeon. Abner proposed a kind of tournament, with twelve champions on each side. The whole story suggests comparatively friendly relations between the two lines; Abner certainly had no enmity in his heart for Joab. The twenty-four were so eager that they killed one another, with the result that both parties flew to their arms and a general engagement followed. Abner and his men were defeated, and in the

---

[1] The passage in question is taken from the appendix, and occurs in a list of David's mighty men. There is no reason to doubt its historicity, though we may be uncertain as to the date to which this and other exploits of the mighty men should be assigned. A comparison with v. 17 suggests that the incident referred to took place before the capture of Jerusalem. So H. P. Smith, *Samuel*, p. 290; Budde, *Samuel*, p. 224; Kennedy, *Samuel*, p. 214.

[2] 2 Sam. ii. 1.

[3] 2 Sam. iii. 1, but the passage may be a redactor's insertion in the original narrative. So Kennedy. But for the fact that the battle between David's men and Abner's is located at Gibeon, we should be inclined to suspect that the list of places acknowledging Ishbaal, as given in 2 Sam. ii. 8 f., was a later idealizing of his power.

pursuit Asahel, brother of Joab, was killed by Abner in self-defence. The pursuit continued, till at last Abner persuaded Joab to call a halt, and David's party made a forced march all night to Hebron. The tragedy of the incident lay in the fact that blood now lay between Abner and the brothers of Asahel, and they felt themselves bound to take vengeance sooner or later.

Such strength as Ishbaal had was based on the personality of Abner. The soldier had no illusions as to his importance to his nominal master, and began to display an arrogance which was, perhaps, not unnatural in a man of his day. He took liberties with a certain Rizpah, a concubine of Saul's, in a fashion which could be interpreted only as a claim to the throne.[1] Ishbaal remonstrated, was met with a harsh response, and dared pursue the matter no further. But Abner felt insulted by the very challenge, and determined to transfer his allegiance to David.[2] An arrangement was made, David's wife Michal was restored to him,[3] thus giving him some claim to the allegiance of the followers of Saul, and Abner undertook to bring all Israel over to David's side. Joab heard of the negotiations, though he had been absent on a raid at the time of Abner's visit to David. He had already the duty, as it seemed, of blood revenge for Asahel, and his religious scruples may have been quickened by fear lest Abner should take his place in David's mind. He therefore caught him treacherously and stabbed him.[4] David made it clear, by his elegy and by his public lamentation, that he had no part in the murder, and Abner's work lived after him. Ishbaal, whose 'court' was, if anything, simpler than even his father's, was assassinated by two of his adherents, and the murderers, bringing the news to David, received the treatment meted out to the slayer of Saul.[5] But there was now none left to maintain the cause of Saul's house, except the lame Meribaal, Jonathan's son, and some children of Saul's secondary wives whose claim would have been admitted by no one.

The result was that the adherents of Saul's house saw that their cause was hopeless, and that it would be better to give up

---

[1] The universal rule in the ancient east was that the whole of a dead king's harem became the personal property of his successor. Cp. the action of Absalom in 2 Sam. xvi. 22, and Solomon's reception of Adonijah's request for Abishag, 1 Kgs. ii. 22 ff.

[2] 2 Sam. iii. 6–11.

[3] 2 Sam. iii. 13–16. She had been given to a certain Phalti, after David's flight from Saul's court, 1 Sam. xxv. 44.   [4] 2 Sam. iii. 22–7.   [5] 2 Sam. iv.

the struggle. David had always been a favourite in Israel, and his behaviour to Saul's family had done nothing to shake this popularity, even among those who were devoted to the other cause. Very wisely, then, they approached David, and offered him the kingship of all Israel. He accepted the crown, and his accession was solemnly ratified, on the basis of a formal constitution, and for another five years he continued to rule the country from Hebron.[1]

It is during these five years that we must place the greater part of David's struggle against the Philistines.[2] As long as he was a local dynast, ruling over the southern portion of the land, with his formal authority probably limited by Jerusalem, he was tolerable, and was even an asset to the Philistine power. But as king of the whole country, with the military reputation which he had secured, he can have been regarded only as a serious menace to the suzerain, and the issue fully justified those who suspected him of being a danger to the newly-won Philistine empire. And, as the story goes, it was not he who took the initiative, but the enemy, probably feeling that they must act and crush him at once, if they wished to assert their dominion over Israel in any real sense.

Strangely enough, we have very few details of this war. In the accounts of David's mighty men we have several instances of feats of arms done on individual Philistines, usually men of gigantic stature, and a reference to the one campaign of which we have an extended account. Thus, we hear of Abishai saving David's life when he was threatened by Ishbi-benob, of Sibbecai who slew another giant at a place called Gob in our present text,[3] of Elhanan who slew Goliath, of Eleazer who, with two

[1] 2 Sam. v. 3.

[2] It is clear that the order of the events as given in the succeeding chapters of 2 Samuel cannot be that of the actual history. The capture of Jerusalem there follows immediately on David's acceptance of the throne, and, as has been hinted above (p. 210), at least one period of conflict with the Philistines must have intervened. Moreover, the time given for the reign of Ishbaal is only two years (2 Sam. ii. 10; the grounds on which the text has been suspected seem hardly adequate), as compared with David's seven and a half years' reign in Hebron. The capture of Jerusalem must rather be regarded as the decisive action of the war against the Philistines, who can have given David comparatively little trouble when once the strongest fortress which favoured them had fallen into the hands of the enemy.

[3] The reading in 2 Sam. xxi. 18 is very uncertain; the MT. of the parallel in 1 Chron. xx. 4 has Gezer, the LXX and Pesh., Gath. Nob has been suggested as a possible reading, cp. EB., cols. 1,745 and 2,210 f. (art. 'Ishbi-Benob'). But the locality is a matter of minor importance to the narrator of such a story.

others, defeated a whole host of Philistines, of Shammah, who held an army at bay single-handed, and of the three who drew water from the well of Bethlehem in spite of the enemy.[1] The single campaign which is recorded[2] opened with an advance by a Philistine army, which made its way up the Vale of Sorek and took up its position in the Valley of Rephaim, to the south of Jerusalem, evidently intending to move south, through Bethlehem, on Hebron. Hebron may have been ill defended; at all events, David felt that he could not await the enemy there, and withdrew to Adullam, where for the time he occupied the cave which had sheltered him in his early days. The absence of a hostile force may have led the Philistines to relax their vigilance, and have left them unprepared for David's action. At length he struck, and attacked the enemy at a place known as Baal-perazim, which has not been identified; in all probability it lay not far from Bethlehem. His victory was complete, and the Philistine army was swept away. It is to this battle that the tradition preserved in 2 Sam. xxiii. 13–17 assigns the feat of the three heroes who fought their way through the Philistine army to bring David water from the well of Bethlehem.

This defeat, nevertheless, was not decisive, and the Philistines made another attempt by the same route. This time David seems to have advanced immediately against them, without retreating to Adullam. He did not, however, make a direct attack, but came on the Philistines in the flank and rear, with his assault probably masked by a grove of balsam trees. To him and to his men the wind in the tree-tops sounded like great footsteps approaching, and they recognized in it the advance of Yahweh to fight for them. The result was a victory even more complete than that of Baal-perazim, for the Philistine host was driven in headlong rout as far as Gezer. The site of the engagement is given as Geba or Gibeon, a name so common as to make identification practically impossible.

Another incident to which the narrative calls attention is the capture of the Philistine gods. As Yahweh had been taken prisoner by the Philistines two generations earlier, so now His people held their deities. 2 Sam. v. 21 does not tell us what Israel did with them; the Chronicler[3] states that they were

---

[1] These exploits will be found in 2 Sam. xxi. 15–22, xxiii. 8–19.   [2] 2 Sam. v. 17–25.
[3] 1 Chron. xiv. 12. The A.V. of 2 Sam. v. 21 is an unjustifiable inference based on the Chronicler's account.

burnt. This, no doubt, is what *ought* to have been done with them, from the view-point of a pious Jew of the third century.

Both these Philistine movements were made through the Valley of Rephaim, which lies to the south of Jerusalem. It was the point from which the Hebron district could most easily be assailed, since the approaches to the south were probably too easily defensible by a force holding the hills above. But the Vale of Sorek, which leads up to Jerusalem via Rephaim, was not in David's hands, and the Valley of Rephaim itself was dominated by Jerusalem. It may have been these considerations which led David to an attempt which might well have seemed impossible, the capture of Jerusalem itself.

The site of ancient Jerusalem is, fortunately, outside the wall of the present city, and is therefore available for archaeological research. The hill on which the city stands is set among higher mountains, to the western side of the deep valley of the Kidron. To the south it divides into two ridges, with a valley between known as the Tyropoeon, and these ridges end in steep knolls. That to the east, known as the Ophel, is the site of the old Jebusite city of Jerusalem, and it forms one of the strongest places in Palestine. To east, south, and west, the ground falls steeply away, and comparatively slender defences are sufficient to resist any attack. To the north there is a lower saddle between the knoll and the main ridge, and it was here that the strongest walls were built. The remains that have been unearthed during the last few years show that these walls were one of the finest examples of the ancient art of fortification. The Jebusite walls[1] were built of roughly hewn, ill-fitting blocks, the spaces being filled up with chips from the larger stones. Every five or six courses the wall was slightly recessed, giving a series of steps, several feet in height and five or six inches in width. There were two of these walls on the north side, forming a double line of defence, and the fact that no Canaanite pottery has been found between them shows that the intervening space was deliberately kept clear, or in time it would have been filled up and rendered useless.[2]

---

[1] For an account of the fortifications of early Jerusalem as discovered on the Ophel see J. Garrow Duncan, 'Millo and the City of David', *ZAW*. xlii. (1924), pp. 222–44, especially the plan of the buildings excavated on the northern side of the Ophel, p. 242.

[2] Duncan regards this space as the 'hold' of 2 Sam. v. 17, judging from the formation of the towers that it was the citadel. That may have been its purpose,

The water supply has always been one of the main problems of Jerusalem. The only spring in the neighbourhood is the so-called 'Virgin's Spring', lying under the Ophel, on its eastern side, and the city has, in later days, always had to depend on large tanks where rain water is stored. The ancient Jebusite city, however, derived its supply direct from the Virgin's Spring. A tunnel led the water under the rock, and a vertical shaft was sunk from above ('Warren's shaft'). Another sloping tunnel was cut to the head of this from inside the city, so that water was at all times available, even though the city might be closely besieged. It is probably this tunnel that is indicated by the 'watercourse'[1] of 2 Sam. v. 8, and it proved to be the vulnerable point in an otherwise impregnable city. The walls could safely be manned by the blind and the lame;[2] they alone were sufficient

but it is not likely to have been the retreat of David before the battle of Baalperazim, for (a) the verb 'go down' would not have been used of it, (b) the mention of Adullam and of Bethlehem in 2 Sam. xxiii. 13–17 implies that David made his attack from the south.   [1] Heb. צִנּוֹר.

[2] We may, however, ask ourselves what the blind and the lame had to do with the original form of this passage. The text is obscure and probably corrupt, making very little sense as it stands, especially in 7b and 8. Even if we take הסיר‎ך as a future perfect or a perfect of certainty 'will have repulsed thee', we have not solved the difficulties of verse 8. These are to some extent avoided by the LXX, which makes צנור a weapon with which the blind and the lame were to be attacked. But we are practically certain that it means a tube or channel, and we cannot easily surrender the identification with Warren's shaft. We may get some help from the parallel in Chronicles, whose compiler seems to have had before him an earlier form of the text represented in Samuel. Here we have no mention whatever of the blind and the lame, while 1 Chron. xi. 6 (corresponding to 2 Sam. v. 8) runs: ויאמר דויד כל מכה יבוסי בראשנה יהיה לראש ולשר ויעל בראשונה יואב בן צרויה ויהי לראש: 'And David said, Whosoever smiteth the Jebusites first shall be made chief and captain. And Joab the son of Zeruiah went up first, and was made chief.' We note the omission of any reference to the צנור, but this may have been due to the compiler's inability to fit the shaft into the story as he understood it. It looks as if in 2 Sam. we had a conflation of two narratives, of which one only was before the compiler of 1 Chron., though he had it in a more complete form than that which has survived in our present text of 2 Sam. Could it have run something like: ויאמר דוד ביום ההוא כל מכה יבוסי בראשונה יהיה לראש ולשר ויעל יואב בן צרויה בראשונה בצנור ויגע ביבוסי ויהי לראש: 'And David said on that day, Whosoever smiteth the Jebusites first shall be made chief and captain. And Joab the son of Zeruiah went up first through the watercourse, and smote the Jebusites and became chief.' This would at least give an intelligible sense, and the archaeological evidence would be satisfied. The reference to the blind and the lame seems to be a fragment of a narrative which explained a forgotten *taboo*. The LXX actually renders הבית as 'the house of the Lord', apparently taking it as a reference to the regulation which forbade service in the Temple by priests who suffered from any physical disability. If we have to assume the originality of the text as it stands, however, the explanation given above seems to be the best.

defence, so the Jebusites thought. But David made some de-
monstration outside, to attract all the inhabitants to the walls,
whence, no doubt, they freely mocked him, while a select party
made their way up the tunnel, scaled the shaft, and so won the
city from within. The tradition preserved in 1 Chron. xi. 6
ascribes this feat to Joab, and the text of 2 *Samuel* at this point is
so corrupt that there is no difficulty in supposing that, in its
original form, it also contained a mention of Joab's name.

David broke down a considerable length of the outer northern
wall, and some portion of the inner wall.[1] It seems as if his first
intention was to destroy the fortifications altogether. But he
may have found the task too laborious, or he may suddenly have
reached his decision to transfer his capital to Jerusalem. Certainly
he did break down the walls, and it is not likely that this took
place in the course of the assault. He made no attempt to rebuild the old defences, but strengthened the north-east corner of
the outer wall ('Millo'?), and ran a wall, far from being as
strong as those built by the Jebusites, diagonally across to beyond the point where the old inner wall had been broken down,
thus closing the breach. This wall was never brought up to the
same strength as the others. David's successors patched up the
wall to the east, overlooking the Kidron valley, but they did not,
except at Millo, add to the new northern wall, probably because
the city very soon extended northwards to the main ridge on
which the Temple stood later.

No single act of David's did so much to exhibit his high qualities of statesmanship as his transference of his capital to Jerusalem. It was the strongest fortress in all Palestine, even after the
changes David made in its northern fortification. It stood at the
head of the best of all the passes into the hill country, and any
power which would be absolute in the land must hold it. As far
as we know, the Philistines made no effort to capture it from
David, and its occupation by the Israelites meant the definite
end of their hopes of a Palestinian empire. We may take it that
the war continued, and that it was by slow stages that David
proceeded to the conquest of the rest of the country. His
occupation of the hills would be secure from the time when

---

[1] Thus proving that the adoption of Jerusalem as his capital was no part of his
original plan in attacking the city. Clearly his primary object was military, not
political, and it was only later that he realized the value of the position for his own
purposes.

Jerusalem was captured, but the Philistines were not likely to give up the fortresses of the plain of Esdraelon without a severe struggle. Yet these, even Megiddo and Beth-shean,[1] must have fallen, and it is possible that the tribes to the east of Jordan had some hand in their reduction. The decisive and critical point, however, was the occupation of Jerusalem.

David's choice of Jerusalem as his capital had, however, still more important results as an act of domestic policy. The two main sections of Israel, the northern and eastern on the one hand, represented by Ephraim and Gilead, and the south, now Judahite, on the other, had always stood apart from one another. It is true that they had a tradition of common ancestry, and a common religion, but they had never tried, as yet, to enter into a political unity. Saul had some freedom in moving through the south country, and his authority may have been admitted by the Judahites, but, as far as we know, he effected no serious organization of the land. It was inevitable that there should be jealousy between the two groups, and only the most careful and considerate statesmanship could avoid disruption when the external pressure should be relaxed. David himself belonged to the southern group just as Saul had belonged to the northern, and while his personal popularity and the need for his military leadership might have kept the whole country loyal for a time, there was no guarantee of permanence in the situation. For him to have transferred his capital to some spot on northern territory, to Bethel or to Gibeah, might well have alienated the south. But here was neutral ground, which neither side could claim. It had been the centre of the barrier between the two groups, and was now to be used as a link between them. Just as Washington and Canberra stand on soil which belongs to no state in their respective Unions, so David needed, and saw that he needed, a site which could not be assigned either to Judah or to Joseph.

To this we may add a personal aspect of the matter. Jerusalem was the greatest of the conquests of David. In all its long history, Nebuchadrezzar and Titus are the only other commanders who have captured the city by direct siege, though it has often been surrendered to a force which has conquered the

[1] Archaeological evidence suggests that Beth-shean was destroyed by fire at the end of the second millennium B.C. Cp. C. S. Fisher in *University of Pennsylvania Museum Journal*, 14 (1923), pp. 227 ff.

rest of the land. No stronger testimony to generalship and personal prowess could be offered to the nation, and by adopting it as his capital, David held before the people a constant reminder of his own skill as a soldier. In a very real sense the adoption of Jerusalem as the capital marks the beginning of the Kingdom of Israel.

To military and political considerations, David added the influence of religion. We need not doubt that he was actuated by truly religious motives in bringing the Ark to Jerusalem, but at the same time his action made the city, more completely than ever, the centre of the national life. There were other sanctuaries—many of them—and each had a fame of some kind, partly through its traditions and partly through the sacred objects which it possessed. But the Ark had a unique importance, and the bull and snake symbols[1] could not seriously compete with it. Tradition carried it back to the days of Moses, and made it the outward and visible sign of that covenant on which the Israelite nationality and faith were based.

David's first attempt to introduce the Ark was unsuccessful, as an accident resulting in the death of one of the attendants took place, not far from Jerusalem, near the house of Obed-edom. Three months later, however, it was transferred with due ceremonial to its resting-place in the city of David, whence it was removed in Solomon's day to its final home on the hill to the north of Ophel.

The selection of that site is recorded in 2 Sam. xxiv, which, in spite of its position, describes events which probably belong to an early point in David's reign. The story goes that David compelled Joab, much against his will, to take a census of the people. This was held to be sin, possibly because 'it was regarded as a sinful ambition on the part of the creature to possess a secret which the Creator intended should be His alone',[2] or because the census was a preliminary to an organized taxation of the people, and to their being called upon to supply forced labour for David's building works. When it was too late, David repented, and as a punishment was given the choice between three forms of calamity. He chose a three days' pestilence, and on the third day he saw the destroying angel approaching Jerusalem from the north. Probably by this time he had already

---

[1] Possibly the latter was connected with the local cult of Jerusalem, and was taken over by Israel with the city.   [2] Kennedy, *Samuel*, p. 314.

taken up his quarters on the hill to the north of the Ophel, though it is not clear that his palace was yet built. The destroyer halted, as it seemed to David, at the threshing-floor of Araunah the Jebusite—this hill would be the natural spot on which an inhabitant of old Jerusalem would make a threshing-floor, outside his city and on a fairly high hill—which must have been close by the great natural outcrop of rock, which clearly was used in ancient times as an altar. It was probably near the 'high-place' of Jerusalem[1] in pre-Israelite days and retained its sanctity, like so many other sacred spots, after the conquest, though it was now dedicated to the service and use of Yahweh. David erected an altar and offered sacrifice, and the plague went no further. Thus was indicated the spot on which the later Temple was to be built.

David was now firmly established, but his work of conquest was far from complete. He had not only to enlarge the borders of the territory he possessed, still small, so as to include all of the Israelite name and faith, but also to extend his dominion, beyond the boundaries of Israel proper, so far as to protect his frontier against possible invaders. To give his people that peace which they needed, there must be a ring of subject or of friendly states about them. Four conquests of neighbouring peoples are recorded, though we are not sure as to the order in which they were subdued. To the south David reduced Edom in a campaign of which we have no reliable details[2] beyond the fact that the decisive battle was fought in the Valley of Salt, not far from Beer-sheba.[3] Moab also was reduced, and all we know of this conquest is the cruelty with which it was marked,[4] for David is said to have put to death two-thirds of the fighting men of the country. The two conquests that are described in detail are those of Ammon and Syria. It is noticeable that in these wars the Hebrew historian is careful to represent David as always being attacked, never the aggressor. The war against Ammon and that against the Syrians were intimately connected. The first move was made by Ammon. On the death of Nahash, who may be the king defeated by Saul at Jabesh-gilead some twenty-five or thirty years previously, David sent messengers to condole

---

[1] For a discussion of the relation between the rock, the threshing-floor, and the altar, see G. B. Gray, *Sacrifice in the Old Testament*, pp. 130 ff.

[2] Our present text of 1 Chron. xviii. 12 ascribes the victory to Abishai, the tradition preserved in 1 Kgs. xi. 14 ff. to Joab.

[3] 2 Sam. viii. 13 f.   [4] 2 Sam. viii. 2.

with his son Hanun, on the ground that Nahash had rendered
David good service. Hanun, so the story runs, prompted by his
arrogant councillors, took the opportunity of offering David a
deadly insult. Realizing that he would take vengeance,[1] the
Ammonites summoned as their allies certain Syrian princes. It
would seem that the Israelite army, under Joab and Abishai, was
already about to besiege Rabbah, when the Syrians appeared
to their relief. The Israelites were caught between the two
forces, but one body of them, under the command of Joab
himself, faced about and confronted the Syrians, a manœuvre
similar to that performed in like circumstances by Alexander at
Arbela and by Julius Caesar at Pharsalus. The Syrians were
unable to withstand the charge of Joab's veteran troops, and
fled from the field, pursued by Joab. The Ammonites, finding
themselves deserted by their allies, also fled and took refuge in
the city.

The siege was not pressed, but in the following year[2] Joab led
an army against Rabbah. The city made a stout resistance, and
the story of the death of Uriah shows that the besiegers suffered
some loss. At length the 'water city', probably a fort or
bastion built about the chief well, was captured, and the end
could not long be delayed. David himself came to superintend
the final operations, and we have an account of the booty he
secured from the city. The inhabitants were reduced to slavery,
being employed on various royal manufactures. There is no record of wholesale slaughter of the Ammonite captives, though
perhaps they may have found their lot little less terrible than
death.[3] It is a significant fact that the Ammonite king was among
those who succoured David in his flight to Transjordania during
Absalom's rebellion.

It is the Ammonite war which introduces the struggles with
Syria.[4] The Ammonites were always much more like a Bedawin

---

[1] The full account of the Ammonite war is contained in 2 Sam. x–xii, and includes the story of David's sin with Bathsheba and the death of Uriah. This latter
occurs in the section chs. ix–xx, which is otherwise concerned with details of David's
family life, and the story of Ammon is probably introduced in order to explain the
circumstances of David's sin.

[2] Cp. 2 Sam. xi. 1.

[3] 2 Sam. xii. 31 has been held to imply that the captives were tortured to death
with various instruments, or roasted in brick-kilns. But this is to strain the text,
which more naturally implies hard labour. See the commentaries *ad loc.*, and
Driver, *Notes on the Hebrew Text of the Books of Samuel*, pp. 294–7.

[4] See note at end of chapter.

people than the other neighbours of Israel, and at this time it would seem that a number of wandering Aramaeans owed some kind of allegiance to one Hadadezer, son of Rehob, 'king' of Zobah. The narratives in the text suggest that his authority extended even as far as the Euphrates, and that he was able to control a number of other tribes of the same type as his own. It will have been noticed that in the first campaign against Ammon, Joab is said to have returned to Jerusalem, leaving Rabbah intact, though his victory was won under its walls. It is difficult to avoid the impression that he was not so successful as the narrative implies, and that he considered he had done well to rout the Syrians and escape without disaster. Before Rabbah could be attacked with real hope of its capture, it was necessary to neutralize the power of Hadadezer. To judge from the narrative of 2 Sam. viii. 3, 5, the Syrian king was trying to summon various vassal states to his help when David fell upon him. He had not yet gathered the forces from the Euphrates district, though the contingents of Damascus were already under arms, and before they could effect a junction with Hadadezer, David threw himself between them and defeated them separately. He seems to have been content with the defeat and spoliation of Hadadezer, but he occupied Damascus in the way that the Philistines had occupied Palestine, i.e. by placing officers in all important towns and exacting tribute.

These conquests presuppose a complete victory over the Philistines, which confined them to the coastal plain and the lower Shephelah, and drove them out of the plain of Esdraelon, though it is strange that we have no reference to fighting to the north of Jerusalem. It is possible that the Philistine power was so weakened that the maintenance of garrisons in the cities was found to be impracticable, and that David simply occupied them peaceably.[1] In any case, it is clear that the defeat of the Syrians was the final stroke needed to consolidate the Palestinian empire. David's authority now reached on the south and east to the desert itself. The north was not a dangerous frontier, partly because of the nature of the country, and partly because after the Syrian victory the king of Hamath was friendly to David. Probably there was a considerable extent of territory between the two kingdoms for which neither had much use, and neither found

---

[1] But cp. the archaeological evidence as to the destruction of Beth-shean, cited on p. 217, n. 1.

it to his interest to extend his borders. The traditional extent of the Israelite kingdom was to 'the entering in of Hamath', and this must refer to the dominions of the king of Hamath rather than to the city on the Orontes itself.

To the north-west, again, David secured himself by peaceful means, making a treaty with the king of Tyre.[1] This is easily intelligible. Throughout her history Phoenicia never, as far as we know, made any attempt to establish a continental empire. Her eyes were always turned westwards, and she depended largely on the Mediterranean trade and on her western colonies for her prosperity. At the same time she had an eastern commerce, for which she relied on the merchants of other lands coming to her markets, and there were times when she was threatened by those who wished to secure this trade for themselves by taking possession of the harbours. Few cities of antiquity offered more serious problems to a besieging enemy than did Tyre, and even Jerusalem was not more difficult to capture. But it was eminently to the advantage of the Phoenician cities to be protected from the east, so that caravans should have free access to her. She must have suffered from the migration of the Philistines, and she would naturally welcome an alliance with a strong military power which could protect her trade routes to the east, and which was not likely to embark on any scheme of conquest. Some such consideration must have lain behind the alliance, for it was not merely a commercial agreement. Tyre sent to David workmen and building materials, and erected the royal palace, but we hear nothing of any payment made in return, as we do in Solomon's day, and we are left with the hypothesis of the protection of trade routes as the most probable recompense that David could offer. For this purpose the control of Aramaean territory was of vital importance, for while communication with Egypt could be maintained by sea, the great eastern road ran through Damascus.

Here, then, at last, is a genuine Palestinian kingdom, estab-

---

[1] The king mentioned is Hiram, Solomon's friend, who came to the throne (according to the accepted chronology) in 969 or 968, and reigned for thirty-three years. This would make the embassy to David late in his reign, and possibly Solomon was already on the throne at Hiram's accession. The implication of 2 Sam. v. 11 is that Hiram sent to congratulate David on his accession to the throne in Jerusalem, and either the received chronology is much in error, or Hiram's name was inserted by a later editor or scribe who found that the king was not identified at all in this verse.

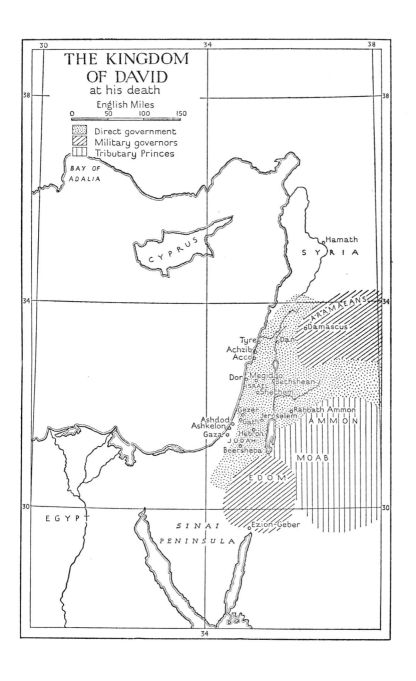

THE KINGDOM
OF DAVID
at his death

English Miles

0   50   100   150

Direct government
Military governors
Tributary Princes

BAY OF
ADALIA

CYPRUS

Hamath

SYRIA

ARAMAEANS
Damascus

Tyre   Dan
Achzib
Acco

Dor   Megiddo
ISRAEL   Bethshean
Shechem

Gezer   Rabbath Ammon
Ashdod   Gath   Jerusalem
Ashkelon   AMMON
Gaza   Hebron
JUDAH
Beersheba

MOAB

EDOM

EGYPT

SINAI
PENINSULA

Ezion-Geber

lished for the first and only time in the history of the land. Its limits may not have extended quite as far as those claimed for it, but they certainly included much more than has ever been under a single native Palestinian monarch, before or since. They did not, it is true, embrace the Philistine cities of the coastal plain, for in that case we should surely have had mention of tribute paid by them, or some other indication of their subjection. But the whole country, 'from Dan to Beer-sheba', recognized David's authority, and on every side, except possibly on the west, the neighbouring tribes were either subject to him or else bound to him by the ties of friendship. As we have seen, there were several factors which contributed to this result, including the weakness of both Egypt and Mesopotamia, the strength which resistance to the Philistines had given to the idea of co-operation, and the unifying influence of Israelite religion; but we must count among the most important the personality of David.

In 2 Sam. ix–xx we have a series of narratives, clearly derived, in the main, from contemporary records, dealing almost entirely with the domestic life of David. Ch. x, which we have already had before us, is the only section which alludes to David's relations with any other people. These chapters are widely and justly held to be one of the finest monuments we have of Hebrew prose style, and they have never failed to kindle the warm interest of their readers. But, for the history of Israel, their value lies less in the events which they record than in the picture they give of David and those nearest to him, the way in which they illustrate certain weaknesses in the Israelite monarchy, even under David, and the light which they throw on his character. In them we see the king presented at his best and at his worst. Ch. ix tells us of his chivalry and fidelity to the house of Saul, and, more particularly, to his old friend Jonathan. One representative of the family is left, a lame son of Jonathan, whom David takes into his own household. He has no reason to fear Meribaal,[1] partly because of his physical weakness, and partly because the king is so sure of the devotion of Israel, and gives him a position of honour at court. This is David at his best.

The next story gives us David at his worst. It is unnecessary to transcribe in detail one of the world's best-known narratives; it will be sufficient to repeat the familiar comment that David's

---

[1] This was clearly the original form of his name, cp. p. 193, n. 1.

action in the matter of Bathsheba and Uriah is quite characteristic of oriental monarchy, and would hardly have excited
remark outside Israel. It would be difficult to find higher
testimony to Hebrew standards of life, and to Hebrew theories
of society, than the condemnation which the writer, and every-
one else, passes on David. To the ordinary eastern mind, for a
king to take the wife of a subject is quite normal and natural, for
the sovereign is well within his rights. Few men in David's
position would have felt it necessary either to conceal the act or
to get rid of the husband. But in Israel a man was a man, even
though he were a subject and of foreign birth, and his rights in
property and person must be respected. Characteristic also are
the rebuke of Nathan and the repentance of the king. Neither
would have been conceivable in any other nation of the ancient
east, and the fact that the story comes to us from a hand which
is practically contemporary, adds to our sense of the very high
standard of religion and morals which is already manifest in
Israel. This we must attribute to the influence of the Aramaean element in the population, which still went far in maintaining the point of view it had brought with it from the nomad
life. We shall have occasion at other points also to notice similar
features appearing in the thought and life of the people.

The perils attaching to a polygamous monarchy are still
further illustrated by the story of Absalom, told in 2 Sam. xiii-
xix. This clearly belongs to the latter part of David's reign, and
it gives a vivid picture of a Hebrew Alcibiades, handsome,
attractive, passionate, ambitious, and unscrupulous. There are
two parts to the story: the first tells of Absalom's vengeance
for the outrage on his sister, the second of the young man's
attempt to supersede his father. Each throws light on the
conditions of the court and of the people. The first shows us the
comparative seclusion of the women of David's harem; Amnon
has to resort to a trick to get speech with Tamar.[1] It lets us see the
size of the royal family—the watchman who sees them returning
after the murder of Amnon beholds a 'large crowd'.[2] It suggests
that members of the king's house might have property of their
own, apart from their ancestral land; Absalom has a 'ranch' in
Mount Ephraim, near Baal-hazor, and not far from Bethel.[3]
The methods of court intrigue familiar to the east are not
wanting; Joab goes about his task of intercession with extra-

[1] 2 Sam. xiii. 1–14.   [2] 2 Sam. xiii. 34.   [3] 2 Sam. xiii. 23.

ordinary indirectness—which deceives nobody, least of all the king.[1] One important legal, or quasi-legal, point is settled; the king has the right to prohibit the operation of the law of blood-revenge.[2] This appears not only in the fact that Absalom is given permission to return to his home in safety, but also in that in conversation with the Tekoan woman David assures her that her fratricidal son shall be spared for her sake. This is not the only illustration we have from the early monarchy of the weakening of the blood feud, and while it undoubtedly continued to operate for centuries, it must have become gradually less stringent and oppressive.

2 Sam. xv–xix contains the story of Absalom's rebellion, and throws a strong light on the conditions of the Israelite monarchy. David was already growing old, and was unable to attend as closely as he had done in earlier years to his judicial functions—always the first duty of an oriental sovereign. Absalom made use of this failure to create dissatisfaction, and was successful especially because the litigants came from many quarters in Israel, and would carry back to their homes a favourable account of his kindness and courtesy. Four years[3] of this steady sapping of his father's authority left him in a position in which he felt strong enough to make an actual attempt. He used as his opportunity a special sacrifice at Hebron, which, he claimed, had to be made as a thank-offering for his return to Jerusalem, in fulfilment of a vow. It is significant that he had to go to Hebron to perform this sacrifice to Yahweh, showing that the sanctuary there was held in high repute. His plan was probably to move in the way his father had done, first securing the south, and then the centre and north of the land. In winning the north he may have relied on the help of the people of Geshur, his mother's original home,[4] where he had found refuge after the murder of Amnon.

At Hebron he openly raised the standard of revolt, and so successful had his preliminary measures been that practically the whole country was ready to rise in his favour. News was brought to Jerusalem, and David hastily fled, accompanied only by a few Israelite soldiers, led by Joab, and his Philistine body-guard. He refused to take the Ark with him, and left the priests, Abiathar and Zadok, together with his friend Hushai the Archite, from

---

[1] 2 Sam. xiv. 1–20. [2] 2 Sam. xiv. 11.
[3] The 'forty years' of the MT. in xv. 7 is obviously corrupt; the LXX is probably right in reading 'four'. [4] 2 Sam. iii. 3.

Mount Ephraim, to work for him in Jerusalem, thus counter-mining the conspiracy of his son.

Several incidents of David's flight have been preserved, particularly the action of Ziba, servant of Meribaal, who believed in David's ultimate triumph, and sought to ensure his own prosperity at his master's expense;[1] and the cursing of the fugitive king by Shimei, of the house of Saul.[2] Once more we have presented to us the real magnanimity of David, who would not allow vengeance to be taken on Shimei.[3]

The scene changes to Jerusalem, where Absalom had assumed the royal state, and we have a vivid account of the debate in his council, in which the advice of Ahithophel, who urged an imme-diate pursuit and assault, was rejected in favour of the treacher-ous advice of Hushai to muster a great army. At the same time Hushai managed to warn David through the sons of the priests, and David crossed the Jordan. To the east he was among friends, and received help and assistance. Making his head-quarters at Mahanaim,[4] he turned on the pursuers. The story of the battle is very familiar, and few scenes in history have more completely aroused the sympathy of men than the picture of David caring more for his rebellious son than for all else. David seems to have been incapable of vindictiveness towards a personal enemy.

David's restoration left him more firmly seated on the throne than ever; but it did not prevent another outbreak, which our text of *Samuel* connects with the rebellion of Absalom. It may be doubted, however, whether the connexion is original,[5] and this event should, perhaps, be ascribed to the time which followed immediately after the death of Ishbaal. Similarly, it is not im-possible that the account of the murder of Amasa by Joab, which seems to have had no motive other than professional jealousy, was originally also entirely independent of the Sheba story. In any case, Sheba is pursued to the far north, and takes refuge in Abel-beth-maacah,[6] a strong city not far from Dan. Here he is

---

[1] 2 Sam. xvi. 1–4.   [2] 2 Sam. xvi. 5–13.
[3] Assuming that 1 Kgs. ii. 8 f. is not strictly historical.
[4] The exact site is uncertain, but the town lay to the north of the Jabbok.
[5] The event is apparently an attempt to revive the kingdom of Saul at the expense of David, and would more naturally have stood near the beginning of David's reign. For a thorough discussion see S. A. Cook, *Notes on the Composition of 2 Samuel*; *AJSL.*, 1900, pp. 145–77; and Budde, *Samuel*, pp. 295 f.
[6] So read as one word, omitting the conjunction.

followed by Joab, and, in order to save the city, Sheba is put to death, and his head is thrown over the wall to Joab.

All the later history of Israel looked back on David, in spite of his admitted faults and sins, as the ideal monarch. It behoves us, then, to try to form some picture of his government, of the theory on which it was based, and of the organization of the kingdom. Our materials are somewhat scanty, but a few salient points may be noted.

In the first place, we may observe that the sovereignty of David over all Israel was based on a 'covenant'.[1] It is difficult to lay too much stress on this fact, for it colours, in a sense, the whole of the later history of the monarchy, and illustrates a remarkable political theory. Normally, kingship in the ancient, as in the modern, east is unlimited, and depends entirely on the will of the sovereign. It may be secured by force, but when once it has been attained, there is no power which can lay down conditions, no means whereby a check can be placed upon it. Monarchy necessarily implies autocracy. In Israel this was not so. Among other gifts that the Aramaean invaders brought into the country was a conception of human relations which we cannot but call profoundly democratic, and this ran through all the dealings of man with man. Israel, like other nations, recognized degrees in rank, but the true ancestral spirit of the people always refused to admit that the sovereign had unqualified and unlimited rights over his subjects. In this respect the prophets were repositories of the Israelite feeling, and the neo-prophetic movement from the first entered its protest against the exercise of an arbitrary authority which disregarded the rights of man. We shall have occasion to notice this more fully when we reach the ninth century, but it is implicit in the view Israel took of the monarchy from the first. Here it may be enough to cite two significant passages, both dating from the seventh century or the beginning of the sixth. The first is Deut. xvii. 20, in the law of the monarchy, where, after the demand that the king shall procure a copy of the Law and study it all his life, the reason given is 'that his heart be not lifted up above his *brethren*'. The second is Jer. xxii. 13, where the prophet denounces

[1] 2 Sam. v. 3. Cp. Desnoyers, *HPH*. iii. 349 ff. Two suggestions are made as to the terms of the covenant, (a) that 1 Sam. viii. 11–18 may be a fragment of an ancient formula (p. 358), (b) that one of its provisions forbade the taking of a census (p. 351, n. 3).

Jehoiakim for his tyrannical ways, and especially because he makes his *neighbour* work without adequate recompense. It is in these words 'brother' and 'neighbour' that we have the key to the true Israelite attitude towards monarchy. Even the divine right conferred by the anointing ritual is limited by law, custom, and covenant, and all these are based on the fundamental fact of equality in the sight of Yahweh. The sovereign does not belong to a different species, he is no semi-divine being, as most oriental kings claimed to be; he has a special position with peculiar privileges, but he is only *primus inter pares*, and his privileges are limited in themselves and balanced by responsibilities.

The Israelite king was thus, if we may use the phrase so early, king by contract, not by natural right. His accession involved a threefold covenant, in which the parties were the king, the people, and Yahweh. What its exact or normal terms were, we do not know; the regulations laid down in Deut. xvii. look like an ideal which men had not yet realized, but which bitter experience had taught them to be desirable, for they have the air of a demand for the redress of grievances. It seems that it was not every king who had thus pledged himself on his accession; we may certainly doubt whether Jehoiakim took any oath, save one of loyalty to his foreign overlord. But the procedure seems to have been normal, and the account of Rehoboam shows that the covenant must have been of the nature of a charter, limiting the royal power. No doubt it bound the subject to render certain customary dues, to come armed for war, if called upon, and to be prepared to give certain national services free. It seems to be equally clear that it laid on the king certain limits beyond which he could not go in making these demands of his people, and the introduction of Yahweh into the transaction was a sufficient guarantee of its observance by both the other parties. There was no set formula for the rules laid down, and they might be varied from time to time. At the beginning of each new reign the terms were subject to revision, as the story of Rehoboam shows, and the people felt that they had the right to refuse a sovereign who would not accede to their demands—unless he could impose himself upon them by force of arms. Here for the first time, though its conditions were not rigidly fixed, we have a formal monarchical constitution, with recognized privileges and established checks on prerogative.

Within the limits thus imposed a fairly high degree of

organization was possible. The three main functions of oriental government are concerned with war, finance and justice, to which commerce and transport may often be added, and for these there will be systematic provision in a well-ordered state.

The organization of the army seems to have been comparatively simple. We have no formal account of it, but in all probability the general levies of Israel were arranged in family and local groups, so that men fought side by side with their neighbours and kindred. The officers had command of bodies of hundreds and thousands, though we must not assume that the numbers were always rigidly fixed. Regular drill does not seem to have been invented, for fighting was for the most part individual and in loose order, the armies depending for victory largely on panic produced by the shock of the first charge. It was a rare thing for any single warrior to stand alone when his comrades fled, and one of David's most famous heroes made his name by holding his ground after his fellows had been driven in terror from the field.[1]

In addition to the national levy, David had at least the nucleus of a standing army. It is interesting to observe that its main strength was drawn from foreign sources, for the Cherethites and the Pelethites are almost certainly Philistines,[2] and they not only formed the mainstay of David's personal force, but their presence in the ranks of Solomon went far to secure his accession —they were to David what the Praetorian Guard was to the Roman emperors. David's army was also distinguished by the presence of two significant groups of 'mighty men'. It does not appear that they held any particular military rank in virtue of their inclusion in these groups (though they may have done so), since this seems to have been a matter settled practically when the troops were about to proceed to battle. Benaiah, however, was the captain of the royal guard. The groups were rather orders of merit, especially the Three. The Thirty may have had some organization among themselves; Abishai is their 'commander'.[3]

---

[1] 2 Sam. xxiii. 11 f.

[2] The two names always occur together, 2 Sam. viii. 18, xv. 18, xx. 7, 23 (where the Kᵉthibh has הכרי for הכרתי—an obvious mistake corrected by Qᵉre), 1 Kgs. i. 38, 44. It will be remembered that Ittai the Gittite commanded a division at the battle of the wood of Rephaim, 2 Sam. xviii. 2.

[3] The lists are somewhat confusing, in spite of the evidence that may be obtained from the copy in 1 Chron. xi. 10–47. The text, as is not unnatural, seems to be in some disorder, and there is an uncertainty as to the number. The total of the names given in 2 Sam. xxiii. 18–39 is thirty-three, including Abishai and Benaiah,

Of the organization of the civil authorities for finance and 'public works' we know very little, save that Adoram was the officer responsible for the supply of unpaid labour.[1] But we may assume that the organization was already in existence, though it was only in the reign of Solomon that its development was completed. We have no evidence at all as to the amount of tribute paid to the king. It is clear that it must have been considerable, for the expenses of the court, though far below those of the next reign, cannot have been small. Nor do we possess any account of the way in which it was assessed or collected. Probably these arrangements were still at an elementary stage of development.

Two names are mentioned as belonging to what we may call the Secretariat. The offices they hold are those of 'recorder' and 'scribe'. The two may have overlapped, but their main functions are easily distinguished. Every eastern court of any consideration kept an official record of events, and there must have been one person primarily responsible for seeing that the royal annals were duly maintained. It was also necessary to have a whole staff of secretaries to deal with the official correspondence. While the art of writing was well known, and had been for many centuries practised in Palestine, it was by no means universal, and was largely confined (as at this day in the east) to a professional class. It would be most interesting to know how this correspondence was carried on, in what kind of script and in what language. Four centuries earlier the cuneiform script and the Akkadian language had been universally used for official correspondence in Palestine, and by the time

who are especially singled out for the mention of their deeds. Verse 39 says that there were thirty-seven, a figure which may be held to be inclusive of all the 'mighty men', attained by adding in Joab and the Three to the list of the Thirty. Still stranger is it to find the name of Shammah the Hararite in both lists—in the table of the Three his father's name is given, but the two must surely be the same person. *Chronicles* adds a further sixteen names at the end of the list; they may be derived from a different source or they may imply that the list in *2 Samuel* has been accidentally mutilated at the end. Probably the number thirty was maintained as the limit, and the larger figure is due to the fact that vacancies were filled up as they occurred. We know nothing of any of them except Abishai, Benaiah, and Uriah, unless 'Elhanan the son of Dodo the Bethlehemite' be identified with 'Elhanan the son of Jaare-oregim a Bethlehemite' mentioned in 2 Sam. xxi. 19 (his father's name is obviously corrupt), and Mebunnai the Hushathite (2 Sam. xxiii. 27), called Sibbecai in 1 Chron. xi. 29, be identical with the Sibbecai whose exploit is recounted in 2 Sam. xxi. 18.

[1] 2 Sam. xx. 24, a late insertion in its present position, but possibly drawn from a contemporary record.

the monarchy came to an end, Aramaic was in use for this purpose. Traces of an early form of the writing known to us through remains in Phoenicia and Palestine have been found in Sinaitic monuments dating from the fifteenth century B.C. (or perhaps the eighteenth?),[1] and it is possible that the medium employed in the Israelite monarchy (as in the Moabite kingdom of the ninth century) was the Hebrew language in this script.

When we turn to the judiciary we have even less direct information than on other points already mentioned. We may suppose that the old methods of settling disputes still maintained themselves, and that the general organization of the village and city communities had undergone little, if any, change. Justice seems to have been still a local matter, as we may see from the story told by the Tekoan woman in 2 Sam. xiv. 5–7, where the whole community rises up and demands the penalty for fratricide. But there was one novel feature. This same story shows that an appeal lay to the king, and that he had the right to set aside even the immemorial tradition and custom of the land, cancel the sentence of a lower court, pardon the condemned criminal—act, in a word, as the final court. His position and duties are brought out clearly also in the story of Absalom's revolt, for the young rebel's method of winning himself a party is to condole with suitors who meet with delay or with an adverse decision, and assure them that if only he had control, they would have far more reason to be satisfied.

Duplicate lists, with slight differences, of the chief officers of the kingdom are found in 2 Sam. viii. 16–18 and xx. 23–6. Each closes with the mention of the priesthood, and the notice serves to show how far from the actual facts is the elaborate ecclesiastical system which a later age attributed to David. In both lists, two priests are mentioned by name, Zadok and Abiathar. How their duties were apportioned we cannot say, nor have we any account of the way in which Zadok attained his position. Abiathar, with the Ephod, had been one of David's earliest followers, having taken refuge with him after the

[1] See H. Grimme, *Althebräische Inschriften vom Sinai* (1923); A. H. Gardiner, 'The Egyptian Origin of the Semitic Alphabet', *JEA*. iii (1916), pp. 1–15; A. E. Cowley, 'The Origin of the Semitic Alphabet', ib., pp. 17 ff.; K. Sethe, *Die neuentdeckte Sinaiinschrift und die Entstehung der semitischen Schrift, Nachrichten v. d. K. Ges. zu Göttingen* (1917), pp. 437–75; D. Völter, *Die althebräischen Inschriften vom Sinai*; H. Bauer, *Zur Entzifferung der neuentdeckten Sinaischrift* (1918).

slaughter of the rest of his family at Nob. Perhaps Abiathar still remained as the priest of the Ephod, while Zadok had special charge of the Ark. But the most remarkable feature of the notice comes at the end. In ch. xx the list concludes with the statement that 'Ira the Jairite was priest unto David', as though he had a private establishment, independent of the normal priesthood of the national sanctuary. This in itself seems strange enough, but stranger still, in the light of the later theory, is the statement which replaces this remark in ch. viii, to the effect that 'David's sons were priests'.[1] There is no reason to doubt the historicity of the statement, and it has even been suggested that in its original form the list contained both Ira and the sons of David. The king himself had acted as priest when bringing the Ark up to Jerusalem, and there can have been nothing unnatural to his mind in putting his sons into that office. No doubt there were others who were required for the service of the sanctuary, but, even so, the ecclesiastical establishment of David must have been a very simple matter compared with that organized by Solomon and maintained by his successors.

The establishment of the monarchy brought with it one important change in national organization. The tribe almost disappeared as an administrative unit. We hear of tribal names in later days; in the eighth century Zebulun and Naphtali,[2] Ephraim and Manasseh,[3] are mentioned, but the first two terms are local rather than tribal, and the two latter suggest primarily the conflict of rival dynasties. From the first days of the settlement the tendency to unification must have made itself felt, but the process was long and slow; to Israelites themselves it may have been imperceptible until the organization of the kingdom by David. But with his reign and that of his son the maintenance of tribal divisions became almost impossible. A strongly centralized monarchy turned men's eyes to the king and to the capital rather than to the local chiefs,[4] whose power and authority

[1] Several problems of text are raised by these two passages, such as the mention of 'Ahimelech the son of Abiathar', a curious confusion of father and son, the naming of Ahitub (really Ahimelech's father) as the father of Zadok, and the variant between the last clauses in the two recensions. For a full discussion see Budde, *Samuel*, pp. 243 f.
[2] e.g. Isa. ix. 1 (Heb. viii. 23). [3] e.g. Isa. ix. 21 (Heb. 20).
[4] The 'Elders' still survived, it is true, though their powers must have been curtailed. They appear to have had an important position during, and after, the Exile, when the disappearance of the monarchy to some extent restored the more primitive conditions.

declined as their subordination to the sovereign became obvious. Increased facilities for communication, made possible by the political union of the country, tended to break down local barriers, and, while the memory of tribal independence was doubtless preserved by peasant tenacity, the movements of individuals were liable in practice to obscure the old distinctions. Numbers of foreigners settling and mingling with the people turned naturally to the monarch rather than to the small group, in whose traditions they had little or no interest. A new aristocracy of wealth (a factor in the life of Israel which, though not prominent till the eighth century, must have originated with the monarchy) sprang up, and its members owed allegiance only to the king whose favour permitted their prosperity. Numbers of officials drawn from all sections of the population found their home at court, and the influence of their activities in the country at large tended to break down differences among the people. The royal cities had very mixed populations, and, as the life of the nation expanded, these places served more and more as centres of local interest. It is significant that in the list of Solomon's administrative districts[1] five tribal names only appear— Ephraim, Naphtali, Asher, Issachar, and Benjamin—and the phraseology suggests that neither the district of Ephraim nor that of Asher represents a single, complete, tribal unit. The distinction between Israel and Judah remained, it is true, but we should observe that the Benjamin country belonged to the latter. There was no tribal affinity between Judah and Benjamin; it was the presence of a centralizing power in Jerusalem which kept them united as against the rest of Israel.

At the same time, among the agricultural, and still more among the semi-nomad elements in the population, the memory of the old organization was preserved. Tribal names are not uncommonly used by the prophets, the natural guardians of the 'lower' classes in the Israelite community, and the ideal reconstruction of the nation always presupposed the re-establishment of the primitive order and relationships. The truth is, that in practice monarchy and tribal organization were entirely incompatible, and it was only in circles which were more or less prejudiced against the idea of human kingship in Israel that the tribal names and ideas persisted. Ezekiel, in dreaming of the perfect Israel some day to be established in Palestine,

---

[1] 1 Kgs. iv. 8–19, cp. pp. 263–5.

went back to the patriarchal names, and, though some of the tribes had perished centuries since, they were all to be revived, and each was to be given its due place in the final polity of the chosen people. But for the time, and for practical purposes, the tribal organization was at least in abeyance.

It was David, then, who was the real founder of the Israelite state. The way had been prepared through generations of struggle against foreign enemies, and sporadic and evanescent signs of a coming royal dominion had manifested themselves in earlier days. The pressure of the Philistine advance had made some valid unity between the divided elements in Palestine imperative, unless she were to remain subject for ever to an alien power. The life and death of Saul, fruitless as they seemed at the time, were not unavailing; there was that about the tragic figure of the prophet-king which made the idea of an Israelite monarchy not only feasible but attractive. Yet, great as he was (and none with any understanding of human nature can deny greatness to Saul), a greater was needed to complete the work that he had begun, and with the need arose the man.

If we would understand the true import of David's work, we can best appraise it by a comparison between the positions of Saul and of Solomon. The glory of the latter stands in vivid contrast to the rustic court of the former. David's predecessor lived a life of battle and of war—much of it, no doubt, due to his own weakness. But Solomon was no stronger a man, and the prestige of the Israelite kingdom, even as a fighting power, gave him a reign in which we have no record whatever of foreign war. His territories were traditionally the largest ever governed by an Israelite king, yet they must have been simply the lands which he inherited from his father. David left all the countries bordering on Israel either subject to him or bound in close alliance by treaties of peace, and had his son and grandson been his equals in intellectual and moral qualities, the kingdom might have endured and spread till it rose to a dominant height in the east. But not for many a generation, perhaps never again in her history, was Israel to produce another David, and that portion of the work which could be achieved only by a long period of wise and humane rule was for ever left undone. David could and did inaugurate a kingdom comprising a united Israel, but it could attain a secure position only when generations had grown accustomed to the situation, and a politically unified people had become as much a matter of national tradition as their oneness in the worship of Yahweh.

It is, after all, on the religious side of Israelite life that David's work proved most enduring. Himself a passionate devotee of Yahweh, in spite of much in his belief that was elementary and 'superstitious', he emphasized and reinforced the conception of a national religion in a fashion which was never forgotten. When he brought the Ark to Jerusalem he laid the foundations of an idea which was to endure for a period whose end is yet in the far future. Of the four great monotheisms which the world has known, two hold Jerusalem the most sacred spot on earth, and a third keeps it scarcely less holy. The days were to come when Israel was to be torn asunder politically, but even in the eighth century a prophet could speak of Yahweh as 'roaring from Zion'[1] when he addressed northern Israel. Judah herself lost her independence, the Ark perished in the flames that devoured the first Temple, but by that time the work was done, and men were ready to learn a new conception of religion, in which no material embodiment of Yahweh was needed more, when men should no longer speak with regret of the Ark of the covenant of Yahweh,[2] nor should it enter their thoughts, but their spiritual life should be built on a new Covenant, placed in their inward parts and written on their hearts.[3]

[1] Am. i. 2.   [2] Jer. iii. 16.   [3] Jer. xxxi. 31-4.

Additional Note C

DAVID'S SYRIAN WARS

THE whole question of David's Syrian wars is difficult and complicated, not only because we are not certain of all the localities mentioned, but also because of problems which arise from the Hebrew text. We have three accounts of the defeat of the Syrians, derived, it would seem, from different sources; as they stand they are difficult to harmonize with one another. The first is in 2 Sam. viii. 3–12. Here David smites Hadadezer, son of Rehob, king of Zobah. The Syrians of Damascus come to the help of Hadadezer and are crushed in turn. David is congratulated by Toi, king of Hamath, who has himself had trouble with Hadadezer.

The second narrative, 2 Sam. x. 6–14, is that which also describes the defeat of the Ammonites, who have hired the Syrians of Beth-rehob, and the Syrians of Zobah, and the king of Maacah, and the men of Tob; all are defeated.

The third passage is 2 Sam. x. 15–19, following immediately after that just mentioned. Hadarezer summons the Syrians who are beyond the river and they come to Helam with Shobak, Hadarezer's commander-in-chief, at their head. David meets them at Helam, defeats them, kills a large number of them, destroys seven hundred chariots, and kills Shobak. The result is that all the kings subject to Hadarezer make peace with David, and are afraid to give any further help to the Ammonites.

It is generally agreed that this third passage is introduced by the compiler of the book in order to explain why it was that the Syrians helped the Ammonites when the latter were first attacked by Israel, but refrained from offering assistance in the second campaign. It is not impossible that we have here the correct interpretation of the actual course of events, but the passage which records the Syrian defeat is, nevertheless, a comparatively late compilation.

It is, however, fairly clear that this third passage is not independent of the first. Hadarezer can hardly be a different person from Hadadezer—the confusion between ר and ד is so common that we can hardly regard the substitution of the one for the other as a conjectural emendation. Further, the suggestion in viii. 3, that Hadadezer held authority over tribes on the Euphrates, is easily understood as the basis of Hadarezer's force mentioned in x. 16. Is it possible that Shobak himself is due to a corruption of Zobah?

Even if we admit the dependence of the third narrative on the first, there remains the possibility that the first has come down to us with a good deal of corruption, both of text and tradition, and that the later form may contain details which were original with the earlier, but have not survived. The greatest difficulty is that offered by the

mention of Rehob, which, in the form Beth-rehob, is mentioned in
Judges xviii. 28 as being in the neighbourhood of Laish-Dan, and
in Num. xiii. 21 (P) in the simple form Rehob, as being the northern
limit of the expedition of the spies. A place Rehob is mentioned on
the Seti stele found at Beth-shean, cp. C. S. Fisher, *University of
Pennsylvania Museum Journal*, 14 (1923), p. 232. It is tempting to
assume, with Winckler (*Geschichte*, i. 141 f.) that 'ben Rehob' does
not mean 'son of Rehob', but 'a man belonging to Rehob', and that
Beth-rehob and Zobah are the same state (see Budde, *Samuel*, p. 239).
On the other hand, the famous inscription of Shalmaneser III concludes the list of kings whom he fought at Ḳarḳar with the name of
Ba'asa, son of Rehob, king of Ammon (see Luckenbill, *ARA*. i,
no. 611, p. 223). This shows that Rehob was not only a place-name,
but also a personal name, and the most probable solution of the
problem presented by our documents is that the personal name
Rehob was understood as a place-name by the editor, who therefore
inserted it as a place-name in the *second* narrative, making it a
separate state alongside of Zobah. 1 Sam. xiv. 47 (see p. 184) is
probably derived from 2 Sam. x. 6.

For further suggestions as to the text see the commentaries, *ad loc.*

Chapter XI

SOLOMON

SUMMARY

[Solomon has achieved a great reputation, mainly as the builder of the Temple and as the wisest man of the ancient east. But he was without experience of the hardships of David's earlier life, and his character made him a strong contrast to his father. He was selfish, ostentatious, and extravagant, while his government was marked by tyrannical oppression.

He continued his father's foreign policy, but the only addition to his territories was the site of Gezer, handed over to him by the Egyptian king as the dowry of the princess whom Solomon married. He strengthened his defences by adding to the fortifications of several border towns, and in more than one place he established a force of chariotry for which the material was obtained from Egypt.

His chief works were carried out in Jerusalem, where he erected the Temple and a number of other palatial buildings, while he considerably enlarged the city itself. Supplies of material and skilled artificers were obtained from Phoenicia, while for labour Solomon relied on forced levies from Israel. His income was derived partly from taxation and partly from trade. For financial and administrative purposes the country was divided into twelve districts, not including Judah, which seems to have had preferential treatment. He organized voyages in conjunction with Hiram of Tyre, and also used Elah as a port.

Solomon's later years were gloomy. He is charged with allowing his foreign wives to lead him into apostasy, and before his death both Edom and the Aramaean tribes had recovered their independence, the latter making their centre at Damascus. At the same time his wastefulness and oppression went far to undermine the position of the crown at home, and prepared the way for the division of the kingdom.]

For the reign of Solomon we have no authority, not even the smallest reference, outside the Biblical record. That is contained in 1 Kgs. i–xi, with perhaps occasional notes in 2 Chron. i–ix, though here, as elsewhere, we often suspect the Chronicler of idealizing the facts, when he differs from, or adds to, the accounts given us in *Kings*. And even the older work shows clear traces of redaction from a later, i.e. a Deuteronomistic, standpoint. The materials from which Solomon's story has been compiled seem to be mainly three in number, (*a*) the royal annals, (*b*) a collection of stories about the king which had become traditional, (*c*) records of the Temple. In addition to these we have from time to time—and here we must include some of the noblest passages in the book—insertions made by the editor, and

expressing, like the 'speeches' in Thucydides, not so much what was
actually said or happened, as what should have been said, or should
have happened, from the view-point of a later generation. The most
conspicuous example is Solomon's great dedicatory prayer (1 Kgs.
viii. 22–53), but it does not stand alone. In spite of this complexity,
however, it is not usually difficult to disentangle from the narrative
those elements on which we may safely rely as giving us, either a
contemporary record, or a sound tradition.

IT was, perhaps, a calamity for Israel that David's successor
was one of his younger sons. Had he been followed by one of
those who knew from experience something of his earlier life, of
his reign in Hebron, and of his struggles for the existence of his
kingdom and his nation, the history of Israel might have taken a
very different course. But Solomon was 'born in the purple',
when David's authority was firmly established over all Israel,
and his career of foreign conquest was nearly, if not quite,
complete. If our records are reliable, he first saw the light at
least a year after the Ammonite war, and the Syrian wars which
are closely connected with it must have taken place before
Solomon was old enough to appreciate their significance. The
only war which he can have seen himself was the struggle
against Absalom, and the victory was so complete as to
strengthen any ideas he may have had previously on the rights
and position of the king in Israel. He thus entered on his reign
equipped with those conceptions of monarchy which are characteristic of the eastern world in general, conceptions which
seem to presuppose that the king is an absolute despot, and that
the people exist purely for his sake.

Solomon's real character has been much overlaid by later
generations. As the builder of the Temple, he had the strongest
claims to approbation from the later theologians and ecclesiastics whose views have coloured all the history of Israel as it has
come down to us. His reputation for wisdom has enhanced the
high position which his piety assured to him, and has made him
a figure of superhuman magnitude and power alike to Jewish
and to Moslem tradition. The magnificence of his buildings and
the splendour of his court have dazzled his own and later ages,
and the theory that the extent of his dominions remained unimpaired until his old age, or even perhaps until his death, has
given him the reputation of governing more lands and peoples
than any other Israelite sovereign.

Yet there is another side to the picture. Raised to the throne by a palace intrigue to be joint sovereign with his father during David's last days, he took, as it seems, no oath, and accepted no covenant. The monarchy was yet a new thing, and men did not realize the need for safeguards against the exercise of arbitrary power. Even had they felt their danger, the absence of any organized resistance—for Adonijah's party collapsed at once— in the face of the royal body-guard probably would have made it impossible for the nation to enforce its will, and Solomon was left free from the restraints which had bound David and were to bind many, if not all, of his successors.

Our records have come to us through men who counted it a king's highest service to his God to maintain the pure worship of Yahweh, and even from the Deuteronomic standpoint, in other ways so typical of the best moral and social feeling in Israel, the builder of the Temple occupied a unique position. But the eighth- and seventh-century prophets might have thought very differently about him, and, had they lived in his day, might have spoken of him in terms like those in which Jeremiah denounced Jehoiakim.[1] His buildings cannot have been erected except at enormous expense for materials, and certainly must have required very large supplies of labour. There can be no doubt that, in spite of other resources which may have been at his disposal, Solomon was compelled to lay the greater part of these burdens on his own unfortunate subjects. It is true that one account represents the king as utilizing for this purpose only men of Canaanite origin,[2] but we must regard this rather as an attempt to justify him than as actual history. The distinction between the two races had long ceased to have any practical significance, and we have direct contradictions elsewhere.[3]

Solomon's enormous harem may be attributed primarily to his desire for magnificence; a man's standing in the east is often to be judged by the number of wives and other women whom he possesses. Later Israelite feeling condemned the practice, probably on social and religious grounds, and the Deuteronomic prohibition[4] is possibly based on traditions of Solomon's life. For even the historian is compelled regretfully to admit that in his old age Solomon did not maintain the high standard with which his reign had opened, but allowed his wives to lead him into

---

[1] Jer. xxii. 13–19.
[3] 1 Kgs. v. 13, xi. 28.
[2] 1 Kgs. ix. 20 ff.
[4] Deut. xvii. 17.

the worship of foreign deities. To the later scribes this was a sin far more terrible than the oppression of his subjects.

Solomon was lauded for his wisdom in his own day and by later generations, but the examples which tradition has recorded suggest that the qualities which he possessed should come under other categories. He may well have had that keenness of wit which would enable him to solve a knotty problem in the administration of justice, and this is always attractive to an eastern community. For many purposes it is necessary, above all things, that a king should not judge according to the sight of his eyes or the hearing of his ears, in a world where the only evidence on which the least reliance can be placed is circumstantial—and that is often manufactured. This smartness in applying a test which will induce a criminal to convict himself has a high value to the oriental, and Solomon may have possessed it. He may have had an elementary interest in science, and have anticipated Aristotle and Theophrastus by his investigations into natural history. He may have had a flair for epigram and a pretty turn for lyric poetry. These are the forms of wisdom and the accomplishments which are ascribed to him, the qualities which attracted the Queen of Sheba, and are still more highly elaborated in eastern, especially Moslem, tradition. But none of these things could compensate for his absolute lack of true wisdom, his inability to see the meaning of facts, his failure to appreciate the eternal laws which govern the relations of man with man, and the principles on which alone a happy and successful kingdom can be established. In these respects he was far inferior to his father, stood even below the level of the average Israelite, and immeasurably beneath the high standards attained by the great prophets of the eighth and seventh centuries.

The new king, then, appears to us as a person very different from his father. He was no warrior, and had never known real hardship. He had some gift for organization, but seems to have been lacking in those magnetic qualities of personality which endeared David to his people. He was utterly vain and selfish, ostentatious and extravagant. He had little or no regard for the feelings of his people, and his reign was one of tyrannous oppression. He did nothing to reconcile the two sections of the people, northern and southern, to the union which his father had brought about, and his character and policy prepared the way for the disruption which took place at his death. It is at his door that we must place the chief responsibility for the weakness of Israel in the generations which followed; a wise and beneficent rule might have consolidated the new-born state, and enabled it to hold its own when pressure from the east was once more brought to bear on the country. As it was, he wasted the resources of the land, both in material goods and in man-power, and gave opportunity for the growth of jealousy and hostility which frittered away what strength the country had left in petty local struggles. If he did not actually destroy the national edifice erected by David, he did at least undermine its foundations.

The circumstances of Solomon's accession are described for us in detail,[1] and prove that his elevation to the throne was a triumph for the principle of autocracy. He was one of the younger sons, and his claim to the crown can hardly have been widely recognized. There was no rule of primogeniture, as it seems, and yet it was natural that David should be immediately followed by one of his older sons. This seems to have been the view taken by Adonijah, and he adopted the state of an heir-apparent. Round him gathered a popular party headed by Joab, the commander of the national levies of Israel, and Abiathar, the priest who had followed David from his early years. The mention of these two men, and the omission of Benaiah, the captain of the foreign body-guard and of Zadok, the new-comer into the priesthood, indicate clearly the general tendency of Adonijah's movement. He expected, and sought to be, such a king as his father once had been, raised to the throne by the enthusiasm of the people as a whole, and resolved to rule with all respect for their prejudices and principles. David, as it seemed, acquiesced in his elder son's actions, and matters came to a head when Adonijah made a great public festival to which all his associates and supporters, including the royal family, were invited. The omission of Solomon is significant, and suggests that already there was strong feeling between the brothers. Doubtless, had Adonijah succeeded his father, Solomon would have been in a difficult, perhaps in a dangerous, position. But, through the influence of Nathan and Bathsheba, the king was induced to order the formal coronation of Solomon as a colleague of his own. Apparently the plans of Adonijah had not taken an armed movement into account, and the presence

---

[1] 1 Kgs. i. 5–53.

of the Cherethites and Pelethites in Solomon's train made resistance impossible. The festal company hastily dispersed, and accepted the new king without striking a blow.

Our records suggest that Solomon took no further steps to strengthen his position while the old king lived. But as soon as David was dead, the young man began to remove all those who might be rivals or were likely to try to organize a party against him. Tradition has ascribed to David a last will and testament,[1] in which he gave Solomon instructions as to how three persons were to be treated. These were Joab, Barzillai, and Shimei. Barzillai had helped David during his flight before Absalom, and his sons were to be rewarded, the other two were to be put to death. Joab had been among the most faithful followers of David from his earliest days, and his very enthusiasm had at times embarrassed the king. More than once, feeling that he knew better than David where his master's safety lay, he had put to death persons whom the king would have spared. In one instance, that of Abner, he had a specious justification in the existence of a blood-feud, but that excuse can hardly be made for his treatment of Amasa and Absalom. The reason assigned for the condemnation of Joab is that the blood of Amasa remained unsatisfied while he lived, and that the whole realm was in danger of some such disaster as had been brought upon it by Saul's treatment of the Gibeonites.[2] Joab was 'girded and shod with blood',[3] and no atonement could be made for that blood save by the blood of him that shed it. Shimei had cursed the king. His imprecation had not yet been fulfilled, and it remained, therefore, alive and malignant, to be a danger to Solomon. The young king could assure his own safety only by guiding the curse on to the head of the man that had uttered it. So David left it to his son to destroy these two men as he thought best.

We cannot but ask ourselves whether our records are accurate in ascribing these injunctions to David. Solomon himself had abundant reason to desire the deaths of Shimei and of Joab. The former represented the house of Saul. Joab had been the great strength of the party of Adonijah, which might be revived, and his influence, as commander-in-chief of the popular levies of Israel made him dangerous. No eastern monarch could have felt safe while such men lived, apart from any peril induced by the words of the one and the acts of the other. David, on the

[1] 1 Kgs. ii. 1–9.   [2] Cp. 2 Sam. xxi. 1.   [3] 1 Kgs. ii. 5.

other hand, had nothing to fear from either. Joab, in particular, had always been loyal to him, and his adhesion to the party of Adonijah was in no sense treason against his king. Shimei had lived for years without proving himself a further danger, and the restriction which Solomon placed on him shows that it was not his curse that was to be feared, but his influence among the disaffected in Israel.[1] We inevitably suspect that the record in its present form is an attempt to remove a slur that might have lain on Solomon, by throwing back the responsibility on to David.[2] But maintenance of personal animosity against his private enemies was not characteristic of David, as his treatment of Saul showed, while we know nothing of Solomon which prevents us from ascribing it to him.

Our record[3] tells us that after the death of David, Adonijah tried, through Bathsheba, to secure for himself Abishag, the latest acquisition to David's harem. Naturally interpreting this as a claim to the crown, Solomon had Adonijah put to death, and Joab fled in fear to the sanctuary, where he in turn was cut down at the very altar of Yahweh. Abiathar was banished to Anathoth. Solomon had thus dealt with the most prominent of his rivals and opponents, though, strangely enough, we hear nothing of the fate of David's other sons. But, as the narrative stands, it raises questions in our minds. It is almost inconceivable that Adonijah should have been so foolish as to make of Solomon the request ascribed to him. He must have known that only one construction could be put on his action, and that, unless he had a party behind him, and was prepared to fight for his life, the result would be fatal to him. And why should Joab's execution have followed immediately after that of Adonijah? Why was it that the death of the prince excited the terror of the old soldier? Joab's fate was decreed on grounds which were entirely independent of Adonijah, and no reason is advanced for the delay in putting him to death.

We may, perhaps, conjecture that the order of events as given to us in the narrative has been somewhat dislocated. Is it not more probable that Adonijah's request for Abishag was preferred before, rather than after, the death of David, and that it was laid before the old king himself? It would be natural for Solomon to remove his rival immediately after his father's death.

---

[1] 1 Kgs. ii. 36.　　[2] So Benzinger, *Die Bücher der Könige*, p. 8; Stade, *GVI*. i. 295.
[3] 1 Kgs. ii. 13–25.

The whole story becomes simple and intelligible if we can assume that Adonijah asked David—possibly through Bathsheba, though this is a suspicious detail—if he might receive Abishag as a legacy. Immediately on David's death Adonijah was put out of the way, and Joab, hearing the news, fled to the sanctuary, only to fall there.

It is nearly impossible to write anything like a history of the reign of Solomon. There are few events to be recorded, and the order in which those few occurred seems quite uncertain. We have a series of pictures, handed down by tradition or inscribed in the annals of the court and of the temple; but the compilers of the books of *Kings* seem to have used much freedom in arranging them, and have not aimed at chronological sequence. This, however, need not prevent us from trying to form a judgement as to his policy abroad and at home.

In his relations with other peoples, Solomon maintained his father's policy. The subject-peoples continued faithful to him for a part of his reign; but in his later years, if not in the early days, it seems that he lost his hold over Damascus and Edom. Not long after his accession, however, he secured a new ally in Egypt, probably by recognizing in some way the suzerainty of the reigning Pharaoh. This seems to be implied by Solomon's acceptance of an Egyptian princess, for it was often an admission of a subordinate position, albeit that of a favourite, to receive a wife from another monarch. Unfortunately we have no means of knowing which of the Pharaohs it was who thus entered into an alliance with Solomon. He was clearly a sovereign of some power, since he was able to claim, and partially to enforce, authority over Palestine. Gezer is said to have 'revolted' against him, and, after destroying the city[1] he handed the site over to Solomon. The natural inference is that he was one of the later kings of the twenty-first dynasty, but unfortunately no Egyptian record of the event has yet been discovered, and until such a reference is available it is impossible accurately to identify him. Sheshonk, the founder of the twenty-second dynasty, reversed the policy of his predecessors, and did all in his power to weaken Solomon. It is, therefore, to his reign that we must ascribe the

---

[1] 1 Kgs. ix. 16. The ruins of Gezer have been excavated, and confirm the statement of the book of *Kings*. Solomon did not actually rebuild the city, but erected his fortress on a neighbouring site. See especially Macalister, *Excavations at Gezer*.

help given to the 'adversaries'[1] of Solomon, Hadad of Edom, Rezon of Damascus, and Jeroboam. It was the first two of these who were responsible for the reduction of Solomon's territory by the establishment of independent kingdoms in Edom and in Damascus.[2] In the end he gained nothing by his Egyptian alliance.

Solomon's defensive measures for his kingdom are important, and in this matter he certainly followed the policy of his father. Four fortresses are mentioned as having received his special attention. The first is Jerusalem, and here he continued and strengthened the work begun by David. His new city embraced a great deal more than the original Jebusite town, for it seems to have spread across the Tyropoeon, to the western hill, and to have extended northwards to include the Temple. Only small portions of his walls have yet been excavated, but they are sufficient to illustrate his work here. In particular, he added to the tower at the north-east corner of the Ophel, known as Millo,[3] and his masonry can still be distinguished from that of his predecessors. David, as we have seen, did little more to defend Jerusalem than to run a wall across to cover the breaches in the two Jebusite walls, and Solomon must have felt that the city, especially with its extensions, needed a more stable protection.

The other three places mentioned are all in a sense border towns. Hazor is in the far north, and would serve to protect the country from any invader who tried to enter over the rising ground which separates the valley of the Litany from that of the Jordan. Megiddo is, of course, one of the key positions, and a fortress there would serve to protect the plain of Esdraelon from invasion by Philistines, and to supply a base from which the great caravan route could be controlled. Gezer is, again, a border fortress, and stands in a position from which it can defend the entry into the hills either by the Valley of Aijalon or by the Valley of Sorek. Three other cities are mentioned in 1 Kgs. ix. 17 f., Lower Beth-horon, Baalath, and Tamar. Unfortunately the sites of the last two are not known, though Tamar has been

---

[1] 1 Kgs. xi. 14–40, and see below, pp. 258–60.

[2] Stade, *GVI*. i. 301, places these events at the beginning of Solomon's reign, and attributes the revolts to the deaths of David and Joab, the latter having been the real subjugator of Edom (1 Kgs. xi. 15 f.). But this is to reject unnecessarily the whole connexion of the revolts with Egypt, for it is hardly likely that a Pharaoh would thus diminish the territory of his son-in-law.

[3] Cp. J. G. Duncan, 'Millo and the City of David', *ZAW*. xlii (1924), pp. 222–44.

confused with Tadmor, i.e. Palmyra, but we may take it for
granted that they were a part of the king's scheme for surrounding the whole country with defensive fortresses.

It is not improbable that Solomon made considerable additions to the standing army. Particularly, he raised and maintained a force of chariotry. This, it seems, had been inaugurated
by David after the defeat of the Syrians, for it is said that he
kept a hundred of the captured chariots with their horses.[1] We
may suspect that Solomon had a force of chariots at each of his
main fortresses; recent excavations at Megiddo have revealed
buildings which were apparently chariot-stables, giving accommodation for over two hundred vehicles with their horses.[2]
This establishment became traditional, and it is significant that
at the battle of Ḳarḳar, 853 B.C., the largest chariot force contributed to the allied army which fought against Shalmaneser
was that of Ahab—2,000 chariots.

It is as a builder that Solomon himself would probably have
desired to be known. Not only did he undertake the works of
fortification to which allusion has just been made, but he set
himself to make of Jerusalem a city worthy of royalty. The Ophel
was too small for his projects, and he extended the city northwards so as to include the ancient Jebusite high place by the
threshing-floor of Araunah.[3] Here he erected the Temple which
has made his name so famous. The account of it is given in
1 Kgs. vi, a passage which is certainly based on contemporary
records, probably preserved in the Temple itself.[4] The site of
the old high-place was an irregular rectangle, which was possibly
modified artificially by Solomon. Towards its northern end,
rather to the west of the middle line, stood the great outcrop of
rock which at one time served as an altar, and it would seem
that the Temple itself was erected to the west of this, where

---

[1] 2 Sam. viii. 4.

[2] See Guy, *Bulletin of the Oriental Institute of the University of Chicago*, No. 9.

[3] For a description of the way in which the site was prepared, cp. Wilson and
Warren, *The Recovery of Jerusalem*, and Desnoyers, *HPH.* iii. 72 ff.

[4] The text of this chapter is often difficult to understand, partly because of the
number of technical terms employed, unintelligible even to the ancient translators,
and partly owing to the corruption of the text, which is one of the worst preserved
sections of the Old Testament. The ideal Temple of Ezekiel, however, which is largely
a programme of restoration, sometimes throws light on obscure passages. Cp. the
leading commentators, especially Benzinger, *Die Bücher der Könige*, pp. 25 f.;
Skinner, *1 and 2 Kings*, pp. 103 f.; also T. W. Davies in the *DB.*, art. 'Temple', cols.
694–710.

there is just room for such a building. Its interior length was roughly about 100 feet,[1] its breadth about one-third of its length, and its height about 50 feet. It was divided into two portions, of which the western, or inner chamber, was a square, and the eastern, or outer chamber, twice as long as it was broad. In front, i.e. to the east, was a 'porch', or entrance chamber, half the width of the main building, and one-third of its length. The thickness of the wall is not stated in *Kings*, but in Ezekiel's ideal Temple, which in this feature probably reproduced Solomon's building, it was six cubits on the ground floor.[2] At the height of five cubits, however, it was recessed by half a cubit, a style of building which appears in the old Jebusite walls of Jerusalem excavated on the Ophel, and five cubits higher the same device was used, giving the form of a series of very high and narrow steps. These ledges were used in the construction of a series of chambers, whose floor beams rested on the ledges, thus avoiding penetration of the wall. The outer wall containing these chambers was[3] five cubits thick at the base, and was similarly recessed, giving three tiers of chambers, each one cubit broader than that immediately below it, the breadths being five, six, and seven cubits in the successive tiers. Probably the chambers communicated with one another, each tier thus formed a continuous passage round three sides of the building, north, west, and south. The lowest tier of chambers was reached by a door on the south side of the building, and access was gained to the upper chambers by some kind of staircase.[4] In front of the porch on either side stood twin pillars named Jachin and Boaz, with swelling capitals, adorned with carved reticulations. These probably had some mystic significance which we can no longer recover with any certainty.[5] The porch of the Temple on the east side

[1] There is some uncertainty as to the exact dimensions, as two 'cubits' were in use in Israel, one the ordinary cubit, about the average length of the forearm, the other a handsbreadth longer. Cp. Ezek. xl. 5, xliii. 13.

[2] Ezek. xli. 5.

[3] Again according to Ezekiel, xli. 9.

[4] The Hebrew word used in 1 Kgs. vi. 8 does not occur elsewhere, but was understood by the ancient translators to mean a winding staircase. Stade, however (*ZAW.* 1883 (iii), pp. 136 ff., in the course of an article entitled 'Der Text des Berichtes über Salomos Bauten'), points out (*a*) that there is no trace of a winding stair in the architecture of the ancient east, (*b*) that in Rabbinic Hebrew the word לוּל means 'a trap-door'. He admits that a trap-door alone would not suit the present passage, and therefore supposes that ladders were implied in the term.

[5] Robertson Smith (*Religion of the Semites,*[3] p. 487 f.) believed that one of them was the altar of burnt-offering, and that sacrifices were actually consumed in its

was approached by a flight of ten steps. These are not mentioned in *Kings*, but Ezekiel (xl. 49, LXX) alludes to them, and we may accept his evidence as applying not only to his ideal future Temple, but to that which he remembered from the days of his youth. Air, and a certain amount of light, were supplied by a kind of loophole, guarded by lattice work. Each of the side chambers had one such aperture, and above them were similar openings in the wall of the outer room. The inner room or *Debir*[1] seems to have been in complete darkness,[2] unless, as in the Shiloh Temple, a lamp was kept burning continuously before the Ark.[3] The *Debir* itself formed a cube, being only twenty cubits in height, and it is not clear whether a false roof ran above it at a height of twenty cubits from the floor, thus leaving an empty space of ten cubits in height above it, or whether the roof above the *Debir* was ten cubits lower than that of the front part of the building.[4] Even the lower roof would still leave five cubits above the outer chambers at the side.

The style of architecture thus presented to us is, as Skinner

brazen capital. Cp. Gray, *Sacrifice in the Old Testament*, p. 136. Cheyne held that they were representations of the widely spread conception of the 'mountain of the gods', properly Mesopotamian, but transferred to Israel, *EB*. ii, cols. 2,304 f. Others have suggested that they simply called attention to the truth or the prayer implied in their names; S. A. Cook has mentioned the possibility that the names represent Baal and Yahweh. Others have thought they may have been an elaboration of the Maṣṣebah; for these and other explanations see Benzinger, *Die Bücher der Könige*, pp. 46 f., Skinner, *1 and 2 Kings*, pp. 125 f. Perhaps further light may be obtained from the form and decoration of the capitals. Skinner remarks (*op. cit.*, p. 123): 'If the reader will think of two enormous pineapples, with the leaves removed, he will perhaps have some notion of the form and reticulated appearance of these strange objects.' That suggests inevitably the curious pear-shaped object held in the right-hand of so many of the sculptured genii discovered in Mesopotamia. Barton (*Sketch of Semitic Origins*, p. 91) is undoubtedly right in interpreting these as the staminate palm flower, and the genii themselves as fertility spirits. In that case the *original* import of the two pillars will be emblems of fertility, possibly even phallic, though we need not suppose that either Solomon or his Israelite contemporaries were conscious of this meaning. Similar objects were to be found beside many eastern temples, and Solomon may well have borrowed the form as a symbol of deity from Phoenicia without laying stress on the primary significance. The average Hindu, revering the Linga, is seldom conscious of its implications; to him it is but a sacred object.

[1] The rendering 'oracle' found in the English Versions is quite incorrect, and seems to depend on a false etymology.

[2] This is suggested by the opening words of Solomon's dedicatory prayer, 1 Kgs. viii. 12. Though the prayer itself is comparatively late, its compiler may have known the Temple.

[3] Cp. 1 Sam. iii. 3.

[4] The latter seems to the present writer the more probable alternative, cp. Kittel, *GVI*. ii.[3] 260.

remarks,[1] 'massive rather than elegant', and he adds that 'this, perhaps, reflects the character of the Phoenician architecture', and appends a suggestion of Renan's, that the architectural principle is that of the hewn rock. This is doubtless correct, but it leads us to seek further for the origin of this Phoenician style, and though the Mesopotamian sacred buildings were equally massive, yet the *ziggurat* is of a totally different form. We naturally carry back this type of building to the rock temples of Egypt, and in the last analysis it was probably an Egyptian ideal that lay before the builders of the Jerusalem Temple, though it came to them, not directly, but through Phoenicia.

The inner decorations, according to our text, were all characterized by a profusion of gold plating. This, though not impossible historically, is questioned on critical grounds, and, for most of the building, may be neglected.[2] Even without this extra adornment, the interior was sufficiently magnificent, for the whole was covered with wood, the walls with cedar, and the floor with cypress;[3] 1 Kgs. vi. 29 states that the walls were carved with figures of Cherubim, palms, and open flowers. The inner doors which led to the *Debir* were of carved olive wood, and the outer doorposts were of the same material, while the doors themselves were of cypress. They seem to have been of the type usual in the ancient world, consisting of two leaves, each leaf turning on pins in the middle, which fitted into sockets in the threshold and the lintel.

The furniture of the Temple is elaborately described. Within the *Debir* stood the two Cherubim, with a space for the Ark between them. We have no details as to the exact form of these figures, save what we can derive from Ezek. i, though some of the features of Ezekiel's Cherubim will not fit the record in *1 Kings*, e.g. the prophet's statement that each had four wings[4] does not suit the account in 1 Kgs. vi. 24–9, which seems to imply that each had two only. We may, perhaps, think of them rather as taking the form of the winged bulls and lions so characteristic of Mesopotamian sculpture, or, still more probably, of that mixed Mesopotamian and Egyptian form of which we have evidence from Phoenicia.[5] Their outstretched wings

[1] *1 and 2 Kings*, p. 105.
[2] See Stade, *ZAW.*, 1883, pp. 140 ff.; Benzinger, *Die Bücher der Könige*, p. 35; Skinner, *1 and 2 Kings*, p. 113; Stade, *GVI.*, p. 329.
[3] 1 Kgs. vi. 15, 18.
[4] Ezek. i. 6.   [5] Cp. Volz, *Die biblischen Altertümer* (1925), Tafel 1.

filled the whole space from wall to wall, and the inner wings formed a canopy over the Ark.[1] Immediately before the door of the *Debir* stood the table of shewbread,[2] overlaid with cedar, and there seems to have been no other furniture within the building itself. Outside, in the main court, the chief objects seem to have been the great bronze sea, whose use is not clear; it may have had a cosmic significance.[3] As in the case of Jachin and Boaz we may have here a foreign symbol whose use and meaning are not fully understood in Israel. There were also ten 'lavers', large cauldrons placed on wheeled stands, which could be used to carry water from one part of the building to another. A mass of minor utensils is mentioned, and we may be sure that in all such matters the Temple was well equipped.

There is one outstanding omission. Nowhere have we in 1 Kgs. vi any reference to an altar of burnt-offering in Solomon's Temple. Yet a Temple without such an altar is inconceivable, and various attempts have been made to supply the deficiency by conjecture. An altar stood before the Tent of the Ark, and that may have sufficed for ordinary purposes, the natural rock altar being used for special occasions such as the dedication of the whole building. Yet 1 Kgs. ix. 25 speaks of an altar which Solomon built, apparently of stone. When Ahaz introduced an altar of foreign pattern, he removed an older bronze altar to make room for the new one,[4] and we have no account of the construction of this bronze altar either in the reign of Solomon or at any later period. Solomon's is, however, the most likely time for its erection; had any later king been responsible for it, we should have had mention of it in the records, for it would be too important an event to be overlooked altogether. On the whole, the suggestion just made seems to be the most probable solution of the difficulty. We have reason to suspect that the holocaust became much more common as time passed, and for the burning of the small portions of victims reserved for the altar in the

---

[1] The exact significance of the Cherubim is as obscure as their form. They sometimes appear as guardian spirits (e.g. in Gen. iii. 24) or as bearers of Yahweh (Ezek. i, Ps. xviii. 10 (Heb. 11)). Possibly they have here a third character, that of attendant spirits.   [2] Called an 'altar' in 1 Kgs. vi. 20, cp. the commentaries, *ad loc.*
[3] For a discussion of its purpose see Benzinger, *Die Bücher der Könige*, p. 48, and Skinner, *1 and 2 Kings*, p. 127, together with the authorities quoted by the latter; also, with reference to Babylonian parallels, Lods, *Israël*, p. 481; *Myth and Ritual* (ed. Hooke, 1933), p. 178.
[4] 2 Kgs. xvi. 14. For a discussion of the various theories that have been propounded see Gray, *Sacrifice in the Old Testament*, pp. 136 ff.

'peace-offering',[1] the 'horned altar' which stood before the 'tent of Yahweh'[2] sufficed. For the extraordinary occasions on which the holocaust was offered the rock itself might have been employed.

The Temple, though by far the most famous of all Solomon's buildings, was but one element in a comprehensive scheme of royal edifices which he erected on the hill to the north of the Ophel. Of these a description is given in 1 Kgs. vii. 1–12. It seems that the buildings are mentioned in order from south to north, since Ezek. xliii. 8 implies that the king's own house, the last to be mentioned in the series, was the nearest to the Temple. The order, proceeding upwards and northwards was probably (1) the 'house of the forest of Lebanon', (2) the hall of pillars, (3) the hall of justice, (4) the king's own house, attached to which was (5) the house of Pharaoh's daughter. The first is the only one to be described in detail, the construction of the rest was similar. The architecture seems to have been of the simplest; a single great hall, with rows of cedar pillars, and a ceiling of cedar wood, light being obtained from openings in the walls. Yet simple as these structures may have been, they must have appeared stately and impressive, and they were certainly very costly.

The mention of Solomon's buildings naturally leads us to think of his financial and other civil arrangements. The timber was procured from Lebanon, and it would seem from 1 Kgs. v. 10 that Hiram, king of Tyre, had some claim to it, though parts of the Lebanon were included among the nominal territories of Israel. It is clear that Hiram had a large supply of competent workmen whom he lent to Solomon, and that he controlled the transport. Land carriage would have been too slow and too costly, even for such resources as those ascribed to Solomon, and

---

[1] References to the עֹלָה, or burnt-offering, which can be assigned with certainty to the period before the middle of the ninth century, are rare. There is one in the story of Gideon (Judges vi. 26), one in the story of Samson (Judges xiii. 16, 23), one in the account of the restoration of the Ark by the Philistines (1 Sam. vi. 14 f.), one in the narrative of the events which led up to the battle of Michmash (1 Sam. xiii. 10, 12), one in the record of the bringing of the Ark to Jerusalem (2 Sam. vi. 17), and the description of the dedication of the Temple, in addition to the two references to human sacrifice in Gen. xxii and Judges xi. Though the references to the other type of sacrifice are not numerous, they suggest that it was familiar and regular, while the burnt-offering was exceptional. As time passed the relative positions changed, till, after the exile, it seems that the burnt-offering was the more common.

[2] Cp. 1 Kgs. ii. 28.

the wood was therefore brought by sea. We do not know for certain what port Solomon could command on the Mediterranean, for the southern coast was in the hands of the Philistines. He may have been able to land his materials at Dor, just to the south of Mount Carmel, but even from there the road to Jerusalem was of some length. To these expenses we must add the gold and bronze—a hundred and twenty talents of the former (1 Kgs. ix. 14), and an unspecified amount of the latter—together with ornamental stones of various kinds.

Both the original cost and the transport of the wood and other materials for building must, therefore, have been enormously expensive. In other ways, too, the royal exchequer must have been subjected to serious drains. In 1 Kgs. iv. 22 f. we have the daily ration required for the royal household. The figures appear to be derived from contemporary court accounts, and the total included over three hundred bushels of fine flour, twice that quantity of coarser meal (probably barley), ten stall-fed oxen and twenty from the pastures, in addition to unstated supplies of game. All this, or the greater part of it, must be regarded as unproductive expenditure. This total does not seem to include more than what was needed for the royal household, and to it must be added the maintenance of the countless officials and workmen employed on the various luxury undertakings which are ascribed to Solomon. Some apology might be made for the establishment of the chariotry, since that could be regarded as a form of national defence. Solomon had fourteen hundred chariots—less, however, than those ascribed to Ahab by Shalmaneser III—and twelve hundred horsemen, distributed among the 'chariot cities', of which Megiddo is the only one at present excavated. Probably Gezer was another chariot station, and perhaps also Hazor, and other places. Solomon does not seem to have bred horses, but procured his supplies from Egypt,[1] paying for each horse and chariot a sum equivalent in weight of silver to about £94, but enormously more valuable in purchasing power. The maintenance of this force must have

---

[1] Cp. Dt. xvii. 16, Isa. xxxi. 1; but it is possible that they were obtained elsewhere too. In 1 Kgs. x. 28 it is said: 'The export of horses which Solomon received from Muṣri, even from Ḳoa . . .' (reading מִמְּצָרִי וּמִקְוֶה for מִמִּצְרַיִם וּמִקְוֵה—the best solution of a difficult textual problem). Ḳoa (Ḳue) and Muṣri were in northern Syria, near Asia Minor, south of the Taurus mountains; in this district horses were bred, cp. Ezek. xxvii. 14, where Togarmah, in northern Syria, is named as a place from which the Israelites obtained their horses.

been expensive, and was probably met in part by the exercise of certain rights on grass; in the eighth century we hear of the 'king's mowings', which seems to be the first of the crop,[1] any that came up later being left to the farmer. Hay does not seem to have been used at all, and other kinds of fodder cannot have been cheap.

To meet these demands on his purse Solomon had two main sources of revenue. The first was taxation. Under this head we must include, not merely actual money or goods taken from his subjects, but also the unpaid services which he demanded of them. This latter, especially, must have been burdensome, and, more than anything else, contributed to the unpopularity of the government. In 1 Kgs. ix. 20–22 it is stated that only Canaanites were impressed into these labour gangs, but there is a direct contradiction in v. 13 and xi. 28, and it seems clear that the distinction between Israelite and Canaanite had practically vanished. Moreover, we can hardly believe that the people who, at the accession of Rehoboam, demanded a lightening of burdens and revolted because they could not secure it, were all Canaanites rising against Israel. In 1 Kgs. v. 13 we hear of a levy of thirty thousand men for work on Lebanon alone, each man having one month's work in the mountains and two months at home, attending to his own business. Four months in the year is a great deal for the peasant farmer to give up from his regular labours. These thirty thousand, it seems, were occupied solely in transport, for another eighty thousand are mentioned as hewers of wood in the mountains, and seventy thousand unskilled labourers—'coolies'. These last may have been practically slaves, and the total of men employed for the twenty years during which Solomon's building operations were in progress must have been between 150,000 and 200,000 men. We can understand the need for 3,300 overseers and gangsmen.[2]

For the recruitment of this labour a special official, Adoniram (Adoram?) was responsible. We have no definite information as to the system on which he worked, but it is clear that he must have had a large and efficient organization under him. We may suspect that the division of the country into twelve districts,[3] primarily intended for the supply of the royal household, furnished a useful basis for other forms of taxation also, and the

---

[1] Am. vii. 1.
[2] These figures, however, are very possibly exaggerated.   [3] 1 Kgs. iv. 8–20.

same organization might well have served more than one purpose. The officers who had charge of these districts were clearly men of rank and importance; two of them were married to daughters of Solomon. Three of the administrative divisions were to the east of Jordan, and of the others only four in any way coincided with Israelite tribes. It is noticeable that Judah proper —Bethlehem, Hebron, Tekoa, &c.—was not included in the list, a fact which suggests preferential treatment.[1]

Direct taxation in money seems to have been rare in Israel, for the country necessarily still lived on a rather primitive plane, and money was not common. There was, of course, no coined silver, and it had to be paid out by weight. We hear of a money-tax being raised in the middle of the eighth century,[2] and in the cities the medium of exchange was silver, but we may doubt whether there was much that entered the country districts. Taxation, therefore, was usually in kind, and took the form of a fixed proportion of the products of the farm or of the ranch. Even as late as the ninth century, the tribute rendered by Moab to Israel was paid in wool and lambs, and such archaeological evidence as we have bearing on the subject indicates that the Israelite paid his taxes in corn, wine, and oil. This would suffice for the upkeep of the royal household and body-guard, for all, indeed, that a normal sovereign, ruling over a self-contained and self-supporting country, would ordinarily require.

Solomon's ambitions, however, were far from being satisfied with so natural and so simple a position. He required a large number of imports not only for his buildings, but also for the maintenance of the magnificent display for which he became proverbial. It was therefore necessary for him to find sources of wealth in addition to those supplied by the land and the people of his kingdom. He is distinguished as the first great commercial king of Israel—perhaps the first great Israelite merchant. We gather from 1 Kgs. x. 15 that some of Solomon's money was derived from tolls, which he exacted from merchants passing through his territories, and since the occupation of Damascus and the possession of territory both to the east and to the west of Jordan gave him command of practically all the trade routes, we can understand that this would be a valuable source of income. 1 Kgs. x. 29 suggests that he dealt profitably in Egyptian horses with Anatolia and Syria. But, further, he emulated the Tyrian

---

[1] See Additional Note D, pp. 264 f. [2] 2 Kgs. xv. 20.

king in undertaking voyages[1] himself, and made a port of Eziongeber, on the Gulf of Akabah. This was rendered possible by the occupation of Edom by Israel, and it proved one of the most important sources of Solomon's income. Voyages were made to Ophir, whose site has never been determined with certainty,[2] but is generally placed in the Persian Gulf. If we may trust alike the text and the historicity (both are questioned) of 1 Kgs. x. 22, Ophir was valuable, not merely as a place whence gold could be procured, but as a mart where articles from the farther east could be purchased. That verse mentions ivory, apes, and peacocks, and the only country which produces all three is India. Moreover, the Hebrew word for peacock seems to be derived from the Dravidian name of the bird. Gold and ivory were employed in the construction of Solomon's great throne.

Even so, the immense quantities of gold which are said thus to have found their way into the country did not satisfy Solomon's passion for display, and he was forced to draw on his capital. In return for 120 talents of gold he ceded to Hiram a district in the north which is given as Galilee. Hiram was displeased with the villages handed over to him, and gave to the district the contemptuous name Kabul, which still survives as that of a village not far from Acre. If this be the district mentioned in 1 Kgs. ix. 11–13, the 'Galilee' is not the region which bore that name in later times, but a section of coast-land, stretching from Phoenician territory down to Carmel.

A still more sinister suggestion comes to us from Deut. xvii. 16, where the king of Israel is forbidden to send men back to Egypt in order to procure horses. This seems to imply that, since ancient Palestine produced hardly any exportable commodities, the kings of Judah and Israel had been in the habit of paying in men for the horses and chariots which they got from Egypt. The direct evidence that we have of this practice comes from much later times, but there is reason to believe that Israelite mercenaries were sent to Egypt under the monarchy, and Solomon may have been the originator of the practice. There is, unfortunately, nothing known of him which would make such conduct inconsistent with the rest of his character and behaviour.

[1] Much has been written on the location of the Tarshish referred to in 1 Kgs. x. 22 and elsewhere; perhaps the fullest discussion is to be found in Desnoyers, *HPH.* iii. 66 ff., where a site on the Black Sea is suggested. But the term 'Ship of Tarshish' refers, of course, to the class of vessel, not to its destination.

[2] For various theories see Price in *DB.*, pp. 626–8; Cheyne, *EB.*, cols. 3,513–15.

The list of Solomon's officials[1] shows an increase on the establishment of his father. We have two new offices, that indicated by the obscure title 'the king's friend', and the superintendent of the district officers, while the numbers of the officials are slightly larger. Thus, we have two scribes instead of one, and there appear to be four priests instead of two. But we still have no trace of the elaborate ecclesiastical order which later generations attributed to Solomon.

Solomon's religious policy is represented as falling away from the high standard set by David. The number of wives, especially of foreign wives, whom he took into his harem made it imperative that some kind of arrangement should be made for the introduction of their cults that they might offer the worship with which they were familiar. But it was not merely the presence of foreign women which made this necessary from the ancient point of view. A treaty between two nations nearly always had a religious side, and it involved the mutual adoption of the gods of the two contracting parties. Thus, Wen-amon's treaty with Byblos[2] implied the installation of the Egyptian god Amon in the city, and this was especially true when one of the two parties was much the stronger. Even apart from his marriages, Solomon's commercial relations would have involved the introduction of foreign cults, and so have earned the condemnation of the later compilers, who did their work under the influence of the great reform of the late seventh century. There is no need for us to assume that Solomon was conscious of any apostasy in establishing 'chapels' for his wives and traders, especially since these were located outside Jerusalem, on the Mount of Olives; he would probably have felt himself to be still the whole-hearted and faithful servant of Yahweh. It was not till men learnt how far the character of Yahweh stood above that of all other gods that they realized how utterly incompatible was His worship with that of any other deity.

Apart from all question of apostasy, the reign of Solomon, which had begun with such hopes, and continued in such splendour, closed in gloom. He was unable to hold all the territory that had been left to him by David,[3] and lost first Damascus and

---

[1] 1 Kgs. iv. 2–6.   [2] See Gressmann, *ATAT.*, pp. 72 f.

[3] It is often held that the defection of Syria and Edom must have taken place early in the reign of Solomon. This may possibly be true of Syria, but it is improbable of Edom. The text of 1 Kgs. xi. 14–22 is admittedly in disorder, and almost certainly includes two interwoven narratives. But both assure to Hadad

then Edom. The Syrian revolt[1] reminds us in some ways of the story of David. Rezon escaped from the defeat inflicted by David on Hadadezer, betook himself to the wilderness, gathered a troop of outlaws about him, and took possession of Damascus. As far as our records have to tell us, Solomon did not even make any attempt to prevent the capture of Damascus; the narrative has no word of any military expeditions whatever undertaken in his reign. The loss of these two dependencies must have meant a serious diminution of Solomon's income, not only in direct tribute, but also in levies on passing merchandise.

While the revolt of Damascus meant the establishment of a power which was in later days to be the sharpest thorn in the side of Israel, the defection of Edom had a different significance. Joab's extermination of the Edomite people[2] was not so complete but that some fugitives escaped to Egypt, among them a small child named Hadad[3] who was brought up in the household of Tahpenes, queen of Pharaoh—perhaps in the first instance bought as a slave, a kind of Edomite Joseph. After the deaths of David and Joab he obtained permission to return to Edom. Except for the reference to Joab and David there is no indication of the date of Hadad's return to his own land, but the fact that Solomon was able to occupy Ezion-geber makes it almost certain that the complete revolt is to be placed later rather than earlier in his reign. It is clear, however, that Edom

the favour and the help of Egypt, and though the Pharaoh does not encourage him to return, it is difficult to imagine him lending support of any kind to a man who could be regarded only as a rebel against his own son-in-law. The Pharaoh who aided and abetted Hadad must surely belong, not to the twenty-first, but to the twenty-second dynasty, which reversed the old policy towards Israel, and showed decided hostility to the house of David. Further, it is difficult to see how Solomon could have established a port at Ezion-geber, and have transported enormous quantities of gold and other valuable commodities thence to Jerusalem, if the country had been in the hands of a hostile ruler.

[1] 1 Kgs. xi. 23–5.   [2] 1 Kgs. xi. 16.

[3] 1 Kgs. xi. 14–22. It is generally agreed that two accounts of the adventures of Hadad have been interwoven, cp. Winckler, *Alttestamentliche Untersuchungen*, 1 ff., followed by most later scholars. According to one account Hadad was a small child who was adopted by Tahpenes, and when he grew up he was allowed to return to his own land, under protest from the Egyptian court. According to the other account he escaped from Joab's massacre as an adult, made his way through Midian and Paran to Egypt, won the favour of Pharaoh, and received the sister of Tahpenes as his wife. She bore him a son named Genubath, who was brought up at the court of Pharaoh. Chronological reasons give a decided preference to the former account, and Winckler himself (though others have not followed him so readily here) believed that the second account had originally no reference to Edom, but dealt with a Midianite prince.

secured its independence before the death of Solomon, and that
the dominions of David were thus reduced in the south. The
narrative suggests that this was a part of the policy of the Egyptian royal house, and if so, it must indicate a change of dynasty.
Exact dates are difficult to ascertain, but the end of the twenty-
first dynasty and the beginning of the twenty-second may be
placed somewhere about 945 B.C.,[1] which must fall within the
reign of Solomon. The Pharaoh who had favoured Solomon
was probably one of those princes of the Delta who maintained
themselves in practical independence through the later reigns of
the twenty-first dynasty, or was perhaps Siamon, glad enough to
have some support for his weak throne outside Egypt. Sheshonk,
the founder of the twenty-second dynasty, was a stronger character, and may well have seen a danger, not a source of aid,
in a powerful kingdom on his northern frontier. This conjecture
is borne out by the events which followed on the death of Solomon; but it is not very probable that his interest in Palestinian
politics originated with his own assumption of the Egyptian
crown.

The external outlook during the last years of Solomon's reign
was thus sufficiently serious. But the results of his domestic
policy were even more disastrous. David seems to have built up
a united kingdom, stable enough for the time, and to have left
behind him a well-filled treasury and a people who were, on the
whole, content with his rule. Solomon's wasteful extravagance
had not only dissipated David's accumulated stores, but had
left the realm practically bankrupt. It may be true that he
enriched Jerusalem with precious metals, magnificent buildings,
and costly works of art, but these things were utterly unproductive, and, in the end, the only purposes they served were to
excite the cupidity of contemporaries and to be used in buying
off the enemies of Judah. The truth was that the economic basis
on which the royal house of Israel had to rely for its resources
was too small. Even the revenue obtained at the height of
Solomon's prosperity was barely sufficient for the satisfaction
of his vanity and ostentation. With the loss of control over the
trade routes, which the independence of Damascus involved, and
the cessation of the sea-borne traffic, which the liberation of
Edom inevitably imposed, the royal income must have fallen far
below the requirements of Solomon's luxurious tastes and habits.

[1] So Breasted, *HE.*, pp. 527, 600.

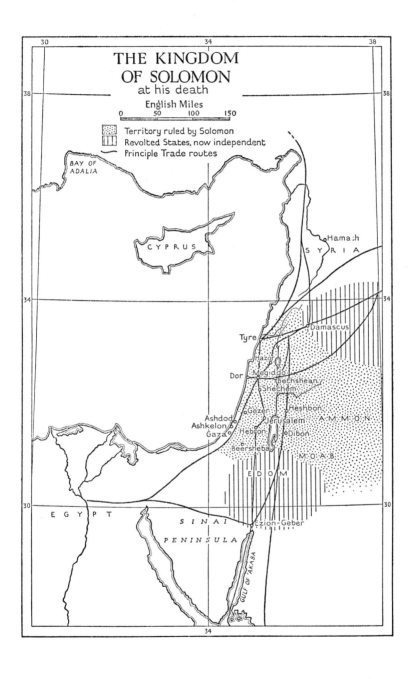

THE KINGDOM
OF SOLOMON
at his death

English Miles

0   50   100   150

Territory ruled by Solomon
Revolted States, now independent
Principle Trade routes

BAY OF
ADALIA

CYPRUS

Hamath

SYRIA

Damascus

Tyre

Hazor

Dor   Megiddo
Bethshean
Shechem

Ashdod   Gezer   Heshbon
Ashkelon   Jerusalem   AMMON
Gaza   Hebron   Dibon
Beersheba   MOAB

EDOM

EGYPT

SINAI

PENINSULA

Ezion-Geber

GULF OF 'AKABA

We have already had occasion to notice and comment on the demands made by his building operations on the man-power of the country, and this, taken with the regular supply of provisions for Hiram's workmen and the unproductive crowds that thronged the court, must have bled the country white. The agricultural districts of Palestine were never very extensive, and though, under modern methods of culture, she has valuable exports, especially in various fruits, yet she has seldom been able to produce more foodstuffs than are necessary for the upkeep of her own working population, and in ancient times such natural accidents as famine and drought brought her to the verge of starvation. The life of the Israelite farmer in the reign of Solomon must have been far from pleasant, in fact hardly tolerable.

Men may be induced to suffer hardships, even under an autocratic government, if they realize the necessity and see that their rulers share their difficulties. But no nation can continue indefinitely enduring what Israel had to endure, simply in order that one man or one group may live in extravagant luxury. The moral effect of Solomon's policy was yet more serious than its economic results. A weak people, a submissive slave race, accustomed to long generations of despotic rule, may dully acquiesce in oppression for centuries, though in the end an explosion is certain, and will be the more terrible the longer it is delayed. But in Israel there was still that strong and vigorous democratic feeling which refused to admit any essential superiority inherent in the royal house, and held the doctrine, strange enough in the ancient east, that the sovereign had duties as well as rights, responsibilities as well as privileges. The men who had fought for David, who had made possible the establishment of the monarchy, who had behind them the immemorial tradition of the free nomad—such men were not likely to yield without protest to Solomon's régime. Nowhere else have the value and importance of human personality and its rights received more stress than in Israel, and the methods employed by Solomon were such as to reduce men to the level of machines. In prosperity the sturdy peasants might have been content to accept a benevolent despotism, but the combination of repression and of hardship made an outbreak almost inevitable.

Additional Note D
SOLOMON'S ADMINISTRATIVE DIVISIONS

FOR a discussion of the list in 1 Kgs. iv. 7–20 see especially Albright, 'The Administrative Divisions of Israel and Judah', in the *Journal of the Palestine Oriental Society*, vol. v (1925), pp. 17–54. The map on p. 264 is based on that given by J. W. Jack, *Samaria in Ahab's Time*, p. 91 (1929), and is practically identical with that of Albright, a few slight changes having been made in modification of some of Albright's opinions. Strangely enough, both Albright and Jack assume that the twelfth district included Judah, in spite of the direct statement in 1 Kgs. iv. 19 that it lay to the east of Jordan. The actual list of districts in *Kings* is as follows:

1. Hill country of Ephraim.
2. Makaz, Shaalbim, Beth-shemesh, Elon-beth-hanan.
3. Arubboth, Socoh, Hepher.
4. Naphath Dor.
5. Taanach, Megiddo, Beth-shean, Abelmeholah, beyond Jokneam.
6. Ramoth-gilead, including Havvoth-Jair, Argob (Bashan).
7. Mahanaim.
8. Naphtali.
9. Asher and Bealoth.
10. Issachar.
11. Benjamin.
12. Gilead and the Sihon country.

To the last clause of verse 19 the first word of verse 20 should probably be attached, and the whole read וּנְצִיב אֶחָד אֲשֶׁר בְּאֶרֶץ יְהוּדָה—'and one officer who was in the land of Judah'. Other suggestions have been made, notably that of Klostermann (*ap.* Benzinger, *Die Bücher der Könige*, p. 22), who would read וּנְצִיב אֶחָד אֲשֶׁר עַל־הַנִּצָּבִים אֲשֶׁר בָּאָרֶץ —'and one officer who was over the overseers who were in the land'. The division is no longer exactly that of the tribes, but most of the districts are easy to identify. They seem to be given in no sort of order, for after No. 1, which is the country lying between Benjamin and Manasseh, we have in No. 2 a district to the west of Judah, towards the Shephelah. No. 3 is a district in western Manasseh, in which Shechem and the site of the later Samaria were probably included. No. 4 is the coastal plain between Carmel and Philistia. No. 5 the plain of Esdraelon with an extension down the western side of the Jordan valley. Nos. 6 and 7 are to the east of Jordan. No. 8 is in the extreme north, including probably Dan and Hazor. No. 9 includes the coast district between Carmel and Phoenicia, much of which seems to have been sold by Solomon to Hiram. Jack

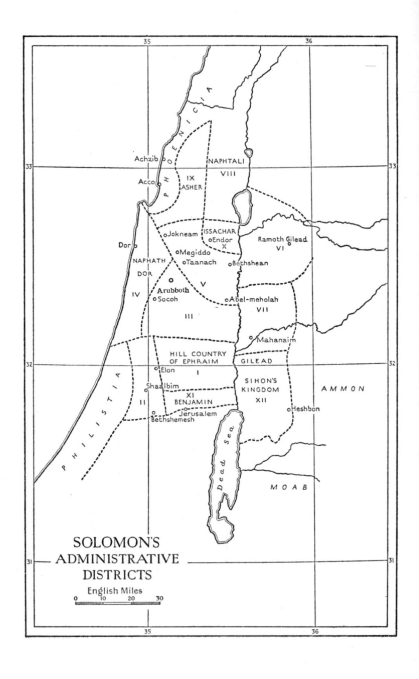

SOLOMON'S
ADMINISTRATIVE
DISTRICTS

English Miles

0   10   20   30

(*Samaria in Ahab's Time*, p. 96) believes that וּבְעָלוֹת is a corruption of זְבוּלֻן, and Alt (*Israel's Gaue unter Salomo* in *Alttestamentliche Studien— Rudolf Kittel Festschrift*, p. 13) suggests that possibly בְּעָלֹת is a place in Zebulun, a district not mentioned elsewhere in the list. No. 10 is what was afterwards known as Galilee. No. 11 is self-explanatory, and No. 12 is the southerly of the three districts to the east of Jordan (the mention of Og, king of Bashan, in verse 19 may be regarded as a later gloss; some Israelite writers could not think of Sihon apart from Og). The only name that has been connected with Judah proper is Bealoth, which Albright places in the south and makes a separate district. But it is rather a curious way of identifying Judah, and the name may well have been used of more than one place. Moreover, the list in *1 Kings* places Bealoth in the same district as Asher. We have to admit that, in all probability, Judah was never included in the list, for there is no mention of places like Bethlehem, Hebron, Tekoa, or even Beer-sheba. Preferential treatment given to Judah in this matter would certainly arouse the jealousy of the rest of the land, and may well have been one of the contributory causes of the disruption. Strangely enough, S. A. Cook (*CAH*. iii. 359) and Lods (*Israël*, pp. 430 f.) are almost alone among modern students in adopting this view. The doubtful clause at the end of verse 19 may well be read as in the first emended form mentioned (so, apparently, the LXX), and regarded as an addition by an editor or scribe who failed to understand why Judah should be omitted, and therefore inserted it as a *thirteenth* district, though he had no name of an overseer in his sources and the number thirteen is very awkward to fit into a twelve-month year.

B. THE DIVIDED KINGDOM

THE period that we have before us in this section of the history of Israel is that in which the results of the great secession worked themselves out. We are shown a seething mass of little kingdoms, all jealous one of another, and each seeking to prey upon its neighbours. No great principle manifests itself, and no national tendencies are to be observed. It is in some ways, until we draw near to its close, the least inspiring time in the whole history of the land. The age of heroic conquest is over, that of heroic defence has not yet come. All that lies before us is the slow attrition of the strength of these little peoples in struggles which, in the light of larger history, wear almost the aspect of civil war. Except for the Philistines, all the tribes and princedoms involved recognized a certain kinship one with another, though only two had the uniting bond of a common worship. Damascus, Israel, Judah, Ammon, Moab, and Edom all belonged to much the same racial group, and the traditions preserved in Israel (which may have extended also to the other peoples, or to some of them) asserted a common ancestry for all.

We are, however, primarily concerned with the two political groups which recognized Yahweh as their God. In a certain sense these two do stand apart from the rest and acknowledge a closer tie of blood one with the other. Intercourse between the subjects of the two realms seems to have been at all times free and unrestrained, and though their citizens necessarily acknowledged a different political allegiance, they felt themselves to be essentially one. Prophets whose home lay in the one section might, and did, speak clearly of the other, and though the references to which we can point belong, as a matter of fact, to the next period, we have no reason to doubt that they reflect the conditions of an earlier age, as well as of their own. We naturally think of 'the divided kingdom' rather than of 'the two kingdoms'.

The outstanding fact of the whole period is the absence of interference from the outside. The invasion of Sheshonk was, as far as we know, the last attempt made by an Egyptian king to assert his authority over Palestine before the end of the seventh century B.C.[1] The truth is that Egypt had once more fallen

---

[1] 2 Chron. xiv. 9–13 speaks of an invasion made by a certain Zerah, king of the Cushites, whom Champollion identified with Osorkon I (924–895 B.C., Breasted).

on evil days, and the history of the twenty-second dynasty after Sheshonk I depicts for us 'a dynasty rent asunder by family feuds and constantly threatened by revolt of this or that powerful mercenary commander who feels himself aggrieved or able by force of arms to improve his position',[1] and in the confusion it is difficult to be sure even of the order in which the kings followed one another. There is no possibility of foreign conquest in the midst of domestic anarchy such as this.

Assyria in turn had not yet embarked on her career of conquest in the west. In so far as her kings contemplated foreign acquisitions, they were compelled to fight on their nearer frontiers, for they had dangerous neighbours both to the north and to the south. The Armenian mountains sheltered a number of sturdy tribes, who had to be reduced to submission before the country could be safe from that quarter, and there was a tendency for inroads to be made from the hills as well as from the desert into the fertile plains. To the south lay Babylon, always the most difficult and dangerous spot in the Assyrian empire. She had to be kept in submission, and throughout their history the Assyrian kings do not seem to have discovered an effective method of securing Babylonian loyalty. Not till the year 876 B.C. do we hear of a great advance towards the Mediterranean under Ashur-naṣir-pal, and even then his line of march carried him far to the north of Palestine. The invasion of Shalmaneser III in 853 B.C. was the first occasion on which Assyria came definitely into contact with Israel, and we may take that date as closing the first stage of the history of the Hebrew monarchies.

After the disruption, the period falls into two main sections. In the first, including the dynasties of Jeroboam I and Baasha in northern Israel, there is constant war between the two parts of the people. In the second there is not merely peace, but a close alliance—with the north as the dominant partner. One striking difference between the two kingdoms appears: while the south is constantly faithful to the house of David, the north shows no such continuity. There are no less than three families in succession on the throne within eighty years, and the house of Omri is the first to number more than two kings. Though to outward

But the identification is philologically doubtful, and we do not even know that the 'Cushites' were Egyptians. Moreover, events which are described in *Chronicles* and omitted in *Kings* are always a little doubtful, and most moderns are slow to accept them without some further reason or evidence—in this instance entirely lacking.

[1] Breasted, *HE.*, pp. 532 f.

appearance the north is a united realm, there are clearly rival
factions and mutually jealous districts. Even within the kingdom
there is no real unity.

Except for the inscriptions of Sheshonk and of Mesha, which fall
at the beginning and at the end of this period respectively, our only
sources of information are those which we find in the Bible itself. Of
these the main, if not the only reliable, document is *1 Kings*. The
records are very scanty, more so here than in any other part of
the monarchy, being confined for the most part to the names of
the kings and a few personal details. The compiler tries to keep the
records of the two kingdoms abreast of one another, and uses an
ingenious system of synchronisms, which, however, does not always
give satisfactory chronological results. After describing the reign of
Jeroboam, he goes back to the beginning of that of Rehoboam, and
then continues the story of Judah until he reaches a king who survived Jeroboam. Then he turns back to the north, and continues
the history of that kingdom till he has reached the end of the last-
mentioned Judahite reign. He is thus able to keep the two narratives to some extent level with one another.

The compiler is plainly drawing on original sources. He makes
references to the royal annals in a way which shows that these were
still extant in his day, and he supposes that his readers may possibly
have access to them. This implies a date before the exile, and parts
of the work in its simplest form were completed before the fall of
Samaria. But if so it has been very thoroughly revised in the interests
of a Deuteronomic theology, and it is to a writer or to a school of
writers belonging to this party that the book owes its present form.
Like the book of *Judges*, similarly revised and edited, it has a series of
formulæ which serve as a framework. For the kings of Judah this
runs: 'And in the *x*th year of A, king of Israel, B became king over
Judah. He reigned for *y* years, and his mother's name was C.' Then
follows a judgement on the moral and religious quality of the reign—
'B did (or did not do) that which was right in the sight of Yahweh'—
the actual phrase varies a good deal. Any details of the reign worth
recording are then inserted, and at the close we have: 'And the rest
of the acts of B and all that he did, are they not written in the book
of the annals of the kings of Judah? And B slept with his fathers, and
was buried in the city of David. And his son D reigned in his stead.'
A similar form is used for the kings of Israel, with some modifications (e.g. the name of the king's mother is not recorded). In no
instance is it stated that an Israelite king did that which was right in
the sight of Yahweh. The standard of judgement is primarily the
observance of the law of the central sanctuary. A king of Judah who
did not patronize the local shrines is commended, while, of course,

THE DIVIDED KINGDOM 269

no king of Israel insisted on Jerusalem as the only place of sacrifice, and therefore all were condemned.

We have occasional references to the work and influence of the prophets, especially at the end of the period, when Elijah comes into prominence; but, for the most part, there is little that the historian has to record. A few further details are sometimes given in *2 Chronicles*, but that work is seldom a safe guide to history, though it may in places rely on an ancient tradition which has escaped the compilers of the book of *Kings*.

Mention has already been made of the inscription of Mesha. This is carved on a slab of black basalt, found at Dibon in 1868. The story of the deeds of Mesha belongs to the reign of Ahab, at the end of the period immediately before us, and it confirms and in part corrects the impression produced by the Biblical narrative. It is written in the old 'Phoenician' character, and the language is a dialect of Hebrew, so close to that of the Bible (though there are differences) as to be easily intelligible to any reader of Biblical Hebrew.[1]

[1] The inscription is best known to English readers through the discussion contained in Driver, *Notes on the Hebrew Text of the Books of Samuel*,[2] pp. lxxxiv–xciv (1913), but there are also two very handy little editions for the use of students, one by Compston, published by the S.P.C.K., the other by W. H. Bennett, *The Moabite Stone* (1911).

Chapter XII

THE DISRUPTION

SUMMARY

[David had taken advantage of the temporary weakness both of Assyria and of Egypt to establish a single kingdom in southern Syria. Solomon's policy went far to neutralize the advantages thus gained, and after his death the discontent provoked by his oppression broke into open revolt. Rehoboam, required to accept a covenant on terms which would limit the royal prerogative, refused, and the malcontents found a leader in Jeroboam, whom they made king of northern Israel.

Rehoboam tried to recover his lost territory, and, it seems, met with some success, but Sheshonk of Egypt invaded the country, subdued Rehoboam, and carried away much of the treasure left by Solomon in the Temple and the palace.

Jeroboam is best known for the fact that he established two sanctuaries in northern Israel, one at Dan and one at Bethel, where Yahweh was worshipped under the form of a bull. He thus set up serious rivals to the Temple at Jerusalem, and so completed the severance of the two kingdoms.

The disruption rendered for ever impossible a great Hebrew empire. A united realm, such as David achieved, might in the long run have become a first-class world power. As it was, the strength of Palestine was wasted in petty local conflicts, and in the end she failed, not only to achieve wide dominion, but even to maintain her own independence.]

For our knowledge of the events which immediately followed the death of Solomon, including at least the reign of Rehoboam, we are indebted almost entirely to the record in 1 Kgs. xii–xiv. There is, however, an important inscription of Sheshonk on the wall of the temple at Karnak which we cannot neglect, as it serves to throw light on the attitude of Egypt, and may suggest details which are not found in the book of *Kings*.

The relevant chapters in *1 Kings* are composite, being clearly derived from different sources. The compiler had at his disposal the royal annals of both kingdoms, and probably took extracts from each. The account of the disruption itself, in xii. 1–24, seems to have been taken from the north, though this is disputed. Wellhausen and Stade[1] assign it to the south, mainly on the ground of similarities in style to 2 Sam. ix–xx. Kittel and Benzinger, however, feel that no southerner could possibly have admitted the right of the people to

[1] *GVI.*, pp. 344 f.

choose their own king when once the dynasty of David had been seated on the throne. Neither reason seems to be finally decisive, and, fortunately, from the historian's view-point, the question is of little moment. There are, of course, other elements involved. The account of Jeroboam's establishment of the sanctuaries at Bethel and Dan clearly owes its present form to Deuteronomic influence. We have also excerpts from a collection, or possibly from a whole literature, which dealt with the lives and acts of the prophets, while the story of the unnamed prophet who foretold the overthrow of the altar at Bethel (1 Kgs. xii. 33–xiii. 32) is probably a piece of Midrash appended to the prophetic histories.

The text of this section is sometimes uncertain, and the LXX often represents a totally different recension. This is particularly obvious in the story of Jeroboam himself, where two texts seem to have been interwoven, since the LXX gives the whole story over again in a new form after xii. 24. It is unnecessary to enter here into a detailed discussion of the originality of the two texts or of the preference to be assigned to the one or to the other, since the question has been thoroughly worked out in the more recent commentaries. See Burney, *Notes on the Hebrew Text of the Books of Kings*, pp. 163 ff.; Benzinger, *Die Bücher der Könige*, pp. 86 f., 97 f.; while the clearest statement for English readers is to be found in Skinner, *1 and 2 Kings*, pp. 443 ff. Whatever be the literary-critical view of the LXX text here, it certainly seems to present us at times with a sound historical tradition, and where it is employed as a valid source in the following pages, the fact will be indicated.

IT is clear that even during the reign of Solomon there had been signs of dissatisfaction, especially in northern Israel. The Joseph tribes, in particular, had never forgotten their ancient supremacy. Ephraim had been the traditional leader of the people, and the first king had arisen from Benjamin. In two of the narratives in *Judges*[1] we have Ephraim depicted as proud of its hegemony, and very jealous of any other who dared to take a leading part in fighting the enemies of Israel. In 2 Sam. xx. 1–22 we hear of an attempt made, even in the reign of David, to induce northern Israel to secede, led by one Sheba, a Benjamite. The personal popularity of David and his military fame naturally made such an attempt hopeless from the first, but Solomon was not the successful warrior his father had been, and the irritation produced by his government was more exasperating.

---

[1] In the Gideon story, Judges viii. 1–3, and in the Jephthah story, Judges xii. 1–6.

The discontent focused itself round a certain Jeroboam, the son of Nebat. There are conflicting accounts of his early years, but the most probable reconstruction of events seems to be as follows. He was an Ephraimite,[1] who found service with the king in the construction of the fortifications of Jerusalem. His abilities won the royal favour, and he was promoted to the over-seership of the labour recruiting in 'Joseph', i.e. in Mount Ephraim. Here he was in his own country and among his own people, and while his duties must have been highly unpopular, we must assume that he carried them out in a manner which did not irritate the people against him personally. He used his position to place himself at the head of the malcontents, and fortified a city called Sareida[2] or Sareira—according to 1 Kgs. xi. 26 his birthplace. He raised a force of three hundred chariots and, perhaps openly, rebelled against Solomon.[3] The rebellion was a failure—if it ever actually took place—and Jeroboam was compelled to flee for safety to Egypt.

In telling the story of Jeroboam, the text of 1 Kings introduces[4] a narrative which may be unhistorical, but is certainly true in other ways. It tells of a prophet, Ahijah the Shilonite, who met Jeroboam as he was leaving Jerusalem one day, and, with symbolic action, foretold his future accession to the throne. We are thus early introduced to an instance of prophetic inter-ference in domestic politics, and this is by no means an isolated example. The prophets, even the earlier $N^{e}bi'im$, stood for a pure Yahwism, and, drawn as they normally were from the proletariat and the unofficial classes,[5] they strongly maintained the popular view of society, law and politics. We have no other instance of a class of men in any state in the ancient east who thus represented the common people and were at the same time

---

[1] The MT. makes him the son of a widow, the narrative peculiar to the LXX calls him the son of a harlot.

[2] Identified by Albright (*Bulletin of the American School of Oriental Research*, No. 11 (Oct. 1923), pp. 5 f., with the modern Ain Ṣeredah, on the Wadi Deir, among the hills on the western slope of the central range.

[3] This seems to be the meaning of the account given in the extra verses of the LXX, though the text is somewhat obscure. Cp. Skinner, *1 and 2 Kings*, p. 443. As Skinner remarks, it is much more probable that there was some overt act of rebellion which would account for Solomon's hostility, rather than suspicion based on an interview between Jeroboam and a prophet, which was a secret to all except the two of them. At the same time, Kittel's suggestion that the conspiracy was discovered before there was any open outbreak (*GVI*. ii.[3] 248) is not impossible, though it lacks the support of any direct statement from either form of the text.

[4] 1 Kgs. xi. 29–39, cp. Benzinger, *Die Bücher der Könige*, pp. 82 f.   [5] Cp. 1 Sam. x. 12.

immune from royal punishment owing to their sanctity. We cannot doubt that, as later illustrations help to show, they maintained the strongly democratic spirit which the Aramaean invaders had brought into the land, thus keeping alive a point of view which was one of Israel's great contributions to human progress. An oppressed Israelite community was always liable to find a mouthpiece among the prophets, and more than once their protest against tyranny and injustice proved effective.

Jeroboam's flight to Egypt must have taken place not long after the seizure of the throne by Sheshonk, at a point when the policy of the court towards Solomon was undergoing a change. It is clear that he was kindly treated, though we may regard the tradition that he married a daughter of Sheshonk[1] as an imitation of the story of Hadad. All forms of tradition agree that he returned to his home on the death of Solomon, though it is not clear how far he was responsible for the actual revolt. He was, at all events, available when a leader was needed, and his previous history must have marked him out as a suitable candidate for the throne.[2]

The story of the events at Shechem is very familiar and, allowing for a modicum of later redaction, reliable. The people were determined to exercise the right of election on definite conditions. It seems that this had been omitted on the accession of Solomon, perhaps because he was associated in the kingship before his father's death. The consequences had been disastrous, and men did not intend to let the matter go by default a second time. So Rehoboam was required to grant a charter, in which he would undertake to reform the worst abuses of his father's reign, and to revert to the old standard of David. This, on the advice of the younger of his counsellors, he refused to do, being apparently determined to stand on his royal rights from the first. His refusal was the signal for revolt; the people as a whole repudiated the house of David; the chief officer in charge of labour recruitment was stoned to death, and Rehoboam saved himself only by

[1] So in the additional passage in the LXX.
[2] The MT. of 1 Kgs. xii. 2, 3, 12 speaks of Jeroboam as being present at the gathering which had met for the coronation of Rehoboam. But the LXX omits verse 2 altogether and does not include his name in verses 3 and 12. He is mentioned, it is true, in the LXX of verse 15, but only as the man to whom Ahijah's oracle had been given, not as among those present at Shechem. And verse 20, which is identical in both texts, except that the LXX adds Benjamin after Judah, assumes that he was not at Shechem.

hurried flight. Then, and not till then, was Jeroboam fetched and made king over all Israel, giving, we may assume, the required pledges. It is worth noting that the genuine Israelite conception of monarchy prevailed in the northern kingdom at least down to the middle of the next century.

Rehoboam still held a throne. He made his way to Jerusalem, and retained his authority over the country to the south. Probably the possession of Jerusalem and the presence of the royal body-guard were enough to prevent any serious revolt, even if the people had wished to get rid of the king. Jerusalem offered a barrier difficult to pass over, and effectually secured Rehoboam against a combination of north and south. But the northern frontier of his kingdom lay not far from the city, and, in spite of many changes in the actual border-line, Bethel, only some twelve miles from Jerusalem, was reckoned in the northern kingdom as long as that kingdom existed.

Rehoboam was not prepared to lose his kingdom without a struggle, and prepared for war. To him the defection of the northern tribes must have appeared as a revolt like that of Sheba, and he seems to have believed that it could easily be quelled by force. A prophetic insertion in 1 Kgs. xii. 21–4 tells us that he received an oracle through a certain Shemaiah, forbidding him to proceed further, and that he therefore abandoned the campaign. But 1 Kgs. xiv. 30 states that there was war between Rehoboam and Jeroboam continually, and it is generally held that the other presentation is not historical.[1] We may conjecture that Rehoboam, having at his disposal a trained force and experienced leaders, was not wholly unsuccessful at first. We have no evidence of the fact in *Kings*, and, indeed, no details of the struggle are anywhere supplied for us in the Biblical narrative, but some light may be thrown on the course of the war from Egyptian sources. In 1 Kgs. xiv. 25 we read that in the fifth year of Rehoboam, Shishak king of Egypt came up against Jerusalem. This is clearly Sheshonk, and we have a mutilated account of his campaign from his own annalists recorded on the wall of his great temple at Karnak.[2] Here the god Amon and

---

[1] Cp. Benzinger, *Die Bücher der Könige*, p. 89; Skinner, *1 and 2 Kings*, p. 189; Stade, *GVI.* i. 350; Kittel, *GVI.* ii.³ 317.

[2] See Breasted, *HE.*, pp. 529 f., *ARE.* iv. 348 ff., §§ 709–22. Professor Breasted makes the curious mistake of supposing that *1 Kings* xiv. 26 definitely records the capture of Jerusalem. It is not expressly stated even in 2 Chron. xii. 2–12, though the language of the Chronicler may be held to suggest it.

the presiding goddess of Thebes lead named captives, one hundred and sixty-five in all. Unfortunately, not more than seventy-five names are now legible, and of these all that can be recognized belong to Palestine. They include chiefly cities belonging to northern Israel; the limit seems to be the plain of Esdraelon, where Tanaach, Megiddo, Beth-shean, Shunem, and other places, are mentioned. Socoh and Arad are the only well-known towns in Judah whose names have been read, and even the former may be the northern town of that name. What does this invasion of the north imply? Jeroboam was Sheshonk's protégé—according to one account his son-in-law. It seems highly improbable that the Egyptian king should have attacked a person whom he so favoured, and whom he had, apparently, allowed to take his place in Israel in order to check the power of the house of David. Nor can the cities mentioned be simply those which were tributary to Egypt. If that were so, they would not have been represented as captives taken in war, and the list would surely have included Israelite places farther north. The natural assumption, since no Palestinian kings' names are mentioned, is that places are now in the hands of Rehoboam,[1] whose attacks on his rival have thus far been successful. This makes the whole expedition intelligible; Jeroboam, confined to the far north and in desperate straits, is rescued by his patron and overlord, Sheshonk, who recovers his cities, and at the same time inflicts a severe punishment on Rehoboam. Jerusalem is not captured; probably, like Sennacherib more than two centuries later,[2] Sheshonk found it too strong to be taken by assault, especially if he secured all that he wanted by the voluntary surrender of Rehoboam. No doubt both Sheshonk and Sennacherib would have pressed the siege of the city if they had failed to secure the submission of the Judahite king otherwise, but it must always have been a slow enterprise, costly both in money and in men. As it was, Rehoboam, like Hezekiah after him, saw no chance of ultimate success, with his whole country in the hands of the enemy, his cities captured, and his lands ravaged, and made composition with the victor. Sheshonk exacted an enormous tribute of which the details have not survived on the Karnak inscriptions, but which is described in

---

[1] It has been objected to this view (cp. Lods, *Israël*, p. 435) that Rehoboam's success is not mentioned in *Kings*. But our records are so unequal in fullness that this is not a serious difficulty. [2] Cp. pp. 395 ff.

1 Kgs. xiv. 26. The terms are quite general, only the golden
shields used in the ceremonial are expressly mentioned, and it is
clear from the later history that some of the rich ornamentation
of Solomon was left behind. But the greater part of the old
king's treasure was carried off and dedicated to an Egyptian god.

Seldom in history have despotic oppression, careless luxury,
and selfish vanity met more swiftly with the nemesis due to them.
David, as it were, collected and laid in place the materials for a
noble kingdom which might have been expanded into an empire.
But it inevitably lacked that cement of habituation which time
alone could supply, and for its endurance it needed a succession
of rulers who would maintain his spirit and carry on his tradition. But the two kings who immediately followed him were
cast in another mould, with the result that first the outlying
portions fell, and then, at the touch of a real test, the whole
fabric crumbled away. Perhaps we should not blame Rehoboam
overmuch. He was not the frivolous youth that we so often
picture to ourselves,[1] and if tradition is right in attributing his
action at Shechem to his younger counsellors,[2] they did at least
represent the feeling and outlook of Solomon's régime. Golden
shields, a gold and ivory throne the like of which existed nowhere else on earth, cedar pillars, costly marbles, apes and
peacocks—these were but the iridescent colours on the surface
of a bubble. The bubble was pricked, and the house of David
was left with territories scanty and unfertile in themselves,
suffering from the ravages of despotism and of war, with
an empty treasury, and with no hope of realizing those promises of empire which had once seemed so bright. The
prosperity and durability of a nation or of a society are not
to be measured by external magnificence, they depend on
the maintenance of spiritual principles. A recognition of the
rights and demands of personality is indispensable, and neglect
of sound social relations is ever fatal. So the Aramaean ancestors of Israel had believed, and so her later prophets taught,
while the lesson is reiterated on every page of the history of
Israel. She had been offered her first illustration of this truth,
and while she never grasped its meaning as long as she main-

---

[1] He was forty-one years old when he came to the throne (1 Kgs. xiv. 21),—a
well-matured age in the East.

[2] We may, perhaps, suspect this to be an attempt to whitewash the Solomon
period; David's advisers would doubtless have given saner counsel, but hardly men
trained in Solomon's court.

tained her national independence, yet, paradoxically enough, in later ages it has proved to be not the least important element in the message she had to give mankind.

Jeroboam, either before or after the Egyptian invasion—probably after it—set about the organization of his kingdom. His most important political act was to rebuild Shechem.[1] When it was destroyed we do not know. It is possible that it never recovered from the exploits of Abimelech,[2] but, on the other hand, it is mentioned as the place where the tribes met to make their bargain with Rehoboam.[3] Perhaps the mention of the locality is due to a late and unreliable tradition, or it may be that it had been restored under David or Solomon, and that it was once more laid in ruins by Sheshonk. There is no reference to the place in the Karnak inscription—at least in those parts of it which have been read—though it may be among the names which are 'mutilated and unrecognizable'.[4] Possibly, again, the statement that Jeroboam built it simply refers to additional fortifications. Some support for this view may perhaps be found in the further statement that Jeroboam built Penuel,[1] thus making himself a strong fortress on either side of the Jordan. Shechem, however, was his capital.[1]

But this was not enough. Jeroboam saw clearly that a merely political severance of the two districts was inadequate to maintain the independence of the north;[5] as always in the ancient east, there must also be a religious basis for the the new régime. It is quite clear that he had no intention whatever of abandoning the national God, Yahweh; that would have been inconceivable. But men must not be compelled to go up to Jerusalem to worship Him;[6] while the prestige conferred by the Temple and the Ark gave that sanctuary a leading position among the holy places of Israel, it was by no means the only spot where the name of Yahweh was revered. Nor was the Ark the only symbol of His presence which Israel believed herself to possess, for there were shrines of many sorts scattered up and down the country, and wherever the old Canaanites had carried on a cult of their local

---

[1] 1 Kgs. xii. 25.
[2] Judges ix. 45, where it is said that Abimelech broke it down and sowed it with salt. [3] 1 Kgs. xii. 1. [4] Breasted, *ARE.* iv. 350.
[5] 1 Kgs. xii. 26–33, xiii. 33 f.
[6] Stade fails to appreciate this point, and attributes Jeroboam's action merely to a desire to appear as a 'patron' of Yahweh (*GVI.* i. 352). Kittel (*GVI* ii.[3] 364 ff.) takes a much sounder view.

Baals, there Yahweh had taken His seat and might be met. Two places in particular attracted Jeroboam. One was Dan, in the far north, and the other was Bethel. Both were centres of bull-worship, and both had traditions which were valuable for the king's purpose. Bethel claimed to be a site of theophany dating from the days of Jacob, and, as we have seen,[1] there were probably traditions which carried back the bull-cult to Moses. Dan similarly had a bull-cult, and though its sanctity was not referred to the patriarchal age, its legends told of a close connexion with the family of Moses.[2] This would serve the northern tribes, while any who wished to go to Jerusalem would have to pass not far from Bethel on their way.[3]

The severance of the two kingdoms was thus complete. The north now had an establishment, both political and religious, which gave it total independence of the south. The house of David did, indeed, retain its authority over a part of the land, and was so secure that it not only kept the crown in the one family, but also survived the end of the northern kingdom by a century and a half. This may be attributed to several causes. In the first place,

---

[1] pp. 108 f.   [2] Judges xviii. 30.

[3] A later age thought of Jeroboam's action as a piece of deliberate apostasy, and ascribed to him the actual foundation of both cults. This, however, is inconceivable, for an entirely new establishment could never have won the assent or adherence of Israel. It is not impossible, indeed, that he added the figure of the bull to the existing divine emblems at Dan, but he must have had the strongest authority for the assumption of this form of Yahweh. The presence of bull-worship in pre-Israelite Canaan makes it quite unnecessary for us to suppose that this was a form of the Apis cult, imposed by Sheshonk on his vassal. It is clear that Rehoboam was as much a subject of Sheshonk as was Jeroboam, and we have no suggestion anywhere of the establishment of such a form of worship in Jerusalem. Just as David had adopted the Ark as the Yahweh symbol about which the king's cultus at Jerusalem was to centre, combining an ancient object with an ancient shrine (the artificial markings on the Jerusalem rock altar are pre-Israelite), so Jeroboam combined the bull-symbol with the Bethel sanctuary. It had never attained to the highest rank in Israel, being eclipsed by Shiloh in pre-monarchic days, probably by Ramah in the time of Saul, and by Gibeon in the days of David and Solomon, but there must have been that about it which made it a plausible centre of worship for all Israel.

The theory that Jeroboam's action implied grave apostasy illustrates the jealousy of the Jerusalem priesthood, further exemplified in the contemptuous description of Jeroboam's priesthood (1 Kgs. xii. 31, 32, xiii. 33). We have also a strange story of a prophetic protest against the altar, told in 1 Kgs. xiii. 1–32. This must be regarded as pure Midrash which cannot be dated earlier than the end of the seventh century (cp. Stade, *GVI.*, pp. 350 ff.; Benzinger, *Die Bücher der Könige*, pp. 90 f.; Skinner, *1 and 2 Kings*, pp. 193 f.). On the other hand, the story of the death of Abijah (1 Kgs. xiv. 1–18), though much expanded by Deuteronomic redaction, contains very ancient elements which may be authentic, though of no importance for the history of Israel.

Jerusalem remained faithful to Rehoboam, perhaps because it could not help it. And with a fortress of this strength to guard the northern frontier, the southern clans were once more cut off from the north even more effectually than they had been before the time of David. To the north of Jerusalem the frontier was ill-defined, and Baasha's attempt to build Ramah[1] shows how near a successful northern king could come to Jerusalem. But the country to the south lay open to the city, and it required a very strong force, with control of the Philistine plain, to take the city in the rear. In the second place, Rehoboam still had, presumably, his body of mercenaries, a strong, trained, fighting force. They were unable, it is true, to face an Egyptian army; probably their numbers were too small. Normally they would serve as the nucleus of any army employed against an enemy from outside Palestine, but without the help of the general levies of the country they were too weak to hold their own against a large, well-organized, and well-equipped invader. But they were quite sufficient to overawe and control so small a body of troops as that which a Judahite revolt could put into the field, even if Judah had been so minded. However, it is far from clear that there was any movement towards revolt in the south. After all, the house of David was of Judahite origin, and had a special claim on the allegiance of David's own tribe. Further, as has been hinted already, even under Solomon it seems that Judah may have received some preferential treatment. The list of Solomon's overseers for the household supply[2] does not include any place known to have been in Judah proper. The second district[3] impinges on Judah, it is true, but the places mentioned there (e.g. Beth-shemesh) lay on the lower hills to the west, overlooking the Shephelah. There is no reference to Bethlehem, Tekoa, Beer-sheba, or, most striking of all, to the Hebron district. While this apparent exemption from one of the most burdensome of Solomon's exactions would tend to mark the distinction between north and south, it would also have the effect of reducing the irritation felt by Judah at Solomon's methods of government, and deprive the south of one of the worst of the grievances which led to the great secession.

We may allow ourselves to pause for a moment to consider the practical bearing which the disruption of the Hebrew kingdom had on history. Had the policy of David been maintained for a

---

[1] 1 Kgs. xv. 17.   [2] 1 Kgs. iv. 8–20; cp. pp. 263 ff.   [3] Verse 9.

few generations, Israel would have had time to be united and consolidated into a real nationality. With the outlying and neighbouring subject lands, which would in no long space of time have lost their individuality, she would have formed a solid block between Asia and Africa, controlling all commerce between the two continents, and in no small measure dictating the international policy of both. As long as the kingdom remained united, even in the days of Solomon's decadence, Egypt found it good policy not to attack her with open force; and when, a century later, a hastily formed alliance of the western states (the more important of whom had been included in David's dominions) faced the might of Shalmaneser III, it was able to check his advance, though at frightful cost, and even he might have found the subjugation of the Syrian and Palestinian countries impossible but for the breaking-up of the alliance. No people of the ancient world made better warriors than the Israelites, with their higher skill and training directing the natural courage and *élan* of the old Aramaean blood, as yet unspoiled by the social calamities of the ninth and eighth centuries. A nation of peasant farmers with the fighting qualities of Bedawin, they might well have proved formidable to the strongest of existing world-powers.

The kingdoms came into existence at a time when there was no great rival in the world to contest their power. Had it not been so, they could never have been formed at all, and there was full time for complete consolidation before Assyria recovered the position of a first-rank empire. With Palestine as a basis, the dominions of Israel might well have spread north and east, embracing the whole of Syria and keeping Assyria within narrow limits to the east. Eight centuries earlier Egypt had been over-run by Semitic tribes, and the empire of the Hyksos might have been revived by Israel. There is nothing impossible or fantastic in the supposition that, in favourable circumstances, an Israelite kingdom might have arisen which should have stood in history among the world's great empires and have made an epoch in the political story of mankind.

Solomon (and, to a lesser degree, his successor) made this achievement for ever impossible. Grasping at the shadow of splendour, he lost the reality of power, and, with the need for generations of the welding process still before him, behaved as though the world lay already firmly knit into a unity beneath his throne. The nascent kingdom broke at once into its component parts; the dream—if it ever was so much as a dream to the early Hebrew kings—fled with the dawn, and Israel awoke to find herself but little better than the old Canaanite princelets whose authority she had superseded. From now onwards her history is a record of petty struggles between minute states, with endless waste of effort, of men, and of material, which might have served a grander cause. Edom, Moab, Judah, Israel, Damascus —to say nothing of the Philistine cities—rent each other's vitals and drained each other's blood, till the time came when a real enemy appeared, and all alike fell before the Assyrian and Babylonian kings, never again to achieve independence, much less empire.

Yet, when we see the facts in the light of the larger history of the race, when we measure the import of events, not by centuries but by millennia, we cannot regret the failure of Israel to establish a great political kingdom of the east. To her was reserved a far nobler task than ever fell to military conqueror or to imperial statesman. She had to teach, and in the end she did teach, lessons which none other ever taught, and to bring home to mankind truths that have outlasted all the evanescent empires of her day. The little peoples about her, once as great as she, are lost and forgotten by the majority of mankind. The great world-powers of the distant past are of interest only to the specialist in archaeology and ancient history, save where they impinge upon and help to determine the life of Israel. She and her thought have endured because they dealt, not with material things, but with the deeper interests of the soul. From her has come forth a Law, and from that which was best in her has emanated a Spirit, which the world could ill have spared. In and through her very political failure she achieved a yet more notable triumph, and her ethic and her faith, albeit in modified form, to-day dominate the thinking of the world's leading nations. This she owes—and we owe—to her political insignificance. Had she succeeded in attaining the goal to which the life and work of David seemed to point her, she might have been another Assyria; as it was she became—what she did become.

Chapter XIII

HOSTILITY BETWEEN ISRAEL AND JUDAH

SUMMARY

[Hostility between the kingdoms continued for two generations. Abijam, son and successor of Rehoboam, appealed for help to Damascus, which now entered for the first time into conflict with Israel. But an attempt was made to extend Israelite territory at the expense of the Philistines, while Asa of Judah, saved from the attack of Baasha of Israel by Syrian intervention, repelled a serious raid from the desert. Asa's long reign is also noted for an attempt at religious reform.

The siege of Gibbethon, abandoned on the assassination of Nadab, was renewed under Elah, son of Baasha. He, however, was murdered by Zimri, who, in turn, fell before Omri, the founder of the first strong dynasty in the north.]

For two generations the bitter feeling arising out of the disruption kept the two sections of the country apart from one another. No doubt active hostilities were suspended after the invasion of Sheshonk, for Judah was certainly in no case to make further war for a time. One notice only appears in the record of Rehoboam, his attempt to restore something of the ceremonial of Solomon by providing bronze shields to take the place of the golden shields removed by Sheshonk. Of Jeroboam, too, the historian is silent, save for the mention of his son Abijah's death. This has been introduced probably from some early form of the narratives about the prophets, considerably expanded by a Deuteronomic editor. It has no practical bearing on the history of Israel, save that it shows Jeroboam to be still faithful to Yahweh in spite of the condemnation passed on him by the later historian. It is to a prophet of Yahweh that he turns in his trouble, the same who had originally foretold his elevation to the throne.

The war dragged on through the reigns of the successors of Jeroboam and Rehoboam, and with varying fortunes. A new element was introduced into the struggle by Abijam, son and successor of Rehoboam, who, finding Israel too strong for him, appealed to Damascus, and made a treaty with Tab-rimmon, king of that city. There can hardly be any doubt that the agreement involved the submission of Abijam, and the recognition of

Tab-rimmon as his overlord.[1] No further detail is furnished for us of the reign of Abijam[2] (the reference to the treaty with Damascus comes accidentally in a note belonging to the next reign) in *1 Kings*, but we have mention in 2 Chron. xiii. 3–20 of Abijam's success in war. Some parts of the story are obviously Midrashic, but the Chronicler seems to have had an early document on which to rely, and his main narrative may be substantially correct. He describes a battle in the Ephraimite hill-country between the forces of the two kings, in which Jeroboam skilfully outmanoeuvres his opponent, and surrounds his army. But Yahweh intervenes and smites Jeroboam's troops with panic, so that they are driven far in flight. Thereupon Abijam advances his frontier northwards, capturing Bethel and other cities in that region. We may take it for granted, however, that the success was not quite so complete as is suggested; it is extremely unlikely that Bethel fell into the hands of Judah, either now or at any time before the fall of Samaria.[3] In view of the Syrian alliance, however, we can well believe that the pressure on the frontier was reduced, and that Abijam was able to make some progress northwards.

At the same time, the north steadily aimed at larger conquests, and we hear of a siege of Gibbethon, north-west of Bethel, on the lower hills overlooking the Shephelah. This was undertaken by Nadab,[4] son of Jeroboam, but was not pressed to a conclusion owing to the assassination of the king by Baasha.[5] The new royal line made its home at Tirzah, and, apart from this fact, there was no change in policy. Abijam was now dead, and had been succeeded by his son Asa,[6] of whom we have an unusual amount of information, partly because of his long reign, and partly because of his religious measures. Thus, in 2 Chron. xiv. 9–15 we have an account of an invasion by Zerah the Cushite king.

---

[1] 1 Kgs. xv. 18. The MT. makes Tab-rimmon the son of Hezion, for which the LXX seems to have had Hazael. Some have suspected that Hezion is a corruption for Rezon, the founder of the kingdom of Damascus. This, however, is not necessary, for it does not follow that Tab-rimmon's father was actually king. Damascus was as liable to dynastic revolution as was Israel, and the kings mentioned in 1 Kgs. xv. 18 may well belong to a new house.

[2] See 1 Kgs. xv. 1–8.

[3] It is, as we have seen, possible that Rehoboam temporarily recovered much of the territory of northern Israel, and the mention of Abijam's success may reflect a tradition which originally referred to the reign of his father.

[4] See 1 Kgs. xv. 25–31.

[5] See 1 Kgs. xv. 33—xvi. 7.   [6] See 1 Kgs. xv. 9–24.

It does not seem probable, or even possible, that this story has been wholly invented by some theologian who thought that Asa's piety should be rewarded by a victory; it may quite well be that a raid from the desert was successfully repelled, and that this grew into a great victory in process of transmission.

Elsewhere Asa does not appear as a successful warrior. Baasha was much too strong for him, and even began to fortify Ramah, seven or eight miles north of Jerusalem. The completion of this enterprise would have been an important step towards the blockade of Jerusalem itself, and that is said to have been Baasha's ultimate purpose.[1] Asa appealed to Damascus, where Ben-hadad had now succeeded his father Tab-rimmon, and the latter took prompt measures to relieve his ally. The extreme north of Palestine was invaded, and the country round the Sea of Galilee and northwards was ravaged. Baasha was at once called away, and Asa took advantage of his withdrawal to use the building materials collected by Baasha at Ramah to erect forts of his own at Geba and Mizpah, thus advancing and strengthening his frontier.

Asa's reign, however, is chiefly remarkable for his religious policy. He is one of the few kings of whom the compiler of the book of *Kings* expresses strong approval, though in his case there is one limitation. The full programme of the Deuteronomists required that there should be no sanctuary whatever on Israelite soil save at Jerusalem itself. It condemned the worship of the 'high places', the old Canaanite shrines, which had been converted to the cult of Yahweh, though probably the old rites persisted. *A fortiori* it condemned still more strongly cults introduced later, especially such as might involve immoralities in worship and ritual. A number of these had made their appearance during the last three reigns[2]—we cannot hold Abijam responsible for them all—and Asa swept all these away, including especially the sacred prostitutes attached to some of the shrines (though these were no new feature of the religion of Canaan) and even a cult which had been favoured by his own mother. What precise form this took we do not know, but it was clearly connected with the worship of Astarte,—possibly also the sacred pole, or Asherah.[3]

---

[1] 1 Kgs. xv. 17.   [2] Cp. 1 Kgs. xiv. 22–4.

[3] The whole question of the Asherah is difficult and complicated. On the one hand, it seems clear that it was a wooden post, unshaped and unworked, perhaps a simple tree trunk, corresponding to the Maṣṣebah, which was a natural stone, a *menhir*. Passages like Jer. ii. 27, where the 'wooden thing' is called the father and

Asa is said to have reigned for forty-one years, and to have seen, not only the close of the reign of Jeroboam, but the rise and fall of three other northern kings and the establishment of a third dynasty. Israel maintained a certain vigour, even after the disruption, and her kings, in spite of Aramaean pressure from Damascus, never lost the ideal of a larger kingdom. Twice we hear of a siege of Gibbethon,[1] and it is introduced on both occasions, quite casually, as the scene of a dynastic revolution. Had we not reason to believe that the compiler had before him authentic contemporary records of the kings whose reigns he describes, we should be tempted to believe that there was some confusion between the two narratives. The latter of the two is the more circumstantial, and tells us how the expedition had gone down to Gibbethon under the command of Omri, leaving Elah, son and successor of Baasha, behind in the capital, Tirzah. Here, so we gather from the narrative, he spent his time in feasting and luxury, while his men were enduring all the hardships of war and of siege. A conspiracy was formed against him by Zimri, second in command of the chariotry, and, probably also by Arza, the royal chamberlain. At a drinking bout in the house of Arza, Zimri[2] surprised and slew Elah, making himself king. But this was simply a palace revolution, and clearly Zimri had no support among the people at large. The army elected Omri as soon as they heard of Elah's death, and, leaving Gibbethon, moved on Tirzah at once. So swift was their action that Tirzah was immediately surrounded, and seven days after the murder of Elah, Zimri, seeing that all was lost, set fire to the

the 'stone' the mother, show that the distinction between the two emblems did not necessarily depend on the sex of the deity symbolized—we cannot say that the Maṣṣebah always represented a god and the Asherah a goddess. On the other hand there seem to be references, e.g. 2 Kgs. xxiii. 7, where it is practically certain that the Asherah is regarded as a goddess, probably to be identified with Ishtar, to judge from the passage cited. To the Hebrew ear there was seldom confusion between א and ע, and if the two words go back to the same original, the identification must have been made in Mesopotamia, for in Akkadian there is no apparent distinction between the two aspirates. It is just possible that we have two distinct senses of the word, (a) the old Canaanite meaning, an upright wooden post, and (b) a later signification, introduced from Mesopotamia. The Akkadian pronunciation of Ishtar, owing to the א having taken the place of the ע, might well sound to the Palestinian ear nearer to Asherah than to Ashtoreth. The matter is still further complicated by the appearance of other meanings for Asherah, e.g. a room appropriated to certain sacred purposes. For a discussion see Moore, EB. i, cols. 330-2; Allen, DB. i. 165; and Cooke, NSI., pp. 50, 51.

[1] 1 Kgs. xv. 27, xvi. 15. [2] See 1 Kgs. xvi. 8-14.

palace and perished in the flames.[1] This is remarkable as one of the three (possibly only two)[2] instances of suicide in the Old Testament.

Yet Omri had still to fight for his throne. A certain Tibni, son of Ginath, appeared in opposition to him, and succeeded in winning the allegiance of a large section of the people.[3] From the fact that Tibni's father is mentioned while Omri's is not, we should gather that the former belonged to a noble family, and therefore had a certain prestige, while the latter owed his position solely to his own talents and exertions. Tibni and his brother Joram[4] maintained, as it seems, a long struggle, but they gradually grew weaker, and at last met their death, when Omri became king without a rival.

[1] See 1 Kgs. xvi. 15–20.

[2] The other two are, of course, Saul and Ahithophel, and if we accept the tradition which makes an Amalekite kill Saul, one other instance alone remains.

[3] Cp. 1 Kgs. xvi. 21–2.

[4] So the text of the LXX in 1 Kgs. xvi. 21, generally accepted as original.

Chapter XIV

ALLIANCE BETWEEN ISRAEL AND JUDAH

SUMMARY

[Omri was one of the greatest of Israelite kings. Judah was subordinate to him, and Damascus seems to have been too weak to attack him. He renewed the old Israelite dominion over Moab, and followed David in allying himself with Phoenicia. This league was cemented by the marriage of Jezebel, daughter of the Sidonian king, to Ahab, son of Omri, a step which had serious consequences for Israel. Ahab did not meet with the same success as his father. Moab revolted, perhaps because the fighting strength of the kingdom was being drained by the Syrian wars. For Damascus had recovered her strength, and the border between the two countries was the scene of endless raids. Sometimes the Syrian *razzias* penetrated far into Palestine, and at length formal war broke out. Our records tell us of two striking defeats suffered by Benhadad of Damascus, ending in his virtual submission to Ahab. The war was eventually renewed, Jehoshaphat of Judah fighting on the side of Israel, and Ahab met his death in an attempt to conquer Ramoth-gilead.

This reign witnessed the first contact between Israel and Assyria. Shalmaneser III led an army into the west in order to conquer Palestine, but met with determined resistance from a coalition headed by Benhadad and including Ahab, who actually contributed the largest contingent of chariotry. The Assyrians were checked at Karkar, though the allies suffered very heavily, in the year 853 B.C. Ahab cannot long have survived this battle. During this period Jehoshaphat reasserted the old Judaean supremacy over Edom.

The reign of Ahab is best known to us through the struggle between Jezebel and Elijah. Israel still preserved much of the old Aramaean democratic feeling and the old nomad enthusiasm for Yahweh, especially in districts where the pastoral life had not yielded, and could not yield, to the agricultural. The first of these instincts was outraged by Jezebel's treatment of Naboth, the second by her attempt to impose the cult of the Tyrian Baal, Melkart, on all Israel. Resistance found leaders in the prophets, especially in Elijah and his successor Elisha, who succeeded in checking the movement towards apostasy, though their protests against social injustice were comparatively futile.]

UNDER the house of Omri[1] Israel rose to a height which she had not attained since the death of Solomon. The first two kings of the dynasty were strong men, with personal vigour and

---

[1] For Omri see 1 Kgs. xvi. 23–8.

real statesmanship. Had Jeroboam and his successors been such
men as they, it is possible that the political harm done by the disruption might have been to some extent repaired, but now it
was too late. The Assyrians were already near at hand, and
there was no time for the consolidation of the kingdom before
the blow fell. The Assyrians themselves call Israel 'Land of
Omri'. He was possibly the first Israelite king of whom they had
heard, and, in any case their use of his name is a real tribute to
the greatness which they recognized in him. The one Moabite
record which has come down to us attests his conquests to the
east of Jordan. It is extraordinary that we have so little space
given to him in the book of *Kings*, and what we have is mainly
devoted to condemning him for his religious policy—and even
there we have hints rather than details.

Fortunately we can learn a good deal from the silence of the
writer of *1 Kings*, and we have also information from outside
sources. In the first place we observe that there is no longer any
mention of war between Israel and Judah. On the contrary, the
house of Omri is closely allied with the house of David, and in
later years there is even a marriage between the two families.[1]
Jehoshaphat of Judah, the son and successor of Asa, appears
more than once in the company of an Israelite king, and his
grandson Ahaziah[2] follows his example. The circumstances,
however, do not suggest a complimentary visit of state paid by
one king to his equal. In particular, we receive the impression
that Jehoshaphat joins in the military expeditions of Ahab[3] and
Jehoram,[4] not from pure friendship, but under some form of
compulsion. This is especially obvious in the story of the battle
of Ramoth-gilead, where we can hardly imagine Jehoshaphat
falling in with Ahab's plans willingly. Ahab is to go into battle
disguised as a common soldier, in order to escape the notice of
the enemy,[5] while Jehoshaphat is to wear all the royal insignia,[6]
thus making himself a mark for every hostile weapon. Such an
arrangement would have been accepted only by a man who was
in no position to refuse. Elisha's speech to the king of Israel,[7]
when the joint armies are in difficulties in Moabite territory,
suggests that he holds the higher rank, and it is a surprise to
hear that the prophet will help the allies because of his respect

---

[1] 2 Kgs. viii. 18, 26.   [2] 2 Kgs. ix. 16.   [3] 1 Kgs. xxii. 4.
[4] 2 Kgs. iii. 7.   [5] Perhaps also to avoid the effects of Micaiah's prophecy.
[6] 1 Kgs. xxii. 30.   [7] 2 Kgs. iii. 14.

for the lesser king. It is obvious that the strife between the two kingdoms is at an end, and it is hardly less clear that it was ended by the practical submission of Judah and her recognition of Israelite suzerainty.

It is worth noting, too, that, for a time, we hear nothing of the hostility of Damascus. She has hitherto appeared mainly as an ally of Judah, but the *rapprochement* between Judah and Israel has deprived her of the right of interference which the old league had given her, and she seems to be too weak to do serious damage to Omri. There is no question here of vassalage; on the contrary, Damascus is quite independent, and holds much territory to the east of Jordan which Israel had always claimed as her own. And when the western princelets unite to face Shalmeneser III, it is Benhadad of Damascus who stands at their head, though the force brought by Ahab must be counted as being practically of equal strength.[1] But at least we are forced to assume that throughout the reign of Omri the relative strengths of the two kingdoms were such as to make each unwilling to attack the other.

In one direction, moreover, Omri achieved a direct conquest. Moab, which had been free ever since the days of Solomon, was invaded and overcome. A number of Moabite cities were taken and occupied by an Israelite population, and the whole country was laid under an enormous tribute payable in kind—sheep and wool. It is true that the frontier was not pushed back to its ideal position on the Arnon, but the Gadites occupied much of the country between the northern end of the Dead Sea and the Arnon, including the cities of Mehedeba,[2] Ataroth, and Yahaṣ. It is clear that it was not the whole of the land that was occupied, for the royal house still maintained itself at Dibon, whence it moved to the recovery of the country in the next reign.[3] With

---

[1] Inferior in infantry, but much stronger in chariotry, the more important arm.

[2] The spelling of this name varies a good deal, partly because the Mesha inscription includes a ה instead of the ׳ which appears in the Hebrew Bible (cp. Num. xxi. 30, Josh. xiii. 9, 16, 1 Chron. xix. 7, and Isa. xv. 2), and partly because the inscription is written without vowels.

[3] Cp. MI.: 'Omri, king of Israel oppressed Moab many days, for Chemosh was wroth with his land. And his son succeeded him and he also said "I will oppress Moab"' (ll. 4–6). 'And Omri possessed the land of Mehedeba and dwelt in it, his days and half the days of his son, forty years' (ll. 7–8). 'And the men of Gad dwelt in Ataroth from of old, and the king of Israel fortified Ataroth for himself' (ll. 10–11). 'And the king of Israel built Yahaṣ and dwelt in it while he fought against me' (ll. 18 f.).

the Moabite territory as a base, no doubt Omri planned to recover the Gileadite cities which had fallen into the hands of Damascus, and, indeed, he handed this enterprise on as a legacy to his son.

Like David and Solomon, Omri was glad to secure himself by peaceful means where possible, and, like them also, he entered into a close alliance with Phoenicia. This was cemented by the marriage of his son, Ahab, to a Phoenician princess, Jezebel, daughter of Ethbaal (Ishbaal?) king of Sidon.[1] The marriage may have been highly politic, but it failed to take into account certain elements in the feeling of the Israelite people, and in the end it contributed, more than any other one event, to the downfall of the house of Omri. For the time being, however, it secured for Omri and his son a safe alliance and a valuable outlet for trade. As of old, an alliance between Israel and Phoenicia was profitable to both parties, for while the one had command of the sea, the other could control, or partly control, the caravan routes. Omri went further than David and Solomon had done, and built himself a new capital, looking outwards towards Phoenicia and the sea. The site of his city, Samaria— 'the watch-tower'[2]—was well chosen. Standing on a conical hill, three hundred feet above the surrounding valleys, with still higher mountains about it on three sides, it faces the west, and is easily accessible from that region only. In itself it was nearly impregnable, and stood more than one notable siege. The recent excavations show it to have been splendidly built, and to have been a capital worthy of a great kingdom.[3]

The death of Omri practically coincided with the great expedition of Ashur-naṣir-pal to the west. He marched through the neo-Hittite kingdom of Carchemish into the valley of the Orontes, and then through the Lebanon to the sea, receiving tribute from many peoples, including Tyre, Sidon, Byblos, and the Amurru. This latter term may include Palestine; a century and a half later it is used by Sennacherib to distinguish certain parts of Palestine from 'the land of the Hittites'. These events have left no mark on our records, and probably Ashur-naṣir-pal was content with a formal acknowledgement of his authority and with the presentation of tribute.[4] But the event does, in any

---

[1] 1 Kgs. xvi. 31.

[2] For a description of the site and an estimate of its importance, partly followed above, cp. G. A. Smith, *HGHL.*, pp. 345 ff.

[3] See especially Reisner, Fisher, and Lyon, *Harvard Excavations in Samaria* (1924); Jack, *Samaria in Ahab's Time* (1929). [4] Cp. Luckenbill, *ARA.* i. 164–7, esp. § 479.

case, mark the beginning of a new epoch in the history of Palestine. The last Egyptian forces had appeared in the land just fifty years before this time, though for two centuries previous to the expedition of Sheshonk Egypt had exercised no practical authority over the land. As we have seen, it was this age of non-interference from the outside that had permitted the growth of the Israelite state, but now the great interval was over. It is true that only once again in the pre-Alexandrian age did Egypt make an attempt to reassert her ancient dominion, but another power had arisen to the east, and henceforward the country was never wholly free from the threat of foreign invasion. The Egyptian period in Palestinian history, which had begun with the invasion of Tutmose III, was now definitely at an end; the Mesopotamian period had begun.

For over twenty years, however, the kingdoms of Israel and Judah were not seriously affected, and for practical purposes the reign of Ahab belongs to the earlier and not to the later age. For the Hebrew state the dividing line comes with the battle of Ḳarḳar, fought in 853 B.C., probably the last year, or the last but one, of the reign of Ahab. Until the invasion of Shalmaneser III Israel seems to have been unaware of the great power that was one day to overwhelm the people, or at least our Biblical records show no trace of acquaintance with it. Even Ḳarḳar is not mentioned, and the modern world was aware of the facts only when Shalmaneser's own account of them was deciphered.

Yet for the history of Israel the reign of Ahab[1] is critical, and marks a definite turning-point. More space is given to it in our Bible than to any other since Solomon, and we have traditions from several sources. Both internally and externally events took place which proved to be of the highest importance, and in no small degree determined the fate of the Hebrew race. We may glance at these one by one.

Ahab was unable to maintain the full extent of the kingdom which had been won by his father. In particular, Moab revolted. In 2 Kgs. iii. 5 this is assigned to the reign of Ahab's successor, but the inscription of Mesha himself shows this to be an error, for it was the son of Omri against whom he revolted, and the language employed makes it unlikely that the word 'son' is used in the general sense of 'descendant'. For the time being complete independence was secured, and not only so, but the

---

[1] 1 Kgs. xvi. 29—xxii. 40.

territories of Moab were considerably extended beyond their usual limits. The places captured by Mesha include Nebo, well to the north of the normal frontier, which was put to the ban.[1] Here was a sanctuary of Yahweh, and its sacred vessels were removed and dedicated to Chemosh. Mesha's conquests extended far enough north to enable him to threaten the fords of Jordan, though he does not seem to have made any attempt to push his frontiers farther north or west. The rebuilding of Jericho[2] may have been due to fear of Moabite invasion. But Moab was lost to Israel, and it is a significant fact that the king of Moab, unlike the king of Ammon, is not mentioned among those who sent contingents to the allied armies that fought Shalmaneser at Ḳarḳar.

Throughout the latter part of the ninth century, the most serious of Israel's rivals was always Damascus. The Syrians were first introduced into Israelite politics by Abijam,[3] who applied to Tab-rimmon for help against Jeroboam, and accepted Syrian sovereignty. But probably Damascus would have been willing enough to interfere in any event. Israel held one section of the great trade route, that which passed through the plain of Esdraelon, and ever since the acquisition of her independence, Damascus must have desired control over country so important to her commerce. Even Omri, great and successful soldier as he was, found himself compelled to grant special privileges to Damascus, and to assign a quarter in Samaria to the Aramaean traders.[4] It is also possible that the latter secured rights over the caravan roads, and they may even have held the great cities.

The story of Ahab's wars with Damascus is contained in 1 Kgs. xx and xxii.[5] It presents him in a light which is far from

---

[1] i.e. the *ḥerem*; Mesha (l. 17) uses the word that is familiar to us in Hebrew, e.g. in connexion with the destruction of Jericho (cp. Joshua vi. 17, &c.).

[2] 1 Kgs. xvi. 34.   [3] 1 Kgs. xv. 18 ff.   [4] 1 Kgs. xx. 34.

[5] The origin of these stories has received close attention from students of the text. They seem to be derived from a series of narratives describing events in the reign of Ahab, written in a popular rather than in an official, annalistic style. In this respect they resemble the narratives which deal with the prophets, but their main interest is not in prophecy; Elijah is nowhere mentioned, and the prophets, even Micaiah, are not the most prominent figures in ch. xxii. The writer's attitude towards Ahab is interesting and significant. The official view of the prophetic and of the later Deuteronomic parties is sufficiently represented by the statement that he 'did that which was evil in the sight of Yahweh above all that were before him' (1 Kgs. xvi. 30). But here we have no hostility, and little that we can call disapproval. There may be criticism in the account of Ahab's treatment of Micaiah, but, on the whole, the tone is friendly and sympathetic. The narratives seem, therefore, to be due to some popular history of the reign of Ahab, which resembles those of the life and court of David, and were, doubtless, an amplification of the official annals.

unfavourable, especially when it is compared with pictures which we derive from other sources. He was subject to the king of Damascus, who had also at his disposal thirty-two kings,[1] and with this united force was determined to take possession of Israel so completely that, though Ahab might retain his throne nominally, yet in fact he should have nothing that he could call his own. Benhadad threatened Samaria with all his force, and demanded that Ahab should lay everything he had at the disposal of the Syrian king. The demand was a personal one, and involved none but Ahab himself and his family. It amounted to practical deposition, and Ahab was prepared to accept the terms stated. But a second demand was made, involving not only the king but all the people as well; they were to be treated as a conquered enemy, and to be plundered as freely as the Syrians might desire. Glad as Ahab was to save his people the horrors of the siege and sack of his city, he could not accede to this demand, and, encouraged by a prophetic message, he made a sortie. The time chosen was noon, when all the world was at rest,[2] and Benhadad himself was drinking with his officers in his tent. The assault was completely successful, the Syrians were routed and slaughtered, while Benhadad himself with a few mounted men managed to escape.

The victory was attributed by the Syrians to the power of the God of Israel, who was assumed to be a God of the hills—among which Samaria lay. Further, it was suspected that the subordinate kings were not so whole-hearted in the Syrian cause as Benhadad's own subjects would have been. Therefore a year later a fresh army was prepared and equipped, officered by native Syrians, and it made its way across the plain of Esdraelon to Aphek.[3] An Israelite force, so small that it is pathetically described as being 'like two little flocks of kids',[4] moved down into the plain opposite to the great Syrian host, and, after six days' inaction on both sides, a battle took place. We have no

---

[1] The figure is possibly exaggerated; at Ḳarḳar there were only twelve, and these included Ahab himself.

[2] The heat of noon in the east is so great as to make the middle of the day almost as much a recognized period of rest and inactivity as the night itself. Cp. Jer. vi. 4.

[3] The name is so common that it is difficult to be reasonably sure where the exact locality was. It is, however, quite possible that the place mentioned here lay at the northern end of the plain of Sharon, threatening both the passage through Dothan into the plain of Esdraelon and the valley leading up to Samaria. It also covered the route between Samaria and Dor, and between Samaria and Phoenicia, in case Ahab should seek aid from that quarter. [4] 1 Kgs. xx. 27.

details of the fighting, beyond the statement that enormous numbers of Syrians were slain, but it resulted once more in the complete overthrow of Benhadad, who took refuge within the walls of the city of Aphek, and surrendered at discretion, with every outward sign of submission and, indeed, of humiliation. Ahab, to the annoyance of the more fiery elements in Israel, represented by an unnamed prophet, granted Benhadad life and liberty, on condition that the old situation should be reversed, that Damascus should now be the subject city, and should make an Israelite quarter within its walls.

The result of this battle was that hostilities were suspended for three years.[1] It is clear that even though the supremacy claimed by Ahab may not have been fully recognized, yet he was in a far stronger position than ever before, and was able to turn his attention to the task of further conquest. Perhaps it was during these three years that he reached an understanding with Jehoshaphat, king of Judah, either by war or by negotiation. The alliance was cemented by the marriage of Jehoshaphat's son, Jehoram, to Ahab's daughter, Athaliah,[2] which in itself would imply the subordination of Judah, and, in spite of the disastrous consequences which this marriage was to have within a few years, it was at least a gain that the eighty-years' old hostility between the two sections of Israel was at an end. It is a full century before we hear of it again.

Ahab's strength was now reinforced by the addition of Jehoshaphat, and, probably, of Judaean levies. He therefore determined to try to recover Ramoth-gilead, one of the cities to the east of Jordan which had long been in the hands of Damascus. The story is told in 1 Kgs. xxii. 2–40, where we have a vivid and illuminating picture of the two kings, of the court, and of the prophets. There is much in the scene which is of the highest importance for the study of Israel's religious development; but this cannot be elaborated here. Suffice it to remark that the whole story brings out Jehoshaphat's dependence and Ahab's authority. Ahab seems to have suspected that the Syrian policy would be to try to break the strength of the Israelite army by destroying him, and therefore ordered Jehoshaphat to assume the insignia of royalty, while he himself went disguised as a common

---

[1] 1 Kgs. xxii. 1. The Biblical narrative is here followed, and the reconstruction of the history will be considered when the battle of Ḳarḳar is discussed.

[2] 2 Kgs. viii. 18, 27.

soldier. As he had foreseen, the attack was concentrated on the undisguised king, and ceased only when it was discovered that he was not Ahab. Ahab had taken his place among the chariotry, and a chance arrow, passing between the breastplate and the lower armour, inflicted on him a severe wound. He would have been driven out of the fighting, but the line moved steadily forward, and he could not leave it without danger of throwing it into confusion. So he remained all day, sorely wounded as he was, in the thick of the fighting, and died with the evening. We do not know what the result of the battle was in a military sense, though the narrative suggests that Israel was not defeated, but the death of the king made further progress impossible, and it was nearly a century before Israel actually recovered her lost territory to the east of the Jordan.

No mention is made in the Hebrew records of any other war in which Ahab took part, and, curiously enough, the book of *Kings* is silent as to the most important military event of his reign. This was the invasion of Shalmaneser III, undertaken in his sixth year, with the object of reducing the whole of the Mediterranean coast of Syria and Palestine. Shalmaneser[1] crossed the Tigris, received the homage and tribute of several cities on the route, and devoted himself to the overthrow of the king of Hamath. A coalition of western peoples came to the assistance of the threatened state, as Ḳarḳar, the 'royal city' of Hamath, was attacked. They mustered between them a force of from 50,000 to 60,000 or more, distributed as follows:

	Chariots.	Cavalry.	Infantry.
Hadadezer of Aram . . .	1,200	1,200	20,000
Irḥuleni of Hamath . . .	700	700	10,000
Ahab the Israelite . . .	2,000	..	10,000
Gueans	..	..	500
Muṣreans	..	..	1,000
Irkanateans	10	..	10,000
Matinuba'il the Arvadite . .	..	..	200
Usanateans	..	..	200
Adunuba'il the Shianean . .	30	..	?ooo
Gindibu' the Arabian . . .	..	1,000 camels	..
Ba'sa, son of Ruhubu the Ammonite	..	..	?ooo
	3,940	1,900	53,900[2]

[1] The story is told by the Assyrian king on the well-known 'black obelisk', which records a long series of his triumphs. For a translation see Luckenbill, *ARA.* i. 211 ff., especially §§ 610, 611, on pp. 222 f.

[2] A minimum figure; the numbers of the troops of Adunuba'il and Ba'sa are illegible, all that remains being the word for 'thousand'.

The list contains only eleven contingents, and Shalmaneser speaks of twelve, probably a round number. It will be seen at once that Ahab contributed just over half the chariots, and that, next to Hadadezer (Benhadad), his was the largest force supplied.

Shalmaneser claims to have routed his enemies utterly, and to have slain 14,000 of them, describing with regal hyperbole the way in which the land was filled with corpses and the valleys ran with rivers of blood. He adds that he captured chariots and horses. No doubt the slaughter was enormous, but the significant fact is that the Assyrian king pushed this expedition no farther. This does not point to a decisive victory, and the probability is that he received a definite check. At the same time, it must be remembered that his main objective was Hamath, and he says that he reached the coast. But it is clear that the coalition headed by Benhadad was formidable to the Assyrian power, for Shalmaneser mentions further conflicts with the same group of kings in his tenth, eleventh, and fourteenth years, i.e. 849, 848, and 845 B.C. He gives few details beyond the formulae characteristic of a claim to victory, but it was not till his eighteenth year (841 B.C.), after the death of Benhadad, that he defeated the enemy so completely as to be able to besiege Damascus.[1]

There is nothing in all this which is inconsistent with the Biblical records, though no mention whatever is made of Assyria. We even have some light thrown on the chronology of the period. The battle of Ḳarḳar took place in 853 B.C., and we cannot date the death of Ahab later than 852 B.C.[2] The coalition must be placed within the three years' peace mentioned in 1 Kgs. xxii. 1, for it can hardly have been before the battles described in 1 Kgs. xx. We must, then, suppose that the alliance was always liable to be restored at short notice, and that after the death of Ahab the war between Israel and Syria languished, the latter being once more the predominant power. Immediately after the battle of Ḳarḳar Ahab may have felt that Damascus was too weak to defend her possessions, and it is a little surprising to find that he suffered so much less than Benhadad. Perhaps he sent only a small portion of his available infantry into the field. But the narrative testifies to the fact that Ahab was no weakling, that he could rise to a great occasion, and that the Israel of

---

[1] See Luckenbill, ARA., pp. 239, 240, 243, §§ 652, 654, 659, 672.
[2] See Additional Note I, pp. 454 ff.

his day could fight desperately and not wholly unsuccessfully against the greatest military power of the age. The partial revival of Israelite strength is also illustrated in the southern kingdom. While Jehoshaphat was, as we have seen, almost certainly a vassal of Ahab, he was free to undertake expeditions on his own account, and for some time succeeded in asserting his authority over Edom. We do not hear of a war, but the fact is certain, inasmuch as the Edomite royal house was superseded and its place taken by a governor appointed by Jehoshaphat.[1] This officer, possibly with support from Ahaziah of Israel, attempted to organize a naval expedition on the model of those ascribed to Solomon, but his ships[2] were wrecked and no fresh attempt was made. Some change must have taken place in the status of the governor of Edom, or Jehoshaphat may have decided to try another method of maintaining his hold on the country, for in 2 Kgs. iii. 9 a king of Edom participates in the expedition against Moab. At the same time, this notice makes it clear that Edom was not independent, and it may be added that the expedition against Moab was made through Edomite territory. Further, a final revolt is recorded as having taken place in the reign of Jehoram, son of Jehoshaphat,[3] and this implies that the country remained subject to Judah throughout the reign of Jehoshaphat.

2 Chron. xvii–xx contains a long and elaborate account of the reign of Jehoshaphat, recording his defensive measures and the respect in which he was held by all the neighbouring peoples. In xx. 1–30 we have a circumstantial account of a victory over the joint forces of Moab and Ammon in the Tekoa district. The narrative may contain a substratum of fact, though it must be remembered that later ages thought of Jehoshaphat as a model king, and ascribed to him a great cultic reform. This would tend to make the priestly historian give to him success of every kind—so good a king must have been rewarded by great prosperity. It is, however, very difficult to explain the omission of

---

[1] 1 Kgs. xxii. 47 f. (Heb. 48 f.), reading וּנְצָב הַמֶּלֶךְ יהו״ בֶּאֱדֹום : for נָצָב ב׳ מֶלֶךְ יהו״: The LXX has this passage after xvi. 28, and the emended text seems to have been that before the translators, though it may have omitted the king's name. But since the whole section deals with Jehoshaphat there is no doubt as to which king is intended.

[2] Possibly we should read the singular, which the LXX has throughout. The Kethibh of the MT. has the singular verb (נשברה) in verse 48 (Heb. 49).

[3] 2 Kgs. viii. 22.

the events from the book of *Kings*, whose compilers were equally enthusiastic over Jehoshaphat's character, and such a victory as that of 2 Chron. xx can hardly have been omitted from the royal annals. Further, it is clear that many of the details in these chapters are due to a comparatively late hand. At the same time, we ought not to assume as a definite conclusion that these events have no basis whatever in fact, since there may have been reasons unknown to us for their omission from the record in *Kings*.

Ahab's dealings with peoples outside Israel, while not wholly unsuccessful, tend to show that a decline was already beginning to set in, and that the country was threatened with dangers from which it might escape only with difficulty, if at all. Still more serious, however, was the effect of the Tyrian alliance on internal politics. As we have so often seen, Israel still retained in a very high degree the outlook of the Aramaean nomads, the traditional ancestors of Israel, who had made good their footing centuries earlier. Even when they settled down and took to the operations of agriculture, they still maintained much of the old tradition, and the popular mind cherished the stories of the pastoral ancestors of Israel, while it forgot the history (if there were any history) of the Canaanites who formed the bulk of the population.[1] They loyally accepted a king, but on conditions, and the very existence of the northern kingdom had depended on the recognition of the legitimate limitations of the royal prerogative. A yet stronger factor in the national life was supplied by religion. Israel was the people of Yahweh; He had given them their land, and He alone must be admitted as their God. They must have no other gods before Him—that was one of the basic rules of their religious life. It may well be that many in Israel failed to observe this condition, and we have repeated complaints of apostasy, though most of these seem to be due to a later interpretation of the history. But the tendencies were there, and the two principles, democracy (to use a term convenient if not quite exact) and Yahwism, had a strong hold on the popular mind of Israel.

It must never be forgotten that there were two Israels all through the period of the monarchy. This has no reference to the political division into two kingdoms, but to the social and economic position, and to the religious outlook, of the people

---

[1] It is possible that we have in *Genesis* a few 'Canaanite' traditions; the most obvious of them is the story of Tamar in ch. xxxviii.

concerned. On the one hand, we have those who settled in Palestine and made their home on the land, becoming just ordinary eastern peasants, and, on the other, we have men living on a very different plane, that of the shepherd. There were wide tracts of territory, especially to the east and south, which could never grow crops at all, though the herdsman could find there sufficient pasture for his animals, and so continue the life common to all the Aramaean ancestors of Israel before the conquest. It was here that the old traditions in Church and State were most strongly held, and at the same time all felt themselves to be one and the same people with their brethren in the arable lands of western Palestine. In western Palestine, too, we have occasional manifestations of the same feeling; the proper life and standards of Israel were those of the nomad, not of the farmer. We hear vaguely of Nazirites, and with more detail of Rechabites (a party or group which first comes into prominence just at this period); both represent a protest against the life of the peasant, especially in their rejection of the use of the vine and of all its products. The Rechabite, too, would not live in a solid house; the home of the wilderness was a tent, and in a tent, therefore, he would dwell.[1] This quasi-nomadic element was reinforced by the prophetic, standing for Yahweh, and when the combination of the prophet and the man of the wilderness arose, there would certainly be a strong protest against the appearance and development of non-Israelite ways of thinking in politics and religion.

To men with these instincts, the point of view represented by Jezebel was utterly abhorrent. She was a foreign princess, and brought with her the worship of her own deity. A chapel was set up for her convenience, and if the matter had stopped there,[2] though the stricter minds in Israel might have objected, yet it is unlikely that there would have been any serious consequences. But Jezebel does not seem to have been content with having her own forms and objects of worship for herself, and the evidence suggests that she tried to popularize the cult of the Phoenician Baal among the people at large. She maintained an establishment of ecstatics, over four hundred in number,[3] as fiercely

---

[1] To these illustrations we should add the fact that the patriarchal traditions, which probably reached a written form during this period, clearly imply that the nomad life is the true national ideal.

[2] 1 Kgs. xvi. 32.   [3] 1 Kgs. xviii. 19.

devoted to Baal as the Israelite *Nabi'* was to Yahweh. To the
ordinary mind in the ancient east there was no incongruity in
worshipping any number of deities at one and the same time,
and Jezebel must have failed entirely to understand the unique
position of Israel.

Still more serious was her political outlook. She had the
usual eastern conception of monarchy, an absolute despotism
in which the ruler had unlimited privilege, and the ruled no
rights whatever. To her the king was the master and his subjects
were his slaves;[1] he could do with them or with their property as
he would. She was a woman of striking personality and of strong
will, and her presence was a source of real danger to the peace of
the realm. Both in politics and in religion she was sure, sooner
or later, to arouse the most bitter antagonism and the fiercest
hostility in those who clung to the old traditional ways of Israel.

It seems that Israel first realized fully the meaning of Jezebel's
influence through the murder of Naboth. The story is very
familiar as told in 1 Kgs. xxi,[2] and is most instructive for the kind
of impression that Jezebel must have made on the genuine
Israelite mind. We see first the sturdy figure of the peasant
farmer, who owns his little plot of land and refuses to surrender
it on any terms whatever. He is, no doubt, obstinate, foolish,
and objectionable, but he is within his rights, and the spirit of
the nation will uphold him. In the second place, we have the
king himself. He is consumed with a passion for this little plot
of ground, and the refusal of the owner to let him have it throws
him into a fit of despair. He sulks in a fashion which to-day
would be esteemed quite unworthy of royalty, but men thought
differently in ancient times. He recognizes, however, that
the refusal of Naboth is final; the owner has said that he will
keep his farm, and it does not occur to Ahab that there is any
alternative but to let him keep it. He, at least, has no thought
of violating the rights of the Israelite peasant, however obsti-

---

[1] Cp. the language ascribed to Jezebel in 1 Kgs. xxi. 7.

[2] The chapter clearly belongs to a group of prophetic stories such as we have
found elsewhere in the book of *Kings*, and, no doubt, it followed originally after
ch. xix, a position which is still assigned to it by most MSS. of the LXX. Kuenen
(*Historisch-Critisch Onderzoek naar . . . de Boeken des Ouden Verbonds*, i. 407–9, esp.
§ 25, note 7) and Stade (*GVI.*, p. 527, n.) regard the story as a legend which has
no foundation in history, invented by writers of the Deuteronomistic school. For
this view there seems to be no reason at all, when it is recognized that the latter
part of the story has suffered a good deal from Deuteronomic redaction, cp. Benzinger, *Die Bücher der Könige*, p. 114; Skinner, *1 and 2 Kings*, pp. 254 f.

nately and stupidly those rights may be claimed.[1] Finally we have the foreign queen. To her the problem is no problem at all; the king is the king, and if he wants the land, then he may take it. But she knows enough of the feeling and tradition of Israel to see that the thing cannot be done purely with the high hand of omnipotent autocracy, and she has to devise means which will observe the outer semblance of law. It is interesting to notice that this manipulation of the courts of 'justice' appears to be a new phenomenon in Israel. It is only too common elsewhere in the east, and nothing is easier than to manufacture a case, especially if the party has enough money to spend on the evidence. And the result is that Naboth is convicted of high treason and blasphemy, and is executed, his estate thereupon falling vacant, or, perhaps, being appropriated as a right by the Crown. Ahab has his 'garden of herbs'. But the native feeling of Israel, finding a mouthpiece in Elijah, has seen through the whole process, and calls it simply a murder, which entails blood-revenge. It is true that there is no human kinsman left who is in a position to carry out the demands of the feud, but Yahweh is the guardian of the rights of the helpless, and He will see that at long last justice is done. Ahab has laid a mine beneath his own throne which will one day explode and bring his house to a terrible end.

Jezebel's religious policy was equally obnoxious to the Israelite tradition, though, unfortunately, we have no clear account of any of its details. Her method seems to have been a double one. On the one hand, there are hints of actual violence,[2] and it is said that Jezebel put the prophets of Yahweh to the sword and desecrated His sanctuaries. If this tradition be trustworthy, then the queen did make a definite attempt to supersede the cult of Yahweh altogether by that of Melkart, and, as a first step, tried to destroy that class of men which was most closely identified in the popular mind with Yahweh. Her action had the further effect of being a direct challenge to Yahweh Himself. None could touch the devotees of a god, or destroy his altars, without calling down on himself the divine anger, and Jezebel was saying to the people in effect, 'Yahweh is futile; He can neither protect nor avenge His chosen servants or His holy shrines.'

---

[1] It is important to observe that Ahab is represented as being entirely ignorant of the steps his wife is taking, and that he hears of her actions only after Naboth is actually dead.   [2] 1 Kgs. xviii. 4, 13; xix. 10, 14.

The other method may have been more peaceable, and yet had, possibly, the threat of force behind it. We do not know what inducements Jezebel offered or could offer to the average Israelite to adopt the cult of Melkart, but there is good reason to believe that it was widely accepted. The whole of Elijah's challenge on Mount Carmel is based on the assumption that the mass of the people are in a state of uncertainty, with their minds wavering between Yahweh and Melkart.[1] Probably most of them were prepared to accept both deities, and to divide their allegiance impartially between them. But it must be remembered that Jezebel's Baal was not the old Canaanite fertility spirit, who had been so largely absorbed into Yahweh, but a foreign national god, and there must have been misgivings in the minds of many. A clear lead by a strong spirit was all that was needed, even though there were only seven thousand faithful souls in all Israel.[2]

To the ancient mind politics and religion were inseparable. The relation between a people and its neighbours was connected with, sometimes dictated by, its national god. He was the protector of all elements in the community, and one of his duties was always the maintenance of the social standards accepted by it. While, then, the conflict between the Tyrian theory of life and that which had been inherited by Israel from its Aramaean ancestors may seem to us to involve distinct issues, as either politics or religion were concerned, to the normal Israelite they were one and the same thing. Yahweh was the God of nomad Israel, and His supremacy in Palestine involved the imposition of nomad ideas of social relations on the body politic. It was, therefore, only to be expected that the privilege of the subject, so outraged by Jezebel, should find champions among those who adhered most strictly to the old Aramaean traditions of worship.

Men of the type needed were not to be found at the shrines. Many of these had been sites of old Canaanite worship, and the traditions had not wholly perished with the arrival of a new deity. The interests of their priesthood lay in the maintenance of the outward forms of worship, and in the punctual payment of the sacred dues which every Israelite owed his God. If cases were brought for legal settlement, there is no doubt that the sacred oracle, whatever it might be, was invoked, but it was no part of the ecclesiastics' duty to go out of their way to impose

---

[1] 1 Kgs. xviii. 21.   [2] 1 Kgs. xix. 18.

moral and social rules upon the laity. Indeed, if we may judge
from the practices of the eighth century, the attendants at the
sanctuaries were themselves largely indifferent to moral considerations, and we hear complaints that some of the worst
abuses are to be found in connexion with the official worship of
Israel. The most famous of the shrines, e.g. that of Bethel, were
directly under the royal control, and the treatment which Amos
received at the hands of Amaziah a hundred years later[1] suggests
that in such a place it would be the king's prerogative and not
the people's rights that would be most strenuously upheld.

It was among the prophets that the needed leadership was
most likely to be found. Though, as we have seen, ecstatic
prophecy itself was a phenomenon which Yahwism may well
have borrowed from Baalism, the fact remains that the *N^ebi'im*
were always wild Yahweh enthusiasts. It is true that a body of
them seems to have been kept at Ahab's court, and to have been
in the habit of giving him such messages as would please him.[2]
But these did not by any means exhaust the whole body, nor
were they typical of their order. The tradition of prophecy had
always been to stand for the rights of the subject, even against
the king. The narrative which tells of Nathan's rebuke to David[3]
can hardly be later than the middle of the ninth century in its
present form and is most probably to be ascribed to a contemporary writer. It offers us a picture of what Israel had a right to
expect from a prophet, even when he was attached to the court.
It is significant, as illustrating especially the social aspect of
the question, that the popular revolt against the oppression of
Solomon, so drastically manifested in the division of the kingdom, had behind it the prophet Ahijah.[4] We shall have occasion
to notice again the leading role played by the prophetic party
in political affairs, especially in the years that immediately
followed the death of Ahab.

It may well have been that even the prophets of western
Israel were to some extent blinded by their familiarity with, and

---

[1] Cp. Am. vii. 10–17.   [2] Cp. 1 Kgs. xxii. 6, &c.   [3] 2 Sam. xii. 1–14.
[4] 1 Kgs. xi. 29 ff. We cannot, however, assume that Ahijah also represents the
religious side of the protest. It is true that the narrative of 1 Kgs. xiv. 1–18 seems
capable of that interpretation, but the sections which contain the denunciation,
verses 7–11, 13–16, are clearly due to the seventh-century editor, and represent the
Deuteronomic attitude towards Jeroboam. The earlier elements in the story rather
suggest a deep sympathy felt by the prophet for the unfortunate mother to whom
he has to give the news that her son must die.

their nearness to, the actions of the court. Whether that were so or not, the first strong protest against the Tyrian influence came from the east, and was made by Elijah. In him we have one of the best-known figures in the whole of the history of Israel, and he has received the admiration—more than the admiration—of many generations, both of Jews and of Christians. It is not only the part that he played in the political and religious life of Israel which has attracted men; as a matter of fact, this is seldom appreciated at its full worth. But his personality made a deep impression on his contemporaries, and the narratives which were written under that impression have transmitted it to all later readers of the story. He is a strange figure, introduced without mention of father or mother or any genealogy, and comes suddenly on the stage. His aspect in itself is wild and striking; he is a 'lord of hair',[1] either because, like the true Yahweh devotee, he refrains from cutting his hair, or because he wears a cloak of skins. In either case his appearance is un-usual. When under the influence of the Spirit he is absolutely fearless, and neither king nor queen has any terrors for him. It is true that when the high moment is past there comes a re-action, and he flees in terror of what Jezebel may do to him, but that is not unexpected. We do not recognize in him the cold and calculating politician; he is highly strung, intense, vigorous. It is characteristic of him that he seldom stays long in the same place. He is not to be found unless he wishes to be found, and seems to have an almost miraculous power of concealing him-self.[2] His appearances are sudden, and usually unexpected, and each means a crisis of some kind. It is not surprising that tradi-tion said of him that in the end he was taken up into heaven in a chariot of fire. That may be regarded as being originally pictur-esque language describing a thunderstorm, and Elijah himself is a kind of human lightning flash. So great was the impression his unique personality made on the thought of Israel, that he de-veloped into an apocalyptic figure, and our New Testament—to say nothing of such a passage as Mal. iv. 5[3]—attests the place he came to hold in Jewish eschatology.

Elijah[4] appears so suddenly in 1 Kgs. xvii. 1 that some have

---

[1] 2 Kgs. i. 8.   [2] Cp. 1 Kgs. xviii. 10.   [3] Heb. iii. 23.

[4] The narratives found in 1 Kgs. xvii–xix, xxi, seem to be drawn from the collec-tion of the prophetic lives to which we have had occasion so often to refer. As we have seen, doubts have been raised as to the historicity of ch. xxi, and Hölscher (*Die*

supposed that the narrative has been mutilated at the beginning. His task is to prove to the king and the people of Israel that Yahweh, not Melkart, is the God of the land. He announces, therefore, that there is to be a three-years' drought, and we need to remember that the word comes in the name of Yahweh, and that if it proves effective—it is the word of power that produces the event—that in itself will be evidence of the power of Yahweh, for none save the God of the land can give or withhold rain. The drought duly follows,[1] and a series of incidents—not without later accretions, possibly—describe the fearful sufferings which men endure. At the end of the stated time Elijah once more goes to meet Ahab, who addresses him (with some reason) as the troubler of Israel. After all, it is Elijah who has caused the drought, and so has brought the whole kingdom to the verge of starvation.

The time was now ripe for a yet greater challenge to a trial of strength between Yahweh and Melkart. We need not enter into the details of the contest on Mount Carmel, which is told in one of the finest pieces of prose in any literature. It is enough to remark certain features of the scene. The prophets of Baal are of the ordinary ecstatic type, and behave as such men might be expected to behave. When Elijah's turn comes, he exhibits none of the extravagances of his opponents, and is represented as taking all precautions to ensure the validity of the test. In passing, attention may be called to the fact that Elijah has no compunction about rebuilding and using an old altar of Yahweh which stood on the mountain, and that he, though in no way connected with the tribe of Levi, still less with the house of Aaron, feels himself competent to offer the sacrifice single-

---

Propheten, p. 177 (1914)) is of opinion that there is little reliable record of Elijah, but that most of the stories relating to him are reflections of narratives originally belonging to Elisha. Elijah was, of course, just the kind of personality about whom tradition gathers, but it is remarkable how little of what is said about him rouses suspicion in itself. It seems clear that chs. xvii–xix, at any rate, are fairly early, and reached their present form within a century of the events which they describe. The reasons usually given for this view are two: (*a*) the bull-worship of Bethel and Dan is not condemned; Elijah seems to have been willing to admit that this is worship of Yahweh; (*b*) Elijah complains (1 Kgs. xix. 10, 14) that the altars of Yahweh have been broken down. This complaint could not have been attributed to him after the time of Josiah's reform. See Benzinger, *Die Bücher der Könige*, pp. 105 f.; Skinner, *1 and 2 Kings*, pp. 221–3.

[1] The drought is independently attested by Menander (cp. Josephus, *Ant.* viii. 13²) as having occurred in the reign of Ethbaal of Sidon, though its duration is there given as one year.

handed. The climax is reached when the prophets of Baal are taken away and put to death. Here is the final challenge to Baal, and it is a direct answer to Jezebel's challenge to Yahweh. This is no land of Baal's; in this country his writ does not run, and his servants may be destroyed with impunity. Then, while Ahab eats and drinks, Elijah goes up to the top of the hill, looking out towards the west, and enters on some rain-making ritual, crouching into the shape of a rising cloud. At last the real cloud comes, and Elijah, with the abnormal strength of the ecstatic, runs before Ahab's chariot all the way to Jezreel.

A reaction sets in. Jezebel threatens to treat Elijah as she has treated other prophets of Yahweh, and as he has treated the prophets of Baal. Elijah flees for his life to the holy mountain of Horeb in the far south, and there, in the sacred cave among the wild crags, after the majestic passing of wind, earthquake, and fire, he receives in the silence[1] his message. He is not to stand alone, for the vengeance of Yahweh will be executed by three persons, Hazael, Jehu, and Elisha, who will between them utterly root out the worship of the Phoenician Baal, and will leave only the faithful remnant, amounting to seven thousand. An awful sentence, which Hazael and Jehu, at least, did their best to fulfil.[2]

Thus Elijah made his protest against the double peril with which the foreign queen was threatening the life of Israel. Neither element in it was immediately effective. The cult of Melkart received a definite check, as appears from the fact that a few years later Jehu was able to collect all the Melkart devotees into a single building[3]—but perhaps these were only the foreigners or foreign priests resident in the country. It was the sword of Jehu that completed the work, but Elijah had struck the first blow. Still less effective was the political and social protest. The course followed by Jezebel in destroying Naboth set a precedent only too often followed during the next century, and the example which she offered played no small part in bringing about the final ruin of the kingdom.

Thus closes the first half of the history of the Israelite monarchy, that in which the country, free from external molestation until

---

[1] The passage is commonly misunderstood. דְּמָמָה means *silence* rather than *whisper*. xix. 12*b* should run '. . . and after the fire, hark! a fine silence'. So also Job iv. 16 '. . . Silence!—and a voice I began to hear', and Ps. cvii. 29 'He settleth storm into silence, and its waves are dumb.'   [2] 1 Kgs. xix.   [3] 2 Kgs. x. 21.

the end, was left to work out her own salvation. We have seen how far Israel was from establishing any valid polity. The kingdom of David had disintegrated, and there were two states in Israel proper. So much organic unity had been secured. But Israel had no political instincts, and it fell to her to be governed by men who, in this respect, were typical of their race. In David we saw how she had her chance of growing into a great empire; in his successors we have seen how she lost it. A century and a half had passed since Jerusalem had become the capital of a united Israel, and the country was further from political safety and unity than she had been when Joab stormed the Jebusite citadel. The kingdoms of the world were never to be hers, and there were signs that she would not remain indefinitely mistress in her own house.

Chapter XV

LIFE IN ISRAEL UNDER THE MONARCHY

SUMMARY

[One of the outstanding features of Palestinian life was the city. Several Israelite cities of this period have been excavated, and we can to some extent reconstruct them. Houses were built partly of stone and partly of brick, the latter mostly sun-dried.

Dress was usually simple, though the wealthier people wore more elaborate costumes. The main articles of diet were cereals, fruit, and milk.

Commerce was both local, involving traffic in ordinary articles of daily use, and general. The latter was, till the middle of the ninth century B.C., largely in royal hands. Palestine had few commodities to export, but profited by her position on the great trade route.

Village life was simpler than that of the city, and retained most of the old features—the 'gates', the wells, the fields, the cemeteries, and the sanctuaries. The backbone of the Israelite nation was the small farmer, whose independence was maintained by the ownership of his land, while his personal vigour was reinforced by a constant struggle with Nature.

Slavery existed in two forms, temporary and permanent. The governmental administration probably followed the lines laid down by Solomon.

The religion of Israel in this period presents several interesting features. Mention has already been made of Jezebel's attempt to introduce the Tyrian Baal. Among the prophets Micaiah and Elijah are important since they stand alone, and do not work or live with the companies of prophets. It is further to be noted that the prophets now take a prominent part in politics, exercising their influence for the maintenance of the traditional principles of the old Aramaean nomads.

The age is rich in literature, and to it we owe, not only (as it seems) the older legal codes of our Bibles, but some fine pieces of historical prose, such as the account of David's court life contained in 2 Sam. ix–xx.]

BEFORE we pass on to the story of the decline and fall of the Hebrew kingdoms, we shall do well to glance for a moment at the internal state and organization of the country during the period now closing. Apart from that element which has remained semi-nomad, Israel has become a commercial and agricultural people. In one way or another she has entered into possession of 'great and goodly cities which she builded not, houses full of all good things which she filled not, cisterns hewn out which she hewed not, vineyards and olive trees which she planted not',[1] and, taking up this heritage, she has assumed also the whole civilized order to which these things belong.

The feature of the settled life which first appealed to the wandering Aramaean was the city. In recent years a number of Israelite sites have been excavated, and we can now form a fair picture of the buildings and of their arrangement within the walls. One of the finest examples, if not the finest, of the period we have just been discussing is to be found at Samaria. Here, underlying several later strata, we have the actual fortifications —or remains of them—built by Omri, the founder of the city, together with the palaces of that king and of his son.[2] The first step in building was to mark out the site, and cut away the rock all round it to a depth of several feet, forming a scarp. The walls were then erected on the edge of this, so that they were practically a vertical continuation of the solid rock. Large blocks of stone—a yellow limestone, soft and 'cheesy' when first cut, but with a surface rapidly hardening when exposed to the air—were quarried out of the hill itself for the buildings. For all interior walls a trench was hewn out of the rock, and the lower courses of masonry were laid in it. The floor of the palace itself was level, and was therefore built at some little height above the rock, the distance varying with the inequalities of the natural surface. The main plan of the buildings was that still common in the east, a series of rooms arranged in a rectangle about a court into which all opened, the outer wall being pierced by only a single door or gateway. The palace of Omri, for instance,[3] was built round a central court some twenty-six feet square. From the north-east and south-east corners there ran passages opening into rooms on the east and west sides. To the west of the central court were two little rooms, hardly bigger than cupboards, and to the east a room of the same length as the

---

[1] Deut. vi. 10 f.

[2] For a complete account of Samaria as far as it has been excavated see the magnificent publication of the results of the Harvard expedition (Reisner, Fisher, and Lyon, *Harvard Excavations at Samaria* (1924)); vol. i, pt. iii, ch. 1 (Fisher), contains a detailed description of the buildings of the Israelite period, and numerous photographs are to be found in vol. ii. A most useful summary and discussion of the results has been published by J. W. Jack, *Samaria in Ahab's Time* (1929), and the student who wishes to have an adequate presentation of the facts cannot do better than consult this work.

[3] See the plans in *Harvard Excavations at Samaria*, vol. ii, especially Plan 5.

court and about half as wide. To the north of the main block of
buildings was a large court, about fifty-five feet from east to
west and twenty-six from north to south, extending a little to the
east of the main buildings. This was matched by a southern
wing, which, however, was divided into two rooms. The outer
walls were about five feet thick, and the dividing walls between
the rooms rather less. The palace of Ahab was much more
ambitious, and he included his father's buildings within the
court of his own. But the method of building and the general
plan were much the same, except that in the great court of
Ahab's palace, between the outer wall and the west side of
Omri's palace, there lay a building with a complex system
of rooms containing numbers of *ostraka*,[1] apparently dockets
or invoices sent with jars of wine or oil, possibly as tribute. The
city wall was, of course, lower down on the hill-side, and was
very much thicker, having an average width of about thirty feet.
Unfortunately, little of this has survived, and it may be conjectured that it was almost completely destroyed by the Assyrians in 721.[2] As in all ancient cities the streets were very
narrow, though we have evidence of wider spaces in certain
parts. Foot-passengers and mounted men might make their
way through without much difficulty, but wheeled vehicles can
seldom have secured an easy passage. The streets were not only
narrow, but tended to be choked with the paraphernalia of
various trades and occupations. There may have been shops of
some kind, but a large part of the trade was probably done (as
in the east to-day) by men and women who simply brought
their wares into the street and spread them out to catch the eye
of the people as they went to and fro. We have as yet had no
evidence of a system of drainage such as that which was developed in some of the ancient Mesopotamian cities, and the
probability is that refuse of all kinds was left in the streets to be
consumed by dogs and other natural scavengers.[3]

Houses were built of several materials. Those most in use
were stone and brick, burnt or unburnt. As a rule it would
seem that in country districts unburnt brick was the commonest
material; in the cities the lower courses were formed either of

---

[1] See below, pp. 321 f.

[2] Some idea of Israelite building may be obtained from the section of Ahab's
masonry shown on pl. 27 and other plates in *Harvard Excavations at Samaria*.

[3] Cp. 2 Kgs. ix. 35 f.

stone or (less frequently) of burnt brick, and the upper parts—
from three or four feet upwards—of sun-dried clay. This latter
material readily disintegrates in wet weather unless attended
to, with the result that most ancient cities are now simply
mounds of earth, beneath which the stone and burnt brick may
be disinterred. The houses of the peasantry were probably
single-story huts, with no windows beyond a hole through which
the smoke of the fire could escape. In the city, and on the estates
of the wealthier farmers, they were more elaborate, having two
or more stories, with a flat roof above them which could be used
as a promenade or might even have another small building
erected on it. Windows were protected by lattice-work; glass
was not used for this purpose.

The dress of the people varied with their wealth and station.
Men at work probably wore little more than a loin-cloth, but in
addition even the poorest had a 'cloak', apparently a kind of
woollen blanket such as that still used by the eastern peasantry,
and turned to a number of different uses. The dress of the
shepherd peoples and of the city dwellers probably much resembled that worn in Palestine to this day. Women's garments
were ampler and might be more elaborate, and some simple
jewellery was usually worn, if it were only a metal anklet or
bracelet. For ceremonial occasions, such as weddings, a very
complicated costume might be assumed.

The principal articles of food were cooked cereals and fruits,
fresh or dried. The former might be ground into meal in a
hand-mill, or might simply be parched by the fire. The chief
fruits used for food were figs and grapes, the latter frequently
dried. Curiously enough, dates are not mentioned in the Old
Testament at all, though the date palm was common. It has,
however, been suggested (on the analogy of modern Arabic
usage) that the word generally rendered 'honey' sometimes,
though clearly not always, meant a kind of syrup derived from
dates. Pomegranates were also eaten, but apples seem to be
mentioned only in passages which are comparatively late.
Milk—presumably goats' milk in most cases—was made up in
a number of different forms, liquid and solid, especially among
the nomads, and cows' milk seems hardly to be mentioned at all.
Meat can hardly have been a daily article of diet; it was either
the produce of hunting, or, if the flesh of domestic animals were
eaten, confined to sacrificial occasions.

Commerce was of two kinds. There was, on the one hand, the traffic in useful and necessary articles produced by craftsmen in the neighbourhood—pottery, food-stuffs, and the like. This was probably carried on in the streets of the city, and it seems that there were quarters appropriated to particular trades. More characteristic of the period, however, was the growth of international commerce, practically a royal monopoly as far as our evidence goes. There were two attempts to form a mercantile marine, one made by Solomon,[1] and the other by Jehoshaphat.[2] The latter was a complete failure, and it is clear that no private person could have undertaken such an enterprise. Trade with foreigners, apart from commodities brought by caravans from distant countries, was secured by the assignment to Israelite merchants of certain quarters in foreign cities, and such merchants seem to have been strictly in the king's service. We find, on the other hand, that in Samaria itself similar arrangements were made for the accommodation of the 'servants' of the king of Damascus.[3] We may assume, too, that the control of the caravans was also very largely a royal prerogative.

This larger commerce played a most important part in the life and policy of Israel. Palestine to-day has several exports which bring income from outside, especially in various kinds of fruit and minerals. But the former were not grown in ancient times, while the value of the latter was not realized, and the country had little or nothing which could be offered in exchange for the characteristic produce of other lands. It is true that there was plenty to satisfy the simpler needs of life, and the Israelite could rely on adequate supplies of corn, wine, oil, flax, wool, and other articles needed for his own use. But practically every country of the ancient world could normally produce these things; it is only when we come to fifth-century Athens that we find a population depending on imports from abroad for its daily food. It was not worth while loading caravans to cross the desert spaces simply in order to carry these commodities to markets already sufficiently stocked with native products, and the consequence was that the Israelite trader, king or subject, had little or nothing which he could offer in exchange for the goods of foreign peoples. This difficulty has met us already in considering the reign of Solomon, and we have seen[4] how that

---

[1] 1 Kgs. x. 22.　　　　　　　　　　　[2] 1 Kgs. xxii. 48.
[3] Cp. 1 Kgs. xx. 34.　　　　　　　　　[4] Above, pp. 253 ff.

extravagant king was put to most serious straits to pay for the
ostentatious magnificence in which he delighted. While it is
true that Hiram accepted certain quantities of corn and oil,
probably for the maintenance of his Lebanon workers, in the
end the Israelite king was compelled to liquidate his debts by
the cession of territory.

On the other hand, some of the great trade routes of the world
led through Palestine,[1] and this gave to the Israelite the only
opportunity he had of securing an income from without. If
caravans passed directly through the country, a toll might be
levied—and we may be sure that it was levied. But a great deal
of material was brought to the Syrian markets and sold there,
no doubt at a profit to the native trader. It became, then, a
primary object of the policy of the Palestinian and Syrian kings
to secure for themselves as many of these markets as they could.
Phoenicia had succeeded Byblos as the principal centre for the
overseas exports of Asia, and the safer route to Egypt still led
through Damascus, across the plain of Esdraelon, and down the
Philistine coast. The possession or control of Damascus had been
in no small measure responsible for the comparative prosperity of
the reign of David and the early years of Solomon, and the loss
of that city must have been a very severe blow to Israel. The
alliances and conquests of the house of Omri clearly have as their
object the maintenance of control over a section of the great
trade routes. Hence his alliance with Sidon, and Ahab's acceptance of Benhadad's offer of 'streets in Damascus',[2] however
unacceptable it may have been to the prophetic party, was quite
in accord with the political and economic advantage of Israel.
We can hardly suppose that the privilege thus granted to Israel
(a reversion of that previously claimed by Damascus) simply
meant that the Israelite merchant had the right to sell Palestinian produce in Damascus; that city could supply for herself
all that she needed without importing from her neighbours. It
must have had reference to international trade, and have implied that Ahab's officials were free to make their profit from
the goods brought by eastern caravans for the south and west,
or from Egypt and Phoenicia for the east.

It is just here that we find the outstanding difference between
the position of the northern kingdom and that of Judah. The

---

[1] See above, pp. 21 f., especially map on p. 23.
[2] 1 Kgs. xx. 34; cp. above, pp. 292, 294.

latter never, after the time of David, had the least claim to control the trade route which ran through the Philistine plain,[1] and the result was that, while agriculture was practised in some parts of the country (though not to the same extent as in the north) the southern kingdom was far less commercialized. In one direction only was there an opportunity for foreign trade, and that lay to the south-east, through the Red Sea. The use of this route demanded the occupation of Edomite territory, and for the greater part of the period we have just been considering, this route was barred to Israel by the independence of Edom. It is significant that it is only in the reign of Jehoshaphat, when there was close alliance between the two Hebrew kingdoms, and when the north to no small extent controlled the south, that an attempt was made to revive commerce through this route. If Ahab—and we may assume that the policy was dictated by him to Jehoshaphat, and that he, rather than his subordinate, would have reaped its benefits—had succeeded in reopening trade communications with the south-east, Israel would once more have reached that high condition of commercial prosperity which she had enjoyed only in the last years of David and the early days of Solomon. But the attempt failed, and Judah, at least, remained shut out from the great world of international commerce.

It seems very unlikely that in ancient Israel any family lived in an isolated house, whether large or small. It is true that we hear from time to time of single houses, but this is simply due to the fact that the neighbours are not involved in the narrative. At no time, over the greater part of the territory of Israel, was the country secure enough from occasional raiders to make it safe for men to live alone. Houses were grouped into villages, where they were sure of mutual protection. The site chosen was frequently on or near the top of a hill, and was determined partly by the amount of arable land in the neighbourhood, partly by the supply of water. In modern Palestine—and we have no reason to believe that custom has changed in this respect—the steepness of the slope often makes one house look out directly on to the roof of that immediately below it. Only the

---

[1] The routes leading from the north seem to have been fairly easy to traverse, and Jerusalem was always accessible from that direction. But south of Hebron the country was dry and travelling comparatively difficult. Hence Jerusalem did not lie on a through route.

smallest hamlets were unprotected, and the community always tried to surround itself with a wall, which, though not an elaborate fortification such as that which defended the larger towns, was yet protection enough against a mere raid. Within this the houses were very closely packed together, and traffic facilities must have been even smaller in the country towns and villages than in the large cities. The houses seem to have been of the same general type as those found in the cities, though there can have been comparatively few of larger size.

One of the most important spots in the whole place was the gateway. It was usually the only means whereby a village might be entered or left, and it had, for other reasons as well as this, a unique position in country life. In the seventh century the term was equivalent to 'city' or 'town'. Here was the gathering of the elders, and of others who wished to talk together, forming an assembly much like those which are to be found in the chief tent of an Arab encampment at this day. Here business, both legal and commercial, might be done, and the place served the purposes of a Town Hall. We may suspect that it was one of the few spots in the Hebrew village or country town where there was any fresh air, and where there was room for people to meet.

Another of the centres of the village life was the well. It goes without saying that every inhabited spot, large or small, must have its water supply. This was more particularly the meeting-place of the women, since the carriage of water is always a woman's task in the east. The position of womanhood makes it unlikely that much serious business was transacted there, but all the gossip and much of the social life of the place would be concentrated about the well. In some places the water does not run freely, it takes some time for each vessel to be filled, and there is plenty of opportunity for extended conversation. The occasional references call up before us a charming picture of simple, happy life and society.

Many, probably all, of the Hebrew towns and villages had cemeteries at no great distance. The treatment of the dead, based as it seems to be on animistic ideas which die hard, with its elaborate ceremonial and variety of rites and customs, is a subject too large to be discussed here. It would seem that bodies were always interred, even in those rare cases where a human victim was offered up as a holocaust. If possible, a corpse was buried within the house occupied by the dead during life. Thus

Joab, Samuel, and others found their last resting-place 'in their own house'. A tomb outside the town or village might be either a pit dug in the ground or a cave hewn out of the rock. It does not seem that the body was usually placed in a coffin of any kind; the fact that Joseph's corpse was thus treated is thought worthy of special mention.[1] It was, however, only the well-to-do who could look forward to a special tomb or burial-place of their own, for we hear of the 'graves of the common people', probably larger pits in which numbers of bodies might be laid. In any case the exposure of the body was regarded, in Israel as elsewhere, as one of the most terrible calamities which could befall any man.[2]

Among the essentials of life was a sanctuary. Usually this would seem to have been built on the top of the hill on whose slopes the town lay, and its structure would be elaborate or simple in proportion to the fame and influence of the shrine. Here sacrifice would be offered and the sacred dues paid. A conspicuous tree might also serve as a suitable site for worship, and there may have been places so small as to have no sanctuary. But the food regulations[3] were such as to make it imperative that every man in Israel should have within comparatively easy reach of his home some place where he might offer sacrifice.

Round the village proper lay the cultivated lands belonging to it. Palestine is a stony country, and the farmer, in ancient as in modern times, must gather together the loose stones from the ground he wishes to till. They might be used to make walls, and sometimes seem to have collected into tall heaps which would serve the purpose of watch-towers.[4] Each family in the village had its own plot, though these were not necessarily marked off from one another except by trodden paths and landmarks, whose removal was held to be a heinous offence.[5] Vineyards and vegetable gardens needed rather more elaborate

---

[1] Gen. l. 26. The story, in its present form, comes to us from the period immediately under discussion, and this detail probably represents the feeling of the time of its compilation.

[2] See further, Oesterley, *Immortality and the Unseen World* (2nd ed. 1931), and cp. Deut. xxviii. 26.

[3] In particular, the flesh of the domestic animals might be eaten only when they had been offered in sacrifice, and could be consumed only within the precincts of a sanctuary. Cp. e.g. 1 Sam. i., ix. 22–4, &c.

[4] Cp. Elihu Grant, *The People of Palestine*, p. 39 (2nd ed. 1921). Dr. Grant's book forms an admirable account of modern Palestinian life, and may be taken as offering some indication of conditions in ancient times.   [5] Cp. Deut. xxvii. 17.

care than the grains (of which barley was the chief). Often a small shed of some kind, perhaps a rough hut of stone or of branches (where trees were plentiful enough), was built, in which a permanent watcher could be placed. This was especially necessary during the early autumn, when the grapes were beginning to ripen, for the vinedresser has many enemies, both animal and human. We have little direct evidence as to the housing of the draught animals. To this day in the east the smaller cattle, usually goats, live freely in the rooms occupied by their owners, but oxen and asses would take up too much space. As far as our excavations can tell us, there was hardly room in the ordinary village houses for stalls or sheds, and occasional references[1] seem to suggest that accommodation was provided outside the circuit of the village. The larger establishments may have had special buildings of some kind, but there is no evidence to suggest such extensive provision as that supplied, for instance, by Solomon, for horses and chariotry.

The basis of Israel's economic life was the small peasant farmer, the 'crofter', who lived on the plot that had belonged to his family in the past and would be handed down to his descendants. There were larger farms, but a person who owned one was regarded as exceptionally wealthy. Whether the farm were large or small, it was worked almost entirely by the owner and his household; we hear nothing of the absentee landlords receiving rent until the eighth century. The owner's children, if he had any, took their share of the work, and the women of the family also had duties out of doors. In the larger families slaves, temporary or permanent, and also, possibly, hired labourers, might be included. As long as there were men with strength and vigour to do the work of the land, and provided that the season were favourable, and that no other untoward accident (such as a foreign raid) occurred, a comfortable living could be made in the fertile lands of Palestine. But the failure of any one of these conditions meant hardship. A solitary woman had a bitter struggle at any time, and any additional trouble almost certainly spelt ruin.[2] Drought brought famine in its train, and if it were

---

[1] Cp. e.g. Gen. xxxiii. 17. While the events described are referred to the nomad age, the passage dates from the monarchy, and the mention of the 'house' suggests that the writer is thinking of the conditions of a settled community.

[2] In the prophetic stories of the ninth century we have one or two very

serious it must have cost countless lives and gravely impoverished the survivors.[1] In those parts of the country which were most exposed to foreign invasions life must have been very precarious, and even in this period we have hints of a cruel border warfare between Israel and Damascus, which must have ruined large numbers of households lying within reach of plundering bands. Yet, in the main, the picture we have of Naboth may be taken fairly to represent the general type of the agricultural Israelite, the small man with undeniable faults and obvious weaknesses, but with a sturdy independence of spirit and a conservative outlook, one who would fight to the death for his property and for his rights. It was of such men that the backbone of the Israelite nation was composed.

The methods of agriculture seem to have been of the simplest. The soil was turned up and prepared with a plough, apparently not a very large or effective instrument. It was such as one man might easily carry, and though it was shod with metal, it was probably of the general type described by Virgil, somewhat resembling that still used in the east. The draught animals were normally oxen, though asses might be used; it is interesting to find the Deuteronomic law forbidding the yoking together of the two species.[2] As far as our evidence goes, there was no rotation of crops, and the same produce was probably grown year after year in each field, but a fallow year was regularly observed, though, perhaps, rather from religious motives than from a knowledge of the principles of agriculture. Little seems to have been known of methods whereby the soil might be rendered more fertile, and we have no reference in these early times to the use of manure on the ground. The farmer probably depended on the natural richness of the soil and on his regular fallow year. For working smaller patches of land, a hoe or mattock of some kind was used, and there was clearly some method of harrowing it. The gathered crop was taken to the threshing-floor, a space of hard earth, usually on the hill-top. There the grain was beaten out from the ear with a sledge, a flat instrument made of

---

illuminating references to the hardships which might befall a poor widow, cp. 1 Kgs. xvii. 8 ff., 2 Kgs. iv. 1–7. The former of these concerns a Phoenician woman, but the same conditions would prevail in Israel.

[1] The stories of Ruth and of the Shunamite woman (2 Kgs. viii. 1–5) show how even wealthy families might be reduced through famine. In these cases the sufferers were compelled to migrate, but that was their only hope of surviving, and it normally meant the loss of their land. [2] Deut. xxii. 10

heavy boards and studded beneath with stones and pieces of metal. This was dragged over the corn by draught animals, usually oxen. The grain was winnowed with a 'fan', a large shovel which was used to toss it into the air, when the wind would blow away the chaff and allow the grain to fall back to the floor. Grit and dust were cleaned out of it with a sieve. Some minor crops were beaten out with a flail.[1]

We have fewer references to the work of growing vines and olives, the other two most important products of the soil. Vines, however, we know to have been grown in rows, and the grapes, when gathered, were trampled out in a winepress, whence the fresh juice was drawn off and allowed to ferment. We have no direct information as to the details of its manufacture. Olives were either crushed or beaten; the latter process was supposed to supply the purer and better oil. The importance of the olive lay in the fact that its oil was the only form of fat commonly in use in Israelite cooking, as we see, not only from such passages as 1 Kgs. xvii. 12, but also from the sacrificial regulations.

Baking was done in an oven, which might be one of two kinds. The first was an inverted bowl under which the leavened dough was placed, the hot coals being raked over it, the other was a dome-shaped structure which was placed over the fire, and the cakes of dough laid upon it. Probably Hos. vii. 6 refers to an oven of this kind. In the cities the art of confectionery attained a high standard, and probably owed something to foreign, especially Egyptian, influence.

It is a striking fact that there is no distinctive Palestinian pottery. The forms, indeed, are graceful, especially in the period we are now considering, but they are clearly borrowed from other sources, perhaps mainly Philistine.[2] Three general classes may be distinguished. We have first of all the common pottery, vessels that were made on the wheel, but without much art except the mere form. They are made, for the most part, of a brown clay, burnt red; others are made of a 'grey ware, burning drab or pink when well baked. Bowls and jugs usually bear a thick haematite wash.'[3] These include two-handled jars of various sizes, jugs with a single handle, bowls, dishes, and lamps.

---

[1] Cp. Isa. xxviii. 27.
[2] For a summary discussion see J. W. Jack, *Samaria in Ahab's Time*, pp. 26–33.
[3] *Harvard Excavations at Samaria*, i. 275

They were of a kind that might be used by ordinary people, and were probably very cheap.

The second type is of a finer make altogether, and is highly burnished. Examples are naturally not so abundant, but the shapes are similar to those of the last class. The third type, which includes decorated pottery, is suspected of being Greek, and may belong to a period as late as 400 B.C.—at least as far as the specimens and fragments found in Samaria are concerned. In any case, they do not seem to belong to the time of the early monarchy.

In addition to these a large number of *ostraka* have been found. These are simply broken pieces of pottery which have been used as a writing material, and the collection in Samaria is interesting as many of them bear the names of the places whence they emanated. We can thus see that the type was not peculiar to Samaria itself, but was found in other parts of the country as well.

Remains in metal are rare, and seem to be confined to iron spear and arrow heads. A few objects of ivory have been recovered, usually of Egyptian provenance.

In these circumstances it will be readily understood that finance was normally a simple and, indeed, an elementary matter. In the country most of the trade was evidently done by barter, and even in the cities this method may have been adopted in many instances. There was no regular currency; money, such as it was, took the form of silver bullion, and had to be weighed out whenever payments were made.[1] Thus, the equipment of every trader included small scales for the appraising of the customer's money as well as the measures needed for estimating the quantity of goods supplied. It seems, however, that in this period the use of money was considerably extended, and that it was making its way into the country as well as into the cities. A farmer's difficulties might compel him to borrow, and the money-lenders formed a regular and familiar profession. Money would be lent on some security; for a small loan a man's 'cloak' might be taken, but if so it must be restored to the owner for use at night.[2] For larger debts the peasant could offer only

[1] Cp. Amos viii. 5, where the dishonest tradesman cheats his customer in two ways over a single purchase, 'making small the ephah'—giving short measure, and 'enlarging the shekel'—securing more than a fair quantity of silver in exchange for his goods.

[2] Exod. xxii. 26. The 'Book of the Covenant' almost certainly belongs to the

his land, his own person, or some member of his family, and if
the debt fell due and was not paid, the person pledged was
liable to be sold into slavery.[1]
Slavery was of two kinds, permanent and limited. The first
type affected captives taken in war, women, and those born
in the household of slave women. Israelite men taken for debt
or for some other reason belonged to the second type. The slave-
period was six years, and at the end of that time the master was
bound to let the slave go free, unless the latter expressed a
preference for slavery, when he would be transferred to the
class of the permanent slave. The Israelite rule in this matter
was similar to that which prevailed all over the ancient east,
though the period varied, being only three years instead of six
in Babylonia. Apart from the distinction between slave and
free, there is practically no trace of a system of 'caste' or of
social orders in Israel,[2] and, indeed, such a division of society
would be entirely at variance with the normal sense of
brotherhood and equality which the genuine tradition of Israel
maintained.

The actual processes of government were doubtless carried on
along the traditional lines. Justice would be administered by
local officials, or by the informal court of the elders of the
locality, though in the larger towns some more formal and
definite appointments must have been made. As always in the
east, the principal business of the local administration was the
collection of taxes, payable in kind. For this purpose the country
was divided up into districts, and we may suspect that the old
arrangement of Solomon was generally observed. We have a
certain amount of contemporary evidence, both from Israel and
from Judah in the *ostraka* and royal jar-handles of which so
many have been found. It would seem that the latter, which are
characteristic of Judah, belong without exception to the eighth

---

first half of the monarchy, though it is clear that some of its provisions were honoured
in the breach rather than in the observance.
    [1] Cp. 2 Kgs. iv. 1, where the use of the article (הנשׁה) implies that the money-
lender was a regular feature of Israelite life.
    [2] The attempt of M. Lurje, *Studien zur Geschichte der wirtschaftlichen und sozialen
Verhältnisse im Israelitisch-jüdischen Reiche* (1927), to show that there was a class of
'gentry' in Israel as in Mesopotamia, is hardly successful. The evidence adduced
is very scanty and can all be explained in other ways. Moreover, the distinction in
Babylon is so obvious and has left so clear an impress on the legal system, that if it
had existed in Israel some unmistakable traces would surely have shown themselves.

century.[1] But this probably means only that a new method of registration was then introduced, while the old divisions were retained. The four districts seem to have had as their administrative capitals the towns of Socoh, Hebron, Ziph, and Mamshath. If Mamshath is correctly identified with the Roman Mampsis[2] and with the modern Qurnub,[3] then it would seem that the four districts ran practically longitudinally east and west across Judah, though it is possible that the Hebron district extended as far north as Jerusalem and that the Socoh district included all the Judaean Shephelah.

The exact meaning and purpose of the Samaritan *ostraka* have been disputed, but the most probable solution (seeing that they were all found preserved in a special room in the palace of Ahab) seems to be that they were dockets or invoices sent with wine and oil paid as tribute. In that case the names will include the prefects of the district. A number of the places mentioned have been identified, and all are to be found in western Manasseh, in the third of Solomon's administrative districts. Even these seem to have been subdivided, inasmuch as we find the names of more than one officer from the same locality in the same year. It seems to be a curious accident that has preserved these dockets belonging to a single district, and, as far as the places have been identified, to no other, but we may assume that the rest of the northern kingdom was similarly apportioned, and that officers were appointed for the regular collection of tribute.

The administration of the army, again, does not seem to have developed far beyond that of the united kingdom. A somewhat larger establishment may have been needed, owing to the increase in the force of chariotry, which was nearly half as large again under Ahab as it had been under Solomon, even if the forces of Judah are included in those of Israel. There was in addition a standing force of cavalry and infantry, conveniently subdivided, though we must suppose that the great armies which were raised on special occasions—e.g. to meet Shalmaneser in 853 B.C.—were largely based on local levies. As to the officers we hear expressly in 2 Kgs. i. 9 ff. of captains of fifty. This is

---

[1] For a discussion of the whole subject see Alt, *Israels Gaue unter Salomo* in *Alttestamentliche Studien* (Kittel Festschrift), pp. 1–19 (1913); Albright, 'The Administrative Divisions of Israel and Judah', in the *Journal of the Palestine Oriental Society*, v (1925), pp. 17–54; J. W. Jack, *Samaria in Ahab's Time*, pp. 84–105.

[2] Hommel, *Expository Times*, 1901, p. 208.

[3] Hartmann, *Journal of the Palestine Oriental Society*, iv (1924), p. 153, n. 1.

a small unit, and must have been included in larger bodies, probably thousands.

Religion in this period seems to have advanced little from that of Solomon's day or even earlier. One effect of the monarchy was undoubtedly to give prestige to the shrines which were especially patronized by the kings, but there seems to have been very little attempt to secure any actual centralization of worship—none at all in the northern kingdom. Even Asa, who secures the approval of the Deuteronomic editor of *Kings*, is expressly stated to have allowed worship at the local sanctuaries to continue. His son, Jehoshaphat, however, does seem to have made a tentative effort at a reform in this direction, and though he did not venture to remove the sanctuaries themselves, he did seek to purify their cult by eliminating the hierodules. If we may judge from the silence of the record, however, his action did not extend to the female prostitutes who appear to have been a regular feature of these local cults.[1]

The period is, however, remarkable for the definite protest made by Elijah against the introduction of the Tyrian Baal as an object of worship in Israel. We have already discussed this from its social and political aspects, and it remains to notice the exact extent to which Elijah seems to have wished to go. As far as we know, he made no attempt whatever to remove, or even to protest against, the Israelite cultus as carried on at Bethel and other sanctuaries. He seems to have had no objection to the worship of the bull, and certainly does not appear to have suggested that there was anything wrong in the presence of more than one altar. On the contrary, one of his complaints of his people is that they have thrown down the altars of Yahweh,[2] and he himself took pains to repair the ruined altar on Mount Carmel, and offered sacrifice upon it.[3]

It is, further, clear that, when Ahab acquiesced in the promotion of the cult of Melkart, he had no intention of eliminating the worship of Yahweh. The names of three of his children are known to us—Ahaziah, Jehoram, and Athaliah, and all three are compounds including the name of Yahweh. This in itself should acquit their father of the charge of deliberate apostasy. The activities of his wife were, no doubt, more drastic, but even so, we may well believe that there was a point beyond which the king would not be prepared to go.

[1] 1 Kgs. xxii. 46 (Heb. 47).   [2] 1 Kgs. xix. 10, 14.   [3] 1 Kgs. xviii. 30–8.

The development of prophecy during the period is interesting and important. Perhaps owing to Tyrian influence, there grew up the custom of maintaining a number of devotees about the court. Jezebel had a large staff of Melkart ecstatics—estimated at four hundred and fifty by the historian[1]—who were maintained at the queen's expense. Later[2] we hear of about four hundred prophets of Yahweh who similarly attended the king, and took the place of the old priestly lot when he wished to inquire of Yahweh. The assumption of this function is interesting, for in earlier days it was usual for the prophet to act and speak purely on the impulse of his own experience, and, except in the case of Ahijah,[3] we have no reference before this time to the formal consultation of a *prophet* (as distinct from a *seer*).

Still more striking are the positions of Elijah and Micaiah. Each stands entirely alone. The infection which the ecstasy conveyed tended to make the prophets gregarious, and we have already seen in the stories of Saul how they were normally to be found in companies. The narratives which concern Elisha belong properly to the next period, but they show tendencies that were not new in his day. It is clear that the ecstatics were now beginning to form communities (if they had not previously done so) and to settle down on favourable sites in the country. Prophecy became a profession, and was no longer the irresistible impulse of a man who had other occupations, such as Saul. In stories which deal with the second half of the ninth century we find the phrase 'sons of the prophets', which implies a special caste and community. Much of the work of Elisha is said to have been concerned with these communities, but he was clearly not their founder, and their development is not unnatural from the ecstatic bands of the pre-monarchic days.

But Elijah and Micaiah are in no way connected with these professional establishments; Micaiah, at any rate, has sufficient independence of spirit to remain unaffected by the prophetic crowd about him. We do not hear of the professional prophet's inner experience; he does not claim to have received his message through the 'second sight'. It is Micaiah who exhibits that combination of ecstatic and seer which later became typical, and details to the king[4] that which he has seen

---

[1] 1 Kgs. xviii. 19. [2] 1 Kgs. xxii. 6.
[3] 1 Kgs. xiv. 1–18. [4] 1 Kgs. xxii. 17–23.

on two different occasions. It does not appear that he actually sees the visions as he stands before Ahab; he describes them as in the past, and tells the king what his experience has been. Yet Ahab recognizes him as a genuine prophet of Yahweh, and, hot as is his feeling against him, he does not dare to have him put to death. It is these men of genuine personal inspiration who are the forerunners of the great ethical prophets of the eighth and seventh centuries.

Next, we note another symptom in the prophetic movement. This is the tendency to take a practical part in political life, and to stand quite definitely in opposition to the monarchy. We have already had a hint of this in the story of Jeroboam and Ahijah, but it may have been projected backwards into the history from a later age. There is, however, no doubt as to the attitude taken by Elijah, and tradition tells us that Elisha was his true successor in this respect. In prophets of this type it was especially the common people whose views and feelings found expression. The prophets were socially and politically insignificant, save in so far as they were the spokesmen of the great mass of the people. They were in a very real sense the inheritors and the guardians of that democratic principle which Israel had preserved from nomad days, and within twelve years of the death of Ahab their feelings had grown so strong that they were able to engineer a dynastic revolution.

Before we pass on to the next period in the history of Israel, we should note that the early monarchy was a time of great literary activity. Whether this was the work of the prophetic circles or of some other groups, it is impossible to say; but the former alternative appears far less probable than it did a generation ago. There was a professional class of scribes, and the sanctuaries themselves may have done something to contribute to the general literary output. There was, of course, no such thing as publication in our modern sense of the term, but part of the business of scribes, especially of those attached to the royal courts, was to make copies of the annals and of other documents. We do not know whether any Israelite king ever sought to establish libraries such as those of the Assyrian kings, especially of Ashur-bani-pal. But a fair amount of material now found in our Old Testament must date from this age.

We need not consider poetry. Poetry is older than prose, as speech is older than writing, and it takes shape long before men think of committing it to a visible record. We have Israelite poetry which goes back to much earlier days than those of the kings,[1] and we have occasional pieces from the men of their time. Unless, however, portions of the Psalter are to be assigned to this early date (which appears very unlikely, though many may come from the later monarchy), we have no religious poetry from this period, and it was naturally religious poetry that had the best chance of survival. The poems attributed to David in 2 Sam. xxii, xxiii, are almost certainly later compositions, but there exists no reasonable doubt as to his authorship of the great elegy over Saul and Jonathan.[2] This, and the elegy over Abner,[3] however, seem to be the only pieces which we can confidently assign to this age, and they help us to feel how much we may have lost, for they must rank high in the history of the world's literature.

The period was, however, the golden age of Hebrew prose, and its literary remains include some of the noblest pieces of writing in any language. It is probably true that no book of the Old Testament reached its present form till long after the ninth century, and many students would say that such comprehensive works as those indicated by the symbols J and E belong to a later age. But they embody a great deal of earlier material, some of which must have had written shape, and not a few continuous and fairly long pieces can be isolated from the final form.

Broadly speaking, the prose of this age falls into two main classes, legal and historical, and both present features of interest and importance. The Law (even in the narrower sense), as we have it now, is clearly a compilation containing elements from several sources and from different stages in the development of the people. It is to be noted that the difference between *jus* and *fas*, between laws which regulate the behaviour of man to his fellows on the one hand, and laws which are concerned with his relation to his God on the other, is not strongly felt. This impression, however, is probably due to the later compilers, and it is possible to trace an earlier stage in which we have definite codes of civil laws.[4] There is a certain amount of overlapping as

---

[1] The best example, of course, is the song of Deborah, Judges v.
[2] 2 Sam. i. 17–27.   [3] 2 Sam. iii. 33 f.
[4] The whole subject of the legal codes of Israel has been recently discussed by Jirku; see his *Das weltliche Recht im Alten Testament* (1927). Jirku observes that the secular laws as they stand fall into ten groups, distinguished by the

between these codes, even in the portions which the compilers have preserved, and we may be sure that the correspondence was once much more extensive than it now appears to be. The *lex talionis*, for example, appears both in Exod. xxi. 23–5 and in Deut. xix. 21, and the prohibition of adultery is found, in very similar language, in Deut. xxii. 22, Lev. xviii. 20, and Lev. xx. 10, the varying formulae in each case showing that the separate citations were derived from different codes. We may conjecture that these codes were inherited by Israel from their predecessors in Palestine, and that each had an independent local origin. The disorganization and disintegration of pre-Israelite Palestine make it probable that each city and district, perhaps each great sanctuary, would have its own stereotyped code, and, if that be so, we have in the combination of them which is presented to us in the Pentateuchal laws one more illustration of the way in which Israel unified the whole land.

Four other codes from the ancient east are known to us. We have first, in a fragmentary form, a Sumerian body of laws.[1] The best known is the code of Ḥammurabi, dating from the end of the third or the beginning of the second millennium B.C.,[2] but we have others from Assyria,[3] and from the Hittite kingdom.[4] A comparison of these with the Israelite codes shows that they cannot be independent of one another. All reflect the same general type of society, though with local variations, and all

formula with which they are introduced. These are: (1) 'if' usually כִּי, but אִם in Exod. xxi. 23, xxii. 1, Deut. xxii. 25 (perhaps because these particular passages do not represent the whole of laws, but fragments of which the first part has not been included); (2) 'Thou shalt'; (3) Law introduced in the 3rd person, often by אִישׁ or אִשָּׁה; (4) Law in the form of a curse; (5) 'Ye shall'; (6) Laws introduced by a Jussive; (7) Laws introduced by a participle; (8) 'If thou'; (9) 'If ye'; (10) 'If a man' ('2nd If'). It is not impossible that closer examination may reduce the number, e.g. the distinction between 3 and 6 is slight, but the larger bodies are clearly distinguished. Jirku maintains that each group of laws is derived from a single code, and devotes careful study to a comparison between these codes and others known to us from the ancient east. His general conclusion is that the Israelite codes, especially the first mentioned, exhibit an earlier form of general oriental law than do those of Mesopotamia and Anatolia, and he supposes that the first, together with the earliest elements in the Decalogue, were derived by Moses from the sanctuary and settlement at Kadesh.

[1] Cp. especially Langdon, in the *JRAS.*, 1920, pp. 489 ff.

[2] Cp. e.g. C. H. W. Johns, *The Oldest Code of Laws in the World* (2nd ed. 1913); S. A. Cook, *The Laws of Moses and the Code of Ḥammurabi* (1903); D. H. Müller, *Die Gesetze Hammurabis*, which includes a close comparison with Hebrew law and with the XII Tables.

[3] Cp. esp. Jastrow, 'An Assyrian Law Code', *JAOS.* xli. 1 ff.

[4] Cp. esp. Hrozny, *Code Hittite provenant de l'Asie mineure* (1922).

exhibit the same general principles of law. There are, of course, differences, and while the resemblances are so great as to make a theory of independent origin impossible, it is quite clear that none of them is directly derived from one of the others. It is strange, but apparently undeniable, that it is the Old Testament types of the laws which have retained the more primitive form. Even the Mesopotamian codes, ancient as they are, have been adapted to a more highly developed community, and must have passed through a long history, during which they have been considerably modified. We are therefore compelled to assume that the general type of law reached the Mediterranean coastlands not later than the middle of the third millennium B.C., and that it retained its primitive character there long after the more highly cultured nations of the north and east had developed new features.

As compared with these other codes, those of Israel were clearly adapted to an agricultural community rather than to a commercial people, to peasants rather than to city-dwellers. It is interesting to note that in most respects the Israelite laws are the harsher; the death penalty is far more often inflicted, and (to take a single illustrative detail) the period of legal slavery is six years instead of three. We also observe, however, that this severer tone is manifest in Israel most frequently in cases of injury done to persons; where property is damaged, the position is reversed, and it is the other codes which tend to be the more stringent. This change in the ratio of personal to material values is what we should expect in a community which was developing an elaborate commercial system.

A further difference is to be found in the suggestion of a primitive, almost animistic, outlook offered by the Old Testament codes. This is most obvious in the laws relating to bloodshed. It is clear that the primitive reason for executing the murderer lay in the fear that blood spilt by violence might injure the living unless it were covered by the blood of the slayer. While this does not seem to have had any material influence on the actual provisions of the Old Testament codes, it clearly had not wholly died out. In the other codes bloodshed demands a penalty, either in accord with the principles of the *lex talionis*, or in compensation for damage suffered by the kindred of the dead. This is, perhaps, more obvious than elsewhere in the case of a man who has been killed when there is no clue to the murderer. In the Old Testament law[1] a ceremonial is prescribed which is clearly designed to free the nearest inhabited spot (on which responsibility would naturally fall) from danger resulting from the murder. In the code of Hammurabi there is nothing said about ritual purification, but the city has to pay the dead man's relatives a *mina* of silver. Obviously the whole outlook of the latter code is characteristic of a higher culture.

Another feature to which attention may be called is the social and political organization which is assumed. The Old Testament has a law defining and restricting the powers of the crown,[2] which is in itself eloquent testimony to the democratic spirit prevailing in Israel throughout the whole history of the monarchy. But the king is nowhere else mentioned in any of the Israelite codes. Now, more than once, we find in other codes that the king stands in a privileged position. Criminals may be sentenced to become 'slaves of the king' for a period in the Assyrian law. Among the Hittites the king has authority to pardon certain offences, especially those against the laws relating to sex. In Israel, on the other hand, we hear of a 'prince',[3] of judges,[4] officials,[5] and elders, but their function is always to administer the law, and they have no special privilege or position.

Finally, we must repeat what has often been said, that, in spite of a harshness which appears in certain instances, on the whole, there is a humanitarian tone in the Old Testament codes which is almost entirely lacking elsewhere. Conspicuous is the kindly treatment demanded for the slave, and for the depressed classes. The fugitive slave is to be sheltered, not to be handed over to his master.[6] Particularly instructive are the laws of Ex. xxii. 25-7,[7] Deut. xxiv. 6, 10-13, which restrict the action of the money-lender in taking and keeping his pledge. These have no parallel elsewhere, and they serve as illustrations of a general tendency which may be observed in the whole of the Israelite attitude. It was not without some justification that a seventh-century writer took pride in the 'statutes and judgements' which Yahweh had given His people.[8]

---

[1] Deut. xxi. 1–9.   [2] Deut. xvii. 14–20.
[3] נשיא, Exod. xxii. 28 (Heb. 27).   [4] שפטים.   [5] שטרים.
[6] Deut. xxiii. 15 f. It should be noted, however, that in this passage the slave is apparently one who has escaped from some foreign country, while the parallels in the Sumerian and Hammurabi codes think of one who has fled from a fellow-countryman, and is therefore still his property.   [7] Heb. 24–6.   [8] Deut. iv. 8.

It is in the realms of history and biography that we have the finest literary specimens of the prose of this age. Amid much else that may date from this period, we have almost certainly a contemporary document describing events in the personal life of David.[1] This is, perhaps, the first great piece of historical writing that the world has known.[2] We have annals, simple records of events, from a far earlier period, both in Egypt and in Mesopotamia. We have the novel, a creation of fancy, in Egypt at least as far back as 2000 B.C. But here, for the first time, it seems, we have the attempt to take annals, the dry narrative of events, and create real history out of them. And, in spite of many corruptions of text, due to careless and ignorant copyists, such a piece of writing as this story of David's court must retain a very high place in historical work. The style is simple, yet dignified, making no pretension to eloquence, yet demanding and holding attention. The action is swift, and there is no trace of labour in the finished product. There is no complicated syntax and no attempt at epigram; the Hebrew author writes *sans phrase*, and his very language expresses the straightforward simplicity of his mind. There is a great rhythm in his style, and there is a reticence which makes us see more than is said. These are characteristics which seem to spring out of the nature of the Hebrew language itself, for (unless philological tradition has grossly misled us) the great strength of its accent makes it the most musical tongue ever spoken by human lips, its paucity of adjectives gives it a stateliness rare in any literature, and its simple syntax carries forward the movement of the story in a straight line, making no strain either on the ingenuity or on the memory of the reader. It is no accident that the noblest monuments of English prose are nearly verbatim translations of the Hebrew text—often reproducing the style more exactly than the meaning.

[1] 2 Sam. ix–xx.

[2] There is, doubtless, much else in the *Hexateuch* and *Judges* which can be traced back in literary form to the period under review, and a large proportion of it shares the qualities of the long section here mentioned. But this comparatively early material has been so much interwoven with later writing that it is difficult to reconstruct narratives of any length. Of course, if we were *sure* that either J or E was to be ascribed as a whole to a time before 850 B.C., we should have at least two long continuous books of this early date. But the utmost that we can assert dogmatically is that the *sources* of these two documents go so far back, and we do not know how far they have been modified by the later writers and compilers.

BOOK IV
THE ISRAELITE MONARCHIES: THEIR DECLINE AND FALL

INTRODUCTORY REMARKS

WE have now followed the story of Israel to the point at which the nation may be said to have reached its political zenith. We have seen how the comparative peace accorded to the land by the weakness of the two older centres of civilization (Egypt and Mesopotamia) gave opportunity to the genius of David to form a strong state, through the overthrow of the Philistines, the one power that might have proved a rival to Israel. We have watched how the chances presented to Israel were wasted through the prodigality, vanity and ostentation of Solomon and the folly of Rehoboam. We have traced the growth of power in the hands of Omri, which, in spite of the division of the land and its impoverishment by his predecessors, might, in happier circumstances, have led to a re-establishment of the former glory of the country; and we have observed the rising of the cloud in the east which was one day to overshadow the whole of western Asia, and even to pass beyond the borders of Egypt. And now it falls to us to mark the collapse of Israel as an independent people, to trace the slow process by which she slipped more and more into the power of the great eastern empire, until first, the north lost its independence, and finally, three centuries after the time of Omri, the last stronghold of Hebrew national life was destroyed, and Israel, as a political unit, ceased to exist. Already, even in the reign of Ahab, it is clear that the seeds were being sown which would lead to disaster, and that there were elements within the nation which might constitute a grave peril. For Israel perished, not merely because of the power of Assyria, but also because of her own inherent failure to maintain her standards. There was a social and political cancer within the body politic which made ruin sooner or later inevitable. It is possible that an internally healthy Israel might, in the end, have had to succumb to Assyria, but, as the clearest minds in her midst saw, she was suffering from diseases which must in any event have proved fatal.

Thus, externally, the outstanding feature of the period was the power of Assyria. The long age of comparative eclipse had come to an end, and she was now ready to take her place as the world's dominant nation. Her own immediate frontiers had been strengthened, and the dangerous tribes on the north and north-east thoroughly quelled. Babylon, always the weakest point,

was more or less quiescent, and though she broke occasionally
into revolt (the most serious movement is at the end of the eighth
century), she was never so powerful that a few campaigns could
not repress her. The way was open for a great advance westward, where the timber stores of Lebanon and the sea-borne
trade of Phoenicia offered strong inducements to conquest. Yet
her progress was not uniform, and during the first hundred
years of the period is hardly to be noted. The power of such an
empire as that of Assyria necessarily depends on the personality
of its kings, and the successors of Shalmaneser III fell below the
standard required for their task. Between 841 and 745 B.C. there
was no serious Assyrian menace to Israel, though Damascus was
struck down in 805 B.C., and if the Palestinian states had been
masters of sufficient political insight, they might have used their
respite to band themselves together into a firmly knit unit, which
would have had an opportunity of resisting the encroachments
of their great enemy.

But none of the little kings of the west seems to have had the
slightest understanding of the trend of contemporary history.
Instead of co-operating and allying themselves one with another,
they continued the old ruinous policy of perpetual conflict. The
border warfare knew no cessation, and all the countries about
Israel and Judah were given to sending out bands of plunderers
and slave-raiders.[1] Thus impoverished and decimated, the
people were also steadily losing their *moral* through the grave
economic and social changes that were passing over them, with
the result that when at last the danger obviously threatened, and
an attempt was made to form a political alliance which might
offer some resistance to the advancing enemy, there were no
longer the reserves of man-power and of courage which alone
could have given the slightest hope of success to the defence.

To these causes of decline must be added the intrigues of
Egypt. This country, too, had fallen on evil days, yet from time
to time she passed into the hands of some king, abler and
stronger than his immediate predecessors, often a foreigner, and
so won a short space of new life. She never (save for a brief
interval at the end of the seventh century) made any serious
attempt to claim sovereignty over the Palestinian states, but she
could not forget that she had once been great. She lived, too,

---

[1] For pictures of the conditions prevailing in the eighth century cp. e.g. Amos
i. 3–ii. 3.

especially towards the end of the period, when the possibilities of Assyrian conquest became more and more obvious, in perpetual fear lest she herself should be overcome and absorbed into the great empire that threatened to swallow the world. She was in no position to meet the threat with armed resistance; only once did she make the attempt, as far as we know, and its issue was disastrous for her. She relied rather on intrigue, and sought to keep the Assyrian at bay by stirring up disloyalty and rebellion in the states which she could reach without difficulty. She did not want an Assyrian army in the Delta, and it seemed to her that the best plan to avoid this calamity was to keep her enemy busy elsewhere. The policy was futile, for it led in the end to the complete annexation of these little principalities, and brought the Assyrians on to the very frontiers of Egypt; but it was beyond the power of the Egyptian politicians to foresee even so obvious a result as this. 'A broken reed, on which if a man lean it shall pierce his hand'[1] was the judgement of an acute observer, and it serves as a summary of her history for these two centuries. The Hebrew monarchies, torn by local dissensions, demoralized by new social conditions, falling into anarchy and political confusion, and snared by the cunning intrigue of a futile Egypt, went their road to destruction.

The Israelite kingdoms did not fall into ruins together. Within the space of a few years in the second half of the eighth century the northern monarchy came to an end, but the southern endured for nearly a century and a half longer. This seems to have been due to two causes. In the first place, Judah was more submissive than Israel, and had, at the same time, a more stable government, and therefore a more consistent policy. When once she had accepted the suzerainty of Assyria, she remained faithful to her overlords, except for one short interval at the end of the eighth century, when her disloyalty came within an ace of destroying her independent existence. As a matter of fact, the kingdom of Assyria came to an end nearly thirty years before the kingdom of Judah. The second cause may well have been her comparative insignificance. Samaria was a province which stood on one of the world's main highways, and the country was in touch with most of the great movements of the day. An eastern king who wished to control the trade routes to the south, or to prepare the way for an ultimate advance upon Egypt, was

[1] Language ascribed to the Rabshakeh, 2 Kgs. xviii. 21.

compelled at least to neutralize Samaria, and could not feel that the end was in sight until the city was reduced and the country placed under more or less direct Assyrian rule. But Jerusalem lay away in the hills, far above the great roads. No doubt she could make herself unpleasant to caravans or to armies marching along the Philistine plain, but she could not seriously menace the safety of communications, and the policy of Sargon shows him far more anxious to reduce the cities of the maritime plain than to meddle with Jerusalem and her people. There was less plunder, too, to be got from the little mountain state, and on all accounts the armies of Assyria did well to let Jerusalem alone, unless the folly of her government compelled them to interfere. When she did fall, the Chaldeans were the instruments of her destruction, and it was her own insistent meddling with international politics which made it necessary for Nebuchadrezzar to suppress her if he would maintain his position in the west.

Few periods in ancient history are better documented than this, especially after the middle of the eighth century. For the first hundred years, it is true, we have little outside the book of *Kings* on which to rely. Our external sources are confined to the inscriptions of Shalmaneser III, and after his death there is a gap in the dealings between Assyria and Israel. But from the beginning of the reign of Tiglath-pileser III (745 B.C.) we have abundance of material for history. The last kings of Assyria, from Tiglath-pileser down to Ashurbani-pal, have left us fairly detailed accounts of their reigns, and we know more about this section of Assyrian history than we do of many periods in the story of medieval Europe. For events which took place in the outer world during the last Judahite reigns, we have the Babylonian Chronicle, though, unfortunately, we have, as yet, no complete copy. We are fairly well acquainted with events in Egypt, though these throw only an indirect light on what was happening in Palestine.

But from the middle of the eighth century we have from Israelite sources a wealth of material of a kind only too rare in the ancient world. This is to be found in the prophetic literature of the Old Testament, or at least in the utterances of the pre-exilic prophets. *Amos, Hosea, Isaiah, Micah, Zephaniah, Nahum, Habakkuk,* and *Jeremiah* are extraordinarily illuminating, partly from their references to contemporary events (though these are often allusive and uncertain of interpretation), but still more from the fact that they do not represent the official court view, as nearly all other ancient records do. The prophetic literature is essentially popular, in the sense that its pictures are those of life as seen through the eyes of the ordinary citizen, who has no temptation or inclination to glorify a king or to extol a dynasty—often the contrary. Thus the light they throw on the conditions of their day is almost without parallel, and affords us opportunities of seeing the life of Israel at this period as we can seldom see it at any other time.

Chapter XVI

THE PROPHETIC REVOLUTION

SUMMARY

[In spite of repeated Assyrian assaults the border warfare with Syria continued through the reigns of Ahab's sons. Occasionally formal war broke out, and once Samaria was besieged and nearly starved into surrender. But Israel retained enough strength to attempt once more the subjugation of Moab. That country was laid waste, but the capital did not fall, and Moab retained its independence. Edom, too, revolted from Judah.

In 842 or 841 B.C. a revolution was brought on by the prophetic party in Israel, Jehoram, and Ahaziah of Judah being murdered by Jehu, who destroyed Baal worship in an act of horrible massacre. He deserted the general Palestinian alliance, and Damascus, left alone, was unable to resist Shalmaneser III. But the city soon recovered from the destruction wrought in 841 B.C., with the result that Jehu and his successors still suffered from Syrian rivalry and oppression. In Judah the throne was usurped on the death of Ahaziah by his mother Athaliah, daughter of Ahab, but she was put to death by a priestly revolt in 835 B.C., and was succeeded by her young grandson, Jehoash. The cult of the Tyrian Baal was definitely and finally uprooted, though on its social and moral side the prophetic protest seems to have passed unheeded.]

SHALMANESER III had been repulsed by a coalition of most of the kings of the west, but the alliance hardly survived the withdrawal of the Assyrian armies. Within a year, the old state of frontier warfare broke out again. The aggressor was Ahab, who may have seen in the weakening of the power of Damascus, through losses sustained at Ḳarḳar, an opportunity for the recovery of parts of that Transjordanic territory which had always been claimed by Israel, but had been so long in Syrian occupation. The policy was short-sighted, but the Assyrians had gone, and Israelite statesmen were seldom able to see beyond a very limited horizon. A real understanding of the Assyrian ambition and power would have told the western princedoms that the day of reckoning was only postponed, and that it behoved them, if they would face it with any hope of success, to make every preparation for a further united resistance, instead of sapping their strength by petty but wasteful border strife. Ahab may have had further plans. Mesha was still independent, and there can have been little country to the east of Jordan that was not held either by Moab or by Damascus. It is possible that the Israelite king hoped to use the northern part of this territory as a base from which an attempt could be made to reduce the south. Moab sent no contingent to Ḳarḳar, and was, presumably, still strong. The story of Ahab's effort to recover Ramoth-gilead has been mentioned in Chapter XIV, and here demands no further reference. Its importance lies in the fact that it marks the revival of local warfare, which continued throughout the reigns of Ahab's two sons. We have few details, and what we have comes to us in the main from the stories of Elisha. In the narratives no king is named, but we must assume that he was generally Jehoram, the second of Ahab's sons, since the former, Ahaziah, is given a reign of only two years.[1] While we cannot always trust to the details of these stories, which are essentially folk-tales about a national hero, they do serve to give us an extremely interesting and reliable general picture of the conditions of the time. Three or four of them bear directly on events whose historicity need not be questioned, though we may suspect that Elisha's part in them has been somewhat exaggerated. It must, however, be remembered that it was only because he was held to have been one of the actors in the scenes depicted, that the narratives themselves have come down to us.

Two of the narratives allude to raiding bands. The first is the well-known story of Naaman, the leper, who hears of the possibility of a cure from a slave-girl taken in such an expedition.[2] The second[3] tells of an attempt made by the king of Syria (unnamed, as usually happens in these stories of Elisha) to seize the person of the prophet himself, who is suspected of frustrating the plans of the raiders by revealing them to his own king. The story of Naaman is important inasmuch as it implies that there was no formal war between the two countries concerned. The king of Syria is able to send a letter to the king of Israel, and the latter's comment is that the sender is seeking an opportunity for war. In modern phrase, diplomatic relations have not been broken off; the governments are at peace if the people are at war, and the

---

[1] 1 Kgs. xxii. 51 ff. (Heb. 52 ff.). We must, however, leave open the possibility that, since no Israelite king is ever named, the Elisha stories *all* belong (as some of them certainly do) to the reigns of Jehu and his successors.   [2] 2 Kgs. v.
[3] 2 Kgs. vi. 8–23.

situation recalls the relations between Spain and England during the first thirty years of the reign of Elizabeth. Much the same impression is given by the story of Elisha's capture of the powerful band sent out to seize him. When he has them safely in Samaria, the king desires to destroy them, and the prophet saves them by reminding him that they would not have been put to death if they had been prisoners of war—how much less when the situation is what it is?[1] This suggestion of free intercourse between the two peoples, implying the absence of formal war, is further brought out by the story of the visit of Elisha to Damascus mentioned in 2 Kgs. viii. 7 ff. Not only is he free to come and go—in spite of the fact that the king has once sought his life!—but he is recognized in Damascus, and his advice is sought there as eagerly as in his own country. It may be that the story is to be attributed to a desire to magnify the Israelite prophet as honoured in the eyes of all the world, but even if it be unhistorical, it does at least show that free communication was held to be possible at the time when the narrative was compiled.

But though there was no formal war between the two governments, this irregular series of raids by the one people on the other must have tended to the steady weakening of the national resources. While nominally maintaining peace the king of Damascus is represented as being interested in these attacks, and as directing their operations to some extent, until the skill of Elisha makes them useless.[2] And we may take it for granted that, though it is only Syrian forays that are described for us, the Israelites were not prepared to accept the position tamely, and there must have been retaliation, more or less effective. We need not doubt that the Syrians were the stronger, as is uniformly represented in our stories, but it is unlikely that Israelite reprisals were a complete failure, and the Syrian border country must also have suffered. The extent and seriousness of some of the more ambitious expeditions are attested by the story which brings a large Syrian company as far as Dothan, which is in the pass connecting the plain of Sharon with the plain of Esdraelon.

Elisha is introduced into another story, in which, perhaps, he played originally a smaller part than he does in its present form.[3]

---

[1] 2 Kgs. vi. 21 f.   [2] Cp. 2 Kgs. vi. 8–23.
[3] 2 Kgs. vi. 24–vii. 20. The narrative has suffered in course of transmission. In particular, it must surely have given a reason why the king should have regarded Elisha as the source of the nation's troubles. The messenger of vi. 32 f. seems out of

This time we have a regular war, for the whole armed force of the Syrians is collected, and, not content with attacking small and undefended villages and carrying off plunder and prisoners, they invest Samaria. The horrors of the siege are vividly brought out by a story of cannibalism,[1] and the city is evidently at the last extremity when the Syrians fall into a panic and flee, leaving everything behind them. The reason given is their sudden fear that the king of Israel has hired Hittites and 'Muṣri'[2] to rescue him. There may well be an historical fact lying behind their fear, for it is quite possible that such an expedition to the south was made by these powers in the interval between the two main Assyrian expeditions to the west. We may, then, assume the accuracy of the general picture presented to us by these narratives, viz. constant hostility between Syria and Israel, normally confined to raids by one party or the other, but sometimes breaking into open warfare. The Israelite king is either Jehoram or Jehoahaz,[3] for nowhere is it suggested that the activity of Elisha is to be placed in the reign of Ahab, and for some time after 841 B.C. Damascus was almost certainly too weak to take the vigorous action which these narratives presuppose. But it is clear that both kingdoms were suffering and both were drawing nearer to the edge of calamity.

Another expedition described as occurring during the reign of Jehoram[4] is certainly historical. This is the joint invasion of

place in the story, which in other ways assumes that the king comes himself. Cp. Skinner, *1 and 2 Kings*, pp. 308 f. The *provenance* of the story is also disputed, Wellhausen, Kittel, Driver, and others ascribing it to a collection of narratives dealing with the wars of the kings of Israel, whilst others (e.g. Benzinger) find close similarities with other passages taken from the narratives about the prophets. Perhaps Benzinger is right (*Die Bücher der Könige*, p. 142) in regarding it as composite, drawing elements from both sources. [1] 2 Kgs. vi. 26-30.

[2] Probably *not* Egypt, as our translations have it, but a north Syrian or Cappadocian kingdom. Cf. Winckler, *Alttestamentliche Untersuchungen*, pp. 166 ff.; Hommel, *Geschichte Babyloniens u. Assyriens*, p. 610 (1888). The 'Hittites' also are not to be identified with any certainty. The old Hittite empire of the fourteenth and thirteenth centuries had long since vanished, but the term is used in Assyrian documents for a number of states, even as far south as Ashdod. Perhaps the Hittites in the writer's mind are the people of Hamath and the neighbourhood, or the term may be used more generally for 'north Syrian'. On the 'obelisk of Nimrod', which gives a summary account of the campaign of Ḳarḳar, Sargon groups all the allies of Hamath under the name 'Hittite'.

[3] For the official notice of Jehoram's reign see 2 Kgs. iii. 1-3, for that of Jehoahaz, 2 Kgs. xiii. 1 ff.

[4] This is not certain. The opening verses of the passage (2 Kgs. iii. 4-27), which mention Jehoram, are drawn from the royal annals, but in the story itself the king is not named after verse 6, and may well have been Ahaziah.

Moab by the king of Israel, Jehoshaphat, and the king of Edom.[1] The expedition was made by way of Edom, round the southern end of the Dead Sea. This was necessary if an attack were to be made on Moab at all, because so much of the territory to the east of Jordan was in Syrian hands, and it is clear that the attempt on Ramoth-gilead or other cities of Transjordania had not been renewed. The route had the further advantage of delivering an attack on Moab from a side whence Israelite invasion was not likely to be expected.

The whole narrative illustrates the methods and character of warfare between these little states. An invading army might be victorious in the field, and if so would devote itself to the work of destruction; but sieges were a different matter. Evidently the Moabites were reduced to desperate straits, and therefore had recourse to human sacrifice, the king offering up the noblest victim in the land as a burnt-offering to Chemosh. The god, as the Israelite writer seems to imply, and as Mesha himself would certainly have explained, had been angry with his people, and so had delivered them into the hand of their enemies. But the sacrifice appeased him, or rather it diverted his wrath, and turned it against the invaders, so that they were compelled to return to their own land, leaving Ḳir-hareseth, the temporary capital, unsubdued, and the king of Moab still independent.

This ineffectual attempt to reduce Moab must be placed rather early in the reign of Jehoram if not actually in that of Ahaziah, though the whole chronology of this period is uncertain.[2] It seems that Jehoshaphat died not long after it, and was succeeded by his son Jehoram,[3] son-in-law of Ahab. Perhaps encouraged by the change of kings and by the Israelite failure in Moab, Edom now revolted, and, though an attempt was made to subdue the land, it failed. As our text stands, it seems as if

[1] Again we have a narrative whose origin is not easy to determine. It is assumed by some, e.g. Wellhausen, Kuenen, Cornill, and others, that it belongs to a collected account of the wars of Israel, and is connected with 1 Kgs. xx, xxii. On the other hand, Benzinger has given reasons against this view, and supposes it to be taken from the prophetic stories. This also creates difficulties, and the best solution is, perhaps, that of Skinner, who believes that an ancient history of the same type as 1 Kgs. xx, xxii, has been worked over in order to show the influence and miraculous powers of Elisha. As history, the narrative would not lose in consecutiveness or in value if the passage involving Elisha, 2 Kgs. iii. 9b–24, were omitted altogether. We should miss the interesting details of the Israelite victory, but we should still have the main fact, that the whole of the Moabite territory was laid waste.

[2] See Additional Note I, pp. 454 ff.

[3] For the official notice see 2 Kgs. viii. 16 ff.

Jehoram had won a considerable victory,[1] but this must be due to textual corruption of some kind, and it is clear from the sequel that the revolt was wholly successful. In the meantime, the house of Omri had not given up the hope of the reconquest of eastern Palestine. The death of Jehoram, king of Judah, made no difference to the political situation, for his son and successor, Ahaziah,[2] maintained the close connexion with his uncle, Jehoram, king of Israel, and shared with him in the enterprise of reducing Ramoth-gilead. From the short-sighted view-point of the Israelite monarchy the occasion was particularly favourable. Damascus was once more threatened by invasion from the east. In one form of his annals[3] Shalmaneser records victories over Benhadad and his twelve confederate kings in 849, 848, and 845 B.C., but the language he uses is summary and he achieved no greater success than in his victory at Ḳarḳar. In 841 B.C., however, he records an invasion which was for the time decisive. Hazael of Damascus met him on the slopes of Mount Hermon, and Shalmaneser claims to have slain 16,000 of his troops, and to have captured 1,121 chariots and 470 horses.[4] Damascus was besieged, and though the city itself was not captured, the whole country was laid waste as far as the Hauran. The record adds that tribute was received from 'Tyre, Sidon, and Jehu, son of Omri'. Shalmaneser can hardly be expected to have concerned himself with the dynastic struggles of these petty states, and, important as it was from the Israelite point of view, the supersession of the house of Omri by Jehu was unknown to him.

---

[1] 2 Kgs. viii. 20-2. Verse 21 is clearly in some confusion, for the last clause וַיָּנָס הָעָם לְאֹהָלָיו must refer to Israel. It is generally supposed (cf. Benzinger, *Die Bücher der Könige*, p. 147; Skinner, *1 and 2 Kings*, p. 318) that a clause or sentence has dropped out, explaining that the Edomites had surrounded the Judahite army, in which case the account of the battle will refer to a successful attempt on the part of Jehoram and his chariotry to cut their way through. On the other hand (though this involves rather serious alteration of the text), we might read וַיָּקָם לַיְלָה וַיַּכֶּה אֶת־אֱדוֹם וַיָּסָב אֵלָיו וְאֶל־שָׂרֵי instead of וַיְהִי הוּא קָם לַיְלָה וַיַּכֶּה אֶת־אֱדוֹם הַסֹּבֵיב אֵלָיו וְאֵת שָׂרֵי, thus avoiding the awkward suggestion that the Israelites, whose camp is already surrounded, fled to their tents. In any case, it is clear that the victory lay with Edom.

[2] Cp. 2 Kgs. viii. 25 ff.

[3] 'On two huge bull-colossi, from the centre of the mound at Nimrud . . . (text published in Layard, *Inscriptions*, plates 12 f. and 46 f.). See also Delitzsch, *BA.* vi, 144 f. . . .' (Luckenbill, *ARA.*, p. 236). The colossi are at Calah.

[4] Luckenbill, *ARA.*, p. 241, § 663, and a fuller account in another inscription, p. 243, § 672.

Already, in or about 842 B.C., the prospects of Assyrian invasion must have been manifest to Damascus. Hazael reached the throne by the assassination of his predecessor,[1] apparently at the instigation of Elisha. Unless we are to reject the whole of this story as pure Midrash—and it is difficult to account for its origin unless there were some historical fact behind it—there is a connexion between the revolution which took place in both Damascus and Israel about the same time. We need not suppose that there was a kind of international society of prophets, representing always the democratic element among the peoples, and that they united in a general conspiracy against the reigning houses of the three countries, Damascus, Israel and Judah, but it is quite possible that the Israelite prophetic party were interested in the internal politics of Damascus, and saw an opportunity of gaining certain ends of theirs through the death of Benhadad. Be that as it may, the revolution took place, and the result was a weakening of the military power of Damascus. Still more serious was the breaking up of the old general alliance. We hear no more of the twelve kings, and at the battle of Mount Hermon Hazael had to fight alone. This may have been due, in part, to the failure of these western kings to realize the profound importance of standing together against eastern aggression, and to the internecine warfare of which the siege of Ramoth-gilead forms a striking instance; but we may attribute it, in at least equal degree, to the revolution which took place in Israel while that siege was actually in progress.

The story told in 2 Kgs. ix and x is explicit, and, probably, fairly accurate. Ahaziah and Jehoram were fighting together at Ramoth-gilead, and the latter, wounded in a sortie (apparently), retired to Jezreel while his wounds healed. We may assume that for the time Ahaziah was regarded as the commander of the besieging army, but he paid a complimentary visit to Jehoram, to enquire after his progress. The revolutionary party took advantage of his absence to carry through their project. It seems that the breach between them and the house of Omri was too serious to be overcome. The appearance of Jezebel on the stage of Israelite politics had brought to a head the division within the nation itself. On one side stood the party of the court, including the commercial community. They held broad views, and were anxious to see their country taking her place among

---

[1] 2 Kgs. viii. 15.

the nations of the world. They accepted, and indeed sought, alliance with the great commercial powers, and were prepared to fall in with the ways of the peoples round about them. Religion especially was affected. These men were, doubtless, loyal to Yahweh in their own fashion, but that loyalty did not imply to them the exclusive worship of the national God. Everywhere else a multitude of deities was permitted, and they could not see why Israel should be an exception to the general rule. The usage of the world made it impossible for them to enter into close business relations with others, unless they were prepared to give some place to the gods worshipped by their customers; the presence of the foreign god was the sign and seal of friendly relations between the two nations. Jezebel, it is true, went further than this, and made a determined effort to secure the supremacy of her own deity in the land of Israel. She came, perhaps, with a contempt for this comparatively uncultured folk, and to her the dominance of Melkart may well have seemed to imply the dominance of the higher culture of her own home. In a certain sense her position appears to have been not dissimilar to that taken up by Antiochus Epiphanes centuries later,[1] though she was not so obviously trying to impose the faith of a conqueror on a subject people. Certainly her activities stimulated the same kind of reaction as did those of the Seleucid king.

In the second place we may mention the agricultural elements in Israel. With the conservatism natural to their class and type, they feared and resented innovations of any kind. It is true that they had, some centuries earlier, nominally accepted the God of the Aramaean nomads, though even this at times appears doubtful,[2] but they had continued to maintain, for the most part, the old ritual. Nevertheless, they had been deeply affected by the social principles of the Aramaean element in their tradition, and they would not willingly accept the supersession of Yahweh and all that for which Yahweh stood.

Finally, we have a third type, that of the section in Israel which still clung to the old wilderness standards in religion, economics, and social theory. It is clear that this element lent strength to the religious conservatism and to the democratic feeling of the peasants, but it went also much further. To the shepherd community of the east and south no god but Yahweh

---

[1] Cp. vol. ii, chap. xvi.   [2] Cp. such passages as Hos. ii. 2–13 (Heb. 4–15).

could be permitted upon the sacred ground of Israel. Everything foreign was evil and dangerous. Yahweh alone must be worshipped within the borders of His land, and the true Israelite must have no dealings whatever with other deities. While this feeling was proper to Transjordania and southern Judah, it had champions in the fertile lands as well. Foremost stood the popular prophets, who maintained the old conception of Yahweh, and would brook no divergence from His standards. But with them were also the Rechabites, and the participation of Jonadab[1] in the revolution is significant of the forces working in favour of the older and simpler faith. It is true that the Rechabites would have abolished all signs of the higher culture, and would have returned to the external manner of life familiar to the nomad, but this extreme attitude was bound up with their enthusiasm for Yahweh, and they could look on Jezebel and her foreign religion only with horror and detestation.

Jehoram did take measures which should have appealed to them, for he removed certain emblems of the cult of Melkart, and made it clear that he did not propose to follow in detail the religious policy of his father.[2] When we remember that neither Elijah nor any of his immediate successors is represented as protesting against the current worship of Israel, it seems to us as if Jehoram's policy should have done something to conciliate the prophets. At the same time, it is clear from the account given of the revolution, that the Melkart cult was not wholly extinguished, and that relics of it continued to exist; Jezebel, who still remained in Jezreel, about the court of Jehoram, probably was allowed to retain her own chapel and worship. But the truth is that the religious protest was only one side of the objection taken by the prophets to the house of Omri. They were in a very real sense at this period the repositories and the representatives of the popular feeling in social and national matters. No doubt their actions show them to have been entirely destitute of insight into the meaning of international politics, but they felt with intense keenness the claim of the average Israelite, and they stood for the rights of man against the power of the Crown. To them, the house of Omri was stained with blood, and, in their primitive way, they felt that the blood of Naboth—and possibly of others as well—cried out from the ground for vengeance. In other words, Israel, the genuine

---

[1] Cp. 2 Kgs. x. 15 f., Jer. xxxv. [2] 2 Kgs. iii. 2.

people of ultimate Aramaean descent, had, as it were, a blood feud against the reigning house, which could be quenched only by the complete elimination of the guilty family. Judging from the way in which the story is told, that was by far the more prominent element in the complex feeling which led to the revolution, and in a certain sense the revolt was an illustration of the law of blood-revenge.

As we have already seen, an opportunity was given to the revolutionary party by the absence of both kings from the army. The story is graphically told, but it clearly implies more than it says. A prophet (unnamed, but instigated by Elisha) enters an assembly of the leading officers, calls Jehu out, anoints him, and flees. To all appearance this is already arranged, for when Jehu returns to his comrades, they ask if all is well, and he replies that they know who the man is and what his objects and standpoint are. He explains in further detail, but obviously all are prepared for the final announcement, and at once hail Jehu as their sovereign. The army is there, and is on the side of the revolution, but there may be isolated individuals who hold to the cause of Jehoram, and a strict guard is placed on the camp, that no news of what has happened may precede Jehu to Jezreel. The new king himself is famed for his swift driving, and hastens to Jezreel. Jehoram and Ahaziah, warned of his approach by the watchman on the city wall, go out to meet him, and both are shot down by Jehu. He enters Jezreel; Jezebel's deliberate defiance ends in her own death, and the scene changes to Samaria. There the surviving members of the families of Ahab and of Ahaziah are put to death, and finally the 'worshippers of Baal'—probably priests and the Phoenician establishments—are destroyed in a wild orgy of blood.

It seems impossible to defend or excuse Jehu's methods by any known moral standard, ancient or modern. The law of blood-revenge may have required the destruction of the family of Ahab, and this feeling would be reinforced by the view that all the relatives of a deceased king were better out of the way. This was normal in ancient times, elsewhere than in Israel, but it is characteristic of the Hebrew kingdoms that a new sovereign seldom resorted to such extreme measures for establishing his throne. But nothing can justify the murder of Ahaziah and his brothers, still less the wholesale slaughter of the followers of Baal. So strongly was this felt in later days, even in prophetic circles, that Hosea[1] went so far as to threaten destruction to the kingdom of Israel on the ground of the bloody day of Jezreel. Nevertheless, for the time being the work was done, and there was no longer any likelihood of the establishment of a cult, rival to that of Yahweh, in Israel. It is possible also that the more democratic feeling of Israel was conciliated, and that Jehu and his successor were compelled to accept the kind of limitation that Hebrew tradition ever sought to impose on its monarchs.

Politically, however, the revolution was a disaster. It is true that the collapse of the alliance of western states was probably complete before the rising of Jehu, but he seems to have made it clear at once that he did not propose to offer any resistance to Shalmaneser. His name appears among those of the tributaries who voluntarily proffered their submission on the crushing of Damascus. He may have felt his own position to be less secure than he would have liked, and thus have tried to assure himself of Assyrian support in case he met with opposition in his own country. It is clear that this payment of tribute must have taken place at the beginning of his reign, and even if fear of Assyria were one of his leading motives his action must have had the effect of strengthening his throne—for the time. In the long run, however, it served once more to emphasize the divisions between the little kingdoms and so to prepare the way for their final ruin. Politically, this was the result of the policy of the prophetic party and of their interference in the government of the country.

The damage inflicted by Shalmaneser on Damascus seems soon to have been repaired. Shalmaneser was in southern Syria again in 837 B.C., when the territory of Hazael again suffered, and the Phoenician cities paid tribute.[2] But his main object in the west was control of the route through Tarsus. After his death his son, Shamshi-adad V, was compelled to fight for his kingdom against rival claimants to the throne. Damascus rapidly recovered, and was soon in a position, not merely to prevent Israel from recovering the lost cities of northern Gilead, but to occupy the whole of Transjordania as far south as the frontier of Moab.[3] For in addition to the fact that Jehu, in spite of his military training, seems to have been no leader in war, he was now, it seems, bereft of allies. Even Judah, as we shall presently see, could no

---

[1] It should be said that though this is the usual interpretation of Hos. i. 4, it has not passed unquestioned in recent years.   [2] See p. 354.   [3] 2 Kgs. x. 32 f.

longer be relied upon to give him help, and his violent eradication of the Tyrian cult must have cut him loose from all hope of a real alliance with the Phoenician cities. His reign probably marks the lowest point reached by the northern kingdom, until the years that immediately preceded its fall.

Though Ahaziah lost his life at the same time as Jehoram, the prophetic revolution in Judah was delayed for half a dozen years. We do not gather that the situation in the southern kingdom was ever as acute as it became in the north. We hear little, if anything, of prophets in and about Jerusalem, and the particular evils of which Elijah had to complain seem to be less prominent under the house of David in the ninth century. While Jehoram and Ahaziah are said to have admitted the Tyrian cult, their action does not seem to have aroused the same protest among their contemporaries,[1] and probably did not play so large a part in the national life. Judah was less exposed to hostile invasion and to the raiding bands of her neighbours than was Israel, and the greater part of her population, being still largely a shepherd people, was accustomed to harder conditions, lived more simply, and was less liable to the oppression of its rulers than were their brethren in the north. It is not till we come to the end of the eighth century that we hear complaints of social injustice in Judah, though then the cry is bitter enough, and suggests that the treatment which the country folk are receiving is nothing new. And the affection of the people for the house of David seems to have been extremely strong; they would not lightly have overthrown their dynasty to set a stranger on the throne. At the same time, no one city dominated northern Israel as Jerusalem dominated Judah. It was by far the most important place in the land, both as a fortress, a commercial centre, and a religious capital. A sovereign who could control this city by means of the royal bodyguard could be fairly sure of the allegiance of the rest of the country.

This supremacy of Jerusalem was clearly illustrated in the events which followed the murder of Ahaziah by Jehu. As soon as the news reached Jerusalem, his mother, Athaliah, daughter of Ahab,[2] realized that she might be in danger of sharing her

---

[1] 2 Kgs. viii. 18, 27.
[2] She does not seem to have been the daughter of Jezebel; her mother is nowhere mentioned, and it is unlikely that Jezebel's children would have borne names in which Yahweh was an element.

son's fate.[1] In order to secure herself, she massacred all members of the royal family on whom she could lay her hands, and the story tells us that only one escaped, a baby barely a year old, who was rescued by his aunt Jehosheba, wife of Jehoiada the priest, and hidden in the Temple. Athaliah's conduct could not fail to arouse antagonism among the people at large, but it was perforce silent and helpless until time brought an opportunity for its expression. We may take it for granted that in practically every direction Athaliah's policy was that of her own kinsmen, though we have to admit a complete absence of details. Instead of a revolution in Judah corresponding to that of Samaria, the old position was still more strongly maintained than before.

The reaction in Judah, however, was only temporary. There was, it seems, no great prophetic party or prophetic order like that of the northern kingdom, nor do the Rechabites seem to have established themselves yet in the south.[2] The place of the prophetic party is taken by the priesthood, and it is Jehoiada who is the hero of the Judaean revolution. It may be supposed that he was of a conservative type of mind, and resented the intrusion of foreign elements of worship into the Temple and, perhaps, still more, of the maintenance in Jerusalem of a rival Baal Temple.[3] We do not know how far he was able to resist innovations, for the Temple was essentially the royal sanctuary. The priests held office at the will of the king, and felt themselves compelled to carry out his policy and instructions. The same body of foreign mercenary guards was on duty both in the palace and in the Temple. Yet, while all may have felt that there was no alternative, for a time, to carrying out Athaliah's wishes, it is clear that there was a strong feeling against her, which only awaited a suitable opportunity to break into open revolt.

It seemed to the malcontents that the right time had arrived when the rescued child, Jehoash,[4] or, to use the common abbre-

---

[1] See 2 Kgs. xi. 1–3.

[2] The Rechabites, first mentioned in connexion with Jehu's *coup d'état*, seem to have been a revolutionary group which aimed at the restoration of the conditions of the nomad age even in the agricultural community. Thus they eschewed the use of the vine and all its products, and refused to live in any kind of house except the tent of the nomad. They were enthusiastic Yahwists, as the connexion between their founder, Jonadab, and Jehu shows, and represented that type of thought in Israel which insisted that the pure Yahwism was that of the pastoral age. Cp. also Jer. xxxv.

[3] 2 Kgs. xi. 18.   [4] For the official notice of his reign see 2 Kgs. xii. 1 ff.

viation, Joash, had reached the age of seven years.[1] Jehoiada
secured the allegiance of the bodyguard and arranged the details.
It seems that one-third of the guard was on duty in the Temple
every day, except on the Sabbath, when two-thirds were present,
perhaps because the number of worshippers was much larger.
Jehoiada arranged that the decisive act should take place at the
hour when the Sabbath guard was about to be relieved, and
therefore, for the moment, the whole guard would be in the
Temple. They then took their positions covering the whole of
the court between the Temple and the palace, with the king in
their midst, and the ceremony of proclamation was performed.
The crown was placed on the boy's head and the 'testimony' in
his hand,[2] and he was acclaimed king by all present. From a
later, but, on the whole, reliable narrative we have the account
of the death of Athaliah, who, hearing the noise, came down
into the court, only to find that the young king was standing by a
pillar,[3] probably one with a special covenant significance, and
cried out against the treason. She and her followers—a few men
seem to have remained faithful to her—were taken outside the
sacred precincts and executed. The covenant, probably that
customary among kings of Judah, was now solemnly ratified,
Jehoiada answering on behalf of the king. The paraphernalia of
Melkart worship were then destroyed in much the same way as
they had been eliminated in the north six years earlier, though
with far less bloodshed. The only person who lost his life, apart

[1] The story is told for us in 2 Kgs. xi. 4–20. It would seem that there are traces
of two narratives in the record, the main body of the account being taken from the
royal annals of the court of Judah, and a section (verses 13–18a) from some other
source, in which the leading part is played by 'the people of the land', not by the
royal guard under Jehoiada's directions. The main motif in the former is political,
in the latter religious. See Stade, ZAW., 1885, pp. 280 ff.; Benzinger, Die Bücher
der Könige, pp. 155 f.; Skinner, 1 and 2 Kings, p. 337. Benzinger ascribes a higher
historical value to the former narrative, though there are elements in the latter
which must surely be original. The whole is a little difficult to understand, owing
to the fact that we do not know enough of the topography of the Temple. Wellhausen's reconstruction is generally followed above.

[2] This item in the narrative has not been generally understood, and most editors
would alter the text, reading עֵדְיוֹת for עֵדוּת, or making some similar change.
But it is not impossible that the MT. is right. As the later source shows, the ceremonial included the acceptance of a 'covenant'—the combination of the sources is
fairly early, since the Chronicler had the whole in its present form—and the עֵדוּת may
have been some material symbol of the covenant—perhaps a written document
or charter, containing the conditions upon which the covenant was made.

[3] Cp. the mention of a pillar in the narrative of Josiah's covenant of reform,
2 Kgs. xxiii. 3.

from Athaliah and her attendants, seems to have been Mattan, priest of Baal. But the revolution was as effective in the south as it had been in the north, and there was no more danger of the general spread of the foreign cult. As a matter of fact the danger had probably never been very great. The simpler life of the Judaean peasant and his stronger conservatism made him less willing to accept a novelty, while his contact with the outside world was far less complete or continuous. The short reign of Athaliah gave little opportunity for the spread of her religion beyond the immediate neighbourhood of Jerusalem, and it is clear that the restoration of the old régime was so popular as to make violence unnecessary.

With the revolution in Jerusalem we may connect the story of the repair of the Temple, which is assigned to the twenty-third year of the reign of Joash.[1] It would seem that from the days of Solomon onwards the repairs of the Temple had fallen upon the royal exchequer, and the policy of Joash was to change this system, and to make the Temple, as it were, self-supporting. For this purpose the king issued instructions that all moneys paid into the Temple funds, hitherto the perquisite of the priests, should be set aside for maintaining the fabric of the building. This order may have been given early in his reign, or at any rate soon after he was old enough to assume the government for himself. Time passed, and no repairs were executed, so that at length it became clear that some other method must be adopted. The priests had not been a success as administrators of the Temple funds. Accordingly a new method was tried. A box was placed in the Temple, with a hole in its lid, and all dues were deposited in it, except such moneys as were paid as fines for breaches of law recognized by the ecclesiastical authorities. These remained the perquisite of the priests, and formed, in fact, the chief basis of their livelihood. The sums found in the box were placed in the control of lay administrators, whose honesty was so well recognized that no audit was felt to be necessary, and the plan proved a success. This was, in all probability, the method pursued as long as the Temple stood, and the narrative is intended to explain the origin of the custom prevalent in the days of the historian. One of its effects must have been to

---

[1] 2 Kgs. xii. 4–16. The narrative is clearly taken from the Temple archives, perhaps from a continuous history of the Temple, as Wellhausen suggests, and it may be trusted as an accurate account of what actually happened.

stimulate a desire that the Temple should become more and more the great popular sanctuary of Judah, not merely the king's private chapel. It was in the interest of the priesthood, and of all connected with the Temple, even of the king himself, to secure as large a number as possible of worshippers who might contribute to the upkeep of the fabric and to the maintenance of the priestly establishment.

Thus the prophetic revolution was carried through, both in north and south. There was never need to repeat it. Foreign cults were from time to time imposed on the courts of Israel and Judah either by treaty or by conquest, and we hear again and again of the worship of foreign deities. But there was no more danger lest these should take hold on the nation at large. They were confined to the court and to the circles immediately about the kings, and had little or no influence on the general religious attitude of the nation. So it came to pass eventually that the royal sanctuaries, by a curious perversion of the ideals of the reformers, became probably the most corrupt of all the shrines of Israel, and accumulated masses of strange and foreign cults in which the people as a whole did not participate. At the same time, there seems as yet to have been no attempt to go beyond the ideals accepted by Elijah. It is expressly stated of Joash, though he wins the mark of approval from the Deuteronomic editor, at least for his earlier years,[1] that the local sanctuaries were not superseded, and the old syncretistic religion continued to hold its own. There was no thought of apostasy in the minds either of king or of people; in spite of many reprehensible elements in the cult, it was genuinely Yahwistic, and remained the normal faith of Israel down to the last years of the monarchy.

The other side of the prophetic protest, that of social morality, did not by any means meet with the same success. It may be true that the power of the crown was curtailed, and that the rights of the average Israelite as against the sovereign were adequately asserted. But there were other dangers in the situation, which, perhaps, the prophetic party failed to observe. For this they were hardly to be blamed. Israel had been for the last few centuries entering on a new social order, and its meaning and its perils were not as yet appreciated. The danger no longer lay in the excessive use and abuse of the power of the king, but in the rise of a wealthy class which stood apart from the

[1] 2 Kgs. xii. 2–3.

great mass of the people, and constantly kept them on a lower level.[1] It was this situation which the prophetic movement had to meet in later years, and, unfortunately, the leaders of popular and religious thought in the ninth century failed to anticipate it and provide against it. Perhaps, even if Elijah and his immediate successors had foreseen the future, they might have been helpless to persuade Israel to follow a safe course. No lesson seems harder for mankind to learn than that of an altruistic commercialism, yet there is no other basis on which a mercantile community can build its social order. It is hard enough for kings to recognize the claims of human nature and the rights of man, but all history tends to show that the task is immeasurably harder for a business world.

[1] It is noticeable that, while the prophets occasionally attack the king (e.g. Am. vii. 10 ff., Jer. xxii. 13–19, &c.), such denunciations are comparatively rare, and it is the wealthier citizens who are the special object of their anger.

ADDITIONAL NOTE

Page 348, note 2. For Assyrian campaigns in the west after 841 B.C. cf. *CAH.* iii. 24, 373; Olmstead, *History of Palestine and Syria*, p. 399.

Chapter XVII

THE ISRAELITE REVIVAL

SUMMARY

[The renewed supremacy of Damascus was vigorously maintained until the city was conquered and plundered in 805 B.C. by Adadnirari III. From this she never so far recovered as to be a serious rival to Israel, and with the reign of Jeroboam II the northern kingdom reached a height of prosperity which it had not attained since the death of Solomon. At the same time, Judah revived, and it seems that Edom was once more subdued. These conquests and a revival of trade led to a considerable influx of wealth into the country. A class of rich capitalists grew up, with whom luxury took the place of comfort.

At the same time, it is clear that a fatal change had taken place in the social and economic order, for the old peasant farmer had been almost eliminated. Large estates had accumulated, worked mainly by slave labour, and those who remained nominally free suffered terribly from the exactions of their landlords. The process was probably carried out largely through the laws of debt, and accelerated by gross injustice in the law courts.

Such a condition could lead only to ruin, and the official religion gave no help—rather intensified the evil. But protests were made by such groups as the Rechabites, and still more by the canonical prophets, whose first representative, Amos, appeared about 760 B.C. He laid special stress on Yahweh's demand for justice, and insisted that unless Israel understood and met this requirement she must perish.]

THE generation which followed the prophetic revolution saw Israel reduced to lower depths than any other that she touched throughout the history of the monarchy. The new policy involved an isolation from her neighbours which was practically complete, and it is clear that Jehu placed all his reliance on support to be obtained from Assyria. That was not forthcoming. As we have seen, the invasion which temporarily wrecked Damascus in 841 B.C. passed, and left no appreciable effect on the position and strength of Syria, except in so far as it meant the separation of the other states one from another. Israel must have lost control even over Judah, for it is difficult to believe that, if Jehu had been strong enough to enforce his will, he should have left Athaliah for six years upon the throne. In Damascus, on the other hand, Hazael and his son Benhadad were steadily gaining in strength. Transjordania fell completely into the power of Syria before the death of Jehu,[1] and the invasion of Israel was pushed still further in the reign of his son Jehoahaz.[2] Of this phase of the struggle we have no details, and it is worth noting that the later compiler dates the beginning of Israel's recovery in this last reign.[3] This, however, is generally held to be an anachronism; there is no reason to believe that there was any alleviation of the position until the time of Jehoash.[4] Jehoahaz was completely subdued, and was subjected to conditions which recall to us those of the Philistine occupation. The Israelite king's fighting force was reduced to fifty horsemen, ten chariots, and ten thousand infantry.[5] Further, it is clear that the Syrian forces dominated the country, and that they had free passage through the dominions of Jehoahaz. In 2 Kgs. xii. 18 f. we have a notice of a Syrian attack on Gath, which Hazael captured. Now of all the Philistine cities, Gath, though it does not seem to have been satisfactorily identified, lay obviously closest to Judah, and the Syrian army must have passed right through the centre of the land of Israel to reach it. We could hardly have had a more telling illustration of the weakness of Jehoahaz. From Gath Hazael marched up into the hills and actually threatened Jerusalem, being bought off by the gift of all the gold that was left in the Temple and the royal palace. Joash of Judah seems to have been in little better case than Jehoahaz, and Damascus had attained to a position of complete dominance over the whole of Palestine.

But this supremacy was not destined to last, for it was made possible only by the comparative weakness and non-interference of Assyria. As we have already seen, we have no record of a western expedition by Shalmaneser III after 841 B.C., and though he reigned till 823 B.C., he seems to have left this part of the country alone. His successor, Shamshi-adad V, was too much occupied in securing his throne against nearer enemies to concern himself with the outlying posts of his empire, and it was not till Adad-nirari III came to the throne in 805 B.C. that an Assyrian force once more played a part in Palestinian life. The new king's inscriptions[6] show that the western principalities had

---

[1] 2 Kgs. x. 32 f.   [2] Cp. 2 Kgs. xiii. 1 ff.   [3] 2 Kgs. xiii. 4 f.   [4] Cp. 2 Kgs. xiii. 10 ff.

[5] 2 Kgs. xiii. 7. Verses 4–6 are either due to the compiler or are derived from another source; verse 7 follows naturally on verse 3, and its subject seems to be Yahweh.

[6] Cp. Luckenbill, *ARA.*, p. 261, §§ 734 f., p. 263, § 740. The language is somewhat high-flown, and we may guess that the king's conquests were not so extensive as he claims.

felt themselves free during the reign of Shamshi-adad, for they had 'rebelled and withheld their tribute'. His attack was directed against Mari', king of Damascus, and he gives details of the spoil he took from this city—'2,300 talents of silver, 20 talents of gold, 3,000 talents of copper, 5,000 talents of iron, coloured woollen and linen garments, an ivory bed, an ivory couch, inlaid and bejewelled', an enormous booty, showing something of the pitch of prosperity which Damascus had reached since 841 B.C.[1]

So ended the supremacy of Damascus. It does not seem that other lands were seriously affected by this new Assyrian inroad, and when Hazael was succeeded by Benhadad[2] and Jehoahaz by Joash, the Israelites began once more to assert themselves against Damascus. Details are almost entirely wanting, and more space is given to the scene in which the dying Elisha secures the promise of triumph for Joash with the magic arrows of victory[3] than to the story of the fulfilment of the prediction. But the statement is clear enough, and tells of three victories won by Israelite troops over those of Damascus, and of the recovery of the cities which Hazael had taken from Jehoahaz. This refers in all probability to territory west of Jordan, which must have been occupied by the Syrians during the reigns of Hazael and Jehoahaz. The territory to the east of Jordan[4] had been in Syrian hands at least since the days of Jehu, and can hardly be referred to here. We have no direct statement as to cities in western Palestine occupied by the Syrians in this reign, but we may suppose that the conquests of an earlier Benhadad in northern Israel may have been repeated.[5] The Syrian occupation of Israel, as we have already seen, may be taken as an accepted fact, and the first step towards the recovery of independence was to expel the foreign forces.

The revival in the north was accompanied by a similar recovery in the south. Joash of Judah was assassinated by two members of his own household, and was succeeded by his son Amaziah.[6] A more detailed account of the reign of Joash is given by the Chronicler, who states that the king's character deteriorated after the death of Jehoiada, and that he gave himself to strange cults. For this he was rebuked by Zechariah, Jehoiada's son, whom he caused to be put to death in the Temple

---

[1] 'Bit-Ḥumri' and Edom are also mentioned, though not Judah.
[2] 2 Kgs. xiii. 24.   [3] 2 Kgs. xiii. 14–19.   [4] 2 Kgs. x. 32 f.
[5] Cp. 1 Kgs. xv. 20.   [6] Cp. 2 Kgs. xiv. 1 ff.

court.[1] It is said that the murder of the king was perpetrated in revenge for the death of Zechariah. There is nothing improbable in the story, and the Chronicler may well have had access to a sound tradition which escaped the notice of the compiler of the books of *Kings*.

Amaziah's reign has but two events ascribed to it. The first is a great victory over Edom, which, however, does not seem to have reduced that country to complete submission, though it was a welcome sign of the revival of the power of Judah. Flushed by this success, Amaziah issued a challenge to Joash of Israel, and, in spite of the latter's attempt to persuade him not to fight, he insisted on seeking the test of battle. It may be that Israel was still claiming sovereign rights over Judah, and Amaziah's action was an effort to shake himself free. Whatever his motive, the issue was disastrous, for he was utterly defeated, and taken prisoner. The conqueror brought him back to Jerusalem and broke down a stretch of the wall on the north side of the city, thus laying it open to any assault from the side of the northern kingdom. The city was despoiled of all its treasures, and Joash went back to Samaria, apparently leaving Amaziah on the throne as a vassal. This conquest must have left Israel nearly as strong as she had been in the days which preceded the prophetic revolution.

With the accession of Jeroboam II, son of Joash,[2] Israel entered on her last period of prosperity. Once more the tide of Assyrian invasion had receded, for Adad-nirari III, who died in 782 B.C., was succeeded by weaklings, and for our knowledge of them we are dependent mainly on the chronological lists and the dating of contract tablets. By 750 B.C. Assyria had fallen lower than she had been for over a century, and it was only with a change of dynasty and the accession of Tiglath-pileser III, who came to the throne in 745 B.C., that the country recovered its old prestige and power. Once more the opportunity had come to the western states to expand without danger of interference, and this time it was Israel, not Damascus, which was in a position to take advantage of the situation. Damascus had been too thoroughly crushed in 805 B.C. to revive swiftly, and before she had a chance to re-establish herself, Joash and his son had made good their standing.

We have little direct information as to Jeroboam's achieve-

---

[1] 2 Chron. xxiv. 15–26.   [2] 2 Kgs. xiv. 23–9.

ments in the political world. The record states in summary
fashion[1] that in fulfilment of his divine mission Jeroboam
restored the border of Israel from the entry to Hamath to the
Dead Sea. How much that says, and how little! The limits are,
excepting the territories of Judah, the ideal boundaries of the
kingdom of David and Solomon, and no king of northern Israel
had ever ruled over such wide realms. Yet we have no details,
and no account of any act of conquest. In one small point the
narrative may be supplemented from another source. In Am.
vi. 13 we have a picture drawn by the prophet of Israelites
exulting over Lo-debar[2] and saying, 'Have we not captured
Karnaim for ourselves by our own prowess?' Lo-Debar is
mentioned in 2 Sam. ix. 4, xvii. 27, as one of the cities to the east
of Jordan, and Karnaim is probably an abbreviation for Ashtoreth Karnaim, roughly in the same district. The mention of
these two names throws a strong light on the history, for it shows
that Jeroboam undertook with success a campaign of conquest
to the east of Jordan, and recovered territory that had been
for many years in other hands than Israel's. It may quite well
be that practically the whole of Transjordania came back to its
old proprietors, and that the capture of these two cities simply
represents an incident which happened to be much on men's
lips at the moment when Amos spoke.

Judah, too, revived under Azariah or Uzziah,[3] a younger
contemporary of Jeroboam. His father Amaziah was assassinated, as the result of a court conspiracy, much as Joash had been.
But the conspiracy must have been more extensive, for the king
had notice of it, and was able to escape as far as Lachish, where

---

[1] 2 Kgs. xiv. 23–9 is all that is given to one of the greatest kings of Israel, a most
illuminating instance of the way in which the compiler was dominated by theological preconceptions. In these few verses we have two diametrically opposite
standpoints represented. In verse 24 we have the Deuteronomic compiler's condemnation of Jeroboam for maintaining the schismatic worship of his namesake,
just as we have it applied to every king of Israel. But verses 25–7 give us the view
of an earlier compiler of the records of Israel, who saw in Jeroboam the instrument
of Yahweh's pity and mercy. Israel's God had seen the distress to which the country had been brought during the recent reigns. He did not purpose its complete
destruction, and had therefore raised up for it a deliverer, just as the old Judges
had been raised up. This must have been written before 734 B.C.

[2] It is generally agreed that this is the correct pronunciation of the words לֹא
דְבָר in our Hebrew text.

[3] For the official notice see 2 Kgs. xv. 1–7. The former name is that given to the
king in the book of *Kings*; in 2 Chron. xxvi and in Isa. vi. 1 he is called Uzziah.
No satisfactory explanation of the two names has ever been given.

he was overtaken and put to death. The circumstances show
that there must have been a mutiny in the royal bodyguard
rather than a popular insurrection. A king in Jerusalem might
be suddenly attacked and cut down in spite of his guards, but
he could hardly be pursued to a distance unless they had for-
saken him. We have no inkling as to the reason for the conspiracy, and it may have been some trifling matter of military
discipline. The popular vote without hesitation installed his
son, then only sixteen years of age. A very long reign is ascribed
to him, though the actual figures (fifty-two years) may need
some modification when the whole subject of chronology is
taken into account. But for the last thirteen or fourteen years
of his reign he was incapacitated by leprosy, and his son Jotham
acted as regent.[1] The Chronicler ascribes the king's disease to
his presumption in entering the Temple and undertaking
priestly duties,[2] but this is not generally accepted as a piece of
actual history. It may well be that he did offer sacrifice in the
Temple, but it seems improbable that this was regarded as a
serious crime at this period.

Throughout the history of the divided monarchy there is one
test of the power of a king of Judah which is seldom wanting to
a successful king: he conquers Edom. We find, accordingly, in
2 Kgs. xiv. 22 the statement that Azariah built Elath and
restored it to Judah. And though this is the only conquest
ascribed to him in the book of *Kings*, the Chronicler has a whole
list of his triumphs, as well as an account of the organization and
equipment of his army. It seems quite improbable that such a
tradition should have been entirely invented, and we are led to
accept in broad outline the tradition there preserved.[3] If reliance may be placed upon this section,[4] then Azariah made a
successful expedition into Philistine territory, and seized Gath
and other cities, including Ashdod, breaking down their walls
and rebuilding cities where he saw fit. We may suspect that the
original element in this story is the capture of Gath, which, as
we have seen, lay nearer than any other Philistine city to the
Judaean border, and had already been weakened by Hazael.
It is not impossible that it was still nominally Syrian, and that
Azariah's expedition was undertaken in conjunction with

---

[1] 2 Kgs. xv. 5.   [2] 2 Chron. xxvi. 16–21.
[3] For a justification of this view cp. Kittel, *GVI*. ii.[3], 516 f.
[4] 2 Chron. xxvi. 6–15.

Jeroboam's campaigns against Damascus and Transjordania. Arabs and Ammonites are also included among his conquests, and it is clear that the Chronicler thought of him as having recovered the whole of the territory lying between Palestine and Egypt. A significant omission, however, is Moab, which is not mentioned among his new acquisitions. Extensive additions to the fortifications of Jerusalem are ascribed to Azariah, and we have an interesting account of the organization of his forces, with a special nucleus of 'raiders', and the stands of arms required for them.

But if our references to detailed events are but scanty, we have abundant evidence from the contemporary prophets, especially from Amos and Isaiah, as to the general level of prosperity in the age of Jeroboam and Azariah. The conquests had not only led to an increase of territory; they had brought into the land stores of goods plundered from the captured cities. We have no record of the amount seized in any place, but such an extension as that which we may safely ascribe to these two kings[1] could not fail to supply them with copious booty. To this we may certainly add a revival of trade, due to the recovery of the great caravan routes on both sides of the Jordan valley, and to the comparative security which could be assured to travellers (probably at a price) as they passed through the dominions of the two kings. Samaria seems to have become one of the world's great emporia for the time being, goods from north and south and east being found in her. The palaces of Omri and of Ahab were still further extended, and we gather from references in Amos (though the Samaria excavations have not been carried far enough either to confirm or to refute this view) that the royal house no longer maintained a monopoly of trade. There grew up a class of merchant princes, who seem to have emulated the king in their building and in their style of living, though probably on a smaller scale. We hear of 'summer houses and winter houses'[2] and of 'houses of ivory and houses of ebony'.[3] The former probably refers to houses built of two stories, of which the upper, being more exposed to the air, was used in summer, and the lower, being more easily heated with braziers, was occupied in winter.[4] There were terrible natural disasters—

---

[1] Even without Damascus and Hamath itself, which the Deuteronomic editor of Kings includes among Jeroboam's conquests, 2 Kgs. xiv. 28.   [2] Am. iii. 15.
[3] Ib., reading בָּתֵּי הָבְנִים for בָּתִּים רַבִּים.
[4] Cp. J. W. Jack, *Samaria in Ahab's Time*, p. 20.

earthquake, famine, drought, blight, plague,[1] but these failed to discourage or to deter the wealthier classes from pursuing their ends. The cheap house, constructed of sun-dried brick, might be worn by weather and shattered by earthquake, but in its place they would erect the costly palace of hewn stone.[2] The coarse and common fig-trees, with their poor timber, had been cut down by raiding bands of Aramaeans and Assyrians; in their place luxurious and extravagant Israel would plant cedars.[2] Samaria was full of great houses—palaces, as Amos calls them,[3] and no expense was spared on their construction and their adornment.

Within the homes of the richer people were to be found costly articles of furniture. The days were past when a room prepared for an honoured guest contained a simple pallet, a table, a stool, and a lampstand. These things implied a high degree of comfort and dignity for their own time,[4] but they were much elaborated in the generations that followed Elisha. The couch must be ornamented with ivory, if not made entirely of that material, and the rest of the fittings must correspond. There was free indulgence in the pleasures of the table, and the Samarian magnate would have his own farm, whence he could rely on supplies of veal and lamb.[5] Wine was drunk in quantities, and though some of the descriptions of the wild drinking-bouts seem to refer to sacred festivals,[6] it is clear that large quantities were consumed in private houses, where people drank it in great bowls.[7] No delicacy or dainty that could be produced or imported was lacking in the Samaria of Jeroboam II.

Personal adornment kept pace with other features of the luxurious life in Samaria and in Jerusalem. We hear little or nothing, strangely enough, of men's clothing, but mention is made of the unguents they used.[7] And more than once we have allusions to the women of the day. Amos seems to have believed—and, on the whole, Isaiah was with him—that in the last resort it is the women who set the standards of comfort and of social life generally. They would have wine, whatever it cost,[8] and would dress themselves in gorgeous robes and quantities of jewellery.[9]

---

[1] Am. i. 1, iv. 6-11. [2] Isa. ix. 10 (Heb. 9).
[3] Am. iii. 10. [4] 2 Kgs. iv. 10. [5] Am. vi. 4.
[6] e.g. Am. ii. 8, Isa. xxviii. 7 f. [7] Am. vi. 6. [8] Am. iv. 1.
[9] Isa. iii. 16-26. The list of garments and trinkets in verses 18-23—a regular milliner's catalogue!—is, doubtless, a later insertion, but the rest of the passage gives us a picture sufficiently vivid.

It seemed that the day of unending prosperity had dawned, and men and women lived this life of extravagant luxury without a thought of disaster or a suggestion of danger. If they looked forward to any startling event, it was to a great Day of Yahweh, in which He would finally overthrow all the enemies and rivals of Israel, and establish for ever the régime which they found so pleasant, adding thereto the spoils of all the conquered world. Solomon in all his glory was the model which the age of Jeroboam II set before itself, and it came nearer to realizing that ideal than any other period in Israel's history, before or since.

At the same time an economic and social change had passed over the land, and probably involved neighbouring countries as well as Israel and Judah. The small peasant proprietor disappeared, and his place was taken by the wealthy landlord, while the little farms were absorbed into large estates.[1] The type represented in the ninth century by Naboth vanished, and the result was a complete change in the character of the country. From time to time we have hints as to the method by which this transfer of property was effected, and it seems that it was often, if not always, carried out through the laws of debt. Even in the days of Elisha the money-lender was a familiar element in the Israelite community, and in 2 Kgs. iv. 1–7, whether we regard the whole story as historical or not, we have a vivid picture of the life of the common people. The widow, unable to farm her land without help, has mortgaged her two sons, and as she is unable to discharge the debt, they are about to be sold as slaves.[2] There is no suggestion of hostility to the money-lender. He is simply pursuing his trade, and it is taken as a matter of course that if the debt is not paid and the mortgage liquidated, it will be necessary for him to enslave the children and sell them in order to avoid losing his money.

[1] Cp. Isa. v. 8–10.

[2] Several points in this story are worth close consideration, inasmuch as it clearly represents a scene only too familiar in the life of Israel. We note the helplessness of the woman who has no adult male to protect her. The land is there, but it must be worked if she and her children are to get a living; she has no resources on which to call, and no neighbours who are willing to save her from the dangers of her situation. Her only resource is the money-lender, and he is mentioned with the definite article—הנשה—as a modern story might speak of 'the baker' or 'the milkman', indicating one of the normal factors in daily life. Everywhere there are money-lenders, and comparatively few escape all their lives without dealings with them. The poor woman has no property on which she can raise a mortgage, except her own person and those of her children. They are the first to go, and she will be left helpless.

We can thus catch a glimpse of a community which contained indeed persons like the famous woman of Shunem and her husband, wealthy and successful, owning and working their own land, with an efficient staff of labourers. But there is another side to the picture, which was inevitably accentuated by the new wealth of the period of revival. The small farmer, his resources already exhausted by generations of a cruel border warfare, nevertheless is tempted by the ostentation and the new standards of comfort which he sees on his occasional visits to the big cities. He is liable to spend beyond his means, and, living as he does on the verge of calamity, he is reduced to the most serious straits by the first bad season or unusual call on him. He has none to help him except the money-lender, and no security to offer save his land and himself. Sooner or later the mortgage is called in, he fails to pay, and the ground becomes the property of the capitalist. It may be that the man is not ejected, but if he remains his status is changed, and he is now a tenant, paying a burdensome rent. The new owner takes no money but receives a proportion of the crops, often a large one, and Amos denounces bitterly the landlord who exacts load after load of corn from his poor tenant.[1] The amount left for the worker and his family, to say nothing of what is required for seed, must often have been ruinously small. The result is fresh borrowing, and now the man has to mortgage himself or the members of his family. Again the debt remains unpaid when demanded, and this time the poor peasant loses his freedom and passes into actual slavery.

The process is thus bad enough when the usual forms are observed, and when substantial justice is done. Many agricultural countries, notably Rome, have had to face a similar stage in their history, and to see the change in the social and economic order take place. But all may be done under the forms of law, and if a change is to be made it must be in the law itself. It is true that Israelite slavery was technically limited to a six-year period, but to many that provision can have brought little relief For what was there left to a man when his legal term of service was over? He had no land on which he could make a living, and no home to which he could go. As a slave he was fed and cared for at least well enough to keep him fit for work; liberty might offer him nothing except freedom to starve. Not a few must

---

[1] v. 11, reading מַשְׂאוֹת with LXX.

have preferred the alternative of permanent slavery when the time came at which they must choose between the life of a slave and the death of a free man.[1] Such as preferred their liberty, even though there was but little hope, only added to the growing mass of the destitute which, as so often in history, appears alongside of the class of immoderate wealth.

In a certain sense, then, the system as it stood was responsible for the new social order. But from time to time we receive sinister hints that the system itself was being abused, and that the process was a faster one than even the law could justify. It would seem that against the money-lender there must always have been some sort of appeal to a court of law, whether it be to officially appointed judges, or to the little group of the elders of the place. We may doubt whether any creditor would be permitted by popular opinion to take possession of land or of people, unless he could prove his case before some kind of tribunal. And it seems that the forms of law were made to serve the interests of the capitalist class. The corruption of justice is one of the standing causes of complaints in all eastern countries, and the repeated demands for fair dealing in the law-courts, for the absence of preferential treatment for the wealthy and for the powerful, show how deeply the need for judicial impartiality was felt—and how seldom that need was satisfied. The ideal ruler was one who would judge the cause of the poor and lowly, the fatherless and the widow, disregarding the face of the wealthy and the great. But it seems clear that the precedent set by Jezebel was only too readily followed. A man of substance could always secure a verdict in a court, whether his case were good or bad. Again and again Amos pleads for justice,[2] and laments its absence.[2] For a poor man to carry a case into court is fatal; he will lose all he has, and might as well swallow poison.[3] A trumped-up suit against the poor farmer or tenant is sure of success. There need not have been any actual loan; it is enough for the rich man to swear that there has been, and to give a small present to the judge—a pair of sandals will be enough[4]—and the unhappy peasant passes into slavery, literally bought and sold for a pair of shoes.

This basic change in the social constitution of Israel necessarily brought with it the gravest perils. The old order had many

---

[1] Cp. Exod. xxi. 5 f.
[2] Cp. Am. ii. 6 f., v. 7.
[3] Am. v. 7, vi. 12.
[4] Am. ii. 6, viii. 6.

disadvantages. Not every economist would concur in Isaiah's dictum that the small holding is the most successful agrarian arrangement.[1] The peasant himself has many obvious weak points in his character, and is often a difficult and stubborn person to deal with—as Ahab found. But he has a sturdy vigour and a passion for his own land, which will lead him to fight to the very last for his country and for the existing order. The stable societies of the world have hitherto been, for the most part, built up on these lines. But, beneath the fair surface of the age of Jeroboam, this solid substratum of vigorous and independent humanity had been drawn away, leaving a mass of seething want and corruption. Cheating in the markets, perjury in the law courts, selfish and arrogant luxury on the one hand facing ragged and loathsome squalor on the other—all these things meant that the very heart of the nation was rotten, and at the first shock she must perish.

Israel's situation in the eighth century is by no means unique in the history of civilization. A striking parallel is found, for instance, in the change which took place in Roman society between 250 and 150 B.C.[2] In modern times we get much the same impression from accounts of French society in the eighteenth century, or of Russian in the nineteenth, though, in both these last instances it must be admitted that the repression of the lower orders does not seem to have been as complete as it was in the ancient world. And whenever a society is found in such a state its doom is certain, unless it can remake itself. The catastrophe may be delayed for generations, perhaps for centuries, but in the long run it must fall—'as if a man were to flee from a lion and a bear meet him, and he enter a house and lean his hand on the wall and a serpent bite him'.[3] There is always a 'day of the Lord' in wait, and that people must 'prepare to meet its God', sooner or later.[4] One of two things must happen; there is no third alternative. It may be that some spark of human self-respect and personal vigour still remains unquenched within the oppressed, and smoulders unseen until it burst into a devouring blaze. So it was with France in the eighteenth century and with Russia in the twentieth. Or, on the other hand, the nation may be reduced to a spiritual, if not a legal, slavery. The great mass of the people

---

[1] Isa. v. 8–10. [2] Cp. Mommsen, *History of Rome*, ch. xii.
[3] Am. v. 19. [4] Am. v. 18–20, iv. 12.

may cease to regard themselves as true personal entities, and may be accounted as being but living machines by the classes above them. This means a national emasculation, a total loss of power of resistance, and the land will fall a victim to the first serious enemy who attacks it. So, in the end, ruin fell upon the old classical world, which perished through its slavery, for sheer lack of free men, and so, on a much smaller scale, but, in its way, not less fatally, did Israel meet her doom. It may remain an open question as to whether, if she had continued a free people, and had maintained the social ideal and standards she had inherited from her nomad ancestors, she could have held her own against foreign invasion; even so she might have failed. But the state into which she fell between the middle of the ninth century and the middle of the eighth left no room for uncertainty or for hope; destruction was now inevitable, and had it not come through Assyria it would have met her by some other road.

In all this it may pertinently be asked whether the religion of Israel had no hope and no direction to offer. As far as the official cults are concerned, the answer must be a decided and categorical negative. The religion of Bethel, Gilgal, Beer-sheba, even of Jerusalem and other great shrines, had made no change for the better during the century between Ahab and Jeroboam II. We still have the syncretistic faith, Yahweh worshipped as an old Canaanite Baal. One of the spiritual heroes of Israel, with unique insight, goes so far as to see through the outward forms and to declare that the nominal worship of Yahweh is in reality no more than the revival of an old Baal cult.[1] But by the great mass of the people it was undoubtedly felt to be the genuine worship of Yahweh which was carried on at these sanctuaries. Men were more devout than ever, and more scrupulous in their religious observances. The temple courts were trampled by reverent crowds, and the altars smoked with victims. Tithes were most punctually paid; the sabbath and other solemn occasions observed with meticulous accuracy. In time of need men would make costly pilgrimage to distant shrines, and would seek by every means in their power to propitiate their God and learn His will. The pious Israelite would offer his gift of blood by day, and stretch himself by night at the side of the altar itself, that he might be the more sure of entering into

---

[1] This seems to be the most probable interpretation of Hosea's denunciation of Israel's worship as a Baal cult, Hos. ii. 2–13 (Heb. 4–15).

communion with Yahweh. We may be certain that the great
establishments shared in the outward prosperity of the realm.
But none of this touched the real evil; religion, as understood by
the official leaders, had no concern with social morality. In
certain respects Yahweh's name stood for righteousness, e.g. in
the oath, yet perjury became only too familiar a fact in daily life.
But, for the most part, religion not merely condoned immorality,
it often enjoined it, and we have the spectacle, too common in
the history of religions, of God and moral goodness standing on
opposite sides. One or two illustrations rise at once to our minds.
The common law of Israel permitted a creditor to take a poor
man's outer garment only on condition that it should be returned for use at night,[1] but if the creditor could claim that he
needed or was going to use the cloak for some sacred purpose,
such as 'incubation', the ecclesiastical custom was allowed to
override the humanity which underlay the civil law, and the
latter was suspended.[2] Still more startling is another feature of
Israelite ritual which has a counterpart in almost every agricultural religion in the east. Sexual promiscuity was most strongly
condemned by the true Israelite feeling, and there were few
offences on which the old nomad tradition spoke with clearer
voice. Yet the practice of ritual fornication was by no means
unknown, and may have been a regular feature of the cult at
the great sanctuaries.[3] So far from giving help and guidance to
the people in the great moral and social crisis of her history, the
established religion was much more likely to have thrown all its
weight into the other scale, and to have fostered those very
tendencies which threatened the life of the nation.

But the official religion was not the only force at work. It is
true that the organized worship of Israel seems to have been
almost entirely of that syncretistic type which made Yahweh the

---

[1] Exod. xxii. 25 f.　　　　　　　　　　　　　　　　[2] Am. ii. 8.

[3] Cp. e.g. Am. ii. 7. Attempts have been made, on the basis of the word נַעֲרָה,
which has no necessarily religious connotation, to relieve the sanctuaries of the
charge in this instance, and to suppose that Amos was speaking of secular, not of
religious life. But the concluding words of the verse surely make it clear that this
must have been held to be an act of worship. Iniquity committed outside the range
of Yahweh's immediate interests could hardly have been said to 'profane' His 'holy
name'. It is possible also that the tragedy of Hosea's life was due to religion. There
was in Babylonian religion at least one class of temple prostitute, the *Kharimâti*,
whose position carried no social slur, and, after a period of service in the Temples,
such women normally married, and settled down to respectable family life. (See
CAH. i. 538 ff.)

Baal *par excellence*, but other tendencies made themselves manifest. Once more we need to remember the two Israels, the agricultural and the pastoral, and to remind ourselves that in the east and the south, and possibly at isolated spots elsewhere, there were those who clung to the conception of Yahweh as the wilderness God of a shepherd people, and did all that lay in their power to maintain the traditions which had come down to them from the earliest days of their national existence. This fact cannot be too strongly emphasized, for it was vital to the whole of Israel's religion, and proved to be the decisive factor in the complex situation which gave rise to the later Judaism. On the basis of the agricultural syncretism there could be no progress, and all experience has tended to show that such a body of beliefs has ever deteriorated, save where it has given birth to a philosophy which has ultimately overshadowed or even extinguished the religion. The nature of the Hebrew mind was such that no refuge was to be hoped for in that direction, and Israel's spiritual life was saved only by that element which looked back on her bridal days, when she followed Yahweh in the wilderness,[1] as offering the ideal towards which she must once more strive.

There was more than one class of holy person who felt, though perhaps, but dimly, the peril in which the nation stood. We hear of the Rechabites, that strange group which, in the midst of an agricultural community, insisted on living by the standards of the nomad life. There were also Nazirites. In spite of much uncertainty as to the true nature of the early Nazirites, it is clear that they were in a special sense consecrated to the service of Yahweh, and that, like the Rechabites, they utterly eschewed the use of wine. We may suspect that they resembled the Rechabites in other ways also, differing from them mainly in the fact that they were normally isolated individuals, and never formed an organized community.[2] But, best of all, there were the canonical prophets, perhaps the most extraordinary, original, and important group of men whose labours history records. No other class has ever exercised so profound an influence on human thinking about God as did Amos and his successors.

---

[1] Jer. ii. 2.
[2] Cp. Am. ii. 12. The originality of the sentence has been disputed, but the most likely solution of the critical problems involved is that 11*b* has been misplaced, and should follow rather than precede 12*a*.

To their own generation these men were indistinguishable from the popular *N^ebi'im*, save, perhaps, that each of them stood alone, and that they were not connected with the companies into which the professional ecstatics tended to group themselves. They were thus the true successors of Micaiah and of Elijah, and it is not an accident that the first of them, Amos,[1] came also from a non-agricultural community. In his shepherd life he, like Elijah, had learned to know Yahweh as the God of the wilderness days,[2] and he came into the complicated life of the great cities with a profound sense of the contrast between his ideal and Israel's actuality. His critical faculties were unimpaired by familiarity, and undimmed by a knowledge of involuntary complicity in the society whose evils he so obviously beheld, and to this detachment we may attribute that amazing clarity of vision which enabled him to understand, estimate, and condemn the life of Samaria and of Bethel as no citizen of the north could have done. While his detachment robbed him of that power of sympathy which is essential to the most effective rebuke of sin, it gave to him a unique perspective. Tradition and experience taught him to see the facts with full sympathy for the poor and the lowly, the depressed classes, and the moral standards and democratic principles which men of his standing associated with Yahweh were outraged at every turn by what he saw in agricultural Israel.

Amos thus stood in a certain sympathy with the Rechabite and the Nazirite. But his true greatness and significance are to be observed only when we contrast him with them. Like him, they seem to have been conscious of the rottenness of the state of Israel, and their solution was economic, social, political. They said in effect, 'Civilization is a fearful and a wicked thing; let us get rid of civilization and go back to the simple ways of our distant forefathers'. Amos had no political scheme to offer. He did not condemn the agricultural and commercial order *per se,* nor did he call for a revolution, as his ninth-century predecessors had done. It was not the system that was wrong; at worst the system was no more than a symptom of a graver disease, more deeply seated in the body politic. He bade men recover the

---

[1] Amos's prophetic utterances certainly fall within the reign of Jeroboam II (vii. 11) and are probably to be dated about 760 B.C. In viii. 9 he seems to allude to a solar eclipse, suggesting that he had experienced that of June 24, 763 B.C.

[2] Cp. e.g. v. 25.

ancient principles which had been associated with Yahweh in the early days, in times before elaborate ritual and costly sacrifice were allowed to become a substitute for nobler and purer theories of living. He besought them to seek Yahweh, not the sanctuaries, if they would save their country. Let them realize that the God of Israel demanded, first and foremost, fair and right dealing between a man and his fellow, let conduct in the new order be based on the principles which had found expression in the older law, above all let men realize that what seemed morally evil to them could not seem right to Yahweh, and there might be a chance of safety.

It was in this insistence on the ethical character of Yahweh that Amos made his supreme contribution to the religion of his people, and, ultimately, to that of the whole world. It was a new idea for men, and one that proved most fruitful. Yahweh was not the whimsical, capricious, non-moral being that men thought all gods to be. It is one of the tragedies of religion that men's faith so often presents them with an object of worship who is ethically their inferior, and they ascribe to their deities a character and a conduct which they would most strongly condemn in themselves and in their fellows. That Israel, too, shared this belief is beyond dispute, and this fact makes all the greater the miracle of the prophetic doctrine. In so far as there is any explanation it must lie in that double line of thought and tradition to which attention has so often been called. The nomad religion did carry with it an ethical content which was adequate to the needs of a simple shepherd people. Amos and men like him, recognizing their oneness with agricultural and commercial Israel, and the common faith which all professed, saw that the moral principles expressed in the precepts of the past must be applied to the new conditions of a changed social order. Israel's permanence would depend on her knowledge of Yahweh's moral demands and on her conformity to them. She must seek Yahweh if she would live.[1]

[1] Am. v. 6.

Chapter XVIII

THE FALL OF SAMARIA

SUMMARY

[With the death of Jeroboam II began the collapse of Israel. Its first sign is the succession of usurpers, each of whom assassinated his predecessor. Menahem paid tribute to Tiglath-pileser III in 738 B.C., but Pekah, the murderer of his son, tried, with Rezon of Damascus, to revive the old alliance of 853 B.C. They tried to force Ahaz of Judah into the coalition, but he refused, and, when attacked, appealed to Tiglath-pileser for help in spite of Isaiah's advice and warning. In 732 B.C. Tiglath-pileser brought the kingdom of Damascus to an end and replaced Pekah by Hoshea. Some form of foreign cultus seems to have been imposed on Ahaz, but he suffered no loss. On the death of Tiglath-pileser, Hoshea, incited by the intrigues of Egypt, rebelled against Shalmaneser V. He was put out of the way and the Assyrians besieged Samaria, which fell in 721 B.C., after the death of Shalmaneser. The greater part of the territory of northern Israel had been organized into Assyrian provinces in 732 B.C., and Sargon now applied the same method to Samaria itself. Many of the inhabitants were deported, and their places taken by immigrants from Mesopotamia. It is to this event that the Hebrew historian traces the mixed and heretical Samaritan people.]

THE reign of Jeroboam II was apparently prosperous, but, nevertheless, the country was rotten to the core, and the first impress of an external force pierced the thin skin of prosperity and revealed its true condition. The generation which immediately followed the appearance of Amos at Bethel saw the total collapse of the northern kingdom, and, forty years after the utterances of the pioneer prophet, the kingdom of the north for ever ceased to exist. All forms of evil seem to have been let loose. King followed king with bewildering rapidity, and one only after Jeroboam was succeeded by his own son. Again and again a king reached the throne only by the murder of his predecessor, and held it just so long as he could avoid being murdered by his successor.[1] The political fabric of the kingdom had fallen apart, and, with her man-power exhausted, her lands harried by war, her national vigour sapped by economic oppression, Israel inevitably fell an easy prey to the Assyrian invader.

A certain melancholy interest attaches to the spectacle of this

---

[1] Cp. Hos. vii. 7*b*, viii. 4*a*.

swift collapse, and we have a fair number of details. Jeroboam's son, Zechariah, had no more than six months on the throne,[1] before he was assassinated by a certain Shallum, whose home is probably to be placed at Jibleam, in the plain of Esdraelon.[2] But another faction was already in the field, with its centre at Tirzah, advocating the claims of one Menahem, son of Gadi. Shallum was soon disposed of, being killed in Samaria a month after the murder of Zechariah, but it seems that a garrison belonging to the same party held out at Tiphsah.[3] Menahem besieged and captured this city, treating its inhabitants with a cruelty characteristic of oriental warfare.

Menahem is assigned a reign of ten years,[4] and it is remarkable, not so much for what the king himself did in Palestine, but because the Assyrians appeared once more in the west. The stage of weakness through which the empire of Nineveh had passed came to an end in 745 B.C., when the throne was seized by a usurper, Tiglath-pileser III.[5] His first ten years were spent in reducing the east to submission and order, and he then turned his attention to the west. In 738 B.C.[6] he made an expedition to the shores of the Mediterranean, receiving homage and tribute from a number of the local princes, among whom was Menahem. The list also includes Rezon of Damascus and the kings of Tyre and Byblos,[7] and it seems that in all these cases the tribute was given without resistance. It has been suggested that Menahem was paying for Assyrian support in the civil war which gave

[1] 2 Kgs. xv. 8–11.

[2] So read with LXX ᴸᵘᶜ in verse 10 MT. עַם קָבָל, a very curious and un-Hebrew phrase.

[3] The best-known place of this name is Thapsacus on the Euphrates, which can hardly be the spot. It has therefore been proposed to read Tappuach, which was the name of a city some miles to the south of Shechem. But there seems to have been a Tiphsah to the west of Tappuach, which may be the place intended.

[4] 2 Kgs. xv. 17.

[5] He is sometimes known in the Old Testament (cp. 2 Kgs. xv. 19, but cp. also verse 29) by the name of Pul, the title accorded to him in Babylon. It was not an uncommon thing for an Assyrian king to bear a separate name in Babylon, and he may have used this also in the west. Another explanation offered is that Pul was his personal name, and that, on attaining the throne he adopted the name of a great Assyrian king of the past. If so, he was worthy of the title, for he was one of the greatest kings who ever sat on the throne of Nineveh. We may also remember the possibility that the final redaction of *Kings* was made in Babylon, and the editor might be more familiar with the name used there.

[6] This is the first date in the history of Israel that we can place with accuracy since the tribute paid by Jehu to Shalmaneser III in 841.

[7] Cp. Luckenbill, *ARA.* i. 276, § 772

him the crown, but that would give him a very short period on the throne, and it seems more likely that his reign was nearing its close.[1]

One interesting feature of this tribute lies in the means by which it was raised. A sum of a thousand talents was demanded, and was secured by the imposition of a poll-tax amounting to fifty shekels on every well-to-do Israelite.[2] This indicates a fairly large number of persons in a position to pay, for at least forty thousand must have contributed to make up the required total. It is also clear that, at least among the wealthy classes, the use of silver as a medium of exchange was becoming well established, no doubt as a result of the commercial activities of the last few generations.

One of Tiglath-pileser's inscriptions has a good deal to say about a certain Azriyahu, king of Yaudi, who is identified by some scholars with Azariah, king of Judah.[3] But, if that be so, it is curious to find that the record makes no reference to any place or person known to be connected with Palestine. Azriyahu seems to have been the head of a strong coalition of the peoples of his district (wherever that was), and his allies included Hamath and other places to the north of Israel. We have no reason to suspect that Azariah ever exercised control over an empire which stretched so far north, and no place south of the Lebanon is mentioned in this inscription. More probably he was king of some district in the north of Syria.

Menahem was succeeded by his son Pekahiah, who was murdered after a short reign[4] by Pekah, the son of Remaliah, who appears to have been a Gileadite, since his fellow-conspirators come from the east of the Jordan. If so, we may conjecture that he had behind him the support of Damascus, for the outstanding feature of his reign was a close alliance between the two states.[5] It would seem that both Samaria and Damascus had come to the conclusion that the Assyrians might be and ought to be resisted. It may be that they recalled the stand made

---

[1] For further discussion see Additional Note I, pp. 454 ff.

[2] 2 Kgs. xv. 19 f.

[3] Luckenbill, *ARA.* i. 274 ff., § 770. The identity of this Azriyahu with Azariah is strongly maintained by Luckenbill, Hall, and others. But names in -yah(u) are found elsewhere in northern Syria, and the fact that no other place in southern Palestine is named in the Assyrian record seems decisive.

[4] The period given in 2 Kgs. xv. 23 is two years, but all the figures in this part of the narrative are open to some suspicion. See Additional Note I, pp. 454 ff.

[5] Cp. Isa. vii. 1 f.

by a general coalition over a century before their time, and were determined to renew the attempt. They used every effort to secure the co-operation of the king of Judah. Azariah had died some years previously, and the throne was occupied by his young grandson, Ahaz,[1] son of Jotham.[2] We have in the book of *Isaiah* a vivid picture of the consternation produced in Jerusalem by the attempt to force Ahaz into the coalition. He was determined to resist, and the confederates planned to dethrone him and to place a certain Syrian, Ben-Tabeel, on his seat.[3] A siege was foreseen, and it appears that the scantiness of the water supply was a source of grave anxiety.[4] We may conjecture that Jerusalem was actually invested, and that the city was reduced to dire straits. In 2 Kgs. xvi. 3 it is stated that Ahaz 'caused his son to pass through the fire', and the strongest condemnation was passed on this action by the later compiler of the book. Human sacrifice had long since passed out of use as a regular form of offering; indeed it may be doubted whether it is to be found in historic times in Israel at all, a surrogate being accepted even for the consecrated first-born.[5] But a human victim might be offered at a time of peculiar stress, as was done by Mesha,[6] king of Moab, when besieged by the joint armies of Israel, Judah, and Edom. It is unlikely that Ahaz would have resorted to this extreme measure except in the very gravest peril, and we know of no other point in his reign at which he is likely to have been so threatened as he was by the Pekah-Rezon coalition.

Another step which he took in order to protect himself was to appeal for help to Tiglath-pileser,[7] promising submission in spite of a protest made by the best known of the prophets of Israel, Isaiah. The contrast between the two points of view is significant. Ahaz can see nothing but the political situation, and the peril in which he is placed by the armies approaching from the north. Isaiah is confident that the movement cannot be finally successful. He is so sure of Yahweh that he cannot believe Him

---

[1] This is the form his name takes in our Bible, but, to judge from the Assyrian records, it is a contraction for Jehoahaz. Possibly his reputation for unprecedented wickedness led the Jewish scribes to eliminate the divine element from his name.

[2] 2 Kgs. xvi. 1 ff.   [3] Isa. vii. 6.

[4] This is suggested by Isa. vii. 3, where it appears that Ahaz was inspecting one of the aqueducts.

[5] The practice seems, however, to have been reintroduced by Manasseh, cp. below, p. 403.   [6] 2 Kgs. iii. 27.   [7] 2 Kgs. xvi. 7.

capable of abandoning His city and His home to a pair of up-
starts such as these. The enemy has no power of endurance and
must soon fall; the two kings are like bits of stick drawn from the
fire, still smoking, but to all intents and purposes already extinguished.[1] The prophet offers to put the matter to the test,
and since Ahaz will not issue the challenge Isaiah suggests, he
makes a prediction: 'If a woman were to conceive now, and the
child were born in due time, then, before it could tell the difference between good and bad, between pleasant and unpleasant, Jerusalem would be safe, and the two threatening kings
would have perished.'[2] But expostulation and promise were
alike useless; Ahaz would have his way, and sent his message to
the Assyrian court, with such offerings as could be collected
from the depleted treasuries of the royal house and of the
Temple. Such a step was quite unnecessary, for the action of the
two kings was such as no Assyrian sovereign, least of all Tiglath-
pileser, could possibly overlook. In 734 B.C. an Assyrian army
was again in the west,[3] and Tiglath-pileser exacted full vengeance on his enemies. Syria was struck down and depopulated,
and we hear no more of the kingdom of Damascus in the Assyrian annals. Northern Israel likewise suffered. Naphtali is the
only district mentioned in Tiglath-pileser's extant inscriptions,
but the record in 2 Kgs. xv. 29 adds practically the whole of
northern Israel, whence a large part of the population was
removed to Assyria, and other documents attest the formation of
several provinces to the north and east. It seems that Tiglath-
pileser was the first Assyrian king to make this extensive deportation one of his regular methods, but his example was followed
by all his successors. The expedition extended as far as Gaza,
and even the Egyptian frontier was threatened. Tiglath-pileser
says that Pekah was deposed; 2 Kgs. xv. 30 states that he was
murdered, but both agree in making Hoshea his successor.

In the meantime Judah had suffered severely, probably owing
to the attack of Pekah and Rezon. Not only was the land
ravaged and the city of Jerusalem attacked, but Edom found its
opportunity to revolt and recover Elath.[4] Though Ahaz submitted as a vassal to Tiglath-pileser, the latter does not seem to

---

[1] Isa. vii. 4. [2] Isa. vii. 10–16.

[3] Cp. Luckenbill, *ARA.*, pp. 279 f., 292 f., §§ 777, 779, 815 ff.

[4] 2 Kgs. xvi. 6. The MT. seems to make 'Syria' the victor over Judah in this
verse, but probably we should omit the name רְצִין and read אֱדֹם and אֲדֹומִים for
אֲרָם and אֲרֹומִים.

have felt any obligation to recover the lost seaport, and the historian remarks that it remained in Edomite hands down to his own time.

There was one incident of this campaign which had important results for the religious life of Judah. It seems that it was the custom for the Assyrians to introduce some form of cult into every city which they conquered, and to impose it on their subjects as a sign of their supremacy. The normal token of authority was the veneration of a green branch or bush, or the winged disk symbolizing Ashur,[1] but it is possible that in some instances some further cult was imposed. Whether for this or for some other reason, Ahaz made certain innovations in the Temple ritual.[2] While Tiglath-pileser was in Damascus, settling the affairs of that kingdom, Ahaz paid him a visit in order to do homage, and there saw a pattern of an altar which he arranged to have copied for use in Jerusalem. This can hardly have been a Syrian altar; there was no reason why he should have adopted any element from the cult of a ruined state. On the other hand, there may have been strong inducements for him to copy an altar of the Assyrian type, especially if, in addition, he had to introduce some element from the Assyrian cultus. The king still had complete control over the Temple and all its furniture, and was able to dictate to the priesthood there whatever forms he chose for use in worship. The new altar was placed in front of the eastern door of the sanctuary, and the bronze altar, which had previously occupied that position, was moved to the north. It is possible that this old altar, which, as far as we know, was still that which had originally stood before the door of the Ark-tent in David's time,[3] had now become rather small for all that was required of it. Possibly the practice of the burnt-offering had increased with the passing of time, and it may have been felt that a larger article was needed. The old altar, however, was not entirely superseded, but was still used for special purposes, particularly for divination. What form of divination was intended, we are not told, but the obvious suggestion is that it should be used for the inspection of entrails. No other form of divination is known which could not better be carried on without an

---

[1] Cp. Smith in *CAH*. iii. 91.

[2] 2 Kgs. xvi. 10–16. The previous verses may have been taken from the court annals, but this section clearly comes from the history of the Temple which we have had occasion to notice elsewhere. [3] See pp. 252f.

altar than with it; the traditional Israelite method of casting the lot required no altar. Divination by inspection of entrails was developed and studied more completely in Mesopotamia than anywhere else in the ancient world, and the introduction of this method into Jerusalem may well have been one of the innovations which Ahaz owed to the Assyrian supremacy.

Here for the first time Judah entered into direct relations with the great Mesopotamian power which remained the chief factor in politics as long as the Hebrew monarchy endured. For the most part the alliance was not wholly disadvantageous to Judah, for, with the exception of a single period in the reign of Hezekiah, the kings of Jerusalem were faithful to their overlord.[1] We hear little on the Jewish side of the interference of Assyria, and little on the Assyrian side of the revolts of Judah. But in the long run the association was bound to be disastrous, and though the kingdom of Judah actually outlived that of Nineveh, there came a time when the successors of Assyria felt themselves compelled to bring the Hebrew monarchy to an end.

The Mediterranean coast-lands of Asia were still far from realizing the true position of Assyria. To them the important factor was not the people but the king, and an empire governed as that of Assyria was, necessarily depended for its cohesion, almost for its existence, on the personality of its ruler. Most of the kings had to fight for their dominions against revolting cities and states immediately on their accession. Tiglath-pileser was succeeded in 727 B.C. by Shalmaneser V, and at once there began a series of intrigues covering the whole country from the Orontes valley to Egypt. 2 Kgs. xvii. 3 speaks of an expedition made by Shalmaneser in the course of which he reduced Hoshea to obedience, but verse 4 tells of a rebellion, and of treasonable correspondence with 'So, king of Egypt', who is almost certainly to be identified with the Sib'u or Sib'e[2] of Sargon's inscriptions. His position in Egypt, however, is far from being clear; he has been identified with Shabaka, but it is not certain that we ought to accept this view. The chronology is awkward and the philology doubtful, and since Sargon's records lead us to suspect that Sib'u was not at this time king of Egypt;[3] it is possible that

---

[1] It seems that Judah was implicated in the revolt which led to the capture of Ashdod (711 B.C.), but for some reason or other no penalty was inflicted.

[2] This is the name which, philologically, is nearer to So (Sewe?) than any other known to us from Mesopotamian or Egyptian inscriptions.

[3] The evidence of Sargon's own inscriptions appears to be inconsistent. The

he was one of the minor princes of the Delta, acting under the orders of his overlord, the king of Egypt for the time. Hoshea broke into open rebellion in 725 or 724 B.C.,[1] and Shalmaneser marched into Palestine. The Israelite king was captured and imprisoned,[2] but this did not end the resistance. Samaria still held out, though we have no details of the government of the city either from Assyrian or from Hebrew sources— the reign of Shalmaneser is, as far as our discoveries have yet gone, very poorly documented. Samaria was besieged for three years, and Shalmaneser died before the city fell, leaving its capture to be the first achievement of his successor, the great Sargon. Even this did not end the resistance in the west, and Sargon records yet another invasion in the following year. This was due to a general rising organized by Hamath and Sib'u. Sargon moved swiftly, and gave the two groups of rebels no chance to unite. A rapid march southwards brought him into contact with the Egyptian army, whom he defeated at Rapihu (Raphia), some fifteen miles south of Gaza. Sib'u, as Sargon says, fled in panic and was never heard of again—at least by the Assyrians,—while his principal ally, Hanno, king of Gaza, fell into Sargon's hands and was carried captive into Assyria. Sargon then marched northwards, and met the king of Hamath and his allies, including contingents from Damascus and Samaria,[3] at Ḳarḳar. He inflicted a complete defeat on the allies, captured the city of Ḳarḳar, and flayed alive the king of Hamath, who fell

Annals inscribed on the walls of the palace at Khorsabad state 'Sib'u ordered his *turtan* to go to his [Hanno's] aid, and he came forth against me, offering battle and fight. At the command of Ashur my lord, I defeated them and Sib'u ran off alone like a shepherd whose sheep have been carried off, and he died' (Luckenbill, *ARA*. ii. 3, § 5). On the 'Display Inscription', on the other hand, the same events are recorded in these terms: 'Hanno, king of Gaza, with Sib'e, *turtan* of Egypt, who had come out against me at Rapihu to offer battle and fight, I defeated. Sib'e became frightened at the clangor of my weapons and fled, to be seen no more. Hanno, king of Gaza, I seized with my own hand. The tribute of Pir'u (Pharaoh), king of Egypt . . . I received' (Luckenbill, *ARA*. ii. 26 f., § 55). This last quotation suggests that Sib'e was *not* the king, but the officer who bore the title of *turtan*, while in the former inscription he *sent* the *turtan*, with whom, therefore, he cannot be identified. Mr. Jacobsen, of the Oriental Institute of the University of Chicago, informs me, however, that the text of the Annals is uncertain, and partly illegible, so that it may well have run: ' . . . ordered Sib'u, his *turtan*, to go to his . . . ' This will explain the apparent discrepancy in Luckenbill's rendering of the text, and will make it clear that Sib'u was not actually king.

[1] Cp. the Eponym list printed by Luckenbill, *ARA*. ii. 437.   [2] 2 Kgs. xvii. 4.

[3] It may be worth pointing out that this does not necessarily imply that Samaria still existed; these may have been Israelite fugitives who had taken service with the king of Hamath.

into his hands.[1] But there is no further mention of Samaria, and it seems clear that Israel had ceased to trouble the Assyrians.

From this point the story of the northern parts of Palestine ceases to belong to the political history of Israel proper. The land is an integral part of the Assyrian empire, and is no longer strictly Israelite. It is possible that some part of the more southerly hill country was handed over to Ahaz, for we know that the Assyrian monarchs did take this means of rewarding vassals who had remained faithful when those around them were in revolt. And we shall find that, twenty years after the fall of Samaria, Sennacherib claims to have captured forty-six fortified cities from Judah, which is a very large number for Judah alone as it was in the days of the divided monarchy. Perhaps the old territory of Benjamin, including the Bethel and Gibeah districts, was handed over to Ahaz, and incorporated in the kingdom of Judah.

Wherever possible the Assyrians seem to have tried to govern through native princes, whom they held responsible for the loyalty of their realms, i.e. for the payment of tribute. Where this system failed, as it failed in the cases of Damascus and Samaria, the country was divided into administrative districts, and suitable officials were appointed. Their duties were judicial, military and financial, and each district seems to have had at least one officer for the performance of each function. The official title of the district governor was *bêl paḥâti*, abbreviated in later times to *peḥah*, the name still preserved through the Persian period. After the conquest of Damascus and the dethronement of Pekah in 734 B.C., Tiglath-pileser had organized a considerable part of their territories, establishing new districts and appointing district governors.[2] To the east of Jordan lay the provinces of Damascus, Qarnini (comprising the country lying immediately to the east of the Jordan valley, between the Lake of Huleh and the Sea of Galilee, with its capital at Ashtoreth Karnaim, while to the west of this lay the province of

---

[1] Sargon left a number of inscriptions recording his triumphs, and nearly all have some mention of this campaign. Cp. e.g. Luckenbill, *ARA*. ii. 3, 27, §§ 5, 55. The king of Hamath is variously called Ia'u-bidi'i and Ilu-bi'di. This is not the only instance of a north Syrian name which appears to contain the divine name Yahweh. In the absence of other evidence we may conjecture that the friendly relations between David and the king of Hamath (see above, pp. 221 f.) had involved the introduction of a Yahweh-cult into the dominions of the latter.

[2] For the whole subject see Forrer, *Die Provinzeinteilung des Assyrischen Reiches,* especially pp. 56–70, which deal with the south-western provinces in detail.

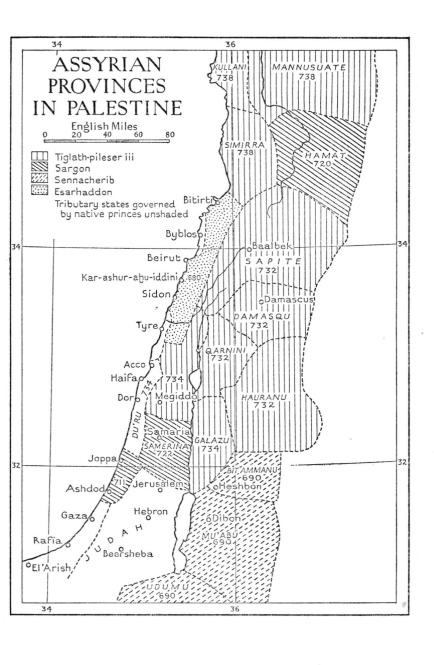

ASSYRIAN
PROVINCES
IN PALESTINE

English Miles
0   20   40   60   80

▦ Tiglath-pileser iii
▨ Sargon
▧ Sennacherib
▨ Esarhaddon
Tributary states governed
   by native princes unshaded

KULLANI
738

MANNUSUATE
738

SIMIRRA
738

HAMÁT
720

Bitirti

Byblos

Baalbek

Beirut

SAPITE
732

Kar-ashur-abu-iddini 680

Sidon

Damascus

DAMASQU
732

Tyre

QARNINI
732

Acco

Haifa 734

Dor DU'RU 734

Megiddo

HAURANU
732

Samaria

GALAZU
734

SAMERINA
722

Joppa

BIT AMMANU
690

Heshbon

Ashdod 711 Jerusalem

Gaza

Hebron

Dibon

MU'ABU
690

Rafia

J U D A H

Beersheba

El'Arish

UDUMU
690

Hauran. To the south lay Gilead (Gal'azu), bordered by two
kingdoms which retained their independence, Ammon and
Moab. To the west of Jordan it seems that the land of Naphtali
was made into a province, and to the south of this was the
district of Megiddo, which embraced southern Galilee and the
plain of Esdraelon. Carmel and the coastal plain, from Akko to
the northern borders of the Philistine territory, were formed into
a province whose capital was at Dor, and this included the city
of Rashpuna, the later Apollonia. It will be seen that the extent
of country over which Hoshea was allowed to rule was thus very
small indeed, containing little more than the hill country of
Ephraim, and northward as far as the plain of Esdraelon. The
insignificance of it may be judged from the fact that Sargon
organized it as a single province after the capture of the city
itself. The only additions made after 721 B.C. were the province
of Ashdod (on the capture of the city by Sargon in 711 B.C.) and
the two kingdoms of Ammon and Moab, which fell into the
hands of Esarhaddon in 690 B.C., but were never held long
enough to be organized as regular provinces of the empire.

The hold that the governors had upon their provinces was
probably adequate at ordinary times. They almost certainly
had some kind of military guard, though it cannot have been
large, and they were in some danger of being isolated. It is
clear that the forces at their disposal were sufficient to hold
their own provinces, for in the great rebellion which broke out
on Sennacherib's accession we hear nothing of any revolt among
the organized Assyrian districts—Sennacherib does not mention
one of them. But it is equally clear that they were not strong
enough to undertake other conquests, for none of the governors
made the slightest attempt, as far as our records tell us, to
reduce the rebellious cities at that critical time, and no progress
could be made until Sennacherib himself appeared with an
Assyrian army.

One most important step was taken by Sargon. Tiglath-
pileser had removed large numbers of the people, and Sargon
himself carried away fifty chariots and 27,290 of the inhabitants,
though he does not tell us where he took them. For information
on this last point we are indebted to the statement in 2 Kgs.
xv. 29 that Tiglath-pileser's prisoners were removed to
Assyria, while in 2 Kgs. xvii. 6 we are told that Sargon's
deportees were settled in various parts of Mesopotamia—

Halah, Habor, and Media. But it was no part of the Assyrian policy to leave the land desolate, and it was a convenient spot on which to settle rebels from other parts of the empire who had shown themselves too truculent to be allowed to stay in their old homes. More than one Assyrian king used Palestine for this purpose. Sargon himself, in 715 B.C., placed there a number of Arabs from different tribes.[1] Ezra iv. 2 speaks of settlements made by Esarhaddon, and Ezra iv. 10 of immigrants similarly introduced by Ashur-bani-pal, while in 2 Kgs. xvii. 24, 30 f., we have a list of the nations represented among the new-comers. They include men from Babylon, Cuth, Sepharvaim, Hamath, and Avva. It is practically impossible to reconstruct any history of the immigrations from these data, if only because the Assyrian kings prided themselves on being protectors of Babylon and Cuth, and claim to have restored exiles to these cities. Their policy was to conciliate the people of Babylonia, while making war on their rebellious rulers, and it seems quite unlikely that they should have transported colonists to Palestine from Mesopotamia. Nevertheless, allowing for some inaccuracy in details, it is clear on all accounts that foreigners were settled in the land, and that further elements were thus added to the racial mixture already in the country.

The story of the religious difficulties of the new colonists has every mark of truth,[2] even if we find it improbable that the settlers were drawn from the cities actually named. War and the removal of the people (though Sargon's figure for the exiles is not very large) must have left the land somewhat thinly populated, and in such circumstances wild animals readily multiply. Naturally the ancient mind attributed this to the anger of the local deity, now defrauded of his due worship, and took steps to secure correct instruction. At the same time the immigrants were unwilling to abandon the cult of their own ancestral gods, and they combined the two. The situation does not differ very greatly from that of Israel in the first generations after their entry into Canaan, save that the new creeds lacked that exclusiveness which in the end reduced all the local spirits of Canaan to forms or agencies of Yahweh. The old cult and the new continued side by side, and helped to accentuate the age-long division between the north and the south. It is no wonder that in the long run the adherents of a purer Yahwism than

---

[1] Luckenbill, ARA. ii. 7, § 17.   [2] 2 Kgs. xvii. 29–41.

ever pre-Exilic Israel had known repudiated the northern peoples as heathen—or worse. It is true that eventually the worship of Yahweh did overshadow and supersede all other cults in the north, and it is a striking fact that to this day it is on the site of Samaria alone that the Passover, most ancient and characteristic of all Israel's ritual forms, is still faithfully observed.[1]

[1] Cp. Gray, *Sacrifice in the Old Testament*, pp. 340 n., 341, 372 ff., together with the authorities cited by Gray; also Jeremias, *Passafest der Samaritaner* (1932).

Chapter *XIX*

ASSYRIA AND JUDAH

SUMMARY

[Sargon captured Ashdod in 711, but Judah remained faithful to Assyria till the accession of Sennacherib in 705 led to a general revolt throughout the empire. This seems to have been organized by Marduk-apal-iddina of Babylon, and the only western vassal who remained faithful to Assyria was Padi king of Ekron. He was deposed and imprisoned in Jerusalem. Hezekiah was severely criticized by Isaiah, who felt that Judah was profaning herself by meddling in world politics, but he refused to take the prophet's advice. As a gesture of independence he inaugurated a reform of the cultus, putting down the local sanctuaries and destroying the bronze snake worshipped in Jerusalem. He also secured the water supply of the city by cutting the Siloam tunnel, and took other measures to strengthen the defences of Jerusalem.

Sennacherib dealt first with the Mesopotamian rebels and then marched westwards, completely overthrowing his opponents. Jerusalem was besieged, though not taken, and all Judah laid waste. Hezekiah was compelled to restore Padi and pay an enormous tribute, while his territories were curtailed. Sennacherib's return to Mesopotamia was probably hastened by a fresh revolt in Babylon and an outbreak of plague which decimated his army.

This was the last revolt of Judah against Assyria, but the reign of Manasseh was a period of religious reaction. The old local sanctuaries were restored and foreign cults were introduced. Human sacrifice was practised and tradition tells of massacres of the prophets.

It was in the latter half of the monarchy that the canonical prophets first appeared, teaching that Yahweh was a God of Law, of Creation, of History, yet especially the God of Israel.]

THE list of Assyrian provinces in Palestine and the neighbourhood, which we have already noticed, contains no mention of Judah. As a matter of fact Judah never was a province of the Assyrian crown, and remained one of the few states which, to the end of the Assyrian dominion, preserved a nominal independence under her own king, though paying tribute regularly and homage when it was required. From 734 B.C., when Ahaz first appealed to Tiglath-pileser, down to 626 B.C. when, as it seems, the last traces of Assyrian power in the west were swept away, Judah continued to be a faithful vassal of

Assyria, except for one outbreak,[1] which, indeed is one of the best-known events in the history of Israel.

The capture of Samaria and the organization of the province were not the end of Sargon's advance in the west. By this time it seems as if the Assyrian government already had designs on Egypt, and the slow occupation of Palestine was a necessary preliminary to a conquest which would make Assyria the sole mistress of the civilized world. Sargon states that he received tribute from Pharaoh, king of Egypt in 714 B.C.,[2] though he makes no claim to have occupied the land. But in the campaign of 720 B.C., following on the capture of Samaria, he overran Philistia, in particular subduing Gaza, the most southerly of the Philistine towns. Apparently at this time he left all the cities under native rulers, who continued to pay their tribute regularly for some years. At length, however, Philistia broke into revolt, and in 711 B.C. Sargon was compelled to undertake the reduction of its chief cities.

An abortive attempt at rebellion had been made by Azuru, king of Ashdod,[3] who was accordingly deposed by Sargon, his brother Ahimitu being placed on the throne. But the people of Ashdod (whom Sargon calls Hittites) refused to accept the Assyrian nominee, and elected a certain Iatna or Iamani[4] in his place. Sargon promptly brought an army into Philistia, and reduced, not only Ashdod, but also Gath and Ashdudimmu. The Ionian escaped before the arrival of the Assyrian forces, and took refuge in upper Egypt, on the borders of Ethiopia. The Philistine cities seem to have suffered very severely, for Sargon states that he rebuilt them. Ashdod was now converted into an Assyrian province, with a regular governor, who ruled over the greater part of Philistia, though Gaza and Ekron still remained under tributary kings of their own. Egypt and Assyria were now practically face to face.

It is worth noting that Judah played little part in these events. Sargon speaks of her as sharing in the 'revolt', but there

---

[1] It is true that Sargon mentions Judah among the states which rebelled in 711 B.C., but neither he nor the Hebrew historians mention any campaign against Jerusalem or any punishment inflicted on Hezekiah.

[2] Luckenbill, *ARA*. ii. 77 f., 26 f., §§ 18, 55.

[3] Date uncertain, but probably not long before 711 B.C.

[4] The former seems to be the form on the 'Annals' inscription (Luckenbill, *ARA*. ii, p. 13, § 30), the latter is that of the 'Display Inscription' (Luckenbill, *op. cit.*, ii, p. 31, § 62); it appears that the word simply means 'Ionian' or 'Cypriote'. Sargon does not know and does not care what the man's own personal name was.

is no account of any expedition against Jerusalem and the whole incident passes without reference in the Old Testament, unless it be in an oracle pronounced over Philistia by Isaiah[1] and in a symbolic action performed by the same prophet, indicating the danger to Egypt.[2] He saw clearly that now, with Ashdod an Assyrian province and with Gaza dependent, there was nothing to prevent the further advance of the Assyrians southwards. But these are the judgements of a keen observer looking at the state of the countries about him, and do not involve his own people further than his implied warning against any reliance on Egypt. Rather do they testify to the fact that Judah was not directly affected by the fresh Assyrian advance.

The terror of Sargon kept Palestine quiet for the remainder of his reign, and we hear of no further expeditions to the west after 711 B.C. But on his death in 705 B.C. it seemed as though the whole of the Assyrian empire might break up into small fragments. There was always the probability of sporadic revolts on the death of an Assyrian king, but never before or since (save after the death of Ashur-bani-pal) was the disturbance so widely spread. This was due to the fact that behind it lay a man of real ability, almost of genius, Marduk-apal-iddina (in our Biblical texts called Merodach-baladan), who was to Assyria much what Hannibal was to Rome. As king of the 'Sealand', i.e. of Chaldaea proper, a district near the northern end of the Persian gulf, Marduk-apal-iddina had paid tribute to Tiglath-pileser[3] in 731 B.C.[4] On the accession of Sargon he made a successful attempt to secure Babylon, where, it seems, he was permitted to remain for twelve years on payment of tribute,[5] as it seems from

[1] Isa. xiv. 28 ff. The occasion is almost certainly the death of an Assyrian king, but the date given, the year of the death of Ahaz, makes Tiglath-pileser much the most likely of the three possible kings. The date of Hezekiah's accession has been much disputed, but neither 721 nor 705 B.C. has been seriously suggested. Of course the reference to the death of Ahaz may be a compiler's guess—but it is the most direct evidence we have, and is not to be discarded without some reason.

[2] Isa. xx. 1.   [3] Luckenbill, *ARA*. i. 285, 794.   [4] Olmstead, *History of Assyria*, p. 250.

[5] Sargon's account is not very clear (Luckenbill, *ARA*. ii. 14, 31), but this seems to be the best interpretation of his statement. The events are dated in his twelfth year—'In my twelfth year Marduk-apal-iddina ... withheld his tribute. ... He prepared for battle and descended upon the land of Sumer and Akkad. For twelve years, against the will (heart) of the gods, he held sway over Babylon, the city of the lord of the gods, and ruled it.' Sargon goes on to say that he was the deliverer of Babylon appointed by Marduk, and describes the way in which he fulfilled the divine commission. Obviously we cannot add the twelve years to the twelfth year of Sargon's reign, for he reigned only from 722 to 705 B.C., and we are forced to conclude that the two periods synchronized.

Sargon's records. In 709 B.C., however, he revolted, and succeeded in forming an extensive alliance against Sargon in southern Mesopotamia, including the Elamites in his confederacy. Both the principals prepared armies, but before they could unite Sargon flung himself between them and prevented the Elamite forces from coming to the help of the Chaldaeans. Marduk-apal-iddina was compelled to withdraw to Sippora, and early in the following year he was so thoroughly defeated that he had to take refuge in the marshes at the head of the Persian gulf.

The death of Sargon in 705 B.C. gave Marduk-apal-iddina a new opportunity. This time he determined to organize a general revolt over the whole of the Assyrian empire. He secured support at once from practically all the tribes, Aramaean, Arab and Akkadian, in and about lower Mesopotamia, and entered once more into an alliance with Elam. But he was not content with a local rising, and did his best to stir up trouble for Sennacherib in the far west. Messengers were sent to Palestine and, probably, to Egypt; whether the Egyptian movements were concerted with those of Mesopotamia or not, Shabaka certainly took his share in the enterprise. All the tributary states of the west seem to have been involved, including Judah,[1] Ammon, Moab, Tyre and others. Three vassal kings remained faithful to Sennacherib, Mitinti of Ashdod, Silli-bêl of Gaza, and Padi, king of Ekron, but the last was deposed by his own subjects and sent to Jerusalem, there to be kept in prison by Hezekiah. Jerusalem was probably selected by the confederates partly because it was close to Ekron and partly because it was one of the strongest fortresses in the country—probably the strongest of all. We have no mention of any of the Assyrian provinces, except Ashdod. Here it seems that the method of government had undergone a change. Sargon distinctly states that he made

---

[1] It is almost inevitable that we should connect with this revolt the visit of Marduk-apal-iddina's embassy to Hezekiah, described in 2 Kgs. xx. 12–19. The Hebrew historian places it, it is true, after the deliverance of Jerusalem in 701 B.C., but he must have been misled as to the order of events. Marduk-apal-iddina disappeared from Mesopotamian history even before Sennacherib's invasion of Judah, and may have been finally defeated before his envoys actually reached Jerusalem. Some scholars, e.g. Skinner (cp. *1 and 2 Kings*, p. 403), connect this embassy with the revolt of Marduk-apal-iddina against Sargon in 710–709 B.C. But is it likely that Hezekiah, who seems to have been implicated in the movement which led to the fall of Ashdod in 711 B.C., though he escaped serious consequences, would so soon have lent his support to a rising against Sargon?

the district into a province of the empire,[1] but Mitinti the Ash-dodite is mentioned among the kings of Amurru who brought tribute to Sennacherib in 701. Apparently the city was allowed to revert to the status of a tributary principality during the last few years of Sargon's reign, or he may not have carried fully into effect his intention of making a province in this part of Palestine. It seems strange to a modern reader that we hear nothing of the provinces from either side. They took no part in the revolt, and their governors do not seem to have done anything to restore the Assyrian dominion in the rebellious principalities.

Hezekiah's policy in joining the revolt did not pass without criticism from within Judah. At least one man, the greatest man of his age, and one of the greatest Israelites of all time, Isaiah the son of Amoz, believed that the king was making a mistake, and, with that boldness which characterized the Israelite prophet, did not hesitate to say so.[2] When the first embassy came from Marduk-apal-iddina, he took up a strong position, and insisted that the king had done wrong in giving a favourable reception to the envoys. As reported to us, his condemnation was based on the ground that Hezekiah, by showing them all his resources, would only arouse the cupidity of Babylon, and bring down in the long run a Babylonian king who would carry off all his treasures as spoil to Babylon. This, of course, was not literally fulfilled, for though Hezekiah's wealth was transported to Mesopotamia, it was not to Babylon but to Assyria that it was taken. And we may well believe that the prophet had also other reasons. But there are other prophecies of Isaiah which may come from this same period. In Isa. xviii we have an oracle which is concerned with a visit from certain Ethiopian envoys, and the impression we receive from the attitude of the prophet is that they wished to form an alliance with Israel, the object of which can have been no other than a combination against Assyria. These are surely the ambassadors of Shabaka, the first king of the twenty-fifth dynasty, which was Ethiopian or Nubian in origin. The answer to be given to these messengers is courteous in tone, but the prophet's utterances to his own people

---

[1] Luckenbill, *ARA.* ii, p. 14, § 30, 'Their cities' (i.e. Ashdod, Gath, and Ash-dudimmu) 'I built anew and settled therein the people of the lands my hands had conquered. My official I set over them as governor. I counted them with the people of Assyria and they drew my yoke.'   [2] 2 Kgs. xx. 12–19, Isa. xxxix.

on the subject of an Egyptian alliance are vigorous and almost violent. In Isa. xix. 1 ff. we have a pronouncement of doom against Egypt which touches on the failings of the country—its weakness and internal division, combined with the short-sighted folly of its chief statesmen. In ch. xxx the alliance itself is bitterly denounced; trust in Egypt shall be the shame and reproach of Judah. With this we may compare the words ascribed to the Rabshakeh in 2 Kgs. xviii. 21—'Thou trustest upon the staff of this bruised reed, even Egypt; whereon if a man lean, it will go into his hand and pierce it'. Isaiah and the Rabshakeh were at one in their estimate of Egypt, and both were right. Again, in Isa. xxxi. 1–3 we have a further denunciation of the pro-Egyptian policy, and again the Rabshakeh is with Isaiah in mocking at the Judahite passion for cavalry and chariotry,[1] and once more we can easily see that both were right; a country like Judah had no use for chariots. The northern kingdom had possessed a terrain in which there were plains where they could practise and manœuvre, but they would be useless among the Judaean hills.

What lay behind Isaiah's attitude? Was he convinced simply that Assyria was destined to become the mistress of the world? When the blow which he foresaw had fallen, and the armies of Sennacherib were actually in the land, he was as vigorous in advocating a firm resistance as he had been in denouncing the anti-Assyrian alliance a few months before. Are we to assume that he had changed his views, and that from being pro-Assyrian he had swung over to the opposite standpoint? Those who would see in him nothing more than a practical statesman, with a wider outlook than his contemporaries and a keener insight into the relative strengths of the different parties to the struggle, may find it difficult to explain this apparent *volte-face* on Isaiah's part. The truth is that though he had these powers of statesmanship, and though doubtless he could estimate the relative forces of the combatants more justly than any other man of his day, his real interests and his true basis of reasoning lay elsewhere. His attitude to life and politics was primarily religious. To him Yahweh was essentially the Holy God, and Yahweh's people also must be holy. To secure this end it was needful that Judah should have as little to do as possible with other nations. Egypt in particular was a people which, to the mind that inherited the

[1] 2 Kgs. xviii. 23.

genuine prophetic tradition, stood, now as always, most clearly in contrast to Yahweh. Yahweh was 'spirit', the Egyptians and their horses were but 'flesh', and the latter could have no power and no real value as compared with the former.[1] Judah, if she wished to remain the holy people of Yahweh, must not allow herself to be contaminated by that close association with Egypt which would be inevitable if they were to fight side by side against Assyria. No doubt the policy was sound from other points of view. Judah, now hardly touching the edge of the Shephelah, was a little hill state of no importance, and might well have escaped notice if she had refrained from interfering in world politics. But, while Isaiah may have felt this, it lay in the background of his mind. Nowhere does he offer the slightest hint that such reasons are actuating his advice; the only motives which find expression in his language are purely religious, and are based on his persistent demand on Israel for complete, whole-hearted, and exclusive consecration to Yahweh.

The same principles lay behind Isaiah's optimism when Sennacherib was actually in Palestine and his messengers were summoning Jerusalem. The prophet felt most keenly the desolation of the countryside: 'the whole head is sick and the whole heart faint; from the sole of the foot even unto the head there is no soundness in it, but wounds and bruises and putrefying sores; they have not been closed, neither been bound up, neither mollified with ointment. Your country is desolate, your cities are burnt with fire; your land, strangers devour it in your presence, and it is desolate, as overthrown by strangers. And the daughter of Zion is left as a cottage in a vineyard, as a lodge in a garden of cucumbers, as a besieged city. Except the Lord of hosts had left unto us a very small remnant, we should have been as Sodom, and we should have been like unto Gomorrah.'[2] This might be the punishment of Judah for her sin, and it caused the prophet the bitterest anguish. But when it came to an actual attack on Jerusalem, he could not believe in its success. Yahweh was a Holy God, and Jerusalem, where He dwelt, was a holy city. He needed a city and a people for His self-expression in the world. Isaiah had not risen to that higher conception which characterizes the noblest utterances of Jeremiah, who saw that with or without Israel, Yahweh could still establish His word among men.[3] He felt that there must be a remnant, a surviving

---

[1] Isa. xxxi. 3.   [2] Isa. i. 5–9.   [3] Cp. Jer. xliv. 28.

fraction of Israel which would carry on the tradition, a city in which Yahweh had His home, and that therefore Jerusalem, His city and the seat of His shrine, could not possibly be suffered to perish. But the deliverance would come from Yahweh Himself, not from any human power, Egyptian or another.

Hezekiah entirely failed to appreciate either Isaiah's policy or the reasons for it. He has been, perhaps, over-glorified by that Deuteronomic tradition whose sole test of righteous kingship lay in the royal attitude towards the local sanctuaries. It is not suggested that Hezekiah was a bad man or a bad king, but he certainly did not rise above his fellows in practical statesmanship, and still less could he attain to the height of Isaiah's religious convictions. He was bent on rebellion, and, indeed, it seemed for the moment as if the whole Assyrian empire must crumble to pieces. His decision once taken, his measures were wise and energetic. They fall into two classes, (a) those intended to consolidate his own authority and centralize the interest of Judah in Jerusalem, (b) those aimed at securing the material defences of the city.

The first class of measures may be summed up in the reform of the cultus which is attributed to him. It has been doubted whether he really did carry through all that is ascribed to him in 2 Kgs. xviii. 4,[1] but in that case we still have to explain how the tradition arose. There must have been some ground for it, and the Deuteronomic approval must have had an historical basis of some kind. It is, then, not impossible that Hezekiah did carry out measures which aimed at the suppression of the local sanctuaries, though we may suspect that his objects had a strong political element in them. For one thing, it is not unlikely that, since the days of Ahaz, the chief sanctuaries of Judah had contained some symbol of an Assyrian cult. This was probably true also of Jerusalem, and we may be sure that the reforms included the removal of such objects and the suppression of any cult connected with them. The destruction of the brazen serpent, however, tends to show that Hezekiah's object was the

---

[1] The passage contains serious syntactical difficulties which can be solved only in one of two ways, either (a) by radical emendation of the text, or (b) by assuming that the verse is a very late insertion, dating from a time when the characteristic grammatical features of classical Hebrew had begun to break down. But the passage, though late in its present form, may well embody an ancient tradition. Perhaps the original basis lay in the elimination of Assyrian objects of worship and the breaking of the bronze serpent.

concentration of worship at the true sanctuary of Yahweh—that which sheltered the Ark.[1] Yahweh was the God of Israel, and all Judah would worship Him, whatever forms they might use, and wherever they might bring their offerings. If the Jerusalem Temple were the only spot left at which gifts might be brought to Him, then it would follow that the national enthusiasm would be concentrated on an effort to preserve this spot from the invader. We need not doubt Hezekiah's sincerity if we see in this reform a political gesture, for patriotism and religious loyalty naturally went hand in hand in ancient Israel. But it is a noteworthy fact that nowhere have we the slightest reference to this reform in the extant work of Isaiah, and it is hardly credible that it should have passed entirely without notice if the prophet had seen that it was based on purely religious motives. The only person in the story who makes any use of it is the Rabshakeh.[2]

The most important of Hezekiah's measures for the defence of Jerusalem concerned its water supply, the greatest source of weakness for the city, ever since the time of David. There is only one perennial fountain in the immediate neighbourhood of Jerusalem, that known as the Virgin's spring, to the south-east of the Temple hill. Otherwise the city has to depend on reservoirs of rain-water. From the time of David the spring had been outside the walls, and Hezekiah took steps to bring the water within the city in a way which would not expose it to being cut off by a besieging enemy. Accordingly he cut through the rock the famous aqueduct, known as the Siloam tunnel, and so gave Jerusalem a water supply which may have been satisfactory for his day,[3] at least for a garrison in what was then still the citadel, on the Ophel. This cannot have been done simply while the revolt was in progress, as it must have been slow work,

[1] Serpent-worship in Jerusalem was also probably a form of Yahweh-cult, and it is worth noting that in the great vision of Isaiah (ch. vi) the divine attendants have applied to them the term (שׂרף) used to describe the 'fiery serpents' of Num. xxi. 5–9. [2] 2 Kgs. xviii. 22.

[3] The tunnel is famous, among other reasons, for the inscription which was found cut upon its walls, explaining the final steps by which it was completed. It seems that the engineers started piercing the rock from both ends simultaneously, but made a slight miscalculation, with the result that the two shafts were being driven past one another when the workmen in one of them heard the picks of those in the other through the rock, and cuttings were made sideways. The text of the inscription has been frequently edited; it may be seen, for instance, in Driver, *Notes on the Hebrew Text of the Books of Samuel*, pp. viii ff. The tunnel runs for something over 1,700 ft., winding considerably, from the Virgin's spring to the pool of Siloam, which was within the old city, though now outside the walls of Jerusalem.

and even the three years which elapsed between the first outbreak and the arrival of Sennacherib's armies would hardly
have been sufficient. Probably Hezekiah undertook the task
early in his reign, and the knowledge of a safe supply of water
may have been one of the considerations which led him to
participate in the revolt.

In that revolt Hezekiah played an important role. Not only
did he make himself responsible for the safe keeping of Padi, but
he made a raid on so much of the Philistine territory as remained
faithful to Sennacherib, and carried his arms up to the walls of
Gaza.[1] It seems, however, that he made no serious attempt to
capture the city, and, indeed, it was probably much too strong
for any successful assault unless delivered by people as skilled in
siege warfare as were the Assyrians themselves. It is significant
that the only city which fell into the hands of the insurgents was
Ekron, and that was surrendered by its own inhabitants. Apart
from such help from the inside, the allies were probably unable
to make a serious impression on any of the walled cities which
refused to join them.

Sennacherib was not the man to linger when his dominions
were thus threatened. In one swift campaign he crushed the
resistance of southern Mesopotamia. On his approach a large
army, including the Elamite and Aramaean contingents, together with a number of Chaldaean troops, occupied the city of
Kutha, to the north-east of Babylon, while Marduk-apal-iddina
himself, with the remainder of his army, held Kish, east of
Babylon and nearly due south of Kutha. A strong detachment
was sent forward to deal with Kish, but found the task too great
for them, and it seems they suffered a defeat. But they did
prevent Marduk-apal-iddina from uniting his forces with those
of his allies at Kutha, and while he was winning his victory,
Sennacherib met the Elamites and others under the walls of
Kutha and utterly defeated them, capturing the city with many
prisoners and large booty. He then turned on Marduk-apal-
iddina, who saw that all was lost, and made his escape from Kish
to the marshes. He collected all the men and property he could
get together, and made his escape into 'the city of Nagite-rakki
which is in the midst of the sea'.[2] Sennacherib's difficulties with

---

[1] 2 Kgs. xviii. 8.
[2] See Sidney Smith, *The First Campaign of Sennacherib*, and Luckenbill, *ARA*.
ii, pp. 128–33, §§ 256–67.

Babylonia were by no means at an end, but for the time there was no organized resistance, and he was able to devote himself to other parts of his dominions in the next two years. The king's second campaign was devoted to the reduction of rebellious cities to the east of the Tigris, but he then felt himself free to attend to the west. The story is one of the best known among the Assyrian annals,[1] and gives a clear account of Sennacherib's movements. We may probably supplement this from the Biblical records[2] which, after describing the general issue of the campaign, give us additional details of it from the standpoint of Jerusalem.

Sennacherib dealt first with Phoenicia, whose cities submitted without serious resistance, and, at the same time, received the tribute of a number of other states, including Ammon, Moab, and Edom. But Ashkelon had extended its borders, and seems to have stretched its authority as far north as Carmel. Ashkelon and its territories were reduced by force, and Sennacherib turned his attention to the cities of Judah. To judge from what he himself has left us, he found Lachish the most difficult place to capture,[3] but he seems to have divided his force into a number of smaller detachments while the siege was being pressed. One such body of troops certainly came to Jerusalem, under the leadership of Sennacherib's chief officer, the Rabshakeh. It seems clear that neither the king nor his general expected to capture the city by this move, but it was advisable to prevent Hezekiah from coming to the help of his allies, and there was always the possibility that the city might be surrendered, either by the frightened king, or by some popular movement within the walls. The narrative does not suggest that the Rabshakeh brought siege engines with him, and Sennacherib's language implies merely that the place was blockaded for a time. Even an Assyrian army had little chance of capturing Jerusalem without the best mechanical equipment of the day.

This force, it seems, left the main army as it passed through

---

[1] Two copies of the annals are known: one being the famous Taylor prism, dating from 691 B.C., the other, two years later, being in the Oriental Institute of the University of Chicago. For the latter see Luckenbill, *ARA*. ii. 115–28, §§ 233–54.

[2] See Additional Note E, pp. 409 f.

[3] For Lachish see Bliss, *A Mound of many Cities*. One of Sennacherib's reliefs from Nineveh, now in the British Museum, represents the siege of this city, cp. Gressmann, *ABAT*., figs. 138, 141.

the province of Samaria, and approached Jerusalem from the north. In Isa. x. 28–31 we have a striking description of the enemy's movements, and the route is traced. It lay through the territory of Benjamin, and the way in which place after place is named in quick succession gives us a sense of the speed with which the Assyrian troops moved. At length Jerusalem was reached, and the story of the parley is vividly told in 2 Kgs.

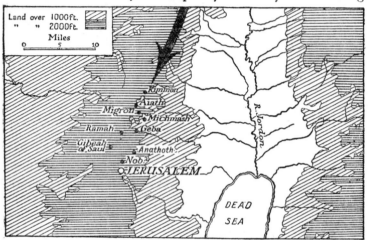

The Assyrian advance in 701 B.C., showing the localities mentioned in Isa. x. 28–31.

xviii. 17–xix. 8. The Rabshakeh delivered his message in Hebrew, standing outside the walls and speaking up to the officers who were upon them. The human voice carries far in the clear air round Jerusalem, and to this day a conversation can be held between a speaker on the Ophel and another in the village of Silwan, or even on the hill above. Fearing the effect of the Rabshakeh's words on the civil population, the officials asked him to speak in Aramaic, but he refused, on the ground that he had no quarrel with the people themselves, but only with Hezekiah, and it was his desire that they should discard their king and submit to Assyria. It is clear that the Rabshakeh would have been glad enough to have secured the city without having to fight for it, and he hoped that the loyalty of the inhabitants would be no stronger than that of other places with which Sennacherib had had to deal.

Hezekiah was assured by Isaiah that there was no danger to the city from the Assyrians, and the people remained faithful to their king. Judah is the only state of the nearer east which, in ancient times, never suffered a change of dynasty, a remarkable testimony to the impression that David had made. But it would seem that the people of Jerusalem itself were never put to the worst strain. We gather, both from Sennacherib's account of the events, and also from the Biblical record, that Hezekiah agreed to all that was demanded of him, even while the siege of Lachish was still in progress. 'I have offended,' the Israelite record makes him say, 'return from me; that which thou puttest upon me I will bear.'[1] The burden thus accepted was not light. Sennacherib claims to have received 30 talents of gold, 800 talents of silver, thrones, stools of ivory, elephants' skins and teeth, and the king's sons. All that is mentioned in *Kings* is the 30 talents of gold and 300 talents of silver, though we should, perhaps, add to this the silver that Hezekiah stripped from his buildings.

It is not unlikely that the Rabshaketh and his force remained encamped about Jerusalem until all the spoil had been handed over. By the time the Assyrians were able to leave, Lachish had fallen, and Sennacherib was besieging Libnah. Ekron was threatened, and at last Egypt showed signs of interference. Sennacherib, it seems, did not feel sure of Hezekiah's loyalty, and sent a message, this time, to judge from the record in 2 Kgs. xix. 9, without a serious force, threatening Hezekiah with utter ruin. The terms of the letter which was brought to Jerusalem do not expressly make the threat conditional on Hezekiah's disobedience, and the king himself seems to have feared that his pardon had been revoked. He was reassured by Isaiah, who, instead of waiting to be consulted as he had done on the earlier occasion, spontaneously offered the king an assurance that the armies of Assyria would not again appear before Jerusalem.

The expectation of an Egyptian advance was fulfilled. Shabaka collected some sort of an army, gathering together the princelets of the Delta and the king of Meluḫḫa, perhaps under the leadership of that Tirhakah who succeeded to the Egyptian throne some ten years later. Sennacherib raised the siege of Libnah, and met the enemy at Eltekeh, in the south of Judah, where he inflicted on him a crushing defeat, though it seems that his own forces suffered from the ravages of disease, perhaps bubonic plague. Eltekeh and a place named Tamna

[1] 2 Kgs. xviii. 14.

fell into his hands, and he returned to complete the subjugation of the land. On his first arrival in southern Palestine he had laid the whole country waste, and claims to have captured 46 fortified cities, besides innumerable villages, taking no less than 200,150 captives. It appears that the last conquest[1] was that of Ekron, to which Padi was restored. The final settlement involved a considerable reduction in the territories of Hezekiah, for parts of his dominions were divided among the few local kings who had remained faithful to Assyria.[2] From the number of the captives and of the cities taken we may suspect that the kingdom of Hezekiah had extended beyond the normal borders of Judah proper, and we may conjecture that Sargon had rewarded the fidelity of Ahaz with a gift of some of the land formerly included in the kingdom of Israel. But we may be sure that Judah, as an individual state, was now reduced to its narrowest limits.

Jerusalem, however, was not taken, and its escape had a profound influence on Israelite thought. It seemed to the people of the city and of the country that Yahweh's presence was a guarantee that no evil could befall His home, and that as long as He remained within its walls the place was inviolable, and could defy any enemy who attacked it. In a certain sense this view was held by Isaiah, but along with it he would certainly have postulated a genuine appreciation of the demands which Yahweh would make on His people—demands, not of ritual service, but of moral conduct. He was entirely at one with Amos, Hosea, and Micah—a contemporary Judaean who saw the evils of the Jewish countryside as even Isaiah did not—and would have endorsed the opinion which found expression more than a century later in the visions of Ezekiel,[3] that Yahweh could be driven from His Temple and city by the iniquity of the people. But for the time the policy advocated by Isaiah seemed to triumph, and men were brought to a feeling of security in their God.

Sennacherib probably had more than one reason for leaving the city intact. He had all that he really required, and he may not have thought it worth while to spend the time and strength

---

[1] This is not the order of the Taylor prism, but it seems that the events there recorded were not necessarily set down in chronological order.

[2] Cp. Alt, *Territorialgeschichtliche Bedeutung von Sanheribs Eingriff in Palästina*, *Palästinajahrbuch*, xxv (1929), pp. 80 ff.   [3] Cp. Ezek. x. 19, xi. 23.

necessary to depose Hezekiah and organize Judah as a province of the empire. Jerusalem was a fortress of great strength, and its reduction would have been very expensive to him. Hezekiah had learnt a lesson which he was not likely to forget, and the prospects of another revolt were remote. Egypt had received a crushing blow, and, still more, had been shown to be incompetent to help her own allies. For a generation at least, no Palestinian state, remembering Eltekeh, would be likely to lend the slightest consideration to Egyptian intrigues. Isaiah and the Rabshakeh had spoken the truth about her.

Allusion has already been made to an event which probably assisted Sennacherib to determine his course of action. In the two accounts we have of the Assyrian messages to Jerusalem, Isaiah appears with a promise of safety, but gives different predictions. When the prophet hears of the words of the Rabshakeh, he tells Hezekiah that a spirit will be put into Sennacherib, and he will hear a rumour, and he will return to his own land, where he will perish by the sword. The Assyrian king did hear a rumour, which proved to be true, that Babylon had once more broken into revolt, and he evidently had to bring his western campaign to a hurried close, and move where he and his troops were urgently needed if the empire was to stand. Marduk-apal-iddina was still alive and active, though the Chaldaean leader seems to have been a certain Shuzubi—perhaps a commander operating under the orders of Marduk-apal-iddina. He was utterly defeated, and the arch-rebel, gathering together all the gods of the land, with their shrines, took refuge once more on the island of Nagite-rakki, where it seems to have been hopeless to pursue him.[1] His name is not mentioned again, and though Babylon was never wholly pacified, it is Shuzubi and Nabu-shum-iskun, son of Marduk-apal-iddina, of whom we hear as the leaders of the patriots. But for a number of years Sennacherib was kept fighting in the east, where the Elamites seem to have played a part not unlike that of Egypt in the west, though with far more vigour and success.

The invasion of 701 B.C. is the last we hear of Assyrian armies

---

[1] Luckenbill, ARA. ii. 121 f., § 242. Needless to say, Nagite-rakki has not been identified, nor is it likely to be. The Persian Gulf in ancient times extended a good deal farther north than it does to-day, and included all the country through which the Shatt-el-arab now passes, the Tigris and the Euphrates reaching the sea by different mouths. The island in question has probably long ago been included in the alluvial land which the two rivers have thrown up in the course of centuries.

in Judah. The policy of Sennacherib was justified, for never again did a king of Jerusalem seriously waver in his loyalty to the court of Nineveh. Hezekiah was succeeded by Manasseh,[1] Manasseh by Amon,[2] and Amon by the boy Josiah.[3] In Josiah's thirteenth year there befell a calamity which swept away the last remnants of Assyrian authority, already weak, from Palestine, and through the whole period there is no instance in which the Assyrians claim that Judah was rebellious, or in which Judahite historians record an invasion of their country. There is, it is true, one apparent exception, for it is stated in 2 Chron. xxxiii. 10 f. that the Assyrians invaded Judah and carried Manasseh away captive to Babylon. There is no hint of such an event in the book of *Kings*, however, nor is there in any known Assyrian document or inscription the least suggestion of rebellion on Manasseh's part. But we have an account of the building of a new suburb at Nineveh, since Esarhaddon found the city too small for him. Twenty-two kings were summoned to offer their homage and to bear their part in the construction, ten of them from Cyprus, and twelve from the Mediterranean coastlands.[4] The latter list includes all the independent or rather tributary sovereigns of Syria and Palestine, and it is interesting to compare the names with those mentioned in Sennacherib's account of his campaign in 701 B.C. The event must have taken place early in the reign of Esarhaddon (680–669 B.C.), since three of the kings of Sennacherib's day, at least twenty years earlier, are still living, and occupy their old thrones. These three are Silli-bêl of Gaza, Mitinti of Ashdod, and Budu'ilu of Ammon. The rest of Sennacherib's contemporaries have gone, and others now hold their places. Prominent among these is Manasseh, who has now succeeded his father Hezekiah, and clearly follows that policy of submission to Assyria which marked Hezekiah's later years. We can easily understand that the tradition of Manasseh's journey to Nineveh grew into a legend of his captivity in Babylon; so wicked a king ought to have suffered some terrible punishment. The story of his restoration, however, lends strength to suspicion. No record suggested anything other than that he held the throne till his death, and he had to be brought back to fit the known history. We note,

---

[1] 2 Kgs. xxi. 1 ff.　　　　[2] 2 Kgs. xxi. 19 ff.　　　　[3] 2 Kgs. xxii. 1 ff.
[4] The record is contained in Esarhaddon prisms S and B, cp. Luckenbill, *ARA.* i. 265 f., § 690.

further, the entire absence of any mention of a substitute or any other means of carrying on the government in his absence. Had he really been deported as a rebel, some one would certainly have been put in his place, for it could not have been foreseen that he would repent and be restored to his own land. As a matter of fact, the omission of a campaign against Judah from the Assyrian annals is decisive. We have a really detailed account of the story of Assyria and of her kings from the beginning of the reign of Tiglath-pileser III down to the thirtieth year of Ashur-bani-pal. For the last thirteen years of the latter reign, it is true, we have no direct annals, but they fell within the time of Josiah, and allow no opportunity for events which affected Josiah's grandfather.

Sennacherib never had to fight in the west again, save for an expedition (which cannot have been a difficult one) against the Arabs and Edomites in 691 B.C. But when he was murdered in 680 B.C. by two of his sons, it seemed once more as if the empire were in danger of falling to pieces. Esarhaddon was in Babylon, where he had been governor under his father, and by prompt action succeeded in destroying some of his rivals and forestalling others. It seems that he was less unpopular in southern Mesopotamia than his predecessors had been, and he was far more free to devote his attention to the west. A 'revolt' in Sidon was first suppressed, and the king then devoted himself to the foundation of a new city on the Phoenician coast, and to the organization of a fresh province in Phoenicia. He does not seem to have carried this out very completely, perhaps because it was impossible for him to capture Tyre, and he had to be content with a treaty, mainly commercial, with Baal, king of Tyre. 'It was somewhat one-sided, for Esarhaddon often speaks in the first person and enforces the penalties; notwithstanding there is a very substantial quid pro quo. If Esarhaddon is able to insist that he may appoint a resident to watch over the Tyrian territory, that Baal is to obey any message sent by the king, that he is to appear when summoned by the resident, the commercial clauses are those of equals',[1] and it must be remembered that we have Esarhaddon's version of the treaty, not Baal's.

There followed a series of expeditions in which the tribes of the wilderness were reduced to submission, and, finally, in 671 B.C. Esarhaddon invaded Egypt and seized Memphis. The

[1] Olmstead, History of Assyria, p. 375.

Assyrian dominion was short, and unstable while it lasted. Esarhaddon died in 669 B.C. as he was on the point of marching to suppress a rebellion, and more than once in the reign of Ashur-bani-pal the land had to be reconquered. The last of these expeditions took place in 661 B.C., and culminated in the sack of Memphis, but nine years later Egypt recovered her independence, never again to fall beneath the yoke of Assyria, and in 640 B.C. Psammetichus I even invaded Philistia and tried to capture Ashdod.

The reign of Manasseh, then, was not one of general peace in Palestine and the neighbouring countries. Armies were passing to and fro; down the great road that led to Egypt there came again and again the forces of Assyria. Her soldiers were never very far from the land of Judah, and yet the little hill state, as far as we know, enjoyed a period of uninterrupted peace. Doubtless tribute had to be paid, and the constant presence of Assyrian forces may have done something to keep Judah loyal. But, whatever the reasons were, there was no attempt at rebellion, with the result that Judah did not suffer from invasion. The practical policy of Isaiah was at last realized; Judah was refraining from interference with her neighbours, great and small, and she reaped at least one reward of her conduct in freedom from outside attack.

In other respects, however, the reign of Manasseh was very far from corresponding to the ideals of Isaiah or of any other prophet. It is known in Israelite records as the great age of reaction, and there seems to have been no other time in her whole history when Judah was guilty of so great and complicated an apostasy. We ought, perhaps, to modify our records to some extent, and to discount somewhat both the picture of Hezekiah's righteousness and of Manasseh's wickedness. But when all allowance of this kind is made, the reign stands out as one of the darkest periods in the religious history of Israel.[1] From the standpoint of the genuine enthusiast for Yahweh, the pure Israelite who clung to the traditions of the old Mosaism of the wilderness, the reign of Ahab had been bad enough, but that of Manasseh was immeasurably worse. 'Backsliding Israel' had committed sin enough, but 'her treacherous sister Judah' had far outdone her in spiritual crime.[2] The sins of Manasseh were partly cultic and partly moral. He restored the old sanctuaries

---

[1] Cp. 2 Kgs. xxi. 2–6, 16.   [2] Cp. Jer. iii. 6–11, Ez. xxiii. 11.

which Hezekiah had destroyed—not, apparently, the snake shrine in Jerusalem itself—and allowed their worship to be reorganized. He may have felt, as many in Judah certainly did feel, that these shrines were legitimate centres of the worship of Yahweh, and that even Hezekiah had no right to overthrow them. Not a few must have traced the calamities which befell the land during Sennacherib's invasion to Hezekiah's sacrilege, and have welcomed the restoration of the old ways.

This, however, was not all. He was not content with restoring the position as it had existed before Hezekiah's changes; he made fresh additions to the cultus. He is charged with having set up altars in the Temple itself, to other deities, especially to Baal—apparently the Tyrian Melkart. An Asherah also he erected in the sacred precincts, and though in earlier days this would have been regarded as innocuous, the later theology of the Deuteronomists (to whom we owe the whole story of Manasseh's reign as told in *Kings*) looked upon this emblem with horror. As if this were not enough, he established an astral cult in the Temple itself, probably taking it from Mesopotamia, and adopting it as a compliment to his overlord. He reverted to the older necromancy, which, often suppressed, yet constantly reappeared in Israel. It is perhaps to this that reference is made in Isa. viii. 19 f., though, as Gray remarks,[1] 'such a warning would have been timely at most periods of Israel's history'. The cult of the dead was held by the strict Yahwist to be one of the most dangerous forms of apostasy, not because the 'medium' defrauded his or her clients, but because men believed the whole thing to be true, and it therefore involved the recognition of some other superhuman power than Yahweh. It would seem that it was put down finally only when the orthodox doctrine of a She'ol from which the departed could not reach the living at all replaced the belief that the dead remained in their tombs, and could be summoned thence at the call of the properly equipped and skilled person.[2] More revolting still was the introduction of human sacrifice, for which, as far as we know, Manasseh had not the same excuse as Ahaz, since he does not seem to have been faced with such perils. The statement may mean no more than that the regular offering of the first-born was restored— though that is terrible enough.

To these acts of apostasy Manasseh is said to have added

[1] *Isaiah, ICC.*, p. 157.   [2] Cp. Oesterley, *Immortality and the Unseen World.*

wholesale slaughter of persons against whom no crime could be proved. Tradition believes this to have been an organized persecution of the prophets and of their followers, and most people are familiar with the story that Isaiah was sawn asunder[1] in this king's reign. This, however, is not expressly stated, and it may be doubted. A prophet, no matter how unpopular he was, or how unwelcome his message to the authorities, was still a person who stood in a very special relation to Yahweh, and even those who had most cause to wish him put out of the way would hesitate to strike the blow that should deprive him of life. On no other ground can we explain Amaziah's expulsion of Amos from Bethel,[2] or the fact that Jeremiah was left to starve in an old cistern.[3] Had either not been protected by the sanctity of his prophetic office and nature, there is not the slightest doubt that he would have met with a swift and sudden doom. The slaughter of a prophet could be regarded only as a challenge to, or a repudiation of, the God who had inspired him, and while Manasseh was certainly guilty of many things contrary to the known will of Yahweh, there is no reason to believe that he desired to discard the national God altogether. Rather he sought to add others alongside of Him—though this was far enough from the true ideals of Yahwism as understood from the days of Moses onwards. It will be noticed, too, that this charge against Manasseh is not placed with the other words of condemnation for ritual and ecclesiastical sins, but stands by itself. It seems more probable that it refers to persistent acts of cruelty and injustice in the administration of civil law, one of the worst crimes of which an Israelite ruler was capable. So great was the loathing felt by the next few generations for the general régime of Manasseh, that men did not hesitate to lay on him alone the blame for the punishment which befell Judah in the Exile.[4] Even when all allowance is made for the theological and other presuppositions of the historian, it is clear that the reign of Manasseh was one of the darkest times through which Judah ever passed, in spite of the continued freedom from foreign invasion.

We cannot leave this age without reminding ourselves once more that, while it may have contributed nothing to the

---

[1] Cp. Heb. xi. 37.   [2] Am. vii. 12 ff.

[3] Jer. xxxviii. 3 ff. There is but one instance of an accredited prophet of Yahweh being put to death by a king of Judah—that of Urijah, see Jer. xxvi. 20-3. The incident is a striking example of this king's reckless arrogance.

[4] Cp. e.g. 2 Kgs. xxiii. 26 f.

development of Jewish culture, and while the condition of the average Judahite was much what it had been during the eighth century, the period from 750 to 700 B.C. witnessed the rise of the great canonical prophets, a body of men who stand alone in the history of the world's religion. We have already observed the contribution made by Amos in his insistence on morality as the supreme demand of Yahweh. While this was the most striking innovation in ordinary thought about God, and was equally maintained by Hosea, Micah, and Isaiah, there are other features of their teaching which call for special remark. These men were, perhaps, the first to hold a doctrine whose modern analogue is the conception of God as Law.[1] The whole trend of human religion was to think of the objects of their worship as beings who might be good-natured and friendly if well treated, but were essentially whimsical and on the whole unreliable. It was never possible for the layman to forecast what attitude the deity would take to a particular action or mode of approach. Against this view the prophets held strongly to a doctrine of the consistency of Yahweh. It is true that all believed in miracle, i.e. in the unexpected and unprecedented interference of God in the world of nature; it would hardly have been possible for them to have held Him to be the creator of the universe and the formulator of the laws by which it moves, if they had not also held that He could at will supersede those laws. It was no violation of his fundamental principles which led Isaiah to believe that the shadow could go back ten degrees on the dial of Ahaz,[2] for only in such terms could he understand Yahweh as the Lord of Nature. But what the Hebrew prophet had to tell the world was that this miraculous power would be exercised only in accordance with certain easily recognizable principles. If men sinned they would be punished, and the punishment would be that appropriate to their sin, that, and no more and no less. They believed that it was possible for every man, by consulting that law of conscience which lay within him (though they would not have used such terms nor shaped their thoughts in quite this mould) to foresee Yahweh's reaction to each and every type of conduct, and so to judge of His pleasure and of His anger.

---

[1] It may not be superfluous to remark that this phrase itself would have been quite unintelligible to the ancient Hebrew. Cp. O. and R., *Heb. Rel.*, pp. 195 f.

[2] 2 Kgs. xx. 9.

It is equally obvious that the prophets thought of Yahweh as the Creator of the universe. This was no novelty, and the doctrine would probably be shared by every Israelite. All over the peoples of western Asia there was spread the old creation myth, according to which some god had fashioned the world after the defeat of the opposing powers of chaos. The myth is familiar to us in the Mesopotamian story of Tiamat, and has come down to us in Sumerian, Babylonian, and Assyrian forms. The interesting feature of these various forms is that each takes the national god of its own people and exalts him as the triumphant hero. Thus in the Sumerian form it is Enlil who achieves the triumph, in Babylonian literature it is Marduk, while the Assyrians ascribed the same victory and the same achievement to Ashur. We cannot doubt that a similar story was current in the mouth of Israel, and that here it was none of the eastern deities but Yahweh who was the conqueror of chaos and the architect of the cosmos. As early as Amos we find repeated snatches of poetry which celebrate the work of Yahweh in creation, and other prophets are in full harmony with him.

The Lord of Creation is also the Lord of History. Other nations claimed to be under the control and direction of their own gods who through their own might could subdue the feebler deities of other nations and give victory and dominion to their own folk. The appearance of this belief in earlier Israel is very clearly marked, e.g. in the stories of the Ark. But the Hebrew prophet of the eighth century went still further, and asserted that Yahweh was the controller of the destinies, not of Israel alone, but of all the nations of the world. It was He who had brought Israel out of Egypt, but He had also brought the Philistines from Caphtor and the Syrians from Kir[1]—He and not the gods of the peoples themselves. The Assyrians might seem to be the greatest nation on earth, and to act in accordance with their own will. They themselves claimed to be carrying out the orders of Ashur their god in the various expeditions they undertook. Isaiah saw that this was a false statement of the case. Assyria was not a free agent, nor was she administered by Ashur; she was but 'the rod of the anger of Yahweh',[2] used by Him for the vindication of His own laws upon his rebellious people and others. As soon as the task of Assyria was performed, and she became no more than an empire based on selfish aggrandizement, she would be super-

[1] Am. ix. 7.   [2] Isa. x. 5 ff.

seded and ruined, and in her place another would be raised up to do the will of Yahweh, albeit unconsciously. Yahweh was Lord of history, as well as Lord of the physical world. Yet, in a very special sense Yahweh was the Lord of Israel. While it is clear to us that such doctrines as those of Amos and of Isaiah must lead in the long run to a pure monotheism, men are slow to perceive the logical conclusions of their own creed, and we have no right, in the absence of any very definite and express statement of a monotheistic doctrine (such as we have in the utterances of *2 Isaiah*), to assume that these men were conscious of the existence of no God other than Yahweh, and denied reality to the rest. They might pour scorn on the ineffective and futile 'godlings'[1] of the nations round them, and exalt Yahweh to a position high above all the rest, they might insist on the unreality of idols and the stupidity of worshipping mere things instead of persons, but if they had been challenged, they would almost certainly have admitted the existence of these other gods and goddesses. Otherwise they and their successors would not have been so fierce in their denunciation of apostasy. To each nation its own god; the gods of other peoples were inferior beings, but Israel's God was the supreme Yahweh.[2] Surely the proudest boast that could have been made by an insignificant hill state in western Asia! It meant that He stood to them in a relation different from that He adopted to the rest of the world. We have seen how Isaiah felt that He needed a people for His own self-expression, and would therefore see to it that Israel did not utterly perish. But Hosea draws another lesson; to him Yahweh was a God so great that He could destroy, and would destroy—for love's sake.[3] Yet both would have agreed with one another and with Amos that Yahweh had taken cognizance of Israel alone out of all the world's nations,[4] and that He had made her in a very special sense His peculiar people. All three would have gone further and have insisted that this special privilege implied a special responsibility. Just because of it would Yahweh punish Israel for *all* her transgressions.

---

[1] Cp. Isaiah's contemptuous use of the term אֱלִילִים, ii. 8, 18, &c.

[2] This seems to be the thought underlying Ps. lxxxii. 1, 6, which may be pre-exilic.

[3] We have to allow for the possibility of development in Hosea's doctrines, and admit that in his later years he cherished the hope of restoration. But the fact remains that certainly at one point in his life he believed in destruction as the final act of love. [4] Cp. Am. iii. 2.

In a very real sense she was His representative in the world, and she must be holy to Him if she would do her task. If she failed there, she failed everywhere.

The Deuteronomist who writes the history of Manasseh is thus in the direct line of the tradition of the great prophets of the eighth century. The reign of Manasseh to him meant the surrender by Israel of all that which made her what she was and gave her a place and a function in the universe of man. She had to stand for Yahweh and for Him alone, and when she gave herself to the worship of other deities she was traitor to her very being. Her excuse for existence was her fidelity to her God, and in the conduct of Manasseh (in which, in accordance with the common view of the solidarity of the nation, all Judah was involved, whether particular individuals were personally guilty or not) it seemed as if she had taken this excuse with both hands and hurled it from her. 'Traitor' was the word which Jeremiah flung at her two generations later,[1] and so also might the eighth-century prophets have spoken. Alone among the nations she knew, or might have known, her Lord's will, and she did it not. Therefore her punishment must fall upon her with many stripes.

[1] Cp. Jer. iii. 7, 8, 10, 11.

Additional Note E
SENNACHERIB'S INVASION OF JUDAH

THE account of Sennacherib's invasion given in 2 Kgs. xviii. 13—xix. 37 has aroused a good deal of discussion. It falls obviously into three parts, (a) xviii. 13–16, a short notice, taken, apparently, from the state annals, (b) xviii. 17—xix. 8, (c) xix. 9–37, the two latter being derived from some collection of incidents occurring during the life of Isaiah. With some modifications, the two latter appear also in Isa. xxxvi f. Of the three, (a) is entirely in accord with Sennacherib's own account of the affair, save that it remains uncertain whether the spoil was sent to him before or after his return to Nineveh. But the other two are detailed accounts which have no parallel in the Assyrian record, except for the statement that an army appeared under the walls of Jerusalem.

The difficulties involved in these two passages are mainly concerned with their relation to one another. Each tells of a summons by Sennacherib, but the first is given through the Rabshakeh, who appears with a large force, though, apparently, without a siege train. In the second instance 'messengers' are sent with a letter. Its language recalls that of the Rabshakeh—at least in part of his speech —and there is no mention of any military force sent with the messengers. A further difference between the two narratives is to be seen in the conclusion. In (b) Sennacherib is to 'hear a rumour and return unto his own land', where he is to fall by the sword (xix. 7), and, in view of the fact that xix. 36, 37 describe his departure and murder, it is usual to take these verses with (b) rather than with (c). In that case (c) will end with the account of the disaster which befell the Assyrian army in xix. 35.

A further difficulty is raised by the mention of 'Tirhakah, king of Ethiopia' at the beginning of (c) (xix. 9). Tirhakah became king of Egypt in 689 B.C., some twelve years after Sennacherib's invasion of Palestine, and it has been objected that this must be an error due to the writer's distance from the events of which he speaks. But it is to be noted that Tirhakah is not called 'king of Egypt', and even if the text had had this phrase, it might be due to a later scribe. Sennacherib does say that an army including 'the kings of Egypt' and the king of Meluḥḥa came against him and was defeated at Eltekeh, and even if we cannot identify Meluḥḥa with Ethiopia, there is no reason why Tirhakah should not have been among the leaders of the army, and mentioned because he did ascend the throne ten years later. But the differences between the two narratives and the allusion to Tirhakah have led some scholars, notably Winckler and Benzinger, to assume that (c) refers to a different occasion altogether, and that Sennacherib made another attack on Palestine in or about 691 B.C.

It is true that in that year he made an expedition against the Arabs and Edom, but he does not mention Judah, nor does he speak of having to meet an organized Egyptian force under Tirhakah. As Sidney Smith has suggested (*CAH*. iii. 74 f.), it is much more likely that this expedition was regarded as a rescue by the Assyrians from tribes who were annoying Judah. We shall understand this passage best if we refer it to the invasion of 701 B.C.

Is it then a variant account of the events described in (*b*)? Not a few readers will feel that the discrepancies are too great to admit of this hypothesis, unless we are to assume that (*c*) is a much later compilation, and partakes of the nature of Midrash.[1] As a matter of fact, there is no difficulty in taking the substance of the narrative as it stands. In spite of the encouragement given by Isaiah to Hezekiah, we may assume that the threatened attack on the city (attested by Sennacherib's own inscription) led the king of Judah to send a message to Lachish implying surrender. The second incident (*c*) may well be due to a rumour of the advance of the Egyptians towards Eltekeh. Sennacherib might have good reason to fear that Hezekiah would throw in his lot with the new enemy, and the primary purpose of the letter was to warn the king of Judah that he must remain faithful. The severity of its language need not prevent us from ascribing this motive to the Assyrian king; the stronger the terms he used, the more likely they were to be effective. The chief difficulties disappear when we realize that the letter was accompanied by no considerable force, and that it may well have been sent after, and not before, Hezekiah's virtual surrender to Sennacherib.

It remains to note the circumstances attending the withdrawal of the Assyrian armies. Two reason are given, (*a*) a rumour, not further specified (xix. 7), and (*b*) a disaster which befell his troops (xix. 35). We may interpret the former as news of fresh danger from Bit-Yakin, where Marduk-apal-iddina was again active. The latter finds support in a story told by Herodotus (ii. 141) to the effect that a great battle took place between the Egyptians and the Assyrians, in which the latter were defeated owing to the fact that on the previous night their bow-strings had been gnawed by mice. A comparison between this and the Biblical narrative has not unnaturally suggested that the Assyrians were attacked by bubonic plague, in the marshes on the Egyptian border. But it is clear that the disaster cannot have been as great as Herodotus and the writer of 2 Kgs. xix. 35 believed it to have been, and the story may be due to an attack of pestilence which affected some small detachment.[2]

---

[1] (*c*) has, apparently, been worked over by a scribe who was under Deuteronomic influence.

[2] For a recent discussion of the subject cp. Rudolph, *Sanḥerib in Palästina*, *Palästinajahrbuch*, xxv (1929), pp. 59 ff.

Chapter XX[1]

THE REFORMATION

SUMMARY

[The last quarter of the seventh century was a period of swift transition. The Assyrian empire had decayed, and its death-blow was given by the raids of the Cimmerians and Scythians. On the death of Ashur-bani-pal in 626 B.C., Babylon recovered her independence under the Chaldaean Nabopolassar. He joined forces with the Medes, and, in spite of help given to Assyria by Necho, king of Egypt, Ashur fell in 614 B.C., and Nineveh itself in 612 B.C., while the last sign of Assyrian resistance disappeared with the capture of Harran in 610 B.C. Necho continued the war, but was utterly overthrown at Carchemish in 605 B.C.

The breaking up of the Assyrian empire left Judah free, and in 621 B.C. Josiah, like Hezekiah before him, carried through a religious reform. Once more the local sanctuaries were abolished, and in Jerusalem itself everything destroyed which was not in harmony with a pure cult of Yahweh. Josiah concluded his work with a unique celebration of the Passover, when all Israel was summoned to the central sanctuary in Jerusalem.

Josiah seems to have escaped the notice of Necho till 608 B.C., but in that year he was killed at Megiddo by the Egyptian king, who was on his way to a Mesopotamian campaign.]

MANASSEH died in 641 B.C., and was succeeded by his son Amon,[2] whose name seems to suggest a revival of Egyptian influence for which there is no other evidence. But Amon followed in the ways of his father, and met with opposition culminating in a conspiracy which cost him his life. In 639 B.C. his young son Josiah,[3] aged only eight, came to the throne. It would seem that no change in the policy of Judah was made by the regents of his early years, and the country continued to stand aloof from the great movements which were taking place about her. It is not till comparatively late in his reign that we have any hint of contact with foreign powers, and by that time the face of the world had changed.

The last fifty years of the kingdom of Judah fell at one of those stages of human history when a crisis has been reached in international relations. Jeremiah, whose long life and activity cover most of the period, saw the fall of the old Assyrian kingdom,

---

[1] For another presentation of the subject-matter of this and the following chapter, cp. vol. ii, chs. 2 and 3. [2] 2 Kgs. xxi. 19 ff. [3] 2 Kgs. xxii. 1 ff.

the final collapse of the power of Egypt, and the establishment of the short-lived but brilliant second Babylonian empire. It is significant that we have no historical inscriptions of Ashur-bani-pal dated later than the year of Josiah's accession. Though he may justly be accounted one of the great kings of Assyria—and the last of such—it is clear that his empire was already beginning to crumble. The acquisition of Egypt, splendid triumph though it seemed to Esarhaddon and to Ashur-bani-pal in his younger days, proved in the end to be too great a weight for Assyria to bear. Her power rested on a comparatively narrow basis, and the extra burden proved sufficient to overbalance the whole structure. Egypt was very far away, and there were signs within her that the old spirit of the ancient Pharaohs was not wholly dead. It is true that until the days of the Ptolemies she never again attained to the rank of a first-class world-power, but she still had enough life and power of resistance to enable her to make one more struggle for freedom, and the effort to meet this drained to danger-point the resources of an Assyria already exhausted by centuries of conquest. Under Psammetichus Egypt recovered her liberty in 652 b.c., and Ashur-bani-pal was unable to attempt the reconquest of the land. As we have seen, the last thirteen years of his reign are wrapped in obscurity, but it is clear that the strength of the kingdom was fast failing, and when he died in 626 b.c. the end was already in sight.

A new factor had appeared in the political and national life of western Asia. From time immemorial the north and northeast had always been a home of mystery and of peril for the peoples of the Fertile Crescent. There dwelt, on the great plains of what is now Russia and on the high lands of central Asia, groups of wandering nomads, of different races, but similar in culture. From time to time economic or other pressure had led hordes of them to break through into the more fertile countries of the south, where some of them were content to plunder and return to their homes, while others made settlements on the land they won. These sudden irruptions have not often effected a permanent change in the population of the southern territories, though once or twice they have assumed the proportions of great racial migrations. Thence came, apparently, the Indo-Aryan peoples who settled in Persia and India on the one hand, and in the lands to the north of the Mediterranean on the other. Thence came the movements of the Germanic tribes, and later of the Goths and the Huns.

To the mixed groups of their day, the classical Greek authors gave the names of Cimmerian and Scythian, and it is by this latter title that they are generally known in history. With the gradual breaking down of the Assyrian empire the northern barriers were weakened, and the barbarian hordes began to make inroads into the south. They did not always come as enemies, or rather they were often found useful as mercenaries (though they must have been rather dangerous allies) by warring kings and princes. Thus it is said that Nineveh was besieged by Kyaxares the Mede, shortly after the death of Ashur-bani-pal, but was saved by the intervention of Scythian armies.[1] But for the most part they seem to have acted independently, and to have formed raiding bands rather than organized armies. They were constantly in the Fertile Crescent during the last quarter of the seventh century, and though they made few if any permanent settlements, in the disturbed state of politics they exercised a decisive influence, for it was they especially who swept away the last remnants of the organized Assyrian empire. It did not much matter to them on whose side they fought; their object was plunder, and they were not concerned with the support or with the overthrow of existing powers, provided that they could secure their end. While in 625 B.C. they were fighting for Assyria against the Medes, the presence of their raiders in the outlying portions of the empire must have brought the Assyrian organization to an end.

It was during the reign of Josiah, roughly about 626 B.C., that they appeared in Palestine. Two prophets, Zephaniah and Jeremiah, testify to their presence and to the terror which they inspired. Both seem to have owed their initial prophetic call to this invasion, and the former saw in it an apocalyptic significance. The latter vividly describes their march,[2] and the impression they made on the inhabitants of Judah,[3] their strange

---

[1] For an account of the Scythians see N. Schmidt, *EB.* iv, cols. 4330–9. There is no mention of this siege of Nineveh from Asiatic sources; our information is derived only from Herodotus. The Greek historian is sometimes suspected, but he seems to have reported faithfully the traditions as they were handed on to him, and we have no reason to doubt the historicity of this event.

[2] Cp. e.g. Jer. iv. 7, 13 ff., 29, v. 15 ff., vi. 1 ff., 22 ff.

[3] The identity of the invaders with the Scythians has been questioned in recent years, especially by Wilke, 'Das Skythenproblem im Jeremiabuch', in *Alttestamentliche*

language, their swift horses—all seem to be mounted—their fierce aspect, their cruel behaviour, their inability to carry out a successful siege. They did, it is true, take Ashkelon, but its fall was due to treachery within the walls, and there is no record of their capturing any other fortified place. Herodotus tells his readers that Psammetichus staved off an invasion of Egypt only by giving the enemy large bribes.

As yet there seems to have been no formal attack made upon the Assyrian empire, either by the Scythians or by other enemies, and the successors of Ashur-bani-pal, though they undertook no field operations, went on with their buildings in their own city. But it is clear that the repeated strokes of these raiding bands weakened the whole state, and Assyria would soon have to face the vengeance of the peoples whom she had so long oppressed. Chief among these was Babylon, which, on the death of Ashur-bani-pal, had been seized by Nabopolassar, king of the Chaldaeans, a people whose home lay to the south, on the edge of the Persian Gulf. Of his reign we have no records until 616 B.C., when the attack on Assyria assumed serious proportions. The dying state had secured one powerful ally in Necho, son of Psammetichus, king of Egypt, but the long distance from his base

Studien für Rudolf Kittel, pp. 222–54, followed by Volz, *Der Prophet Jeremia*, esp. pp. 57 f., and Welch, *Jeremiah*, esp. pp. 101 ff. The grounds on which the view is discarded are mainly these: Herodotus is unreliable—he often admits that he does not believe the stories he reports—and the account of the sack of the Temple at Ashkelon (i. 103–6), which is the sole ground for the introduction of the Scythians as Asiatic rulers, is based on a legend belonging to the Aphrodite cult. In the second place, since the Scythians are represented as being friendly to Assyria, it is inconceivable that they should have attacked an Assyrian province. In the third place the passages in *Zephaniah* and *Jeremiah* which are supposed to refer to this invasion cannot really do so. There is nothing in them which *must* refer to the Scythians, and a good deal which *cannot* apply to them.

The first point may be dismissed; if there are other reasons for accepting the identification, it obviously falls to the ground. The second objection involves a complete misunderstanding of the nature of the Scythian invasions; they were not the formal expeditions of a highly organized empire, undertaken in the interests of an international policy, they were the plundering raids of a miscellaneous horde of savages—noble savages, perhaps, but still savages—who did not care who their victim was. The third difficulty is the most serious, but it disappears when we realize that, even if the interpretation placed on words, phrases, and sentences be correct (and, naturally, it sometimes looks like special pleading) we have no reason to suppose that the whole of the section in which the 'Scythian' oracles appear consists of oracles uttered at the same time. The prophet, as we suppose, had nothing to do with the present arrangement of the oracles; that is the work of a collector, probably living after his time, and he may well have set side by side pieces which originated at very different periods, induced to do so by a certain similarity which exists between them—or some of them.

must have made his help at times uncertain. In accordance with the usual custom, he had to return with his army every year after the campaign, and sometimes, it seems, arrived too late to be of real service. Early in 616 B.C. Nabopolassar marched northwards, and inflicted a severe defeat on the Assyrians at Kablini. But he was to be met throughout the war by a determined resistance, and the first signs of it appeared here. Kablini is on the upper Euphrates, not far from the river Balih, and it was not long before the advancing Egyptian army, stiffening the Assyrian forces, recovered the lost ground and compelled Nabopolassar to retreat. His next movement was up the valley of the Tigris, where he threw the Assyrian army back on the river Zab, not far from Ashur, the ancient capital of Assyria. But once more Nabopolassar failed to hold his ground, and the campaign of 615 B.C. brought him as little success, for after an initial victory he was compelled to retreat, and was actually besieged in the city of Tekrit. A successful sortie, however, drove off the enemy, and the Chaldaean king was able to return safely to Babylon. Early in 614 B.C. the Medes[1] also appeared in the field, and met with better success than Nabopolassar had done, for they captured Ashur while the Chaldaean army was hastening northward to join them. An alliance between Nabopolassar and Kyaxares, king of the Medes, was made when the Chaldaeans came up, outside the ruins of Ashur. In 613 B.C. Nabopolassar was kept busy by an outbreak in the south, but in the following year the allies marched on Nineveh itself. Kyaxares and Nabopolassar combined forces, and an assault was made on the city. The fighting before the walls was most desperate, and three fierce engagements took place before the defences could be stormed. But in the end the allies proved too strong, and Nineveh fell. The scene of its sack has been portrayed for us in one of the most powerful poems in ancient literature by the Hebrew poet Nahum.[2] An attempt was made under Ashur-uballit to

---

[1] On the evidence of Herodotus it was formerly supposed that the Scythians took part in the sack of Nineveh. This led to the identification of the Umman-manda of the Mesopotamian records with the Scythians. But Schnabel (*Zeitschrift für Assyriologie*, *N.F.*, [1924–5], xxxvi, 316–18) has given reasons for the rejection of this view, and has made it clear that in the 'Babylonian Chronicle' which records the fall of Ashur, Nineveh, and Harran, the term Umman-manda is applied to the Medes alone. Cp. also Langdon, *Die neubabylonischen Königsinschriften*, p. 3, n. 2 (1912).

[2] iii. 1–3. Our knowledge of the details of the last struggles of Assyria is derived

reorganize the empire at Harran, but this city too was captured by the combined armies of the Chaldaeans and the Medes in 610 B.C. An Egyptian force tried to recover the city, but failed, and, as far as we know, organized resistance ceased. So ended the empire of Assyria in a welter of blood and fire. She was probably no worse than other peoples of her day, but she had lived by the sword, and by the sword she died.

It is at this point that the 'Babylonian Chronicle' breaks off, and unless and until the remainder is discovered we shall lack direct contemporary evidence as to the events of the next few years. It may be that some effort was still made to preserve the Assyrian kingdom farther west, but of that we know nothing. We do know, however, that Necho did not abandon the struggle, and that year after year he led his armies northwards in order to meet the Chaldaeans. We cannot tell what success he had, nor do we know whether he felt there was still a chance of reviving the old Assyrian kingdom, or whether he was simply fighting for his own hand, in the hope of establishing such an empire as that of Tutmose III. Such a hope would probably have been vain in any case, for Egypt could no longer depend on her own man-power, and her armies were now composed very largely of Greek mercenaries. And any expectation of success that Necho may have cherished was finally dissipated by the fateful battle of Carchemish in 605 B.C. Here, on the banks of the Euphrates, he was utterly overthrown, and there perished the last chance Egypt ever had of claiming the hegemony of civilization. The date marks the end of an era in world history. Till this point there has always been the possibility of the recrudescence of Egypt, as the story of Necho himself shows. Now that possibility definitely vanishes. It is true that the Babylonian empire never made a serious attempt to include Egypt among its subject states, and that the country remained nominally independent till near the end of the sixth century, but its day was over, and from the time when Cambyses established the Persian government there, Egypt has seldom been able to claim autonomy, and has never, save in the period following Alexander, begun to approach the position of a world power.

Needless to say, these events had a profound influence on the kingdom of Judah. The storms of the Scythian raids passed,

from the continuation of the so-called 'Babylonian Chronicle', edited by Gadd in *The Fall of Nineveh*. See also Luckenbill, *ARA*. ii. 417–23, §§ 1167–86.

and the damage was soon repaired. But it was at once clear that Judah need no longer consider herself bound in subjection to Assyria. We have no evidence as to the point at which Josiah ceased to pay tribute to Assyria, but the probable break is the Scythian invasion. For a time the country must have been disorganized, and since no fresh demands came the king would feel a growing sense of security. And we may be certain that the bond between Judah and Assyria had been practically severed before 621 B.C., or the events of that year would have taken a very different course. At these we must now glance, since they constitute the main importance of the reign of Josiah.

The Temple had fallen into a state of disrepair. It is not likely that there was any neglect during the reigns of Manasseh and Amon, for these kings did not sin in failing to use the Temple, but in using it for the wrong purposes. Probably there had been lax oversight during the time of Josiah's minority, and the first few years after he reached man's estate had been occupied with repairing the damage wrought by the Scythian raids. But in 621 B.C. he was in a position to start renovating the building.[1] This in itself implied a growing interest on the king's part in religion. It is difficult to say how far he and his councillors were affected by the preaching of the eighth-century prophets, or by those who were contemporary with themselves. It seems unlikely that Jeremiah had made any impression on the court; he was still a minor prophet, living among the priests at their ancestral shrine of Anathoth. Judah was full of prophets, and one, yet as young as Jeremiah was, could hardly have been noticed, important as his message and his personality were to become in later years. But the tradition of the words of Isaiah may well have lingered in certain circles, and the young king may have had opportunity of coming into touch with those who cherished his oracles. It is certain that Josiah was in most respects a strong contrast to his grandfather, and, probably, to his father. He stands out among the kings of Judah for the simplicity of his spirit and for the geniality of his manners. When, after his death, Jeremiah uttered a panegyric on him in condemning his son Jehoiakim,[2] it was not his religious policy, curiously enough, that he eulogized, but his democratic feeling and his equitable administration. He was one whom his subjects could love, for he made them feel that he was one with

[1] 2 Kgs. xxii. 3–7.   [2] Jer. xxii. 15 f.

them. He had no desire to play the Sultan; it was David who was his model, not Solomon. Here he was fulfilling the ideals of the true Israel as they had been held of old from the wilderness days, and as they had been kept alive in prophetic circles. To him his subjects were brethren, not slaves. In this attitude and spirit we may, perhaps, find evidence of a devotion to the old tradition, which made him the more ready to accept demands which were certainly made in the interests of that tradition, though possibly none of the great canonical prophets would have endorsed them *in toto*.

During the process of the repairs a roll was found, purporting to be a copy of the Law. It was read before Josiah, and he realized at once how far he and his people had fallen from the ritual standards it enjoined. The book is normally identified with *Deuteronomy*, or with an early form of that work,[1] mainly on the ground that it is here for the first time that we meet with that centralization of sacrifice which is so conspicuous a feature of the reform, and it is clear that neither Josiah nor any of his predecessors (except, possibly, Hezekiah) had made any attempt to carry out the principles expressed in the book. Josiah sent at once to find out what the will of Yahweh was in the matter, and his messengers had recourse to a prophetess, Huldah, who was the wife of one of the palace officials. She reported that, while destruction was inevitable for Jerusalem as a whole, yet Josiah's penitence had earned him a personal respite, and the calamity should be postponed till after his death.[2]

Thereupon the king and the priesthood set about the task of carrying the injunctions of *Deuteronomy* into effect. The first step was to gather a general assembly of representatives of the whole nation, and to enter with them into a solemn covenant to observe the conditions laid down in the newly found law. The ritual was performed in ancient form, with the king standing by the royal pillar in the Temple, and the people by their action symbolizing their acceptance of the terms laid down.[3]

---

[1] See Additional Note F, pp. 425-6. [2] 2 Kgs. xxii. 14-20.

[3] Skinner (*1 and 2 Kings*, pp. 416 f.) suggests that this was not an agreement into which two parties entered, whether they were the king and the people or the king and Yahweh—since the covenant was made *before* Yahweh, not *with* Him. But surely the phrase וַיַּעֲמֹד כָּל־הָעָם בַּבְּרִית, whatever action it describes, implies the acceptance of the covenant by the people? Josiah knew well that he could not possibly carry through such radical changes as those contemplated in the Law unless he had the support of the people as a whole, and it was necessary for him to

He then proceeded to perform the duties laid down therein. His measures fall into two classes, (a) those which aimed at the purification of the Temple itself, (b) those which carried the principles of the reform into the country as a whole. The account which has been preserved for us of the first class of measures shows that the Temple had been the repository of all kinds of strange religious practices. It suggests a museum of curious and varied forms of cult, collected from all the countries with which Judah had come into contact. First we have mention of the Baal and the Asherah.[1] These are probably relics of the old Canaanite worship which had been set up in the Temple in or after the days of Solomon. The Asherah, indeed, seems in this story to have been, not simply the wooden post which might have been the symbol of any deity, even of Yahweh, but a figure of, or at least an object sacred to, a goddess bearing that name.[2] This latter may have been of Mesopotamian origin, or it may have been a form of Ashtoreth especially used in Palestine. Whatever the thing was, it seems to have been made of wood, and it was taken out and burnt in the valley of the Kidron, to the east of the city, and its ashes scattered on the 'graves of the common people'.[3] All vessels consecrated to the service of these objects were burnt, in so far as they could be burnt, and the narrator of the scene states that the ashes were carried to Bethel. Josiah then dealt with the cult of the heavenly bodies, an astral worship which had probably been introduced from Mesopotamia during the period of submission to Assyria.[4] Another form of cultus from the same source was one which involved sacramental fornication, including the homosexual rites which were found in some parts of the ancient east. The women of the Temple apparently had a special establishment, in which they were employed in weaving and preparing sacred garments.[5] Such an arrangement was to be found in Babylonian temples, where the women made sacramental vestures which would be sold to the worshippers for use in certain forms of ceremonial,[6] and it seems that this custom had been introduced into Judah also. One type of votive offering which had been made by his predecessors we cannot trace at all. This was the dedication of chariots

bind them to whole-hearted acceptance of the measures he was about to take before
he could make any attempt to impose them on Judah.   [1] 2 Kgs. xxiii. 4.
  [2] Cp. note on pp. 284 f.   [3] 2 Kgs. xxiii. 6.   [4] 2 Kgs. xxiii. 5.
  [5] 2 Kgs. xxiii. 7, reading כתנים or בדים with LXX for בתים.
  [6] Cp. Woolley in *Antiquaries' Journal*, v. 393 f.

and horses to the sun-god. It may have been taken from Mesopotamia, where the sun was worshipped under the name of
Shamash, or it may have been of Egyptian provenance, for Ra
was one of the great gods of Egypt, and that country was the
place to which Israel generally looked for its supplies of horses
and chariots. There seems to have been a special series of stables
to the west of the Temple assigned to this purpose.[1] All this
Josiah swept away, leaving nothing in the Temple area which
was not directly connected with the worship of Yahweh, and
that in a simple form, and breaking down all the superfluous
altars which various kings had erected, no matter to what deity
they had been consecrated.[2] There is no suggestion that these
additional places of sacrifice were used for offerings made to
other gods than Yahweh, though it is not impossible that this
was their function, but since the Law clearly prescribed only a
single altar of burnt offering, it may well be that even those
which had served the cult of Yahweh—as the new altar of
Ahaz had done—were felt to be inconsistent with the will of
the God of Israel.

Josiah then turned his attention to the city outside the Temple
and to its immediate environs. By one of the gates of the city,
which we can no longer identify, there stood a shrine consecrated to the demons of the wilderness, the 'satyrs', or 'goat-
spirits',[3] an ancient cult dating from the animistic stage in
religion, and finding, perhaps, a survival of some kind in the
legitimate cultus in the 'scapegoat',[4] a piece of primitive ceremonial which was absorbed into the much later ritual of the
Day of Atonement. On the Mount of Olives[5] stood sanctuaries,
attributed to Solomon, dedicated to various deities of Palestine
and the neighbourhood—Ashtoreth, Chemosh, Melek—and
these places were desecrated and rendered for ever unfit for
worship by being defiled with dead men's bones. In the valley
of Hinnom, to the south-east of Jerusalem, lay the fire-pits which
had been used for human sacrifice.[6] Here again Josiah took
measures which so defiled the place as to make it for ever unfit
for sacrifice of any kind,[7] and it became so notorious as a home

---

[1] 2 Kgs. xxiii. 11.   [2] 2 Kgs. xxiii. 12.
[3] 2 Kgs. xxiii. 8 *b*, reading הַשְּׂעִרִים for הַשְּׁעָרִים.   [4] Lev. xvi. 8 f.
[5] 2 Kgs. xxiii. 13, reading הַמִּשְׁחָה for הַמַּשְׁחִית, with Versions.
[6] This seems on the whole the most satisfactory meaning for the obscure תֹפֶת,
cp. Robertson Smith, *Religion of the Semites*, pp. 372, 377.   [7] 2 Kgs. xxiii. 10.

of terrors that its name, in the form 'Gehenna', was used by later Israelites as their title for Hell.

The king now proceeded to carry out the further provisions of the newly found law, and to establish its principles throughout all his territories.[1] This was a more difficult and dangerous task than the purification of Jerusalem and its environs, and it seems that it needed the co-operation of large numbers of people. It is very possible that we have some light on the process in Jer. xi,[2] a chapter which purports to give us an account of the prophet's call to promulgate the provisions of the 'Covenant' among the cities of Judah and in the streets of Jerusalem. We may well suppose that Josiah had to make use of a number of missionaries of the new law, whose business it would be, not only to carry out the destruction of the local sanctuaries, but, still more, to explain to the people in general the reasons why this change was being made. One of the sanctuaries in particular is mentioned as the scene of the king's own activities. That is the ancient shrine of Bethel,[3] which had been, ever since the days of Jeroboam I, the great rival of Jerusalem. Either Bethel was included in the recognized dominions of Josiah, or the Assyrian province had practically disappeared. We may be sure that the king had the hearty sympathy of the Jerusalem priesthood in all these operations, for they would realize at once that their prestige was being immeasurably enhanced by the centralization of worship at the shrine with which they were connected. A distinction was made between two classes of the attendants on the local sanctuaries. Some of them seem to have been more deeply tainted with 'false' worship than others; they are called '$k^e marim$', not '$koh^a nim$' (the ordinary Hebrew term for priests), and were simply suppressed, being left, apparently, without means of sustenance except what they might obtain from land which some of them almost certainly held. Others, admitted to be in a sense legitimate priests of the high places, were brought up to Jerusalem, in accordance with the Deuteronomic regulation which provided for their sustenance in the Temple there.[4] But either the Jerusalem priests made a successful fight against sharing their privileges with these

---

[1] 2 Kgs. xxiii. 8. [2] See Additional Note G, pp. 427–8.
[3] The narrative in 2 Kgs. xxiii. 15–20 is very generally recognized as a late insertion, and is not to be regarded as an account of historical facts.
[4] Deut. xviii. 6–8.

new-comers, or it became clear that they were too numerous
to be supported on the Jerusalem offerings, for it is expressly
stated that they did not come up to the altar, though they ate
unleavened bread among their brethren.[1] This seems to imply
that they were allowed a share in the meal offerings, but not in
those which involved sacrifice upon the altar. Ezekiel probably
represents the feeling of the Jerusalem priesthood, and, in his
ideal reconstruction of the Jewish state, takes an extreme Deuteronomic view. He insists that all these were apostates, who,
as a punishment for their having been linked up with the local
altars, must henceforward perform the menial duties of the
Temple,[2] while the Jerusalem priests, members of the family of
Zadok, who had been faithful to the theory of the one altar,
should exercise the functions of the priesthood proper. It must
be remembered that in pre-exilic days the menial duties fell to
royal slaves, often of foreign blood, and Ezekiel would have none
of these about his Temple, so that it was at least convenient to
have at his disposal a group of men who could take their place.
The economic difficulties under the arrangement contemplated
in *Deuteronomy* would probably have been insuperable, even
had the priests been willing to share their perquisites. A large
part of the priests' living must have come in the old days from
the communion sacrifices, whether at Jerusalem or at other
sanctuaries. *Deuteronomy*,[3] recognizing the fact that the Temple
might well be too far away for those who wished to eat
beef or mutton, secularized the flesh of the domestic animals,
and made it possible for it to be eaten in any circumstances.
This regulation, however necessary, must have gone far to
eliminate the communion sacrifice from the regular life of the
ordinary Israelite, and to confine it to special occasions or forms
of ritual, when it was necessary for him to be in attendance at
the Temple. The result must have been a considerable reduction in the amount of sustenance available for the priesthood as
a whole, and have brought on many distress which *Deuteronomy*
had vainly tried to avoid.

The culmination of the whole movement was a great celebration of the Passover, the oldest festival in Israel, and one which
had probably been observed by its nomad ancestors from their
earliest days.[4] It is clear that in its most primitive forms it
was essentially a domestic ceremonial, as is indicated in our

---

[1] 2 Kgs. xxiii. 9.   [2] Ez. xliv. 9–14.   [3] xii. 20 ff.   [4] 2 Kgs. xxiii. 21–3.

oldest descriptions,[1] and we may conjecture (though direct evidence is entirely lacking) that since Israel had been settled in Palestine, the observance had been a compromise between the ancient nomad household festival and an official sacrifice. Probably the victim had to be killed in the precincts of a sanctuary, and its blood, or part of it, dashed upon the altar, while the flesh might be eaten either in the sacred place or at the worshipper's own home. Josiah's centralization of the festival, in pursuance of the regulation in Deut. xvi. 2, shows that it was not merely domestic, and that its proper observance necessarily involved the presence of an altar for some part of the rite. It is possible, though improbable, that it had not been observed at all since the wilderness days, its place being taken by the purely agricultural festival of the unleavened bread, which fell at the same time of year, and was ultimately combined with it. We hear of no later celebration of the same kind, and it may well be that the attempt to gather all the population of Judah into the Temple at Jerusalem proved so impracticable that it had to be abandoned in after years, and some other compromise reached.[2]

As in the case of Hezekiah, we shall probably do Josiah no injustice if we recognize that this widespread reform had a political aspect. It is true that there was no longer any possibility of the interference of Assyria, but Josiah might have been very reluctant to carry out the provisions of *Deuteronomy* if Assyria had still been in a position to take vengeance on him. His action, whatever else it may have meant to the political world of his day, was certainly a gesture of independence, and it was so far successful that no untoward consequences followed immediately, and he retained his throne for thirteen years longer. But he had clearly proclaimed, especially by his treatment of Bethel, to his own people and to all others whom it might concern, that henceforward Judah stood alone, and owed allegiance to no foreign power. The only king who was now in a position to accept this general challenge was Necho, king of Egypt, and he was too busy, at least from 616 B.C. onwards, endeavouring to save the last remnants of the Assyrian kingdom, to give time

---

[1] Ex. xii. 21–8, E.

[2] For a history of the Passover see Gray, *Sacrifice in the Old Testament*, pp. 337–97. Unfortunately Dr. Gray's lecture on the regulations found in J, E, and D has not survived, or we should doubtless have had a valuable discussion of Josiah's celebration.

and thought to the affairs of Judah. But in 608 B.C. the two met at Megiddo. To judge from the account in the book of _Kings_[1] Josiah was not expecting or intending to fight, and may simply have gone at Necho's summons. Possibly the Egyptian king may have found reason to distrust the neutrality of Judah, and to suspect Josiah of having revived the pro-Babylonian policy of Hezekiah. Whatever the reason, and whatever the circumstances, Josiah lost his life, and his body was brought back to Jerusalem, the popular vote placing his second son Jehoahaz on the throne.[2]

[1] 2 Kgs. xxiii. 29.

[2] In 2 Chron. xxxv. 20–5 we have a circumstantial account of the events which led up to Josiah's death. It is there stated that he deliberately challenged Necho, who would have avoided hostilities, and that a pitched battle was fought in which Josiah was wounded by the Egyptian archers, and taken living to Jerusalem, where he died. Until recently the amount of corroborative detail in this narrative has led practically all students to accept it as historical. Doubts, however, have arisen during the last few years, and there is a growing feeling that the story is not to be trusted. Professor R. H. Kennett was the first to call the present writer's attention to the situation, as long ago as 1916, in conversation, and the position he adopted has since been propounded, quite independently, by Professor A. C. Welch (cp. _ZAW._, 1925 (xliii), pp. 255 ff.). The account given in _Kings_ (xxiii. 29) is quite inconsistent with an armed expedition and a pitched battle; no Hebrew writer ever described such events in language like וַיֵּלֶךְ הַמֶּלֶךְ יֹאשִׁיָּהוּ לִקְרָאתוֹ וַיְמִיתֵהוּ בִמְגִדּוֹ בִּרְאֹתוֹ אֹתוֹ. The Chronicler makes one historical error which must be obvious to every reader when he places the death of Josiah in the campaign which led to the battle of Carchemish (almost certainly the interpretation of 2 Chron. xxxv. 20), and is clearly not writing with a contemporary record before him. We may suppose that tradition spoke of a battle which Necho had to fight in 608 B.C., and in which he was victorious, which the Chronicler connected with the death of Josiah, then adding such details as he thought most probable. Such a battle is mentioned by Herodotus (ii. 159), but he places it at 'Magdolos', in the neighbourhood of a 'Kadytis', i.e. at a 'Migdol' near 'Kadesh'. Commentators have assumed that this was an error for Megiddo on the part of the Greek historian, or have suggested altering the Hebrew text to conform with the Greek tradition. But it is much more likely that the battle to which Herodotus alludes was fought in the neighbourhood of Kadesh on the Orontes since Herodotus regards 'Kadytis' as one of the principal cities of Syria, though both Migdol and Kadesh are such common names that certainty is impossible. Necho's enemies, Herodotus' 'Syrians', may have been a force in the service of the Babylonian king.

The internal organization of Judah in the time of Josiah has been brilliantly discussed by Noth, _Das Buch Josua_ (1938), pp. 58 ff.; see especially the map on p. 67.

Additional Note F

JOSIAH'S LAW-BOOK

THE position assumed on pp. 418 ff. has been almost universally accepted until the last few years. Objections have, however, been raised from two points of view, and there is one small group of scholars who would place *Deuteronomy* later than this time, and another that would date it earlier. This is no place to argue the point, but it is inevitable that the chief considerations of each group should be mentioned. Kennett believes that the obvious dependence of *Deuteronomy* on E rather than on J can best be explained by assuming that it is the product of a union between the priests of Bethel and those of Jerusalem, or rather of an occupation of the Temple site at Jerusalem by Bethel priests, such as could hardly have taken place except during the Exile. Hölscher finds that many of its provisions are unpractical, and that no sensible person could have suggested carrying them into effect as long as Judean territory was as extensive as it remained during the monarchy. It must, therefore, be the work of a group of unpractical idealists, unless it is to be carried down to the post-exilic period, when the territory of Judah was confined to a very small district in the immediate neighbourhood of Jerusalem. It was probably the law promulgated by Ezra. In support of his view Hölscher is compelled to deny the historicity of the greater part, if not the whole, of the narrative in 2 Kgs. xxii. f., and to make radical excisions from the books of *Jeremiah* and *Ezekiel*. In the former case he has the support both of Duhm and of Mowinckel, but in his drastic surgery of *Ezekiel* he stands, up to the present, practically alone, except for the support of Torrey. In other respects the theories of both these scholars raise far more difficulties than they solve, and the problems which have led them to their conclusions have been faced, and to some extent met, by every serious student of the question. In particular, attention may be called to the fact that in several ways *Deuteronomy* is conscious of the difficulties which its provision will present to pious Jews living at a distance from Jerusalem, though possibly the solutions offered for those difficulties may not always have been the most practicable. In one notable instance, that of the Passover, it was certainly found impossible to carry out in detail the injunctions of *Deuteronomy*, and a compromise had to be reached between the new law and the older practice.

Oesterreicher and Welch, on the other hand, believe that *Deuteronomy* is much older than the time of Josiah. Welch, in particular, concurs in much of the criticism which Hölscher passes on the book as a piece of practical legislation. But he reaches a very different conclusion, and holds that *Deuteronomy* does not really enjoin the centralization

of worship, or rather of sacrifice, at a single altar. The one passage
(xii. 1–7) where he finds that no other interpretation is possible he
relegates to a later period, and the earlier prescription he interprets
in a novel fashion, insisting that the phrase בַּמָּקוֹם אֲשֶׁר יִבְחַר יְהֹוָה בְּאַחַד
שְׁבָטֶיךָ (Deut. xii. 14) may imply a number of different sanctuaries,
not necessarily one alone. Since the outstanding feature of the reform of Josiah is the centralization of worship, *Deuteronomy* cannot
be the book on which that reform is based. It is enough to say here
that Welch's treatment of Deut. xii. 14 is unconvincing. Moreover,
in spite of his skilfully argued position (see *The Code of Deuteronomy*),
there is much else in the book, e.g. the secularization of the flesh
of the domestic animals, the appointment of cities of refuge, the
arrangements for the payment of tithes, which suggests an attempt
to adapt the life of Israel to new conditions in which many of them
would find that there was no sanctuary within easy reach. The
traditional view is therefore assumed in the present discussion, and
the origin of the book is assigned to prophetic circles working during
the seventh century.

427

Additional Note G

JEREMIAH xi. 1–14

THE originality of Jer. xi. 1–14 has been keenly disputed by some of the most eminent of modern scholars, especially by Duhm, Hölscher, Kennett, and Mowinckel. It raises two distinct questions, one of which is purely critical, while the other is more strictly a matter of history and religion. It is claimed, especially by Duhm and Mowinckel, that this and similar passages are the work of later scribes, writing under the influence of *Deuteronomy*, and seeking to claim for the doctrines of their school the high authority and support of Jeremiah. It is pointed out that the language of the passage is strongly Deuteronomic, both in vocabulary and in style, and it is claimed that this could not have been written by Jeremiah. Duhm, in particular, confines the genuine work of Jeremiah to a limited number of poetic passages in which he can find (sometimes with rather violent treatment of the text, as in Jer. iv. 23–6) a regular 3 : 2 metre. This is, of course, purely a personal assumption, which no other scholar has yet accepted, but the other aspects of the matter have stronger claims to attention. There can be no doubt that the whole tone and character of the passage are Deuteronomic. Yet there are one or two points in which we find hints of another influence, e.g. the word שֶׁרִ (verse 9) is not found in *Deuteronomy* at all, and the metaphor as a description of apostasy is very rare. And in general it may be pointed out that the presence of Deuteronomic style is entirely consistent with the theory which the passage itself suggests. If the young prophet—and the reform occurred five years only after his call—really threw himself heart and soul into the new movement, it is but natural that his thoughts should be clothed in the language of the document on which the reform was based. Further, in this style, peculiar as it is, we should probably see nothing but the ordinary rhetoric of the latter part of the seventh century. A sounder criticism recognizes that this passage is to be linked up with a number of others, e.g. with iii. 6–18, vii. 1—viii. 3, &c., in which the prophet speaks in prose and in the first person. There is direct evidence to show that where we know that a prophet himself reduced his oracles to writing they took the form of prose, and in one interesting instance we have the same oracle first in its original poetic form and then in the prose redaction (Jer. xxii. 10–12). The classification of the material is well recognized by Mowinckel (*Zur Komposition des Buches Jeremia*, 1914), but there is no reason why we should follow him in assigning all passages of this (his 'C') class to a later age, since comparison with similar phenomena in other prophetic books leads to the suggestion that these are the work of the prophet himself, who was attempting to preserve his words for future generations. See especially T. H. Robinson, *Baruch's Roll*, in *ZAW.*, 1924 (xlii), pp. 209 ff.

It is felt on the other hand that Jeremiah could have had no sympathy with *Deuteronomy*, since it permitted the continuance of sacrifice, an institution to which he was bitterly opposed. Attention is also called to the fact that not he but Huldah was consulted when the book was found. Finally—so this school holds—his reference in viii. 8 makes it clear that he regarded the whole book as a forgery, deliberately executed by the Jerusalem priestly scribes.

None of these points—nor all of them taken together—need be decisive. While Jeremiah did not believe that sacrifice was of Mosaic origin, he may have been prepared to accept it if properly regulated so as to guard against its worst evils. He was still young, and may well have failed to realize all the implications of the new régime. Even admitting that viii. 8 is a condemnation of *Deuteronomy* itself (and it may simply imply tampering with the Law on the part of the priests or their scribes), we have no ground for believing that the words were uttered in 621 B.C. They may have come twenty or thirty years later, when it was obvious that the Law had failed to produce the results which the young prophet had hoped and expected, and it may have been just this experience which led him to the conclusion that a written law was futile, and that it must be superseded by one written on the heart (xxxi. 31–4—the man who wrote this has surely at one time accepted the validity of a code?). Further, we may add that the theory of Jeremiah's acceptance of *Deuteronomy* offers a better explanation than any other of the hostility of his own family (xi. 18–23, xii. 6). They were priests of the local sanctuary at Anathoth, and the effect of the reform was to deprive them at once of their prestige and of one source of their livelihood. They would naturally be incensed against him if he was an advocate of the new order. The reference of the court officials to Huldah is intelligible, indeed inevitable in the circumstances; how should they have heard of Jeremiah? Or how should they have regarded this obscure village prophet as the one to whom alone they should repair? On the whole, then, it seems that we are not justified in discarding the historicity of Jer. xi. 1–14 *in toto*, and a substantial basis of accuracy has been assumed above. For an adequate statement of the position see Peake, *Jeremiah*, i, pp. 11–14 (1910), and Skinner, *Prophecy and Religion*, pp. 97–107 (1922).

Chapter XXI
THE FALL OF JERUSALEM

SUMMARY

[On his return from Mesopotamia in 608 B.C., Necho deposed Jehoahaz and placed his elder brother Jehoiakim on the throne. It seems that he entered into no covenant, for his methods of government recall those of Solomon. After Carchemish he seems to have transferred his allegiance to Babylon, but in 597 B.C. he revolted. Before Nebuchadrezzar could reach Jerusalem he died, and his son Jehoiachin surrendered and was taken to Babylon after a reign of three months. With him were deported many of the nobles and best craftsmen in Judah.

A younger son of Josiah, Zedekiah, was placed on the throne. A weak man, he was unable to assert himself against the pro-Egyptian tendencies of the new nobility. A movement of unrest in 592 B.C. came to nothing, but in 588 B.C. Zedekiah revolted and Jerusalem was besieged.

Much of our information as to this siege comes from the biographer of Jeremiah, who was mainly interested in the fortunes of his hero. But we learn that the advance of an Egyptian army compelled the Chaldaeans to raise the siege for a time. They were soon outside the walls once more, and in 586 B.C. the city was stormed and destroyed. Zedekiah was captured, blinded, and taken to Babylon.

A remnant was left at Mizpah under the government of Gedaliah. But he was murdered by Ishmael, and, in fear of Chaldaean vengeance, Johanan took the last survivors down to Egypt.

So ends the history of Israel as an independent state. But she left behind her a threefold legacy for the world. One was her democratic conception of monarchy, a theory that the king had responsibilities as well as rights, duties as well as privileges. The second was a great literature. The other was her religion. This, in its unique form, was still in its early stages, and it was, in a sense, only after she had ceased to be an independent nation that Israel made her supreme contribution to human welfare.]

For our knowledge of the history of the last twenty-five years of the kingdom of Judah we are dependent wholly on Biblical sources. We have, naturally, no records from Egypt, for with the defeat of Necho at Carchemish Egypt passes into the final cloud. The fragment of the 'Babylonian Chronicle', which has given us such valuable information regarding the fall of Nineveh and the extinction of the kingdom of Assyria, breaks off after the year 610 B.C., and though we may still hope for a more complete text, which shall correct many errors, it has not yet appeared. Nebuchadrezzar, great conqueror as he was, has left us little but building inscriptions, though, again, at any time an historical account of his reign may be discovered. At present it seems as if he had been far more interested in the pious task of restoring the temples of the gods than in making himself king of the whole eastern world, though he did undoubtedly achieve that position. Our Hebrew records, however, offer us a wealth of information, for we have not only the actual historical documents comprised in 2 Kgs. xxiii–xxv, but also a number of passages in the book of *Jeremiah* which relate to the events of the period. These are generally recognized as the work of a contemporary hand, and it is usual to assign them to Baruch, the scribe employed by Jeremiah, who faithfully followed his master's fortunes till the end. They reveal, not only an enthusiasm for their hero, but also an intimate acquaintance with the historical events which were taking place about him, at least after the date of the battle of Carchemish. Here is a source of first-hand importance, and it gives us both details and a general picture of the state of Jerusalem, especially during the days of the last siege, which is of the highest value to the historian.

THE Deuteronomic historian condemns Jehoahaz[1] as having done evil in the sight of Yahweh, in other words, as having failed to continue the policy of the reform inaugurated by his father. The writer lived near enough to the times of which he speaks to have had accurate information as to the general trend of the king's policy, but Jehoahaz himself had little opportunity of showing what his intentions were. Pharaoh Necho's campaign on the Euphrates was not a long one,[2] and in three months he was back in Syria. On the outward march he had not stayed to organize the affairs of Judah, for he had more important work in hand, but now, with the winter approaching, he was near enough to his own home to spare some time. Apparently, even if Jehoahaz was not prepared to carry out his father's ecclesiastical policy, he was one with him in politics, and Necho sent for him to Riblah near Hamath, threw him into chains,

---

[1] Cp. 2 Kgs. xxiii. 31 ff.

[2] His inroads into Mesopotamia generally seem to have been brief. Of the two mentioned in the 'Babylonian Chronicle', that of 616 B.C. is dated in the month of Tashritu (Hebrew Tishri: September–October), and Necho does not seem to have been present at the battle which took place in the following Adaru (Hebrew Adar: February–March). In the attempt to recover Harran, made shortly after its capture by the Chaldaeans and the Medes in 612 B.C., the Egyptian king is said to have been before the city from Duzu (Hebrew Tammuz: June–July) to Ululu (Hebrew Elul: August–September), and from these data we may guess that his campaigns were undertaken only in the summer months, and in the late summer rather than in the spring.

and took him down to Egypt, where he died. It does not seem that there was an extensive deportation, though Necho exacted large booty from the country, and laid it under an annual tribute.[1] In place of Jehoahaz, Necho enthroned his elder brother, whose name was Eliakim.[2] Perhaps as a concession to Israelite feeling, he changed his name to Jehoiakim, substituting for the more general divine term in his name that of the national God. From the first, therefore, the new king was a vassal of Egypt, and he represented an Egyptian policy throughout. He formed a strong contrast to his father in almost every way, except that both seem to have been men of strong character and of determination. The circumstances of his accession placed him in a peculiar position, for he was the first of the kings of Judah of whom we know that he was appointed as the nominee of a foreign overlord. It seems clear, too, that his appointment, being made by force of arms, did not necessitate any kind of royal covenant with the people, and left him free to play the tyrant as he would. The constitutional monarchy, so dear to the Israelite heart, had broken down, and in Jehoiakim Judah had a king who was prepared to take full advantage of his position.

That he was a strong man, almost a reckless one, is beyond doubt. He is typical of the bold but wicked ruler who neither fears God nor regards man. Of him alone among the kings of Israel or Judah is it recorded that he actually put to death an accredited prophet of Yahweh.[3] He was ambitious in his own way, but lacked the resources and the foresight necessary to carry out his own plans. In his dealings with his subjects he was tyrannous in the extreme, and made free use of their forced labour for his building enterprises. He sought to erect magnificent edifices, and to adorn them with costly materials, at the expense of his unfortunate brethren. Justice meant nothing to him, and no man dared oppose him to his face. If his father was the David of the last years of Judah, Jehoiakim aimed at being their Solomon.[4]

[1] There are elegies on Jehoahaz, both in Ez. xix. 2–4 and in Jer. xxii. 10–12, the latter very short, consisting of a few lines of poetry followed by a prose version.
[2] 2 Kgs. xxiii. 36 ff.
[3] Jer. xxvi. 20–3. The slaughter of the prophets in the reign of Ahab may be attributed to Jezebel rather than to her husband, and the murder of Zechariah (2 Chron. xxiv. 21) is hardly well enough attested.
[4] For a powerful picture of Jehoiakim as he really was, and for the contrast with Josiah, see Jer. xxii. 13–19.

We may here pause to dwell for a moment on the greatest
character of this period of Judah's history, and one of the noblest
ever produced by Israel. This was the prophet Jeremiah, who,
though he had probably been inspired to prophetic utterance
nearly twenty years before Jehoiakim came to the throne, and
seems to have taken an active part in the Deuteronomic reform,
now for the first time took his place as the champion of the
genuine Israelite thought and feeling against the royal theory
and policy. Born somewhere about 640 B.C. in the village of
Anathoth, a few miles to the north-east of Jerusalem, he belonged
to a priestly family, probably the attendants at the local shrine
who claimed descent from Abiathar.[1] His activities in and immediately after 621 B.C. caused a breach with his own family,
and plots were laid against his life. Either then or at some earlier
time, he seems to have taken up his residence in Jerusalem, and
he is without doubt the outstanding personality of the last days
of the kingdom of Judah. The message which he had to deliver
was unpopular, and he found few friends. His temperament
was retiring, quiet, and shy; all his ambitions would have been
satisfied if he had been able to live on his ancestral land,
surrounded by wife and children in a peaceful and happy home.
But these things were denied him by the nature of his work, and
he had to live a life of storm, conflict, and distress, a 'man of
strife' to all about him. It is true that the few friends he had—
men like the family of Shaphan and his secretary, Baruch—clung
to him faithfully throughout his life, but most of those with
whom he had to deal showed him only hostility. Yet he was
never turned from his mission, either by the fury of the mob or
the tyranny of the king; in the face of man he never flinched.
It was, however, otherwise in his dealings with his God. The
conditions of his ministry, with its forty years of unfulfilled prediction, made him suspect, both to others and to himself, and
the records of the human spirit contain few pictures of more
poignant agony than Jeremiah's record of his struggles with
Yahweh. It is this, even more than the outward persecution he
endured, which has given him his unique position in history.[2]

It is quite clear that the new king at once reversed the religious

---

[1] See p. 245.

[2] Jeremiah has been more fully studied in recent years than any other Old Testament character. For the best among many accounts of him, the reader is referred
to Skinner, *Prophecy and Religion*.

policy of his father. In Jer. vii and xxvi we have an account of
an utterance delivered by the prophet at the beginning of his
reign, which speaks definitely of the revival of the worship of
the 'Queen of Heaven', i.e. probably Ashtoreth.[1] Ch. vii is the
prophet's own record of the event, and ch. xxvi that of his
biographer, usually identified with Baruch. The sin of Judah is
denounced, and it is foretold that the fate of Shiloh will fall also
on Jerusalem. The message aroused keen hostility on the part
of the religious leaders, the priests and the professional prophets,
and Jeremiah was saved only by the intervention of the lay
nobles, who appealed to the precedent of Micah. The matter
does not seem to have come immediately before the king, though
he heard of a companion of Jeremiah's, Urijah by name, who
had delivered a similar message. Urijah fled to Egypt, but was
handed over to Jehoiakim by the authorities and put to death.
Jeremiah escaped, largely through the protection of Ahikam,
the son of Shaphan. Here for the first time we are introduced
to a member of this family. It clearly stood high in court circles,
and produced more than one man of fine character. Its members are seen from time to time on the stage of Jewish history
during these last years, and we always receive a favourable
impression of them. Jeremiah owed much to them, and found
in them a sympathy which was too rarely accorded to him in
other quarters. There may have been others also who shared
their position, and it is clear that there was a party in Jerusalem
which, though it could seldom carry out its policy, was yet
antagonistic to the Egyptian alliance and all that it involved.

We hear of no outstanding event until 605 B.C., when the
utter defeat of Necho by Nebuchadrezzar at Carchemish put
an end to his hopes of world dominion, and made even his
position in Palestine insecure. Jeremiah, and possibly others,
realized the significance of the battle, and knew that the old
orientation of politics had come to an end. His oracles on the
overthrow of Necho are among the most striking of his utterances,[2] and give us a most vivid picture of the splendour of the
Egyptian army and of the completeness of its panic and defeat.
The prophet went further, and took a step in which he had

---

[1] Or Anath? Cp. p. 173, n. 1.

[2] Jer. xlvi. 3–6, 7–9, 10–12. The present writer cannot agree with the more
drastic critics, e.g. Duhm, who deny the Jeremianic authorship of *all* the 'foreign'
oracles in chs. xlvi–li. These three, perhaps, more than any others, must be Jeremiah's, if style is any test of authorship.

perhaps been anticipated by Isaiah. He summoned to his help
a professional writer, and dictated to him the oracles which he
had delivered during his earlier years,[1] and then had the volume
read in public on a festal day when Jerusalem and the Temple
were thronged with people.[2] Baruch read the roll in the 'chamber of Gemariah, the son of Shaphan', evidently knowing that
Jeremiah's words would win a certain sympathy from a member
of that family. Micaiah, the son of Gemariah, heard what was
said, and felt that he must report the matter. Accordingly he
went down to the palace, where he found a group of nobles,
including his father, and told them what he had heard. They
sent for Baruch and the book, and made him read it to them,
examining him carefully as to the means whereby it had been
produced. They decided that the matter must be referred to
the king, and they took the book from Baruch, giving him the
friendly advice to keep himself and the prophet well hidden.
Jehoiakim was sitting in his winter palace, with a fire burning
in a brazier beside him, and, as the book was read, he slashed at
it with his knife, cutting off every few leaves and throwing them
into the fire, in spite of the protests of Gemariah and others. He
felt that all this prophetic movement was nonsense, and that his
throne was as secure as ever, but the only result of his action was
that the roll was re-written, and that the new form was larger
than the old. Probably Jeremiah and Baruch kept it with them,
and fresh prophecies were added.[3]

A maintenance of the old policy, however, was impossible,
and it soon became abundantly clear that the power had passed
from Egypt to Babylon. Nabopolassar died shortly after the
battle of Carchemish, and it seems that Nebuchadrezzar had to
spend two or three years settling affairs in Mesopotamia and the
neighbouring countries. But in or about the year 601 B.C.[4] the
Chaldaean armies were in Palestine, and reduced the country as
far as the Egyptian frontier. Jehoiakim transferred his allegiance
without delay to the new authority, and for three years accepted

---

[1] Isaiah's use of this method of preserving his words is mentioned in Isa. xxx. 8,
but this probably refers only to the oracles contained in chs. xxviii–xxx, perhaps
only to the name at the end of verse 7.

[2] The story is told in Jer. xxxvi.

[3] Many attempts have been made to define the contents of this book, most of
them assuming that it contained the earlier oracles in the form in which we have
them. This, however, in view of other facts seems unlikely. See T. H. Robinson,
Baruch's Roll, in *ZAW.*, 1924 (xlii), pp. 209 ff.　　　　[4] Cp. 2 Kgs. xxiv. 1.

Babylonian domination. But in 598 B.C. or 597 B.C. he withheld tribute, possibly owing to Egyptian intrigues. Necho must have known that he had no hope of recovering his empire, and that there was a very real danger lest his own country should be invaded by the Chaldaeans. It probably seemed to him that he would be safest if he could see one or two independent kingdoms between himself and Babylonia, and that even if he could not achieve this end, he would at least give Nebuchadrezzar some trouble. For some reason or other, the Babylonian king was unable to make an immediate expedition to the west, but stirred up raiding bands from the neighbouring tribes.[1] Before his armies could be set in motion, Jehoiakim died. Though one of the worst and most tyrannous of the kings of Judah, he was yet the only one of the last six to meet with a comparatively peaceful end. Amon had been assassinated by his own people, Josiah had met a violent end at Megiddo, Jehoahaz died a prisoner in Egypt, Jehoiachin was carried in chains to Babylon, and the punishment of Zedekiah was, perhaps, to be the most terrible of all. Here we have unmistakable evidence of the collapse of the kingdom of Judah, whose final dissolution was now not long delayed.

Jehoiakim was succeeded by his son Jehoiachin,[2] a lad of eighteen. He is said to have done evil, but he had little opportunity to show what his real policy would have been. Hardly had he taken his seat on the throne when the Chaldaean army appeared under the walls of Jerusalem, and when Nebuchadrezzar joined his forces, Jehoiachin surrendered at discretion. He was carried to Babylon, and with him were taken many of the best people in the land. The Temple was despoiled and other treasure was carried off,[3] though it is clear that the city as a whole was allowed to remain, and that Nebuchadrezzar had no desire to see it utterly destroyed.

Nebuchadrezzar's measures at Jerusalem in 597-596 B.C. display less than his usual political wisdom. The success of his policy required a strong government which should be devoted

[1] 2 Kgs. xxiv. 2. [2] 2 Kgs. xxiv. 8 ff.
[3] 2 Kgs. xxiv. 13-14 and 15-16 seem to be alternative accounts of the deportation. The former of the two represents the spoliation as being complete, which it clearly was not, and it has been plausibly suggested that it is really an account of events which took place in 586 B.C., and has been misplaced by the compiler. See Skinner, *1 and 2 Kings*, p. 430; Stade, *ZAW.*, 1884, pp. 271 ff. Benzinger (*Die Bücher der Könige*, p. 197) regards the passage as a simple gloss.

to the Babylonian cause, and should have enough stability and insight to stand firmly against the wiles of the Egyptian court. Nothing was to be gained by reducing the country to abject poverty, and he would have done well to leave behind many of the artisan class whom he actually removed. But his worst mistake was in his treatment of the nobles. He placed a younger son of Josiah on the throne, changing his name from Mattaniah to Zedekiah,[1] and, since the old nobility had been largely removed, there stood about the king a court with no stable traditions and with little experience of statecraft. One or two of the old families remained—that of Shaphan has several representatives during this period—and these probably formed an anti-Egyptian party; such influence as they had might be expected to weigh on the side of loyalty to Babylon. But they were not numerous enough or strong enough to control public affairs, and the national policy—if it can be called a policy—was mainly in the hands of the new nobility. We have from time to time illustrations of the stupidity of these people and of the futility of their plans. With no traditions behind them, swayed by the appeal of the moment, exposed to the lowest ideals and the meanest motives, they lacked both firmness and consistency of purpose. In ch. xxiv Jeremiah tells us what impression they made on him. At the gate of the Temple he saw one day two baskets of figs, one of good, rich fruit, the other so rotten as to be utterly unfit for food. As the prophet gazed on them, with that fixed intent which sometimes came upon him, the Divine Hand mastered him, and he heard the Voice telling him that here was a picture of the contrast between the exiles on the one hand and those who had remained in the country on the other. That is the opinion of the most clear-sighted man of his day, and from that time onwards Jeremiah tended more and more to find the ultimate hope of Israel in the exiles.

Zedekiah, too, was a bad choice. He was not a wicked man, and proved in every way a strong contrast to his elder brother. He seems to have had sound human instincts, and to have possessed more than a trace of true religious feeling. In his dealings with Jeremiah he showed himself always inclined to the side of the prophet against his persecutors, and he respected him and would have liked to rely on him, recognizing the ultimate soundness of his advice. We hear no complaints of oppression

---

[1] 2 Kgs. xxiv. 17 ff.

or of unjust dealings, and that selection of the oracles and dirges
on the kings which we find in the book of *Jeremiah*[1] has no word
of condemnation for Zedekiah, though the prophet bitterly
denounced the men who thronged his court and directed his
actions. But if Zedekiah was no Jehoiakim, he was no Josiah
either. He was essentially a weak man, unable to exercise the
slightest control over his reckless and turbulent nobles. Few
sentences in our Old Testament carry a deeper pathos than
Zedekiah's reply to the princes who demanded that Jeremiah
should be put out of the way: 'the king is not he that can do
anything against you'.[2] He lacked the moral courage to resist,
and perhaps feared (with some reason) that if he tried to assert
himself against the unscrupulous courtiers by whom he was
surrounded, he would meet with the fate of his grandfather. In
happier and more tranquil days he might have proved a mild
and beneficent ruler, but he was utterly unfit to battle with the
storms which raged about Jerusalem at the beginning of the
sixth century.

Within the state there were two parties, the one favouring
Egypt and the other pro-Babylonian. To the former belonged,
as it seems, the greater number of the new nobility, and to the
latter men like Jeremiah, the family of Shaphan and, perhaps,
the king himself—could he but have been king in reality and not
in name alone. The intrigues of the former class were incessant;
Egypt was very near, and Babylon was far away, and it was
natural for such people to look no further than a limited horizon.
It may well be that the death of Necho and the accession of
Psammetichus II in 593 B.C. seemed to the dominant party in
Jerusalem an opportunity for a fresh movement. It may be true
that Psammetichus himself had no desire to resume the task in
which Necho had failed,[3] but it is clear that the appearance of a
new and vigorous king aroused the hopes of all who resented the
Babylonian authority. Unrest made itself manifest in Edom,
Moab, Ammon, and Phoenicia,[4] and an attempt was made to

---

[1] xxii. 10–xxiii. 6.   [2] Jer. xxxviii. 5.   [3] So Breasted, *HE.*, p. 585.
[4] Jer. xxvii. 3. In verse 1 the reading צִדְקִיָּהוּ for יְהוֹיָקִם should certainly be
adopted, and the term בְּרֵאשִׁית מַמְלֶכֶת must be broadly interpreted. It
is inconceivable that a revolt should have broken out immediately after the
appearance of Chaldaean armies in Palestine, and we must regard the date given
in xxviii. 1 (where the LXX correctly reads לצ׳ הָרְבִיעִית בַּשָּׁנָה for בַּשָּׁנָה הַהִיא
בְּרֵאשִׁית מַמְלֶכֶת צ׳) as applying to the incidents of ch. xxvii also.

secure the adherence of Zedekiah. But, perhaps owing to the influence of Jeremiah and his friends, perhaps because it was discovered that Psammetichus did not intend, after all, to take the matter up seriously, perhaps because the facts of the intrigue became known at Babylon, and prompt measures were taken to forestall rebellion, the threatened storm passed off.[1] But with the accession of Apries (the Hophra of the Old Testament) in 588 B.C., the revolt broke out afresh, and this time matters were more serious. The two peoples chiefly involved were Judah and Ammon, for the rebellion was not universal, and it seems that both Edom and Philistia remained faithful to Babylon.[2] Certainly the rebels had good grounds for relying on Egyptian support.

Nebuchadrezzar hastily gathered an army and marched westwards. He seems to have been in some doubt as to which of the two rebellious states to attack first, and it was only after consultation with his oracles that he decided to march on Jerusalem.[3] It would seem that he had trouble also with northern Syria, for he made his head-quarters at Riblah on the Orontes, while a detachment was sent against Jerusalem under his chief military officers. They, however, were quite adequate to their task, and early in 587 B.C.[4] the city was closely invested.

Our most detailed source of information for the events of the siege is the biographer of Jeremiah.[5] Naturally his interest is centred on the person of the prophet, but he inevitably touches on a number of matters which affect the people as a whole. The city appears to have been fairly well supplied with food, and, thanks probably to the measures taken by Hezekiah, we

[1] Jer. li. 59 alludes to a visit paid by Zedekiah in person to Babylon. While the passage as a whole is certainly late and historically worthless, it may possibly preserve in this detail a reliable tradition. In that case we may suspect that Nebuchadrezzar was aware of the threatened conspiracy and summoned the king of Judah to give an account of himself, thereby ensuring his loyalty for a time. In any case the rebellion proved abortive, though, unless and until more is known of the political events of the reign of Nebuchadrezzar, it is impossible to be sure of the details.

[2] References, especially to Edom, are always a little uncertain, since they may apply either to the part that Edomites took in the desolation of Judah in 596 B.C. or to the treatment that the country received from them after the fall of Jerusalem. But the denunciations of these two peoples in Ez. xxv. 12 ff., 15 ff. seem to imply that they took some share in the actual sack of Jerusalem in 586 B.C.

[3] Ez. xxi. 18 ff.

[4] The date given in 2 Kgs. xxv. 1 is the ninth year of Zedekiah, on the tenth day of the tenth month, i.e. about the beginning of January 587 B.C.

[5] We have also a vivid picture of its horrors (which included cannibalism) in Lam. ii and iv.

hear of no shortage of water. But it is clear that there was some fear of scanty rations, and many of the wealthier inhabitants at once took the step of dismissing their slaves, thereby relieving themselves of the responsibility of finding them food. At the same time, while all the fortified places in Judah were seized by the Chaldaean army, it seems that no attempt was made to plunder and ravage the country at large. Nebuchadrezzar wanted peaceful possession of a flourishing land, not nominal authority over a desert. The smaller places were left to some extent untouched, though they probably had to supply the needs of the invading army, and so near to Jerusalem as Anathoth the village life was apparently continued with the minimum of interference. The policy of comparative mildness was not without effect, and the pro-Babylonian party in the country, headed by Jeremiah, continued to advocate an unconditional surrender. We can imagine the fury with which this advice was regarded by the dominant pro-Egyptian politicians, and we can understand their feeling that it was the basest treachery, especially since there were constant desertions, both from within and from outside the city.

There was some ground for the confidence which was felt in Egypt, for the intentions of Apries towards his suffering allies were good, even though in practice Egypt was still 'a broken reed'. An Egyptian force moved across the frontier, and the Babylonian generals at once raised the siege of Jerusalem. The respite was marked by a dastardly act of tyranny on the part of the upper classes.[1] Slaves had been manumitted, without waiting for the end of their six-year period of service, in order to save their masters, but now that the danger seemed to be past, the masters insisted on recalling the slaves. So far were the men of Jerusalem from having adopted sound moral standards, and from being actuated by motives of real humanity. At the same time Jeremiah lost his liberty. Some difficulty had arisen about the ancestral property at Anathoth, and there was a small plot to which the prophet had the right of 'redemption'. He attempted to leave the city in order to return to his estate, but was arrested on the ground that he was proposing to desert to the Chaldaeans.[2] His protests were disregarded, and, in view of the advice he had consistently offered to his fellow-countrymen, it is difficult to see how they could have been accepted. He was

[1] See Jer. xxxiv. 8 ff. [2] Jer. xxxvii. 11 ff.

thrown into prison, but not into close confinement, and though deprived of personal liberty and limited to the one house and courtyard, he was still accessible to any who wished to hold converse with him. It is at this point that we have the record of an incident which exhibits the magnificent optimism of the man. He had been, and was still, consistently proclaiming the return of the Chaldaean army and the final destruction of Jerusalem, yet he did not despair of Judah, and beyond the disaster he foresaw a time when she would once more be able to hold her own land. In prison, free as he was to receive visits, he met members of his own family, and concluded the purchase of the plot of ground which he had been unable to attend to in person. He gave the most careful instructions for the preservation of the title deeds, in the full conviction that the time would come when they would yet be valid, and that after the last calamity had befallen Jerusalem, Israelites would still be able to claim and to live upon their own land.[1] The incident is really one of those 'prophetic symbolisms' which do in miniature that which Yahweh will do on a greater scale, the whole land will be 're-deemed' by Yahweh.

Jeremiah's forecast as to the resumption of the siege was only too accurately fulfilled. We do not even know that the Egyptian forces awaited the issue of battle, but if they did they were decisively beaten, and the Chaldaean army renewed the siege. Jeremiah continued to urge on king and people his policy of surrender, and the dominant party determined to get rid of him.[2] Not daring to put to death directly one who was the inspired possession of Yahweh, they let him down into a cistern from which the water had been drawn off, leaving a deep deposit of mud at the bottom.[3] The object was to allow him to starve to death, but he was rescued by a certain Ethiopian slave, Ebed-melech by name, and returned to his former condition, though not, it seems, to the actual scene of his old confinement. Here he was repeatedly consulted by Zedekiah, and gave the same unvarying advice: 'Surrender, and you will be safe; resist, and you are ruined.' But the king could not make up his mind to follow the advice, clearly as he saw its excellence. He was afraid

---

[1] Jer. xxxii.   [2] See Jer. xxxviii. 1–13.

[3] The mud must have been several feet deep, for not only did it require most strenuous efforts to get Jeremiah out of the cistern, but mud which is less than knee-deep excites no comment in an eastern city.

of the courtiers, and afraid of the mockery of the deserters who were now in the Chaldaean camp, and, unable to reach a decision, he drifted to his end.[1]

Jerusalem was one of the strongest fortresses of the ancient world, and in spite of the scientific siege works which the Chaldaeans (and others) had learnt from Assyria to erect, it held out until it was practically starved, and its defenders were no longer able to withstand the assaults of the enemy. A breach was made in the walls,[2] and the Chaldaean generals entered the city. Zedekiah, with such of his guard as remained, fled through a gate which seems to have opened out from the passage which lay between the two old Jebusite walls,[3] and tried to escape across the Jordan, evidently with the intention of taking refuge with Ammon. But the party was pursued and scattered, Zedekiah himself being taken prisoner. He was carried to Riblah, where sentence was passed on him by Nebuchadrezzar. His sons, together with all the nobles of Judah who had been captured, were put to death in his sight,[4] and this scene of horror was the last he was permitted to behold, for his eyes were put out and he was taken blind to Babylon, where he remained a prisoner till his death. Once more the punishment of weakness was more terrible than that of deliberate and high-handed crime.

The settlement of the affairs of Jerusalem was entrusted to a Chaldaean officer named Nebuzaradan, who reached Jerusalem about a month after its capture. He carried out a deliberate work of destruction, pulling down the walls and the buildings within the city, and setting fire to all that was inflammable. It was clearly the Chaldaean intention to make Jerusalem utterly waste, so that it should never more serve as a focus of rebellion. The patience of Nebuchadrezzar was long, but it had been tried beyond its limits, and there were those, even in Israel, who recognized that the punishment of the city was just. All that was worth removing was removed, the larger objects of bronze

[1] Cp. Jer. xxxviii. 14–28, esp. vv. 19, 25.

[2] The date given in 2 Kgs. xxv. 3 is the ninth day of the fourth month of Zedekiah's eleventh year, i.e. about the beginning of July 586 B.C. From verse 8 we learn that this was the nineteenth year of Nebuchadrezzar.

[3] See p. 214.

[4] 2 Kgs. xxv. 7 does not mention the execution of the nobles, but the note is added in Jer. xxxix. 6 and lii. 10. 2 Kgs. xxv. 21, however, speaks of the execution of certain officials at Riblah after the settlement of Jerusalem by Nebuzaradan. Possibly the Jeremiah passages are a combination of the two records.

being broken up. The Chaldaeans did not value these things as
works of art; they probably felt that they had among them men
who could produce better work. We feel the loving regret with
which the narrator lingers over the list of the objects round
which Jerusalem's worship had centred since the days of Solomon.[1] With the material property were taken also all the people,
except the very poorest. The peasants were left in order that
the land might not lie waste, but every person of authority,
wealth, or family, who might serve as a centre for discontent,
was removed.

Some kind of arrangement had to be found for the government of the land, and Nebuzaradan appointed Gedaliah as
governor in the Babylonian interest. He was of the family of
Shaphan, which had consistently advocated submission to
Babylon, and his appointment was a piece of wise policy. He
had no direct claim on the crown, but belonged to the older
nobility, and while his loyalty to Nebuchadrezzar was unquestioned, he was likely to be treated with respect by the
people who remained in the land. Further, his own personal
character was a guarantee of good and faithful government.
Brave, loyal, and unsuspicious, he stands out as one of the really
chivalrous characters in the Old Testament story, and his
presence inspired a confidence in the good intentions and bona
fides of the Chaldaean government which might otherwise have
been difficult to secure. He made his home at Mizpah, and set
about the task of building up a new community out of the
wreckage left by the war. He was so far successful that there
gradually gathered about him a body of men who had made their
escape from the last calamities of Jerusalem and taken refuge
among the various tribes of Palestine, chief among them being
Johanan the son of Kareah.[2] Jeremiah, clearly recognized as an
important influence on the pro-Babylonian side, was permitted
to go where he would, and decided to cast in his lot with
Gedaliah, whom he evidently held in high esteem.

A superficial reading of the Biblical text suggests that the
settlement at Mizpah lasted but a few months. There are,
however, reasons for believing that the little company was able

---

[1] The account in 2 Kgs. xxv. 13–17 has been condensed, but we have the fuller
original in Jer. lii. 17–23.

[2] The accounts given both in 2 Kgs. xxv and in Jer. lii are mere summaries,
but fortunately we have more details from the biographer of Jeremiah, in
Jer. xl.

to hold its own for three or four years,[1] and achieved a success which aroused the jealousy of its neighbours. In particular the Ammonites, who do not seem to have suffered in the campaigns of 587–586 B.C., still maintained their hostility to Babylon, and felt that they could vent their hatred on the new province. Ishmael, a scion of the royal house of Judah, was instigated to carry out the designs of the king of Ammon, and seems to have been a fit instrument for the purpose. Gedaliah was warned against him, but his noble spirit could conceive of nothing so mean in any man, and when Ishmael came with other refugees, he was courteously entertained. But, as Gedaliah and his officers sat together eating with Ishmael, the latter and his ten men fell upon them and slaughtered them, following up their crime by wiping out all whom they could find at Mizpah. Johanan and others were not present, and it was some days before the crime was known. All who passed through Mizpah were put to death, and one recorded incident was the slaughter of a company of pilgrims on their way to Jerusalem to offer sacrifice.[2] Ishmael's position was, of course, untenable, for he could not hope to withstand the inevitable vengeance which would be taken by Nebuchadrezzar, to say nothing of other Jews who were beyond his reach, so he seized all who were left, including the royal princesses of Israel, and tried to escape to Ammon. But he got no farther than Gibeon, when he was over-taken by Johanan and an armed company, and had to flee for his life, leaving his booty and prisoners to be taken back to Mizpah by Johanan.

To the survivors the situation appeared desperate. They knew that Nebuchadrezzar could not possibly overlook the matter, and they feared that indiscriminate vengeance would fall upon them. It seems, as a matter of fact, that the Chaldaeans did make an expedition to Judah in or about the year 581 B.C., and deported a few hundreds of the people.[3] If Johanan and his companions had held their ground and been able to show on

[1] The general impression we get from the narrative is that the community was well established, and that an attempt was even being made to restore the Jerusalem cultus. Moreover Nebuchadrezzar deported Judahites in 581 B.C., and we may most naturally explain this expedition as a result of the murder of his governor.

[2] Incidentally the narrative shows that though the Temple was a heap of black-ened ruins, yet some kind of altar still existed and was regarded as a holy spot by the Israelite survivors. It further attests the fact that a state of comparative peace-fulness and security had been attained, since these people are, apparently, unarmed.

[3] Jer. lii. 30.

an impartial investigation (which the Chaldaeans would almost certainly have granted) that they were in no way responsible for Ishmael's crime, it is probable that they would have been confirmed in their position. But they dared not run the risk, and determined to make their way to Egypt. They consulted Jeremiah as to the route they should take, and, after ten days waiting, they received through him an oracle which forbade them to go at all.[1] This they disregarded, and even accused Baruch of having tampered with the old prophet in order to secure their ruin. They went to Egypt, taking Jeremiah with them, in spite of his protests. Once there they fell back into their old idolatrous ways, reorganizing the cult of the Queen of Heaven. Jeremiah remonstrated, but they replied that as long as they had carried on this cult, all had been well with them, and it was only after its abandonment that calamity had fallen upon them. The only answer the prophet could make was: 'If you must do this, you must. But it is the end of your union with Yahweh; he will no more be your God, and you shall no more be His people. Yet at the last you shall know whose word shall stand, His or yours.'[2]

This was the real end of the Israelite nation, as Jeremiah well saw. What actually became of the fugitives we do not know They may have been absorbed among the Egyptian population, or they may have wandered far to the south up the Nile, and become the ancestors of that strange Jewish community which left documents behind it at Elephantine, dating from the fifth century. But, as the inheritors of Israel's past and as the founders of Israel's future, these men have no place. They are of the greatest interest to the historian and to the antiquarian, because of the light they throw on the religion and on the thought of their age, but they stand outside the stream of the genuine Israelite tradition. Israel had come into being with the great Covenant at Sinai, and when once that Covenant was dissolved, Israel ceased to be. More truly than any other nation in history, she existed in virtue of her faith.

Thus, then, ended Israel's career as an independent political entity. We have tried to trace the story from its earliest phases, watching the growth of the people and its decline. We have seen how Israel owed her being to the impact of certain Aramaean

---

[1] The story is told in Jer. xlii. [2] Jer. xliv, esp. vv. 26–8.

nomads on the agricultural community of Palestine, and how, starting far below the cultural level attained by her neighbours in the land, she yet reached a position of supremacy, and absorbed into herself all that she found in the country before her. In attempting to estimate the causes of her ultimate leadership, it has seemed to us that they are to be sought in her superiority in the defence of the land against foreign aggression, and that this in turn must be ascribed to her unity (at least to the theory of her unity) in blood and faith and to her greater vigour in war. We have tried to give due place to the comparative quiescence of the great world powers to the east and to the south during the period of the struggles against the Philistines, and have seen therein the opportunity Israel needed, alike for her own consolidation and for the establishment of a free and independent state covering the whole of the land-bridge which leads from Asia to Africa. We have watched successive generations fritter away in small and mean jealousies the chance that was offered to them, until it was too late for the nation to hope for the achievement of a great political empire. There were times of temporary recovery, but the leaders of Israel too seldom had the perspective of the statesman, and the few great kings whom she produced were followed in almost every case by men of shorter views and weaker personality. Not only did foreign conquest on a large scale become impossible—that was true from the days of Solomon himself onwards—but even Israel's power to maintain herself gradually disappeared, and both kingdoms sank into the position of provincial areas in the great eastern empires.

But the place of a nation in history is not to be judged by the extent of the territory which it has occupied or by the length of time for which it has endured. Some of the peoples of the ancient world still live, in the sense that the contribution which they have made to human life is so valuable and so permanent that its effects are visible among us to this day. And in three chief ways the nation whose story we have followed has left a great legacy. It has created a profoundly influential literature. It has inspired a valid conception of human personality. It has offered a basis for the one and only conception of God which can hold the thought of the modern world.

There is a continuous history of art and of literature, in which the high peaks of national achievement stand out before us, and assure a deathless memory to the age and to the people that

attained them. Here Israel played her part, and though she
had no artistic sphere save that of literature through which to
contribute to human culture, she stands in a position almost
unique among the races of the ancient east. What has come
down to us can be no more than a scanty relic of the writings she
actually produced, but its influence has been incalculable. The
nations about her spoke languages similar to hers, and yet the
contribution of Moab, once almost her equal, is a single annalistic inscription. Phoenicia, the wealthiest and most powerful
part of all Syria, has left us little more than a few notices on the
coffins of her kings,[1] while Damascus, once Israel's successful
rival, has given us nothing. Yet, to take a modern instance of
the effect of Hebrew writing, the ideal style of two great modern
literatures, those using the German and the English languages,
is based on renderings of our surviving Hebrew authors which
faithfully represent both their vocabulary and their syntax.

We have already glanced[2] at the literature of the first part of
the monarchy, with special reference to its legal and historical
prose. The latter half of the period of the kingdoms was far
richer in literary activity, and the same characteristics are manifested throughout. We may divide our extant works into three
distinct classes. We have first of all liturgical poetry. Unfortunately it is not easy to determine how much of our extant
Hebrew poetry is to be dated before the Exile. Some of that
which has come down to us (including the greatest piece of all,
the book of *Job*) is certainly post-exilic, and it is probable that
a large proportion of the poems contained in the Psalter come
from the same period. But during the last thirty years there has
been a growing tendency to throw more and more back into the
age of the monarchy, and even though the traditional ascrip-
tions contained in the Psalm titles are not generally accepted by
Old Testament scholars, signs of pre-exilic authorship are now
far more widely recognized than they were a generation ago.
Naturally, the Psalms vary a good deal in artistic quality, but
in the best of them we find some of the noblest products of
the poetic art. They are characterized by dignity, beauty of
expression, fertility in imagination, stateliness and restraint in
diction, in a word (to use a term of Lowth's) by sublimity. They
have too, in the highest degree, that quality without which no

[1] This statement needs correction in the light of the Ras Shamrah discoveries.
[2] See above, pp. 325 ff.

great literature can exist, a profound sincerity. They touch the depths of human nature and experience, and it is no accident that all the generations who have known them have responded to them, and have found them fit their own need. They are songs of the human soul, timeless and universal; it is the sacred poets of Israel who, more than any others, have well and truly interpreted the spirit of man.

As a second class we may mention lyric poetry of a unique type, that of the prophets. We need not here consider the many and complicated questions which beset us when we come to discuss its origin and the way in which the books as we now have them were compiled. Suffice it to say that what has come down to us is a collection, or rather a series of collections, of short pieces, often very short, and, perhaps, often mutilated. Each is a sudden and usually passionate outburst, which, nevertheless, takes the form of a complete poem—at least in its original state. No less than eight pre-exilic prophets, whose names are known to us, have left us some portion of their utterances in poetic form, and it is practically certain that our prophetic books include pieces by an indefinite number of unknown authors. But though we may not be able to assign names to them, we can appreciate and treasure their work.[1] Here, then, we have all the features which we have observed in the liturgical poetry of Israel, with, if possible, greater intensity and wealth of imagery. Amos and Jeremiah give us clear and true pictures of the outdoor world of beast and bird; Hosea and Isaiah, while they are not unfamiliar with nature, see life rather from the town-dweller's point of view. Often the force of the prophetic message is too direct and overwhelming even for metaphor, and it falls upon us with the speed and brilliancy of lightning. Isaiah is a master of concise descriptive poetry, surpassed only by Nahum, whose terse yet vivid picture of the sack of Nineveh stands alone in literature of this class. There is, too, a shadow over all the pre-exilic prophets. There may be moments when it is lifted, and a beam of hope falls across the outlook, but for the most part the substance of their work was gloomy and oppressive. For, in spite of the high artistic level on which they stand, artistry was not their primary concern; they had a God-given task to perform, and a divine message to deliver. It is no small part of the value of their style that they forgot it in the larger interest. They never uttered

[1] An example may be seen in Isa. ii. 2-4 (= Mic. iv. 1-4).

poetry for its own sake, and a poem, like a man, finds itself only when it loses itself.

We have thus the fierce denunciation of sin, coupled with the passionate demand for that righteousness and purity which alone can satisfy Yahweh. The threats with which these attacks are pointed are couched in terms which should bring home, not merely to the nation at large, but to the individual member thereof, the issue and goal of evil ways. Again and again the prophet is overwhelmed with the tragedy of the doom which he foresees, and his language becomes a dirge of unspeakable pathos. In two lines Amos brings before us the unutterable sorrow which surrounds the last rites paid to the corpse of a young girl.[1] Isaiah makes us see his country desolated by the Assyrian invasion as a tortured body, with the life yet in it, but torn, bruised, and festering.[2] In Hosea we cannot but feel the breaking of a heart that gave all for love, and saw that love trampled in the mire. Micah is possessed by a fury which breaks the bounds of conventional language at the thought of the unhappy peasants whom he has seen pass beneath the harrow of the landlords' tyranny. In Jeremiah we have something of all the rest, the passion of Hosea, the swift movement and descriptive power of Isaiah, the moral indignation of Amos and Micah, while the bitterness of his inner experience adds a poignancy all his own. Few passages can compare for majestic horror with his vision of 'chaos come again',[3] and in his revelation of his personal dealings with Yahweh he has plumbed the lowest deeps of spiritual agony.[4] If (from the literary point of view) we find the utterances of Zephaniah and Habakkuk less impressive than those of their contemporaries, it is only because we have so high a standard by which to measure them. Taken as a whole, the prophetic lyrics of Israel occupy a unique position in the history of the world's poetry.

We pass to prose. Here we have, what we have found in the earlier period, an attempt to write real history, constructing out of bare annals a genuine record of national progress. We have also, at the end of the period, a new legal compilation, fairly comparable, from a literary point of view, with the 'Book of the Covenant'. But we have two types of prose writing which emerge for the first time clearly during this period. The first is the simple story, usually dealing with some well-known character,

---

[1] Am. v. 2.   [2] Isa. i. 4–9.   [3] Jer. iv. 23–6.   [4] Cp. e.g. Jer. xx. 7 ff.

and describing events in his life. This is the raw material for
true biography, or rather, perhaps, a primitive form of biography.
It springs out of the tales that men would tell one another in the
city gate, or by the camp fire in the open grazing lands. Our
surviving literature of this class nearly always has one or other
of the prophets for its subject; the collections of these stories
dealing with Elijah and Elisha have been freely employed by the
compilers of the books of *Kings*, and it is clear that there was a
body of such narratives whose subject was Isaiah. We have a
number of similar pieces concerning Jeremiah, though these
appear to differ from the general type in being, in their present
form, the work of a contemporary and an eyewitness of the
events he describes. In all we have the characteristic features of
good Hebrew writing, though it is rather more flowing and, if
anything, simpler in construction than the narrative prose of
the earlier monarchy. Its most striking feature—indeed the
feature which gives it unique importance—is that it is all written
from the standpoint of the common people. It helps us to see
the life of the average Israelite, not simply the conditions and
the fortunes of kings and nobles. In this respect it has few if any
parallels in the east, ancient or modern. Nowhere else do we
gain such insight into the hopes and fears, the little concerns of
little people, which, after all, are the essential elements in any
true national life. There is in these narratives a naïve presentation of the experiences and of the motives of the ordinary and
insignificant folk, the man who is in despair because he has lost
a borrowed axe-head,[1] the woman whose debts threaten her
children with slavery,[2] the child carried off by foreign raiders.[3]
It is true that we hear of kings and courts in these stories, but
they are seldom named; the personality of the people in upper
walks of society did not concern either the teller of the story or
his audience, and they appear as a rather vague background to
the incidents which really interest men. In this, as in so much
else, Israel was the great democratic nation of the ancient world.

Finally we have, probably late in the seventh century, the
growth and development of rhetorical prose. The opening chapters of *Deuteronomy* mark an era in the history of literature, and
we can see something of the effect this type of writing produced
on its own age by studying the prose oracles of Jeremiah. The
style forms a marked contrast to that of the Hebrew narrative.

---

[1] 2 Kgs. vi. 5.   [2] 2 Kgs. iv. 1–7.   [3] 2 Kgs. v. 2.

Instead of the simple, usually short, co-ordinated sentences
which we find in the historical books, we have long periods with
a syntax as involved as the structure of the Hebrew language
will allow. This class of writing is still in its infancy in *Deuteronomy*, and a hypercritical eye may detect a certain crudity
in the construction of the style, but the fact remains that the
earnestness of the writers confers a real dignity and impressive-
ness, and there are good judges of literary excellence who would
place the 'Deuteronomic' prose very high in the list of the world's
oratorical efforts.

Yet it was not in literature that Israel's greatest contribution
to human thought was made. Small and insignificant as she
was, there were two directions in which she had something of
profound importance to convey to those who should come after
her. The first of these lay in the realm of political theory, and it
has attracted comparatively little attention, partly because it
seems so obvious to our minds. Israel exhibited a passionate
insistence on the value of human personality, a refusal to recognize that any social order or political institution could be valid
and permanent if it conflicted with the rights of man. Religion
itself must be judged by this standard, and a theology or
a ceremonial must stand or fall by its attitude to humanity.
Not the most orthodox of theologies, not the most scrupulously
accurate observance of cultic rite, could for one instant compensate for the absence of human justice and human sympathy.
Again and again the people fell from the high standard which
their most ancient tradition had set before them, and were
recalled by the preaching of their prophets to first principles.
It was, indeed, only in the teaching of Jesus that those principles
found their highest and unique expression, but it must not be
forgotten that in this matter Jesus was but 'completing the Law
and the prophets'.

And this leads us to the second and the greater of Israel's
contributions to human thinking. A comparative study of the
world's religions shows us that there is a regular and normal
evolution in the world's faiths. As far back as actual observa-
tion will take us, we have a doctrine which we call Animism, a
belief in a multitude of spirits, without personal names, recognized in groups—spirits of the upper air, spirits of the earth,
spirits of the dead. As time passes individuals are identified in
each group, and gradually they are elevated into the position of

'High Gods'. The old animistic ideas still persist, it is true, but they fall into the background, and the stress is laid on the Pantheon. This is a stage to which we give the name Polytheism. But history has shown that a Polytheism is always unstable; on the one hand it tends to drift back into the older animism, and on the other it tends to develop a philosophy which is normally atheistic. The metaphysical demand for unity and the ethical demand for morality are never satisfied by numbers of gods and goddesses, among whom some may be good but others are certainly wicked. Thus the noblest spirits are often faced with the choice between religion and truth, and choose the latter. God and goodness are incompatible, and the best men have tended to discard religion in favour of righteousness. In Israel, almost alone among the nations, God was conceived as supremely righteous. Here, more than anywhere else, we trace the effect of the impact of the nomad ideals on the settled community, and it was the old faith, originating with Moses and interpreted by the prophets, which ultimately gave to Israel her place in human history.

But when Israel ceased to be a political entity she had not yet begun to give the world her supreme message. She had, indeed, not really grasped it herself, and still stood near the beginning of her spiritual history. Nearly a century of varied experience was to pass before she had made the truth her own and was in a position to transmit it to the world about her. It is true that her prophets had proclaimed the moral character of Yahweh, but men are slow to realize the implications of their own beliefs, and we have little justification for holding that men like Amos and Isaiah were monotheists in the strict sense of the word. No doubt it was inevitable that their teaching should lead to the conviction that all the gods of the nations were idols, but Yahweh had made the heavens. But we miss that note of splendid certainty which rings through the utterances of the great anonymous prophet of the Exile,[1] when he insists that there is no God but Yahweh, and that the other objects of worship are nothing or less than nothing—nonentities or minus quantities. It is, further, only at the very end of Israel's history as an independent nation, in the thought of Jeremiah and Habakkuk, that we find

[1] For reasons which cannot be discussed here, the writer is unable to accept the conclusion reached by C. C. Torrey (cp. e.g. *The Second Isaiah*, 1928) that Isa. xl–lxvi must be attributed to a single prophet living in the age of Alexander the Great.

the question as to the righteous government of the universe which led in the end to such rich discoveries in the relation of man and God, and ultimately taught Israel to believe in a valid life after death, a state in which communion was possible with the God whom men had adored while still on earth.

So it came to pass that all was not lost for Israel in her political ruin. There still remained the exiles in Babylon, and they maintained in unique fashion, and with almost miraculous results, the faith of their ancestors and their national sense. In them the tradition lived, and by them it was handed down to later ages. It was due to impulses originating among them that the Temple was at length restored, and eventually a new community grew up about it, which maintained and carried on that which constituted Israel's true message to the world. Paradoxical as the statement seems to be, it is nevertheless true that Israel's work began only when to the superficial eye she had just ceased to be.

But the long story of Israel as an independent political unit, which we have followed from its first beginning at Sinai, is ended. Save for a brief period under the Hasmonean princes, she was never again to enter the arena of world politics as a sovereign people. For, of all the forces which had gone to make her a nation, it was her faith in Yahweh which was primary and fundamental. She lived in virtue of a covenant made with Him, and with the breach of that covenant she ceased to have either a reason for her existence or the means of maintaining it. Those who went down into Egypt with Johanan were the last in the line of tradition. In a political sense this was true; they were the last survivors of the old kingdom of David, as it had grown up on the soil of Palestine, and the nation itself ceased to be when they said in effect, 'Not Yahweh, but the Queen of Heaven will we worship'.

Additional Note H

THE NUMBERS OF THE EXILES

FIGURES relating to the deportations of Nebuchadrezzar are furnished by Jer. lii. 28–30. The passage is omitted by the LXX, and is not found in *2 Kings*, but there seems to be good ground for supposing that it was drawn from some early and reliable source. The very modesty of the figures suggests accuracy. Three deportations are mentioned:

[1] 8th year of Nebuchadrezzar	(597 B.C.)	.	.	3,023
[1] 19th	„	„	(586 „)	.	.	832
23rd	„	„	(581 „)	.	.	745

Total 4,600

This is a very small figure when compared with the 200,150 whom Sennacherib claims to have deported in 701 B.C., but it may be that he there included all the Palestinian captives taken in his expedition, though he ascribed them to Judah. It is particularly surprising to find the total of 832 for those carried away in 586 B.C. But it must be remembered that a month elapsed between the storm of the city and the arrival of Nebuzaradan to settle affairs, and we may suppose that nearly all the survivors made their way into the open country to procure some means of living. The greater number of those removed at this time were probably deserters who had joined the Chaldaeans before the siege was over. The deportations of 581 B.C. suggest that a final expedition was undertaken after the murder of Gedaliah.

[1] The figures in the text are 7th and 18th, but all the other data make it necessary to assume that each deportation is here placed a year too early.

Additional Note I

THE CHRONOLOGY OF THE REGAL PERIOD[1]

ONE of the main difficulties which confront the student of Israel's history is that of securing any degree of accuracy in the dating of events. It is, obviously, impossible to get more than a rough approximation to the date of such occurrences as the Exodus and the Conquest, nor can we expect any exact date before the foundation of the monarchy. With the kings, however, the number of their regal years is always stated, and there is an ingenious scheme of synchronisms as between the kings of Israel and the kings of Judah. This, however, is taken by the compiler from the figures he found already in his sources, and is not to be regarded as independent evidence.

But, in any case, our Biblical data would hardly be enough to give us any certainty, and we are compelled to rely to some extent on the dates which we find in other literatures, especially when they refer to Israel. We have two main sources, those

---

[1] This baffling and complicated subject has attracted the attention of nearly every serious student of the Old Testament. It will suffice to mention the names of Wellhausen ('Die Zeitrechnung des Buches der Könige', *Jahrbücher für deutsche Theologie*, Jahrg., 1875, xx. 607–40); Krey, *Z. für wissenschaftliche Theologie*, 1875, xx, pp. 404 ff.; Rühl, *Deutsche Zeitschrift für Geschichtswissenschaft*, Jahrg., 1894–5 (Bd. xx), pp. 44–76 and Nachtrag, p. 171; Mahler, *Handbuch der jüdischen Chronologie*, 1916; Thilo, *Die Chronologie des Alten Testaments*, 1917; Kugler, *Von Moses bis Paulus*, 1922, ch. iii; Lewy, *Die Chronologie der Könige von Israel und Juda*, 1927; and Begrich, *Die Chronologie der Könige von Israel und Juda*, 1929. The last is the fullest, most thorough, and most acute of all the discussions which have yet appeared, and cannot be overlooked. Begrich finds in the synchronisms in *Kings*, in the actual figures given for each reign, in the figures given in the LXX and in Josephus, no less than five different complete schemes of chronology, and from these, which he works out carefully in detail, comparing them with the definite dates ascertained from Mesopotamian documents, he develops what seems to him a satisfactory scheme. To these should be added Mowinckel, *Chronologie der israëlitischen und jüdischen Könige* (1932).

On two important points it seems to the present writer that Begrich's work is open to criticism. In the first place, Wellhausen is surely right in believing that the synchronisms in *Kings* are worthless, being merely a late compilation from the actual figures given. The parallel of such documents as the Mesopotamian synchronistic lists does not seem to apply, for they were the result of a single government over the two peoples concerned. In the second place, it is hardly justifiable to take the evidence of the subordinate versions and writers as giving anything like independent schemes. They must all go back to the same source as the MT., and each figure can be used only as evidence for the original text of the passage in which it occurs.

The truth is that we are largely dependent on conjecture. The grounds on which various conclusions are accepted are usually subjective, and a study of the opinions of different writers will show how hopeless it is to try to obtain uniformity, still less certainty. The attempt has been made in the following pages to reconstruct a scheme which has no claim whatever to authority, but shows one way, at least, in which the relevant data may be satisfied.

which we derive from Egypt, and those which come to us from Assyria. The latter are usually the more reliable and accurate when we can obtain them, because the Assyrians kept a careful record of the years, following a system not unlike that which prevailed later at Athens. Every year was known by the name of an official whose title was *limmu*,[1] and we have *limmu*-lists practically complete from the end of the twelfth century. From 860 B.C. onwards a note is attached to each year indicating the most important event by which it was marked, and in the year of a certain Bur (Ishdi)-Sagale it is stated than an eclipse of the sun took place in the month *Simanu*.[2] This can only be the eclipse of June 763 B.C., and we are thus enabled to date the whole series with perfect accuracy.

We are on far less certain ground when we are dealing with Egyptian dates, and we have to rely on a kind of 'dead reckoning', based on the regnal years of successive kings, a method which always leaves room for some error, owing to the accumulation of odd months which are not specified. In the whole range of Israelite history there seems to be but one date which can be certified on astronomical grounds from Egypt, and that is the death of Shabaka in the year 700 B.C. Even the eclipse of 763 B.C. was only partial so far south as Egypt, and is not mentioned. The approximate dates of the kings mentioned in Israelite records are: Sheshonk 945–924, (Osorkon I 924–895) (Shabaka 712–700), Tirhakah 688–663, Necho 609–593, Apries 588–569.[3] Osorkon and Shabaka are, of course, only doubtfully identified with Zerah king of the Cushites (2 Chron. xiv. 9 ff.) and with So (2 Kgs. xvii. 4).

Our Assyrian records enable us to identify with certainty the dates of the following events:

B.C.

853 Battle of Ḳarḳar; Ahab the king of Israel.

841 Jehu pays tribute to Shalmaneser III.

738 Menahem pays tribute to Tiglath-pileser III.

734 Assyrian expedition against Philistia (probably that in which Pekah lost his throne).

---

[1] Winckler (*KAT.*[3], pp. 222 f.) and J. A. Montgomery (*JBL.*, 1930, XLIX, iv, pp. 21 ff.) have suggested that similar lists existed in Hebrew, and that fragments survive in the O.T. Unfortunately we cannot use them, if they existed, because they are so fragmentary. The difficulties in O.T. chronology are due, not so much to errors of the authors, as to inaccuracies in the transmission of the text.

[2] Luckenbill, *ARA.* ii, p. 435, § 1198.   [3] Breasted, *HE.*, pp. 600 f.

B.C.

733 Assyrian expedition against Damascus.

732 Assyrian expedition against Damascus.

721 Capture of Samaria, and organization of the Assyrian province of Samaria, by Sargon.

(711 Capture of Ashdod by Sargon.)

701 Expedition against Judah by Sennacherib.

To these we may add:

679 Manasseh does homage to Esarhaddon at Nineveh.[1]

We may also regard as certain the date of the battle of Car-chemish, which took place in 605 B.C., and Nebuchadrezzar's accession in that same year. There does remain, however, a margin of error in dating the fall of Jerusalem. That is dated in 2 Kgs. xxv. 8 as taking place in the nineteenth year of Nebuchad-rezzar, and verse 3 more exactly dates it on the ninth day of the fourth month.[2] We may assume that it is the Babylonian calendar on which the figures are based, and this made the year begin with Nisan—March to April. The date of the capture of Jerusalem, then, will be early in July.

But we cannot be absolutely certain as to the year. The Babylonian chronology dated the regnal years of a king, not from the day of his accession, but from the next Nisan. If Nebuchadrezzar came to the throne in January, February, or March, then the first counted year of his reign began in the spring of 605 B.C. If, however, it was after the beginning of Nisan in 605 that Nabopolassar died, then Nebuchadrezzar's first year would begin in the spring of 604 B.C. In the former case the fall of Jerusalem is to be dated 587, in the latter 586 B.C. We do not know in what month Nebuchadrezzar ascended the throne, though June–July seems probable, but it will be seen at once that the probabilities are three to one in favour of his reign being dated 604, making the fall of Jerusalem 586 B.C.[3] We know that Nebuchadrezzar did not become king till after the battle of Carchemish, and Necho's expeditions to Mesopotamia

---

[1] There is some uncertainty as to the exact year, though the event clearly belongs to the early part of the king's reign. But it is not dated in the inscriptions, cp. p. 432.

[2] The Hebrew text of *Kings* omits the number of the month, but most editors would restore it from the parallels in Jer. xxxix. 2, lii. 6.

[3] It should be pointed out that in the figures of the captives given in Jer. lii. 28–30, each date is a year earlier, and the fall of Jerusalem is assigned to Nebu-chadrezzar's eighteenth year. But this seems at present to be a less probable date, and may be treated as a slip.

did not usually take place until the year was well advanced, which also points to the late summer as the probable time of Nebuchadrezzar's accession. When we find, as we do, that this date fits our general chronological scheme better than 587 B.C., then we are justified in assuming it to be correct, unless and until we have contradictory evidence from Babylonian records.

We turn now to the figures supplied in the book of *Kings*. The two lists for the north and the south run side by side, and it is convenient to divide the period of the monarchy into four sections, because of certain obvious synchronisms. We may regard the reigns of Rehoboam and Jeroboam I as beginning at the same time, and also those of Jehu and Athaliah, while the fall of Samaria is dated in the sixth year of Hezekiah (2 Kgs. xviii. 10), though, as we shall see, the date is open to some suspicion. The period during which the kingdom of Judah survived that of Israel, however, makes a convenient section for study.

The figures given for the four periods are as follows:

A. *The early kings of all Israel.*

Saul . .	?[1]
David . .	40 years
Solomon .	40 ,,
Total .	80+years

B. *The Divided Kingdom.*

Israel.		Judah.	
Jeroboam I .	22 years	Rehoboam .	17 years
Nadab	2 ,,	Abijam .	3 ,, (LXX 6)
Baasha	24 ,,	Asa . .	41 ,,
Elah .	2 ,,	Jehoshaphat .	25 ,,
Omri .	12 ,,	Jehoram .	8 ,,
Ahab .	22 ,,	Ahaziah .	1 year
Ahaziah	2 ,,		
Jehoram	12 ,,		
Totals .	98 years[2]		95 years (LXX 98)

[1] A figure has obviously dropped out in 1 Sam. xiii. 1; Saul clearly reigned more than two years.

[2] The seven days' reign of Zimri has not been included in the above, as it is obviously of no importance for the chronology. But it should be remarked that the historian's synchronisms place the accession of Zimri in Asa's twenty-seventh year (1 Kgs. xvi. 15) and that of Omri in Asa's thirty-first year (1 Kgs. xvi. 23), thus assuming an interregnum of four years. We can, however, hardly take these synchronisms seriously, and we may suspect that the compiler has simply assumed

If we can accept the figure given by the LXX for the reign of Abijam, we thus have identically the same period for the two kingdoms.

C. *Accession of Jehu and Athaliah to the fall of Samaria.*

Israel.			Judah.		
Jehu .	.	28 years	Athaliah	.	6 years
Jehoahaz	.	17 ,,	Jehoash	.	40 ,,
Jehoash	.	16 ,,	Amaziah	.	29 ,,
Jeroboam II .		41 ,,	Uzziah	.	52 ,,
Zechariah	.	½ year	Jotham	.	16 ,,
Menahem	.	10 years	Ahaz .	.	16 ,,
Pekahiah	.	2 ,,	Hezekiah	.	6 ,, (down to
Pekah .	.	20 ,,			fall of Samaria)
Hoshea	.	9 ,,			
Totals	.	143½ years[1]			165 years

D. *Kingdom of Judah alone.*

Hezekiah .	.	23 years (after fall of Samaria)
Manasseh .	.	55 ,,
Amon .	.	2 ,,
Josiah .	.	31 ,,
Jehoahaz .	.	¼ year
Jehoiakim .	.	11 years
Jehoiachin .	.	¼ year
Zedekiah .	.	11 years
Total .	.	133½ years

Since the dates nearer to the compiler's own time are less likely to have suffered from textual corruption, we may consider the last period first. The fixed date is the battle of Carchemish, in Jehoiakim's fourth year,[2] which places his accession in 608 and his death in 597. Allowing for a margin of

---

that Omri's reign is to be dated, not from the death of Zimri, but from that of Tibni, and has allowed four years for the struggle. The LXX has no synchronism at all in 1 Kgs. xvi. 15, suggesting that in the MT. it is a later addition.

[1] The one month assigned to Shallum is omitted as it obviously has no bearing on the chronology.

[2] Jer. xlvi. 2, further attested by the fact that Jeremiah's outlook underwent a definite change in that year, cp. xxv. 1, xxxvi. 1.

error due to uncounted months, we thus get the following dates
for the kings of Judah after the fall of Samaria:

B.C.

Manasseh	. . .	696
Amon	. . .	641
Josiah	. . .	639
Jehoahaz	. .	608
Jehoiakim	. .	608
Jehoiachin	. .	597
Zedekiah	. .	596
Fall of Jerusalem	. .	586

(According to 2 Kgs. xxv.
8 the nineteenth year of
Nebuchadrezzar.)

We are, however, in difficulties when we come to deal with the
reign of Hezekiah. He is credited with a reign of twenty-nine years,
and Samaria is said to have fallen in his sixth year, which would
make the latter date 719 or 720 B.C. at the earliest. But we cannot
put the fall of Samaria later than 721 B.C., as it occurred in Sargon's
first year. On the other hand it is stated in 2 Kgs. xviii. 13 that
Sennacherib's invasion of Judah took place in Hezekiah's fourteenth year, which would imply that he did not become king till
715 B.C.[1] But this figure stands alone in the record, and, knowing
what we do of the transmission of figures in ancient documents,
it is not difficult to conjecture that the original figure was
twenty-four.[2] This would make the date of the accession of
Hezekiah 725 B.C., which is by no means out of the question. We
are still left, however, with the statement in 2 Kgs. xviii. 9 that
it was in Hezekiah's fourth year that Samaria was attacked by
Shalmaneser, and that it was in his sixth year that the city
succumbed. But it is quite clear that in reporting the last days of
Samaria, the compiler has misread or miscopied his sources, for
the Assyrian record itself suggests that Hoshea was not in the
city when it was captured (Sargon does not mention his name),
while 2 Kgs. xvii. 4–5 seems definitely to imply that Hoshea
was captured and imprisoned *before* the siege began. Only so

[1] Some scholars accept this date as correct. Box, *The Book of Isaiah*, pp. 9, 168,
places the accession of Hezekiah in 720 B.C.—another way of meeting the difficulty.
[2] Reading וְעֶשְׂרִים for עֶשְׂרֵה. Others would regard the number as a conjecture, based on the statement in xx. 6, that Hezekiah was to live fifteen years after
his sickness, and the theory that this sickness coincided with the invasion of Sennacherib. But the Babylonian embassy must be before 701 B.C., and the sickness earlier
still. See Skinner, *1 and 2 Kings*, p. 388; Benzinger, *Die Bücher der Könige*, p. 179.

can the chronology of these years be understood, for on any calculation at least eleven years (which, owing to looseness of reckoning, might be twelve) elapsed between the appointment of Hoshea and the fall of Samaria. The 'ninth year' of Hoshea mentioned in 2 Kgs. xvii. 6 is a natural miscalculation on the part of the compiler, and need not be taken as evidence.[1] If we can assume that the original account stated that it was in the fourth year of Hezekiah that Samaria actually fell, we can understand that this might be interpreted as meaning that it was in that year that Hoshea ceased to reign, and the knowledge that the city held out for two or three years after his deposition would introduce the sixth year as the date of the fall of the city. The compiler himself would—very naturally—be confused as between all these figures, and produce the statement we actually have in his effort to harmonize them. If, then, we may suppose that Samaria fell in the fourth year of Hezekiah, and that Sennacherib's invasion took place in the twenty-fourth, we arrive at the consistent date of 725 B.C. for the accession of Hezekiah, which agrees with the twenty-nine years ascribed to him and the dates already reached for his successors on the basis of the Biblical figures.

This carries us back to division C. Here we are at once met by an obvious discrepancy of at least twenty-one years between the figures given for Israel and those of Judah, the latter being the longer. By placing the fall of Samaria in the fourth year of Hezekiah instead of the sixth, we reduce this discrepancy to nineteen years, but that is still too long to be ascribed to looseness in reckoning odd months. One obvious resource is to reduce the reign of Jotham, and assume that the total figure, sixteen, includes the years during which he was co-regent with his father. Thus we might obtain a superficial harmony between the two lists by assuming that Jotham's independent reign lasted only seven years and that his father reigned forty-two instead of fifty-two years. But while we might thus reach a scheme which would produce internal consistency in the Biblical figures, we should still be far from a final solution, for we should have to take into account the Assyrian evidence, which is decisive where it can be found. Since Ahab was still alive in 853 B.C., the date of Jehu's tribute to Shalmaneser III, i.e. 841, must be very near the beginning of his reign. Hoshea was

---

[1] Cp. Skinner, *1 and 2 Kings*, p. 374.

deposed in 723 B.C. at the latest, possibly in 724, giving, at most, a period of 118 years between the two events, as against the 143 which is the minimum offered by the Biblical figures. How are we to get rid of these twenty-five years? Some light is thrown on this problem by a further discrepancy. Menahem paid tribute to Tiglath-pileser in 738 B.C., and Pekah was dethroned in 732 at the latest. Yet twenty-two years are assigned to the reigns of Pekahiah and Pekah together. It seems fairly clear that we must reduce the reign of Pekah to two years instead of twenty, and it is more or less a matter of taste as to where we deduct the other seven or eight. Perhaps Menahem reigned for two years only, or perhaps Jehu's figure should be twenty or that of Jehoahaz ten. Jehu's is, perhaps, the reign in which reduction can most readily be conjectured. This has the advantage of bringing the accession of Jehoash into the year following the great Assyrian raid on Damascus which apparently so reduced its strength as to facilitate the recovery of Israel which began under Jehoash. We thus reach the following table:

	B.C.		B.C.
Jehu . . .	841	Pekahiah . . .	737
Jehoahaz . . .	821	Pekah . . .	735
Jehoash . . .	804	Hoshea . . .	733[1]
Jeroboam . . .	788	Deposition of Hoshea	724
Zechariah⎫		Fall of Samaria . .	721
Shallum ⎬ . .	747		
Menahem⎭			

We are still left with the task of adjusting the reigns of the kings of Judah. We have already seen that one resource is the assumption that Jotham's years as co-regent with his father have been reckoned into the total years of his reign, and that possibly the reign of Uzziah himself is too long. The only *necessary* synchronism between the two kingdoms (apart from the beginning of the period) lies in the fact that the reigns of Jehoash of Israel and Amaziah of Judah overlapped. Of the other reigns those of Jehoash and Uzziah were clearly long, and must not be too greatly reduced; even on the Biblical figures Jehoash was only

---

[1] The *limmu*-lists show that there were expeditions to Palestine in 734, 733, and 732 B.C., Damascus being expressly mentioned as the objective of the two latter, and Philistia as the aim of the first. It is, then, quite reasonable to suppose that while Pekah was removed in 734, Hoshea was not formally appointed till the following year, while the expedition of 732 resulted in the organization of the Palestinian provinces.

forty-six when he was assassinated. The simplest solution, therefore, is to reduce Amaziah to nine years and Uzziah to forty-two, assuming that Jotham was co-regent with the latter for twelve or thirteen years. We thus get:

			B.C.				B.C.
Athaliah	.	.	841	Jotham (co-regent)	.	757
Jehoash	.	.	835	Jotham (sole rule)	.	744
Amaziah	.	.	795[1]	Ahaz	.	.	741
Uzziah	.	.	786	Hezekiah	.	.	725

In division B the attractive solution of the discrepancy between the two lists is to accept the LXX figure for the reign of Abijam—six years instead of three, thus reducing the whole period for both kingdoms to ninety-eight years. But this will not allow for the adjustment to the Assyrian date of 853 B.C. for the battle of Ḳarḳar, which means that some reduction must be made in the reigns of Ahaziah and Jehoram of Israel. The simplest plan—though this involves a textual emendation which is not so easy as some that have been proposed—is to cut the three years off the reign of Jehoram, and to keep the figures of the MT. for Judah. The necessary synchronisms are two; Baasha must overlap Asa, and Jehoshaphat Ahab and one of his sons. These conditions are fulfilled by the following table:

Israel.			B.C.	*Judah.*			B.C.
Jeroboam	.	.	936	Rehoboam	.	.	936
Nadab	.	.	914	Abijam	.	.	919
Baasha	.	.	912	Asa	.	.	916
Elah	.	.	888	Jehoshaphat	.	.	875
Zimri ⎫				Jehoram	.	.	850
Tibni ⎬	.	.	886	Ahaziah	.	.	842
Omri ⎭							
Ahab	.	.	874				
Ahaziah	.	.	852				
Jehoram	.	.	850				

Apart from the simple calculation which places Solomon's accession in 976 B.C. and that of David in 1016, we can go no further in identifying dates.[2] We may guess that Saul reigned about

---

[1] The statement in 2 Kgs. xiv. 17 that Amaziah survived Jehoash of Israel by fifteen years is obviously a compiler's deduction from the figures of xiii. 10, xiv. 2.

[2] The system of reckoning adopted by several scholars (e.g. Skinner, *1 and 2 Kings*, pp. 40 ff.) which makes the Hebrew chronology include the same year as the last of one king and the first of his successor, thus reducing every reign by one year, can hardly be applied here. It would bring the death of Solomon down to 930 B.C. Now

twenty years—it can hardly have been much less, but before his time all dates are a matter of conjecture, and, as we have seen in discussing the dates of the Exodus and Conquest, there are margins of several centuries in extent. But we may venture to restore tentatively the following general scheme:[1]

B.C.	Kings of Israel.		Kings of Judah.	Outstanding events.
1036 (?)		Saul		
1016		David		
976		Solomon		
936	Jeroboam I		Rehoboam	
931				Invasion of Sheshonk
919			Abijam	
916			Asa	
914	Nadab			
912	Baasha			
888	Elah			
886	Zimri, Tibni, Omri			
875			Jehoshaphat	
874	Ahab			
853				Battle of Ḳarḳar
852	Ahaziah			
850	Jehoram		Jehoram	
842			Ahaziah	
841	Jehu		Athaliah	Jehu's tribute to Assyria
835			Jehoash	
821	Jehoahaz			
805				Adad-nirari III subdues Damascus
804	Jehoash			
795			Amaziah	
788	Jeroboam II			
786			Uzziah	
757			Jotham (co-regent)	
747	Zechariah, Shallum, Menahem			
744			Jotham (sole rule)	
741			Ahaz	
738				Menahem pays tribute to Tiglath-pileser III
737	Pekahiah			
735	Pekah			

the invasion of Sheshonk took place in the fifth year of Rehoboam's reign, i.e., on this reckoning, in 926 or 925 B.C. But Sheshonk seems to have died in 924 B.C. at the latest, and the date suggested would not allow time for the erection of the Karnak inscription which describes the Palestinian campaign.

[1] This table must be accepted as being, at many points, approximate and conjectural—any table of Israelite dates must be so. The figures are bound to be affected by various ways of reckoning the regnal years and by the odd months more or less than the full number of years given. But it may be assumed that these will average against one another, and will not materially affect the general conclusion. The attempt has been made simply to achieve the best result possible with the maximum probability and the minimum departure from the Biblical figures.

B.C.	Kings of Israel.	Kings of Judah.	Outstanding events.
734			Tiglath-pileser III subdues Damascus
733	Hoshea		
732			Assyrian provinces organized in Palestine
725		Hezekiah	
724			Deposition of Hoshea
721			Capture of Samaria
701			Sennacherib invades Judah
696		Manasseh	
641		Amon	
639		Josiah	
608		Jehoahaz, Jehoiakim	
597		Jehoiachin, Zedekiah	
586			Fall of Jerusalem
581			Nebuchadrezzar's third deportation from Judah

H h

INDEX: MODERN AUTHORS CITED

INDEX: GENERAL

Aaron makes golden calf, 108.
— priesthood of, 98, 110, 305.
Abdikhiba, 76.
Abel-beth-maacah, 227.
Abel-meholah, 263.
Abiathar banished to Anathoth, 245.
— escapes to David with Ephod, 207, 232 f.
— in Absalom's rebellion, 226.
— joins Adonijah, 243.
— possible ancestor of Jeremiah, 432.
Abigail, 207.
Abijah, death of, 278, 282.
Abijam, date of, 457 ff.
— reign of, 283.
— subordinate to Damascus, 282, 292.
Abimelech (b. Gideon), Kingship of, 151, 153.
— — mixed ancestry of, 146, 148, 150.
— — occupies Shechem, 128, 151 ff.
— — sacks Shechem, 152, 277.
— — wars of, 151 ff.
— (king of Gerar), 57.
Abiram rebels against Moses, 98.
Abishag, Adonijah asks for, 211, 245.
Abishai at battle of Rabbah, 220.
— rank of, 230 f.
— saves David's life, 212.
— would kill Shimei, 204.
Abner at pool of Gibeon, 210.
— David's elegy over, 326.
— Ishbaal's chief supporter, 193, 211.
— killed by Joab, 211.
— kills Asahel, 211.
— quarrels with Ishbaal, 211.
— Saul's commander-in-chief, 194, 195.
— treats with David, 211.
Aborigines of Palestine, 32.
Abraham called out of Harran, 55.
— called out of Ur, 54.
— defeats Mesopotamian kings, 56.
— founder of sanctuaries, 55 f.
— life of, 51.
— traditional date of, 46.
Absalom, 204, 220, 240, 244.
— appropriates David's harem, 211.
— rebellion of, 225–7.
Achan, sin of, 124.
Achish, 101.
— assigns Ziklag to David, 208.
— David flees to, 188, 207.
— dismisses David, 190.
— his friendship with David, 204.
Achshaph, 129, 130.
Achzib, 132.
Acre, 257.
Adad-nirari II, 11.
— III, 356.
— crushes Damascus, 11, 358.

Adam, 24, 121.
Administrative districts of Israel, 255 f., 263 ff., 321.
— — of Judah, 322.
Adoni-bezek, 125, 169.
Adoniram (Adoram), 255.
Adullam, David retreats to, 207, 213.
Adum-ba'il, 295.
Aegean peoples and culture, 9 ff., 33, 191.
— — destroy old Hittite empire, 142, 175.
— — represented by Philistines, 42 f., 142.
— — repulsed from Egypt, 9 f., 74.
Agag, 184.
Agricultural festivals, 96.
— life, conditions of, 18 f.
— religion, 138, 167, 345.
Agriculture, beginnings of, 17, 26, 104.
— methods of, 316.
Ahab, 11, 78, 291 ff., 325, 366, 431.
— alliance with Judah, 288, 294, 297.
— alliance with Tyre, 298.
— and Elijah, 305.
— and Naboth, 300 f.
— at Karkar, 289, 295 f.
— at Ramoth-gilead, 288, 294 f., 339.
— date of, 455 ff.
— death of, 295.
— loses Moab, 291.
— marries Jezebel, 290.
— massacre of his family, 347.
— palace of, 310, 361.
— prophets of, 303.
— religious attitude of, 323, 402.
— secures commercial privileges in Damascus, 313.
— wars with Assyria, 295 f.
— wars with Damascus, 295 f.
Ahaz, 375 ff.
— and Isaiah, 375.
— appeals to Tiglath-pileser III, 375 f., 385.
— date of, 455 ff.
— dial of, 405.
— his full name Jehoahaz, 81, 375.
— receives territory from Tiglath-pileser III, 380.
— reign of, 375 ff.
— religious innovations of, 377 f., 392, 420.
— sacrifices his first-born, 375, 403.
Ahaziah (king of Israel), 297, 323, 339 ff., 342.
— — — date of, 457 ff.
Ahaziah (king of Judah) allied with Israel, 288, 343.
— — — at Ramoth-gilead, 344.

PRINTED IN GREAT BRITAIN
AT THE UNIVERSITY PRESS, OXFORD
BY CHARLES BATEY, PRINTER TO THE UNIVERSITY

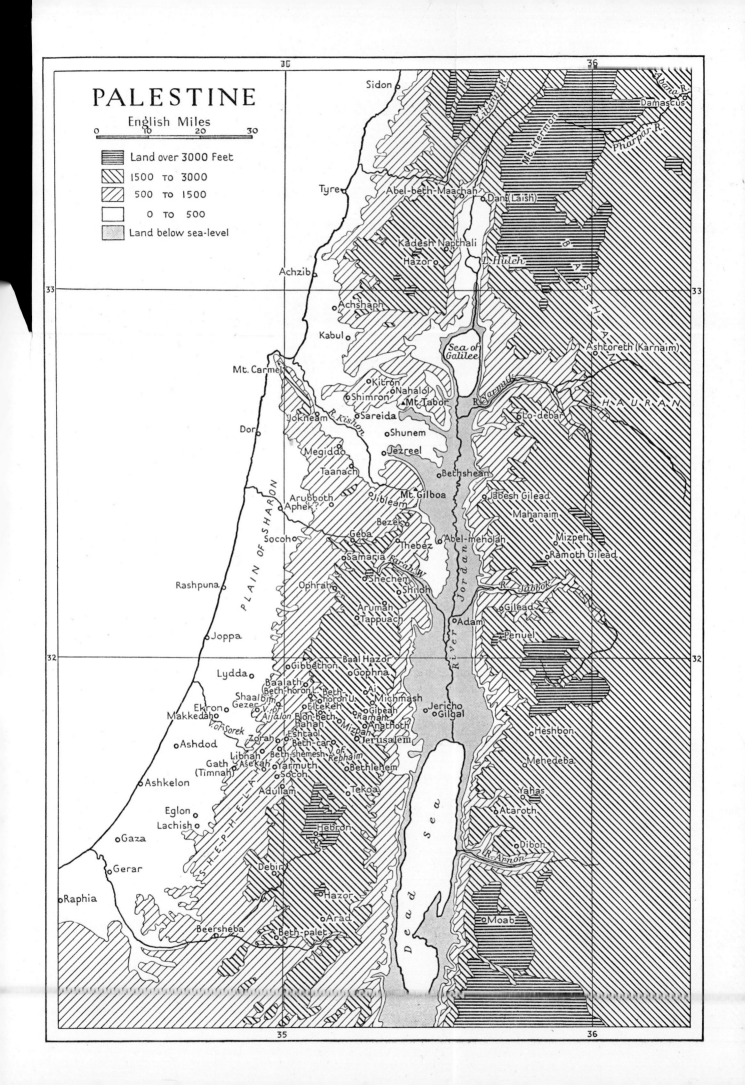